WARRIORS OF THE WORD

The World of the Scottish Highlanders

Michael Newton

BIRLINN

First published in 2009 by
Birlinn Limited
West Newington House
10 Newington Road
Edinburgh
EH9 1QS

www.birlinn.co.uk

ISBN: 978 1 84158 826 1

British Library Cataloguing-in-Publication Data
A catalogue record for this book is available from the British Library

Designed and typeset by Iolaire Typesetting, Newtonmore
Printed and bound by MPG Books Ltd, Bodmin

WARRIORS OF THE WORD

MICHAEL NEWTON is a lecturer in the Celtic Studies department of St Francis Xavier University in Nova Scotia. He was awarded a PhD in Celtic Studies from the University of Edinburgh and is a leading authority on the literature and cultural legacy of Scottish Highland immigrant communities in America. He has written several books and numerous articles on many aspects of Highland tradition and history, and was the editor of *Dùthchas nan Gàidheal: Selected Essays of John MacInnes*, which won the Saltire Society's Research Book award of 2006.

CONTENTS

Celtic Beginnings • The Highland–Lowland Divide • The Lords of the Isles •
Linn nan Creach and the Stewarts • Jacobites, Hanoverians and Religion •
Clearance, Empire and Evangelism

The Invention of Celticism • Territory and Identity • Language and Identity •
Ancestries and Genealogies • Inter-ethnic Relations and Perceptions

Oral and Written • Historical Developments • Professional Poets • Vernacular
Oral Tradition • Interpretative Methods • Interpreting Prose Narrative •
Interpreting Poetry • Literature and Identity

Clanship • Leaders and Leadership • The Diverse Bonds of Clanship • Territory
and Ownership • Law and Morality • Feasting and Fighting • Cooperation,
Obligation, and Reciprocation • Gender Roles

Names and Naming • Family and Clan Life • Stages of Life • Sustenance •
Health and Happiness • Clothing

Sacred and Secular in Gaelic History • The Otherworld of the Sìdh • Goddess of
Life and Landscape • Cosmology and Social Order

Contents

LIST OF ILLUSTRATIONS

ACKNOWLEDGMENTS

I have been fortunate to have received the encouragement and support of many friends and colleagues over the years in which I have been collecting and researching Scottish Gaelic matters, too many to name here. It is my hope that this work honours the generosity I have received from innumerable people who have offered me help, hospitality, and encouragement in the conviction that it would be for the greater good.

This volume draws in a number of places on the research I carried out in the course of my doctoral degree in the Celtic department of the University of Edinburgh. I received formal supervision and instruction during my training from Ronald Black, Thomas Owen Clancy, William Gillies, Allan MacDonald, and Roibeard Ó Maolalaigh, as well as informal guidance and inspiration from Margaret Bennett and John MacInnes. To them all I owe an immeasurable debt of thanks. I would also like to thank the Clan Donald Educational and Charitable Trust, the Overseas Research Scholarship, and the Richard Brown Scholarship, whose contributions supported my training.

I also owe thanks to a host of readers who provided comments, corrections, suggestions and information of all sorts on this manuscript, including Hugh Cheape, Rodger Cunningham, John Gibson, Peter Gilmore, Tad Hargrave, Russell Johnston, Allan MacDonald, John MacInnes, Alastair McIntosh, Sharon Paice-MacLeod, Robin Edward Poulton, Barry Shears, and Christopher Thompson. I particularly appreciate the substantial contributions and assistance offered by Iain MacKinnon of Sleat (Iain Dhomhnaill Dhomhnaill Dhomhnaill Nèill Dhomhnaill Iain), Wilson McLeod, and Keith Sanger. Thanks to Susan Johnston for the enormous task of proof-reading the manuscript. Any and all shortcomings are of course my own.

I must acknowledge and thank the libraries whose resources I used in collecting the material which appears in this volume, including the Celtic Collection of the Angus L. Macdonald Library of Saint Francis Xavier University, the National Library of Scotland, Edinburgh University Library, the libraries of the Celtic department and School of Scottish Studies at Edinburgh University, Glasgow University Library, the library of the Celtic department of Glasgow University, Widener Library at Harvard University, the Edinburgh City Library, and the library of Sabhal Mór Ostaig.

Thanks to the Breadalbane Folklore Centre for permission to print photographs of artefacts in their holdings, to the School of Scottish Studies (University of Edinburgh) for permission to reprint the song 'Sann a' bhruadar mi raoir', to Elaine Dunn for permission to reprint the 'Christening Song' collected by the late Charles Dunn, and to the Scottish Gaelic Texts Society for permission to reprint William J. Watson's Gaelic edition of the poem 'Ríoghacht ghaisgidh oighreacht Eòin' (poem one of Appendix A).

Thanks also to Andrew Simmons of Birlinn for many vital services necessary for the creation of this volume, not least of which was providing me with several highly useful Birlinn books.

I am grateful, finally, in many ways to my beloved wife Stephanie who provided encouragement, support, advice, love, and patience during the long gestation of this project. Tha mi fada 'nad chomain.

FOREWORD

A personal epiphany played its part in opening up new dimensions for a wider understanding of time and space in Scottish history and culture. For me, this was an insight of such simple, instantaneous and profound significance. On a summer's evening in 1980, I was walking from the main north-south road in South Uist up to Hogh Mòr, sited as it is on the Atlantic coast. I met a man within sight of the ancient building cluster and we stopped and conversed. In that kindly and naturally curious way of the indweller, he asked me my business, to which I replied that I had come to look at the old structures there and to discover something about the site as a whole. My interlocutor told me that I was standing at a place of great significance, that this was once a place of learning with its churches and chapels and associated buildings, and that this was indeed a medieval university of considerable status. I did not doubt him although I could not immediately envisage the literal meaning of what he was telling me. Having looked at the scatter of ruinous structures and stones enveloped within the big precinct wall, I moved on towards a high dune from which a great deep sound was coming. Until I topped the dune, the sea was invisible but, from that point, a huge vista of murmuring ocean opened. I was overwhelmed by the immensity of the scene and the locus of Uist in a wider world, stretching across the Atlantic of course, but more significantly tied intimately into seaways north – the 'northern common-wealth' of the Viking centuries – and south, into Europe and the Mediterranean, and into the streams of culture which fed places of learning and vitality such as Hogh Mòr. Behind me as I stood there, the world of medieval and modern Scotland dropped away into relative insignificance.

The intellectual refreshment afforded by such a 'change of mind' is comparable to the material, ideas and interpretation offered by Michael Newton. He is a highly original scholar who has established a well-deserved reputation for himself in Celtic Studies, with a number of excellent books and articles which have put teachers and researchers in his debt. His own diligent and detailed research has ranged widely over history, geography, ethnology, anthropology, sociology and ecology, but returning always with his findings and intuition to the Gaelic language and culture. By putting language at the core of his synthesis, he is adding immeasurably to issues of identity and culture which, in the case of Scottish Gaelic, have invited considerable speculation and hypothesising over the generations but which are doomed to failure without a thorough knowledge of the language itself. This was of course our author's starting-point and it lends weight to his findings and value to their authenticity and significance.

Warriors of the Word presents us with an insightful account of social and economic life, its cultural and intellectual framework, the practical skills and experience of life and survival, and the dynamic and imperatives of the community, Highland and Hebridean. Language, as the author stresses, is the glue which gives coherence, intelligibility and sustainability to a complex mix. Michael Newton's detailed exploration of eras, players and episodes draws with it insights into the realpolitik of community leaders, their aspirations, cultural interests and horizons. Behind these lie one or two big issues or distinctive histories whose most significant sources of evidence lie within Gaelic language and literature.

The time that separates us today from the time of Cromwell's Commonwealth approximates to the era of almost 350 years of predominance of the Lords of the Isles, between 1146 and 1493. The 'Lordship' formed a third axis in high medieval power struggles between England and Scotland. This was a remarkable dynasty of rulers in the north and west of Scotland, emerging from (and active in) the weakening and collapsing Viking and Norwegian rule in the Hebrides in the twelfth and thirteenth centuries. They consolidated their power following the Wars of Independence in the fourteenth century. Though related to Vikings leaders, they established a kingdom in which Gaelic culture ruled. From their head-house at Finlaggan in Islay, successive Lords controlled vast areas from Ulster to the Butt of Lewis and held them together by control of the sea and innate skills such as we learn from the sea epic, *Bìrlinn Chlann Raghnaill*. The extent of Lordship power in the Hebrides and claims to large areas of the northern and eastern mainland, particularly in the earldom of Ross, led in time to the kings of Scots removing the Lordship at the end of the fifteenth century. This process tends to be described from a centrist and monarchical point of view which makes the outcome of this clash inevitable. Perceptions of the power and reputation of the Lords of the Isles may be sought within Gaelic sources. A Gaelic charter of 1408 by Donald, Lord of the Isles, is couched in distinctive terms of European kingship: 'And in order that there may be meaning, force and effect in this grant I give from me, I again bind myself and my heirs for ever under covenant, this to uphold and fulfil . . . to the end of the world'. A traditional saying that the Lords of the Isles possessed half Scotland and a house – *taigh is leth Alba* – reflects the confident threat presented by the majority shareholder to the status quo.

In the intangible cultural heritage of Scotland, religious belief occupies a firm if presently unfashionable position. Religious belief is strongly characteristic of human nature and religions such as Christianity, Islam and Buddhism have been successful and powerful. Grass-root beliefs and practices, considered to be outside mainstream religion, have also been powerful and compelling, and Gaelic culture manifests these in abundance. Living in the wild places with a strong oral culture keeps beliefs alive and ensures their transmission from generation to generation. The monumental collection of charms and prayers in the *Carmina Gadelica* shows how distinctively spiritual as well as realistic and practical was keeping faith in the Highlands and Islands.

Christianity came to Scotland about sixteen centuries ago, probably in the closing years of the Roman occupation of Britain. After Ninian built a church at Whithorn, Columba and his fellow missionaries from Ireland settled in Iona about AD 563. Over the next 300 years, Irish and Scottish churchmen moved through Scotland and into England, to Lindisfarne and through the Anglo-Saxon kingdoms, and then took their Christianity into Western and Central Europe. The missionary church of Colm Cille thrived on kinship and political links, essentially secular imperatives. It has left a material culture of unique splendour in objects such as the Book of Kells, the Monymusk Reliquary, and standing crosses which were and still are the admiration of the western world. At home, Columba, Latin scholar and Gaelic poet, and patron saint of the Gael, has left a map of devotion in chapels and churches and place-names of native saints.

From the twelfth to the sixteenth centuries, the 'church' in the Highlands was part of the European Church of Rome, sharing the *lingua franca* of Latin. But Gaelic churchmen used their own language to compile manuscripts and treatises and to write down poems and songs and stories of Fionn and the Fianna. This intermixing of the 'spiritual' and the 'worldly' sustained a rich literature and language, unrealised until caught up in Celtic philology and historical linguistics. A further dimension of the richness of the language emerged when John Francis Campbell of Islay published his collection in the remarkable four volumes of *Popular Tales of the West Highlands* in 1860–1862, establishing the international significance of Gaelic traditions of prose narrative. The Protestant Reformation of 1560 cut church links with Europe and was followed over the next three hundred years by political efforts to extend the rule of church and state over the Highlands and Islands and destroy their culture.

Warriors of the Word offers a counter-thrust to concepts of the destruction of Gaelic culture or of its irrelevance to a complex and 'globalised' culture bestowed on us as members of today's society. More than this, the work offers a distillation which makes its continuing value clear and explicit. It must be symbolic of Gaelic's resilience that a term for 'complex' is *ioma-fhillte* or 'multi-folded', figuratively representing an abstract in material terms; such imaginative handling is typical of the directness and subtlety of the language. The author breaks the mould of conventional discourse, treats Gaelic culture in its own right and discards the defining and retrospective lenses of Romanticism and 'Clearance' and of too-often suffocating accounts of historical and economic determinism.

Hugh Cheape
Sabhal Mòr Ostaig
Colaiste Ghàidhlig na h-Alba
An Inid 2009

NOTES ON LANGUAGE

Translation between languages is an inherently complex challenge that usually leaves me with a sense of dissatisfaction: double entendres and deliberate ambiguities in the original require tediously long explanations; words are not discrete units but bundles of associations which seldom correspond to those of words in other languages; phrases carry with them allusions to items in the greater corpus of literature and oral tradition which cannot be carried into translation; the union of sound and sense in one language is inevitably broken when being transformed into another. Nonetheless, I have attempted to provide translations for the readership without a knowledge of Gaelic, rendering the text in modern colloquial English and reordering phrases as necessary, rather than attempting a literal translation that follows too closely to the abstruse style preferred by many other translators. Accordingly, I have chosen to provide translations in chunks rather than common approach of following the Gaelic text line by line.

Gaelic names themselves present complications. Gaelic words and names operate according to their own logic which ideally should be followed in any serious study of Highland society. Unfortunately, anglicised forms of names have become so deeply entrenched that it may seem unreasonably pedantic to many readers to see 'Mac-Dhomhnaill' rather than 'MacDonald', 'Caimbeul' rather than 'Campbell', and so on. As a compromise I have attempted to provide first names and epithets in their original Gaelic form but surnames in their anglicised equivalents. Similar problems exist with clan names, such as Clann Domhnaill or Clann Ghriogair. Here again, despite strong reservations, I have generally used the anglicised forms.

This book includes Gaelic texts from both Scotland and Ireland spanning some fourteen centuries. I have attempted to spell Gaelic names and words according to the conventions of the time and place whence they originate. Although there are many names and words that are attested throughout that time span, they are represented differently, depending on whether they have been rendered in Old Gaelic, Classical Gaelic, Modern Irish, or Modern Scottish Gaelic, for example. While it may be jarring for some readers to encounter *síd* from an eighth-century text next to *sìdh* from recent Scottish Gaelic oral tradition, differences in orthography are inevitable over such a long period of linguistic development and are respected in this volume.

Gaelic words have been misspelled in many early sources, not least in those texts written by outsiders attempting to render Gaelic sounds with English spelling (a system not even consistent or logical for writing in English). I have frequently corrected the Gaelic words in such sources, placing them in square brackets, for the convenience of modern Gaelic speakers and scholars.

Gaelic terms are set in italics the first time they appear; after being defined, however, they usually reappear in unmarked form. Short phrases, quotations, and the names of songs and tales are usually given in the body of the text in single quotes and given in translation in round brackets; longer quotations and excerpts from literature are given first in Gaelic (marked with italics) and followed by a full translation in English.

MAPS

1. Kingdoms and Important Sites in Scotland in the eighth century AD

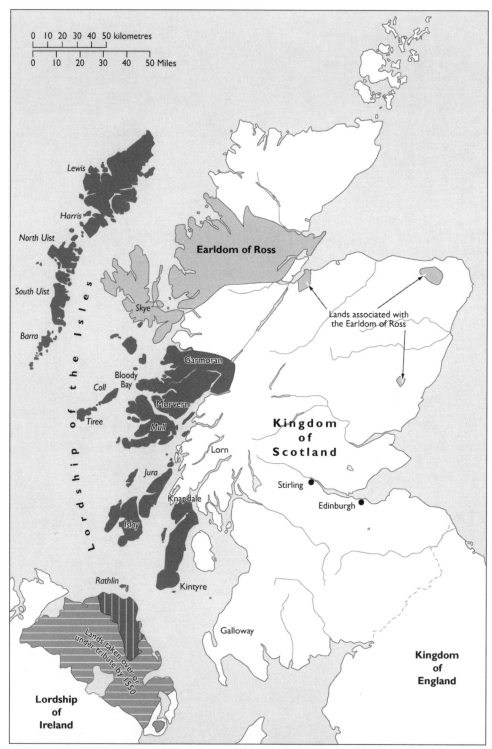

0 10 20 30 40 50 kilometres

0 10 20 30 40 50 Miles

Lewis

Harris

North Uist

South Uist

Barra

Earldom of Ross

Skye

L o r d s h i p   o f   t h e   I s l e s

Lands associated with
the Earldom of Ross

Garmoran

Bloody
Bay

Coll

Morvern

Tiree

Mull

Lorn

**Kingdom
of
Scotland**

Jura

Knapdale

Stirling

Edinburgh

Islay

Rathlin

Kintyre

Lands taken over or
under tribute by 1550

Galloway

**Kingdom
of
England**

**Lordship
of
Ireland**

2. Lands claimed by Clan Donald from the thirteenth to the sixteenth centuries

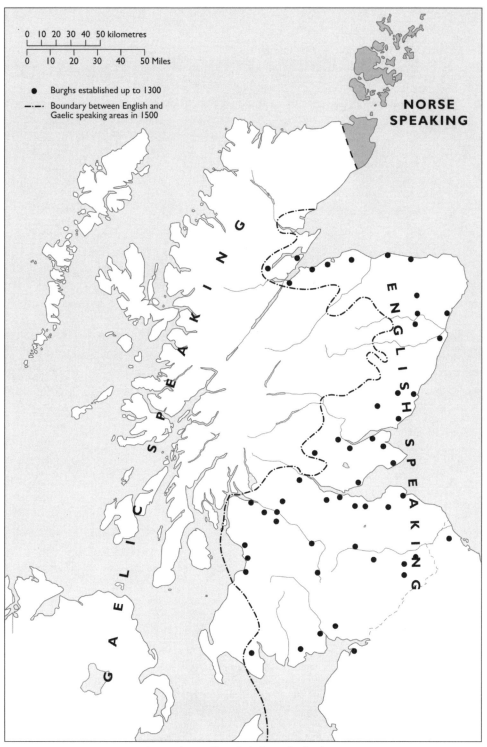

3. *Approximate linguistic boundaries in 1500*

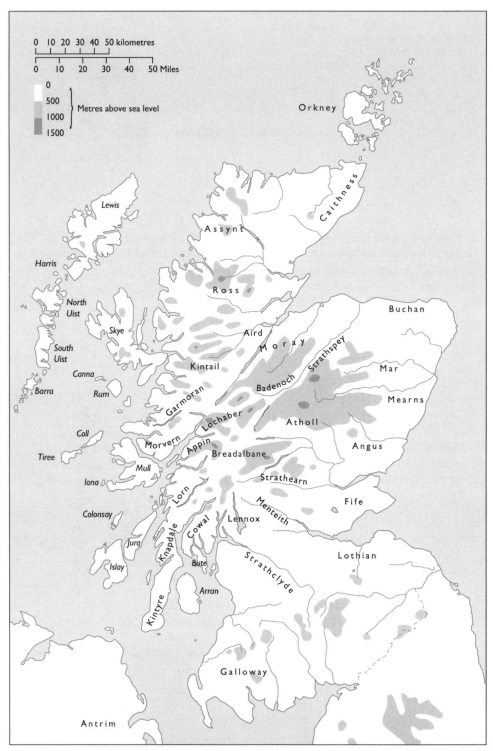

4. *Some Island and District names*

INTRODUCTION

When Scottish scholar John Lorne Campbell visited Nova Scotia in 1953, he was amazed to find that in the forests of Canada seventy-eight-year-old Angus MacIsaac kept alive verses from a medieval Gaelic song well after they had been forgotten in Scotland. Here in 'New Scotland', where Highlanders first settled in 1773 with little more than their oral traditions to sustain them, MacIsaac chanted a dialogue in verse that recalled the far-off days when Saint Patrick first encountered Ossian,[1] the poet of the pagan warriors known as the Fian:

> One night Patrick went to the dwelling
> Where there was revelry, song and drink
> To see Ossian of the Fian,
> For he was the most eloquent of them.
>
> (*Ossian*)
> O Cleric who sings the psalms,
> You are but a fool to me!
> Will you not listen for a while to my tale
> Of the Fian, which you've never heard?
>
> (*Patrick*)
> I will not idle away my time for your tale
> Which I have never heard
> While the flavour of the psalms lingers on my lips:
> Those are much better for me than your music!
>
> (*Ossian*)
> If your psalms mean so much more to you
> Than the Fian of Ireland, bearing naked blades –
> I wouldn't give a second thought
> To severing your head from your body!
>
> (*Patrick*)
> Oh, but you are welcome alas for me!
> It is for your company I came:
> Tell me, what was the hardest fight that the Fian
> Ever fought, since you were born?[2]

1

The song goes on to describe how the Fian fought off an invasion of Vikings led by the son of the King of the Norse. Campbell, who had already spent decades travelling around Scotland to record Gaelic tradition-bearers, was surprised that such songs could still be heard in the second half of the twentieth century:

> I knew of the existence of this ballad, of course, before I met Angus, but he was the only person I ever met who knew any of it, and who sang it. [. . .] Finding this relic of the ancient tradition in Nova Scotia, when no one had been able to sing it to me in Scotland, was a matter of great interest.[3]

It was not just a matter of survival against time, it was a matter of survival against the authorities themselves. Medieval Gaelic scholars found a way to accommodate pagan lore within Christian society by the creation of such literature as the song-dialogues of Ossian and Patrick, but it was an uneasy relationship that was never entirely resolved. For clergymen such as John Carswell, the author of the first book ever printed in Gaelic, these secular works detracted from the Christian message. His 1567 translation of the *Book of Common Order* into Classical Gaelic decried those who would rather sing the praises of warriors than the praise of God:

> And great is the blindness and darkness of sin and ignorance and of the mind among composers and writers and patrons of Gaelic, in that they prefer and are accustomed to maintain and improve vain, hurtful, lying, worldly tales composed about the Tuatha Dé Danann, and about the sons of Milesius, and about the heroes and Fionn mac Cumhaill with his warriors [the Fian], and about many others whom I do not recount or mention here, with a view to obtaining for themselves vain worldly gain, rather than to write and compose and to preserve the very Word of God and the perfect ways of truth.[4]

Disapproval of the Ossianic ballads[5] followed Highlanders into Nova Scotia when the Rev. James MacGregor immigrated in 1786.[6] Despite such condemnations, however, Highlanders continued to identify with Fionn mac Cumhaill and his warrior band as heroes of their culture and even ancestors.[7] This was as true in late eighteenth-century Argyll, the stronghold of Highland Protestantism, as it was in Catholic Barra. John Francis Campbell, a pioneer of folklore in the nineteenth century, commented that the Ossianic traditions 'pervade the whole traditions of the country and are interwoven with each other'.[8] Proverbs featuring members of the Fian set standards of behaviour and offered advice on matters profound and mundane. Another nineteenth-century folklorist, John Gregorson Campbell, said that the heroes were so much a part of daily conversation 'that it became a saying, that if the Fians were twenty-four hours without anyone mentioning them they would rise again'.[9]

The oral traditions of the land of their birth were valuable possessions to the exiles in Canada, just as they were to Highlanders who had remained in Scotland and fought for the dignity of their language and culture. Songs such as those recalling how the Fian had withstood the scorn of Patrick and the onslaught of the Vikings were vessels which carried cultural identity and the message of self-worth from generation to generation. In the later literary tradition, the Fian became exemplars of heroic ideals, a band of warriors defending the borders of Gaelic Scotland and Ireland against Viking invaders with a seer-warrior, Fionn mac Cumhaill, to guide them, and a poet, Ossian, to record their achievements in verse for posterity.

The songs of the Fian sparked a war of words, and a battle for hearts and minds, that lasted for over a century and still rumbles on in muted form. In 1760 James Macpherson, a young Highlander from Badenoch, anonymously published *Fragments of Ancient Poetry, Collected in the Highlands of Scotland, and translated from the Galic or Erse language*. Macpherson took certain elements from the Gaelic ballads about the Fian – characters, themes, plot-lines – but reworked them considerably in new forms to meet the aesthetic expectations of his contemporary anglophone audience. Rather than own up to his own hand in these creative adaptations, however, he claimed that the epic poetry in this and several subsequent volumes was a literal translation of the Gaelic verse of the poet Oisean, who Macpherson renamed 'Ossian'.

Macpherson enjoyed success beyond his wildest dreams: Napoleon carried a copy of *Ossian* in his breast pocket and commissioned Jean-Auguste-Dominique Ingres to paint a colossal scene from the epic in his palace; Thomas Jefferson was such a devotee of the 'bard of the North' that he wished to learn Gaelic in order to read it in its original form; the poetry and sentiments of *Ossian* stirred the hearts of young poets across Europe and America, from Wordsworth and Blake to Goethe and Tennyson. Highlanders were glad to be the objects of admiration for a change, even if those familiar with Macpherson's 'translations' had misgivings about his claims.

Sceptics were having none of it, especially in England: Highlanders were already stereotyped as ignorant savages, but the general atmosphere of anti-Scottish prejudice which pervaded England in the eighteenth century soured the reception of anything about which a Scotsman could boast.[10] The controversy gained further prominence after the publication of *A Journey to the Western Isles of Scotland* by the renowned English lexicographer and author Samuel Johnson in 1775. Johnson went to the Western Highlands and Islands to investigate the matter of *Ossian* first-hand. He concluded that Highlanders did not have a literary tradition in their native language, then commonly called 'Erse' rather than 'Gaelic':

Of the Earse language, as I understand nothing, I cannot say more than I have been told. It is the rude speech of a barbarous people, who had few thoughts to express, and were content, as they conceived grossly, to be grossly understood. After what has been lately talked of Highland Bards, and Highland genius, many will startle when they are told, that the Earse was never a written language; that there is not in the world an Earse manuscript a hundred years old. [. . .] the Bard was a barbarian

3

among barbarians, who, knowing nothing himself, lived with others that knew no more.[11]

Johnson was factually wrong (as Chapter Three will demonstrate) and insulting to boot; these were fighting words and the literary dispute became a matter of national pride for some Scots. Withering satires of Johnson were composed in Gaelic (only one of which has been edited and translated to date[12]), and several extensive treatises defended *Ossian* and Highland literature in general against Johnson's charges. Such was the confident bombast of Johnson's words, however, and the authority afforded to him in the annals of British literature, that his appraisal of *Ossian* as a 'hoax' and a 'fraud' is still unthinkingly repeated by respectable authors to this day, ignoring the subsequent research of Gaelic scholars who have traced the trails of authentic Highland sources employed by Macpherson in his work.[13]

Macpherson's *Ossian* is not the direct translation he claimed it to be, but neither is it the 'forgery' which it is still reported to be by the uninformed. The Ossianic controversy spurred the documentation of Gaelic oral tradition by literate members of Highland society, but it also cast a long shadow of suspicion and cynicism over Gaelic tradition which continues to the present.

The Ossianic legacy offers a compelling metaphor for the history of Gaelic culture. Oral tradition has been a primary vehicle for the sustenance of Highland culture; it has absorbed external influences and influenced foreign literary canons; it has been a site of resistance to cultural imperialism and an entry point of cultural colonisation; it has been a centre of contention over origins, identity, meaning, and significance in which the voices of the Gaels themselves have usually been drowned out by their more assertive and self-assured neighbours.

~

Storytelling has a special place in human consciousness and culture. The creation and interpretation of stories has enabled humankind to make sense of ourselves and the world around us during the eons of human development. The most natural and effective way for people to understand culture is to represent it in the form of a narrative. Verbal narratives allow us to simulate, manipulate, play with, and ask questions about the basic premises of our culture better than any other media or genre. They allow us to pose questions and dilemmas about our own lives in a safe verbal laboratory. They allow us to coordinate concepts and reimagine possibilities that might otherwise be difficult to actualise. They can help to reaffirm old patterns as well as form new ones.

> People live by stories – they use stories to organize and store cultural traditions. Changes in people's stories not only reflect changes in cultural reality; they can actually create them. That is why politicians are traditionally said to distrust poets. A story or poem or song allows ordinary people – the traditional 'Everyman' – to see

4

things anew, even to detect and avoid cultural traps. With stories and poems, people can work cultural changes in areas that they cannot even think about *except* as stories.[14]

The world is shaped and governed by narratives: government ministries create stories that justify political policies and economic decisions by reference to the biography of the nation; educational authorities create stories about the past, about what we are supposed to value in the present, and about what we are supposed to expect in the future (in a kind of self-fulfilling prophecy); industry creates stories about wealth, value, progress and the individual. But who is in charge of creating the stories? Whose purposes do they serve? What stories are not being told? For too long Scottish Highlanders have been ill-served by the stories told to them and about them but have lacked the institutions to become the authors of their own narrative.

During the medieval period, Gaelic culture flourished in Scotland and enjoyed significant intellectual, cultural, social, material, musical, and artistic achievements. Scottish Gaeldom was closely connected to Ireland and Lowland Scotland, exporting and importing new ideas, but maintained a high degree of independence and distinctiveness. While Gaels sometimes make stereotyped cameo appearances in books about Scotland or Scottish subjects – as early founders of Scotland, 'wild, wicked Highlanders' causing mayhem in the Lowlands, or 'ill-fated' Jacobite 'rebels' – surprisingly few volumes attempt any sustained examination of their culture and historical experience from their own point of view.

This book has stories at its core: although I offer interpretations and analyses of many aspects of Scottish Gaelic culture, I have endeavoured to allow oral traditions – stories, songs, and proverbs – to be star witnesses to their own realities. I begin every chapter with a brief story that illustrates some key points discussed in the chapter, and I offer an anthology of Scottish Gaelic poetry at the end of this volume. I have made liberal use of the most recent and insightful research in Scottish Gaelic studies, little of which is easily accessible to the general public, in order to synthesise a broad overview of Scottish Gaelic culture. I hope that my modest efforts can help to bridge the chasm that yawns between academic discourse and the wider world.

This is not primarily a history book. Although out of necessity it contains enough historical material to put the rest of its contents into context, it is more concerned with the biases of previous generations of historians than with the minutia of historical facts whose interpretations are being rapidly transformed by a new wave of scholarship in any case. Nor is this book primarily concerned with archaeology, agriculture, economic means of production, or other forms of material culture of which there were many regional variations across Gaeldom, although I draw upon certain aspects of these topics where appropriate.

This book is primarily about the mental and social world of the Gaels, focusing especially on the period when independent clans held sway in the Highlands, from the twelfth century to the eighteenth. Even when the social institutions of clan life had been made forfeit by the central government, the values and mores of clan society – especially as encoded in and transmitted by oral tradition – have continued to inform the inner life of Gaelic culture. These cultural resources still hold promise for those who are willing to reclaim them as their own and retell them to succeeding generations.

Chapter One

THEMES IN SCOTTISH HISTORY

It is certainly a legitimate function of history to produce, as the cliché goes, a usable past. But there is a danger in our obsession with mapping out the routes to the present, because in doing so, we slice off all that is not 'relevant' and thus distort the past. We eliminate its strangeness. We eliminate, most of all, its possibilities. History should do more than validate the inevitability of the present.

– Richard White, 'Other Wests'[1]

During their heyday in the ninth and tenth centuries, the Norse enjoyed military and political supremacy along the coastal areas of much of western Europe; they unsettled the existing political order, imposed their own leaders and developed their own settlements. Yet, in most locales, within a few generations they were beginning to lose their dominance and Gaelic culture proved resilient enough to assimilate the would-be conquerers. By the late medieval period, the Gaels of the west of Scotland, most of whom had a mixture of Norse and Gaelic ancestors, were recounting legends of how Gaelic warriors such as Somerled had liberated their lands from Viking usurpers. The alienation of Highlanders from their own Scandinavian ancestry once they had become Gaelicised is one of the many ironies of history that alert us to the dangers of assuming that ethnic identity reflects 'racial' origin.

Gaeldom's comeback is celebrated in tales such as the following legend from Argyll. Like many local legends, it explains the origin of a significant place name, which adds a sense of historical weight and veracity to the tale. The place name Gleann Domhainn ('Deep Glen') may symbolise how Gaeldom withdrew after the Viking attacks to inland sanctuary until it regained strength. Despite several generations of dominance in the west, the narrative implies that the only legacy left by the Norse is a series of place names signifying their defeat.[2]

~

The Norse once made a sudden descent from their ships on the lower end of Craignish. The inhabitants, taken by surprise, fled in terror to the upper end of the district and didn't stop until they reached Slugan ('the Gorge') in Gleann Domhainn.

Once there, they rallied under a brave young man who took their leadership and slew the leader of the invading Norse with a spear. This inspired the Craignish men with such courage that they soon drove back the disheartened Norse across Barr Breac river. As they retreated they carried off the body of their fallen leader Olav (*Amhladh* in Gaelic) and buried it on a place on Barr Breac farm which is still called Dùnan Amhlaidh ('Olav's Mound'). The Craignish men also raised a cairn at Slugan to mark the spot where Olav was slain.

~

The old adage 'History is written by the winners' acknowledges that people experience events differently, according to their own perspectives and circumstances, and that the writing of history has frequently favoured one party to the detriment of others. The labels used for political movements, factions and players often betray biases: whether a person has been represented as a rebel or a hero has been determined not so much by the deeds he has done as whether or not his story was written by someone sympathetic to his cause.

The writing of history is inevitably a matter of interpretation: not all of the innumerable people and actions over a space of time can be accounted for, so the scholar must decide which factors are most responsible for the outcomes of social processes and how people are affected by the results. He must decide whose story to tell and how to tell it.

The story told about the Highlands has long been dominated by the assumption that the region has always been an isolated and remote backwater, and by a negative appraisal of the Gaels themselves as a people. Both of these biases have served to marginalise the Gaels in the writing of Scottish history. Documents portraying Highlanders as primitives naturally inclined to resist the rule of law and principles of progress have often been taken at face value. The perspectives of the Highlanders themselves have been too easily ignored, especially when pitted against those of others assumed to be more 'civilised'. The author of the Sleat history of the MacDonalds complained in the mid seventeenth century about the anti-Gaelic prejudices which distorted the way in which Scottish history was written in the Lowlands:

> These partial pickers of Scotish chronology and history never spoke a favourable word of the Highlanders, much less of the Islanders and Macdonalds, whose great power and fortune the rest of the nobility envied [. . .] he relates that such and such kings went to suppress rebellion here and there, but makes no mention of the causes and pretences for these rebellions. [. . .] Although the Macdonalds might be as guilty as any others, yet they never could expect common justice to be done them by a Lowland writer.[3]

When Gaelic folklorist J. G. Mackay addressed the Glasgow Highland Association in 1882, he observed that 'to many Highlanders the extraordinary antipathy and determined antagonism with which they have been treated by pragmatical historians has long been a most unaccountable mystery'. While historians made an effort to understand the motives, circumstances and affiliations of English and Lowland subjects, 'the Highlander could have no such sentiments, he could only be activated by his love of plunder and bloodshed'.[4] Even near the end of the twentieth century, the accomplished scholar John Lorne Campbell, who spent his life recording and publishing Gaelic materials of all kinds, remarked that Highlanders were still grossly misrepresented in historical scholarship:

> Unless a historian possesses some knowledge of the Gaelic language and its written and oral literature, and has the insights that that knowledge bestows, it is very difficult not to be borne down by the accumulating weight of official assertions and propaganda, and arrive at the mental state of accepting them without question. [. . .] Far too long have the Scottish Gaels been treated by historians as non-persons with no legitimate point of view.[5]

We can better understand a society when we have examined the forces, events, and agents that have influenced its experiences and development. This chapter attempts to provide a summary of the history of Scottish Gaeldom: the people and events which provide the subjects and topics of Highland literature; the circumstances and trends which have influenced the forms and functions of its culture; the conditions and constraints which have affected the allegiances and political decisions of Highland leaders; the factors that have influenced the living conditions, social institutions and roles of the generality of Highlanders. This outline is intended to provide a context for specific aspects of Gaelic culture explored in depth in following chapters.

CELTIC BEGINNINGS

The term 'Celtic' has become popularly associated with particular people, places, art styles, musical styles, and so on. There are many difficulties with using the term 'Celtic' in these imprecise ways, however; scholars use it to refer to a family of languages belonging to the greater Indo-European family. Celtic languages are ultimately related, albeit at several removes, to other languages familiar to us in Europe and Asia, such as French, Italian, Hindi, and Persian.

In theory, the many Celtic languages (and their associated cultures) are derived in some way from a Celtic parent. The relationships between 'parent' and 'child' cultures, however, are complex and prevent us from making simplistic assumptions about a unified Celtic culture existing anywhere at any time. Earlier generations of scholars, living during an imperial epoch, assumed that the spread of Celtic languages and cultures could only be explained by an invasion of Celtic-speaking people who conquered new lands because of superior technology. The newer paradigm of Celticity instead proposes a long period of cultural development beginning in the late Bronze Age, from 1200 to 700 BC, driven by the influence of trade and networks of a Celtic-speaking élite.[6] The diffusion of Celtic languages and cultures happened in such a loose way (rather than being imposed by a centralised state from a prescribed standard) that we cannot speak of a single Celtic people, way of life, or identity, but rather a family of inter-related languages and cultures. 'Celtic', then, is an abstraction of convenience for a set of features which are found in concrete form in specific times and places, even though not all 'Celtic' tribes shared all of the same characteristics.

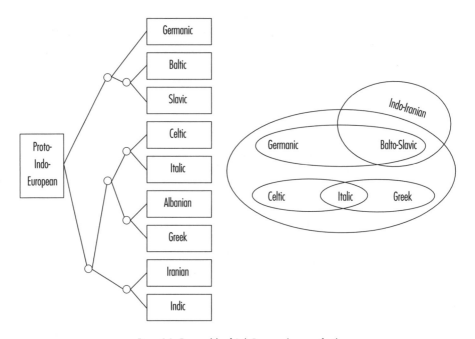

Figure 1.1: Two models of Indo-European language families

Although we get different kinds of evidence from archaeology, place names, inscriptions, and historical sources, it is safe to say that for several centuries before the birth of Christ Celtic-speaking peoples were living across a large section of Europe.

> Originally they extended in a broad swath from south-western Iberia, through Gaul and the Alpine region, into the Middle Danube, and one group of settlers, the Galatians, introduced Celtic into central Asia Minor.[7]

Britain and Ireland were occupied by Celtic-speaking peoples at the dawn of recorded history and had been for some time. This conclusion is confirmed primarily by personal names, tribal names, and place names recorded in early documents and by the testimony of early Classical authors. Archaeological evidence also allows us to interpret some features of surviving material culture – houses, forts, burials, clothing, artistic styles, etc. – in relation to other cultures classified under the rubric 'Celtic'.

Pytheas, a Greek writing as early as 325 BC, referred to the 'Pretanic Isles'; the Romans referred to the island as 'Britannia'. These territorial names are based on the Celtic tribal name *Britanni*. An earlier and purely territorial name for the island, **Albiu*, survives to the present day in Gaelic in the form *Alba*. In the second century AD the Greek geographer Ptolemy preserved a list of the names of Celtic tribes in various parts of Britain and Ireland. Some tribal names recur in several parts of the Celtic world: there are 'Brigantes' in eastern Ireland and northern England; 'Parisi' in eastern Yorkshire and 'Parisii' in France. Similarly, there was a 'Cornavii' in Caithness and a 'Cornovii' in the English mid-lands, a 'Damnonii' in the Clyde valley and a 'Dumnonii' in Cornwall.[8] It is not clear if these were branches of the same tribe that migrated to different areas, or simply names based on similar origin legends or mythological founders.

The Insular Celtic languages (those spoken in Britain and Ireland) are generally classified as P-Celtic (or Brythonic) and Q-Celtic (or Goidelic) because of how the 'Q' consonant inherited from the theoretical linguistic ancestor, Proto-Celtic, evolved in two descending branches: it was simplified as a hard 'c' consonant in Goidelic languages, while in Brythonic languages it became a 'p' consonant. There were speakers of both branches of Celtic on both islands (as the tribal names above suggest) during the late Iron Age, but on the whole most of Ireland was Goidelic and most of Britain was Brythonic.

Roman troops under Claudius invaded the south of Britain in AD 43 and after consolidating their victories, Gnaeus Julius Agricola, Roman governor of Britain, moved armies north to invade Scotland in AD 79. His ability to march as far as the Tay suggests that he had already formed relationships with the tribes of southern Scotland before the campaign. The Romans were expert at military strategies such as proxy warfare and servitor imperialism: it was common for them to form pacts and client relationships with native tribes (and displaced élite) along the frontier at each stage of territorial expansion to make subjugation easier.

Lasting military conquest and occupation in Scotland, however, proved elusive for the Romans: several strings of forts were built to control territory and assert authority, but by AD 165 the army had withdrawn to Hadrian's Wall. Such was the ability of the northern tribes to harass the Roman forces that they bribed the Maeatae (a tribe that occupied the area around modern Stirlingshire) in exchange for a cessation of hostility and the release of prisoners. The Romans were under attack by a broad 'barbarian conspiracy' in the fourth century which they were never able to contain. Problems within the empire itself precipitated the collapse of its occupation of Britain in the early fifth century; by AD 410 the forces at Hadrian's Wall were dispersed.[9]

Despite the inability of the Roman Empire to control and assimilate the Celtic tribes of Scotland, particularly north of the Antonine Wall, the Roman presence had significant consequences. South of the Forth–Clyde line tribes such as the Votadini (later known as the 'Gododdin') who aligned themselves with the Romans were able to flourish while others collapsed. Direct Roman influence was considerable in the 'buffer zone', not least because it brought Christianity to the Brythonic peoples perhaps as early as AD 200. Continued connections between the Brythonic peoples of the Lothians, Cumbria and Wales seem to have been encouraged by Roman leaders.[10]

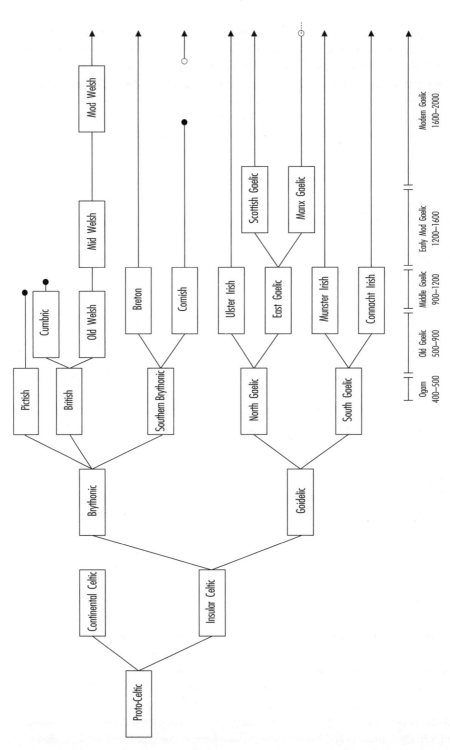

Figure 1.2: Family tree of Insular Celtic languages with stages of Goidelic[11]

The Celtic tribes north of Hadrian's Wall coalesced into ever larger political federations, at least in part as a way to counter the Roman threat. These peoples, commonly referred to as 'Picts', seem to have united under a single king in the late seventh century. The term 'Pict' was first recorded by the Romans in AD 297; we aren't certain if this was a Roman nickname for the non-Romanised northern tribes or if it corresponded to a name they used for themselves. The Picts were long assumed to be a shadowy and mysterious people about whom little could be known, but more recent research argues convincingly that they are P-Celts, that is, another kind of Brythonic-speaking people. They probably called themselves 'Priteni' in their own language; they are called 'Prydyn' by the Welsh and 'Cruithne' by the Gaels, all which correspond to the early ethnonym 'Britanni'. During the reign of Caustantín, king of the Picts (862–76), the list of Pictish kings was extended back in time to begin with 'Cruithne', the mythical founder who gave his name to the people.[12]

The personal names, tribal names and place names of the Picts confirm that they spoke a P-Celtic language. The names of rivers and lochs are usually the oldest names in any country, surviving changes of language and population, and many river and loch names in the ancient 'Pictish heartland', such as the Tay, the Dee, and the Lossie, are definitely Celtic. A number of place-name elements, such as *aber, perth, tref, mynydd* and *cardden*, occur in Pictland as well as other parts of Britain, showing it to be part of a continuum of Brythonic speech.[13] The second elements of place names which begin with *aber-* 'river confluence' have Celtic roots with close correspondences in Gaelic: Aberbervie 'the boiling water' (Gaelic *berb*), Aberbothrie 'the deaf (silent) one' (Gaelic *bodar*), and so on.[14] The personal names of Picts which appear in Roman and early Christian sources are clearly Celtic: Agricola mentions Calgacus 'the Swordsman' and Dio Cassius mentions Argentocoxos 'Silver Leg'. Claims that the Picts practised matrilineal kingship have been discredited by recent scholarship; their inheritance patterns appear essentially the same as those of their neighbours.[15]

Roman writers used the ethnonym 'Scotti' to refer to the Gaels as an ethnic group, regardless of whether they lived in Ireland or Britain.[16] According to Roman sources, Scotti and Picti acted in concert in attacking the Brythonic kingdoms in the south of Scotland and the Romans themselves as early as the third century. The Gaelic kingdom of Dál Riata emerged in the sixth century, joining a dynasty in Antrim to Gaelic settlements in Argyll. A tradition recorded in the tenth century claimed that Fergus mac Erc and his sons were the first Gaels to settle in Scotland after leaving Ireland *c.*AD 500, ruling a Gaelic population which was divided into three tribal territories: the Cenél nOengusa in Islay, the Cenél nGabráin in Kintyre, Gigha, Jura, Arran, and Cowal, and the Cenél Loairn in Lorn, Mull, Tiree, Coll and Ardnamurchan. Until recently this legend of Gaelic origins in Scotland has been taken by most historians as literal truth.

There is cause to doubt the claim that Gaelic only arrived in Scotland with these Irish colonists at this time, however; it is more likely that Gaels had been in Argyll for a considerable time longer. The chain of islands in Argyll form an archipelago between

Scotland and Ireland; the modern political boundaries that we impose around Scotland and Ireland now were probably insignificant then and no serious obstacle to travel. The archaeological evidence argues for a continuity of material culture in Argyll before and after Dál Riata, and no evidence of typically 'Irish' features suddenly appearing in the archaeological record. The legend of this late colonisation may have been promoted later in order to allow the Gaels of Scotland to share in the high cultural achievements of Ireland in the early medieval period and help to legitimate the Cenél nGabráin's rise to power.[17]

During the centuries of Gaelic–Pictish interaction, 'bilingualism' of the two varieties of Celtic languages must have been the norm, with a gradual shift from Pictish to Gaelic. Place names provide evidence for this linguistic transition. The Pictish element *aber-* was translated to Gaelic *inbhear-* in a number of place names and some place names in Scotland which were coined by Picts were translated (or transliterated) into Gaelic. Some Pictish terms borrowed into Gaelic demonstrate that distinctive administrative concepts from Pictish culture survived the linguistic shift. Ogham (an early script for writing on stones) inscriptions in Pictish territory record names which seem to become increasingly Gaelic.[18] Gaelic, as it is spoken in Scotland, bears the influences of the masses of Pictish speakers who learnt it as a second language.[19]

The capital of Scottish Dál Riata was Dunadd. Far from being a remote outpost in a backwater, excavations have shown it to be at the hub of an international trading route bringing luxury items from France and the Mediterranean. The peak of Dunadd, where its kings were inaugurated, commands an impressive view of a landscape rich in prehistoric monuments, emphasing the dynasty's roots in an ancient and glorious past. Gaelic, Pictish, and Anglo-Saxon nobility and their artisans mingled at Dunadd, making it one of the primary crucibles for the creation of the 'Insular' art style (see Plate 2).[20]

Colm Cille, better known as 'Columba' from the Latin form of his name, was a member of the most powerful kindred then in Ireland, the Uí Néill; his noble origins allowed him to play a powerful role in the church and in secular society. Columba and a group of his followers left northern Ireland and settled on the island of Iona in the 540s. Iona's location allowed access to Gaelic, Pictish, and Brythonic kingdoms; indeed, the clerics of Iona were to play prominent religious and political roles throughout the British Isles and beyond in the next several centuries. According to his biographer Adomnán, Columba presided over the inauguration of Aedán mac Gabráin, king of Dál Riata, in 574. If this claim is true and not just church propaganda, it would be the first Christian ordination of a king in Europe. In any case, it indicates an early recognition of the ties between religious and secular authority. Aedán's intention may have been to create ties to Columba's kindred in Ireland; Adomnán, on the other hand, was promoting the ideals of Christian kingship and the right of the church to be involved in the affairs of state. While there were many other missionaries in Scotland during the Age of the Saints, few were as influential as Columba and his successors. The figure of Columba continued to play a role in the inauguration of Scottish kings until the thirteenth century.[21]

Christianity deliberately sought to disenfranchise druids and defeat paganism, collaborating with political leaders to do so. Druidism as a religious institution was defunct in Ireland by the ninth century and not long afterwards in Scotland.[22] Christianity inevitably took on features of local culture and local scholars deliberately elevated the status of native learning and history to that of the Classical world. At the level of the common folk, the Celtic saints were a vital link between the old faith (paganism) and the new (Christianity). Some of the oldest surviving folklore in Gaelic oral tradition concerns the activities of the saints; the biographies of saints contain ample evidence of the affirmation of the power of Christianity by recourse to native Celtic beliefs and values. The cults of saints took over the sanctity and traditions of pre-Christian sites all around Scotland.

The development of secular society and the consolidation of political power in Scotland was heavily dependent upon the Christian church. As the intellectual heir of the Roman Empire and Classical learning, it provided learned professionals with the administrative and literary skills needed to build and run a sophisticated kingdom. Adomnán himself was a paragon of scholarly achievement: he and his disciples composed reference works that remained influential in Europe throughout the Middle Ages, including *Vitae Columbae* (the Life of Columba), *De Locis Sanctis* (a guide to Jerusalem), and *Collectio Canonum Hibernensis* (a collection of church laws). He also created the world's first international human rights treaty, *Cáin Adamnáin* (also known as 'The Law of Innocents'), which protected women, children and clergy from the ravages of warfare. It was ratified in 697 by over fifty Irish kings, the kings of the Picts, the king of Dál Riata, and the king of the Strathclyde Britons. This attests to the growing role of the Columban church in political affairs and its extensive territorial reach. Monks from Iona and other Gaelic centres of learning went even further afield, taking up positions in the courts of Charlemagne and other European rulers.

Dál Riata was not the only Scottish kingdom that Columba and his followers transformed: from the late seventh century, the Columban church played a central role in the efforts of the rulers of the Pictish kingdom of Fortriu to create a single, unified Pictish dynasty. The penetration of Gaels into the upper echelons of political and religious institutions accelerated the Gaelicisation of the Picts. Abernethy, probably the episcopal centre of the Pictish kings, was dedicated to St Brigit. Atholl, the power base of the Pictish kingdom, seems to have been teeming with Irish churchmen by the early eighth century; it contains an early concentration of Gaelic church names and stone sculpture of Ionan style. The Gaelic name for Atholl, *Ath-Fhodla* 'New Ireland', was recorded in 739. The fact that some 90 per cent of compound place names beginning with the Pictish element *pit-* 'parcel; estate' end in a Gaelic name or word suggests that Gaels became the élite in former Pictish territory and dominated land-holding.[23]

Pictish, Brythonic and Dál Riatic dynasties became entangled at an early stage: the 'Pictish' king Gartnait of the late sixth century may have been a Gael; three Britons from the kingdom of Strathclyde held the Pictish kingship between 631 and 653; by the eighth century many Pictish kings had Gaelic names and held Pictish and Dál Riatic kingships at the same time.[24]

Surviving annals first record the raids of the Vikings on exposed coastal monasteries and settlements in the 790s, although the Norse may have attacked northern parts of Scotland even earlier.[25] Continued Viking assaults across the British Isles brought about social turmoil and an almost complete reconfiguration of political structures. The kingdoms of Dál Riata and Northumbria collapsed in the chaotic conditions of the ninth century; the Picts of the far north seem to have been completely overrun and conquered by Norse invaders. The inland Pictish kingdom of Fortriu was exceptional in being relatively unscathed by Viking aggression.[26]

The kings of Gaelic Dál Riata and Pictish Fortriu joined forces in a massive battle against the Vikings in 839. They and their followers were defeated by the Norse and slaughtered in great numbers. During the ensuing civil war, a Gaelic warrior from the west, Cinaed mac Ailpín ('Kenneth MacAlpine' in English), seized the Pictish kingship *c.*AD 842 (he may have ruled Dál Riata for two years before that).[27] With Dál Riata beleaguered by the Vikings, Gaelic interests turned inland and eastward, away from the Norse threat. Cinaed transferred holy relics associated with Columba from Iona to Dunkeld, an ancient stronghold of the Picts; this act confirmed his territorial claims to Pictland and his commitment to the Columban church. Cinaed chose as his royal palace Forteviot, a location with the most impressive landscape of prehistoric monuments in eastern Scotland. This further signified his control of locations symbolic of Pictish sovereignty and his desire to be associated with the deep past of Pictland.[28]

Folkloric elements took the place of factual details as the Picts were Gaelicised and receded into the historical horizon.[29] The Irish tale 'Braflang Scóine' records that Cinaed mac Ailpín slaughtered the Pictish nobility during a banquet to which he invited them, but this is a retelling of a legend first recorded by Herodotus in the fifth century BC and reused in many later stories about peoples who were conquered and assimilated.[30] Later legends make them out to be brewers of heather ale, or small and secretive people, which again are folklore motifs commonly attached to the dim recollections of vanished peoples.

Important shifts in political power, dynastic pretensions and cultural perceptions are visible in the records of the ninth and tenth centuries. Domhnall mac Custantín (reign 889–900) was the first king whose Gaelic title *Rí Alban* signified his claim of a territorial entity divested of its previous connection with the Picts. The Gaelic-speaking population of this kingdom were referred to in contemporary sources as *Albanaig* or *fir Alban*: 'Presumably the Gaelic-speakers of "Scotland proper" in the tenth century were the first people to think of themselves as "Scots" in any way ancestral to today's sense.'[31]

The Gaelic dynasty of Cinaed mac Ailpín was secure in Pictish territories, but the Norse were settling the west coast and Hebrides, once in the orbit of Dál Riata, by the middle of the ninth century. Norse settlement was heavy enough in the Northern Isles to replace Pictish; most of the Western Isles and west of Scotland, on the other hand, seems to have retained some Gaelic population. Even so, the Outer Hebrides was renamed *Innse Gall* 'the Isles of Foreigners' due to the Norse there. Regardless, those who settled in the Irish sea province soon began to intermarry with Gaels and create a hybrid Gaelic-Norse culture described by the term *Gall-Ghàidheal* 'foreign Gael'.

The first Norse dynasty to dominate the Irish sea province was established by Ivar (†873); this ruling kindred, the Uí Ímair, formed a loose federation of lordships from the late ninth century and into the early tenth century which included the Outer Hebrides, Islay, the coast of Antrim, the Rhinns of Galloway, the Isle of Man, and Dublin. Even these ambitious Norse-descended kings needed the approval of their Gaelic peers: Olaf (*Amhlaibh Cuaran* in Gaelic), the king of Norse Dublin, rewarded a poet for a Gaelic eulogy sometime between 945 and 980 and was a supporter of the Columban church. When he died in 981, he was buried in Iona. The Gaelic language enjoyed a resurgence by the eleventh century as the descendants of the Norse assimilated to Gaelic linguistic and cultural norms.[32]

The Gall-Ghàidheal Somerled, married to the daughter of the king of the Isle of Man, first appears on record in 1140 with the title *regulus* 'king' of Kintyre. When in 1153 both David I (king of Scotland) and Amhlaibh, king of the Isle of Man, died, Somerled seized the opportunity to extend his rule and in 1158 he controlled territory from the north of Lewis to the south of Man. Despite his ancestry, Somerled has been remembered in oral tradition to the present day as the hero who liberated the Gaelic west from the Vikings.

After Somerled's death in 1164, his territories were fragmented between three of his sons and the sons of his brother-in-law, Godred son of Olaf of the Isle of Man. For several generations these leaders vied for supremacy and split nominal allegiances between the king of Norway and the king of Scotland. King Hakon of Norway mounted a naval expedition in 1263 to re-establish his control of the Hebrides, but failed. The last king of the Isle of Man died in 1265 and in 1266 Hakon's son Magnus signed the Treaty of Perth, which formally ceded the Hebrides to the Scottish kings. Apart from the Northern Isles and the tip of Caithness, the Norse were absorbed into Gaelic society and are remembered in Gaelic tradition by their own descendants only as the Other, the archetypal enemy.[33] Somerled's grandson Domhnall was the founder of Clan Donald, which became the ruling dynasty of the Lordship of the Isles.

THE HIGHLAND–LOWLAND DIVIDE

At the time of the Norman invasion in England, Gaelic was at its high-water mark across Scotland: it was the tongue of the courts of the king and most of the native élite; it was used by church clergy and national intelligentsia; it was spoken in communities in the south of Scotland, and even south of the Tweed.[34] The battle-cry of Scottish soldiers in 903, 918 and 1138 was '*Albanaigh, Albanaigh!*' (Gaelic for 'Scotsmen, Scotsmen!'). 'There can be little doubt that the prevailing ethos of the kingdom of Alba from the time of Kenneth mac Alpin to that of Malcolm Canmore was Gaelic.'[35]

From Cape Wrath to the Clyde–Forth line [. . .] was a land whose inhabitants, the Scots, were overwhelmingly Celtic, speaking almost universally the 'Scottish', e.g. the Gaelic, language, and observing social and religious customs that must be explained largely in Celtic terms.[36]

The Battle of Hastings in 1066 had repercussions throughout the British Isles, although the influence of the Anglo-Normans was spread in different ways in different places. In England, Ireland and Wales, the Anglo-Normans imposed their language and culture at sword-point. The situation in Scotland is more complex. Many English nobles refused to submit to William the Conqueror and some sought refuge in the Scottish court. King Malcolm III (also known as Malcolm Canmore, whose reign was 1058–93) married the young princess Margaret, daughter of Anglo-Saxon prince Edward and Hungarian princess Agatha; she had been exiled from England with her brother in 1072. While she did show some support for existing Gaelic institutions, Margaret disliked many practices she found in Scotland and attempted to alter them according to the cultural standards of her English and Continental background. She set a number of church reforms into motion, including the resettlement of Benedictine monks from Canterbury in Dunfermline.[37]

The floodgates of change opened dramatically under the rule of David I, the youngest son of Malcolm Canmore and Margaret. David had been raised as a hostage in the French-speaking court of Henry I, the son of William the Conquerer, and was said to have been a paragon of Norman knighthood. David had ruled as 'the prince of the Cumbrian region' (Strathclyde, Tweeddale and Teviotdale) during the reign of his older brother Alexander I, bringing new forms of secular and religious government into this area which he relied heavily upon after ascent to the Scottish throne in 1124.[38]

David introduced into Scotland a broad range of political, economic and religious reform that is neatly bundled up in the term *feudalism*. Feudalism is epitomised by the use of formal charters, the power of the knight, the building of castles, and the creation of centres granted specific commercial privileges. In theory, all land was owned by the king, who granted favoured vassals the right to occupy land in exchange for unswerving loyalty and military service. Throughout society, previous positions inherited through kinship were to be replaced by legal contract and formal appointment.

Previous generations of historians simplified 'feudalism' to imply a uniform set of prescribed cultural, economic and political norms. In fact, behind fixed feudal conventions in Europe lay a diverse set of social structures and practices. This was true for Scotland as well, as native traditions could be expressed in terms of 'feudal' concepts.[39] Rather than representing entirely new developments, the Anglo-Norman settlement intensified trends already under-way in Scotland: an English-speaking population in the south-east was established and growing, fixed settlements trading internationally were of increasing economic importance, church institutions were in the process of being reformed by mainstream, European religious orders, and the Scottish Crown had long been trying to monopolise power and downgrade regional leaders and national rivals.[40]

Some of the native Gaelic élite themselves were quick to adapt to David's innovations. The MacDuffs, a leading Gaelic kindred in the eleventh and twelfth centuries, were granted the earldom of Fife by David *c*.1136 as well as positions as national justiciars.[41] This may have encouraged other Gaelic leaders to accommodate themselves in the new order. In fact, up to the first War of Independence (*c*.1290), seven of the thirteen ancient earldoms of Scotland remained in the hands of native families, and four of the others had come into 'foreign' hands by marrying into native families.[42]

Nonetheless, the impact of the Anglo-Normans was significant. From David's reign to the end of the reign of Scottish king William I (1165–1214) the native élite in some areas were dispossessed in favour of incomers. Extensive grants to Anglo-Norman lords forming a circle around Galloway look like a deliberate strategy of containment. A similar pattern appears in the land grants of the firth of Clyde, controlling access to the Gaelic west, given to the Stewarts and others.[43]

The dominance of Anglo-Normans in Britain was not achieved solely through military might, but by the conspicuous display of the trappings of feudal culture in the royal courts of England and Scotland. The impact of the Anglo-Normans was greater than their numbers because they were associated with a cosmopolitan and international movement with political, social, economic, and religious dimensions which local élites aspired to emulate. Such was the vogue that an English chronicler remarked in the thirteenth century, probably over-emphatically, that 'more recent kings of Scots profess themselves to be rather Frenchmen, both in descent and in manners, language and culture; and after reducing the Scots to utter servitude, they admit only Frenchmen to their friendship and service'.[44]

The unity of Scotland in the twelfth century and the absolute authority of the descendents of king Malcolm Canmore should not be overstated: there was still a strong sense of regional identity and political independence in 'peripheral' lordships. While the 'Canmore kings' formed a network of alliances in the east, another network of relationships emerged in the west, centred around the Norse dynasty of the Isle of Man. The lineages of the Norse sea kings, Somerled of the Hebrides, Fergus of Galloway, and MacHeth of Ross, all of whom showed opposition of various forms to the Canmore dynasty, became entwined.[45]

The northern regions of Moray and Ross, then effectively frontiers outside of the control of the Canmore dynasty, were springboards for uprisings against them from the 1110s to 1230. In 1215 armies led by Domhnall Bàn MacWilliam, Kenneth MacHeth, and a son of a king of Ireland, invaded Moray as the first stage of an uprising against King Alexander II. A man named Ferchar Macintsacairt (in Old Gaelic), of whom we know little now, defeated the 'rebellion' and executed its leaders. Ferchar was the first Gaelic leader to serve the interests of the Scottish Crown in the north. By 1230, the king rewarded him for his loyalty by making him Earl of Ross, in turn extending royal authority and integrating the north into the mainstream of the kingdom.[46]

In the 1220s Ferchar settled Premonstratensian canons to the religious community in Ross at Mid-Fearn. This was not just an act of piety, but a statement about keeping pace with new ideas. The patronage of new monastic orders – Augustinians, Benedictines, Cistercians, Premonstratensians, and others – increased the status of local élite, projected their authority into new realms, and confirmed their interest in keeping up with developments in the wider world. It also had the consequence of demoting the prestige of native saints and traditions, introducing alien clergy with negative views of local culture, and strengthening the power and authority of the Scottish Crown in the area.

These effects have been documented in the role of the reformed monastic orders in the 'civilising' of Galloway. Galloway is named after the Gall-Ghàidheal who dominated the area; in fact, Gaelic-speaking communities may have survived there even into the late seventeenth or early eighteenth century. English writers from the Cistercian and Augustinian orders generally portrayed the people of Galloway as savage and barbaric. The utter destruction of the Galloway army at the Battle of the Standard (1138) reinforced the conceit that English civilisation – its moral standards and its military resources – were superior. Fergus (†1161), ruler of Galloway, began the establishment and patronage of new religious orders within his realm in 1142 by bringing monks from the abbey of Rievaulx (in Yorkshire) to Dundrennan.

Ailred (c.1110–1167), a Northumbrian who spent several years at the court of King David I before leaving c.1134 for the Cistercian monastery at Rievaulx Abbey, connected spiritual transformation with agricultural improvement. He linked David's godly leadership with the general well-being of the nation: 'a land uncultivated and barren [was made] pleasant and fruitful'. The Cistercians saw twelfth-century Europe as a wilderness that they would cultivate commercially and morally. The economic development which they promoted in Galloway further integrated it into southern Scotland and northern England, while at the same time giving the Scottish Crown cause to become more directly involved in local matters.[47]

The reformed orders in Galloway acted to strengthen the power and authority of the Scottish Crown in the region and to assimilate Galloway's aristocracy within four generations. The church's conquest of the 'primitive' aspects of native culture is graphically depicted by a thirteenth-century sculpture in the ruins of Dundrennan Abbey: an abbot with a partially concealed dagger looms over a kilted tribesman who he has partially disembowelled, pinning him down to the ground with his staff.

Economic reform was an aspect of feudalism that had long-lasting consequences. A *burgh* was a legal entity recognised by the king which privileged a community of burgesses with the right to trade and gave them exemption from toll charges throughout the kingdom. About fifteen burghs were founded during David's reign

(1124–53), largely populated by Flemish immigrants, and later, King William the Lion (reigned 1165–1214) granted the first burghal charters. Most Scottish burghs were in the south and east, where they had access to natural resources and sea routes where they could trade with the continent of Europe. By the mid fourteenth century burgesses had a place inside the Scottish Parliament alongside churchmen and the nobility, making them one of the 'three estates'.[48] The economic and political importance of burghs gave them a greater prestige than the Gaelic-speaking country-side. Besides coming to sell raw materials and buy finished products, Gaelic speakers came to the burghs for employment, not least because the high mortality rate in towns from disease, fires, and warfare kept the demand high.[49]

A language then called 'Inglis' by its speakers (but later called 'Scots') emerged from the admixture of earlier Anglo-Saxon settlements, the Flemish mercantile class, Anglo-Norman élite, and Northern English dependants who were brought in during the 'feudal' reform. The use of Inglis for commerce and administration in the burghs enabled its spread through Lowland Scotland at the expense of Gaelic. These processes are illustrated in a study of linguistic change in thirteenth-century Fife. Most of Fife was Gaelic-speaking in the twelfth century. Incoming Anglo-Normans accrued economic and political advantages, which caused Inglis to displace Gaelic around the area of their settlement:

> As a burgh, Crail was the centre of a new mercantile economy, with its necessary nucleus of administrators, clerks, traders, merchants and others, most of whom will have had their roots not among the local families of Fife, but elsewhere, among Scots speakers or further afield. [. . .] Many of these folk, and the community as a whole, will have had a higher economic status, and perhaps social status, than the Gaelic-speaking communities around them.[50]

Despite Anglo-Norman settlement and the diffusion of English, many Gaelic influences survived in the Lowlands, sometimes from later borrowings during centuries of coexistence. This is well illustrated in the realm of legal terminology and practices in Scotland. Scots law incorporates concepts and procedures which are inherited from Celtic law. Assythment, the system of compensation for wounding or slaughter, survived at least into the fifteenth century in national law and may have even survived in nineteenth-century Fife at a community level. A number of Scots terms for social offices and practices come from Gaelic, such as 'tocher' meaning 'dowry' from Gaelic *tochradh*, 'dewar' meaning 'keeper of relics' from Gaelic *deòradh*, and 'cain' meaning 'tax' from Gaelic *càin*.[51] Ossianic stories and characters, moreover, were well known in the medieval Lowlands and appear in Scots literature such as Barbour's *The Bruce* (1376) and Sir David Lindsay's *Ane Satyre of the Thrie Estatis* (*c.*1540).[52] Goll mac Morna, one of the better-known Ossianic heroes in the Lowlands, appears as the place name Gowmacmorran in Carnwath, Lanarkshire.[53] Hector Boece (*c.*1527) wrote that Fionn mac Cumhaill was a Scotsman 'of quhome ar mony vulgar [i.e., popular] fabillis amang us, nocht unlike to thir fabillis that ar rehersit of King Arthure'.

The Scottish Crown did not yet interfere with the internal affairs of regions if they did not pose any obvious threat, allowing even the élite in many areas to maintain Gaelic traditions. The Kennedys of Dunure in Carrick, for example, maintained Gaelic social practices and titles into at least the mid fifteenth century without disapproval of the king.[54]

The acculturation of personal identities went both ways. Anglo-Normans assimilated in areas where Gaelic culture remained strong. Many of the large clans of the Highlands, such as the Grants, the Menzies, the Chisholms, the Murrays, the Frasers, and the Stewarts, were founded by Anglo-Normans who married into Gaelic communities and had to assimilate to local culture to be accepted by their dependants.

Other than wholesale displacement and replacement of people, change throughout Scotland would likely have seemed gradual. The consequences, however, were such that Lowland Scotland was being assimilated into Anglophone culture and becoming estranged from its Gaelic origins. By the late fourteenth century, Scotland became polarised into two cultural and geographical zones – Highland and Lowland – whose inhabitants viewed each other with suspicion and hostility. The irony of these stereotypes was already apparent in 1390 when the host of the 'Wolf of Badenoch' attacked and burnt Elgin Cathedral: they were described as 'wyld, wikkit, heland men', despite the fact that the Wolf was the son of Robert II, Scotland's first Stewart king, and caused as much destruction to Highland communities as Lowland.[55]

THE LORDS OF THE ISLES

After the line of Gaelic kings came to an end in 1290 with the death of Margaret the Maid of Norway, the sole surviving descendant of Alexander, Scotland was ruled by elected Guardians who asked King Edward I of England for advice in choosing between a number of competitors. Edward was determined to become overlord of Scotland. Attempts to resist English domination were defeated and the regalia that symbolised Scotland's identity as a nation, including the Stone of Destiny – items which originated in the nation's Gaelic past – were taken to England. In 1297 a popular rising aimed at restoring the kingdom was under way. Wallace and Murray were the acknowledged leaders, though it is significant that the MacDuffs, Scotland's premier native nobility, joined the cause.[56]

Battles over Scottish sovereignty rumbled on for decades. The most celebrated hero of these efforts was Robert Bruce. Although the Bruces were a feudal Anglo-Norman family, Robert's mother was of the native Gaelic nobility of Carrick. He was fostered in boyhood with a prominent Irish nobleman. His commitment to the Gaelic identity of the Scottish kingdom was manifest in his harnessing the Gaelic symbols of nationhood, such as the reliquary associated with Saint Columba, the *Brecbennach* (see Plate 3), and Saint Fillan's Bell. Bruce was installed as King of Scots in 1306 at the traditional site of Scone but soon was forced into exile in the Gaelic west. One of his main supporters during this crisis was Aonghus Òg of Islay, the head of the Clan Donald and the great-great-grandson of Somerled, specifically mentioned at the Battle of Bannockburn in Barbour's epic poem *The Bruce*:

> And of Argile and of Kentyre,
> And of the Ilis, quharoff wes syre
> Angus of Ile, and But, all tha.

Origin legends are often created, and fulfil their purposes most effectively, during times of crisis. The English occupation of Scotland, and Scottish attempts to regain political independence, spurred on intellectual efforts to justify Scottish sovereignty. At least two legends of the origins of the Scots produced in the late thirteenth century by reworking earlier materials underscored not only a common identity with the Irish but a continued sense that Ireland was still the ancestral homeland. This reflects the consciousness of the Gaelic origins of Scotland's élite rulers and culture, as well as the prestige of Ireland as a centre of learning to which Scots wanted to maintain a connection. It was not until Baldred Bisset's *Pleading* (1301) that origin legends begin to make Scotland, rather than Ireland, the homeland of the Scots.[57]

The 'Letter from the Barons of Scotland to Pope John XXII' (1320), also known as the 'Declaration of Arbroath', was taken to Rome to convince the Pope, as an arbiter of disputes throughout Christendom, to recognise Robert Bruce's claim of kingship and the right of Scotland to be an independent nation. It emphasised the ancient lineage of the Scottish kingdom by naming Bruce as the 113th king and by recounting the success of the Gaels in conquering previous inhabitants and invaders:[58]

> We know, and from the chronicles and books of the ancients we find, that among other famous nations our own, the Scots, has been graced with widespread renown [. . .] The Britons they first drove out, the Picts they utterly destroyed, and, even though very often assailed by the Norwegians, the Danes and the English, they took possession of that home with many victories and untold efforts; and, as the historians of old time bear witness, they have held it free of all bondage ever since.

Robert Bruce required Scottish lords to relinquish lands that they held in England and he forfeited the lands held by those who had not been loyal to him. Aonghus Òg, the leader of Clan Donald, was rewarded with lands in Lochaber previously held by the Comyns; Duncan Campbell was given lands in Argyll previously held by the MacDougalls. Aonghus' marriage to the Irish princess Áine Ní Chatháin brought a retinue of warriors and learned men who came as her 'dowry' (referred to in Gaelic as *tochradh nighean a' Chathanaich*).[59] From the late thirteenth century onwards, Irish leaders, especially in their resistance to English conquest, recruited heavily from the warriors of the Highlands and Islands, the *gall-óglaigh* (English 'galloglasses').[60]

Eòin (English 'John') inherited the Clan Donald leadership in 1325 and was granted Lewis and Harris by King David II in 1343. His first wife, Àine, was the female heir of Clan Ruairi, whose territories of Knoydart, Moidart, Uist, and Rum came into his possession through her in 1346. In 1350 Eòin left Àine and married Margaret Stewart, daughter of Robert Stewart. He had assumed the title *Dominus Insularum* 'Lord of the Isles' by 1336[61] and in 1376 he received Knapdale and Kintyre from his father-in-law, who had become King Robert II. Eòin and Clan Donald, through marriage and political involvement, were now firmly ensconced in the upper echelons of the Scottish kingdom.

The Lordship of the Isles created, in effect, a 'Gaelic Scotland' in miniature, an infrastructure for Gaelic culture after the Scottish court and Lowlands had become estranged from it. Not only did this subkingdom extend, in its prime, to nearly the entire west coast of Scotland and into the north of Ireland, but its armies could rival those commanded by the Crown itself. The Lordship was most important in its role in maintaining a stable and peaceful order under which traditional culture could flourish. The rejuvenation of Iona, the choice of Columba as patron saint, and its inaugural rites all reflect a pan-Gaelic ethos. The Lordship provided patronage for hereditary classes of literati, lawmen, musicians, artisans and medical doctors, often importing them directly from Ireland, reinvigorating the Gaelic intelligentsia in Scotland, and establishing families of learned professionals which lasted in some cases into the eighteenth century. The success of the Lordship is physically demonstrated by the proliferation of noble residences without defensive fortifications and the restoration of monastic sites.[62]

Domhnall inherited the Lordship from his father in about 1387. In the 1390s his younger brother Eòin Mór married Margery Bisset, heiress of the Glens of Antrim, establishing Clann Eòin Mhóir (called 'the MacDonnells of Antrim' or 'Clan Donald South' in English) in the north-east of Ireland. Both Scottish and English kings attempted to exploit this link between Scottish and Irish Gaeldom in their efforts to dominate the British Isles. Kings Richard II and Henry IV acknowledged the legitimacy of Clann Eòin Mhóir's feudal claims in Antrim, seeing them as a possible tool for restoring English rule as well as a back door into Scotland.

Domhnall married Mariotta Leslie, the daughter of the Earl of Ross. The Duke of Albany, Robert Stewart, was the ruthless regent of Scotland while James I was held prisoner in England. The Duke claimed the Earldom of Ross for his son, attempting to maximise his own control of Scotland. In 1411 Domhnall chose 6,000 of his best warriors and marched into Aberdeenshire to press his wife's better claims to Ross, battling the forces of the Earl of Mar (his first cousin) at Harlaw. Both sides were said to have endured heavy losses and the outcome was unclear, but in 1412 Domhnall paid obeisance to the duke. His son Alasdair inherited the Lordship on his death in 1422.

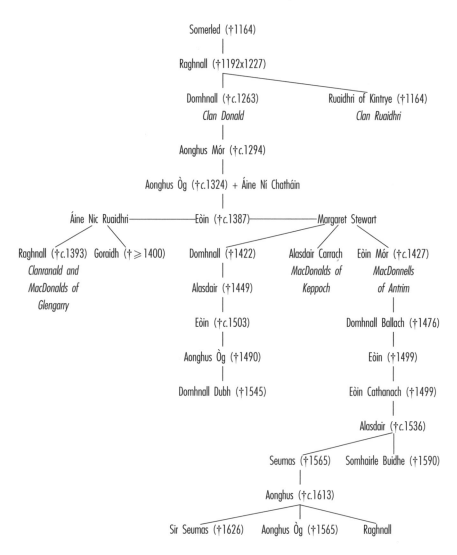

Figure 1.3: Some descendants of Somerled[63]

James I finally returned to Scotland in 1424 with his English wife and aspired to centralise control in the monarchy as much as possible, particularly by reducing the power of regional lordships. He called a meeting of chieftains from the Highlands and Islands in the royal burgh of Inverness, which was a pretext for capturing and imprisoning Alasdair. James promised to release him if he would relinquish the Lordship in return for being a member of the king's courtiers. Instead, Alasdair escaped, burnt the royal burgh and attacked Inverness Castle. James, in turn, forced Alasdair to surrender and imprisoned him again. Clan Donald did not back down, however. In 1431 Clan Donald warriors, led by Domhnall Ballach of Antrim, defeated the king's forces at Inverlochy under the Earl of Mar and by the mid 1430s Alasdair was restored to his former title and lands, confirmed as Earl of Ross, and was granted the Isle of Skye in addition. Attempts to master Ross, however, brought the Lords of the Isles into conflict with others and drew their attention away from their Hebridean heartlands.[64]

Eòin inherited the Lordship in 1449 but was a poor leader. He married Elizabeth Livingston, daughter of Lord James, whose family was close to the Douglases. In 1452, King James II of Scotland murdered Earl William Douglas, sending his brother James into exile in England. In 1462 King Edward IV of England planned to invade Scotland and made a pact with Eòin, his cousin Domhnall Ballach of Antrim, Domhnall Ballach's son Eòin and the exiled James Douglas to divide and rule Scotland between them as subjects of the English crown. The 'Ardtornish–Westminster treaty' came to naught, but when King James III finally learnt of it in 1475, he demoted Eòin to a lord of Parliament and forfeited him of the territories of Ross, Knapdale and Kintyre. The Clan Donald star began to wane.[65]

LINN NAN CREACH AND THE STEWARTS

Eòin's son Aonghus Òg rallied a portion of Clan Donald around him, in defiance of his father and King James' reduction of their status. Although Aonghus and his men managed to challenge the king's authority and troops, he was assassinated in 1490. His cousin, Alasdair of Lochalsh, inherited the now fragmented Lordship, but after raiding in Ross, James IV declared the entire Lordship forfeit in 1493. Deteriorating conditions grew worse, with the power vacuum unleashing the latent rivalries between clans, heralding the era known as Gaelic as *Linn nan Creach* 'The Era of Plundering and Chaos'. Parliament noted in 1504 that 'thair hes bene greit abusioun of Justice in the north partis and west partis of the realm sic as the north Ilis and south Ilis. And therethrough, the pepill ar almaist gane wild.'[66]

Clan Donald's adversaries gained from their losses. Archibald Campbell, the second Earl of Argyll, was appointed lieutenant of the former territory of the Lords of the Isles in 1500, and from 1514 to 1633 the office of Justice General (the chief judge in criminal court) was inherited by successive Campbells of Argyll. Gordon of Huntly's estates were extended into the upper Spey Valley and into Lochaber in the 1500s, where he came into frequent dispute with Clan Chattan and the Mackintoshes, who had held their lands under Clan Donald. Meanwhile, disaffected Hebrideans began migrating to Antrim after the 1475 debacle, spilling into neighbouring regions and consolidating the control of Clann Eòin Mhóir.

Scottish affairs were particularly ill-managed between the death of James IV at the Battle of Flodden in 1513 and the ascension of James VI in 1587: three successive infants inherited the throne, with thirty-three years when the sovereign was a minor. The powers invested in agents of the Scottish Crown in the Highlands were blatantly abused, either with the tacit approval or neglect of king and his council. The Crown freely exercised its powers of eviction, thereby adding to social disruption and the number of 'broken' (landless) men resorting to mercenary activity. The way in which the central government executed its system of justice in the Highlands encouraged the perpetuation of enmities and feuds: afflicted parties were rewarded with 'Letters of Fire and Sword', allowing them to exact vengeance for damages done rather than seeking effective redress or resolution of underlying issues. Nor were there effective civil institutions to administer and enforce law equitably. Agents such as Campbell of Argyll could provoke a criminal response amongst rival clans and then use his position as Justice General to punish them and reward himself with their territory. In short, the 'lawlessness' of the Highlands was as much a matter of inept government policies as the inherent nature of the Gaelic society itself.[67]

> The power of successive earls of Huntly in the north was such that they could play clans off against each other, inciting disturbance or instigating reconciliation when necessary to heighten their position both in the locality and at court. [. . .] The very act of de-militarisation actually drove the clan into a series of military alliances in search of protection and back again, therefore, into the fold of the traditional martial Gaelic mainstream.[68]

When in 1528 King James V came to power, he aimed to curb the growing power of Colin Campbell, Earl of Argyll, by nullifying all previous charters in the Gaelic west. This instead incurred the ire of the MacDonalds; Campbell's enthusiasm for suppressing their revolt confirmed James' fears of his excessive ambition. By 1531 James had replaced Colin with Alasdair of Antrim as his chief authority in the Gaelic west and restored most clan lands in Kintyre and Islay. James also encouraged Clann Eòin Mhóir to maximise their power in Ulster, seeing them as a means of striking at English interests in Ireland.[69]

In early 1539 rumour had it that King James would invade Ireland with a Hebridean army and that the French would attack England simultaneously. Clann Eòin Mhóir and their Irish allies raised what was said to have been the largest force ever seen in Ireland; they attacked the area under English control ('the Pale') in advance of James' arrival. The Gaelic troops were surprised by English Lord Deputy Grey near Carrickmacross, however, and the invasion was aborted. Vexed by matters in Ireland and further unrest and dissent in the Hebrides that year, James became more forceful in the Gaelic west and returned the Campbells to favour.

The remnants of the Lords of the Isles revolted at least seven times after 1493 in efforts to restore their former power. In 1545 Domhnall Dubh, the son of Aonghus Òg by the daughter of the Earl of Argyll, recruited many of the former families of the Lordship to join him, raising an army of as many as 8,000 warriors and entering into a pact with King Henry VIII of England. They sailed to Ireland in some 180 galleys but, after much delay, Domhnall Dubh died without an heir in November. Domhnall Gorm of Sleat hoped to exploit tensions between King James VI and Queen Elizabeth of England in 1598, claiming the title of Lord of the Isles and reminding the queen of the 'favour and friendship shown by the queen's predecessors to his predecessors the Lords of the Isles'. Branches of Clan Donald vied with each other in hopes of regaining supremacy into the seventeenth century, but while Campbell chieftains profited from their favourable relations with the Edinburgh establishment, Clan Donald's poor relations with the Scottish Crown left them to curry favour with the English.[70]

During the sixteenth century the Scottish Crown became more organised, intrusive and demanding, seeking new ways to exert its control and to extract taxes and loyalty directly from subjects. King James VI fashioned a monarchy even more powerful than that of his forefathers. He explicitly stated his divine right over both church and state, and devised new rituals for the Scottish Parliament and Lords which represented his position over them. To fund his grand schemes, James sought greater income from his realm and became convinced that the Highlands contained untapped sources of wealth.[71]

By 1585 the Scottish burghs were sending ships to waters on the northern and western seaboard, already in competition with the king's own efforts to exploit the 'fishing of the Ilis'. Highlanders retaliated against the unsanctioned extraction of wealth from their coasts, but numerous complaints recorded in the Register of the Privy Council convey no motivation for these reactions other than Gaelic habits of savagery and plunder. Most of the Gaelic magnates controlling waters of the north-west – MacKenzie of Kintail, MacDonald of Sleat, MacLeod of Lewis, MacLeod of Coigeach, MacLeod of Assynt, and others – were denounced as rebels in 1586 for merely charging Lowland fishermen with the fees to which they were entitled by Scots law for landing, anchorage, and the use of storage. The Highland chieftains may have had better business dealings with Dutch fishermen, but the Scottish burghs strongly opposed the Earl of Seaforth's attempt to work with the Dutch in 1629.[72]

In 1597 King James VI summoned the Highland élite to come to Edinburgh and show proof of their land titles. This was an early step in an increasingly aggressive campaign to change chieftains from being warlords in a kin-based society to landlords and merchants, replacing oral agreements, local consumption, and customary dues with written records, a cash economy, and normalised economic transactions.[73] The extraction of wealth from the Highlands, it was determined, would happen with or without the cooperation of the Highland élite; in the same year the Parliament passed an act to create burghs in the Highlands as outposts 'of ciuilitie and polecie' in Kintyre, Lochaber and Lewis. Plans in Lochaber came to naught. In Kintyre, the Campbells directed the gradual development of Campbeltown during the 1600s, particularly by importing Lowlanders and explicitly excluding the ability of Mac-Donalds, MacLeans, MacLeods, MacAlasdairs or MacNeills to obtain leases.[74]

King James' book *Basilikon Doron* (1599) expressed his disdain of Gaels and his desire that the isles of Scotland be planted with 'colonies among them of answerable inland subjects, that within short time may reform and civilize the best inclined among them: rooting out or transporting the barbarous and stubborn sort, and planting civility in their rooms'. In 1598 a company of ten Lowland gentlemen, the 'Fife Adventurers', were given a grant to colonise Lewis, subjugate its inhabitants and create a fishing centre in Stornoway. Apartheid was part of the scheme: 'Na marriage or uther particular freindschip to be any of the societie, without consent of the haill, with any Hyland man.' The plan was seen as useful for the subjugation of Ireland as well.[75]

The Campbells continued to manipulate rivalries and social disruption to their advantage. In December 1578 Lachlann Maclean complained that Campbell of Argyll was encouraging Clann Eòin Mhóir to attack them. Campbell was granted commissions of fire and sword in 1593, 1596 and 1601 against the MacGregors, who had acted as their 'shock-troops' when they had expanded into Perthshire. After the Battle of Glen Fruin in February 1603, a short distance from the Highland–Lowland line, the Clan Gregor were outlawed and the Campbells encouraged to apprehend them. Alasdair MacGregor of Glenstrae, before his execution in 1604, claimed that Argyll had tried to persuade him to murder Campbell of Ardkinglass; Argyll probably also encouraged MacGregor's attack on Colquhoun in 1603. In late 1603 Aonghus MacDonald of Clann Eòin Mhóir and Eachann Maclean of Duart were ordered to surrender their strongholds to Campbell of Argyll; a month later, Campbell had a commission of fire and sword against them, which stated that they were 'void of the fear and knowledge of God, delighting in nothing but murder and a savage form of living'.[76]

Little wonder, then, that many clans held animosity against the Campbells and that leaders became increasingly distraught; acts of desperation, however, were generally seen as further proof of their barbarity. King James ascended to the English throne in 1603 and continued his efforts to 'tame' the Gaels. On 8 December 1608 he gave two reasons to the Commission to Improve the Isles for launching a new phase of 'daunting the Isles':

> First, in the case we have of planting the Gospel among these rude, barbarous and uncivil people, the want whereof these years past no doubt has been to the great hazard of many poor souls being ignorant of their own salvation. Next, we desire to remove all such scandalous reproaches against Scotland, in suffering a part of it to be possessed with such wild savages, void of God's fear and our obedience, and herewith the loss we have in not receiving the due rents endebted to us from those isles, being of the patrimony of that, our crown.[77]

The colonisation of Ulster drove a wedge between Irish and Scottish Gaeldom. While the MacLeods of Lewis resisted several attempts of the 'Fife Adventurers' to extirpate them, the threat of overwhelming force from a king who could now command the resources of three kingdoms (Scotland, Ireland and England) loomed over others. In August 1608, Lord Ochiltree (Andrew Stewart) kidnapped leading members of the Hebridean élite and held them in the Lowlands while they negotiated with the Commission for the Isles on the terms of their release. In the early summer of 1609, Andrew Knox, Bishop of the Isles, took the results to King James in London and was commissioned for a new expedition to further the accords. Two important documents were produced in Iona in late August 1609, now often called the 'Statutes of Iona'.

There is little reason to doubt that the Hebridean élite were involved in their wording and intent. King James expected that subjugation and colonisation would be necessary for the reformation of the isles; Bishop Knox sought a compromise which would allow the élite to remain in place, as obedient subjects of the king and agents of the central government who would transform society from the inside. The Statutes of Iona reflect the interests of native Gaelic leaders to retain power and privilege in their territories. They focus on social and economic reform, with both chieftains and king to profit from the proceeds. On 28 September 1609, the day on which Bishop Knox presented the documents to the council, an embargo on the sale of cattle and horses between the Hebrides and Argyll – which the chiefs said had prevented them from being able to pay their rents – was lifted. The Statutes worked well for the next several years, with clan chiefs appearing regularly before the council and paying rents.[78]

That the embargo was lifted when the Statutes were recognised by the council suggests that it had been meant to punish them in the past, but that the cooperation of the chieftains now made them unnecessary. The author and enactor of the embargo could have been none other than Campbell of Argyll, who used his legal and political influence to strangle his competitors economically. The Statutes were likely crafted to benefit the Hebridean élite who had been excluded by Campbell's jealous monopoly. Argyll thus had an interest in bringing about the downfall of this settlement.[79]

In 1603 Aonghus MacDonald of Clann Eòin Mhóir handed his eldest son Sir Seumas MacDonald over to Campbell of Auchinbreck, having fallen out with him and renounced him as heir. Sir Seumas was imprisoned. Before his death in late 1612 or early 1613, Aonghus relinquished Islay; although Campbell of Cawdor attempted to appropriate it, a short-term lease was instead given to Sir Raghnall MacDonnell of Antrim (Aonghus' cousin). By March 1613, island inhabitants were complaining of Sir Raghnall's handling of affairs and in March 1614 Aonghus' illegitimate son Raghnall seized Dunyveg Castle, which Bishop Knox had left with a small government force. Shortly thereafter Aonghus Òg (Sir Seumas' younger brother) recaptured the castle and asked the government for clemency for offences committed in the process. Bishop Knox landed in Islay in September with a small force that was soon outnumbered, surrendering his son and nephew as hostages while he returned with Aonghus Òg's request to be given possession of Dunyveg Castle and for the lease of Islay to go to himself instead of Sir Raghnall of Antrim. Then, and later, Aonghus Òg claimed to have acted according to the advice of Campbell of Argyll, who would have wanted to limit Sir Raghnall's expansion as well as the success of Bishop Knox and the Statutes of Iona. Those already distrustful of the MacDonalds saw Sir Raghnall's expansion from Antrim into Islay as a reassertion of MacDonald claims and Bishop Knox's additional appointment in Raphoe as reconnecting, rather than disconnecting, pan-Gaelic interests. On 22 October Bishop Knox was dismissed from his role in the affair and Campbell of Cawdor was granted a commission of fire and sword against Dunyveg. On 21 November he was granted a lease of Islay and by early 1615 he had defeated Aonghus and sent him and five of his followers to Edinburgh for execution.[80]

Meanwhile, by October Sir Seumas was proposing his own solution to the crisis, including migrating his kin to Ireland. His offers were ignored, and fearing imminent execution, he escaped from prison in May 1615 with the help of some leading MacDonalds. He began recruiting warriors from MacDonald territories for a rising to regain Islay; that the only signatory of the Statutes to join was MacDuffie of Colonsay, a long-time vassal of Clan Donald, demonstrated the commitment of the Hebridean élite to the Iona contracts. Many rank-and-file MacDonalds joined Sir Seumas, however, and in June he drove the Campbells from Islay and furthered his position of strength by sending forces to Jura and Kintyre. For several months, his troops reoccupied the former territories of Clann Eòin Mhóir. Campbell of Argyll was assigned by the government to orchestrate the reprisal with the aid of two English warships. In September Campbell's forces routed the MacDonalds, carried out executions of 'rebels', sent Sir Seumas into exile in Spain, and claimed ownership of Islay.[81]

From the view of Edinburgh and London the rising of Clann Eòin Mhóir seemed to offer further proof of the intransigence of islanders and the necessity of dealing harshly with them. The remaining Hebridean chieftains who had signed the Statutes of Iona were called before the council on 26 July 1616 to sign an even more stringent bond retrenching and extending the aims of the Statutes of Iona, each acting as guarantor for the lawful obedience of the others. The previous conciliatory tone was replaced by fiercely anti-Gaelic rhetoric which, amongst other things, required them to send their children to schools on the mainland where they were to be taught English. Later that year the Privy Council recrafted the text in an effort to apply the same principles of assimilation to education throughout Scotland.[82]

> Forasmuch as the King's Majesty, having a special care and regard that the true religion be advanced and established in all the parts of this Kingdom, and that all his Majesty's subjects, especially the youth, be exercised and trained up in civility, godliness, knowledge, and learning, that the vulgar English tongue be universally planted, and the Irish language, which is one of the chief and principal causes of the continuance of the barbarity and incivility amongst the inhabitants of the Isles and Highlands, may be abolished and removed; and whereas there is no measure more powerful to further his Majesty's principal regard and purpose than the establishing of schools in the particular parishes of this Kingdom where the youth may be taught at least to write and read, and be catechised and instructed in the grounds of religion.[83]

Thus, by 1616, the mechanisms intended to assimilate the Gaelic élite were in place, even if they did not complete their task until after the Jacobite Rising of 1745–6. Between being educated in English in the Lowlands, frequent and extended sojourns outside of their home territories, and mounting debt, Gaelic chieftains increasingly compromised the social contract of clanship.

JACOBITES, HANOVERIANS AND RELIGION

A national court for the reformed church in Scotland, the General Assembly, was established in 1560. Where conversion to Protestantism in Gaelic areas occurred, it was largely due to the personal choice of clan chiefs. A few, like Campbell of Argyll, were early converts who lent the crucial support to make the operation of Protestantism in the Highlands possible.

Although James VI had been subtly promoting the Episcopalian form of Protestantism throughout his new United Kingdom, his son and successor Charles I was far more aggressive. In 1638, the National Covenant was signed by leaders agreeing to defend the king himself but to oppose his pro-Episcopalian policies. A Covenanting army marched into England and forced the king to accept the Scottish Parliament's abolition of Episcopalianism and the right of Parliament to challenge the king's authority. In this flux of authority, the Gaels of Ulster attacked British colonists in 1641, aiming to regain control of Ulster and the English colony of Dublin and build a 'Catholic Confederacy' which could demand religious rights. Alasdair mac Colla Chiotaich, whose father had been one of the leaders of the rising of Clann Eòin Mhóir, joined the insurgence.

The Scottish Covenanters entered into a Solemn League and Covenant with the English republicans in 1643. The rising in Ulster joined the king's Royalists when Alasdair mac Colla led an army from Ireland to Scotland. Under the leadership of Alasdair and James Graham, Marquis of Montrose, the Royalists won battles and terrorised Campbell lands for over a year. When their army was finally defeated, King Charles gave himself up to Scottish Covenanters. They handed him over to the English Parliament when he rejected their demand to make Presbyterianism the religion of England and was executed in 1649. As the reign of Cromwell began military garrisons at Fort William and Inverness were built. The sustained conflict between Covenanters and Royalists escalated the intensity and scale of warfare in Gaeldom. It sowed bitter division between clans as they were inexorably drawn into British politics and forced to choose sides. The news of these violent clashes reinforced the stereotype of Highlanders as rebellious, bloodthirsty savages.[84]

The eighth Earl (and first Marquis) of Argyll, an ardent Covenanter, was beheaded for treason when Charles II was restored to the monarchy in 1660. It came, then, as a bitter disappointment to the majority of Highland clans, who had been loyal to the king, that the restored regime did not reward them for their loyalty but instead gave its support again to the house of Argyll, who continued territorial expansion. In 1662 the

Scottish Parliament restored bishops to the national church and the authority of the Crown over them. Charles II, who had no interest in Scotland, suppressed the dissension of committed Presbyterians.

When Charles II died in 1685, his Roman Catholic brother James VII succeeded him. James fled to France in 1689 to escape growing hostility to Catholicism; those who continued to support his claim to the throne (and those of his descendants) were called 'Jacobites'. His son-in-law Prince William of Orange took the throne through his marriage to James' daughter Mary. As part of the 1690 revolution settlement, the Presbyterian Church became the national Church of Scotland (albeit tied to the political interests of the London government). Ministers in Scotland were required to demonstrate their loyalty by praying publicly and explicitly for William and Mary, and in 1693 ministers were additionally required to take an oath of assurance which acknowledged the right of William and Mary to the Crown. Most bishops were unwilling to take these pledges, however, and instead maintained their loyalty to the Stewart kings, proving effective propagandists for the Jacobite cause.

The Established Church made renewed efforts to win the Highlands for Presbyterianism, the Williamite reign, and the English language. In 1646 the General Assembly passed a resolution to implement the provision of the Statutes of Iona calling for an English-language school in every parish. One of William's first acts was to force Highland tenants to pay unpaid rents for the 'erecting of English schools for rooting out the Irish language, and other pious uses'.[85] The General Assembly passed an Act in 1699 to supply all Highland parishes with Gaelic-speaking ministers, who were in very short supply. Although Gaelic was recognised as necessary for missionary activity – and the fear of the Counter-Reformation played no small part in making Protestantism make such concessions – it was clearly the long-term goal to supplant it with English.[86] In 1709 the Society in Scotland for Propagating Christian Knowledge (SSPCK) was established in order to expedite the Act of 1696, which restated the 1646 Act but required that Highland tenants themselves fund the schools. It considered the Highlands a foreign missionary field inhabited by people 'who live in great barbarity and ignorance'.[87]

The Act of Union amalgamated the English and Scottish parliaments in 1707. Disaffection for the policies of the Crown and the London government came to a head on the death of Queen Anne in 1714 and the arrival of George of Hanover to take her place. Shouts of 'God save the King' by burgh officials in Inverness were overpowered by the popular response 'God damn them and their King'. The Jacobites seized the opportunity for a Rising, one which many thought would succeed. The Earl of Mar gathered twenty-six clan chiefs to Braemar under the pretence of a deer hunt in 1715 and raised the banner for exiled King James. The response was, however, mixed. Few of the western clans came and splits within clans were detrimental. Even the Clan Campbell was divided between sides. A stalemate on Sheriffmuir came two months later. Some Jacobites who participated in the Rising had their estates forfeited to the York Buildings Company and some fled into exile for safety. General Wade was appointed commander in Scotland in 1725, building military garrisons and roads to facilitate Hanoverian control of the Highlands.[88]

There are few episodes in Scottish history with as varying and hotly contested interpretations as the Jacobite Rising of 1745–6. Jacobitism was a complex phenomenon with political, religious and cultural dimensions. Each segment of society engaged with it in different, and sometimes contradictory, ways. Jacobitism in Scotland was fuelled in part by national pride in the royal lineage of the Stewarts. Jacobite propagandists interpreted Scotland's travails as the result of the usurpation of the throne by foreign kings. The 1707 Act of Union had negative repercussions in Scotland in the years immediately following and Scottish Jacobitism stated as an express aim the repeal of the union and reinstatement of the Scottish Parliament. Many clans saw Jacobitism as a means of restoring the losses they had suffered from the expansionism of the Campbells. Scottish Gaels as a whole saw the potential of being restored to their rightful place within Scotland by being instrumental in the restoration of their ancestral king.[89]

Knowing that the Highland clans offered the only viable military force available, Charles Edward Stewart and his supporters attempted to appeal to Gaelic sensibilities and aspirations, such as the declaration read at Glenfinnan at the outset of the 1745 Jacobite Rising:

> Having always borne the most constant affection to our ancient kingdom of Scotland, from whence we derive our royal origin [. . .] we cannot but behold with the deepest concern the miseries they suffer under a foreign usurpation [. . .] We further declare that we will with all convenient speed call a free parliament [. . .] so the nation may be restored to that honour, liberty, and independence, which it formerly enjoyed.

Some clan chieftains had been chastised into submission to the Hanoverian line after the 1715 Rising and many had by now become deeply invested in the empire with too much at stake to risk another forfeiture. Many of their followers, however, came out independently to fight for the prince. Amongst the notes of optimism from Gaelic oral tradition of the period are also severe doubts and trepidation.[90] The government army deliberately targeted civilians and domestic property to distract and discourage Jacobite soldiers, brutalising the Highland population in violation of contemporary European conventions of warfare. This forcefully asserted the government's claim on the monopoly of violence, but it was justified by a belief that the Highlanders were barbarians incapable of understanding or acting according to rules of civility. Accordingly, Jacobite soldiers were shown little humane treatment and executed rather than taken prisoner, and sexual violence against Highland women was advocated.[91]

> Long-standing stereotypes of the Highlanders as savages made the adoption of such tactics acceptable to government ministers, military leaders, and the English public; and especially after the battle of Prestonpans and the Jacobite Highlanders' entry into England,

denigration of Highland culture became common and vehement. [. . .] The events of 1745 and 1746 confirmed deep-seated cultural animosities that contributed to an impulse among many in the army to punish Highlanders regardless of their age or sex.[92]

The Jacobite army enjoyed decisive victories early in the campaign, but at Culloden in 1746 a weary and ill-prepared Jacobite army was crushed. The Hanoverian army committed indiscriminate acts of cruelty and destruction throughout the Highlands. While anecdotal evidence suggests that some Gaels in the Hanoverian forces did what they could to soften the violence, every area in the Highlands has its catalogue of brutalities.[93]

The defeat of the Jacobite army at Culloden became burned into the collective memory of Gaelic speakers everywhere, irrespective of religion or political persuasion. [. . .] Important as the battle was at the time in terms of human loss, it became even more important as a symbol – the symbol of something like the end of independent Gaelic action. The bubble of confidence, the conviction that the Wheel of Fortune was on the turn at last, was rudely burst.[94]

The British state brought its full weight and attention to dismantling Gaelic society and replacing its cultural institutions from the ground up with those that would uphold Protestantism, commercial values and 'progress'. For the first time the outside world impinged directly and unrelentingly upon the everyday consciousness of ordinary Gaels. The 1746 Disarming Act forbade civilians from bearing arms and males wearing the symbols of the Highland warrior, the kilt and tartan. In 1747 Parliament annulled the private courts of the aristocracy and the obligations of tenants to provide military service for landlords, seeking to mediate all relationships through cash transactions. In 1749 a survey of fifty-three properties of former Jacobite chieftains was begun, resulting in the sale of forty estates and the direct management of the remaining thirteen by a government commission.

The rents and profits [were] for the Purposes of civilising the Inhabitants upon the said Estates, and other Parts of the Highlands and Islands of Scotland, and promoting amongst them the Protestant religion, good Government, Industry and Manufactures, and the Principles of Duty and Loyalty to his Majesty, his Heirs and Successors, and to no other Purpose whatsoever.[95]

Although Samuel Johnson was not always able to see across the cultural and linguistic divide that separated him from the Gaels when he toured the Highlands in 1773, he confirmed that they were oppressed by all of the official state institutions:

There was perhaps never any change of national manners so quick, so great, and so general, as that which has operated in the Highlands, by the last conquest, and the subsequent laws. [. . .] Of what they had before the late conquest of their country, there remains only their language and their poverty. Their language is attacked on every side. Schools are erected, in which English only is taught.[96]

Johnson displayed sympathy for the suffering of the people, but he also revealed his belief that Scotland would inevitably be civilised by England for its own good, evoking the paragon of imperial civilisation, Rome:

Yet what the Romans did to other nations, was in a great degree done by Cromwell to the Scots; he civilized them by conquest, and introduced by *useful violence* the arts of peace [. . .] Till the Union made them acquainted with English manners, the culture of their lands was unskilful, and their domestick life uninformed.[97]

John Ramsay of Ochtertyre also observed the results of these deliberate policies first-hand:

The whole weight of the Government, for a number of years, was employed to dissolve every tie between the chief and the clan, and to abolish all distinctions between the Highland and Lowland Scots. Even the gentry who had not been engaged in the rebellion found it expedient to drop some of their national customs, which either gave offence, or were prohibited by law. [. . .] their successors have no longer the same attachment either to their people or to ancient modes of life. They affect the manners of the Lowland gentry [. . .] The application of so many violent and bitter remedies at the same time could not be agreeable to the Highlanders. In fact they were treated like a conquered people, whom it is necessary to keep under restraint.[98]

The Jacobite Rising of 1745 and its aftermath influenced the evolution of the British Empire and the capacity of the military in 'reforming' its frontiers. Cumberland and his officers believed that the army's mission was to further 'civilisation' and showed a marked disdain for cultural difference in the Highlands. They voiced their opinions in debates about how to transform Gaelic society, creating ethnographic reports to guide Westminster's policies for the region. William Roy's commission in 1746 to create a military survey of the Highlands established the Ordnance Survey. Many of the leading figures of the ensuing Scottish Enlightenment were involved in or informed by such experiences. Cumberland's protégés went on to apply their experiences in high-ranking positions all over the empire.[99]

CLEARANCE, EMPIRE AND EVANGELISM

The eighteenth century was a period of massive social convulsion all across Europe. Through better diets, reduced famine conditions, and improved medicine, populations everywhere increased by 50 to 100 per cent. Agricultural practices, rural communities and the landscape itself were altered radically in the quest to feed more people and generate surplus wealth for the aristocracy. The idea of *improvement* – re-engineering society and nature for maximum efficiency – spread amongst literate land-owners with many sweeping, and unpredictable, results.[100]

A number of factors made the transitions in the Scottish Highlands more abrupt and dramatic than elsewhere in Britain and most of Europe. The traditional Highland economy maximised the social potential of land – the number of people it could support – rather than economic profits. The Highlands were remote from commercial centres, had limited exploitable natural resources, and did not have the benefit of native industrial development which was able elsewhere to provide work for much of the population displaced by agricultural improvement. It was especially the un-checked, tyrannical power of landlords and the indifference of the government to intervene, however, that allowed the native population to become defranchised and dislocated during the transition of the Highland economy. The benefits of improve-ment everywhere were limited by the aristocratic domination of land-holding: in many parts of Europe, the élite monopoly of ownership was broken to allow rural communities to own land and maintain themselves on it. In Scotland, however, the power of landlords to remove tenants at their discretion was reaffirmed in law in 1555, 1707 and 1756, leaving inhabitants with no legal recourse.[101]

> A substantial part of the logic behind clearance was also to create a large landless population with limited options for the pursuit of a livelihood who could then be compelled to provide cheap labour on various envisioned industrial schemes on the landlords' estates.[102]

Highland communities began to emigrate to North America in the decade before Culloden, some in response to early improvements. It was the men of the middle class – the 'tacksmen' as they were called in English, or *fir-bhaile* in their native Gaelic – who were the first to lead these migrations. They knew that they were, as a class, being squeezed out of existence. Beyond this, they tended to be literate in English and were used to being administrators and leaders. As they anticipated that impending social and economic reform would bring about a reduction in their quality of life, they had the greatest incentive to organise migrations that would take them and their subtenants to new lands.

By the mid eighteenth century, the sturdy sheep of the Scottish Borders had been brought to the Highlands and found to adapt to conditions successfully. Markets for both wool and mutton were on the rise and by 1760 sheep-farming was being introduced into Argyll and Highland Perthshire. Landlords could make four times the amount of profit from sheep than cattle; they therefore began to rent grazing areas to sheep-farmers. Sheep-farming required capital and experience which few Highlanders had, but which was readily available in the Lowlands. Each sheep-farmer displaced dozens of tenants, taking over lands that had been occupied and used by Gaelic communities from time out of mind.[103] The term *clearance* is generally used for the forced evictions of Highlanders from their homes.[104] While many early emigrants left without the use of physical force, especially after famines in 1763–4 and 1772, and rising inflation after the 1770s, they did so because it was their only available option. Patrick Campbell wrote in 1791:

> I knew a great many people from the corner of Scotland I had come from, were in use for some years of emigrating to the American states [. . .] which I knew was not owing to wantonness or desire of change of situation on their part, but principally to the inhumanity and oppression of their landlords, who either distressed them, or screwed up the rents to a pitch they could not possibly pay. Of this I could not be mistaken, as I knew many of the people in this predicament, and some of them I had seen wringing their hands, crying most bitterly, deploring their miserable families, and the state they were reduced to.[105]

The Clearances still evoke a strong emotional response in the Highlands, and in much of Scotland, because of what they symbolise historically and in the present. Accordingly, the interpretations of the Clearances are often the cause of much debate. The focus of many texts is on 'economic conditions', stating them to be objective facts and processes that can be stated to run to logical conclusions, with both landlords and Highland peasantry being equally the 'victims' of forces beyond their control. Such an outlook, however, neglects the fact that the economy is a cultural institution in which human agency is involved; the state always intervenes in the economy when it is in its own interest. Standard interpretations absolve landlords and government from blame and ignore the harnessing of prejudice and racism to justify the forced removal of Gaels from their homes 'for their own good'.[106]

> Scottish Whig historians, who invariably write from an urban point of view, seem unable to grasp that there is nothing inevitable, God-given, or sacrosanct about Scottish land laws, particularly about those land laws before the passing of the Crofters' Act of 1886. If they had not been so shy of making any kind of comparison between Scotland and other northern countries of Europe, they might have asked why the glens and islands of Norway, from which there was voluntary emigration to North America, were never emptied as many of the Scottish glens and islands were.[107]

While Britain was at war, landlords discouraged emigration because they were able to exploit tenants for military recruitment and the gruelling production of kelp. The government spent between 75 per cent and 85 per cent of its budget on military enterprises and Highland landlords benefited from the 'fiscal-military state' by raising regiments and promoting the idea of the loyal Highland warrior. Common Highlanders wished to be redeemed from the stain of 'rebellion' and were promised security of tenure for enlisting. By the end of the American War of Independence

(1783), many descendants of Jacobite chieftains were restored to estates forfeited from their families. Highland soldiers too expected to be rewarded by the Crown for their sacrifices.[108] Clearance, to the contrary, accelerated after wars ended. Highlanders saw the Clearances as a betrayal of a long-standing social contract between chieftains and dependants in which landlords protected the rights and interests of their tenants in exchange for services rendered, especially in military form. The raising of military regiments by landlords for British imperial efforts reinforced such notions and in protest songs Highlanders hoped that Napoleon would exact revenge for them.[109]

Local industries were created in some areas. Fishing, textiles and seasonal migration were means of supplementary income for those who were resettled on *crofts* – small-scale holdings – which were on unwanted, marginal land, often on the seashore. Still, especially in the nineteenth century, most landlords pressured or forced mass emigration. The potato – initially resisted by Gaels when introduced in the eighteenth century – became the staple of the Highland diet as it grew well on what little poor soil they had available.[110] Many sheep-farms became converted into hunting estates, especially after railroads made the Highlands easily accessible in the 1860s and demand for sheep fell in the 1870s.[111]

During the eighteenth century, a British identity was promoted actively by laying special stress on common enemies, especially France and the Catholic Church.[112] Scottish Gaeldom became largely estranged from Irish Gaeldom and many Highland Catholics emigrated to Canada. Involvement in the military gave Highlanders a personal investment in the idea of Britishness and a new focus for their loyalties, especially since Gaelic society itself now afforded few alternative outlets. Religion too was instrumental to the reorientation of identity and traditions.

> If it is true to say that the British Empire and the Highland Regiments recreated the Gaelic view of the world, so that now the enemies of the Empire were the enemies of the Gael also, it is even truer that religion brought a new identity. [. . .] It is not an exaggeration to say that overall it produced something like a cosmological revolution in Gaelic society. [. . .] We can sense in the traditions of the nineteenth century not only bewilderment with the loss of a way of life, with Clearance and emigration, but also an intellectual and spiritual hunger accompanying the physical hunger of economic poverty.[113]

Lacking the moderating influences of healthy secular institutions, the church became the dominant institution in Highland life. The ministers of the Church of Scotland in Highland parishes, commonly called the 'Moderates', were recruited from the upper classes of Highland society. They were well-educated men who were key players in Gaelic literary efforts, but they were members of a state institution and most were appointed by land-owners. They were said to include news about British military victories in their sermons,[114] and were keen promoters of social and moral 'im-provement' for their congregations. The peasantry turned against the Moderates as laymen emerged to lead a grass-roots Evangelical movement. It was by definition an anti-establishment movement which landlords and the clergy looked at with suspicion.

In 1843, when the Church of Scotland divided, over 90 per cent of many congregations in the Highlands went to the newly established Free Church. Gaelic was the language of the Free Church in many places after the Church of Scotland abandoned it. The Free Church could be a 'recluse religion', however, turning its back on the evils of the world by establishing an alternative internal community. Like contemporary Evangelicals, the most extreme rejected worldly 'vanities' and were opposed to secular Gaelic culture, especially music, song and dance. The view that the world was a vale of tears, that justice was for God and that man should resolve his own inner battle, could lead to political indifference and inaction.[115]

A former enemy can be more easily romanticised once they no longer pose a threat. The inferior savages who threaten law and order at the height of their power are often transformed into a 'noble race' once they are effectively subjugated. James Macpherson's *Ossian* facilitated the transformation of the conquered Highland barbarians into noble savages and the once-terrifying Highland landscape into heroic backdrop. It was highly influential in the first stirrings of Romanticism and created an image of Highland culture as misleading as it was popular.

The kilt became associated with the Highland regiments, who were depicted as the imperial offspring of the clans of old. Many of the Scottish upper classes, looking for ornamentation rooted in history that would differentiate themselves from other members of the British upper classes, latched on to tartan. Jacobitism was no longer a threat and tartanism provided pomp at the same time that industrialisation was contributing to the homogenisation of British society. Tartan became a national fashion and symbol of Scottishness after King George IV, the first British monarch to visit Scotland since 1651, came to visit Edinburgh in 1822. Walter Scott decided that the event should be a colourful spectacle featuring Highland dress, Highland clans, and Highland chieftains. The king himself was fitted with kilt, bonnet, and tartan jacket. The Highlands provided the most distinctive symbols of ethnicity from Scotland, invoking a glorious and romantic past that was visibly contrastive from England. This new national mythology – commonly called *Highlandism* – created a space in the collective past for the 'primitive' Highlands at the same time that it accepted the values and institutions of the British Empire.[116] Those who had participated in and benefited from the brutal dismantling of Highland society, moreover, could free themselves of that guilt by adopting Highland symbols and identifying themselves with them. Highlandism tokenised and commoditised certain assets of Gaelic culture for the benefit of a Lowland audience, but did little to validate Gaelic culture on its own terms.

Churches made sporadic efforts in the eighteenth and nineteenth centuries to run free schools which taught literacy in Gaelic, although most restricted education to religion itself and had proficiency in English as the ultimate aim of their work. Gains that had been made for Gaelic literacy were effectively undermined by the Education Act of 1872 which made education mandatory for all children in Scotland and made no provision for Gaelic. Besides reinforcing the conceit that English was the exclusive vehicle for education and progress, the Act shut down the supply of Gaelic-speaking teachers and opened the channel for teachers who were usually hostile to the language. In reaction to the Act, pro-Gaelic agitation brought some concessions, but Gaelic policies were insubstantial and the dominance of English had been established. Furthermore, anti-Gaelic prejudice had been so deeply ingrained that efforts to make use of such measures were limited.[117] In practice, most teachers and school-masters in Highland schools were overtly prejudiced against the Gaelic language or unconsciously passed on a sense of shame and inferiority about it. The acclaimed Gaelic poet Evan MacColl remarked on the psychological terrorism that had been inflicted on school children in the early nineteenth century to alienate them from their mother tongue, techniques which were also well known in Ireland and Wales:

> Another barbarous mode of forcing us to make English our sole vehicle of speech at school was to make all trespassers on that rule carry on their breasts, suspended by a *gad* made to go round the neck, the skull of some dead horse! and which he was by no means to get rid of until some other luckless fellow might be overheard whispering a word in the prohibited tongue. How Highland parents, with the least common sense, could approve of all this is to me inexplicable. Little wonder if, under such circumstances, we could often devoutly wish that the Saxon and his tongue had never existed![118]

It has been argued from experience that educational institutions did more damage to the Gaelic language than any of the other catastrophes experienced in the Highlands.[119]

In the 1880s, Highlanders began organising acts of civil disobedience and political action in hopes of bringing attention to social injustice. Several Highlanders made direct contact with the Irish Land League in 1881, which had similar grievances and goals, and formed the Highland Land League. By 1882, many crofters had stopped paying rents, resisted eviction, and even fought against the police. Landlords became anxious about growing 'lawlessness' coincident with Ireland's agrarian revolt; the government sent an official representative to negotiate with the crofters in Skye. Newspapers had become widely available for the first time and reports of deprivation and inhumanity in the Highlands reached a British general public more sympathetic than in previous eras. Advocates of Highland interests in Lowland Scotland, England, and abroad popularised the case for land reform. In 1883, Lord Napier headed a commission to record evidence from crofters about past evictions and to write a report suggesting recommendations. In 1885, in the first exercise of participative democracy most Highland males had ever enjoyed, five members of the Highland Land League were voted into Parliament. Sufficient pressure existed now to address the 'Highland problem' politically.[120]

The Crofters' Holding Act was passed in 1886 with several key provisions: crofters were given security of tenure, the right to pass on their croft to an heir, and the entitlement of compensation for improvements made to holdings. The Crofters' Commission was established to protect the interests of crofters, oversee the implementation of the Act, and settle rents. The Act is important symbolically as the first concession of the government in centuries to the interests of Highlanders, restraining the totalitarian rule of landlords. The legislation has been criticised, however, for fossilising an already inadequate system, failing to make more land available, and neglecting to redress underlying economic inequalities in the Highlands.

An Comunn Gàidhealach ('The Highland Association') was formed in 1891 to advance the interests of Gaels, with education a particular concern. To encourage the use of Gaelic and other aspects of traditional culture, an annual competition, the *Mòd*, inspired by the Welsh Eisteddfod, was established at regional and national levels with monetary rewards. Unfortunately, however, the association stayed strictly apolitical and the 'improver' mentality of the élite involved in the association meant that traditions were not so much preserved as modernised along contemporary aesthetic notions of urban taste and refinement.

Despite important political gains, Highland society remained vulnerable to forces beyond its control and never regained a healthy sense of self-esteem. The costs of two World Wars were heavy on Highland communities and economic conditions became increasingly intolerable as better opportunities elsewhere in Britain, or abroad, were easily obtained by migrating. Even now, at the dawn of the twenty-first century, emigration levels in the Western Isles are the highest in Scotland,[121] and legislation to protect Gaelic and Gaelic speakers, such as the Gaelic Language Act of 2005, is still in its early stages.

The Gaels were central to the creation of the Scottish nation and have always made important contributions to it. The Highlands have never been entirely cut off from material and intellectual exchange with the rest of the world and in many periods sea travel facilitated better connections than existed in many other parts of Britain. The kingdom of Dál Riata was an international hub of learning, religion and the arts, and the Lordship of the Isles reclaimed this role in the same territory, strengthening the links between Irish and Scottish Gaels. Even the native tartan was brightened by the importation of cochineal from North America as early as the seventeenth century.[122]

Through the ages, Gaelic society produced many of its own innovations and was stimulated by many external developments, but like any people, preferred to accommodate changes on its own terms. As anglophone society became more powerful and more convinced of its privileged role in advancing civilisation, it sought to monopolise political power and impose its own norms upon rivals. By the seventeenth century, Gaeldom's own élite were being increasingly assimilated into anglophone society and had their cultural liberties fatally compromised. Action was restricted to collaboration with or against the state, with resistance portrayed as barbarism and treachery. As native institutions were swept away, Gaeldom was deprived of leadership and the means of negotiating cultural transformation, reducing a sophisticated society with a long history of cultural and intellectual accomplishment to an impoverished shadow of its former self. Exposed to the hostile political, educational and religious institutions of the central state which only saw Gaeldom as 'the Highland problem', a set of primitive and deviant traits to be eliminated and replaced by those of the 'civilised centre', it came to internalise the stigmas projected upon it by its enemies.

Chapter Two

IDENTITY AND ETHNICITY

There can be no identity without memory (albeit selective), no collective purpose without myth, and identity and purpose or destiny are necessary elements of the very concept of a nation. But this is also true of an ethnic community; it too must be felt to have an identity and destiny, and hence myths and memories.

– Anthony Smith, *The Ethnic Origin of Nations*

The debate about which symbols most accurately represent Scottish identity has flared in and out of intensity for over two centuries. There have been many negative reactions to Highlandism as the kilt, tartan, and the Highland bagpipe are poor representatives of the modern Lowlands. It is easily forgotten, however, that the Highlands and Lowlands shared many more cultural elements in the past than are visible today. Highlanders are represented in many tales and traditions, furthermore, as the primeval Scots, the historical ethnic core of the nation who have strived to preserve its traditions and its independence.

The resistance of Gaeldom to the efforts of the anglophone world to overthrow it, despite greater resources and an assumption of superiority, are represented in a children's tale recorded on Loch Lomond-side in the nineteenth century. The tale holds the attention of the listener by imitating of lowing of bulls, an effect almost impossible to render in translation from Gaelic to English. It bears a striking resemblance to the final scene of the ancient Irish tale *Táin Bó Cualgne*, which concludes with a battle between two bulls.

Perhaps it is not surprising that such a stridently ethnocentric tale was told in this southernmost frontier of the Gaelic world, for it was through such reaffirmations of self-worth that culture is able to survive and sustain itself in the face of antagonism and deprivation. For many centuries, Highlanders endured hostility not from the English directly but from their Lowland neighbours, yet the tale tells how a Highland bull defended Scotland's honour from the ill will of an English bull.

～

A big, red bull from England once came to put Scotland to shame. He stood up high on the shoulder of Ben Vorlich and he exclaimed, 'What a pathetic country!'

A black Highland bull was on the far side of Loch Lomond. He shouted back, 'From whence do you come?'

The red bull answered, 'From the land of your enemy!'
The black bull said, 'What food do you eat?'
The red bull said, 'Wheat and wine.'
The black bull said, 'I could push you backwards!'
The red bull said, 'Where were you born?'
The black bull said, 'In the cattle fold of the fortress.'
The red bull said, 'What have you been eating since you were a calf?'
The black bull said, 'Milk and the tops of heather.'
The red bull said, 'This curved horn right into your chest!'
The black bull said, 'I'm coming for you! I'm not afraid!'
The black bull went over around the end of Loch Lomond and the two bulls met each other on the shoulder of Ben Vorlich. They butted their heads and wrestled. The black bull pushed back the red bull up to where there was a huge rock and they caused it to take a tumble. The rock went rolling down the slope until it reached a level spot on the side of the main road five miles away. The black bull put his crooked horn through the chest of the red bull and killed him.[1]

Identity is contrastive by nature: defining who we are is only possible by differentiating ourselves from those who we are not. Although there have been common patterns, *ethnicity* – group identity – has been conceptualised in different ways in different cultures. Human beings are multi-dimensional and society is multi-layered, so identity is necessarily multi-dimensional and multi-layered, depending as much on context as on inherent characteristics.

Ethnicity is closely related to culture in that cultural practices, beliefs and values are often the reason that groups see themselves as being distinctive. Ethnicity does not necessarily have to rely upon differences in culture, however, because ethnicity is about perception and collective consensus of ideas about identity; what may seem to be insignificant to an outsider may be the cause of heated division between groups. Nor is ethnicity the same as race: race is only one idea about identity, and a very specific one tooled to justify the political, economic and social disparities of early modern European societies.[2]

The previous chapter presented an outline of Scottish Gaelic history from the perspective of a modern historian, which often differs from the contemporary percep- tions of the people who experienced it. It is inevitable that our culture and identity influence the way in which we interpret and perceive events, encouraging us to identify with some people and lack empathy for others. While ethnic paradigms and the means of promoting them in the pre-modern world were not the same as what we know today, the 'distorting lenses' of identity and ethnicity had an impact on the ways in which people framed events and comprehended their own history in the past much as happens today. Conflicts are commonly understood in the popular imagination as ethnic oppositions or a clash of cultures, even when a sophisticated analysis by scholars shows them to be otherwise. The currency of such portrayals suggests that they have meaning for their audiences, however, and they are worth investigating on their own right, rather than simply dismissing. This chapter explores the dominant dimensions of identity in Gaeldom and discusses how notions of ethnicity informed relations and perceptions between Gaels and others during the course of Scottish history.

THE INVENTION OF CELTICISM

The idea of the Celts as a single ethnic group of that name is a modern simplification that conflates different historic ethnonyms (names for ethnic groups) and means of classification. The Greek writer Hecatæus of Miletus used the name *Keltoi* to describe the people living near modern Marseille, France. Greek writers called the tribe who invaded Greece and Anatolia from Central Europe in the third century BC *Galatoi*, which was similar to the name *Galli* used by the Romans for the Celtic-speaking people of Continental Europe. Most Classical authors of the first century BC felt that these names were interchangeable: Caesar wrote, 'we call [them] Gauls, though in their own language they are called Celts.' Forms of the name seem to have been used for tribes (e.g., the 'Celtici') and for people (e.g., 'Celtius'), although we cannot now be sure of the origin or meaning of the name.[3]

While the Greeks and Romans left many texts about the Celts, they did not practise ethnography in a modern sense. The depictions of the Celts tell us as much, if not more, about the Greeks and Romans themselves – their fears, ideals, values and contemporary concerns – as they do about the Celts. Classical authors emphasised the exotic and used the Celts as mouthpieces for their own agendas or as allegorical figures. The Romans in particular contrasted the 'barbarians' with their own conception of civilisation, celebrating the triumph of rationality and order (in their own image) over the forces of savagery and anarchy.[4] The Celts had more in common with the Romans than the Romans would have liked to admit: the empire just carried out violence in a more systematic way, and Greek and Roman epics glorify bloodshed no less than the epics of their barbarian neighbors.

The Celtic languages of the European continent died out in the early medieval period. The Celtic peoples of the British Isles do not seem to have called themselves 'Celts' but identified themselves with tribal and regional names. With the triumph of Christianity, the Bible provided legendary lines of descent and a cosmological framework used to explain the diversity of humankind until the Renaissance. The Classical notion of the Celts was rediscovered at the same time as European explorers were encountering 'primitive' people on distant continents and scholars were probing the origins of languages and societies in the creation of national histories. George Buchanan (1506–82), a native Gaelic speaker and the tutor of King James VI, was the first to suggest that the ancient inhabitants of the British Isles spoke Celtic languages, using place names and ethnographic evidence for his argument.[5] He also noted the widespread persistence of Gaelic in his own day:

A great part of [Galloway] still uses its ancient language. These three nations [Wales, Cornwall, Scotland], which possess, the whole coast of Britain that looks toward Ireland, preserve the indelible marks of Gallic speech and affinity. But it is worthy of particular notice, that the ancient Scots divided all the nations who inhabited Britain, into two classes, the one they called Gael, the other [Gall].[6]

The scholarly groundwork for the relationships between the Celtic languages was pioneered by Edward Lhuyd, a Welshman who did fieldwork to sample the existing Celtic languages (and collect manuscripts) in the late 1600s. He published the first volume of his pioneering work, *Archaeologia Britannica: an Account of the Languages, Histories and Customs of Great Britain, from Travels through Wales, Cornwall, Bas-Bretagne, Ireland and Scotland*, in 1707 and used the term 'Celtic' to define the language family. Scholars continue to clarify the relationships between the Celtic language family and its Indo-European relations (see Figure 1.1), and the relationships between the various branches of the Celtic languages (see Figure 1.2). From the evidence of place names, tribal names, and inscriptions, we now know that by about 600 BC Celtic languages were spoken in a wide arc across Europe, from the north of Italy through France and parts of Spain to the west of Ireland, and were brought by Gaulish migrants to Turkey in the third century BC.

Archaeology was maturing as a scientific field in the nineteenth century and a wealth of finds was carefully excavated, recorded and analysed across Europe. In the mid nineteenth century, it was realised that material from the Iron Age in much of Europe had been produced by Celts. Two archaeological sites in particular were important for defining art styles and chronological time periods: Hallstatt in Upper Austria, excavated formally from 1846 to 1863, and La Tène in Switzerland, which was discovered in 1857. In 1871 it was recognised that the styles of La Tène artefacts matched those of other sites associated with the Celts. On the basis of these excavations, the Celtic Iron Age was divided into two main phases, Hallstatt (*c.*1200–475 BC) and La Tène (fifth century BC onwards). Celts, defined archaeologically, were thus believed to leave physical signs of their presence: embryonic towns (commonly called 'oppida'), torcs (neck pieces made of twisted gold and silver), particular types of swords, and various art styles (the 'vegetal' style, the 'plastic' style, the 'sword' style, etc).

There are complexities when attempting to correlate these different criteria of Celticity, however: archaeological, linguistic and historical data don't always match. The largest amount of La Tène artefacts comes from an area not identified as Celtic by Caesar. Although we know that the Celts travelled widely in Greece and created the colony in Turkey known as Galatia, there are few material artefacts that can be recognised as Celtic in those areas. While there were Celts on the Iberian Peninsula from an early period, Celtiberian material culture does not reflect typical Celtic styles, but looks similar to other non-Celtic peoples in Spain and Portugal.[7]

There are also problems regarding the origins and movements of people who are defined as Celtic. The main period of the development of Celtic society on the continent of Europe was 600–250 BC, yet Ireland, commonly seen as the touchstone of Celticity, was cut off from the continent during this key period. Can Ireland be prototypically Celtic if it missed out on the heyday of Hallstatt and La Tène, or is it a pre-Celtic anomaly? We know that Celtic languages were spoken at an early period in Britain, Ireland, and the Iberian Peninsula, but we have no evidence for the mass migration of Celtic speakers to these places during the period when the Celtic languages were emerging.[8] Indeed, the DNA evidence suggests a stable population over many thousands of years.

> Celticity is not racial. Conquest and intermarriage will have ensured that Celtic peoples of the early Middle Ages were far from being pure-blooded descendants of those Celts who had migrated from their old homes somewhere in Central Europe about one and a half millennia before. The continuity suggested is only one of language, social, and culture, and even then only partial. The conquered and the foreigner taken in marriage may well have contributed their share to the inheritance. Even as late as the early Middle Ages, the Irish were well aware of the heterogeneous origins of their populations.[9]

The term 'Celtic' is a convenient abstraction for groups of people identified by language, similar to the terms 'Scandinavian' or 'Slavic', but attention needs to be paid to specific people, places, times and contexts. There was never a single Celtic people living a uniquely Celtic way of life. The field of Celtic Studies makes use of the common roots of the Celtic languages, and the cultural data embedded in these words, as well as literary, legal and social features which derived from a Celtic past. Even so, as a recent study of social structures in Irish and Welsh law reminds us, we can be misled by assumptions of uniformity:

> Early Irish and Welsh kinship may reasonably be termed Celtic. Both inherited major elements from the Common Celtic period, above all the shallow lineage of four generations. Both remained, in very general terms, similar [. . .] On the other hand, it is much less helpful to talk of Ireland and Wales as Celtic societies. In spite of such striking similarities as the position of the poet, the major difference [. . .] is so important as to make the two societies considerably different when considered in the round. One can say of Ireland and Wales in the early Middle Ages only that they were fairly Celtic societies.[10]

The claim that all Celts can be classified in the same category as Other, however, has a long history. The idea that the Celtic subjects of English kings were ethnically different, and markedly inferior, is already apparent in the twelfth century.[11] Concepts of civilisation and savagery in Classical sources reinforced such prejudices during the Renaissance as European powers were forming empires inspired by the Roman model.

When John White depicted the native peoples of Virginia in *The Trve Pictvres and Fashions Of The People in that Parte of America Novv Called Virginia* (1585), he accompanied his illustrations with imagined depictions of ancient Celts.

In the eighteenth century there were attempts to put a positive spin on Celtic identity. This was in part a response of Celtic peoples to reclaim what had been denigrated in the suppression of their native cultures; Macpherson's *Ossian* was in the vanguard of these efforts. Distinctive figures, symbols and art forms from Celtic cultures helped to distinguish the individuality of territories which had been subsumed in the British state. The most widely admired pro-Celtic expressions succeeded because they found an outside audience – a non-Celtic one – who were reacting against the growing strictures of industrialisation, rationality and empire, and 'Celts' were only too happy to be celebrated rather than disparaged. Popular forms of Celticism often reinforced artificial and simplified oppositions between the imperial centre and the 'Celtic fringe'.

Category	'Roman', 'Anglo-Saxon'	'Celtic'
Society	Civilised, Urban, Central	Barbaric, Rural, Remote
Style	Order, Discipline	Anarchy, Misrule
Gender	Masculine	Feminine
Mode	Reason, Rationality	Superstition, Emotion
Genres	Science, Fact	Art, Music, Poetry
Era	Modernity	Timeless Past

Table 2.1: A simplified conceptual schema of Celticism

This set of features was claimed to make the Celts incapable of effective self-government and hence dependent upon 'Anglo-Saxon' paternalism to maintain law and order. Celts were seen as valuable assets in an English dominion given that they were complemented deficiencies of the English character and thus injected colourful ornamentation. Such decoration was not, however, thought the foundation of a stable society:

> The Celtic revival, while sympathetic to Gaelic culture, merely reinforced its disconnection from the reality of industrialisation and empire. It relegated Celtic life to a protected reservation set apart from the main highways of modernity. [. . .] This vision of the Celt emphasised his literary and artistic sensitivity, but tended to reinforce the stereotype of the mystical emotional Gael out of step with the march of economic progress, an image which had limited political appeal in the Lowlands.[12]

Whatever affirmative qualities might have been declared for the Celts, with or without the collaboration of native 'culture brokers', they were marked as different and it was the dominant anglophone society that was in control of deciding what 'Celtic traits' were supposed to be positive or negative.

Today the label 'Celtic' serves as a kind of marketing brand on popular forms of entertainment and spirituality, perhaps unconsciously contradicting the historical and linguistic realities of the Celts. The artistic style which features interlace and inter-twining beasts commonly known as 'Celtic art', for example, is actually a relatively late hybridisation with Anglo-Saxon styles, and while this art form was popular with the élite of the British Isles (including non-Celts), it was not shared by the Celts of the European continent. Much of what passes as 'Celtic music' is usually the least Celtic element of musical traditions. Dance music played on the fiddle, for example, was common to western Europe and took local form wherever it was adapted. While such common European musical traditions may have survived better in Ireland than in England or Germany, for example, they date from only the seventeenth century and are not representative of ancient Irish musical genres.

Playing loosely with the 'Celtic' label enables many writers, especially of books on 'Celtic spirituality', to mix together indiscriminately information separated by millennia and thousands of miles. In short, the term 'Celtic' is often used to refer to things that belong to one particular Celtic community in a specific place and time as though they always belonged to all Celts, or in association with things that survive in Celtic regions but originally had a much larger currency.

Criticism of the misuse and over-generalisation of the word 'Celtic' should not be mistaken as implying that the concept has no relevance to modern Celtic-speaking people, or that the ancient Celts were nothing more than the bogeymen of the Classical imagination. While the concept and label 'Celtic' has utility particularly in terms of linguistic and cultural affinities, in practice more specific terms are generally of greater importance.

TERRITORY AND IDENTITY

The meaning and usage of ethnonyms is complex. They tend to emerge in particular circumstances, as when a new ethnic group is encountered or a new group identity is formed. Over time, the makeup of such groups may change, the ethnonym itself may be reinterpreted or reapplied, or the means by which group identity itself is under-stood may change.

The usual pattern in Celtic languages is for territories to be named after ethnic groups (although the reverse is sometimes the case). The common Gaelic name for Ireland is *Éire* and today an Irishman is called in Gaelic an *Éireannach*. A Scotsman (regardless of his speech, or whether he lives in the Lowlands or Highlands) is an *Albannach* (plural *Albannaich*). England is *Sasann* in Gaelic and an Englishman is a *Sasannach* (contrary to common misunderstandings, *Sasannach* is not used in Gaelic to refer to a Scottish Lowlander).[13] This pattern of ethnonymic formation in Gaelic is also used for more local forms of identity. A person from Lochaber (*Loch Abar* in Gaelic) is an *Abrach*; a person from the Isle of Barra (*Barraigh* in Gaelic) is a *Barrach*; and so forth.

In the High Middle Ages Gaels began to refer to the foreigners who were settled amongst them as *Gall* (plural *Goill*). This initially denoted a person from Gaul – someone from outwith the British Isles – but was subsequently applied to Vikings, Anglo-Normans and Englishmen. It is never used in reference to other Insular Celts. The dominant presence of Vikings (formally called *Lochlannaich*) in the Outer Hebrides caused the islands to become renamed *Innse Gall* 'the isles of strangers' in the tenth century, a name which persists in modern Gaelic. Caithness is called *Gallaibh* in Gaelic for the same reason.

Compounds with *Gall* were formed during the medieval period to refer to specific ethnic groups. The Gaelic compound *Gall-Ghàidheal* 'foreign Gael', used of the mixed Norse-Gaels of the Irish Sea, was noted in Chapter One. The province of Galloway, which must have had some Gaelic communities before Norse settlement, is named after the *Gall-Ghàidheil*.[14] The term *Fionnghall* (*fionn* 'white, fair', with positive connotations) initially referred to Vikings from Norway, while *Dubhghall* (*dubh* 'black, dark', with negative connotations) referred to those from Denmark. 'Fionnghall' was later redefined to refer to the Uí Ímair dynasty of Man and the Isles. The term was inherited by Clan Donald, whose leader claimed the title *Rìgh Fionnghall* 'King of the Fair Foreigners', and was also used in compounds referring to the territory of Clan Donald. The ethnonym fell out of favour in the seventeenth century, however, given its archaism and the reality that Clan Donald (and Hebrideans generally) were in no way 'foreigners' in their own lands.[15] Although the term 'Dubhghall' originally referred to the Danes (who established a kingdom in England with a capital at York), it was redefined by the early modern period to mean 'a Lowlander with no tincture of Gaelic culture'.[16] It seems to have developed this usage as a contrast to Fionnghall – who were, as the Lords of the Isles, the custodians of Gaelic tradition – and because of the negative associations of 'dubh'.

By the early modern period in Scotland, *Gall* came to mean generically the people of the Lowlands who spoke a form of English (in distinction to *Sasannach* 'Englishman'). This terminology indicates a Gaelic perception that the English-speaking peoples who became 'naturalised' in Scotland were different to those who lived south of the Scottish border. 'All we can say from the evidence of Gaelic tradition is that the integrity of *Alba*, Scotland, is never in question. The inhabitants of the Lowlands are unquestionably *Albannaich*. But within that framework, there are more detailed perceptions.'[17]

The equation between the Highlands as a geographical territory and as a Gaelic-speaking region only became fixed in Gaelic terminology in the late eighteenth century. This is not surprising, given that Gaelic-speaking communities existed into the eighteenth century in places now considered 'Lowland', such as parts of Ayrshire,

Dumbartonshire, and Aberdeenshire. In the seventeenth and eighteenth centuries (and probably earlier periods) the geographical Highlands were referred to in Gaelic as *na Garbh-Chrìochan* 'the Rough Bounds' (although this term also has a more restricted application to the area from Moidart to Knoydart). The geographical Lowlands are referred to in Gaelic as *a' Mhachair* or *a' Mhachair Ghallda*.

The term *Galldachd* first appears in fourteenth-century Irish texts to refer to the English-speaking community and was extended in meaning by the sixteenth century to mean 'foreign ways, alien manners'. It appears in Scottish Gaelic sources in the late seventeenth century to refer to both Lowlanders and the Lowlands. The term *Gàidhealtachd* appears in Irish and Scottish sources in the late seventeenth century, referring primarily to people rather than place, although it was already used to mean the territorial Highlands by the early eighteenth century.[18] Up into the twentieth century, the extent of the Gàidhealtachd was said to be *bho Hirt gu Peairt* 'from St Kilda to Perth', an expression whose rhyme makes it easy to remember.[19]

LANGUAGE AND IDENTITY

Language helps to form a culture's worldview and it also has an important symbolic role in marking group identity. The equation between language and ethnic identity is a very old one: 'Since the beginning of recorded history, people have been aware of language as a marker of ethnicity.'[20] Medieval European scholarship was tied to biblical cosmology and the story of the Tower of Babel provided the explanation for the origin of ethnic groups (ethnogenesis). Isidore of Seville (*c.*560–636), whose writings had a profound impact on European scholarship for over a millennium, asserted that ethnic diversity was a product of linguistic distinctiveness: 'races arose from different languages, not languages from different races'.[21] When Bede enumerated the peoples in eighth-century Britain – Britons, Picts, Gaels and Anglo-Saxons – he equated their language and ethnic identity. Already in the Old Gaelic period (*c.*AD 750) *Auraicept na nÉces* 'The Scholars' Primer' declared that Gaelic identity was based on a common language, not on 'blood' ancestry.[22]

The word used in Scottish Gaelic to denote the language – *Gàidhlig* – and the people who speak it – *Gàidheil* – was borrowed from the Brythonic *gwydd*, meaning either 'wild' or 'forest'.[23] This suggests that Gaels did not have a name for themselves until they came into contact with a distinctively different ethnic group, which probably happened in Irish settlements in South Wales after AD 600.[24] The implication seems to be that the Welsh, who had been exposed to Roman civilisation, considered the Gaels to be primitive but that the Gaels themselves did not see the association with the forest or wildness as an insult.

Given that language and identity were so closely related the extinction of a people and their language required creative explanations. The author of *Scalacronica* (*c.*1355), Northumbrian knight Sir Thomas Gray, explained that the Picts disappeared because they took Irish wives 'on condition that their offspring would speak Irish, which language remains to this day in the highlands among those who are called "Scots" '.[25] While this is clearly a myth, it does acknowledge the importance of the mother in transmitting native languages, often called the 'mother tongue' in English for this very reason.

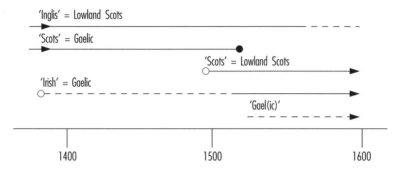

Figure 2.1: A timeline of ethnic and linguistic terms in Lowland Scots

The use of ethnonyms and language labels can be misleading and confusing, given that they often originate in error and diverge in meaning and usage with time. The situation in Scotland can be particularly confusing. The term 'Scot' originally referred to a Gaelic speaker, whether living in Scotland or Ireland, and his language. The form of English spoken in the Lowlands was originally referred to as 'Inglis', a name which continued into the seventeenth century. Shifts in perceptions of identity caused new terms to appear and old terms to be reassigned new usages in the speech of the Lowlands. As the Gaelic-speaking Scots were closely associated with the Irish, on account of the language they spoke as well as their culture and legendary origins, the term 'Irish' (especially in the form 'Erse') began to be applied to them in the 1380s. Although 'Scotice' was used for Gaelic as late as 1505, Gaelic was generally referred to as 'Irish' thereafter. From the 1520s Lowland writers such as Mair and Boece also made occasional use of terms derived from Gaelic's name for itself. The first known use of the term 'Scot' to mean the Germanic language of the Lowlands appeared in 1494 and became the dominant term in the sixteenth century.[26]

The Gaelic word *beurla* refers to language in general, appearing in archaic compounds such as *beurla nam filidh* 'the jargon of the poets' and *beurla na Féine* 'legalistic terminology'. *Beurla Shasannach* is the English of England, while *beurla Ghallda* refers to Lowland Scots.[27] Because of the common presence of English, *beurla* alone implies any variety of English. In the seventeenth century the blanket term *luchd na Beurla* appeared, with a note of disparagement, for speakers of both English and Lowland Scots.

Language is such a strong marker of ethnic identity, it is not surprising that it has figured prominently in cultural allegiances and political rhetoric. When Robert the Bruce and his brother Edward were attempting to extend their dominion from Scotland into Ireland and create a pan-Gaelic alliance against England (in the years

1315–18), they highlighted the language and way of life shared by them (*lingua communis quam ritus*).[28] Campbell of Glenorchy was raising troops at the behest of King James VI in 1601, in order that they be sent to subdue the Irish. One of his potential soldiers refused the offer, noting that 'though the King, [Campbell of] Argyll and he should force them to go, yet they would not serve against that people they were come of and whose language was one with theirs, but be true against them against the Saxons'.[29] Edmund Burt tells us in the 1720s that in the principal town of the Highlands, Inverness, language was a defining feature of identity: 'The Natives do not call themselves Highlanders, not so much on Account of their low [geographical] Situation, as because they speak English.'[30] Finlay Macrae's convictions after Culloden testify that many Highland Jacobites did see the battle as a struggle of Gaels against English in cultural terms:

> [He] is said to have served as a Lieutenant in the Army of Prince Charles in 1745, and who cherished such a hatred of the English, in consequence of the atrocities of the Duke of Cumberland, that he would never speak the English language, but spoke only Gaelic as long as he lived.[31]

Until the late nineteenth century the word 'Highlander' was understood to be synonymous with 'Gaelic speaker', but with assimilation of the élite and the anti-Gaelic policies of schools, the divergence of the meanings of the two terms began to cause controversy.

> What constitutes a Highlander? [. . .] I say those who are born in the Highlands and speak the language of the Highlanders are genuine Highlanders, and none others. To test this position, I venture to assert that the present Lochiel, by descent and birth the chief of a Highland clan, is not a Highlander; he is simply an English gentleman. He can enter into all the ideas, thoughts, tastes and emotions of Englishmen; but he is entirely cut off from any such intimate relationship with Highlanders so long as he is unacquainted with the language in which their thoughts are conveyed.[32]

Language was taking on an increasingly heightened political significance in the later medieval period, with difference understood as deviance and governments becoming less tolerant and more active in imposing uniformity upon their subjects. Edmund Spenser's remarks about colonial efforts in Ireland are well known: 'It hath ever been the use of the conquerer to despise the language of the conquered and to force him by all means to learn his.' As Spenser acknowledged, efforts to convert Irish chieftains to the English language were part of a larger enterprise of political and cultural conquest.[33] Likewise, in Scotland, the central government saw Gaelic as one of the primary causes of the 'barbarity' of Highlanders and used religious and educational institutions to attempt to eradicate it. In 1703, the synod of Glasgow and Ayr stated the wider agenda of linguistic assimilation:

While they continue in their present neglected state Strangers to the Gospell, and bound up to a separate Language and Interest of their own, they are most dangerous to this Church and Nation, ready to assist invading Forrainers, or to break out for plunder in case of Domestick troubles. [. . .] if the People were once brought to Religion, Humanity, Industry, and the Low Countrey Language [. . .] they might yet become a noble accession to the Commonwealth.[34]

Like other minority cultures, the Gaelic community has seen such efforts as attacks on its very existence. There is a continuous tradition from the beginning of the eighteenth century to the present of responding in defence of Gaelic,[35] for these cultural assaults carry with them psychological and social traumas. William Shaw, in the preface to his treatise about Gaelic, wrote in 1778:

The human mind, with great longing, looks back into the past, less interested in many particulars of the present, which it overlooks, and of the future, which it enquires not after. The actions and connections, the fortune and habitations of our ancestors, the fields they walked on, their prudent conduct, and even foibles, we delight to hear recited, with an interested attention. [. . .] But when I look back into the former times of the Gael, whose history a native might be supposed more immediately fond of, finding it so much involved in obscurity, or suppressed and obliterated by the policy of a neighbouring monarch, I could sit down and weep over its fall, execrating the policy of usurping invaders, ever destructive to letters, humanity, and its rights.[36]

ANCESTRIES AND GENEALOGIES

People all around the world have an inherent interest in their origins and display great creativity when attempting to explain the present in terms of the past. Although the specifics of the origin myths of people change according to circumstances, they tend to reflect several common ideas and concerns. First, they are rooted in the deep past to provide a sense of solidarity and historical continuity for people who may be heterogeneous in reality. Second, these myths usually connect their own ethnonym with the name of an historic character on the basis of similarity in sound. Third, origin myths seek to raise the prestige of the group by choosing a high-status legendary founder. Because of their ideological purposes, origin myths always tell us a great deal about the perceptions of the people who create them.

That the pre-Christian Celtic peoples had origin legends is without doubt, but it is only with difficulty that they can be reconstructed even partially.[37] Even before the complete collapse of the druidic order, the Christianised Gaelic literati were attempting to reconcile native names and origin legends with the historical framework of the Bible, Classical literature, and scholarship from Continental Europe. They did this particularly by attaching their inherited ethnonyms – *Scotti* from the Romans, *Gàidheal* from the Welsh, and a native name *Féni* 'nobles' – to characters in these new texts. Their challenge was clearly not to find just any characters, however: the Gaels gave themselves the most favourable ancestry possible, linking themselves to Egyptians, Jews, Trojans and Greeks. This syncretic history made them, at least from the perspective of legend, first-class players on the world stage.

Efforts to provide origin legends for other barbarians within the realms of the former Roman Empire had begun in the sixth century, some of which had a direct impact on Gaelic authors. The work of Isidore of Seville was highly influential on them and probably explains the importation of an ancestral figure *Míl Espáine* 'Spanish soldier' for the Gaels as early as the seventh century. The eighth-century *Auraicept na nÉces* 'the Scholars' Primer' explained that a character named Fénius Farsaid was at the Tower of Babel and created the Gaelic language by choosing the best characteristics of all of them – no signs of an inferiority complex here. This tale connects the Gaelic tribal name *Féni* with the mythological Hebrew figure Fenech. In some texts Fénius Farsaid is said to be the ancestor of the Scythians, which is meant to explain the origin of the ethnonym 'Scotti'. The tract also mentions 'Goídel', a character created in order to give his name (retrospectively) to the Gaelic language; he was said to be a Greek relation of Fénius (variously his grandfather, foster-father or uncle).[38]

Subsequent authors attempted to elaborate on these diverse legends and make them more consistent. The Latin *Historia Brittonum*, previously attributed to Nennius, was compiled by a Welsh writer in 829 or 830 and contains origin legends for the people of Britain. The Britons, it says, were descended from Brutus, the great-grandson of the Trojan Aeneas. There are two different legends for the Gaels, one featuring Míl Espáine and the other, said to have been provided by Irish scholars, featuring a Scythian in Egypt. In later versions of the manuscript the ethnonym 'Scot' gets a second explanation by the introduction of Scota, the daughter of the Pharaoh of Egypt. The persistent elements of the story were in place by the time of the poet Mael Muru of Fahan (†887) but receive extensive literary embellishment in the eleventh-century *Lebor Gabála Érenn* 'The Book of the Taking of Ireland'.[39] This text retained a central place in Gaelic scholarship into the eighteenth century, not least because it provided a rich tapestry of native mytho-history common to the pan-Gaelic intelligentsia into which literary and genealogical endeavours could tap.[40]

Scottish Gaels were connected to these intellectual efforts and used them as the basis of their own national pedigree. The tenth-century *Pictish Chronicle* attempted to integrate Scots and Picts into a single people by tracing them to both the Scythians and Scota, daughter of Pharaoh, explaining that they had white hair and were therefore called 'Albani'.[41] The so-called 'Duan Albanach', composed during the reign of Malcolm Canmore (1058–93) opens with the Brutus origin legend, introduces the Picts, and soon replaces them with the triumphant Gaels. At the inauguration of King Alexander III in 1249, a Gaelic poet recited his genealogy back to Gaidheal Glas, son of Neolius King of Athens and his wife Scota, daughter of Pharaoh. These were not merely idle antiquarian ramblings, but mainstream contemporary political rhetoric.

In a letter to the Pope Boniface VIII, King Edward of England founded his title over Scotland's sovereignty on the Brutus legend (as given in *Historia Regum Britanniae* by Geoffrey of Monmouth *c*.1135). The Scots, in reply, dismissed Edward's claims as 'ancient fables' and countered with the origin legend which paired Scota, daughter of the Pharaoh, with Gaidheal Glas, ancestor of the Gaels. Their case was reviewed favourably in Rome and a plot summary of the legend opens the 'Declaration of Arbroath'.[42]

Elements of this origin legend continued to recur in Gaelic political rhetoric, literature and poetry. When in 1701 the antiquarian Robert Wodrow sent a letter to John Maclean to get information from the learned John Beaton about Gathelus (the Latinised form of 'Gàidheal'), Maclean replied:

> As for Gathelus, [Beaton] avers that indeed he is the progenitor of the Scoti Antiqui, who inhabited Ireland, whose genealogie unto Noah he can shew [. . .] This, he says, is neither fabulous or improbable, seeing there were records left by every generation to their posteritie, and these men were not (as ye suppose) unlearned, but great philosophers, Gathelus being the grandchild of [Fénius Farsaid . . .] to Fergus macRoiss, monarch of Ireland, and progenitor of the kings of Great Brittain of the Steuart race.[43]

It was because of his Gaelic ancestry that many of the Irish literati expected that King James VI would be a more beneficent ruler over Ireland than Elizabeth of England had been. In his reply, Maclean also mentioned Aedh Mac a' Bháird ('Hugh Ward'), a contemporary authority on Gaelic tradition at the Irish Franciscan centre of Louvain (in modern Belgium). In his history of the Gaels (written between 1623 and 1635), Aedh wrote that ancestry through Míl Espáine was considered a prerequisite of leadership:

> the heirs of the Royal blood and dignity who held in contempt all foreign and adventitious claim to nobility if it could not display names and achievements of ancestors going back in a long and ancient line of continuity. Among [the Scoti] no one was permitted to aspire to kingship, to chieftainship, or to a rank of outstanding note or to office who could not reveal family connexion going back in line through grandfathers and great-grandfathers to Milesios or rather Miles.[44]

The lineage of the Scottish monarchs was not just an obscure topic for the literati. Duncan Campbell tells us that when Queen Victoria was inaugurated in 1838

> [my grandmother] and others of her generation enjoyed the liberty this occasion gave them for going [. . .] to the history of Scottish kings as far as Kenneth Macalpin, which had come down by oral tradition. Long afterwards when I read the Duan Albanach I was much surprised to discover that the substance of it was retained to a

remarkable extent in the oral and local traditions which our aged people recalled and told.[45]

An elegy by Eachann Bacach on the death of the chieftain of the Macleans in 1649 flattered him by stating 'Thriall bhur bunadh gu Phàro' ('Your lineage goes back to the Pharaoh').[46] As late as 1777 Gaelic poet Duncan Lothian recounted the Gathelus legend to underscore the injustice of clearing Highlanders for sheep-farms when history demonstrated them to be valuable warriors.[47] The Gaels' belief in their own wholesome pedigree was in contrast to their opinion of the mongrel Lowlanders, as Thomas Morer tells us in 1689:

> We take the Low-landers to be a Medley of Picts, Scots, French, Saxons and English, as their language and habit insinuate, which is the reason why the High-landers, who look on themselves to be a purer race, cannot affect 'em; but on the contrary deal with 'em as a spurious degenerate people.[48]

While a leader's lineage makes an explicit statement about his claims of authority, it can also be read as a symbolic statement about cultural allegiances, especially when ethnic identity is in flux. Clan Donald's posture as the stalwarts of the old Gaelic order is reflected in their claims to Irish ancestry: they use the title *Sìol Chuinn* after Conn of the Hundred Battles (who supposedly lived in the second century AD), and ancestry from Colla Uais, an Irish lord who ruled in Scotland before the establishment of Dál Riata. There are very few direct acknowledgments of their Norse ancestry in Gaelic literature or tradition.[49]

Despite the large numbers of Norsemen who settled in both Scotland and Ireland, the degree to which surviving Gaelic oral traditions in both countries disavows Norse ancestry and instead portrays the Vikings as the archetypal enemy of the Gaels is striking. In many of the Ossianic tales, the Fian protect Scotland and Ireland from Viking raiders and eventually defeat them. The ability of Gaelic culture to not only absorb the Norse but to cause their descendants to disclaim them by the later medieval period again attests to the resilience and self-confidence of Gaeldom: 'these shifts must have been deliberate, with Gaelic identity being consciously promoted and Scandinavian connections consciously discarded and disregarded.'[50] This fact is worth stressing, especially given the current vogue for revising history based on genetic research. Some people wish to 'correct' medieval claims of Gaelic lineage for figures such as Somerled, but this is a misunderstanding of the ideological use of genealogy. It was necessary to validate aspiring leaders by recourse to native tradition, 'plugging them into' the Gaelic mytho-historic matrix with a plausible ancestral connection, but this was not an attempt to find a chain of biological lineage in the same fashion as the work of a modern historian.

The only major clan who regularly acknowledged their Norse ancestry (at least in surviving Gaelic poetry) is the MacLeods, whose Norse ancestors Olbhar (Norse

'Olaf') and Mànus (Norse 'Magnus') are often named in praise poetry.[51] Clans acting as agents of the central government showed their allegiance to Lowland culture by fabricating Anglo-Normans in their genealogy. Foremost in this reformulation of lineage was Clan Campbell. While they were shown as descendants of Míl Espáine in a seventeenth-century Irish genealogical manuscript,[52] which upheld their aspirations in a Gaelic setting, they originally claimed Brythonic descent from King Arthur and used genuine Welsh names to validate that lineage in one Gaelic manuscript.[53] Clearly currying favour on all fronts, Hector Boece lists them among the Anglo-Normans, their Gaelic name being creatively Frankified as 'de Campo Bello'.[54] Finally, in vernacular Gaelic tradition, they are said to descend from the Ossianic hero Diarmaid.

INTER-ETHNIC RELATIONS AND PERCEPTIONS

The conceptual opposition between civilised and savage, and the stereotype of the barbarian, is as old as the conceits of civilisation itself. The depiction of Celts in Classical sources owe much to such associations, and medieval Scottish writers inherited these literary conventions and cultural prejudices. Although writers could insert factual details into these 'blueprints' of the savage, we need not take texts at face value: the ways in which these inherited stereotypes were employed – what was emphasised, elaborated or omitted – depended upon the biases of the writer, his agenda, and the contemporary historical context in which he worked.

English kings were precocious in their creation of a state with expansionist, imperial ambitions. By the tenth century rulers were commonly assuming titles such as 'king of the English and governor of the whole of Britain'.[55] William of Malmesbury's text *Deeds of the Kings of the English*, completed in 1125 and widely copied, espoused the view that the English had become more civilised than their neighbours: 'William looked upon English history as a progress from barbarism to civilisation.'[56] This ethnocentric boast built upon Classical depictions of the barbarian as well as growing psychological distance between the English and the animal kingdom, which he claimed resembled the bestial customs of the Scots, Irish and Welsh. 'The perception of Celtic societies as barbarous obviously functioned in part as an ideology of conquest.'[57]

In his lament for the death of King David I (1153), Ailred, the English abbot of Rievaulx, praised David for his ability to transform Scotland: the landscape was tamed for production, people of 'total barbarity' became refined, and the church was updated according to mainstream orthodoxy. While Ailred's depiction indulged in hyperbole, his aim was to illustrate model Christian kingship by contrasting 'savage Scots' with the godly ideals of the church. Ailred's work was probably well read and influential in Scotland, especially in Rievaulx's daughter house of Melrose.[58]

Most of the early evidence from within Scotland are texts written by monks of reformed monastic communities established in the twelfth century, the majority of whom (especially in the upper echelons) were English in origin. In the twelfth and thirteenth centuries these imported monks generally portrayed 'Scots' (which in this period referred primarily to people north of the Forth who were generally Gaelic speakers) as ignorant of the norms of Christendom and beyond the realms of civilised society in cultural and moral terms. Texts praising King David and his mother St Margaret, however, also hinted that despite Gaelic origins Scots could be improved by the 'civilising influence' of Anglo-Norman culture and the reformed church. The dichotomy between savage and civil thus initially contrasted Gaelic-speaking and non-Gaelic-speaking peoples in Scotland, rather than the regions people occupied.[59]

In the late thirteenth century, however, perceptions of identity within Scotland were shifting. The monks of the reformed orders and their successors came to think of themselves as Scots and needed some way to distinguish themselves (and other 'civilised' Scots) from Gaelic speakers. These circumstances seem to explain the emergence of topographical labels which locate Gaelic speakers in the undomesticated regions, namely the mountains and forests of Scotland. An encyclopedia completed by Bartholomew the Englishman *c.*1245 notes the Irish origins of the Scots, their primitive customs, and the recent arrival of English influences:

> The Scottish people are in origin the same people that were formerly in Ireland, and resemble them in everything including language, customs and character. They are a fickle people, haughty in spirit, fierce towards their enemies [. . .] But in the present time many Scots have changed the manners of the original race in considerable measure and for the better, as a result of intermixture with the English. However the wood-dwelling Scots and the Irish take pride in following in the footsteps of their fathers in dress, language, sustenance and other habits. Indeed in a sense they reject the ways of others in preference to their own.[60]

Bartholomew's text is believed to have influenced another important description of an ethnic division between Highlands and Lowlands previously attributed to John of Fordun (*c.*1385) but now believed to more likely originate in the period from 1260 to 1285:

> The character of the Scots however varies with the differences in language, for two languages are spoken amongst them, the Scottish [i.e., Gaelic] and the Teutonic [i.e., English]. The people who speak the Teutonic language occupy the coastal and lowland regions, while the people who speak the Scottish language inhabit the mountains and outlying islands. The coastal people are docile and civilised, trustworthy, long-suffering, and courteous, decent in their dress, polite, and peaceable, devout in their worship, but always ready to resist injuries threatened by their enemies. The island and mountain people, however, are fierce and untameable, uncouth and unpleasant, much given to theft, fond of doing nothing, but their minds are quick to learn, and cunning. They are strikingly handsome in appearance, but their clothing is unsightly. They are always hostile and savage not only towards the English people and language but also towards their fellow Scots because of the

difference in language. They are, however, faithful and obedient to the king and kingdom, and easily made to submit to law, if rule is exerted over them.[61]

While the two communities were defined in this text in geographical, cultural and linguistic terms, we must keep in mind that this is a simplified schematic depiction that was far more complex on the ground: Gaelic was by no means confined to the Highlands. Down to fifteenth century, the ethnic label 'Scot' on customs, place names and artefacts in the Lowlands testified to the persistence of the Gaelic language and the memory of cultural origins.[62] Still, in the text language plays a role in allegiances and animosities as well as allowing for outward expression of internal characteristics, in which the Lowlanders are given superior status.[63] From this same period comes a poetic statement symbolising the apartheid to which Gaelic was being subjected, with the legendary founder Gaythelos representing Gaelic linguistic identity:

The Scots derive their name from Scota, and all Scota is derived from the Scots,
While increased use of the name of the leader Gaythelos is forbidden.[64]

Barbour's epic *The Bruce* (1376) displays no binary division between Highlands and Lowlands: although Gaels are featured prominently, people are listed by specific regions. This text is the first from Scotland to label Gaelic speakers as 'Irish', but does so without brushing them with any negative connotations or sense of non-citizenship.[65] Walter Bower (*c.*1385–1449) compiled a history of Scotland, the *Scotichronicon*, which reinforced the negative stereotypes of the Gaels. For Bower, all Gaels were caterans, thiefs and rebels who spoke a barbarous language and lived in the forests, beyond the reach of law and order.[66]

Several influential Lowland historians of the sixteenth century emphasised Gaelic origins in order to project Scottish civil virtues, kingship, and a distinctively native church into the deep past. John Mair (1467–1550), writing in 1521, argued for the union of Scotland and England on the basis of the two nations being separate and equal partners of great antiquity. In order to make this case for Scotland, he elaborated upon the history of Dál Riata.[67] Despite admitting the Gaels' role as founders of the nation, Mair continued a primarily negative view of Highlanders (calling them 'Wild Scots'), contrasting them unfavourably with the Lowlanders and explaining to some degree their behaviour as a result of their environment:

Just as among the Scots we find two distinct tongues, so we likewise find two different ways of life and conduct. For some are born in the forests and mountains of the north, and these we call men of the Highland, but the others men of the Lowland. By foreigners the former are called Wild Scots, the latter householding Scots. The Irish tongue is in use among the former, the English tongue among the latter. One half of Scotland speaks Irish, and all these as well as the Islanders we reckon to belong to the Wild Scots. In dress, in the manner of their outward life, and in good morals, for example, these come behind the householding Scots – yet they are not less, but rather much more, prompt to fight; and this, both because they dwell more towards the north, and because, born as they are in the mountains, and dwellers in the forests, their very nature is more combative. It is, however, with the householding Scots that the government and direction of the kingdom is to be found inasmuch as they understand better, or at least less ill than the others, the nature of a civil polity. [. . .] At the present day almost the half of Scotland speaks the Irish tongue, and not so long ago it was spoken by the majority of us.[68]

Hector Boece (*c.*1465–1536), writing in about 1527, was concerned about modern corruption and vice. For Boece, Highlanders retained 'auld virtewis usit sum time amang our eldaris' after the Lowlands were defiled by intercourse with the English, causing them to reject ancestral customs: 'be frequent and daily cumpany of thaim, we began to rute thair langage and seperflew maneris in oure breistis; throw quhilk the virtew and temperance of our eldaris began to be of litil estimation amang us.' The frugal habits and physical hardiness of the Highlanders were the antithesis of urban degeneration.[69]

The ancient Scots were commonly perceived as being 'savage'. Bishop John Leslie (1527–96), writing in 1578, sought to protect contemporary Lowlanders from being vilified by such associations. He accordingly attributed both virtues and vices to the Scots of the past, but asserted that in the present Lowlanders had advanced in political and cultural terms while Highlanders were stuck in a rut of barbarity.[70] Leslie tells us that despite the growing involvement of Gaelic chieftains in Lowland affairs their followers were not willing to see them abandon native customs in favour of Lowland ones:

> They preserve completely unchanged the ancient form of dress and lifestyle, and they are so assiduous about it that their lords and chieftains, when they go to the King's court and dress themselves in more elegant and refined clothes after the manner of the court, always on return to their own people strip off this courtly elegance and dress according to their native style as quickly as possible unless they want to incur the hatred of all, and the gravest insults.[71]

Like Boece, George Buchanan (1506–82) depicted Gaels as retaining primitive virtues uncorrupted by modern vices and luxuries. Buchanan portrayed early Scotland as a Gaelic republic in the Classical mould, pointing out that clan chiefs in the Western Isles succeeded by election and could be deposed by the clan if they did not act in the interest of the clan as a whole. Although this social practice provided him with a living illustration of his political ideals, Buchanan was not a champion of the Gaels for their own sake.[72] In fact, despite being a native Gaelic speaker himself, he advocated that Gaelic be replaced with Latin for the sake of progress:

I can perceive, without regret, the gradual extinction of the ancient Scottish language, and cheerfully allow its harsh sounds to die away, and give place to the softer and more harmonious tones of the Latin. For if, in this transmigration into another language, it is necessary that we yield up one thing or other, let us pass from rusticity and barbarism, to culture and civilisation, and let our choice and judgement, repair the infelicity of our birth.

It is unlikely that the ideological exploitation of Gaelic history increased respect for contemporary Highland culture amongst Lowland readers. Anti-Gaelic prejudices are reflected in much late medieval Lowland literature. A succinct example is a poem attributed to Alexander Montgomerie of Ayrshire (*c*.1540–1611) which mocks the noble pretensions of Gaels and their origin legend in Argyll. It depicts Highlanders as untrustworthy thieves daring to steal from God himself, refusing to be lawful and productive members of society:

> How the first Helandman, of God was maid
> Of ane horss turd, in Argylle, as is said.
>
> God and Sanct Petir was gangand be the way,
> Heiche up in Ardgyle, quhair their gait lay.
> Sanct Petir said to God in a sport word,
> 'Can ze nocht mak a Heilandman of this horss turd?'
> God turned owre the horss turd with his pykit staff,
> And up start a Helandman blak as ony draff.
> Quod God to the Helandman 'Quhair wilt thow now?'
> 'I will down to the Lawland, Lord, and their steill a kow.'
> 'And thow steill a cow, cairle, their they will hang the.'
> 'Quattrack, Lord, of that? For anis mon I die.'
> God then he leuch and owre the dyk lap,
> And owt of his scheith his gowly owtgatt.
> Sanct Petir soght this gowlly fast up and doun,
> Zit could not find it in all that braid rownn.
> 'Now', quod God, 'heir a mervell! how can this be
> That I sowld want my gowly, and we heir bot thre?'
> 'Humff!' quod the Helandman, and turned him abowt,
> And at his plaid nuk the guly fell owt.
> 'Fy', quod Sanct Petir, 'thow sill neuir do weill!'
> And thow bot new maid sa sone gais to steill.'
> 'Umph!' quo the Helandman, and swere be yon Kirk,
> 'Sa lang as I may geir get will I nevir work.'[73]

The poem is replete with the symbolism of rejection of the Other: the Highlander is made of the excrement of an animal, is described as black and compared to 'draff' ('dregs', 'refuse').[74] It contains another clue about ethnic perceptions and pretensions in that the pun 'Lawlands' reflects the psychological distance between the Lowlands and the presumably lawless Highlands.[75] It is ironic if Montgomerie was the author, for he may have spent some of his early life in Argyll, used Gaelic terms in another poem, and was satirised as a Highlander in a flyting with the bard Polwart.[76] In similarly contrasting imagery of the civil-savage/self-Other dichotomy, the celebrations around the baptism of James VI in December 1566 included the dramatisation of an attack on a castle (representing the monarchy) by Moors and 'wyld Hieland men' defeated by the king's men.[77]

The anti-Gaelic prejudices of the Lowland élite can be seen as projections upon the Highlands of what they rejected in themselves in their efforts to become respectable and be seen as 'civilised' in the eyes of the European élite: 'the Scottish lower orders were influenced by a total culture in which an insecure and authoritarian élite articulated an obsessive awareness of its own provincial inferiority and backwardness.'[78] Lowlanders passed on to the Highlanders the derision they felt coming from the English, as Edmund Burt observed in the 1720s: 'For notwithstanding the Lowland Scots complain of the English for ridiculing other nations, yet they themselves have a great number of standing jokes upon the Highlanders.'[79]

Gaels were not unaware of the aspersions cast at them from Lowlanders. A Highlander writing *c.*1543 complained that 'the babalonicall busscheps and the great courtyours of Scotland repute the forsoide Yrish Lordes as wilde, rude, and barbarous people, brought vp (as they say) without lerninge and nourtour.'[80] In an extended, infamous poetic mud-slinging match between William Dunbar and Walter Kennedy (from Gaelic-speaking Carrick[81]) *c.*1500, Kennedy defends Gaelic as Scotland's true native language:

> Thow lufis nane Irische, elf, I understand,
> Bot it suld be all trew Scottis mennis lede;
> It was the gud language of this land,
> And Scota it causit to multiply and sprede,
> Quhill Corspatrik, that we of tresoun rede,
> Thy forefader, maid Irisch and Irisch men thin,
> Throu his tresoun broght Inglise rumplis in,
> So wald thy self, mycht thou to him succede.[82]

Cultural diffusion is facilitated by a common language and cultural developments in England were closely connected to those in Lowland Scotland of this period. Just as the similarities in language and culture formed the basis of a common affinity between the Scottish and Irish Gaels, so does it seem that Lowland Scots and the English saw themselves as sharing increasing mutual interests, one that contrasted with the Gaels. This was especially so after the Reformation in Scotland (*c.*1560). John Mair advocated the creation of 'one sole Monarchy' to 'be called Britain'. Edward Seymour, 1st Duke of Somerset, argued for the union of the English and Scottish crowns in 1547 because the two peoples were 'so like in maner, forme, language, and all condicions'.[83] Scottish commissioners in London advocated the marriage of James Lord Hamilton and Queen Elizabeth in 1560, since Hamilton was

> no straunger, but in a maner your owne countrey man, seing the Ile [i.e., Britain] is a comon countrey to us both, one that speaketh your owne language, one of the same religion. Neither yet neade youe feare any alteracion in the lawes, seing the lawes of Scotland wer taken out of England and therefor booth ther realmes are ruled by one fashion.[84]

Such arguments, of course, entirely ignored the existence of the Gaels, their distinctive language and culture: they were, for the purposes of those in power, non-persons. Before his death in 1568, the Welsh scholar Humphrey Llwyd noted the parallel perceptions between these two sets of people:

> That the Scots are descended from the Irish is well known to themselves as well as to everybody else [. . .] That they came from there seems to be well proven by the fact that they share the same language and customs with the Irish [. . .] For the southern Scots are not true Scots, but are descended from the English, of whom a great multitude arrived in Scotland whilst fleeing from William Duke of Normandy, and to this day they glory in their English origins; at the same time both they and the English look upon the true Scots as barbarous and uncivilised people.[85]

The anti-Gaelic rhetoric in official documents ratcheted up a notch during the reign of King James VI: Highlanders, and especially the more independent-minded Hebrideans, are depicted as pagans, savages, and cannibals. By placing them outside the bounds of humanity, they could thus be dealt with in an inhumane manner. The terms used for natives and colonisers reflect biases: while Lowland colonists sent to the Gàidhealtachd are given the complimentary title 'the Fife Adventurers', Gaels are

> wickit and rebellious [. . .] void of all knawledge and feir of God [. . .] batheing themselffis in the blude of utheris [. . .] everie ane of them exercesing sic beistlie and monstrous cruelteis upoun utheris as hes not beene hard of amangis Turkis or Infidellis.[86]

The English conquest of Ireland was connected in the minds of Lowlanders with the 'Highland problem' in Scotland, and vice versa. George Nicolson, the servant of the English ambassador in Scotland, wrote to Sir Robert Cecil in 1598 that 'the gentlemen of Fife hold their conquest against Lewis: a good [blow] for her majesty to subdue our Ireland with'.[87] Alexander Hay, clerk register of the Scottish Privy Council, advocated that the MacLeod leader of resistance in Lewis be transported to Virginia, for though both Irish and Scottish Gaelic were barbarous tongues, they were mutually comprehensible, whereas he would need an interpreter to conspire with Native Americans.[88] In his *Basilikon Doron* (*c.*1598) King James VI stated that the Gàidhealtachd consisted of subjects of varying states of obedience and 'civility', with the strongest line of demarcation between the Gaels of the mainland and those of the Western Isles:

> I shortly comprehend them all in two sorts of people: the one that dwelleth in our maine land, that are barbarous for the most parte, and yet mixed with some shewe of civilitie: the other, that dwelleth in the Iles and are all uterlie barbares, without any sorte or shewe of civilitie.

There is evidence that Gaels – especially the élite of the clans which acted as agents of the central government – began to internalise this divide. James Fraser of Wardlaw in the late seventeenth century quoted a quatrain condemning the MacLeods (one branch of which, Sìol Torcail, successfully resisted extirpation): 'Sliochd Olbhair sin nach d'fhuair baisteadh / Tha buan masladh' ('Those descendants of Olaf[89] who never received Christian baptism / Who are constantly shameful').[90] In the lament for the ninth Earl of Argyll (beheaded in 1685), the primary vehicle of 'civility' in the Highlands – the Protestant church – is depicted as threatened by the savage natives without his leadership. The irony is obvious, given that the earl was executed by the central government, whose interests he was supposed to be advancing:

> *Có chumas còir ris an Eaglais?*
> *Dh'fhàs i dorcha;*
> *No chumas suas ar luchd teagaisg*
> *Ris na borbaibh?*
> *Có chumas an creideamh cathardha*
> *Suas gu treòrach*
> *Is nach d'fhuair Gille-easpuig cead èisdeachd*
> *An taic còrach?*[91]

('Who will defend the church? She has grown dark; Who will support our teachers against the barbarians? Who will provide the official religion with leadership now that Gilleaspuig has not had the chance to be heard supporting truth?')

Writing in 1605, during King James VI's attempts to colonise the Hebrides, Lowland lawyer Sir Thomas Craig gives a surprisingly sympathetic account of the attacks on Gaelic culture:

> I remember myself the time when the inhabitants of the Lennox and Menteith spoke pure Gaelic.[92] But nowadays that tongue is almost relegated to Argyll and the Hebrides, so that one rarely comes upon any who speak it. There is not a single

chieftain in the Highlands and Islands who does not either speak, or at least understand, English. [. . .] Many also write in that language, and if (as I understand is the case) a London Merchant Company is to be formed to exploit the fishing in Skye and Lewis, and if in consequence troops are sent thither and a settlement is made for the workmen employed in the fishing, and if schools are established, I have not the slightest doubt that before the century is over Gaelic will no longer be spoken on the mainland and islands of Scotland.[93]

By this time explicit evidence of the pressures on the élite for anglicisation is not hard to find. Sir Robert Gordon of Sutherland advised his young nephew John, the thirteenth earl, *c*.1620:

Use your diligence to take away the reliques of the Irishe barbaritie which as yet remains in your countrey, to wit, the Irishe langage, and the habit. [. . .] The Ireishe langage cannot so soone be extinguished. To help this plant schooles in ewerie corner in the countrey to instruct the youth to speak Inglishe. Let your chief scooles for learning be at Dornoche, and perswade the gentlemen of your countrey to bestow lairglie upon ther children to make them schollars for so shall they be fittest for your serwice. Presse to ciwilize your countrey and the inhabitants thereof, not onlie in this poynt.[94]

Edward Lhuyd's treatise on the Celtic languages was expected by the luminaries he met in his fieldwork to vindicate native self-esteem: such is clear from the odes composed by those authorities, printed in his 1707 volume. The Scottish Gaelic poems reflect an anxiety over the precarious state of the language and its vulnerability under a hostile government, but hope for its revival. The piece composed by Maighstir Seathan (the Reverend John Maclean), which displays a broad knowledge of Gaelic history, is worth quoting at length:

Air teachd on Spáin, do shliochd an Gháoidhil ghlais,	A.1, A.4
's do shliochd na Míligh 'nfhine nach budh tais;	A.4, ≠B.9
Budh mhór a nscleó 'sgach fód air cruas a nlánn,	B.2, B.4, D.5
Air fil'gheachd fós, 's air fóghlum nach budh ghánn.	B.8
Nuair a dhfhás a mpór ud mór, a bhos is tháll,	
'Bhi meas is prís fa 'n Ghaoidheilg ans gach báll	B.4
A Teanga líonmhur, bhríoghmhur, bhlasda, bhínn,	
'san chan'mhain thartrach, líobhtha, ghasta, ghrínn.	
A ccúirt na Ríogh, ré mile bliadh'n is tréall	
Do bhí si 'ntús, mun do thog caint Dhúbhghall ceann	
Gach Fili's Bard, gach Leigh, Aoisdán, is Draói,	
Druithnich is Sheanchaoi fós; gach eoladhain sháor.	
Do thug Gathelus leis, on Eighpht a náll,	A.4, A.1
san Ghaoidhelg sgríobh iad sud le gniomh ampeann.	

Na diagh're mór, budh chliu 's budh ghloir don chleir   B.2
   'san lé gu tárbhach 'labhariud briathre Dé.
Si labhair Padric 'nnínse Fail na Riogh,   A.3
   'san faighe caomhsin, Colum náomhtha 'n I.
Na Fráncigh liobhtha 'lean gach tír a mbéus,
   o I na ndeóri, ghabh am fóghlum freimh.   A.3, B.8
B'i bhoide muinte Luchd gach duthch' is teangth'   B.8
   chuir Gaill is Dubhghaill chuic' an tiulsa 'nclonn
Nois dhfholmhsi úainn gu tur, mo nuár 's mo chreach,
   's tearc luchd a gáoil, b' é sud an saó'al fa seach.   øG.2
Thuit í sann túr, maraon le hughdribh pfein,   øC.1
   'sna Flaith' 'mbudh dúth í, ghabh do cumhdach speis.   øG.2
Reic iád san chúirt í, air cáint úir o Nde,   øB.3
   's do thréig le hair budh nár leo ngcán'mhain fein.   øB.3
Air sár o Líath, biodh ádh, is cuimhnu' 's buáidh,
   Do rinn gu húr a dusgadh as a huáimh.
Gach neach 'ta fhréimh on Ghaoidheil ghléista gharg   A.4
   's gach droing don dúth an chánaimhn úd mar chaint.
Gach aoin do chinn, air treabh 'sair linne Scuit   A.4
   An duais is fiach thu, 'scoir gu níocfad dhuit.
On Bhannrighinn air antrás 'a bhfuil an crún,   B.4
   Gu nuig an bochd, do naite nochd a ndún.
'Bhi 'nainm 's a néuchd o linn na ncéud an ál
   Tre meath na Gaoidheilg, dol a cuimhne cháich: øB.2
Nois alla 'ngníomh, chluinn criocha fada tháll   B.4, B.2
   Sdeir síad le cheil, bhi Gaoidhil éin nuáir ánn.[95]

('When the descendants of Gaedheal Glas and of Mílidh – bold folk – came from Spain, the harshness of their blades, and their poetry and learning – which they had in abundance – was the subject of conversation in every land. When their population flourished, here [in Scotland] and across the sea [in Ireland], Gaelic was respected and valued everywhere: a widely-spoken, healthy, lovely, and melodious tongue, a strong, polished, beautiful and articulate language. For a thousand years and more it was topmost in the royal court, before the speech of Southrons raised its head. Gaelic was the language written by every poet, physician, eulogist and druid, craftsmen and storyteller too – every noble art – whom Gathelus brought with him from Egypt. It was in Gaelic that the high priesthood – to the honour and glory of the clergy – proclaimed persuasively the words of God. It was Gaelic that St Patrick spoke in Ireland of the Kings, as did that gentle prophet, the holy Columba, in Iona. The learning of the refined French, influential in every nation, was derived from Iona of the exiles, the mentor of people of every land and language. Norsemen and Saxons sent relations and children to Iona. Now, alas! we have lost it completely: Gaelic has few admirers. What a somersault the world has taken! It has fallen from the Tower, together with the authorities and princes whose inheritance it is, who once took an interest in defending it. It has been sold in the court for an upstart, and scornfully abandoned: people were ashamed of their own language. Good luck, fame and success to the great Lhuyd who has roused Gaelic from its grave; everyone descended from the keen and successful Gàidheal, and all who inherit that language as their own, all who are descended from the family and offspring of Scot, ought to reward you with the prize you have earned, from the queen who now wears the crown to the pauper whose home is the dunghill. Because of the withering away of Gaelic, their name and their achievement for hundreds of generations have been going out of the public memory: now far-off lands will hear the fame of their deeds and say to one another: "Once upon a time there were Gaels." ')

The pattern in Maclean's account of a Golden Age, a decline, and a promised return to former glory for Gaelic, was a common one in Highland perceptions before self-confidence was entirely shattered.[96] Animosities towards Lowlanders were grounded (to at least some degree) in the cultural memory that Gaels were the 'aboriginals' of Scotland who had been unjustly ousted. Edmund Burt, an English officer stationed in the Highlands in the 1720s, observed:

They have an adherence one to another, as Highlanders, in opposition to the people of the Low-Country, whom they despise as inferior to them in Courage, and believe they have a right to plunder them whenever it is in their Power. This last arises from a Tradition, that the Lowlands, in old Times were the possessions of their Ancestors.

Anne Grant of Laggan, who lived in Gaelic communities in both Scotland and North America, described the mutual suspicions and antagonisms that persisted between Highlanders and Lowlanders:

No two nations ever were more distinct, or differed more completely from each other, than the highlanders and lowlanders; and the sentiments with which they regarded each other was at best a kind of smothered animosity. The lowlander considered the highlander as a fierce and savage depredator, speaking a barbarous language and inhabiting a gloomy and barren region, which fear and prudence forbid all strangers to explore. [. . . The Highlanders] again regarded the lowlanders as a very inferior mongrel race of intruders; sons of little men, without heroism, without ancestry, or genius. Mechanical drudges, who could neither sleep without on the snow, compose extempore songs, recite long tales of wonder or of woe, or live without bread and without shelter for weeks together, following the chase. Whatever was mean or effeminate, whatever was dull, slow, mechanical, or torpid, was in the highlands imputed to the lowlanders, and exemplified by allusions to them; while in the low country, every thing ferocious or unprincipled – every species of aukwardness or ignorance – of pride or of insolence, was imputed to the highlanders.

No two communities, generally speaking, could hate each other more cordially, or despise each other more heartily.[97]

On the other hand, there is also the suggestion in Gaelic tradition that as the ethnic core of Scotland, they could form common cause with Lowlanders and regain the status they once enjoyed. Highland advocates of Jacobitism played up such aspirations. The nationality of the people involved on either side of the Jacobite Risings does not inform us as to how contemporary Gaels viewed, or represented, the conflict in cultural terms. Contemporary Gaelic poetry – the overwhelming amount of which is Jacobite, even from Protestant clans[98] – depicts Gaels defending Scottish nationhood and English forces bent on its destruction. It is a simplified binary opposition that left a profound mark on popular representations of Jacobitism, much to the dismay of many modern historians. This is the perspective we would expect of propagandists, such as the master-poet Alasdair mac Mhaighstir Alasdair:

> Nach nàr dhuit féin mar thachair dhuit,
> O Albainn bhochd tha truagh
> Gann làn an dùirn de Ghàidhealaibh
> Fhàgail ri h-uchd buailt'?   øB.9
> Nach smuain thu do chruadal mór,
> 'Shliochd Scota sin nan lann?   A.2, A.4
> Is diùbhlamaid air muinntir Dheòrs'
> Fuil phrionnsail mhór nan Clann.[99]   B.6

('O poor, wretched Scotland, are you not ashamed of what has happened to you, with scarcely a handful of Gaels left to face the battle? Can you not summon up your strength, o descendants of Scota of the swords, and let us take the vengeance of Highland blood on [King] George's forces.')

This perspective pervades contemporary Gaelic poetry at the popular level as well, as in this anonymous woman's song:

> Ailein, Ailein, gabh sgoinn, 's bidh 'g éirigh
> Tionail do chlann, cuimhnich d' fheum orr';
> Bidh Alba mhór fo mheinn bhéistean
> Mur an dìon a muinntir fhéin i.[100]

('O Allan, Allan, take heart and arise, raise your clan and remember their purpose to you; great Scotland will be at the mercy of beasts if her own people will not defend her.')

Hanoverian propagandists demonised Highlanders and entertained fantasies of induced starvation and mass genocide. Such hysteria was generated in England that those billeting the Highland army feared that Highlanders were cannibals and would eat their children. Shortly after news of Prince Charles' reception in the Highlands, some officials called for large-scale forced evictions of entire Highland communities to the American colonies. King George II's second son, the Duke of Cumberland, in charge of the Hanoverian army, proposed in early 1746 that 'whole clans be transported' to the West Indies including 'the entire clan of the Camerons' and some of the MacDonalds. Most post-Culloden reformers envisioned importing 'civilised' foreigners who would help improve Highland society.[101] The Duke of Newcastle received the suggestion in 1746 that 'the now forfeited lands, on which these pernicious Drones [i.e., Highlanders] lived, be planted and cultivated by an industrious and loyal set of People, to be sent thither in their Stead.'[102] While it was impractical to carry out these proposals on a large scale, they demonstrate that ideas of mass eviction and population replacement were in wide circulation well before the Clearances.

Measures taken after Culloden, such as the Disarming Act, intended not just to demilitarise the Highland population but to demoralise them, and the effects were documented by numerous natives and outsiders. During their five week tour of Scotland in 1786, Maximilien De Lazowski and Alexandre de La Rochefoucauld commented that Highlanders had not yet forgotten or forgiven the ignominious treatment they had received from the Hanoverian government:

> They can't speak of Culloden without getting heated, and the thought that they are subjected to the English is one that grieves and torments them [. . .] They preferred to live well and to remain a people utterly apart; not to abandon the smallest of their ways, so much respected in the country, and distinguishing them from all other people. [. . .] They are very proud of their language, and the king of England, seeking gradually to reduce their ideas of separate nationality, has established free schools across the Highlands for teaching English, and there they send their children. [. . .] since English was introduced, they have begun to lose their ancient customs – their music for instance, and what they talk much more about, having been made to wear breeches.[103]

It was particularly disheartening for the peasantry to see their former leaders abandon and betray their cultural norms. The Highland Society's committee in-vestigating the authenticity of Macpherson's *Ossian* received several accounts about Gaelic society from native Highlanders which included internal perspectives on the cultural attack on Gaelic. One was from Ùisdean MacDhomhnaill, a native of South Uist, who perceived Gaelic's decline on a national level:

> *Ach is e buille as truime fhuair a' chànail-sa riamh gun deachaidh an teaghlach rìoghail do Shaghsan, agus gu robh mòr uaislean na Gàidhealtachd 'g an leantainn; bha iad sin aig tabhairt cleachdaidh agus cànail Shaghsan air an ais. Bha barrach coimeasgadh bho*

'n aimsir sin eadar Gàidheil agus Gaill, agus bha riaghladh na rìoghachd uile ag oidhirpeachadh gus a' chànail-sa chur às, gus an robh na Gàidheil, lion beag is beag, ag call an tlachd de ghnàthachadh agus de mhearsalachd cànail neartmhoir an sinnsre, air chor is nach mór nach deachaidh iad air chall gu léir.

But the severest blow which our language has ever received was the removal of the Royal Family to England, and the attendance of our men of rank and influence at Court; who were bringing back to their country the manners and language of England and of the Lowlands. From that period, more frequent intercourse was obtained between the Highlands and the people of the south. The Government exerted its utmost power for the destruction of the Gaelic language, and Highland manners, until by degrees the Highlanders were losing their respect and esteem for the manly and original language of their ancestors.[104]

The backlash against Macpherson's *Ossian* was fuelled not only by English literary critics like Samuel Johnson who were incapable of understanding the nature of Gaelic literature, but Lowlanders who shared similar cultural prejudices and felt threatened that their own literary traditions could be overshadowed. In fact, 'the assault on Celticism was most persistently mounted by Lowlanders of Whiggish leanings who refused to be patronised by "bared-arsed Highlanders".'[105] Adam Ferguson, former chaplain to the Black Watch, native Gaelic speaker and professor of moral philosophy at the University of Edinburgh during the Scottish Enlightenment, remarked to the committee of Gaelic:

It was a language spoken in the cottage; but not in the parlour, or at the table of any gentleman. Its greatest elegancies were to be learned from herdmen or deer-stealers. It was connected with disaffection, and proscribed by government. Schools were erected to supplant it, by teaching a different language. There were no books in it, but the manuals of religion; and these in so aukward and clumsy a spelling that few could read them. The fashionable world in the neighbourhood, as usual, derided the tone and accent of the Highlanders, believing their own to be models of grace and harmony. It was more genteel to be ignorant than knowing of what such a language contained.[106]

Anti-Gaelic prejudices, reinforced by schools and officials, began to be internalised by the Gaels. Arbitrary eviction, loss of self-determination and denigration by the outside world was additionally demoralising. As early as 1811 Anne Grant of Laggan noted:

When a people are taught to despise the modes of thinking, customs and prejudices of their ancestors, and to consider as barbarism and vulgarity all that in their childhood they were accustomed to regard as excellent and elegant – the whole web of thought and feeling is unravelled, and cannot be readily or easily made up in a new form.[107]

John Murdoch, who established the newspaper the *Highlander* to champion the cause of the crofters in the 1870s, connected Gaeldom's internal inferiority complex with its treatment by the anglophone world:

> The language and lore of the Highlanders being treated with despite [*sic*] has tended to crush their self-respect and to repress that self-reliance without which no people can advance. When a man was convinced that his language was a barbarism, his lore as filthy rags, and that the only good thing about him – his land – was, because of his general unworthiness, to go to a man of another race and another tongue, what remained [. . .] that he should fight for?[108]

The first large-scale Clearances were carried out in Glengarry in 1785 against communities who had been renowned warriors. 'The collapse of the Glengarry house was throughout all the Highlands felt to be a whole race calamity [. . .] That disappearance was like the fall of a fixed star from the Celtic firmament.'[109] Highlanders often represented the Clearances as an attack on Gaeldom by the *Gall* or *Sasannach*, whatever the national origins of those actually perpetrating these acts (and it is interesting that many anti-Clearance songs were composed to Jacobite tunes). This may have been, in part, a defence mechanism against the sting of betrayal, as well as an implicit call for cultural solidarity amongst Gaels. Many held on to the hope that the descendants of their former chieftains, having ingratiated themselves with the British establishment (in no small part by exploiting their former clansmen in military regiments) would come to their defence. Others simply gave up hope and saw emigration as the only way out. By the late eighteenth century some Gaels made a causal connection between the defeat at Culloden and the invasion of English norms into the Gàidhealtachd which were hostile to their survival.

This is not to deny that there were proprietors who attempted to maintain a population on their estates. Indeed, the British Passenger Act of 1803 was one attempt to restrict mass emigration. These measures were taken, however, because of landlords' interests in exploiting a subject population in the production of kelp or the raising of regiments, not because of basic human rights or intrinsic value. In his travelogue of 1791, Thomas Newt wrote, 'The case of those men is exceedingly hard and such, I am perfectly convinced, if it had happened in England, would not only have been universally deplored as cruel, but considered as unjust and illegal.'[110]

Despite the lack of capital, security of land-holding and industrial development, Gaels were blamed for the economic failures to which they were increasingly vulnerable. Racist rhetoric was used to claim that the Gaels, and their language and culture, were doomed by natural and irreversible Darwinian laws which were aiding in the inevitable dominance of the Anglo-Saxon throughout the empire. This was true especially in the nineteenth century as the grand narrative of race became more pervasive and economic crisis in the Highlands more endemic. Racialism became a totalising theory that transformed perceptions throughout society, from the arts and sciences to politics and social policy, and some of those most vocal advocates of 'Teutonic' (also called 'Germanic', 'Gothic' or 'Anglo-Saxon') superiority were Scottish Lowlanders. The 'science' of phrenology (interpreting skull structures in racial terms), for example, was developed by two Edinburgh brothers and until its downfall 'its heartland was in Scotland'.[111] By distancing themselves from the Celts and claiming an ancestry even more purely Teutonic than most of England, Lowlanders 'fostered British integration and enthusiasm for imperialism through identification with the greater Saxon mission'.[112] In other words, Scottish Lowlanders acknowledged the superiority of the Anglo-Saxon and claimed descent from them also, which allowed them to portray their participation in the British Empire as the natural amalgamation of a single master race.

> In particular, Teutonism conferred legitimacy on Lowland Scotland's place at the commercial and industrial core of the Empire. Lowland Scots were reassured that as Teutons they were not mere helots of an English Empire, nor a subject colonial people, but a branch of the dominant race which rightly belonged at the imperial high table.[113]

John Pinkerton (1758–1826), a pioneer in the study of Lowland literature who also published works about Scottish history and delighted in attacking Macpherson's *Ossian*, emphasised in 1787 the savagery of the Celts by constantly reiterating an equation between the Celts and subject peoples on the one hand, and the Goths and Classical civilisation on the other:

> The manners of the Celts, as described by Greek and Roman authors, are totally unlike those of the ancient Greeks; the people among the former being slaves, among the later extremely free. [. . .] The Celts had no monuments any more than the savage Americans or Samoiedes. From Diodorus Siculus, and others, it is clear that the manners of the Celts perfectly resembled those of the present Hottentots. [. . .] what their own mythology was we know not, but it in all probability resembled that of the Hottentots, or others of the rudest savages, as the Celts ancient were, and are little better at present, being incapable of any progress in society.[114]

Pinkerton's racial classifications, further elaborated in his 1789 *An Enquiry into the History of Scotland*, attributed the characteristics ascribed to Africans, physical, moral and intellectual, to Scottish Highlanders.[115] By the 1840s the general racial stereotypes of the eighteenth century hardened into genetic determinism. Lowland Scottish surgeon Robert Knox stated in his authoritative work *The Races of Men* in 1850: 'Race is everything: literature, science, art – in a word, civilisation depends on it.'[116] Knox called for the ethnic cleansing of inferior peoples from British colonies, and saw the process already in motion in the Highlands, having begun at Culloden and further by the Clearances.[117] Such prejudices were echoed in the popular press. After several years of the potato blight that struck Europe in 1846, the editorial of the national newspaper *The Scotsman* explained famine in the Highlands as the result of racial inferiority paralleled in Ireland:

> It would be invidious to say what it is that makes a part of the population thus a burden. Some people say that it is the effect of race; and they point to the Celts of Kerry and of Barra, distant some four hundred miles from each other, yet precisely in the same condition of hopeless, listless, actionless, useless penury. [. . .] It becomes clear at once that it is the interest of the productive members of society to get rid of all these classes.[118]

Such racial stereotypes and biases infiltrated young minds via school textbooks and novels.[119] Racialism was not an objective reality but an ideology that could be manipulated in creative ways and as Scottish Gaels became more invested in the British Empire some Highland élite distanced themselves from the Irish by inventing racial divergences. According to some, the Irish had degenerated from the original Celtic stock; according to others Highland blood had been improved by Teutonic admixture. Whatever the rationale for their estrangement, few Highlanders were able to maintain previous cultural allegiances to Irish Gaels when anti-Irish prejudice was rampant and both groups were in economic competition in the cities of the empire.[120]

Highlanders responded to the British military and empire in various ways. Some young men enlisted in the British army zealously under their traditional leaders, expecting that their loyal service would secure land rights for themselves and their families.[121] There are also tales of pressgangs and forced enlistment as well as evasion of recruiters.[122] The deployment of Highlanders as the empire's 'shock troops' is sometimes remarked upon as ironic, but no more ironic than the military's use of Mohawks, Gurkhas, Sikhs, Pathans, and other subalterns. People whose cultural independence has been curtailed and believe that their highest calling is the championing of another people's civilisation make ideal servitor imperialists. The subservience to English norms was self-defeating for the survival of the Gaelic language and culture. No sacrifice was too great to exact from the Gaels in the cause of British interests, but few language or land rights were rewarded in kind.

Gaelic-medium newspapers printed at affordable prices in the fourth quarter of the nineteenth century allowed Highlanders (including those living in England, North America and Australia) to develop some intellectual response in defence of their culture, if only in fits and starts. Some of the response was directed at tartanism's appropriation of Highland identity. The Rev. Archibald Farquharson published *An Address to Highlanders* in 1868 and remarked on the hypocrisy of landlords who hijacked Highland symbols but deprecated Gaelic: 'I am glad, sir, to see you in that dress, but how dare you wear that kilt without speaking the Gaelic?'.[123] A Scottish correspondent wrote in 1896 to the Canadian newspaper *Mac-Talla*:

An Gàidheal aig nach eil meas air cànain a dhùthchadh chan fhìor Ghàidheal e. Faodaidh e dhol gu féill no gu banais ann an trusgan suaicheanta nan Gàidheal, agus toirt air féin a chreidsinn gur fìor Ghàidheal e, ach is iomadh fear air am bheil feileadh beag is sporan donn is còta dearg anns a' chom a labhras gle thàireil ann an comunn nan Gall mun Ghàidhlig agus mu na Gàidheil.[124]

The Highlander who does not esteem the language of his country is not a true Highlander. He can go to a festival or wedding in distinctive Highland clothing, and make himself believe that he is a true Highlander, but there is many a man who wears the kilt and dun sporran and red coat who speaks very disparagingly about Gaelic and the Highlanders in the company of non-Gaels.

When Highlanders came to the Lowlands as emigrants or seasonal workers, they were often treated with disdain; such is a frequent complaint in contemporary Gaelic songs.[125] Emigrants responded by forming organisations, many of them specific to particular islands or districts of the Highlands. Most of these emigrant societies, as well as the Highland, Ossianic, Gaelic and Celtic societies formed from the late eighteenth century, however, lacked the will or commitment to challenge the entrenched anti-Gaelic prejudices of their day or to lead a political movement to redress injustices. As early as 1841 one Gael noted with disappointment that the Edinburgh Highland Society, having reduced its interests to animal husbandry, previously 'had reference to the mental culture of their Caledonian countrymen, instead of as now, unfortunately, to the physical development of the points of the inferior animals'.[126] Complaints about the political impotence of such groups, which many had expected to deliver tangible benefits to Gaelic, were expressed by the more outspoken Gaelic advocates of the nineteenth century, and later in the radical newspaper *Guth na Bliadhna* (1904–25).

By eliminating or assimilating the upper echelons of Highland society, Gaeldom was deprived of intellectual advocates and cultural exemplars, reducing it to an 'aborted civilisation' in the eyes of the outside world. Anglo-Saxon essentialism was claimed to have an exclusive hold on progress and modernity. Efforts to establish a chair of Celtic in Scotland finally emerged in the 1870s. Like many others, the renowned scholar J. F. Campbell wrote in 1872 that the establishment of a chair of Celtic would raise the prestige of Gaelic nationally and the esteem that Highlanders had for it:

I hear that the Rev. Archibald Farquharson is trying to stir up the Highland people to make an effort to establish a Gaelic professorship in one of our Scottish universities. It is high time that a really serious effort were made, and every true Highlander will wish Mr Farquharson God-speed. [. . .] And it is to be hoped that such success will be the means of rescuing the Gaelic language from the contempt in which it is too frequently held by so many of those of whom better might be expected. [. . .] Many

Highlanders, on the contrary, even when residing in their own country, and amongst a Gaelic-speaking people, if they think themselves in any way better than their neighbours, seem (with the most contemptible snobbishness) to consider it quite beneath their dignity to allow their children to learn Gaelic, as if they considered the Gaelic people a conquered and subjugated race; and a most downtrodden and ill-used race they undoubtedly are in many respects.[127]

John Stuart Blackie, professor of Greek at the University of Edinburgh, was an outspoken advocate of Gaelic and campaigned for the establishment of a chair of Celtic as soon as a committee was formed to investigate prospects in 1872. About the anti-Gaelic prejudices which prevailed in Scottish education, he wrote that year:

The objections which are brought forward against teaching the Gaelic language in a Gaelic country, and to a Gaelic-speaking population, are, as might be expected, altogether of that flimsy description which betrays their origin, not in a cool survey of the elements of the case, but in unpurified passion and unreasoning prejudice. The records of the worlds of books, as well as the tone of colloquial discourse, present us with striking instances of the existence of a class of persons who are possessed by a blind idolatry of the Saxon, and a violent antipathy to the Celtic race. [. . .] A certain class of utilitarian philosophers tell us that the Gaelic language is the only existing hindrance to the complete civilization of the Highlands, and that to do anything towards preserving it is only to prolong the period of savagery and isolation.[128]

Such pleas for the recognition of Gaelic as a serious subject at an academic level brought out much antipathy, sometimes mocking Professor Blackie as an eccentric outsider foisting Gaelic upon an unwilling Highland populace, glad to be free of its burden. The *Glasgow Herald* admonished him in 1876 with rhetoric reflecting the racists attitudes of the day:

They will be ready to allow – against the Professor – that the Darwinian law must in the case of the Celt, as in all social and political life, and indeed throughout the whole realm of nature, have full play – all sentiment and even legislation to the contrary notwithstanding. [. . .] It is possible the large, nay, almost total, disappearance of this [village life in the Highlands], the real essence of Highland life, that has already taken place, that leads not over-sentimental Celts to wish for, or at least disposes them to deplore less passionately than the Professor, the completion of the assimilation of Highland to Lowland life. The kernel gone, the mere shell is matter of small enough consequence. Not so, however, thinks the Professor, with the proverbial zeal of the new and late-born converts.[129]

Despite such opposition, the first Chair of Celtic was finally instituted in 1882. Another attempt to reclaim Celtic civilisation, especially through literary reinvention, emerged in the late nineteenth century, usually referred to as the 'Celtic Twilight'.[130] In 1905 Alexander Carmichael, who spent decades collecting Gaelic folklore all around the Highlands which he published in a series of volumes commonly called the *Carmina Gadelica*, saw this sympathetic response as an opportunity to elevate Scottish Gaelic culture:

> Everything Highland is becoming of interest. Let us try to meet this interest and to show the world that our dearly beloved people were not the rude, barbarous, creedless, godless, ignorant men and women that prejudiced writers have represented them. It is to me heart-breaking to see the spiteful manner in which Highlanders have been spoken of.[131]

In a rejoinder in a debate in 1938 over the place of Gaelic in Scottish education, I. A. MacLeòid extended the conversation by decrying the anti-Gaelic biases in the curriculum, embraced by

> men who have drunk so deeply of the imperial springs of English diplomacy that not only can they witness the terrible plight of their own people with sublime equanimity, but they can, with equally supreme indifference, survey disruptive international forces that rock the whole world. [. . .] Does not all this go to show how this corroding poison has eaten in to our very marrow? This insidious virus has permeated our being and has given us an inferiority complex with regard to ourselves and our language, and a false standard of values with regard to everything. And when those to whom we should look for leadership, distinguished men, presumably wise and learned, reveal such distorted views and disseminate such deplorable doctrines, what can we expect from the common herd but confusion of ideas, despair, and inertness?[132]

A poignant essay published in 1986 by the respected author Iain Crichton Smith from the island of Lewis describes the broken world to which Gaeldom found itself heir in the twentieth century.

> There was a period when the language was banned in schools, and when I was growing up there was no Gaelic spoken in the village school even by teachers who were Gaelic-speaking. It was as if an English child were to be taught in French by Englishmen, and to have first to learn French before he could become educated at all. [. . .] There is no question that a language holds a community together in its various manifestations, and that to have to learn a new language in order to be educated at all is a dangerous and potentially fatal attack on that community and those who form part of it. For the imperialist language is imperiously and contemptuously degrading the native one. [. . .] The Gaelic speaker feels himself to be inferior, and his language inferior. [. . .] We are owed – such men are owed – not indifference but at least understanding and care. It is not right that a whole culture should be treated this way,

that like Red Indians and the aborigines so many of our people should have had to leave their homes to inherit the worst aspects of a so-called superior civilisation.[133]

Many features of the stereotype of the barbaric Highlander of the thirteenth century still appear on a regular basis in disparaging statements in the popular press of twenty-first-century Scotland, as does antipathy for the Gaelic language itself. These denigrating remarks would surely not be tolerated if they were made about other minority groups in Scotland as they reek of ignorance and racism.

From the humanists (such as John Mair) defending the Lowlands against the ancient charge that barbarity lies in the North[134] to the modern accusations against 'subsidy junkie' crofters and the 'inferior' Gaelic language, there has been a recurring Lowland rejection of Highland affinities, an Othering of the Gael. The intermediate position of the Lowlands – between 'backwards' Gaeldom and 'progressive' England – made it insecure about its own identity on its own terms, as a position of independent formulation became harder to assert with growing English hegemony.[135] From the violent reactions of the Reformation (more extreme in many aspects than in England) to involvement in the creation of racism, Lowland Scotland frequently overcompensated for its self-doubt by espousing Anglo-Saxonism and rejecting its Celtic elements. This is both ironic and tragic, given its original foundation by the Gaels and the reliance upon the displaced poor who fuelled its industrial revolution and military regiments, a great number of which were cleared from the Highlands or starved out of Ireland.

Chapter Three

LITERATURE AND ORAL TRADITION

But where are we to learn what the manners and customs of the old Highlanders were? We are a thousand fold more dependent upon old Gaelic poems than the Irish. The true history of the Highlanders is to be found in their poems, and nowhere else.
– Rev. Alexander Maclean Sinclair, 1889

The professional poets who were supported by the native nobility are largely responsible for developing Gaelic poetry into a sophisticated art form. Aristocrats expected, in return, to be rewarded with a sort of immortal memory in the work of these poets; if they did not behave magnanimously, however, the poets threatened them with eternal defamation in verse. This self-perpetuating symbiotic relationship, whereby the status of aristocrats was validated by the literati who were in turn employed by them, endured in Scottish Gaeldom into the eighteenth century.

The following anecdote, repeated verbatim from an early-twentieth-century source, illustrates the consequences of being a poor host to a poet, consequences which continue long after death! It also exemplifies the mixture of genres that typically occurs in a single item at a céilidh: in this case a tale explains the meaning of a local proverbial expression and the origin of a song, and ends with the song itself.

~

When the great Clan Campbell was at the height of its power, the estate of Barbreck was possessed by a Campbell, who was the brother or cousin – tradition is somewhat uncertain as to the exact degree of relationship – of another Campbell, the neighbouring laird of Craignish. This latter, the laird of Craignish, kept a piper, while Barbreck did not. Barbreck could afford to keep one, too, as well as his cousin, but he grudged the expense. His stinginess in this respect, or wise economy, if you so like to term it, is still commemorated in a saying common in some parts of Argyll: '*Tha mi as iùnais, mar bha 'm Barr Breac gun phiobaire*' ('I am without it, just as Barbreck was without a piper') – when you would admit that you want a certain thing, such as, for instance, a horse and gig, yacht, or anything else that your neighbour has, and that you might have too, could well enough afford to have if you only liked.

Barbreck was one day on a visit to Craignish, and as he was leaving, meeting the piper, he addressed him, 'The New Year is approaching. On New Year's day morning, when you have played the proper "salute" to your master, my cousin Craignish, I wish you would come over to Barbreck and play a New Year's "salute" to me, for, as you know, I have no piper of my own to do it. Come and spend the day with us.'

The piper promised, and on New Year's morning, after first playing his master into good humour, he went to Barbreck as was arranged. He played and played until the laird of Barbreck was in raptures. After a while the piper felt that he was both hungry and thirsty, and hinted as much to the laird. Food was therefore set before him, but unsatisfactory in every way as to quantity, no less than as to quality and kind. The drinkables were no better, and long ere the sun had set, the piper was anxious to return home.

'Give us one more tune before you go,' said Barbreck.

'That I will,' responded the piper, and he then and there played impromptu the tune, from that day forth so much admired and widely known as 'Taigh 'Bhròinein' ('the House of the Miserly One'). The following are two of some half-dozen stanzas attached to this *port* from the very first, whether by the piper himself or by a brother bard is not known, and having a reference to its origin and history:

> *Bha mi 'n taigh Bhròinein an-diugh*
> *Bha mi 'n taigh Bhròinein;*
> *Fhuair mi cuireadh*
> *'S cha d'fhuair mi gu leòr ann;*
> *Fhuair mi deoch bhrochain ann*
> *As droch aran eòrna;*
> *Fhuair mi cas circ' ann*
> *'S air chinnt gum bi 'm bròn i!*
> *Cuireadh gun dreach a chràidh mi;*
> *Fàgaidh mi nochd*
> *Gun bhiadh gun deoch;*
> *Fàgaidh mi nochd 'm Barr Breac*
> *'S cha phill mi riut tuilleadh*
> *A sheinn do phort fàilte.*[1]

('I was in the House of the Miserly One today, in the House of the Miserly One; I received an invitation but no satisfaction did I have; I had a drink of gruel-water and poor barley bread; I had the foot of a hen and for certain, it was deplorable! The unseemly invitation that vexed me; I will leave tonight without food or drink; I will leave Barbreck tonight and I will not return to play a tune of salute for you.')

~

The nature of literacy and literature in Gaelic is widely misunderstood. People often repeat the belief that 'Gaelic was never a written language' or that 'Gaelic only has an oral tradition'. To the contrary, Gaelic literature was being written before English literature and the Gaels were the pioneers of vernacular literacy in the British Isles. Scottish Gaelic literature has a continuous history as old as any in Western Europe and it has continued to develop to the present despite great adversity.

In pre-modern societies only the élite had any reason to read and write. It was only after the Protestant Reformation that the aspiration to universal literacy became common. While members of the Gaelic élite became literate no later than the sixth century, institutional prejudices and underdevelopment in the modern era made literacy impossible for most Gaels until the eighteenth century and later. Thus, even into the twenty-first century Gaelic has been an oral-dominant literary tradition.

Differing local conditions produced divergent regional material cultures and religious affiliations across the Highlands. What Highlanders most had in common were exactly those forms of culture least visible to the untrained outsider: literature, oral tradition, and other folklore genres. The mythopoeic universe established in texts such as *Lebor Gabála Érenn* continued to resonate in Scottish Gaelic poetry from across the Highlands to the present. Ossianic songs and narratives have been recorded from tradition-bearers from Dunkeld to Nova Scotia, Lewis to Islay. A similar geographical distribution can be seen for a large portion of the corpus of Gaelic oral tradition, including proverbs, hero tales, *puirt-á-beul*, and the work of anonymous and named poets such as Iain Lom, Donnchadh Bàn Mac an t-Saoir, and Màiri nighean Alasdair Ruaidh.

> The Gaelic sense of identity is conditioned and sometimes actually shaped by information that emanates from these historical legends as well as from other, less formally organised categories of tradition. Poetry and legend combine in tradition to create a native view of history.[2]

There is an abundance of approaches to understanding written literature and oral tradition, most of which focus on the function, form, and/or content of the verbal arts. While earlier scholars believed there to be a clean break between oral and literate societies, more recent schools of thought instead observe that orality and literacy operate along a spectrum in which form and content, performer and audience, are deeply intertwined. This chapter will examine the cultural significance and history of the Gaelic literati and their products and discuss some of the most useful means of analysing the verbal arts as literature. Chapter Seven will further discuss the musical and performance aspects of Gaelic poetry.

ORAL AND WRITTEN

The hierarchical and consciously aristocratic nature of pre-collapse Gaelic society is reflected in many aspects of its literary productions. While everyone in society was expected to be an active participant and co-creator of oral tradition, the genres and linguistic registers of verbal expressions that one could create and appreciate varied according to whether one was a *bard baile* 'village poet' or *ollamh rígh* 'king's master of poetry'. Regardless of these distinctions, and the fact that professional poets were literate, even most written texts were meant to be performed orally. To simplify discussion, I will use the terms 'text' and 'literature' to refer generically to verbiage regardless of whether it is recorded from an oral performance or composed on the written page.

The verbal arts are central to the operation of society in oral-dominant societies. The most common themes of oral poetry are praise, blame and lamentation, with the poet acting as a mediator between rulers and dependants, humankind and the gods. In a society without written documents, oral tradition is the primary means of preserving the memory of one's achievements and identity. Patronage of the custodians of poetry was the most effective means of ensuring the immortality of one's ancestors and oneself. The Gaelic word *cliù* means 'reputation, fame' but derives from the word meaning 'what is heard'. It has long been the boast of Gaelic poets that their subjects will live forever in publicly rehearsed verse. In the lament of the death of two Clanranald chiefs, Ailean *c.*1503 and his son Raghnall Bàn *c.*1511, a MacMhuirich poet stated:

Mairidh go bráth buan a chuimhne,	B.2
Cumha a chárad, gidh céim doirbh [. . .]	H.5
Beó bladh a n-aithle gach aoinfhir,	B.2
a Ailín nár [ ] *ngliaidh;*	
gé fior t' éag, is tú nach teasda:	
féach do chlú budh dheasda ad dhiaidh.[3]	B.2

('His memory will live forever, though the grief of his friends is a difficult experience [. . .] A man's reputation outlives him; o Ailean, who shunned death, although it is true that you have died, you have not departed: behold how your fame continues after you.')

In oral-dominant societies, the verbal arts are not just aesthetically pleasing but functional: work and play are accompanied and directed by verbal utterances of various kinds. Songs help to coordinate work, charms are recited for protection, prayers are given in gratitude, lullabies put children to sleep, proverbs guide or justify decisions. In early Gaelic society information was chiefly represented and transmitted in the form of poetry. The tract *Auraicept na n-Éces* states, 'There are five types of poetry: poetry that nourishes, poetry that sings, poetry that impels, poetry that judges, and poetry that establishes.' This suggests how poetry was relevant to every branch of knowledge and every aspect of the operation of society: practical, aesthetic, magical, legal, and ideological.[4]

One way of looking at the verbal arts is to divide them into groups according to the strata of society to which they belong and the time to which they are directed. Items pertaining to the past project continuity into the past and provide exemplars and precedents for the present; items pertaining to the present help to regulate society and encourage stability; items pertaining to the future attempt to secure benefits as well as express ideals, aspirations and goals. While such a classification scheme can be useful, it must also be kept in mind that a single item usually serves more than one purpose simultaneously: stories may teach lessons in morality, for example, but they also serve as entertainment, encourage group solidarity, reinforce language skills, and teach the art of storytelling.[5]

Domain	Past	Present	Future
Sacred	Cosmological myth; Christian scripture; Tales of saints; Tales of Otherworld	Liturgy; Hymns	Supplication to God
Leadership / Politics	Hero legends; Genealogies of kings and chieftains	Inaugural practices; Laws; Charters; Elegies; Eulogy and Satire	Oaths; Poetic advice and pleas
Clan Society	Founding legends; Clan songs; Clan sagas	Gnomic lore; Clan-wide customs; Battle incitements; Work songs; Dance songs; Flyting	Blessings; Battle protection; Poetic debates
Personal	Wonder tales; Anecdotes; Pedigrees	Proverbs; Ritual texts; Invocations; Expressions of emotion	Divinations; Tabus; Charms; Curses

Table 3.1: A schema of the functions of verbal arts in Gaelic society[6]

The differing functions of the verbal arts are reflected in their content and style. Wonder tales focus on the action of the characters and the dialogue between them. While they may implicitly contain a 'lesson', they do not moralise explicitly.[7] Gnomic lore (such as proverbs), on the other hand, exists to provide explicit guidance and deliberately articulates cultural values.

A genre classification attempts to group together verbal expressions according to definitive characteristics such as form (such as prose or poetry) and content (such as comedy, tragedy, or romance). Genre classifications are socially constructed and differ from culture to culture. There is a large store of terms for forms of the verbal arts in Gaelic, some of which are very old. Many of these terms do not form the sort of strict and non-overlapping taxonomy for genre preferred by modern scholars, although they do reflect the functions of native oral tradition and literature, as well as the professional ranks engaged in them.

Three terms which were operative in the medieval period are useful for discussing the verbal arts of Gaeldom's learned professionals. The term *seanchas* means 'traditional knowledge, lore' and includes history, genealogy, and law. The term *filidheacht* refers to the poetry of the filidh as defined by the medieval bardic schools, which most often took the form of verse. The term *sgeul* (in modern Scottish Gaelic) refers in particular to narratives (i.e., tales) but includes history and mythological material and can also refer to knowledge, information or news.[8]

There are many more specific terms for the materials in the learned and vernacular traditions.[9] One fundamental distinction between verbal forms is their relationship to poetry and musicality. Some genres are mostly prose in their form, although it is not unusual for them to also contain features of poetry such as alliteration and rhyme. That there were recognised masterpieces of various genres is suggested by a Highland proverb naming five of them,[10] the first two of which are Ossianic:

> *Gach dàn gu Dàn an Deirg;*
> *Gach laoidh gu Laoidh an Amadain Mhóir;*
> *Gach sgeul gu Sgeul Chonaill;*
> *Gach cliù gu Cliù Eòghainn;*
> *Gach moladh gu Moladh Loch Cé.*

> ('The top-most song: The Song of the Red One;
> The top-most lay: The Lay of the Great Fool;
> The top-most tale: The Tale of Conall;
> The top-most eulogy: The Eulogy of Ewen;
> The top-most praise: The Praise of Loch Key.')

People usually knew and performed a wide range of genre types. These different elements of Gaelic oral tradition often referred to one another and were mutually reinforcing. 'In a culture where the various genres of oral tradition and music complement and support each other, the links between song and oral narrative are of primary importance.'[11] These connections can be seen between other genres as well: the origin and meaning of many proverbs, for example, are often explained by stories; songs make frequent allusion to proverbs. John Francis Campbell noted the wide variety of material carried by the tradition-bearers he met in 1859: 'But though each prefers his own subject, the best Highland story-tellers know specimens of all kinds. Start them, and it seems as they would never stop.'[12]

Oral-derived literature can feel alien to those who have gained literacy in a 'modern education', not least because it tends to flout so many rules: 'Be original', 'Don't repeat yourself', 'Avoid clichés'. These essential principles of modern writing have little relevance in most oral-derived literatures. As in other oral-dominant cultures, the emphasis in the Gaelic verbal arts has been to achieve eloquence on matters relevant to the community within the aesthetic bounds prescribed by tradition.

Gaelic traditional poetry was in the main one of celebration and participation. The poet produced an artefact which enabled his audience to participate in their culture; to act out culturally reinforcing roles. The poetry was largely oral-based; much of it was meant to be sung. In such circumstances innovation was not at a very high premium. The verse had to make an immediate impact, and skill in versification and verbal wit culminating in the well-wrought memorable phrase was therefore the basic requirement.[13]

Most Gaelic poetry has been composed to well-known tunes, choruses or prescribed metrical patterns. The constant recycling of form and content blurs the concept of individual ownership and authorship and reinforces the sense of participation in an inherited, collective art form. This has been particularly true of the vernacular tradition, which has been sustained by active participation of the entire community.

The frequent mention of the author of a song at a gathering was intended to indicate the source and associations; in contrast to some other cultures the concept of ownership did not apply to songs any more than fiddle tunes or stories.[14]

The content, form and performance styles of the verbal arts in oral-derived traditions tend to share certain characteristics. *Metacommunication* refers to the signals (verbal and non-verbal) given by performer about his or her performance and how it should be interpreted by the audience. One of the basic metanarrative devices is the *interpretive framing formula*, which can be used to indicate the beginning and end of an oral performance. When someone says 'Once upon a time', for example, you tend to think 'That person is going to tell a story; I will allow him to continue a monologue and interpret his words as a story.' When he says, 'and they lived happily ever after' you tend to think 'His story is now over and I should interpret his next words as his own.' Interpretive framing formulae occur in many Gaelic poems and narratives, such as in the opening section of 'Laoidh Dhiarmaid': 'Éisdidh beag, madh áil libh laoidh / a chuideachta chaomh so, bhuam' ('Listen a while, dear company, if you wish to hear a lay from me').[15] The formal poetry of the professional poets (*filidheacht*) begins and ends with the same syllable, word, or line, a convention called *dùnadh* 'closure'. This provided both a visual (for the written page) and aural (for the performance) cue for the end of the poem.

Oral performance tends to feature forms of language which differ from the casual, everyday vernacular. The use of archaic words, a special dialect, musical cadences, or dramatic inflections marks the occasion as elevated, lofty, sublime, or special and signals the transformation of the speaker's persona. The text may include many formulaic expressions and kennings which require an inside knowledge of a cultural canon to understand. It is likely to also include a greater number or more sustained stream of figures of speech, such as metaphors, similes, euphemisms, irony, under-statements, puns, and kennings.

Gaelic literature contains many of these features. The style of filidheacht is marked by the use of Classical Gaelic, a specially prescribed form of the language used exclusively by the learned classes during the Middle Ages. Gaelic narratives, and poems in particular, teem with formulae, metonyms, and kennings, not least because they are useful building blocks in poetic construction (such as when a rhyme is needed). John Francis Campbell commented on the stylistics of the tale 'Ridire na Sgéithe Deirge':

> The language of the story is a good example of the way in which these tales are repeated in the Highlands. Words all but synonymous, and beginning with the same letter, or one like it, are strung together; there are strange names for the heroes, roundabout phrases to express simple ideas, and words used which are seldom heard in conversation, and which are hard to translate.[16]

Unlike the permanent record of the written word, performance is transitory and oral tradition-bearers often validate the authenticity of their material with assertions and disclaimers.[17] Many Gaelic storytellers complete their narratives with the state-ment 'Mas e breug bhuam e, se breug thugam e' ('If I have told a lie, it is because I have been told a lie'). Scottish Gaelic tradition places a strong emphasis on verbatim transmission of narratives from one tradition-bearer to the next.[18] Tradition-bearers recorded in the nineteenth and twentieth centuries often recounted from whom they learned each item, and from whom in turn their source had learnt it.

Folklorists who have recorded oral tradition from Gaels have commented on the prodigious memories of such individuals. The volume of poetry by Màiri Mhór nan Òran (Mary MacPherson of Skye), published in 1891, contained about 9,000 lines and she was said to have memorised 'at least half as much more of her own, and twice as much which she is able to repeat, of floating, unpublished poetry, mainly that of Skye and the Western Isles'.[19] Many storytellers, likewise, knew large numbers of tales that took an hour or more to perform. Some stories, such as 'Leigheas Coise Céin', were actually chain tales told over a sequence of evenings, in the manner of the *Arabian Nights*. Over 800 songs, 100 tales and 1,000 proverbs were recorded from Nan Eachainn Fhionnlaigh (Nan MacKinnon of Vatersay, 1902–82) for the School of Scottish Studies.[20]

The accuracy of texts sometimes involved communal effort. Hector Maclean described the deliberation during a storytelling session at Inverary in 1859 when he transcribed the popular hero tale 'Conall Cròbhaidh':

> It was told with the air of a man telling a serious story, and anxious to tell it correctly. The narrative was interlarded with explanations of the words used, and the incidents described. Those who sat about the fire argued points of the story. These were John MacKenzie, fisherman; John MacDonald, travelling tinker; John Clerk, our host, formerly miller to the Duke of Argyll; and some others, whose names I have forgotten.[21]

John Shaw has commented in great detail about the social processes of transmitting Gaelic oral tradition to succeeding generations in twentieth-century Cape Breton and the communal means by which elders of the community offered corrective measures to the young:

> Accuracy was an ideal strictly adhered to, and failure to observe it in reproducing a text would be commented on. [. . .] Individuals from within the culture were able to comment further on questions of accuracy, remarking that many of the most frequent errors in adding or omitting words were related to a lack of verbal listening skills and an inadequate knowledge of the supporting lore and materials [*seanchas*] that serve as verbal and conceptual points of reference for songs.[22]

Oral and written forms of prose and poetry interacted throughout many centuries of Gaelic literature, and prior to the close of the medieval period rigid distinctions between categories of élite and vernacular are elusive. The tale of Conall Gulban was so popular as to be copied into at least fifty-four manuscripts from the seventeenth century onwards (mostly in Ireland, but in Scotland as well), and oral versions have been recorded throughout the Highlands and Islands. Texts in nineteenth-century Gaelic periodicals often took the form of dialogues and sermons in assisting the transition to a written literature and were often read aloud during céilidhs. Even into the twenty-first century oral models of literature have been of primary importance to the form and style of written Gaelic prose.[23]

Lest we dismiss the creative potential and emotional impact of oral narrative, Gearóid Ó Crualaoich has argued that the best performers employing the most resonant themes and primal archetypes were capable of delivering 'oral literature' of high quality which could enable listeners to transcend their ordinary perceptions of reality and explore truths about the nature of the human experience:

> In terms of linguistic excellence and of creative capacity, verbal art affords oppor-tunities to listeners and readers to experience delight and fulfilment in an imaginative, experiential engagement with penetrating shafts of insight into the truth of repre-sentative realizations of human life at its greatest, in the experience of a kind of secular Parousia. In particular, 'literature', whether generated out of written or oral narration, affords the possibility of identification on the part of the listener/reader with characters and with life experiences that are 'true', at depths of consciousness beyond the ordinary and the everyday.[24]

Historical Developments

Like so much of Gaelic culture, the verbal arts show a mixture of continuity, innovation and hybridity. The Greek historian Diodorus Siculus, writing in the century before Christ, described the role of oral tradition in three professions in Gaulish society:

[The Gauls] speak together in few words, using riddles which leave much of the true meaning to be understood by the listener. They frequently exaggerate their claims to raise their own status and diminish another's. They are boastful, violent, and melodramatic, but very intelligent and learn quickly. They have lyric poets called Bards, who, accompanied by instruments resembling lyres, sing both praise and satire. They have highly honoured philosophers and theologians called Druids. They also make use of seers, who are greatly respected.[25]

At approximately the same time the Greek scholar Strabo recorded similar information in his now-lost volume *Geography*:

As a rule, among all the Gallic peoples three sets of men are honoured above all others: the Bards, the Vates, and the Druids. The bards are singers and poets, the Vates overseers of sacred rites and philosophers of nature, and the Druids, besides being natural philosophers, practise moral philosophy as well.[26]

These three terms – bard, vate, and druid – survive in Scottish Gaelic to the present as *bard*, *fàidh*, and *draoidh*, although their social functions and status have changed considerably. An additional title is visible from the earliest Gaelic records, the *fili* (plural *filid*),[27] whose name originally means 'seer'. It is probable that the *fili* originally belonged to the same profession as the *fàtha* (Common Celtic *vate*, Scottish Gaelic *fàidh*), and that both were adjuncts to druids in early Celtic religion. Christianity made an immediate and aggressive assault on druidic institutions and Gaelic kings may have been eager to adopt Christianity as a means of enhancing their status and breaking the monopoly of the druids. There can be little doubt that the considerable oral learning of the druids was in verse and that the filidh acquired some of the status and intellectual tools of the druids as the order was systematically downgraded by the incoming religion. According to early traditions, when St Patrick came to Ireland *c.*AD 433 he granted the right to speak in public to only three classes: the *seanchaidh* (who recited history), the *fili* (who performed praise and dispraise), and the *britheamh* (who made pronouncements on legal matters). Other early traditions relate that the convention of Druim Cett (in County Derry) was held in *c.*AD 575 when the high king of Ireland determined to extinguish the filid. Colm Cille (St Columba) stepped in to save the poetic order, arguing that it should be allowed to reform itself and co-exist with Christianity. This accommodation allowed a remarkable syncretism of native and Latin learning to flourish in the churches of Gaelic Scotland and Ireland;[28] the fact that all known poets between the sixth and twelfth centuries were associated with monasteries demonstrates the church's monopoly on learning.[29]

Ogam, a writing script consisting of sequences of strokes of various lengths and angles, was created no later than the fifth century AD, inspired by the Latin alphabet but not in direct imitation of it (see Plate 6). While ogam was well suited to short inscriptions on stone monuments (such as grave markers), it was not appropriate for documents. With Christianity came Latin learning; education in Ireland grew strong enough to attract a wave of English students in the mid seventh century. The influence of Latin grammar is pervasive from about AD 700 onwards; lest native tradition appear compromised by the ascendancy of Latin learning, scholars asserted the equal weight of Gaelic. Both Latin and Gaelic terms appear in the elegy to Saint Columba (†597) to praise his intellectual accomplishments. The tract *Auraicept na nÉces*, a primer for poets whose core was composed by *c.*750, asserted that ogam was the native Gaelic equivalent of the Roman alphabet, and that Gaelic had been created after the fall of the Tower of Babel (thus freeing it from association with the sin of human pride) by a scholar for learned purposes by choosing the best elements of other languages.[30]

Gaelic society was highly conscious of status and the ranking of poets reflected these distinctions. Research on Gaelic law indicates that in early Christian Ireland, poets belonged to a single institution arranged into grades according to the degree of training, with the fili at the apex of the order and the bard well below. In about the eighth century, the filid and bards were split into two separate institutions, with filid ranked into seven degrees according to education and the bards ranked by social class and function.[31] Copies of the law tract *Uraicecht na Ríar*, which deals with the status of various ranks of poets, were made in Scotland, although it is unclear to what degree it was able to operate effectively outside of Ireland.

By the year AD 600 Gaels were already in the forefront of Latin learning in Europe, but the absorption of Latin learning was balanced by affirming the worth of native tradition and, in many cases, creating Gaelic equivalents of Latin tools. Gaelic scholars created a distinctive script for writing Gaelic in manuscripts. Irish scholar Cenn Faelad (†679) wrote the first grammar for Gaelic (parts of which were incorporated into *Auraicept na nÉces*). Gaelic (or 'Brehon') law began to take written form in the seventh century. Cormac mac Cuilennáin of Munster (†908) was the compiler of the first etymological dictionary for Gaelic and the first for any European vernacular language.[32] Gaelic scholars in Scotland, working in such monastic centres as Iona, shared these accomplishments and achieved many of their own. Although early literary remains in Scotland are scarce, there is enough remaining evidence to demonstrate that Gaelic poets composed texts for and about Scottish subjects. Beccán mac Luigdech of Rum composed Gaelic poetry in praise of St Columba before his death in 677. To Adomnán of Iona (†704) are attributed a Gaelic eulogy to St Columba and an elegy to Bruide (†693) son of Beli king of Brythonic Dumbarton. Other fragments of Gaelic elegies to Scottish nobles survive: Conaing (†622), son of Aedán, king of Dál Riata; Óengus (†761?), king of the Picts; Cináed mac Ailpín (†858), king of the Picts.[33]

Several Gaelic tales preserved in Ireland feature Scottish Gaels or are set, at least partially, in Scotland. These generally portray Scotland as an exotic locale or land of exile. In the tale of Deirdre (known in Gaelic by the title 'Longes mac nUislenn'), continually refashioned from the eighth century to recent times, she and her lover and his brothers escape to safety in Scotland until they are lured back to Ireland. The hero of 'Scéla Cano Meic Gartnáin' probably gave his name to Dùn Cana on Raasay. Conall Corc, who became king of Munster in *c*.AD 400, was banished to Scotland by a jealous rival, according to the tale 'Longes Chonaill Chuirc'.[34] Tales now lost spent more attention on the adventures of the Gaels in Scotland. The tale 'Tochmolud Dáil Riatai i nAlbain' must have chronicled the expansion of the kingdom of Dál Riata in Scotland; 'Argain Sratha Cluada' likely described the siege of Dumbarton by the Vikings in the ninth century; 'Braflung Scoine' portrayed the slaughter of Pictish nobles at a feast held by king Cináed mac Ailpín; 'Echtra Aedain meic Gabráin' dealt with the exploits of the most aggressive king of Scottish Dál Riata, who ruled at the end of the sixth century.[35]

As in Ireland, most early Gaelic scholarly activity in Scotland occurred in the scriptoria associated with monastic centres which depended upon élite patronage to operate. The Latin historical tract *Historia Brittonum* was translated into Gaelic in eastern Scotland during the reign of Malcolm III Canmore (1058–93).[36] Also dating from this period is the 'Duan Albanach', a genealogical poem probably performed at the royal inauguration. The earliest manuscript containing Gaelic surviving from Scotland itself is the *Book of Deer*, written in Aberdeenshire in the mid twelfth century.[37] Documents dating from the reign of Alexander II (1214–49) demonstrate that scribes in eastern Scotland were keeping pace with Gaelic orthographic developments elsewhere and hence maintained contact with the rest of Gaeldom.[38] At the inauguration of Alexander III in 1249 the king's lineage was read in Gaelic, probably by an *ollamh rígh* 'king's master-poet' who resided in Balvaird (*Baile a' Bhaird*), Fife.[39]

The Anglo-Norman transformation of Lowland Scotland reduced the prestige of Gaelic practices and the patronage given to maintain them, especially in the monastic centres where reform from Continental Europe was introduced. Not even Ireland was spared the abrupt upheavals of the era. After the reformation of monasteries in the twelfth century, churches discontinued their support of secular Gaelic learning and for the next century poets understated the pagan overtones of their lore to avoid the censure of the church. There are notable discontinuities during the thirteenth century as poetic patronage and learning shifted from religious centres to dynastic patrons: while syllabic poetry of the twelfth century encoded royal genealogies, territorial claims and legendary lore, the poetry in later periods, while drawing on the versified wisdom of the past, focuses primarily on relations between poet and aristocrat.[40]

The emergence of a new poetic order producing syllabic metres called *dán díreach* in standardised, high-register Classical Gaelic appears to be mostly due to the dominance of the Uí Dhálaigh family of poets. Several Uí Dhálaigh poets of high status are recorded in twelfth-century Ireland, including Maol Íosa, a high-chieftain of Westmeath also described as a chief poet of Ireland and Scotland ('ollam Érenn ⁊ Albann'). The emergence of their leadership, coinciding with the abandonment of secular learning in monastic foundations, suggests that they were instrumental in redefining the practices of the art of poetry. One member of the family who came to be known as Muireadhach Albanach brought the craft to Scotland when he immigrated in the early thirteenth century and founded a poetic dynasty which survived into the eighteenth century. Muireadhach Albanach composed verse for the Earl of Lennox and his son, and was cited as a paragon of poetic skill by later bardic textbooks.[41]

Gaelic Ireland enjoyed a fourteenth-century 'revival' as native lords regained ground that had been lost during the twelfth-century Anglo-Norman invasion. With the increased power of Gaelic lords came new opportunities for patronage and an increased need to validate their social standing by recourse to Gaelic tradition and genealogy.[42] Poets composed Gaelic verse to Gall-Ghàidheal patrons in the west of Scotland such as Raghnall king of Man and the Hebrides (†1229), Domhnall grandson of Somerled (after whom Clan Donald is named), and other Hebridean leaders descended from Somerled.[43] These poems legitimate their social status by associating them and their ancestors with the illustrious Gaelic past. The poem to Raghnall, for example, draws him into the Gaelic cultural matrix by comparing his residence to Tara and the Otherworld and flattering him as the offspring of Gaelic heroes worthy of ruling Ireland.

After having securely re-established their social relevance and system of patronage, the poetic order in Ireland reconsolidated itself into a national institution. In the fourteenth century poets were confident enough to reclaim their 'druidic inheritance'. Such projections into the past obscured the breaks with tradition that occurred, especially during the thirteenth century, and heightened the mystique and aura of antiquity around their craft.[44] The schools of 'bardic poetry'[45] functioned as a sort of trade union that extended in a limited fashion into Scotland primarily by Irish poets working abroad or establishing poetic dynasties, or by sending Scottish students to Irish schools. The normative pressure created by this 'medieval exercise in language planning'[46] was such that a well-wrought poem from twelfth-century Ireland does not differ greatly in terms of language or style from one from early-eighteenth-century Scotland. Bardic poetry was an intellectual art form with political significance in which both Scottish and Irish Gaels participated, but not entirely as equal partners. 'Bardic poetry should be understood as an essentially Irish phenomenon, conceived and developed in Ireland on Irish terms, to which Scottish Gaeldom became attached in a loose and somewhat ambiguous fashion.'[47]

As early as the thirteenth century the descendants of Somerled were beginning to establish or endow religious orders, and in later generations both males and females of the family became leading clergy. By the fifteenth century, the church in Gaelic Scotland had become tightly coupled to secular power. The patronage of the Lords of the Isles was crucial in maintaining the expenses of bardic training and practice in Scotland, as well as that of other learned classes: among the professionals in their employ were MacMhuirich poets, MacMhuirich ('Morrison') lawyers, MacDhubh-Shìdh ('MacDuffie') archivists, MacBheatha ('Beaton') medical doctors, and Mac-GilleSheanaich harpers.[48] Horizontal movement between high status professions was common; members of the MacMhuirich dynasty, for example, also became doctors and clergymen. The Lordship's support enabled Gaelic culture to flourish, an era recalled later as *Linn an Àigh* 'The Golden Age'.

Several other Gaelic magnates followed the lead of the Clan Donald in importing talented filidh from Ireland: MacEòghain ('MacEwan') poets seem to have worked for the MacDugalls of Dunolly in the early part of the fifteenth century before transferring to the employ of the Campbells, for whom they worked into the mid seventeenth century; Ó Muirgheasáin poets appear to be working for the Macleans of Duart by the beginning of the sixteenth century but shifted to working for the MacLeods of Harris and Dunvegan by the early seventeenth century; there were also MacMharcuis filidh in Kintyre and Antrim but the exact nature of their activity and patronage is still unclear.[49] Other professional classes, especially musicians and medical doctors, also found employment in Gaelic Scotland, and sometimes in the Lowlands and royal court as well. The high level of attainment of such men should not be underestimated: in the field of medicine, for example, Gaelic was one of only four languages (besides Greek, Latin and Arabic) in which medical knowledge was formally and systematically studied and taught in Europe during the Middle Ages.[50]

Professionals trained in bardic schools dominated intellectual activity in Ireland, but this monopoly was never as complete in Scotland. The expense of establishing and maintaining bardic schools was prohibitive for all but the largest clans and most chieftains may have considered the lower-order poets to be sufficient for their purposes.[51] These differing environments led to a number of significant cultural and literary divergences between Scottish and Irish Gaeldom. Women, for example, were excluded from education in the Irish bardic schools, but the looser organisation in Scotland afforded a place for major female poets in the seventeenth, eighteenth and nineteenth centuries. The dominance of the syllabic poetry of the filidh eclipsed earlier verse forms in Ireland but in Scotland old poetic forms continued to be used for new compositions into the seventeenth and eighteenth centuries.[52] Interaction with Lowland Scots' scribal activity brought about a tradition of writing Gaelic with Scots orthography which appears as early as the fourteenth century, a major departure from earlier precedents and the standards of the bardic schools (see Plate 12).[53]

The fifth Earl of Argyll (*c*.1532–73) was an early and zealous convert to Protestant-ism. A major tenet of the Reformation was the necessity of allowing all people access to the scriptures in their own mother tongue, breaking the previous exclusivity held by the learned clerics. Campbell sponsored the translation of the *Book of Common Order* into Classical Gaelic, an effort that applied the high-register language of the filidh to advance the Protestant Reformation in both Scotland and Ireland. In 1567 it became the first Gaelic book ever printed.[54]

> Great indeed is the disadvantage and want from which we, the Gaels of Scotland and Ireland, have ever suffered, beyond the rest of the world, in that our Gaelic language has never been printed as all other races of men in the world have their own languages and tongues in print; and we suffer from a greater want than any other in that we

have not the Holy Bible printed in Gaelic [. . .] and likewise in that the history of our ancestors has never been printed.[55]

John Carswell, the translator, demonstrates an early awareness of the institutional disadvantages from which Gaelic suffered even at this early date. Calvin's *Geneva Catechism* was also translated into Classical Gaelic *c.*1631, and both texts presume the existence of a clergy literate in high-register Gaelic operating in the Highland church.[56] As the Gaelic aristocracy diminished their commitment to and patronage of native institutions of learning, the church became one of the few refuges for such professionals.[57]

Unlike the Classical literature of the filidh, vernacular Gaelic literature is almost by definition an oral medium evasive of the documentary record, apart from almost accidental strays, until the systematic collection of verse by ministers in the eighteenth century, especially those spurred on by the Ossianic controversy. There is a clutch of poems that may date from the fifteenth century (mostly incomplete), a somewhat larger selection of more varied material from the sixteenth century, and a broader spectrum of subjects and forms from the seventeenth century onwards.[58] In these texts we see not only the survival of very old metres and the influences of the filidh, but the innovation of new forms and subjects, particularly those connected with instrumental music. Our window into the full diversity of Gaelic verse across social ranks does not open widely until the compositions of the eighteenth century.[59]

In a fully operational Gaelic society, professional poets had been custodians of tradition and the mediators of power; they legitimated or criticised the right of leaders to rule and reinforced social norms through praise and dispraise. From the beginning of the seventeenth century, as the Highland élite derived an increasing amount of their power from authorities outside of Gaeldom, were assimilated into anglophone society, and felt an increasing strain on their financial resources, they became less interested or able to provide the patronage to support the traditional learned classes and artists. Poets begin to hint of the absence and negligence of clan chiefs.[60] Poetry by clerics, clan chiefs and minor nobility modelled on the old syllabic metres but in vernacular language (with some archaisms influenced by Classical Gaelic) appears in the seventeenth century. The title *an t-Aos-Dàna*[61] was given to several prominent men who seem to have functioned as official clan poets, using vernacular forms rather than the more obtuse Classical standards which a decreasing number of people could appreciate.[62]

The increasing role of Scottish Gaels in British political and military affairs reinforced the heroic-age ethos of Gaelic poetry, and rapid changes and tensions in the Highlands gave plenty of cause for social commentary. Royalist movements – Jacobitism in particular – mobilised Gaelic forces of traditionalism, with poets performing a lead part in the promotion of particular perspectives and campaigns, especially MacDonalds, MacKenzies, MacLeans, and MacLeods. The extent to which Jacobite poets could harness Gaelic literature of all genres and registers – from prophetic narrative to mouth-music, from waulking songs of women to sustained, elevated political discourse in verse – is remarkable, attesting to the resilience and adaptability of oral tradition, and its ability to operate across the geographical span and class divides of the Highlands.[63]

The poet Alasdair mac Mhaighstir Alasdair ('Alexander MacDonald') was a key innovator of Gaelic poetry in the eighteenth century, pioneering forms and subjects that resonated well into the twentieth century. Alasdair may have been the first male to compose verses in the predominantly female tradition of *òran-luaidh* ('waulking song') with the explicit purpose of disseminating pro-Jacobite sentiment. He also enjoyed success in imitating the Classical music of the bagpipe (*ceòl mór*) in Gaelic verse and in turning the focus of panegyric to the general rank and file of the clan. In 1751 he became the first Gaelic poet to publish his own work, *Ais-eiridh na Sean Chánoin Albannaich* 'The Resurrection of the Ancient Scottish Language'. This book, the first collection of secular Gaelic poetry to appear in print, was said to have been burnt at Edinburgh's Mercat Cross due to its treasonous Jacobitism (it also contained sexually explicit material). Alasdair's success in stimulating Gaelic poets to experiment with new ideas by adapting them within existing idioms and structures is demonstrated by the many major poets who further developed his ideas, including Rob Donn, Donnchadh Bàn, and William Ross.[64] His son, Raghnall Dubh, published the first anthology of Scottish Gaelic poetry in 1776 (see Plate 24).

The learned tradition, on the other hand, shows a steady decline accelerating throughout the eighteenth century. The use of the traditional Gaelic script (*corra-litir*) is one such indicator. Alasdair mac Mhaighstir Alasdair and his son Raghnall wrote in it, as did a dwindling number of learned men and antiquarians into the late nineteenth century.[65] When the Ossianic Committee interviewed Lachlann MacMhuirich in 1800 about the history of his ancestors, the hereditary poets and custodians of tradition for the Lords of the Isles, and Clanranald after them, he acknowledged his inability to write, signalling the end of the longest-lasting literary dynasty in Europe.[66]

The sensation and debate surrounding the claims of James Macpherson's *Ossian* brought renewed attention to the literary antiquities of the Highlands. Although a few educated men had already begun to collect Gaelic poetry from oral tradition, the controversy about Highland culture and the nature of oral poetry versus written literature spurred systematic documentation, especially by the Moderate ministers of the Church of Scotland. Macpherson's English verses helped to spark the Romantic movement, but had important consequences amongst Highlanders as well in setting new aesthetic expectations in Gaelic literature.[67]

The New Testament had first been translated into vernacular Scottish Gaelic in 1767 and the Old Testament in 1801, and a new edition of the entire Bible was published in 1807. Religious tracts in Gaelic had already begun to appear by 1751, but these were mostly translations of varying quality from English. The availability of the scriptures in their entirety further stirred the educational efforts of religious organisations during the nineteenth century. By 1800, printed texts, especially in periodical format, became the most common means of disseminating popular literature in Britain and Gaeldom was no exception. The first Gaelic periodical began to appear in the 1820s, with notions of improvement, cultural progress and religious reform showing strongly. The emergence of immigrant Gaelic communities in urban settings in Britain and abroad increased the audience for such materials. Archibald Sinclair of Islay established a press in Glasgow in 1848 which served Gaelic literature into the early twentieth century. Print created an effective means of experimenting with new literary forms and ideas and allowed a wider participation in the development of Gaelic intellectual life, but it also made such materials subject to the vicissitudes of economic demands.[68]

Despite the innovation of secular Gaelic literature during the late eighteenth and early nineteenth centuries, religious verse dominated the output of the era, reflecting both the missionary activity in the Highlands and the response to it. The martial focus of the 'Gaelic panegyric code' was refashioned to address Christian ideals: the soul's battle with sin and temptation could be depicted in the traditional imagery of warfare, with Christ displacing the chieftain and warrior as the exemplar of society. Religious bodies established their own Gaelic periodicals in the nineteenth century and ministers continued to serve as writers and editors in a variety of literary endeavours.

Antiquarian research maturing into the modern field of folkloristics found a capable Gaelic representative in John Francis Campbell (1822–85, called *Iain Òg Ìle* in Gaelic, see Plate 27). Campbell and his crew of fieldworkers demonstrated that, despite the hostility of many school-masters and church ministers, Highland story-tellers still remembered a wealth of traditional narrative, much of which remains to this day in unpublished manuscripts. The success of Campbell's 1860 *Popular Tales of the West Highlands* encouraged other nineteenth-century collectors of Gaelic lore, especially Alexander Carmichael, John Gregorson Campbell, John Dewar, Donald Macpherson, and Francis Tolmie. The very effort of recalling such material and presenting it to an interested public must have reasserted the worth of Gaelic tradition at a time when self-confidence was exceedingly low.[69]

Gaelic song-makers continued to compose for and about their own local communities for as long as they had interested audiences, in many cases into the second half of the twentieth century. The energies unleashed by the Land Agitation in the late nineteenth century reinvigorated many genres of Gaelic song, with many new compositions being based on Jacobite antecedents of a century and a half previous. *Baird-bhaile* ('local poets') responded to noteworthy events in their communities and advocated their positions in verse in various public debates. Already in the nineteenth century and increasingly in the twentieth, some writers adopted contemporary mainstream European literary models and diverged from traditional oral genres by composing literature meant to be appreciated on the printed page. The twentieth century saw innovation by numerous literary pioneers who have developed under-represented themes and genres (such as the novel and drama), and applied Gaelic to the full panoply of modern life.[70]

PROFESSIONAL POETS

The file was an integral part of the machinery of a society operating on precedent and pedigree, providing the Gaelic élite with the ideological and genealogical basis of their right to rule. As Cathal MacMhuirich (fl. 1625) stated in verse, the poets sustained the reputation and history of the aristocracy, for without them there would be

Gan neach re cuimhne a gcéimenn	øB.2
do ríomh chreach no caithrémenn	D.1
gan snas ar fíorbhun a bhfis	
glas ar an gníomhrudh d' aithris.	øB.2
Beid a maithe fa mhéala	
do dhíoth lochta a leisgéala	øG.2
's a n-uaisle budh dheacht fa bhroid	

('No one who would recall their deeds, enumerate their forays or exploits, no elaboration on the facts, which will prevent their deeds from being told; their nobles will be at a loss from the lack of advocates, and the aristocracy will surely be repentant.')[71]

The file presided at the traditional inauguration of Gaelic kings and clan chieftains and presented the newly installed leader with his rod of kingship.[72] One of the few glimpses we have of the king's poet in the royal Scottish court is the 'Duan Albanach', which was composed for King Malcolm III Canmore (†1093). In the opening formula, the poet addresses his noble audience and introduces the topic of his verses:

> *A éolcha Alban uile,*
> *A shluagh féuta foltbhuidhe,*
> *Cía céudghabháil, an éol duibh,*
> *ro ghabasdair Albanbruigh?*

('O learned men of Scotland, o noble golden-haired audience, do you know of the first conquest of the land of Scotland?')[73]

It is possible to create a composite portrait of the filidh based on a variety of evidence from Scotland and Ireland.[74] Training was reserved for males born within poetic families who were not only literate but also good at memorisation. Sometimes the training was from father to son, but more often the son was sent away to a bardic school. The master–apprentice relationship was cast in traditional Gaelic form as the bond between foster-father (*oide*) and fosterling (*dalta*). A full degree of filidheacht took six or seven years, during which time the candidate studied a canon of Gaelic literature and history, and tracts on metre and language; exemplars from famous poets of the past were expected to be committed to memory. The literature of the filidh makes frequent allusion to this corpus as well as to Biblical, Greek, and

Latin literature. Poets were assigned poetic exercises in the syllabic metres using Classical Gaelic, composing their verses by memory in the dark and writing them down after they were complete. The school-master critiqued the work of his students and conferred degrees. Some students sought training under several different teachers.

Once a file had completed his training he could be employed as the *ollamh* 'official master-poet' to a king or chieftain, for which he was given rent-free land-holdings close to those of his patron. Such was the stature of the poet, and intimacy between him and his patron, that the metaphor of marriage was used of their relationship. He was expected to compose poems to commemorate significant events in his patron's family, such as marriages, battles, inaugurations, and death, for which he could charge a *duais* 'commission, fee'. The most important of these could be transcribed into a *duanaire* 'poetry book', which formed a kind of family history book in verse. The poems were meant for public performance in the chieftain's hall, but were recited not by the file himself but by a lower-order *reacaire* 'reciter' to the music of a stringed instrument (see Chapter Seven). A significant percentage of the Gaelic élite were literate and accustomed to the formalisms of Classical Gaelic; if this were not the case, such costly performances would have been futile. The ollamh was also responsible for the education of the chieftain's family. Although most surviving evidence states that Scottish poets went to Ireland for their training, the Rev. Donald MacNicol believed that there had been a bardic school near Inverness which may have operated into at least the seventeenth century.[75]

His educational background and freedom to travel made the file a valuable aid and confidant to the chieftain. During his regular *cuairt* 'circuit, tour' the file could visit the courts of other nobles and relay messages between them and his patron, acting as ambassador and diplomat,[76] accompanied by his *cliar* 'poetic retinue'. He could compose a praise poem to the noble he had visited, complimenting him according to his rank and hospitality. He also wrote legal documents and witnessed them. Martin Martin, a native of Skye and tutor to the MacDonalds of Sleat and the MacLeods of Dunvegan, confirms *c.*1695 that such practices continued in parts of Gaelic Scotland into the mid seventeenth century, but hints of conflict between the poets and the increasingly assimilated Gaelic élite:

> The Orators, in their Language call'd [*Aos-dàna*], were in high esteem both in these Islands and the Continent [of Highland Scotland]; until within these forty Years, they Sat always among the Nobles and Chiefs of Families in the [*sreath*], or Circle. Their Houses and little Villages were Sanctuaries, as well as Churches, and they took place before Doctors of Physick. The Orators, after the Druids were extinct, were brought in to preserve the Genealogy of Families, and to repeat the same at every Succession of a Chief; and upon the occasion of Marriages and Births, they made Epithalamiums and Panygericks, which the Poet or Bard pronounced. The Orators by the force of their Eloquence had a powerful Ascendant over the greatest Men in their time; for if

any Orator did but ask the Habit, Arms, Horse, or any other thing belonging to the greatest Man in these Islands, it was readily granted them, sometimes out of respect, and sometimes for fear of being exclaim'd against by a Satire, which in those days was reckon'd a great dishonour: but these Gentlemen becoming insolent, lost ever since both the Profit and Esteem which was formerly due to their Character; for neither their Panegyricks nor Satires are regarded to what they have been, and they are not allow'd but a small Salary. I must not omit to relate their way of Study, which is very singular: They shut their Doors and Windows for a day's time, and lie on their backs, with a Stone upon their Belly, and Plads about their Heads, and their Eyes being cover'd, they pump their Brains for Rhetorical Encomuim or Panegyrick; and indeed they furnish such a Stile from this dark Cell, as is understood by a very few: and if they purchase a couple of Horses as the Reward of their Meditation, they think they have done a great matter. The Poet, or Bard, has a Title to the Bridegroom's upper Gard, that is, the Plad and Bonnet; but now he is satisfy'd with what the Bridegroom pleases to give him on such occasions.[77]

As Martin Martin reminds us, the poets were not just sycophantic flatterers. They could withhold their approval or explicitly disapprove of actions and policies, and wielded considerable influence over the nobility. The tenth-century *Sanas Cormaic* offers a etymology of the word 'fili' which, though incorrect in terms of linguistic history, reflects accurately the two main functions of poetry: '*fili*, that is, *fí* "poison" in satire, and *lí* "splendor" in praise, and it is variously that the poet proclaims.'[78] Poets composed a piece called a *trefhocal* which contained a mixture of praise and threat as a necessary preliminary warning of a satire. Poets were expected to use satire discriminately or they would be discredited; they were to also defend their patrons against unjust satires. Due to the nature of satire and the selection of what was committed to writing, very few survive, although we do have a number of threats. One such was composed to John Stewart of Rannoch, whose poet warns:

> *Ní bhia mé i gcomaoin t' fhaladh,*
> *giodh deacair linn dul fán nós;*
> *acht fá-ríor ar bhéad an bhagair*
> *don mhéad díona tá agad fós.*
> *Déar-sa riotsa, a mheic Shir Roibeirt,*
> *a Ghaoidheil nach críon fán chrodh,*   ≠B.1
> *fa mó an díoth dhuit mo theagmháil*
> *na síoth agus beagán domh.*   B.2

('I will not be beholden to your malice, even though this behaviour is difficult for me; but alas, for the way my threat will damage everything that you own. Let me say to you, o Robert's son, o Gael who is generous with cattle, it would cost you much more dearly to strike me than to grant me peace and some small reward.')[79]

Filidheacht, the verbal art of the filidh, was technically demanding. The basic features of filidheacht are syllable count, word length, rhyme (quality and position), and alliteration. The numerous individually named metres define the length of lines and position of rhymes; there are three degrees of strictness, depending on the adherence to rhyme and alliteration (*dán díreach, brúilingeacht,* and *óglachas,* from most to least strict). Consonants are grouped into six classes, according to phonological principles, with consonance determined accordingly. A stanza from an elegy for Sir Duncan Campbell of Glenorchy (†1631) demonstrates the characteristics of the *séadna* metre, whose syllable count, word length and end-rhyme scheme can be expressed with the formula $2(8^2 + 7^1)^{2+4}$ meaning that there are two couplets; in each couplet the first line has eight syllables and ends with a disyllabic word, and the second line has seven syllables and ends in a monosyllabic word; end rhymes occur on lines two and four. Rhymes are marked in bold and alliteration is marked with underlining in the following *rann* 'quatrain':

> Dob líonmhur ar leirg an locha
> laoch láidir is óigfhear **oll**;
> iomdha um **thriath Tatha taoiseach**
> **sgiath flatha** agus **craoiseach corr.**

The end-rhyme is *oll* : *corr* ('ll' and 'rr' belong to the same consonant group) and internal rhyme is *thriath* : *sgiath, Tatha* : *flatha,* and *taoiseach* : *craoiseach.*

These syllabic metres produce an intricately ornamented texture of words and images and it no surprise that the Gaelic poet was often likened to the weaver. The message of the poet is seldom expressed directly and simply, but is refracted through an array of elaborate rhetorical conventions and formulae demonstrating the poet's command of language and traditional learning. The *synecdoche,* in which a part represents the whole, is frequently used to address the subject: he is the *lámh thréan* 'strong hand' or *gruadh ghlan* 'bright cheek'. Metaphorical epithets associate the subject with suitable animals and plants: he is the *seabhac* 'hawk' or *bile* 'sacred tree'. These are often combined with the names of territories associated with the ancestors of the subject or potentially under his domain, or with family names: he is *ceann-bile Chloinne Cholla* 'the top-most sacred tree of the descendants of Colla', *leómhan Muile* 'lion of Mull' or *seabhag Íle* 'hark of Islay'.

The terms *semi-bardic* and *semi-classical* have been used to describe poetry modelled on the syllabic metres using vernacular rather than Classical Gaelic and 'imperfect' rhyme.[80] People with lesser levels of bardic training and proficiency (including aristocratic amateurs) were composing verse on subjects and for purposes other than those usually within the official remit of the filidh.

By the seventeenth century we also have some of the output of clan bards who acted in some professional capacity, sometimes identified with the title an *t-Aos-Dàna.* These poets composed in vernacular Scottish Gaelic using the *iorram* metre (often referred to as 'strophic metre' – see poem four of Appendix A for an example). Unlike the highly personalised poems of the filidh, the clan poet addressed the larger concerns of the *fine* 'clan élite' and relations between clans. Even poets of 'inferior' rank using demotic Gaelic, however, were influenced by the style and precedents of the filidh. Songs performed in the chieftain's hall entered oral tradition to be recorded in the eighteenth century, and while Gaelic society remained stratified, oral transmission of these texts remained primarily within a small circle of relations.[81]

The *Aos-dàna* 'gifted people, intelligentsia', including the filidh, lawyers, and physicians, were trained in Classical Gaelic for matters within the pan-Gaelic world and in Latin for international communications.[82] In a dynasty where the Gaelic literati were fully supported, the poet and historian held distinct offices. Alexander Campbell drew upon the memories of older *seanchaidh*s when he wrote his history of the Campbells of Craignish *c.*1717. He notes that the end of the MacEòghain poetic dynasty was heralded by the introduction of new media for clan history and political legitimacy:

> Every considerable family in the Highlands had their Bards & Shenachies. The Bard was the Family poet, & the Shenachie their prose wryter, but very oft the Bard supply'd the place of both. These Offices were heretable, & had a pension, commonly a piece of land annexed to that Office. Their work was to hand down to posterity the valorous actions, Conquests, batles, skirmishes, marriages, relations of the predicessors, by repeating & singing the same at births, baptisms, marriages, feasts and funeralls, so that no people since the Curse of the Almighty dissipated the Jews took such care to keep their Tribes, Cadets and branches, so well & so distinctly separate. [Athairne MacEòghain], who lived in Earl Archibald Gruamach's time, & had for his pension the Lands of Kilchoan in Netherlorne, and his son [Niall mac Athairne mhic Eòghain] were the heretable Genealogists of the Family of Argyll. This [Niall] dyed about the year 1650, and was the last of them. Printing of Hystorie becomeing then more frequent, the necessity of maintaining these Annalists began to wear off.[83]

Much ado has been made of ogam and its tree symbolism but it must be borne in mind that literacy was an exclusive privilege of the élite and that ogam was largely obsolete by the High Middle Ages. Ogam, moreover, originally used names other than those of trees, although the arboreal metaphor did dominate ogam later.[84] The scribe Angus Beaton of Skye used ogam to encrypt his name into a Gaelic medical manuscript in 1612,[85] but other than such antiquarian applications, the Gaelic form of the Latin alphabet was dominant amongst the literati by the Classical Gaelic period. This is illustrated by the so-called 'Harlaw Brosnachadh', said by tradition to have been uttered to incite MacDonald warriors before the Battle of Harlaw in 1411: the poet enumerates all of the attributes that he hopes the troops will embody, listing them in alphabetical order according to Latin, not ogam.[86]

Highland life was accompanied by the oral tradition, especially song, from the lullaby of the newborn to the lament of the deceased. Everyone was involved in composition and performance at various levels, participating in a collective tradition that complemented labour and kept minds active and alert. While the verbal arts covered a wide spectrum of occasions and genres, some were restricted by ritual restrictions. Storytelling, for example, was normally reserved for nights during the dark half of the year, 'bho Shamhainn gu Bealltainn' ('from Hallowe'en to May Day').[87] The night-time restriction is implied by the common proverb describing the protocol when a visitor is present: 'A' chiad sgeul air fear an taighe, 's gach sgeul gu lath' air an aoigh' ('The host will tell the first tale; the guest will tell tales until dawn').

A wide variety of sources from nineteenth- and twentieth-century Highland communities testify to the common institution of the *céilidh* 'house-visit, gathering' and its central place in keeping oral tradition alive amongst the common orders of Gaelic society. A native of the Dornoch Firth provides a summary account of the practice of his youth in the early nineteenth century:

> The Céilidh, as a collection of gossiping 'visitors' was named, was a great institution, in the Leathad, where at any house by or without appointment, the lads and lasses would gather of a clear winter night, and gather around the peat fire, and often by the light of pieces of *giuthas*, i.e., fir-root rich with resin, kept burning on a hard wood stump, would tell stories, sing songs, put riddles, play the fiddle and the 'trump' and do some courting too.[88]

In most céilidh houses, the evening typically began with general conversation, followed eventually by storytelling. Each story could provoke discussion and commentary after it had concluded.[89] While in general all sorts of materials – song, dance, music, stories, riddles, etc – were shared at a céilidh, in large and active communities certain houses specialised in particular genres or were dominated by the presence of notable performers.[90] A classic account of the céilidh given by Hector Urquhart, one of John Francis Campbell's fieldworkers, describes how tailors and cobblers, some of the few widely travelled members of the Gaelic peasantry, transmitted stories between communities:

> In my native place, Pool-Ewe, Ross-shire, when I was a boy, it was the custom for the young to assemble together on the long winter nights to hear the old people recite the tales, or *sgeulachd*, which they had learned from their fathers before them. In these days tailors and shoemakers went from house to house, making our clothes and shoes. When one of them came to the village we were greatly delighted, whilst getting new kilts at the same time. I knew an old tailor who used to tell a new tale every night during his stay [. . .] It was also the custom when an *aoigh*, or stranger, celebrated for

his store of tales, came on a visit to the village, for us, young and old, to make a rush to the house where he passed the night, and choose our seats, some on beds, some on forms, and others on three-legged stools, etc., and listen in silence to new tales.[91]

Adults often did simple manual labour while they listened, such as twisting heather into rope or spinning wool. The young men and women might flirt via the messages (explicit or coded) in the songs they sang.[92]

> It was usual for the young women of a *baile*, or hamlet, which consisted of from four to twenty families, to carry their work to the houses of each other's parents alternately. In these societies oral learning was attained without interrupting industry, and the pleasure of instructing and receiving knowledge was mutual. The matron, visited on one evening, perhaps excelled in genealogy; while another was well versed in general history; one may have been adept at poetry, and another an able critic; &c. The Highlander, after his daily occupations, hastened to join the society of the young women, where he met his beloved, or had the pleasure, in her absence, of repeating the last sonnet he had composed in her praise, for which he either received applause or encountered disapprobation.[93]

People challenged each other with riddles, attempting to earn the title *Ridire nan Ceist* 'Knight of Riddles' for the evening. The information discussed was not merely entertainment or escapism: there was lore with great practical value, and people were expected to put the wisdom they absorbed to use. Many Gaelic proverbs, for example, contain utilitarian information (about weather, the seasons, use of resources) and moral advice (how to raise children, how to behave) as well as being pithy encapsulations of wit and humour (see Plate 25).

> Before the year 1800 there was many a one of the Highlanders who could tell the names of his ancestors for many generations back. Also, although they could neither read nor write, they took note of the time, and he who did not always learn the day of the month and the [phase] of the moon, was considered a man void of intelligence. The people who were of old would tell when the new moon would come, when it would be full or in the quarter, as well as though they had an almanac. They trusted much to their memory and when anything remarkable happened, they had a proverb to illustrate it.[94]

It is still good céilidh etiquette to relate the source and background information about an item before performing it so that it can be properly interpreted and appreciated. It is rare for Gaelic songs to be in the form of a self-contained narrative, so explanatory prefaces detailing the author and background history are important.[95] Individual tales and songs are often related to a larger corpus of materials about common characters, clans or events. George Henderson's documentation of storytelling terminology at the end of the nineteenth century provides a rare glimpse into the technicalities of the art at a time when people were aware of its steep decline:

> Ere reciting the incidents of the Fionn or Ossian saga, especially the lays, it is the custom among good Highland seanachies to give a short statement of the facts which are at the foundation of the narrative. Such a concise statement they term *an urspainn*. They often, quite rightly and modestly, regard the lays, as they have them, as very incomplete in comparison with what they once were, and a reciter often regrets he cannot knit the tale well together, saying *cha'n urrainnear an t-seanchas a chur air a ballaibh* ['the lore cannot be reconstructed']. One hears the complaint that there are nowadays only fragmentary tales (*smodail*), and of these a reciter often says, even when he knows a tale very well, *cha b' urrainn domh 'cur air a ballaibh* = 'I could not arrange it consecutively'.[96]

The céilidh house was also a lively venue for the discussion of important social and political issues in the life of the community. Debates were sometimes exchanged in verse between people advocating different sides of an argument, with the audience either immediately signalling their approval or disapproval, or else implicitly support-ing one side by keeping the song active in the local repertoire. During the eighteenth and nineteenth centuries many songs were composed to debate the virtues and vices of items newly come into the Gàidhealtachd from the Lowlands, such as tea or tobacco.[97] Bards were involved in the controversy over whether or not pubs were to be allowed to operate in the north of Skye in the 1960s, and villagers

> looked to their local bards for perspectives on an issue and for articulation of their own feelings. The local song-maker retained this crucial role in Gaelic society as both a medium of and a catalyst for public debate until very recently. He serves as a record of opinion, like the bards of classical Gaelic society, and also expresses his own biases in song. His opinions are often given more credence than those of a 'normal' (i.e., non-song-making) citizen, as he had a reputation for thought, cleverness, and eloquence.[98]

Mary MacKellar's observation of nineteenth-century Lochaber was true of the prolific poetic activities throughout Gaeldom in general:

> Almost every one seemed to be ambitious for either composing a few verses or improvising [. . .] Every little occasion called forth a few verses either in praise or with the more dangerous power of satire. These verses might not be heard of beyond the township in which they were composed.[99]

Good poets were expected to be able to compose verse spontaneously and there are many examples of verses, often satirical or humorous, created on the spot. While conducting fieldwork for the School of Scottish Studies in the mid twentieth century, John MacInnes and a colleague paid an unannounced visit to a poet who improvised a song about them some twenty minutes in length.[100] Martin Martin noted that Hebrideans 'have a Gift of Poesy, and are able to form a Satire or Panegyric ex tempore' and gave a fuller account of one of the many rituals associated with the impromptu composition of song:

> Among Persons of Distinction it was reckon'd an Affront put upon any Company to broach a Piece of Wine, Ale, or Aquavitae, and not to see it all drank out at one Meeting. If any Man chance to go out from the Company, tho but for a few Minutes, he is oblig'd upon his Return, and before he take his Seat, to make an Apology for his Absence in Rhyme; which if he cannot perform, he is liable to such a share of the Reckoning as the Company thinks fit to impose: which Custom obtains in many places still, and is call'd [*Beannachadh Baird*], which in their Language signifies the Poet's congratulating the Company.[101]

Weddings, battles and funerals provided other occasions suitable for impromptu song composition; the keen included praise of the deceased. According to numerous traditions, the *Cliar Sheanchain*, a roving band of poets and songsters infamous in Gaelic tradition for the heavy costs of hosting them, could only be expelled by defeating them in a verbal contest, a feat attributed to several iconic poets.[102] Some cutting and derisive verbal flytings, often between members of rival clans, survive, and well into the twentieth century could not be sung in mixed company lest they rekindle inter-clan animosities.[103]

Although most people today assume that all Gaelic poetry is 'folk song', much of the repertoire sung by common Highlanders and the rhetorical style of their compositions is descended from the élite tradition, inherited by the peasantry after being abandoned by the upper echelons. Amongst the literary jewels that became the common property of the meek were *Laoidhean na Féinne* 'Ossianic ballads'. Prose narratives about the Fian began to be fashioned into verse from the twelfth century onwards and were composed in Classical Gaelic in Scotland as well as Ireland, sometimes localised in Scottish settings. Although 'Laoidh Fhraoich' ('The Lay of Fraoch') was originally a tale in the Ulster Cycle, vernacular versions were reset in several locations in the Highlands, including southern Perthshire (see Plate 14). Veneration for the Ossianic ballads was such that they were used to work magic.[104] Well into the nineteenth century most Highlanders considered Ossianic characters as historically real as those of the Bible, some claiming descent from them.[105]

Vernacular Gaelic poets inherited much of their legacy from their more learned counterparts, the filidh, including the veneration for the word, the supernatural associations of poetry, the power of satire, and the ability to record historical experience in verse. Similarly, some humble storytellers recorded in the nineteenth century were only one or two generations removed from the owners of medieval

Gaelic manuscripts and the recitation of well-polished narratives in the halls of chieftains.[106] This heritage of lore reminded Highlanders that they were members of a society possessed of a high art of ancient and aristocratic origin in which they could directly participate, no matter how materially impoverished they might appear to outsiders.

As the céilidh was a local institution, based in a community, run by and for the members of that community, it could be tailored to their needs, concerns, and resources. People told stories regarding their ancestors, sang songs about events significant in their own communities, created proverbial lore relevant to their own flora, fauna, and sense of place, and engendered an ethos of self-reliance. The school house, to the contrary, especially after the 1872 Education Act, undermined the legitimacy of local oral tradition. Many tradition-bearers recorded in the nineteenth and twentieth centuries testified to the bullying they received from the teacher and fellow students; some quit school altogether. 'Angus MacMillan of Benbecula, one of the most extensively recorded reciters in the twentieth century, ended his school career by thrashing his school-master and forgetting what he had learned there.'[107] In the 1930s the Rev. Calum MacLean attested to the intrinsic value of the céilidh in the life of Gaels before the youth were alienated from it:

> B' e an tigh céilidh an [t-]oil-thigh anns an robh iad a' teagasg a chéile ann an eòlas air gnothuichean mara is tìre. Cha robh foghluim eile aca no ionndrainn air. So mar a thug bodach Thunga a bheachd air an sgoil a bha air ùr thogail 's a' bhaile. Bha na balaich a b' àbhaist a bhi buachailleachd anns an sgoil. Dol seachad leis a' chrodh aon mhaduinn samhraidh, thog e am bata bha 'na làimh agus mhaoidh e air an tigh sgoile ag ràdh, "Is iomadh buachaille math a tha dol dhìth annad-sa."[108]

The céilidh house was their college, in which they taught each other in subjects relating to sea and land. They had no other education nor did they miss it. Here's how an old man of Tongue expressed his opinion about a school which had been newly built in the village. The lads who used to tend the cattle were in the school. As he passed with the cattle one summer morning, he raised his staff and rebuked the school house, saying 'There is many a good herdsman being ruined in you.'

There is a great breadth of diversity in Gaelic song tradition from the perspective of the insider. Nan MacKinnon vaunted confidently, 'If all the music of the world was cut off, the music of the Western Isles would serve the whole world.'[109]

INTERPRETATIVE METHODS

There are several basic terms that can be applied widely to oral tradition. A text's *topic* or *subject* is what it explicitly discusses or describes. A text's *theme* is its emergent idea or message revealed implicitly in the unfolding of the narrative. Themes are usually related to society or to human experience, such as the characteristics of ideal leaders (or the flaws of poor ones), the tensions between the individual and society, and the struggle between altruism and self-interest. Two stories with the same subject can have different themes and two stories with different subjects can discuss the same theme in divergent ways.

Folklorist Stith Thompson defined a *motif* as 'the smallest element in a tale having the power to persist in tradition' which 'may be centered on a certain type of character in a tale, sometimes on an action, sometimes on attendant circumstances of the action'.[110] Motifs serve to develop and move the narrative forward; motifs usually reappear across multiple narratives, sometimes in specific genres; familiarity with a motif aids the audience in interpreting it and its contribution to the narrative and its themes. The jealous step-mother and the assignment of impossible tasks are two motifs which can be found in many international wonder tales. The *geas* – an injunction imposed magically upon the protagonist – is a motif typical of Gaelic heroic tales that has roots in native cosmology.[111]

Most literature employs many different literary devices, not least because they are inherent in language itself. A *symbol* is something that represents something else; there are more specific terms for the many forms of symbols. A *metonym* is an object which represents something else with which it is closely associated, as in using 'crown' to imply 'king'. A *synecdoche* is a part or member which represents the whole, as in saying 'hands' to imply 'workers'. A *metaphor* is a word or phrase used in place of something else because of the implied similarity between them. In a lament to his son, Ó Maoil Chiaráin compares his condition to that of a tree, stating 'I am the branch that shed its nut [. . .] I am the tree that shed its fruit.'[112] An *analogy* is an extended comparison between two things based on a structural parallelism; Gaelic poets often summarised a well-known tale in order to draw an analogy with a contemporary dilemma or situation, such as when the author of 'Ar Sliocht Gaodhal ó Ghort Gréag' recounted how Lugh rescued Ireland from foreign invaders so that he could tell the Earl of Argyll, 'you are the Lugh of the present.'[113]

The *rhetorical mode* of a text (whether in prose or poetic form) is its overall organising principle, driven by its function, that affects the style of presentation and narrative voice. There are Gaelic terms for the most common rhetorical modes: *teagasg* 'teaching, gnomic lore', *sgeul* 'narrative, storytelling', *moladh* 'praise, eulogy, panegyric', *aoir* 'satire', *cumha* 'elegy, lament', *deasbad* 'debate', *agallamh / còmhradh* 'dialogue, conversation', *taisbean / fàisneachd* 'prophecy', *brosnachadh* 'incitement', *beannachadh* 'blessing', and *meòrachadh* 'personal reflection, nostalgia'.[114] A single text can be governed by more than one rhetorical mode.

The questions asked about a text, and the methodologies appropriate for examining it, will vary according to its nature. A proverb yields itself to a different kind of analysis than a love song, a legend, or a joke. Folklorists and literary scholars have developed a range of techniques which answer different sorts of questions about texts. The following table arranges dominant approaches according to their primary focus:[115]

Focus	Kinds of questions asked
Textual	What is the plot of the narrative? What motifs appear in the text? How does the text and its constituent elements relate to other texts? How does the text 'work' internally? Does the plot conform to well-established 'narrative laws'?
Psychological	Does the text provide a symbolic means of mediating the binary structures inherent in the psyche? Is the text a projection of the self or psychological archetypes? Is the text a socially sanctioned means of expressing anxiety?
Ethnological	Does the text contain aspects or elements of the culture which produced it? Does it alternatively express wish-fulfilment or suppressed desires? How does the text relate to deep symbolic systems of the culture? How is the text perpetuated in society?
Functional	Why are certain genres and texts created? Why do they survive? What is the purpose of a given text in a specific society?
Performance	How does a performer remember and reconstruct his text? How does the audience affect the content of the text and the style of the performance? How does the context of the performance affect the content of the text and the style of the performance? How do cultural aesthetics affect the content of the text and the style of the performance? What is the most accurate means of representing the verbal expression?

Table 3.2: Groups of analytical methodologies

Verbal expressions in oral tradition always exist in variation. A story, for example, may be created by one person but by the time it has been retold by a number of different storytellers, and passed through multiple stages of transmission, it will take on changes in different communities, some subtle and some obvious. Each independent form of the story is called a *variant*. Whole narrative plots as well as individual motifs can travel from community to community, across languages and continents. Folklorists describe widely travelled verbal forms as *migratory* or *international*, and have spent great effort tracking the origins of migratory tales such as 'Snow White', which appears in Gaelic oral tradition as the tale 'Lasair Gheug, King of Ireland's Daughter'.[116] Motifs also migrate; migratory motifs first recorded in Homer's *Odyssey* (but probably much older) appear in Gaelic tales such as 'Conall Ruadh nan Car'.[117]

INTERPRETING PROSE NARRATIVE

Two Middle Gaelic lists of tales survive which are arranged according to a native classification scheme, including *táin* 'cattle-raid', *eachtra* 'expedition, adventure', *compert* 'conception, begetting', *cath* 'battle', *togail* 'attack, destruction', *buile* 'vision, madness', *tochmarc* 'wooing, courtship', *aithed* 'elopement', *serc* 'love story', *immram* 'sea voyage', and *aided* 'death tale'.[118]

Many modern folklorists classify oral narratives into categories according to several criteria:[119]

(A) the typical interest or focus of the content,
(B) the characters that appear,
(C) the geographical and chronological setting,
(D) the origin of the narrative type, and
(E) the narrative's primary purpose.

The most common narrative types in Gaelic tradition are:

- **Märchen, Fairy Tale, or International Wonder Tale**: (A) An ordinary human's encounter with the supranatural world, which usually causes him/her to be endowed with extraordinary qualities; (B) Regular people and extraordinary beings; (C) From real world to supranatural world; atmosphere of feudal age, but exact era seldom given; (D) Layers of prehistoric totemism, medieval feudalism, and local context; plots and motifs dispersed internationally across languages and cultures; (E) Entertainment.
- **Myths (Etiological and Eschatological)**: (A) Creation of the world, origins of things, social or geological phenomena, the nature of plants and animals; (B) Usually involve supranatural beings; (C) Usually set in the timeless past; (D) Myths are universal to all societies; (E) Used to explain and justify the social order, cultural institutions, or representations of the world.
- **Historical Legends**: (A) Local historical accounts, which may connect to clan, regional, or national history, believed to be real; (B) Historical persons as primary characters; (C) Definite place and time framed historically; (D) Usually created within the society but often incorporating migratory motifs; (E) Explanation of the origins of kings, local clans, or place names, or to represent historical events.
- **The Religious Tale**: (A) Religious virtues and characters; (B) Saints and supernatural beings; (C) Earth, heaven or hell; (D) Medieval church and preachers, usually in Latin; (E) Teaching of morality and adherence to Christianity and church.
- **The Romantic Tale, or Novella**: (A) Complex tales, more adventurous, pathetic and sentimental than wondrous; (B) Real people; (C) Definite time and location; (D) Literary origins among élite traditions of India, Persia, Arabia, Bible, Greece, Rome and medieval Europe; (E) Entertainment.
- **The Animal Tale**: (A) Can overlap with human tales and etiological legends; (B) Animals; (C) A world analogous to the human world, but no definite time or place; (D) Creation myths and culture legends, on one hand, and literary fables on the other; (E) Teaching and explanation.

In the early medieval period native literature and history was the primary focus of literary activity, but Gaeldom later became more connected to and interested in

Continental European literature. This resulted in the importation and adaptation of romantic tales from the continent into Gaelic manuscripts.[120] There is also later evidence of these tale types in oral tradition. The stylistic features of narratives written in medieval Gaelic manuscripts confirm that they were meant to be read aloud to an audience, from whence they entered oral tradition. The tale of Mànus, a fiction featuring the historical character King Magnus 'Barelegs' of Norway, was probably composed by a member of the MacMhuirich poetic dynasty in South Uist, although the tale has only survived in oral tradition.[121] On the other hand, there are tales in Gaelic manuscripts which seem to have been composed orally first before being transcribed.[122]

Traditional narratives have many characteristics which folklorists observe to be common across cultures: the narrative is not burdened with descriptive passages and elaborate details, but focuses on the actions of the main characters and the dialogue between them; dialogue itself is often the vehicle for progressing the plot; the thoughts and feelings of characters are seldom articulated, except for what is relayed in dialogue; episodes happen three times, with the third time often signalling the success of the protagonist; titles or simple nouns may substitute for the proper names of characters and places (such as 'the king', 'the ogre', 'the forest', and 'the castle').[123]

Migratory tales become transformed according to traditional sensibilities after being 'naturalised' in a Gaelic environment: there is a strong preference for the hero to be an aristocrat, often 'the son of the king of Ireland'; characters and places are frequently given proper names, sometimes those recalling medieval Gaelic lore; Gaelic characters, such as those of the Ossianic cycle, are sometimes inserted; dialogue takes the form of song, especially at moments of intense emotion or drama; stories become reset in the local landscape and associated with unusual place names or prominent features.[124] 'Gaelic wonder tales, too, tend to be longer, more elaborate and poetic than their international counterparts.'[125]

Probably the most elaborate added ornamentation is the *run* (often called *siubhal* or *ruith* in Gaelic), a long, formulaic verbal sequence which embellishes the story's details at certain heightened or transitional moments. Runs consist of clusters of alliterative, onomatopoeic and archaistic words (particularly adjectives) meant to impress the listener; they also aid the storyteller to prepare himself mentally for the next episode of the narrative. There are runs for episodes such as the arming of the warrior, the clash between warriors, the launching of a ship, sailing of the ship, the feasts in the chieftain's hall, and imposition of *geas*. Oral storytellers exercise personal freedom in their choice of run and the means of varying it at particular points in the story.[126] The words rely so much upon the union of sound, sense, association and insinuation as to make them impossible to render in translation. John Francis Campbell commented on the runs that he found in variants of the popular hero tale 'Conall Gulban' which were recorded in Barra, Cowal, Colonsay, Inverness-shire, Benbecula and South Uist:

> There is more incident in the [Cowal variant], which I have followed; but the language of the [Barra variant] is more curious. It is wilder altogether, and savours

more of an old Bardic composition. It is, in fact, the version of a practised narrator, who cannot read. All the fights are described by both men in nearly the same words; but each has a different set of phrases, though sometimes they are very like each other. When these are rapidly given, the effect is that of a kind of chant; something which, with music, would almost be a rude chorus; and might be so uttered as to express the battle.[127]

Besides the migratory tales of various types, there is also a large body of legends in Gaelic oral tradition which purports to record important events and characters from Scottish history. The oldest of these relate to the early Celtic saints, especially Saint Columba. After these chronologically come tales relating to the leadership of Somerled (and associates) in liberating Gaeldom from the tyranny of the Norse. There are also a few scattered narratives from the era of the Lords of the Isles, but the period of chaos and instability unleashed by the dissolution of the Lordship – *Linn nan Creach* – provides the heroic-age background and subject matter of a great many 'clan sagas' (as they have been deemed by John MacInnes[128]).

Exploiting these oral sources for the research and writing of history is not without its own complications: there is not a single, consistent corpus to be gleaned for objective 'facts' but an assortment of diverse and contradictory materials which is coloured by the aspirations and grievances of particular clans and family branches, the tensions between social classes, and the perspectives of individual storytellers.[129] The historical framework and details of these historical legends and clan sagas have been inevitably modified by the verbal artistry of the storyteller: migratory motifs add colourful detail; the 'laws of heroic biography' influence the life story of historical figures (his birth is heralded by omens, he is exiled, etc.); supernatural elements increase dramatic intrigue; and so on. The practice of storytelling allows a community to explain itself to itself, and legends have significance exactly because of the relationship between subject and audience. Stories are not meant to be verbal enumerations of facts: they tend to survive in oral tradition only if they are good stories. They are thus shaped by the aesthetics of Gaelic oral tradition and subject to elaboration or reduction according to the expectations of their audience, amongst other factors.

Although a great deal of Gaelic story and song survives surrounding the MacLeods, MacKenzies and Morrisons of Lewis during the attempted colonisation by the Fife Adventurers, for example, conflicts have been framed simply as clan warfare rather than as local resistance to the machinations of the state.[130] The larger political context and external players (Lowland agents of King James VI, in this case) would have had little lasting meaning or interest to succeeding generations of tradition-bearers or their audience, while personal relationships to landed clans would have maintained interest and attention. The oral history embedded in such popular narratives can tell us much about local attitudes and perceptions, especially those from whom it is recorded, but other aspects of the larger-scale contemporary context must often be recovered from other sources. A comparative study of the history of the island of Tiree attests to the complementary nature of such materials:

> The written sources are mostly connected with the administration of the island by the Duke of Argyll, and tend to reflect the attitudes of the landowner and his agents. [. . .] Sometimes they throw a very clear light on social practices, but in general they do not reflect the attitudes and behaviour of the great mass of the population. The oral traditions of the island record the customs and beliefs of the islanders in considerable detail, and serve to compliment the written record. They provide reliable data on the history of families and communities of occupations and industries and many other aspects of life. But one has to handle oral traditions as critically as written records and be aware of their bias and omissions and distortions.[131]

INTERPRETING POETRY

Until relatively recently, Gaelic poetry was not meant to be read but to be heard. Poetry was always some sort of song, although the metre and musicality of the song varied greatly, from a recitative chant to a fully ornamented melody with regular rhythmic stress. There are native terms to describe the great variety of Gaelic verse forms:[132]

- *Dàn*: Syllabic poetry and its vernacular derivatives, more recitative than musical in performance, with stress shifting according to normal Gaelic speech rhythms. Associated with élite literary traditions.
- *Laoidh*: A narrative song more musical than dàn but of similar metrical form. Some Ossianic ballads and later religious hymns are categorised as laoidhean.
- *Amhran* or *Òran*: A song metre in quatrains with regular stress typified by symmetry and AABA musical phrasing, probably adapted from mainstream medieval European musical tradition.
- *Iorram* ('Strophic'): A song whose units begin with 2 to 8 short lines with two metrical stresses each concluded by a line with three metrical stresses. The theme of all early iorraim is panegyric. This seems to be a survival of an ancient bardic metre (not eclipsed by the filidh).
- *Luinneag*: A song with regular stress in which a soloist alternates singing with the group chorus. The older choral refrains are made up of *vocables* (syllables without semantic content). The surviving Scottish Gaelic repertoire of luinneagan is dominated by work songs, especially *òrain-luaidh* ('waulking songs').[133]
- *Port-à-beul* (literally 'a tune from the mouth'): A song driven by the melody whose text is of secondary importance; the metre and musical style is derived from the instrumental dance music introduced in the seventeenth century played primarily on the fiddle. Not considered 'true poetry' in Gaelic tradition, but a vocal accompaniment to dancing and a mnemonic device for remembering tunes.

The literary conventions of the filidh had a strong impact on vernacular Gaelic poetic tradition, especially in the upper registers of élite practice. Most Gaelic poems were composed with a particular *subject of address*, whether an individual or group, in mind. A rule of etiquette for the file was that he compliment the subject's wife at the end of the piece; if the subject was not his regular patron, the last was also acknowledged towards the end; the poet could reserve his concluding praise to God[134] (see item one in Appendix A for an example). The first of these, the compliment of the subject's wife, is also widely attested in vernacular Gaelic verse when the poem is addressed to a chieftain.

Few Gaelic poems follow a strictly linear narrative. In the poetry of the filidh, succeeding verses often connect via verbal or conceptual links or progressions, or they may be varying restatements of the poem's topic, but each stanza is essentially a self-contained unit. The Ossianic ballads are exceptional in Gaelic tradition in telling a story within the verses sequentially. The expected practice in the vernacular tradition is that the background story is told first and then the song is sung. The non-linearity of Gaelic song becomes more pronounced as one moves away from the élite tradition to the 'sub-literary' register of luinneag. The unfolding images of these song-poems, triggered by association, have been likened to a kaleidoscope,[135] but perhaps the 'hyper-links' of webpages would be an appropriate modern analogy.

The term *iorram* refers to a metre which seems to have a very ancient pedigree: current scholarship indicates that it was the song form of the earliest Gaelic poets and that it survived in Scotland after it was downgraded by the formal syllabic poetry of the filidh in Ireland.[136] The iorram metre was used for vernacular songs about clan concerns and was considered inappropriate for light or romantic topics.[137] Each stanza in the iorram metre consists of a number of lines containing two heavy stresses in regular rhythm, where each of these short lines are linked by end-rhyme. Each stanzaic unit is closed with a line of three heavy stresses. Take, for example, the first stanza in poem four of Appendix A:

'S mi 'am shuidh' air a' chnocan
Chaidh mo léirsinn an olcas
Is mi mar aon mhac an trotain air m' fhàgail.

The first two lines consist of seven syllables of two stresses each (underlined) where the last stressed syllables of each line are connected via assonance (in bold) with 'o'. This assonance rhyme also links to the second stressed syllable of the concluding line, which has an extra three syllables. The vowel of the final stress ('à') connects the final lines of all of the stanzas in the poem.[138] Although most surviving iorraim have three-line stanzas, other examples have as many as nine, and any one poem need not have a consistent number. By the eighteenth century the common usage of the term iorram became confused with the word for rowing (*iomramh / iomradh*), even though the metre is ill-fitted to this task.

The work-song tradition in Scotland has many compositions in a metre in which the single line is the basic unit (see poem five of Appendix A for an example). Series of single lines are connected by the assonance of the last stressed syllable, usually the penultimate syllable of the line. A choral refrain is sung between each line (and sometimes even in the middle of the single line itself). A 'stanza' consists of a sequence of lines containing the same vowel assonance; the transition to a new assonance rhyme (and therefore stanza) is sometimes marked by a variation in the words or melody of the refrain. The new stanza often forms a new statement, sometimes repeating the subject of address or topic. This metrical form seems to be quite old; it is apparently related to metres used for early European heroic poetry, the French carole and English carol, and many early Welsh panegyrics.[139] It may have survived by laying low amongst the tasks and social domains furthest removed from the literary activities of the professional poets, leading one scholar to refer to it as the 'sub-literary song tradition'. Some of these songs contain material about specific people and events, but there are also many formulaic passages which could be assembled spontaneously by members of work parties.[140]

A dominant theme in Gaelic oral tradition, especially poetry, is praise or dispraise.[141] Representative members of the natural world, divided into noble or ignoble categories, provide concrete images in Gaelic poetry to convey praise and dispraise.[142] (There are numerous reasons for these classifications which cannot be generalised across categories.) To call someone an apple tree, for example, is complimentary, while to call him an aspen is an insult.

Category	Praise	Dispraise
Bird	Eagle	Buzzard
Fish	Salmon	Eel
Animal	Deer	Frog
Tree	Oak	Alder

Table 3.3: Examples of symbols used to imply praise or dispraise

Especially since the attention brought by Macpherson's *Ossian*, Gaelic literature has been subjected to a number of foreign literary models and yardsticks ill-suited to it, particularly from anglophone literature, resulting numerous distortions and misrepresentations.[143] One of the most significant developments in the twentieth century for the interpretation of Scottish Gaelic poetry was the recovery of the inner logic of vernacular poetry and its relationship to the cultural context, a rhetorical system called by John MacInnes the 'Gaelic panegyric code'.[144] In his work, MacInnes draws attention to the literary conventions and motifs of Gaelic panegyric poetry and the genres in which they operate. He demonstrates that this panegyric code is pervasive throughout vernacular Gaelic literature, particularly due to the historical experience of Gaels as a disenfranchised community and the primary importance of the warrior-chieftain in defending clan interests. Although 'the stress is on the survival of the group of warrior-hunters at the top of society'[145] this rhetorical system was adaptable to other subjects, such as religion, love, nature and the innovations of technology, to name a few.

> All these evoke different sets of new images interlocking with each other in the same way. Once these conventions were established, even an oblique reference would be intelligible in the very same terms. The commonplaces work thus for anyone who through song has known the rhetoric from childhood; they work with similar effect upon the imagination of a critic who does no more than familiarise himself with the written texts; and we can take it for granted that the audience in the chief's hall was able to respond, though not necessarily in this self-conscious, analytic manner, to all the nuances of each statement. What the bards have produced here is therefore a coherent system of rhetoric of great resonance and evocative power. Nor is it designed to be merely an enclosed universe of poetic discourse. Every commonplace of the system focuses upon a particular facet of aristocratic life, including relation-ships to those who provide imaginative, spiritual, and economic support for the aristocracy.[146]

One of the more important topics, 'Allies', demonstrates the consciousness of the importance of pan-Gaelic solidarity in Scotland, diverging from Irish norms. Whereas Irish bard poetry typically flatters local kings by attributing rule of neighbouring regions or even all of Ireland to them, Scottish poetry (especially vernacular but even bardic) emphasises alliances between clans and their chieftains, often in an idealised manner. This is particularly evident during the divisive politics of the seventeenth and eighteenth centuries. Despite the rivalry between MacDonalds and Campbells, for example, both vied for the claim of *ceannas na nGaoidheal* 'leadership of the Gaels' and often named each other in the 'roll call of allies'. Poets on both sides of this contention were interested in the other's declarations of such claims.[147]

An exhaustive taxonomy of the elements of MacInnes' panegyric code would be tedious, and a blunt and non-holistic instrument for the reading of Gaelic poetry; it is nonetheless one fruitful means of identifying the norms and ideals of Highland society as expressed in literature (as per the 'culture-reflector' approach of literary criticism). The following table is my attempt to identify and group these together; the poetry throughout this book is annotated with these codes.[148]

Code		Meaning
A		**Subject's Territorial, Historical, and Ancestral Credentials**
	1	Identification with place name ('style') (e.g., MacDonald of Glengarry)
	2	Identification with qualifying phrase or adjective (e.g., Black Iain of the Blades)
	3	Place name and qualifying phrase (e.g., Mull of the huge mountains)
	4	Ancestry (personal names, lineage, dynasties, deeds done by ancestors)
B		**Qualities and Characteristics of Subject that Qualify him as Leader**
	1	Providing social support for clan (e.g., mercy, generosity, kindness)
	2	Patronage of poets and subject of poetry
	3	Adherence to tradition and precedent
	4	Perception of outsiders of him (e.g., feared by enemies)
	5	Abilities in leadership, diplomacy and law-giving
	6	*Rìoghail* ('kingly') and *uasal* ('noble')
	7	Personal piety
	8	Intelligent, educated, eloquent and refined
	9	Brave, courageous, fearless
C		**Description of the Subject's Household**
	1	House's grandeur reflects noble status
	2	Hospitality, generosity, feasting (the 'warrior-communion')
	3	Celebration of traditional arts (music, dance and song)
	4	Other noble pastimes (e.g., gambling)
	5	'Cast of extras' (e.g., noble women and visitors)
	6	Leadership reflected in landscape
D		**Subject's Heroic Roles, Deeds and Accoutrements**
	1	Warrior (and associated activities, e.g., cattle-raiding)
	2	Hunter (and associated animals)
	3	Equestrian (and his horse)
	4	Mariner (and his vessel)
	5	Clothing and accoutrements (e.g., plaid, helmet, sword, shield, war-banner)

Code		Meaning
E		**Physical Characteristics of Subject**
	1	Youth, virility, sex appeal
	2	Physical prowess and strength
	3	Face and hair
	4	Body, arms, legs
	5	Carriage, posture, gait
F		**Symbols and Kennings for Subject of Address**
	1	Trees and other flora
	2	Animals
	3	Natural phenomena (e.g., lightning)
	4	Features of sky and landscape
	5	Jewel, treasure
	6	Synecdoche (e.g., hand, cheek, eye)
G		**Subject's Supporters / Social Network**
	1	Dependants (i.e., clansmen)
	2	Allies (especially in war)
	3	The Gaels, the Highlands
	4	Wife and family
	5	God, Jesus, saints
H		**Elegiac Conventions on Death of Subject**
	1	Body of deceased
	2	Coffin and placement in grave
	3	Decay, decomposition
	4	Body lost and can't be buried
	5	Mourning and keening
	6	Nature mourns loss of subject

Table 3.4: A taxonomy of the elements of the Gaelic panegyric code

These elements may appear in this unmarked form or they may be expressed in a periphrastic form:

- **Understatement** ($\neq$): An assertion made as a double-negative. If a poet says 'You were not niggardly with gold', he is praising the subject for his generosity (code B.1).
- **Negation** (ø): An element stated to be absent, thus indicating a break in social norms or relations, and therefore a potential crisis. If a poet says 'There is no music coming from your hall' (code C.3), he is implying that the chieftain's abode is in breach of social conventions, probably due to his death.
- **Reversal** (–): Satire or criticism is effected by stating the opposite.

Many poems open with an interpretive framing formula which describes the mood, location, or position of the poet, such as 'This night seems to last forever' or 'I sit here on the hillock' or 'My mind is greatly troubled.' Less familiar to readers of English literature are the long, dense strings of adjectives which ornament Gaelic verse and describe the subject exhaustively, much like the illumination of manuscripts which fill every possible space with decoration.

Vernacular Gaelic poetry represents and contains vital strains of the continuity of Highland thought, expression and culture, linking the present with the past. The tree, for example, is one of the most ancient and potent of symbols to appear in Gaelic literature, entwined in cosmology, the representation of social structures, the natural world, and literacy itself. The song-poetry tradition and repertoire of the Highlands is even older and more conservative in many respects than that of Ireland due to a number of factors: the relative weakness of the monopoly of the filidh in Scotland, the persistence of the native aristocracy into the mid eighteenth century (lost in Ireland after 1601), and the cultural losses resulting from trauma of the Potato Famine in Ireland unparalleled in Scotland, amongst others.[149]

Recent generations of scholars have moved away from focusing solely on the élite and their associated documentary remains, and instead attempt to reconstruct and interpret the perspectives and perceptions of society as a whole.[150] In the case of the Scottish Highlanders, Gaelic song represents a rich vein of surviving primary evidence to be mined for such purposes. Doing so, however, presents significant challenges to the researcher, requiring the careful study of individual poets, texts and contexts, beyond the obvious matter of translation.[151] It requires being sufficiently acquainted with the literary conventions to understand how statements are framed and to recognise what the poet has left unstated.

Gaelic poets were privileged to speak on behalf of wider Gaelic society and one of the ways in which they exercised this privilege was the composition of poems in the voice of other people (of the same or opposite gender), animals, inanimate objects, features of the landscape, and even abstract concepts (such as love and generosity). This can complicate the interpretation of Gaelic literature for historical scholarship. One of the most popular Gaelic love songs 'Hi ho ró 's na ho ró éile', in the voice of Mary

MacDonald, full of tenderness for and intimate detail of her husband, was actually composed by John MacLean (*Bàrd Bhaile Mhàrtainn*) in Tiree;[152] the researcher armed with the song text alone, without the accompanying narrative, could be easily deceived.

Whatever the technical attainments or historical value of Gaelic poetry, its greatest significance to generations of Highlanders has been as a means of expression for their most personal thoughts and intense feelings, facilitating joy, grief, catharsis and healing. This medium, especially when free of the conventions imposed by the poet-patron relationship, has produced some of the finest gems of literature in any language.

LITERATURE AND IDENTITY

The pan-Gaelic literati fortified common Gaelic cultural values and frames of reference and made them manifest in literature; such impressive artistic forms could not fail to maintain the prestige of native tradition and to have a positive 'trickle-down' effect on lower social strata. The cuairt of the filidh ensured some degree of cohesion across the expanse of Gaelic Ireland and Scotland. Even the oral traditions about the wide geographical operation of the literati strengthened the concept of the Gàidhealtachd;[153] the verbal arts allowed the concept of the Gaelic community to be projected back in time and across the geography of Scotland.

The Fian were literary exemplars for the Gaels themselves; cultural standards and precedents were set by them in oral tradition. While Scotland and Ireland shared the interest in Ossianic ballads, with poets in both countries continuing to compose them into the post-medieval period, the themes and subjects began to diverge; the collapse of the Lordship of the Isles and the de-Gaelicisation of the Lowlands seem to have created an air of nostalgia and retrospection amongst Scottish Gaels and encouraged a greater interest in the elegies of great heroes than exhibited in Ireland; ballads featuring the invasions of Vikings and their subsequent defeat were also more popular in Scotland than in Ireland, probably because of the struggle for cultural survival faced by Scottish Gaels.[154]

Many modern writers imply that non-industrialised peoples enjoy telling stories and singing songs simply because they have no other entertainment, as though the highest form of art can only be found on a television or computer screen. This is to overestimate the superiority of global, electronic mass media and to underestimate the satisfaction that people find in participating in their own local forms of expression. Despite the forces against Gaelic and its oral tradition, tradition-bearers have survived to the present with a great affection for, and dedication to, this heritage, consciously sustaining what they have inherited. Hector MacLean, one of Campbell's folktale collectors, recounted the return to Islay of a tradition-bearer who he knew from youth after a space of over twenty-five years, having lost his leg and much of the lore that MacLean remembered hearing from him:

> When I entered the house he was sitting by the fireside with his wooden leg. The old
> fellow's eyes brightened when he saw me, and I told him I wished to hear some of his

old lore again. 'O,' said he, '*b' àbhaist domh 'bhith 'gan gabhail sin a chumail toil-inntinn riut*' ['I used to recite those to you to entertain you' . . .] I inquired of him about the old people whom he was was wont to hear reciting these stories in his youth, and he enumerated several, and said that the poems were long and beautiful, and that to listen to them was the delight of all. [. . .] '*O, bu lurach an eachdraidh i nuair a bhiodh i air a h-innseadh gu ceart!*' ['Oh, that lore was beautiful when it was told correctly!']¹⁵⁵

There is no hint of inadequacy in the recollections of 'Mac 'ic Eachainn', a native of Ardgour, which seem to date to the late eighteenth century:

*Lasaidh mo chridhe fhathast le sòlas nuair a chuimhnicheas mi air cleachdaidhean agus gnàths nam beann. Cò neach a thogadh anns a' Ghàidhealtachd nach d' fhiosraich an tùs òige, an deòthas inntinn leis an èisdeadh sgeòil na Féinne. Cha dì-chuimhnich mi ri m' bheò an toil-inntinn leis an èistinn ri seanchas nan aosda nuair a labhradh iad mu euchd nan laoch bho'n tàinig iad. 'S cinnteach mi gun do chuidich seo ri clann nan Gàidheal a thogail suas ann am barrachd buaidh os cionn gach sluaigh anns an domhan – mar a bha am beachd air àrdachadh le bhith cluinntinn cliù agus treuntas an sinnsear a ghnàth 'ga luaidh [. . .] Iadsan a dh'fhiosraich an rùn cridhe leis an èist an Gàidheal ri seanchas mu chinneadh, chan ioghnadh leò mar a chumadh air chuimhne iad.*¹⁵⁶

My heart still burns with delight when I remember the traditions and customs of the Highlands. What person, who was raised in a Gaelic community, did not experience in their early youth the mental excitement that comes when the tales of the Fian are heard. I will never forget for as long as I live the enjoyment with which I listened to the lore of the old people when they would speak about the exploits of the warriors from whom they were descended. I'm sure that this enabled the Gaels to be endowed as they grew up with qualities superior to other people of the world – since their ideas were elevated by constantly hearing references to the fame and excellence of their ancestors [. . .] Those who know the love with which the Gaels listen to the lore of their ancestors will not be surprised that they are remembered.

Like other minority cultures whose existence is threatened by hegemonic forces, Gaels have often perceived tradition as an internal cultural resource for the renewal and reassertion of the culture itself.¹⁵⁷ The twentieth-century Lewis poet Murchadh MacPhàrlain remarked on the survival of his Gaelic community with the proclamation 'Yet still we sing!' Calum Ruadh, one of the last active Gaelic community song-makers of Skye, expressed the role he felt poetry had in the maintenance of the language and Highland identity itself:

Had it not been for the bards, over the past centuries, we wouldn't have the Gaelic we have [to]day. [. . .] When you have an interest in those kind of [poets], you like to understand what they've been singing or talking about. I think the bards keep the language going, and the day they go, goes our language, goes our heritage, goes our identity.[158]

A number of related factors have contributed to the decline of Gaelic oral tradition, not least the assault on the language itself. John Ramsay of Ochtertyre stated at the end of the eighteenth century that 'The Highland muses are said to have dropped their wings more since the last rebellion than at any preceding period.'[159] Duncan Campbell noted in the same era that the forced removal to Canada of the fighting men of Glengarry, the subject of so many panegyrics, 'turned war-songs and proud pìobaireachd into hollow mockeries or pathetic laments, took the pith out of the oral traditions.'[160] The recurring complaint of fieldworkers sent by John Francis Campbell in 1859 to collect folklore was that the local ministers had ridiculed and silenced the old people for their tales, and the school-master continued the policy of denigration with the young.[161] The sense of stigmatisation in Campbell's notes is quite palpable.

Both young and old in the Gàidhealtachd were increasingly influenced by evangelical Christianity and institutional education, religious and secular alike. State and church, endowed with the charisma of power, backed by the prestige of print, and employing techniques of individual socialisation through discipline and rote-learning, functioned as innovative, dynamic, even liberating 'communities of memory' promoting new histories [. . .] Promoting coherent narratives of secular and religious progress, these institutions brought individuals into a much more equivocal relationship not just with a 'traditional' past, but also with an unsatisfactory present [. . .].[162]

The incorporation of the Gàidhealtachd into the twentieth-century Anglo-American world of mass-media has accelerated the demise of local oral traditions, an experience paralleled in many other minority cultures. For the older generations the death of these traditions signify the end of community and the end of life itself:

I am reminded, finally, of an old man in Barra who, in 1970, tired of returning home to an empty house as television took over from the céilidh, one night painted THE END in large white letters on the end of his thatched cottage. It remains an appropriate symbol for the passing of one tradition and the arrival of the brave new world.[163]

With the widespread loss of Gaelic in modern times and the neglect of Gaelic literature in Scottish institutions (especially the educational system), the Highlands have been largely denuded of a literary history. The dominant voice of the English language and of prominent Lowland poets such as Robert Burns and Walter Scott have often usurped the place of native Gaelic lore. Anyone wishing to understand Highland history or revitalise Highland culture on its own terms simply cannot afford to ignore the rich resources to be found in Gaelic oral traditions.[164]

Chapter Four

CLAN SOCIETY

[Highlanders] are nothing so barbarous as the Lowlanders and English commonly represent them; but are for what I could find a very hospitable and civil people: and the main reasons for the contrary character I take to be for their adhering too much to their ancient custom, habit [i.e., clothing] and language; whereby they distinguish themselves from all their neighbours; and distinctions always create mutual reflections.
— Edward Lhuyd 1700[1]

In 1688, the MacDonalds of Keppoch and the Mackintoshes confronted one another at the Battle of Mulroy (known in Gaelic as *Cath na Maoile-Ruaidhe*) in Lochaber, the last clan battle to be fought in Scotland. The MacDonalds claimed an hereditary right to the lands of Glenroy and Glenspean, which set them against the Mackintoshes who were given an official charter by the king for these lands. After failing to convince the MacDonalds to leave willingly, the Mackintoshes attempted by hook and by crook to dispossess them. It was humiliating, then, for the MacDonalds to rout the Mackintoshes at this clan battle, especially given that additional reinforcements had been sent by the central government to aid the Mackintoshes.[2]

Alasdair nan Cleas ('Alexander of the Tricks') was the chieftain of the MacDonalds of Keppoch about a century earlier, from the late sixteenth century to the early seventeenth century. He was given this nickname because he was supposed to have learnt black magic while being educated on the continent of Europe,[3] where many of the clan aristocracy were sent for learning in their youth. Clan chieftains were commonly well educated, widely travelled, and fluent in several languages.

⌒

According to tradition,[4] Alasdair was once at an opulent feast in London held by a very wealthy Englishman who boasted of the value of his silver candleholders on the dining table. During the feast, Alasdair overheard one of the guests speaking about the Highlands in very disparaging tones. In a half-serious, half-mocking manner, Alasdair said aloud to the assembled company, 'I could show you a dozen candleholders in my home that are far more valuable than these.' This offended the Englishmen greatly, as they considered the Highlands as nothing but a place of poverty and barbarity. They placed a large bet that there were no candleholders in the Highlands that could compare with those in the present house. Alasdair left his host with an invitation to come visit him and see the proof for himself.

Some weeks later the Englishman and his friend came to visit Alasdair nan Cleas in Lochaber. Instead of a grand castle, they found that Alasdair's chiefly abode in Keppoch was little better than the barns on their estates. When they reached the door Alasdair welcomed them warmly. He invited them in for a feast of the choice offerings of Lochaber: salmon from the river Lochy, venison from Beinne Bhric, fresh fruit from the orchard of Keppoch, and whisky and wine without stint. This pleased his English guests greatly, but there was no sign of any candleholders.

Alasdair noticed that they were scrutinising his possessions and promised them that they would soon see the candleholders. At a motion made by the chieftain, a dozen of his best men entered the room, fully arrayed in their finest clothing, each holding a lit pine-torch in his left hand and a naked claymore in his right.

'You now see the candleholders of Keppoch', said Alasdair, 'and I would ask you without any hesitation if there is enough gold or silver in all of England that could possibly buy them.'

The Englishman arose and admitted to Alasdair that he had lost his bet, for these were the most valuable candleholders that he had ever seen. Alasdair refused to take the winnings of the bet, toasting the health of his friends instead and giving them another week of hospitality in his home.

~

The clans of the Scottish Highlands are popularly portrayed as extended families who were ruled by a chieftain related to them by ancestry, mired in blood-feuds with other clans, and entrenched against the central authorities and all semblance of social progress. Clan books contain lists of family names which are supposed to be septs of particular parent clans, and from these relationships tartans are assigned according to name. Scottish clan maps similarly purport to chart the homelands and territorial extent of clans. The origins of clan lore are often asserted to be 'lost in the mists of time', although some genealogists claim to have traced their pedigree back to Adam.

Such oversimplifications mask a much more fluid, complex, and interesting history. Like many other non-industrial societies, clans were conceptualised as extended families, with familial terms used to describe social structures and relationships. In reality, however, kinship was only one of several different kinds of bonds holding a clan together and often not the most enduring kind. As a result, individuals, families and kin-groups changed their allegiances, home territories, and surnames more often than the static portraits of clan life usually suggest.

The clans were not governed by a unified, coherent, codified 'system' that stretched unbroken to prehistoric times across the Highlands, but were guided by a set of organising principles and practices in constant evolution and subject to local conditions. Although there were many features which originated in Celtic society and had an ancient pedigree, Gaels absorbed new ideas and adapted them when it suited their interests. Most chieftains were related to one another (if not the Scottish king himself) and could not but be affected by the policies and machinations of the central government. The resilience of Gaelic society is demonstrated by its ability to absorb foreigners and outside influences, as well as the adherence of ordinary Highlanders to the values and norms of clan society even after clan leaders were assimilated into the Anglo-British élite and turned their backs on their former followers.

This chapter and those that follow draw not only from songs and stories but from Gaelic gnomic lore and proverbial expressions. These texts offer direct and explicit commentary about life and society. It was not the case that every dilemma and social circumstance could be resolved by reference to a single proverb in an unambiguous corpus of ancestral wisdom: life is too complex for such a system to exist in even the most 'primitive' societies. It would be more accurate to observe that people are indeed guided by the principles embodied in proverbs and other gnomic lore. On the other hand, they often justify their decisions by quoting those that seem to best agree with their own judgments, or reassure themselves with these pithy sayings that their circumstances are within normal expectations. Proverbs are often not only insightful but well crafted in their use of language, employing such poetic devices as rhyme and alliteration. This made them a memorable and functional resource of Gaelic culture for many generations.

CLANSHIP

Gaelic society has been structured in kin-groups for as far back as our sources go. It is well known that the term *clann* literally means 'children' in Gaelic, but it is only one of a series of terms used to name kin-groups. Terms such as *cenél* and *dál* were in use before *clann* became the dominant term in about the twelfth century. In the sixteenth century, *clann* was replaced by *cinneadh*, which remains the normal term for 'kin-group' to this day. Clan names, such as 'Clann Domhnaill' ('Clan Donald') and 'Clann Ghriogair' ('the MacGregors'), were coined during the heyday of the Scottish clans when the Gaelic term *clann* was dominant.[5] Alongside 'clann' the terms *sìol* 'seed' and *sliochd* 'descent group' are also used to refer to groups descended from a common ancestor, although they tend to be used for immediate families rather than larger, functional social groups.

The core of the clan was the *fine* 'clan élite' who adopted a kin-name derived from the founding ancestor. (The term *fine* is sometimes extended to refer to the entire clan.) The descendants of Somerled – Clann Shomhairle – eventually grew large and powerful enough to merit their own separate identities and titles. Within a few generations the three most successful branches – 'Clann Dubhghaill' ('the MacDougals'), 'Clann Domhnuill' ('the MacDonalds') and 'Clann Ruaidhri' ('the MacRuairies'), named after a son and two grandsons of Somerled, respectively – emerged as independent units. This exemplifies how some families could quickly expand and claim their own identity while others became subservient or disappeared altogether. The fine took the kin-name as their surname, and as did those those claiming membership in the clan through a variety of relationships.⁶ The Privy Seal Register, for example, records 'the clan and surname of Macnelis' (the MacNeills of Gigha) in 1531.⁷

Edmund Burt, an English officer stationed in the Highlands in the 1720s, provides a useful description of the composition of ever larger kin-groups from smaller ones and how personal identity and allegiance was affected by these layers of association:

> The Highlanders are divided into tribes, and clans, under chiefs, or chieftains, as they are called in the laws of Scotland; and each clan again divided into branches from the main stock, who have chieftains over them. These are subdivided into smaller branches of fifty or sixty men, who deduce their original from their particular chieftains, and rely upon them as their more immediate protectors and defenders. But for better distinction I shall use the word chief for the head of the whole clan, and the principal of a tribe derived from him I shall call a chieftain.
>
> The ordinary Highlanders esteem it the most sublime degree of virtue to love their chief, and pay him a blind obedience, although it be in opposition to the Government, the laws of the kingdom, or even to the law of God. He is their idol; and as they profess to know no king but him (I was going further), so will they say they ought to do whatever he commands without inquiry.
>
> Next to the love of the chief is that of the particular branch from which they sprang; and, in a third degree, to those of the whole clan and name, whom they will assist, right or wrong, against those of any other tribe with which they are at variance, to whom their enmity, like that of exasperated brothers, is most outrageous.⁸

Clan society is commonly portrayed as a kind of classless democracy; in fact, until its collapse in the late eighteenth century, Gaeldom was stratified and highly conscious of inherited status. Society was ordered and operated according to social rank, especially when exhibited in public form. Judging by the evidence of oral tradition, the aristocrat was the object of attention – and, generally, affection – amongst his peers and dependants. People took pride in their connections, of all sorts, with the élite; many popular songs composed by females of the lower order boast of carrying the love children of high-born men, for example. The literary tradition itself, regardless of the social level at which it operated, was imbued with values, precedents and practices formed for and by the élite. The significance of rank is represented in a proverb employing tree imagery: 'Bidh an t-ubhal as fhearr air a' mheangan as àirde' ('The best apple will be on the highest branch').⁹

Martin Martin describes how important it was that guests were seated at feasts according to their rank:

> Every family had commonly two Stewarts, which in their Language were call'd [*Màrsal Taighe*]: the first of these serv'd always at home, and was oblig'd to be well vers'd in the Pedigree of all the Tribes in the Isles, and in the Highlands of Scotland;

for it was his Province to assign every Man at Table his Seat according to his Quality [. . .] and this was necessary to prevent Disorder and Contention.[10]

An anecdote preserved in the seventeenth-century Sleat history of the MacDonalds, set during the era of the Lordship of the Isles, illustrates how noblemen could be outraged by a violation of rank. This incident is said to have occurred when the Lord of the Isles was hosting a dinner at his castle in Mull in the fifteenth century. Eòin MacDonald assumed the office of Màrsal Taighe for the evening, and took advantage of this by seating others in less favorable positions than his own.

'Now', saith he, 'I am the oldest and best of your surnames here present, and will sit down; as for these fellows who have raised their heads of late, and are upstarts, whose pedigree we know not, nor even they themselves, let them sit as they please.' MacLean, MacLeod of Harris, and MacNeill of Barra went out in a rage, and [. . .] determined, as soon as an opportunity offered, to be fully revenged of John MacDonald for the affront, as they thought, he had given.[11]

The distinction between *uasal* 'high, noble' and *ìosal* 'low, non-noble' is a fundamental one in Gaeldom. The élite are called *daoine-uasal* or *na h-uaislean* collectively, while the commonality are referred to as *tuath*, an old Gaelic term which denoted the entire 'tribe'. As in many other societies, manual labour and agriculture was shunned by the élite of the Gàidhealtachd, being the responsibility of the *sgallagan* 'menial labourers, servile classes'.

Chapter Three examined some of the learned professions in Gaelic society and their responsibilities: poets, historians and lawmen. Professional warriors also constituted a specialised, high-ranking class in Gaelic society: 'They were well train'd in managing the Sword and Target, in Wrestling, Swimming, Jumping, Dancing, Shooting with Bows and Arrows, and were stout Seamen.'[12] The chieftain kept ranks of trained fighting men called *buannachan* and a bodyguard of chosen warriors called *léine-chneas* (or *léine-chnios*). New recruits from the tuath were sometimes taken into this privileged profession on account of their renowned strength or prowess. By about 1600 the social divisions which had discouraged the use of the tuath as soldiers were weakening, particularly as local leaders exploited a growing market for Highland troops.[13]

A powerful chieftain created a network of kinsmen and allies to hold down his territory; this pattern of land-holding essentially superimposed the social structure of a clan upon the landscape. Privileged members of the clan could be offered the office of 'tacksman' (variously called *fear-baile*, *fear-fearainn* or *fear-taca* in Gaelic), the middle managers of one or more townships given such duties as collecting rents, organising military operations, and supervising the exploitation of agricultural resources.[14] As lawyer William Fraser commented in 1772, the role of tacksman provided a place and function for the many clan élite, for a chieftain

gave Leases of their Land to their younger Sons and other Connexions, and very
seldom to any but their own name and Kindred – The Tacksmen formed a kind of
inferior Gentry in the Country and their rents were often little more than an
acknowledgement to their Chief or head of their family.[15]

The lowest-order retainers to be employed by a chieftain were called collectively
(in some areas) the *gillean maola dubha* 'black, bare-headed servants', their lack of
head gear distinguishing them from the nobility.

In the time of peace they were the mere drudges of the castle, but when hostilities
broke out between their master and his neighbours, they were among the first to
follow him to the field, and among the bravest in battle.[16]

Despite differences in status, the interaction and interdependence between classes
was well recognised. The Reverend Norman MacLeod scolded the upper ranks of
Gaeldom for becoming estranged from their humbler relations by reference to this
proverb: 'Ged a b' ubhlan iad air a' ghéig a b' àirde, bu mheanglain sinn uile de'n aon
chraoibh' ('Although they were the apples on the highest branch, we were all shoots
from the same tree').[17] Everyone took pride in their connections with the Gaelic élite
and these ties engendered a sense of innate self-esteem amongst the Highland people
as a whole. The constant intercourse between ranks and Gaelic customs of succession
created a society which had a remarkably high percentage of nobles in comparison
with most of the rest of Europe.[18]

The fluid dialogue between all members of Gaeldom is illustrated by many tales,
songs and anecdotes. When describing how everyone, including the chief, danced
together at the harvest feast, Elizabeth Grant of Rothiemurchus observed in the early
nineteenth century that 'a vein of good breeding ran through all ranks, influencing
their manners and rendering the intercourse of all most agreeable.'[19] John Mair wrote
in 1521 about the pride taken by his countrymen in their pretensions to noble birth:

Most writers note yet another fault in the Scots [. . .] I am not able to acquit the Scots
of this fault, for both at home and abroad they take inordinate pleasure in noble birth,
and (though of ignoble origin themselves) delight in hearing themselves spoken of as
come of noble blood [. . .] Poor noblemen marry into mean but wealthy families. In
this way some of the Scots ennoble their whole country.[20]

Visitors from other nations often remarked at the self-regard of common Highlanders, in contrast to the cringing peasants of their own societies, as when an
anonymous eighteenth-century English visitor noted, 'The poorest and most despic-
able Creature of the name of MacDonald looks upon himself as a Gentleman of far
Superior Quality than a man of England of £1,000 a year.'[21] Regardless of their
economic dearth or the swings of fortune, their cultural self-confidence gave them
buoyancy, as Edmund Burt noted in the 1720s:

The Highlanders walk nimbly and upright, so that you will never see, among the meanest of them, in the most remote parts, the clumsy, stooping gait of the French paisans, or our own country fellows, but on the contrary. a kind of stateliness in the midst of their poverty.[22]

The Rev. Donald MacQueen, minister in eighteenth-century Skye, stated that even the lowest classes aspired to the highest ideals of noble behaviour, as elucidated and celebrated in Gaelic song and story:

A quick sense of honour and shame, which was nourished by their education, being all bred to the use of arms, to hunting, to the exertion of their strength in several amusements, games and feats of activity. The bard celebrated the praises of him who distinguished himself on any of these occasions, and dealt out his satire, but with a very sparing hand, for fear of rousing up the ferocity of men, who were in use to judge in their own cause, when they appealed to the sword, and either retrieved their honour, or died; valour was the virtue most in repute; according to their progress in it were they distinguished by their chieftain and friends. Every one of the superior clans thought himself a gentleman, as deriving his pedigree from an honourable stock, and proposed to do nothing unworthy of his descent or connections; and the inferior clans, the [*bodaich*], as they called them, tread at an humble distance in the steps of their patrons, whose esteem and applause they courted with passionate keenness. The love, affection, and esteem of the community all aimed to procure by a disinterested practice of the social duties, truth, generosity, friendship, hospitality, gratitude, decency of manners, for which there are no rewards decreed in any country, but were amply paid among the Highlanders by that honour and respect of which they had a very delicate taste.[23]

Despite the greater social status of the higher ranks, however, they were little better off materially than the lower ranks; status determined privileges and responsibilities more than economic wealth.[24] The lower orders, moreover, did not always blindly obey their superiors but often demonstrated a surprising independence of mind. When Robert Munro succeeded to the lordship of Foulis in 1540, for example, the tenants of Loch Broom refused to recognise his authority.[25] John Lane Buchanan wrote in the late 1700s that the social and economic changes that happened after Culloden not only estranged the commonality from their former chiefs, but divested the tenantry of their former self-esteem by making them subservient to unsympathetic middle managers, mostly incomers without pre-existing social ties:

The tacksmen and subtenants, formerly, or nearly, on an equal footing, were wont to plead their cause, on equal terms, before a common chief. At present they are obliged to be much more submissive to their tacksmen than ever they were, in former times to their lairds or lords. Formerly, they were a free, animated, and bold people, commanding respect from their undaunted courage, and repelling injuries from whatever quarter they came, both by words and actions. But, now they must approach even the tacksmen with cringing humility, heartless and discouraged [. . .] Formerly, a Highlander would have drawn his dirk against even a laird, if he had subjected him to the indignity of a blow: at present, any tyrannical tacksman, in the absence of the laird or lord, whose presence alone can enforce good order and justice, may strike a [*sgallag*], and even a subtenant, with perfect impunity.[26]

The actions of an individual had a large impact on the rest of the kin-group, so important decisions were often made after consultation with others. The classic example is marriage, as such a union is not merely between two individuals, but between two kin-groups and potentially involved a transfer of wealth and territory. There are many tales and anecdotes about the affront given by gentry who marry without the approval of their families. Hugh MacDonald of Sleat, brother to the Lord of the Isles, was advised against marrying a second time in 1469 without first consulting the Council of the Isles.[27] A woman pleads in a traditional song:

> *Ach mas fear thu a tha air mo thì-sa*
> *Ruig an tìr an còir dhomh 'bhith*
> *Faigh toil m' athar is mo mhàthar*
> *Cead mo chàirdean 's còrdaidh sinn.*[28]

('But if you are a man truly in pursuit of me, go to my native land, find the approval of father and mother, and the consent of my kin, and we'll marry.')

Highlanders were not merely individuals but elements in a network of people with whom they shared responsibilities and rewards. 'Cha duine, duine 'na aonar' ('A person by himself is not a person'),[29] as an old Gaelic proverb has it. There are many sayings which relate the binding force of kinship, such as 'Cha nigh na tha de uisge anns a' mhuir ar càirdeas' ('All of the water in the ocean could not wash away our kinship').[30] Anne Grant commented on the strong social bonds of Gaelic society, noting assertively:

No Highlander ever once thought of himself as an individual. Amongst these people, even the meanest mind was in a manner enlarged by association, by anticipation, and by retrospect. In the most minute, as well as the most serious concerns, he felt himself one of the many connected together by ties the most lasting and endearing. He considered himself merely with reference to those who had gone before, and those who were to come after him; to these immortals who lived in deathless song and heroic narrative; and to these distinguished beings who were to be born heirs of their fame, and to whom their honours, and perhaps, their virtues, were to be transmitted. This might be supposed merely to cherish pride; but, besides this, it had a highly moral tendency.[31]

There were some, however, who fell outside normal clan society. Many landless men (typically referred to as 'broken men') joined bands of *ceatharnaich* 'warriors' (borrowed into Lowland Scots as 'cateran'), who were responsible for much of the disorder in and around the Highlands. Lowland lairds used ceatharnaich as hired thugs to harass and inflict damage on their rivals; such bands also blackmailed Lowland farmers into paying them protection money to ensure against the theft of their cattle. Ceatharnaich contributed to the perception of Highlanders as wild and lawless, even though they existed and operated outside of the normal institutions of clan life.[32]

Leaders and Leadership

In early Gaelic society, the *rígh* 'king' was a semi-sacred figure: his reign was punctuated by ritual activity and constrained by *geasa* 'tabu'. He was as much a figurehead as an administrator, married to the goddess of the territory and duty-bound to secure the needs of his people. A king was considered to have failed in his obligations if he was satirised, maimed, or defeated in battle, or if famine or pestilence came to his land.[33]

The king had officers to assist him, most importantly the *ollamh* 'master-poet' who had inherited many aspects of his office from the druid. The practices surrounding kingship reveal its sacred nature, which is particularly apparent in the functions of the ollamh, who was 'the mediator and the manipulator of the supernatural powers which affected the king and through him his kingdom'. According to early Gaelic laws, for example, 'It is the poet's duty to be with the king at Samhainn and to protect him from enchantment.'[34]

The king was important ideologically as the focus and embodiment of the ideals and identity of his people. This was particularly important in the early history of Scotland, which united a number of different ethnic groups. The *ceann-cinnidh* 'chief' provided a similar focus for the diverse membership of Highland clans.

Leadership existed and operated in Scotland at different levels: at the apex of the hierarchy of authority and power was the Scottish king; immediately below him were regional lords who dominated areas with the sanction and support of the king; below the regional lords were chieftains of clans. Regional lords depended on the cooperation of smaller clans in order to wield power effectively; they often attempted to manipulate local rivalries to their advantage to coerce local leaders into positions of subordination. Local chieftains, on the other hand, could usually only maintain and enhance their power by judicious alliance contracts with regional lords.[35]

Figure 4.1 opens a small window on the hierarchy of leadership in Scottish Gaeldom *c.*1444 from the Scottish king down through several of the dependants of the Lords of the Isles. Scottish kings relied heavily upon regional lords to assert their authority, administer justice and execute their policies in specific areas, which required granting a great deal of power to these magnates. Scottish kings often sought to maintain the balance of power between regional lords so that none became so powerful or independent as to threaten the Crown itself. There are many examples of earls and dukes being created or forfeited by the king, and shuffles of appointments at positions of regional lordship, according to the king's perceptions of the dynamics of power. Clan chieftains, for their part, saw regional lords as important power-brokers between themselves and the king, serving to facilitate (or undermine) regional political stability. Like the king, however, regional lords executed their own political intrigues to prevent subordinate clan chieftains from becoming too powerful.[36]

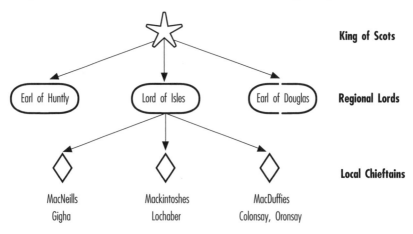

King of Scots

Regional Lords

Local Chieftains

Earl of Huntly

Lord of Isles

Earl of Douglas

MacNeills
Gigha

Mackintoshes
Lochaber

MacDuffies
Colonsay, Oronsay

Figure 4.1: Illustration of a slice of the hierarchy of leadership c.1444

In the Gaelic customs of succession, known in English as 'tanistry', males whose near ancestor had been a leader were eligible to be elected into that position.[37] The *tànaise* (or *tànaistear*) 'heir apparent' was usually chosen during the lifetime of a leader to minimise rivalries after his death, but hostilities often erupted nonetheless. Primogeniture, the system of succession accompanying feudalism, dictated a strict father-to-first-son succession, aiming to limit chaos after a leader's death. It is not always clear from the historical record which system was operating at any particular time in the past: what may appear to us to be a succession by tanistry or primogeniture may have been a result of specific conditions and necessities, and the two systems do not need to be seen as irreconcilable.[38] The royal house of Scotland committed itself to primogeniture in the thirteenth century, but succession to a male other than the oldest son continued in at least some clans into the seventeenth century.[39]

A clan council, consisting of the fine or the leaders of the most important kin-groups, was usually involved in the election of the successor. The Lord of the Isles appears to have been chosen by the Council of the Isles.[40] Even under tanistry, successors tended to be the sons or close relatives of the previous ruler, as one needed to be close to the centres of power to draw upon the necessary wealth, military backing, and expertise to succeed. A nobleman who had a large following of dependants could make a better case, with or without a show of force, than one without such support. Anne Grant, writing in the early nineteenth century, claimed that 'the claimant who had the strongest party in the clan, especially if sanction'd by the will of the deceas'd, was generally acknowledged as heir.'[41] It became common practice in the Highlands for the oldest son of a chieftain to take over running the daily affairs of the clan once he married.[42]

The rites of inauguration were symbolic statements of cultural values and ideals at the highest level of society. Inauguration is referred to as *rígad* in Old Gaelic, although in some accounts the term *banais-ríge* (literally 'king-marriage') drew explicit attention to inauguration as a form of wedding between the leader and the sovereignty goddess of the territory.[43] Although there was no single ritual of inauguration in Gaelic society, there are a number of common elements which recur in accounts of these ceremonies in both Scotland and Ireland, from kings to clan chiefs:[44]

- A poet or cleric conducts the ceremony, enumerating the leader's ancestry and invoking a blessing on him and his reign
- It is on or near a burial mound containing a ceremonial stone, and under or near a *bile* ('sacred tree')
- It includes the leader's horse or chariot (in reality or symbolically)
- The leader's garment or mantle is given to the master of the ceremony
- There is a single footprint, shoe or sandal into which the leader steps
- The leader is anointed
- The leader drinks alcohol from a ceremonial vessel
- The leader is presented with the rod of sovereignty (*slat tighearnais*), sometimes a wand cut from the *bile*

Several of these elements are recorded at the inauguration of King Alexander III at Scone on 13 July 1249, the last for a Scottish king conducted according to Gaelic custom. The moot-hill and the Stone of Destiny seem to have played prominent parts in that ceremony; a Gaelic-speaking seanchaidh addressed the king in Gaelic, 'Beannachd Dhé, Rí Alban' ('The blessing of God, O King of Scotland'), and recited his pedigree back to Gaidheal Glas and Scota, daughter of Pharaoh. The presentation of the sword of state to the king concluded the event.[45]

More elements of the Gaelic rites of inauguration survived amongst the Highland élite much longer. The ceremony for the Lords of the Isles related in a seventeenth-century account reflects much of the archaistic and multifaceted symbolism of Gaelic inauguration and its importance in renewing social bonds:

At this the Bishop of Argyle, the Bishop of the Isles, and seven priests, were sometimes present; but a bishop was always present, with the chieftains of all the principal families, and a Ruler of the Isles. There was a square stone, seven or eight feet long, and the tract of a man's foot cut thereon, upon which he stood, denoting that he should walk in the footsteps and uprightness of his predecessors, and that he was installed by right in his possessions. He was clothed in a white habit, to shew his innocence and integrity of heart, that he would be a light to his people, and maintain the true religion. The white apparel did afterwards belong to the poet by right. Then he was to receive a white rod in his hand, intimating that he had power to rule, not with tyranny and partiality, but with discretion and sincerity. Then he received his forefather's sword, or some other sword, signifying that his duty was to protect and defend them from the incursions of their enemies in peace or war, as the obligations and customs of his predecessors were. The ceremony being over, mass was said after the blessing of the bishop and seven priests, the people pouring their prayer for the success and prosperity of their new created Lord. When they were dismissed, the Lord of the Isles feasted them for a week thereafter; gave liberally to the monks, poets, bards and musicians. You may judge that they spent liberally without any exception of persons.[46]

The potential break in social order between the death (or deposition) of the previous leader and the installation of the new leader could be a cause for anxiety; it was important for the inaugural ceremony to provide proper closure for the previous regime, acceptance for the new regime, and continuity between them. This was one of the social functions of poetry in the procedure, as noted by Martin Martin of the installation of Highland chieftains:

A Heap of Stones was erected in form of a Pyramid, on the top of which the young Chieftain was plac'd, his Friends and Followers standing in a Circle round about him, his Elevation signifying his Authority over them, and their standing below their Subjection to him. One of his principal Friends deliver'd into his Hands the Sword wore by his Father, and there was a white Rod deliver'd to him likewise at the same time.

Immediately after the Chief Druid (or Orator) stood close to the Pyramid, and pronounc'd a Rhetorical Panegyrick, setting forth the antient Pedegree, Valour, and Liberality of the Family, as Incentives to the young Chieftain, and fit for his imitation.[47]

A description of the inauguration of the MacLeods of Dunvegan also highlights the role of the poet in passing the leadership from one generation to the next while reminding the audience of the importance of Gaelic cultural norms:

After the funeral of the late chief, all the clan present sat down to a funeral feast. At this feast it was the duty of the bards to rehearse the genealogy of the deceased, to praise his achievements and to lament his loss. It was then their duty to give an exordium on the qualities of his successor, and express the hopes of the clan as to his valour and other virtues. This done, the new chief then rose in his place, and demanded his predecessor's sword. This was always placed in his right hand by the first man of the clan, and then the new chief was hailed by the acclamation of all present as the leader of the clan.[48]

The MacLeod inauguration culminated with the new chieftain drinking from a very large bull's horn called 'Sir Rory Mor's Horn' (see Plate 15): 'Until comparatively recent times, it was the duty of each Chief, as he succeeded to the Chiefship, to drink the full measure of the Horn in wine.'[49] The ceremonies of the installation of the MacLeod chieftains illustrate how Norse and Gaelic customs could be neatly harmonised: the 'drink of sovereignty' is an ancient idea known to both the Norse and the Gaels.

Inauguration, representing the sacred marriage between leader and goddess of the land, was a ritual that also drew symbolic power by reference to features of the landscape.[50] There are, for example, numerous sacred trees in the Highlands associated with local dynasties that served to reinforce such connections: Tom na h-Iubhraich near Inverness, sacred site of the Frasers; Croit a' Bhile near Inverary, seat of the Campbells of Argyll; Both-Fhionntainn a' Bhile in Glen Roy, home of a branch of the Keppoch MacDonalds; and so forth. This nexus of symbols is reflected in the common motif of Gaelic literature likening the chieftain or king to a noble tree offering shelter to his people (a theme to be further explored in Chapter Six). It also appears in the form of the magical branch held by visitors from the Otherworld who confer blessings upon the leader, and the rod of sovereignty which signifies his supernatural endorsement and connection with the land.

A chieftain had to be an able leader to his people in battle, a common form of which was the cattle-raid and counter-raid. 'Another institution associated with inauguration was the *crech ríg* or royal foray, by which the king demonstrated his suitability for office and acquired not only a heroic reputation but also the wealth in cattle to play the generous lord.'[51] Martin Martin relates information about the survival of this archaic practice in the seventeenth-century Highlands:

Every Heir, or young Chieftain of a Tribe, was oblig'd in Honour to give a publick Specimen of his Valour, before he was declar'd Governor and Leader of his People, who obey'd and follow'd him upon all Occasions.

This Chieftain was usually attended by a Retinue of young Men of Quality, who had not beforehand given any Proof of their Valour, and were ambitious of such an Opportunity to signalize themselves.

It was usual for the Captain to lead them, to make a desperate Incursion upon some Neighbour or other that they were in Feud with; and they were oblig'd to bring by open force the Cattel they found in the Lands they attack'd, or to die in the Attempt.

After the Performance of this Atchievement, the young Chieftain was ever after reputed valiant and worthy of Government, and such as were of his Retinue acquir'd the like Reputation. This Custom being reciprocally us'd among them, was not reputed Robbery, for the Damage which one Tribe sustain'd by this Essay of the Chieftain of another, was repair'd when their Chieftain came in his turn to make his Specimin: but I have not heard an Instance of this Practice for these sixty Years past.[52]

Although the office of the king or chieftain was sacred, the man who filled it was not: he was subject to regulations and obligations and expected to act in the interests of the clan as a whole. The clan council and members of high office offered him advice and criticised him if he did not fulfil his role as protector, provider and patriarch.[53] At least for as long as chieftains derived their position from within Gaelic society and not from the king, they were dependent upon followers for their power and were no stronger than the will of the people to follow them and no more wealthy than the people made them. Many Gaelic proverbs attest to this: 'Is treasa tuatha na tighearna' ('The common people are stronger than a lord'); 'Is àirde tuathanach air a chasan na duine-uasal air a ghlùinean' ('A commoner standing on his feet is taller than a nobleman on his knees'); 'Far nach bi nì, caillidh an rìgh a chòir' ('A king will lose his rights where there is no wealth').[54]

Nothing can be more erroneous than the prevalent idea, that a highland chief was an ignorant and unprincipled tyrant, who rewarded the abject submission of his followers with relentless cruelty and vigorous oppression. He was, on the contrary, the father of his people: gracious, condescending, and beloved, far from being ruled by arbitrary caprice. He was taught from the cradle to consider the meanest individual of his clan, as his kinsman and his friend, whom he was born to protect, and bound to regard. He was taught too, to venerate old age, to respect genius, and to place an almost implicit dependence on the counsels of the elders of his clan.[55]

Surviving evidence from the fifteenth century onwards demonstrates that the clan chief was accountable to his clan and was expected to seek the advice and consent of the fine on clan matters. There were chiefs and chieftains who were deposed and replaced because of they did not execute their duties properly. Iain Àlainn, chieftain of the Keppoch MacDonalds, was deposed in 1498 for having capitulated to the chief of the Mackintoshes, thereby diminishing his authority (and that of the clan) in Lochaber.[56] After some ten years as chief of the Mackintoshes, Farquhar's 'friends of the name of Clanchattan were altogether dissatisfied with his way of managing affairs. Therefore he willingly renounced his inheritance and birthright in favour of his uncle.'[57]

The most powerful regional lords in Scotland, such as the Dukes of Albany, the Earls of Douglas, the Earls of Mar, and the Lords of the Isles, had councils to assist in them in administration and governance. The Council of the Isles accompanied MacDonald on business through his territory; eleven charters were approved by the council in the years 1444 to 1492 in different locations in the Lordship, resolving local legal affairs that needed extra attention.[58] The fine of smaller clans also formed councils which kept a careful eye on the chieftain's actions. The chieftain of the Rosses was warned by fourteen principal gentry of the clan, who signed a document in 1577, that he confer with them for fear that he 'perish his house, kin and friends, and tyne the riggs that his fathers wan'.[59]

It is particularly in this context that we can understand the function of the poet in not only offering advice but also going so far as to threaten the chieftain with satire if he does not fulfil his responsibilities properly. A threat of satire composed by Father Iain Farquharson of Strathglass between 1729 and 1746, warns Simon Fraser, Lord Lovat, in stark terms of the consequences of not freeing a fellow priest whom he had imprisoned.[60] A portion of it reads:

> *Mhic Shimidh, mosgail à d' shuain*
> *Éirich suas is cuimhnich d' olc:*
> *Rinn thu do-bheairt nas leòr,*   –B.1
> *Tha deireadh do sgeòil a' teannadh ort!*   –B.2
>
> *Tha 'n aois a' cur doill air do chéill*   –B.8
> *'S alluidh an dreun a chì mi ort,*   –E.3
> *Fear muinntir fhir muinntir Dhé*
> *Bhith 'n talla breun le neor-thoirt.* [. . .]   –C.1
>
> *'S iomadh donas 's diombuaidh*
> *Chunnaic do shluagh riamh ri d' thìm;*   –B.1
> *B'e siud an donas gun àgh*
> *Chuir sonas gu bràth dhen dìth.* [. . .]
>
> *Tha fàisneachd a' tighinn gu teachd*
> *Gun dèanar ort creach gun tòir,*
> *Gum faicear do cholluinn gun cheann,*   –H.1
> *'S gum bi do chlann mhaoth gun treòir.* [. . .]   –B.5
>
> *Mhic Shimidh, mosgail à d' shuain,*
> *Ge fada an duan, ruigear an ceann,*
> *Tha m' fhàisneachd a' tighinn gu dlighe*
> *'S cha chuir thu i air chùl le d' chainnt.*   –B.2

('O Simon of Lovat, awake from your slumber! Arise and recall your sin: you have done enough mischief – the end of your tale is drawing near you!')

('Old age is blinding your reason; I see a savage frown upon your face: one of God's servants lies neglected in your vile tower. [. . .]')

('During your era your people have seen much wickedness and crime; this evil has banished joy from them. [. . .]')

('The prophecy is coming true, that you will be plundered without recourse; that your body will be seen headless, and that your helpless children will be orphaned. [. . .]')

('O Simon of Lovat, awake from your slumber! Although the poem is long, it will reach its end; my prophecy is doing its duty, and you cannot put it behind you with idle chatter.')

Amongst other misfortunes the poet implies that Lovat will be deposed through his own ill-handling of affairs. This example illustrates the close associations between the functions and privileges of the secular poet and Christian priest in Gaeldom: both tapped Otherworld power with their mastery of the sacred word, could excommunicate members of their society, were held in awe and reverence, were drawn from the same 'aristocracy of learning', and exercised considerable freedom in criticising the actions of secular leaders.[61]

THE DIVERSE BONDS OF CLANSHIP

Kinship was the organising principle of Highland clan society, but in reality not everyone in the same clan was related.[62] A variety of social mechanisms and legal arrangements which maintained the illusion of blood relationship – *fictive kinship* – was used to draw new kin-groups into a clan or allow them to break off and become more independent. As an anonymous, late-seventeenth-century document informs us, 'They reckon him to be their chief, whom they choose for their patron: tho he be not of their name.'[63] Biological relationships did not by any means determine or exclude the range of bonds and arrangements that drew people together. 'Indeed, by the late fifteenth and early sixteenth centuries blood kinship was no longer the principal organising feature of clan society but rather one of a number of factors which contributed to the formation of clannish relationships.'[64]

Fosterage is one of the ancient Celtic customs which endured in Gaelic Scotland into at least the seventeenth century amongst the nobility, and even longer amongst the lower ranks of society.[65] A *dalta* 'fosterling' was to be taught a number of skills, according to rank and gender. A boy was generally returned to his parents between ages fourteen and seventeen, and a girl at fourteen. They maintained close bonds of affections with their *comhdhaltan* 'foster-siblings' and foster-parents (*muime* 'foster-mother' and *oide* 'foster-father'), whom they were obliged to help support in their old age. This practice cultivated interdependence between clans and families within clans.[66]

As a rule one of the chief's sons was handed over as an infant, practically, to one of the tacksmen or other members of the clan, and there he remained, as one of that family, during the years of his pupilarity. The lower classes usually considered this trust a very great honour, and by no means a service for which any direct reward was to be given or expected. So much was the condescension thought of that when a son was born to a chief it was not uncommon to find a contention arising among members of the clan as to who was to be favoured with the fostering of the boy-child. The one who succeeded sometimes had to face a considerable measure of jealousy, and even ill-will, from others less fortunate; and time after time feeling ran so high against him as to cause a feud. [. . .] Against this, however, were to be placed the advantages of a direct family connection with the chief, and the gain therefrom of a higher standing and a more influential position for the lucky one among his fellow clansmen.[67]

There are many Gaelic proverbs which relate to the intense bonding between fosterling and foster-family. 'Is caomh le fear a charaid, ach is e smior a chridhe a chomhdhalta' ('A man's kin is beloved to him, but his foster-sibling is as the pith of his heart').[68] It is telling that the Gaelic terms for foster-parents are related to the English terms of affection 'mummy' and 'daddy'.

Arrangements for fosterage were formal and binding, and some documents have survived to attest to the practice. The natural parents generally paid a fosterage fee in cattle to pay for the service and to guarantee that their children were maintained according to their rank. This fee would be reclaimed by the natural parents if any problem arose.

When the child returned to the parents it was usually accompanied by all the cows given by both the father and the fosterer, with half of the increase by propagation. Those beasts were considered as a portion, and called *Crodh Mhic a Làimh*, of which the father had the produce, but was supposed not to have full property in, but to owe the same number to the child, as a portion to the daughter, or as a stock for the son.[69]

The manuscript history of the Campbells of Craignish offers the example of how the MacEacherns were assisted by the Campbells because of ties of fosterage: 'The MacEachairns [. . .] haveing their force augmented by this new relationship of [co-dhalt]-ship, with the Knights of Lochows Family, a relationship be the by, more binding in these countries, even in my own time, than that of blood.'[70]

Marriage is a nearly universal means of uniting kin-groups and was particularly important as a political arrangement at the upper echelons of Gaelic society; the lower orders enjoyed much more freedom of choice in marriage partners because the political implications were less important. A bride's family contributed a *tochradh* 'dowry' (borrowed into Scots as 'tocher') when she married; brides from aristocratic classes could pull a tochradh of forty to sixty cattle and some were also accompanied by retainers, including fighting men. She was entitled to recover the value of her dowry in the case of divorce.[71] Marriage was one of the ways in which clans sought to gain wealth and territory, and such wealth could be lost when a daughter left her kin-group. A traditional tale from Lochaber describes how the practical concerns of dowry and the common interests of the clan could complicate romance:

The habit of giving cows as a tocher to the daughters of the house made them in the olden time very anxious that they would marry among their own kinsmen, or at least in their own clans, as it would be an enriching of the enemy to give their cows to them, and hence the frequency of elopements in those days. A young man sorely exercised about which was the better thing for him to marry, an old woman who had a tocher, or a young one who had none, went to his father and spoke thus –

> *Comhairle iarram oirbh, an ceò*
> *Cò i feòil is fhearr, a dhuine,*
> *Seann bhò 's i làn saill,*
> *No atharl' òg am feòil thana?*

('Let me ask for your advice, as I am unsure myself: which is the best choice of "meat"? An old cow, laden with lard, or a young one whose flesh is thin?')

And the reply was a sensible one:

> *Cha chuir seann bhò laogh mu chrò*
> *'S i 'n atharl' òg feòil is fhearr [. . .]* [72]

('An old cow will not add calves to the fold: the young cow is the better meat [. . .]')

This 'coded language', in which people are referred to as animals, was very common in the negotiations about marriage for a number of reasons.[73] Women could also find themselves in unsatisfactory marriages with older men because of economic necessity and no small number of songs complaining of this predicament exist.

> *Mur biodh crodh, cha ghabhainn thu,*
> *Mur biodh crodh, cha b' fhiù thu,*
> *Mur biodh crodh 's na laoigh 'nan cois*
> *Cha laighinn air do chùlaibh.*
>
> *Bheirinn comhairle chéillidh ort*
> *Nan éisteadh tu gu ciùin rium*
> *Nan sguireadh tu de d' bheumannan*
> *Bho'n 's tu mo chéile-pùsta.*
>
> *'S an oidhche 'chaidh mo phòsadh leat*
> *Bu deònach air a' chùis mi;*
> *Mus tàinig ceann na madainne*
> *Gum bu mhath leam anns an ùir thu.*[74]

('I wouldn't have taken you, if not for the cattle; you would be worthless, if not for the cattle; if not for the cattle and their calves, I wouldn't lay down next to you.')

('I would offer you sensible advice if you would only listen to me, if you would only stop hitting me, as you are my partner in marriage.')

('The night that I was married to you I was willing in the matter, but before the next morning had passed, I wished that you were buried in the ground.')

Gaelic society remained unusually flexible about the range of reproductive arrangements between men and women, and the legitimacy of their offspring, into relatively recent times.[75] 'Irish law did not distinguish sharply between legitimate and illegitimate sexual unions; rather, it arranged them in a hierarchy from the most honourable to the least.'[76] The most honourable were those which were given with the consent of the woman and her kin, particularly in a formal marriage which created a permanent bond between their kindreds and children who embodied their common interests. The least honourable was rape. Gaeldom came under increasing pressure to conform to the standards of Scots law and church law in rejecting 'unorthodox' practices (such as trial marriage and concubinage) and producing legitimate male heirs with uncontested lines of succession.[77]

The bond of *manrent* was another form of fictive kinship which became increasingly common from the fifteenth century on. Manrent was a form of clientage in which a man (sometimes as a representative of his kin-group) entered into a formal contract with a superior chieftain or regional lord; the dependant offered his loyalty and services (and that of his clan if he was a chieftain) to a more powerful lord in exchange for the latter's protection and leadership. The prevalence of manrent contracts illustrates that kinship by itself was insufficient to maintain the social order of clanship.[78]

Lesser kindreds who were taken under the protection of a greater lord could benefit from the security provided by a more effective corporate body. This was particularly important to kindreds who wished to assert a degree of independence from their former superiors, or who had hostile relations with more powerful neighbours. The superior lord, on the other hand, could use his new dependants to extend his influence and further his ambition in new territories.

Many surviving bonds of manrent state the limits of loyalty in case of conflicts of interest, noting the ultimate authority of the Scottish Crown. Men could even become clients to multiple lords, with explicit clauses in the bonds of manrent to specify how conflicts of interest should be resolved.[79] One of the earliest bonds, granted by Alasdair MacDonald, Lord of the Isles and Earl of Ross, to Thomas Fraser of Lovat in 1442, stipulates a fine of 1500 merks Scots were Fraser to break his oath of loyalty and service to MacDonald. Given that manrent could obligate the entire kin-group, the approval of the clan fine or council is sometimes mentioned in contracts. Campbell of

Argyll offered to transfer his bond of manrent of the entire MacLaren clan to Campbell of Glenorchy in 1559, if the clan chose to have him as their chief and protector. Cameron of Lochiel placed himself in the service of the Earl of Huntly in 1547 'by the advice of his kinsmen and friends and clan', and Huntly in return paid him a fee and officially acquitted the Camerons of past crimes.[80]

The *comh-cheangal* 'bond of friendship' was generally contracted between peers for mutual assistance, usually because of common military and political concerns. They could also be contracted at the resolution of a feud to discourage future conflict.[81] Martin Martin describes the rite of sealing the contract with blood:

> Their antient Leagues of Friendship were ratify'd by drinking a Drop of each other's Blood, which was commonly drawn out of the little Finger. This was religiously observ'd as a sacred Bond; and if any Person after such an Alliance happen'd to violate the same, he was from that time reputed unworthy of all honest Mens Conversation.[82]

The practice of cementing alliances with blood is referred to in the proverb 'Is milis fuil nàmhaid, ach is milse fuil caraid' ('The blood of an enemy is sweet, but a friend's blood is sweeter').[83]

Territory and Ownership

As implied in the tale at the beginning of this chapter, wealth and power in traditional Gaelic society came from the bottom up: a leader needed followers, who needed land and resources; the more followers he had, the more territory he could claim. This structure is conveyed by the Old Gaelic adage, 'Glenad cách a choimdid / comad cách a chrích / barr cáich a choimdiu / bun cáich a chrích' ('Let each man cleave to his lord; let each man protect his territory; the top of each man is his lord; the root of each man is his territory').[84] Similarly, as John Buchanan tells us in the late eighteenth century:

> When the great landholders lived among the husbandmen, who were for the most part allied to them by blood, or at least the sameness of name, the people loved their chiefs: and each laird and lord was accounted rich or poor according to the numbers of tenants that possessed their lands.[85]

A clan's wealth ultimately depended upon the amount of productive territory under its control, but productivity was measured in terms of social value rather than surplus export.[86] Land was necessary for growing crops and grazing livestock which fed the men who defended these lands and sought to expand their holdings. Clans could acquire new land peaceably by marriage or royal favour, or forcibly by conquest. 'Indeed, politics, economy, marriage, kinship, possession of land and of property, were all woven together into an inextricable web in Highland society, to produce a culture which was both dynamic and self-perpetuating.'[87]

The right to land won by conquest occurs in all warrior societies and is usually called *còir claidheimh* 'sword-right' in Gaelic. It is acknowledged in the early Irish law tracts as a legitimate means of acquiring territory[88] and such ongoing rivalry was an expected aspect of life in heroic societies. A poem celebrating the feats of Alasdair mac Colla boasts of military strength in defiance of the central government:

> *dúthchas do shíol Airt an fhoghuil*
> *cairt an chloidhimh.*   D.1

> *Cairt an cloidhimh dhóibh as dúthchas*
> *do droing dhána;*   B.9

> *minic chuirid síos gan séla*
> *cíos is cána.*[89]

('Raiding is the birthright of Art's progeny, the right of the sword; the right of the sword is the heritage of that bold people; frequently do they impose, without official sanction, tax and tribute.')

The use of charters to grant land formally found widespread acceptance amongst the upper echelons of Gaelic society by the fifteenth century; even the Lords of the Isles used charters during their reign. Most of the charters that survive from the Lordship were written in Latin, although there is one fascinating example written in Gaelic in 1408 during the reign of Donald (1387–1422). It grants several townships in Islay to Brian MacKay and his heirs in perpetuity, and they in return are to render to MacDonald and his heirs their services as well as four cows yearly.[90] Donald is also said to be the author of an 'oral charter' recorded in the nineteenth century. According to the tradition explaining the charter, Donald was holding court at Dundonald in Knapdale when a condemned man escaped. He sent a vassal renowned for speed and prowess to bring him back, dead or alive. In exchange for returning the criminal successfully, Donald granted Little MacKay the lands of Kilmochumaig in the following terms:[91]

Tha mise Domhnall nan Domhnall 'nam shuidhe air Dùn Domhnaill a' toirt còir o'n diugh gus a-màireach is mar sin gu Latha Bràth dhut-sa, MhicAoidh Bhig, air Cill MoChumaig – suas gu Flaitheas Dhé agus sìos gu h-Ifhrinn, fhad 's a ruitheas uisge 's a shéideas gaoth; agus seo an làthair Catrìona mo bhean agus Oighrig bhig mo bhanal-tram.

I, Donald of the (Mac)Donalds, seated on Dundonald, hereby grant rights from today until tomorrow and likewise to Judgment Day to you, Little MacKay, to Kilmochu-maig – from the heights of Heaven to the depths of Hell, for as long as water runs and wind blows; here, in the presence of Catrìona my wife and Effie my nurse.

The elements of the natural world are given prominence in the charter, especially in being used to express the idea of eternity ('as long as water runs and wind blows'). It is also significant that the only two witnesses of this contract are women; only one of the 129 surviving legal acts written up during the Lordship had a female witness, who was consenting to her own marriage arrangements.[92] While this oral charter is not likely to reflect contemporary concepts of ownership and territory amongst the élite, it is suggestive of non-élite perspectives on these matters.

Only the most powerful, defiant or desperate of clans dared to continue occupying lands granted by the king (or regional lords) to other chieftains. A recent study of the Campbells suggests that rather than promoting the commercialisation of property, charters in fifteenth-century Argyll 'preserved the overall cohesion and integrity of the wider lordship of which they were a part by creating an inalienable territorial core'.[93] Charters granting land and stating reciprocal obligations were in the interests of both the ruling élite and their subordinates because they explicitly stated the terms under which land was granted, decreasing the threat that a chieftain (or his heir) would dispossess tenants in favour of others at a whim.

Those below the chieftain in the social order – tacksmen, subtenants, landless sgallagan – held land by oral agreement rather than formal charter.[94] Nonetheless, customary practice in the Highlands afforded tenants the right to continue occupying land once they had lived in it for three generations. As Edmund Burt noted in the 1720s, 'the Notion they entertain, [is] that they have a kind of hereditary Right to their Farms; and that none of them are to be dispossessed, unless for some great Transgression against their Chief, in which Case every Individual would consent to their Expulsion.'[95] This inheritance of land is one of the meanings of the Gaelic word *dùthchas*, which seems to have been associated with the words 'kindly' and 'kindness' in Lowland Scotland, affirming a common association with the kin-group.[96] There is a tension in Gaelic tradition between the traditional right to continue occupying ancestral lands and the impetus to win new land through military might, though there is also evidence that hereditary claims had greater weight.[97]

The kin-groups loyal to a chieftain, whether through real or fictive kinship, seldom occupied a cohesive, well-bounded territory; they were often spread out over a patchwork of disparate lands. Some kin-groups were able to expand their territory, while others were forced by circumstances or more successful neighbours to contract or relocate. Some kin-groups occupied land owned by a chieftain other than their own and paid rent to him, on top of the tribute given to their chieftain. Chieftains could also find themselves with a wind-fall of new land because of grants given by the king or regional magnates. Chieftains needed to be able to respond dynamically to fluctuations in their territorial command and those of their subordinates.[98]

When a chieftain suddenly needed to control a new expanse of territory, his first choice was generally to fill it with kinsmen loyal to him as subordinates – brothers, sons, other clan fine. These kinsmen in turn brought their dependants and tenants to occupy and work the land. This could result in mass displacement of the previous population, as when Campbell of Inverawe stipulated in his 1696 takeover of lands in Mull that tacksmen 'remove such of the gentlemen of the name of McLean as are at present tennents and possessors of the island as hereafter he shall be directed'.[99] Pre-existing tenants sometimes resisted these evictions forcibly, even resorting to sustained guerilla warfare that lasted for years.

A chieftain did not always have sufficient 'kinship' resources to impose upon the landscape, however; in such a case he used the social mechanisms of fictive kinship – manrent and friendship in particular – to forge new bonds to provide him with new subordinates whom he could enlist into clan affairs. Some of these could have been tacksmen and their tenants already occupying the land who were willing to accept a new chieftain as their landlord. The territory of a clan was seldom composed exclusively of members of one kin-group, but contained a complex patchwork of tenants of various ancestral relationships and territorial origins.

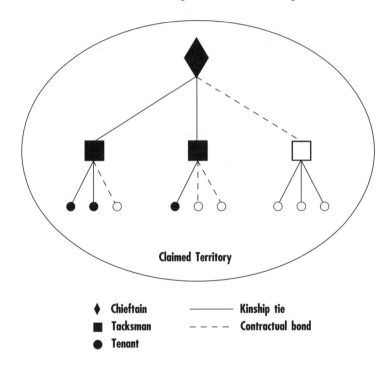

Figure 4.2: Social structure and territorial occupation

Figure 4.2 depicts a hypothetical example of a chieftain's use of social networks to occupy and control territory. Members of the clan who are related are darkened. The chieftain brings in two tacksmen related to him by kinship; some of their tenants were already in the territory and were unrelated to them. The chieftain also forms a bond of manrent with a tacksman already in the territory (the rightmost square) whose tenants give their loyalty and service to the new chieftain.

Many local legends recount how particular families became settled in the area, sometimes on land granted by the chieftain in reward for noteworthy deeds or services. According to a local tradition in Argyll recorded in the nineteenth century, a skilled archer named MacLarty in the retinue of Campbell of Craignish was given land after he repelled an attack from the MacKays of Islay. The tale further relates that he expanded his holdings into nearby unused land:

> MacLarty's services were appreciated by Campbell of Craignish, who rewarded him with the farm of Baile Tarsuinn, so called because it extended across [*tarsuinn*] the whole breadth of Craignish. [. . .] When McLarty took possession of the farm, he formed a plan of cultivating some improvable but [then unused] lands in Ardinarnoch. [. . .] A *seisreach*, or team of six horses, was required to draw the plough.[100]

By the late medieval period many chieftains came to see themselves as the owners of land, but such claims would have been impossible to enforce without the cooperation of their followers. The chieftain was expected to act as a responsible steward on behalf of the clan: he was 'not allow'd to part with territory [even] for the preservation of his life [. . .] the habit of making all private considerations subservient to the good of the community'.[101]

Oral history recorded in Gaelic on Loch Lomondside in the nineteenth century suggests how common clansmen could attempt to impede the changes imposed by the élite if they conflicted with traditional practices of succession and land-holding. After the chieftain of the MacFarlanes was killed at the Battle of Pinkie in 1547, according to the story, his widowed second wife sought a subterfuge by which she could disinherit his eldest son (the progeny of his first wife) and pass the entire patrimony on to her own son. She convinced the eldest son to endorse a contract passing the land to her son if he did not return a prized horse which he borrowed from her. In order to effect the subterfuge she had the horse killed whilst he was riding it to seek an audience with the king in Edinburgh. The fact that she was English seems to be highlighted in the story to cast suspicion on her and her means of subverting customary law:

> When the eldest son of MacFarlane lost his right to the land, the clansmen lost their respect for him altogether and they called him 'An t-Each Breac' ('The Piebald Horse') because he was so stupid as to give the rights to the land as a surety for the piebald horse. He got married and had children. It is from his son that those of the name MacNair ('Mac an Oighre', the son of the heir[102]) were descended. Although the English lady's son got the land in Arrochar, the MacFarlanes never acknowledged him as the leader of the clan. They called his descendants 'MacFarlanes of the land'.[103]

LAW AND MORALITY

For all of the apparent glorification of warriors in Gaelic literature, it may come as a surprise that Gaeldom was a very litigious society and that Gaelic law is the earliest and best-documented law in Western Europe. A formally and extensively trained body of lawyers began writing it down in the seventh century.[104] Elements of this law system, often referred to in English as 'brehon law' (from *brithem,* the early Gaelic word for 'judge'), were in use in Scotland and survived long enough to be recorded in charters of the twelfth and thirteenth centuries.[105] Indeed, many elements were assimilated into Scots law.

Many documents about Gaelic law in early Ireland survive; the degree to which this law system extended into what is now Scotland at an early period is not yet clear. Tracts surviving in Ireland refer to flora and fauna that existed only in Scotland (in any quantity, at least) by the period they were written, such as Scots pine and the bear: the Scots pine may have lingered in small patches in Ireland into the twelfth century but survive to the present in Scotland; the bear was extinct in Ireland after the Early Bronze Age but survived in Scotland into the second millennium AD.[106] Although the laws of Cinaed mac Ailpín are mentioned in historical sources, they themselves do not survive;[107] there is no reason to doubt that they derived from older Gaelic law.

Judges operating under the Gaelic law system were appointed to specific territories and produced legal documents, such as charters. Such legal professions survived in the Hebrides as late as the seventeenth century.[108] The Lords of the Isles sustained the traditional Gaelic legal order, which contributed to the stability and peace of their reign, as recalled nostalgically later in the Sleat history of the MacDonalds:

> There was a judge in every Isle for the discussion of all controversies, who had lands from Macdonald for their trouble, and likewise the eleventh part of every action decided. But there might be still an appeal to the Council of the Isles.[109]

The legendary king Cormac mac Airt, renowned for his just execution of legal matters, provided a literary role model for kings and chieftains. There are a number of Gaelic gnomic texts attributed to Cormac in Classical Gaelic texts and Scottish Gaelic oral tradition.[110] Cathal MacMhuirich composed an elegy to Iain Mór MacLeòid of Dunvegan on his death in 1649, comparing him to Cormac and praising him for his role as arbiter in clan affairs.

Ní bhíodh cúis 'na cúis fhrithir	
Ná diongnadh í d'fhóirithin	
Le breith gceirt sheinrechta a shen	B.5, B.3
Do sheirc eighrechta d' innremh.	
Fá flaith derbhtha an dlighidh ríogh	B.5, B.6
Fá breithemh mhúchaidh míghníomh;	
Fer tighe do bhí ag Banbha	A.1
Rí agus file foghlamtha.[111]	B.6, B.8

('No cause for anxiety arose that he could not address by just pronouncement of ancestral law and from attachment to traditional wisdom.')

('He was a prince who manifested royal laws, who quelled misdeeds, the master of Ireland's house, a king and a learned poet.')

Later clan chieftains maintained courts of law according to wider Scottish practice in order that grievances be heard and justice executed in their territories. These institutions of civil society were inevitably no better than the commitment of particular chieftains to impartiality. When local courts did not settle cases to satisfaction, often because of the biases and vested interests of those involved in decisions, parties could appeal to the system of central courts that operated throughout Scotland. Arbitration allowed parties to choose advocates for their interests; settlements aimed to repair damages done to the clan and to discourage the continuation of hostilities and retribution.[112]

Many social arrangements in Gaelic life, such as fosterage, marriage, and manrent, were agreed by contract. A Gaelic proverb states the importance of such bonds: 'Gach cùis gu cùmhnant' ('Let every business be done by agreement').[113] Such agreements were usually verbal, but this made them no less binding in force in a society where reputation and honour were paramount in relations:

> The provisions upon both sides were easily remembered, and, in case of any dispute, could be adjusted by the witnesses that had been present. Nor did this often happen. A people who transact their business verbally are commonly more tenacious of their word than those among whom writ or oath is requisite. In such a case breach of promise would subject the party that failed to infamy and shame.[114]

Outsiders were often bewildered by the mixture of ferocity and gentility, warfare and courtesy, which they witnessed amongst Highlanders. Although sword-right was an ongoing source of conflict between clans, relations between members of any particular community were generally amicable. As the Reverend Donald MacQueen noted disappointingly in 1774, 'their virtues were too much confined to their own community.'[115] David Stewart explained the difference in conduct in 1822: 'a predatory expedition was the general declaration of enmity [by clearing] the pastures of the enemy [. . . but] in the interior of their own society, all property was safe'.[116] By the time that Sarah Murray visited in the late eighteenth century, she felt that Highlanders were more trustworthy than Lowlanders or her fellow Englishmen:

> I have already mentioned the present amiable manners of the people of Inverness, and the adjacent country; and I must also add, that they are now perfectly secure in their property, as well as polished in their behaviour (which is not always the case in the south), retaining the honest simplicity and hospitality of the patriarchal age, which the rub of refinement has not impaired. Indeed, not only in Inverness, but in

most parts of the Highlands, the manners of the people are pleasant to a great degree; and the poorest of the poor will vie with each other which can most assist, or gratify a stranger, provided it be not on a Sunday. On that day, if a carriage breaks down in the Highlands, there it must lie, for no hand will be found to mend it; not for want of good will, but for conscience' sake. In the Lowlands, in and about large towns, particularly where there are manufactories, or in sea-ports, there are as many depraved folks as in England: but in the Highlands all is safety and security ;– no fear of thieves by night or day. All the doors and windows are left unfastened: and I have even seen sideboards, covered with plate of very great value, stand open in parlours night and day, without fear of it being touched.[117]

Lying, stealing, murder, and other criminal behavior within the clan would lead to swift punishment or banishment, and it was believed that the perpetrator of ill deeds would soon be found out: 'Cha bhi suaimhneas aig eucoir no seasamh aig droch-bheairt' ('Wrong will not rest, nor will ill-deed stand'); 'Cha mhair a' bhreug ach ré seal' ('A lie will not live for long').[118] It was expected that life within one's kin-group was safe and that one's neighbours were trustworthy. Door-locks were considered a sign of evil times: 'Cho mosach ris na glasan' ('As contemptible as door-locks').[119]

The Gaelic word *nàire* is usually translated into English as 'shame' or 'modesty', although it has a wider usage than this in Gaelic, referring to the sense of what is right, proper and honorable. It is a key concept in the operation of Gaelic society. 'Am fear a chaill a nàire is a mhodh, chaill e na bh' aige' ('The person who lost his propriety and his manners lost all he had').[120]

FEASTING AND FIGHTING

Like many other Scottish élite in the pre-modern period, Highland leaders operated largely as aristocrat-warriors who asserted their status and power in public displays of strength and grandiosity. Gaelic culture could be characterised in part as one of 'feasting and fighting' (setting aside the other major cultural preoccupations with law and literature), for it was through such ritualised performances that clan chieftains demonstrated their ability to provide leadership, sustenance and protection for their dependants. Fighting, when it resulted in the capture of cattle from a rival clan, provided the foodstuffs for feasting, which in turn enhanced the prestige of the clan and confirmed its capacity to sustain its members. 'What ultimately underpinned this exchange system was the chief's ability to secure his control over land and to fill it with his own kinsmen or those of allied clans.'[121]

The gathering of disparate branches of a clan was often the occasion for serious business, but also for entertainment and celebration.

The great hunting matches were the means of preserving a social intercourse between tribes who lived far distant from each other. It was a means also of bringing the chiefs and principal men of the country together, and enabled them to adjust differences, settle future proceedings, &c.[122]

Hunts were spectacles of ritualised violence, aristocratic splendour and clan unity that combined the spirit of both feasting and fighting. In such contexts the public-relations agents of the chieftain, his poets, had an opportunity to promote his image, as Rev. John Macpherson wrote in 1768:

When the Hebridean chiefs and captains returned home after a successful expedition, they summoned their friends and clients to a grand entertainment. Bards and [*seanchaidh*]s flocked in from every quarter; pipers and harpers had an undisputed right to appear on such public occasions. These entertainments were wild and chearful, nor were they unattended with the pleasures of the sentiments and unrefined tastes of the times. The bards sung, and the young women danced. The old warrior related the gallant actions of his youth, and struck the young men with ambition and fire. The whole tribe filled the Chieftain's hall. The trunks of trees covered with moss were laid in the order of a table from one end of the hall to the other. Whole deer and beeves were roasted and laid before them on rough boards or hurdles of rods wove together. [. . .] The old and young warriors sat down in order from the Chieftain, according to their proximity in blood to him. The harp was then touched, the song was raised, and the [*slige-creachain*] or the drinking-shell, went round.[123]

In many respects, the 'cult of the warrior' in Gaelic tradition is a genuine inheritance of the warrior ethos of ancient Celtic society. The emphasis of 'heroic-age' warfare was not to create larger political units, such as in the building of modern empires, but to assert status and win honour. There was nothing to be gained by battling with an enemy of low status, or by conquering all of one's enemies, who are the means of maintaining one's fame. As the Gaelic proverb has it, 'Is mairg a chuireadh farran air fann' ('Woe to him who bothers the weak').[124] The warrior-aristocrat instead found lasting fame in song and story by defeating other formidable foes. 'According to the heroic ideal, personal encounter, in which strength and skill counted, is the centre-piece of battle.'[125]

On the other hand, political instability and the machinations of outside forces conspired to foment much unnecessary chaos and bloodshed in the Highlands. The conflicts in which Gaels were involved were not just the result of their own belligerence but were often the schemes of Lowland lairds, regional magnates and British élite asserting themselves on a national, and even international, stage.

James gave Gaels a Lowland problem in the form of more consistent government alliances with certain clans that in turn generated new, more intense forms of warfare. [. . .] Yet while professing qualities of civilisation, the Crown and its agents also adopted tactics which were equally if not more 'barbaric' than the targets of their 'civilitie'. What had been a series of internal feuds and dissension in island kindreds was ruthlessly exploited.[126]

Regardless of the nature of the conflict, honour in battle was paramount and many Gaelic proverbs attest to the achievement of fame through oral tradition: 'Is buaine bladh na saoghal' ('Fame is more lasting than life'). The worst fear of the warrior-aristocrat was to be the subject of shame or ridicule: 'Is beò duine an dèidh a shàrachaidh, ach cha bheò e an dèidh a nàrachaidh' ('A person may live after his harassment, but he will not survive his disgrace').[127]

The emphasis in the heroic ideal is upon personal prowess, so not every method of warfare was equally laudable. Domhnall Cam mac Dhùghaill, a warrior of the MacAulays of Lewis, remarked about the year 1600 when heard about the invention of gunpowder, 'Tha latha a' ghaisgich seachad: tha an duine lag a-nis cho math ris an duine làidir' ('The warrior's day is over: the weak man is now as good as the strong man').[128] Although the Gaels did of necessity adopt firearms, one can find a disdain for such non-heroic weapons even at the end of the eighteenth century, as in this praise of Clanranald.

> 'S iomadh laoch bu gharg an carraid
> Nach iarradh gunna:
> Lann chlaiseach dhubhghorm 'ga tarruing,
> Toirt buaidh urram.[129]

('There is many a warrior, fierce in conflict, who would not want a gun (but rather) a shiny, grooved blade being drawn, achieving victory.')

John Mair, in his 1521 *History*, remarked in defense of the Scottish warrior ethos that 'death in arms and in a just quarrel is a fair end for a man.'[130] John Leslie, a one-time Bishop of Ross, wrote in 1578 that the most noble warrior in the battle company led a charge and those in his command sought to emulate his example and to defend him from harm.[131] Martin Martin observed that the poet (referred to here anachronistically as a druid) provoked warriors for battle by reciting the deeds of their ancestors:

Before they engag'd the Enemy in Battle, the Chief Druid harangu'd the Army to excite their Courage. He was plac'd on an Eminence, from whence he address'd himself to all of them standing about him, putting them in mind of what great things were perform'd by the Valour of their Ancestors, rais'd their Hopes with the noble Rewards of their Honour and Victory, and dispell'd their Fears by all the Topicks that natural Courage could suggest. After this harangue, the Army gave a general Shout, and then charg'd the Enemy stoutly. This in the antient Language was call'd [*Brosnachadh Catha*].[132]

Every male aspired not to be the stooping and sedentary farmer, but the proud and mobile warrior. John Ramsay of Ochtertyre, writing in the late eighteenth century, noted how these attitudes affected economic activity and gender roles:

> Their popular poetry was surely well suited to a country where little more than threescore years ago every person wished to be thought a soldier – husbandry, and even pasturage, being followed no further than necessity required. And till very lately, sheep and goats were regarded as the property of wives, being beneath the attention of their husbands; and the lowest follower would have thought himself dishonoured by entering a byre or assisting at a sheep-shearing.[133]

The most common form of inter-clan aggression was the cattle-raid (*togail creach*), discussed above as an integral part of the inauguration of new chieftains as a demonstration of his ability to lead war-bands. Such activities were originally a customary practice in Gaeldom and were not considered 'thievery'. The Clan Donald is praised by a Classical poet as, 'Clann gan uabhar gan éagcáir / Nár ghabh acht éadail chogaidh' ('A people without arrogance or injustice / Who seized only the spoils of war').[134]

Some Gaels perceived Lowlanders as usurpers of their rights upon the Scottish soil and therefore as legitimate targets for raiding. Lowlanders of course saw such activities as evidence of the lack of civility in the Highlands. Gaelic tradition did not praise needless violence, as the proverb suggests: 'Na sir is na seachain an cath' ('Do not seek out or avoid warfare'). An inscription said to have been on a sword became advice for warriors: 'Na tarraing mi gun adhbhar, is na pill mi gun chliù' ('Do not draw me without a reason and do not return me without honour').[135]

The king (or chieftain) is in fact represented in oral tradition as peacemaker as well as war-leader. In a sixteenth-century poem advocating the leadership of Campbell of Argyll over all of the Gaels, his rule is said to unite the clans and bring an end to warfare:

Ar ngabháil ceannais gach cinnidh	B.5, G.3
Ceangluidh síothchain 'na síth bhuain;	B.5
Congbhuidh ó shin reacht is riaghuil,	B.5
Do bhir ceart gan iarraidh uaidh.	B.5
Ceangluidh sé gan cheilg da chéile	
Curadh-uaisle Innsi Gall.[136]	G.3

('Once he has taken the leadership of all the clans, he will forge a lasting peace; thereafter he keeps law and order; he maintains justice without being asked.')

('He will bind together, without guile, the noble warriors of the Hebrides.')

A MacDonald poet (usually said to have been Aonghas mac Alasdair Ruaidh) asked God to intervene in the troubled political affairs which led to the Battle of Killiecrankie of 1689, remarking that kings should maintain peace and not provoke conflict:

> Dhé 'dh'òrdaich na rìghrean
> 'Chumail sìth ris gach duine:
> Bho is Tu-san as brìoghmhoir'
> Na gach tì dhiubh siud uile
> Casg féin le d' mhìorbhail
> An t-srìth-s' gu h-ullamh;
> Ceartaich robairean Sheumais
> Bàth reubaltan Uilleim.[137]

('O God, who commanded the kings to keep peace between people: since you are the most wondrous of all of those beings, put a lasting end to this strife; correct James' plunderers and the foolishness of William's rebels.')

Violence was mitigated by special times and places designated as sanctuaries, especially because of their sacred associations. Fairs dedicated to saints were recognised as days of truces, even during severe feuds,[138] and churches and sites belonging to 'protected' persons were meant to be safe zones.[139] As the Rev. Donald MacQueen of Skye noted in 1774:

Sanctuaries, called girths, were consecrated in every district, to which the criminal fled; where the superstition of the times, countenanced by the political institutions, secured him from every act of violence, until he was brought to a judicial trial. To this day, we say of a man who flies to a place of security, [*Thug e an* girth *air*]: and whatever party violated the sanctuary, which very seldom happened, brought the terrible vengeance of the church upon their back.[140]

There are, however, a number of Gaelic tales about the violation of the customs of sanctuary, some of which may be best understood as the propaganda of rival clans. Repudiations of such claims are evidenced as early as the seventeenth-century Sleat history of the MacDonalds.[141]

Poets promoted the image of the chieftain as a generous patron and provider for his people; a leader who hoarded the wealth of his people, on the other hand, would be reproached as being greedy and selfish. Rulers are often praised with lines such as 'làmh a liubhairt an airgid 's an òir' ('a hand for bestowing silver and gold').[142] Feasts demonstrated a chieftain's largesse and were intended to impress his current dependants as well as potential clients and allies. One of the heirs of Clanranald was called by his clan *Raghnall Gallda* 'Foreign Ranald' because of having been raised with his mother's clan, the Frasers of Lovat. According to a tradition in Moidart, the clan turned against him during a feast held in his honour when he revealed his miserly and ungenerous disposition.[143]

It is in this context that we can better understand the role of alcohol in Gaelic society as a symbol of the generosity of chieftains to their dependants. The distribution of wealth and alcohol in the chieftain's hall often occur together in poetry, as in this elegy to Sir Seumas MacDonald of Sleat, who died in 1678:

> Bhiodh do ghillean mu seach
> A' lìonadh dibhe b' fhearr blas:
> Fìon Spàinteach dearg aca 's beòir.
>
> Uisge-beatha nam pìos,
> Rachadh an t-airgead 'ga dhìol
> Gheibhte 'n glain' e mar ghrìogan òir.[144]

('Your servants would be taking turns pouring the best-tasting liquor: they had red Spanish wine, and beer.')

('Whisky in silver cups, paid for with silver, glistening like golden beads in the glass.')

Drink was a conspicuous element in the public exhibition of a chieftain's generosity to his subjects. Alcohol could be easily abused, of course, especially after it became more readily available to the general public with the erection of taverns in the seventeenth century; there are gnomic texts and songs warning about the dangers of excessive drink, and songs of complaint about men who drank excessively.[145] Terms like *misgear* 'drunkard' and *misgeach* 'drunken' are generally used negatively in Gaelic poetry.[146]

> Drink was tolerated, as increasing strength of mind, eloquence and gaiety; and its excesses were tolerated, in consideration of those happy results: but if a man drank till he became feeble and stupid, he was considered as exposing the weakness of his mind and body. A man was proud of drinking a great deal, without stuttering or sickening; but beyond that point all was contempt and disgrace.[147]

Drink was an element in many rituals, such as inauguration (as discussed above). As in other nations, alcohol was offered as a toast to others, living and dead, often in commemoration of ancestors; *deoch-cuimhneachain* is a drink taken in memory of the deceased at a funeral.[148] Drink was the communion of the warrior society, connecting the leader with his subjects. These images appear in an ode by Màiri MacLean to Lachlann MacLean (†1687), Lord of Coll:

> | 'N àm bhith triall gu d' fhàrdaich | |
> | --- | --- |
> | Gum b' e d' àbhaist mar bu dual | B.3 |
> | Bhith tarrainn ort am bràithreachas | G.1 |
> | Cur slàintichean mun cuairt. | C.2 |

> *Searragan is tunnachan*
> *Gun chunnart air an luach*
> *Sìor-òl nan corn sinnsearach*
> *A dhìobhradh iad gu suain.*[149]

('When going to your residence it was the custom that you inherited to be drawing together in brotherhood (by) passing around the toasts.')

('Flasks and casks – their costs were of no concern – drinking constantly from ancestral horns that were only put down in order to sleep.')

COOPERATION, OBLIGATION, AND RECIPROCATION

The highest moral imperative in Gaelic society was hospitality to all, regardless of inter-clan hostilities, as the Gaelic proverb intimates: 'Bheirinn cuid-oidhche dha ged a bhiodh ceann fir fo 'achlais' ('I would give him food and lodging for the night even if he had a man's head under his arm'). The demands of hospitality were to be met whatever the cost to the host himself. It is this 'sacred obligation' which has instilled the sense of generosity in Gaels to this day. As the Rev. Donald MacQueen explained in 1774:

> Of all virtues their hospitality was the most extensive; every door and every heart was open to the stranger and to the fugitive; to these they were particularly humane and generous, vied with one another who would use them best, and looked on the person who sought their protection as a sacred depositum, which on no consideration they were to give up. [. . .] Hospitality was founded on immemorial custom, before the thoughts of men were contracted by the use of weights and measures, and reckoned so far a sacred obligation as to think themselves bound to entertain the man who from a principle of ill-will and resentment, scorned upon them a numerous retinue.[150]

It was expected that one's costs would eventually be recovered since generosity was reciprocal: 'Gus an tràighear a' mhuir le cliabh, cha bhi fear fial falamh' ('Until the ocean is emptied with a basket, the generous man will never be empty-handed').[151]

'One of the prime duties of the chief was the extraction of tributes from lesser kingroups.'[152] These payments provided the raw materials and labour needed to sustain the clan and were meant to be redistributed according to need, not hoarded by the élite. These economic practices originated in early Gaelic law and the grounds for them in traditional cosmology recall the sacred attributes of the king and his link with the goddess of the land:

> The ideological basis of the levying of tribute in the form of livestock and agricultural produce, therefore, appears to have been that kings ensured – indeed gifted – fertility, and the ruled were merely returning the products of that fertility, as food-rent, winter hospitality, and other services, to their rightful owners.[153]

The exact form and schedule of *cìsean* 'taxes, tribute' varied according to local custom and changed over time. The Gaelic term *càin* (borrowed into Scots variously as 'cain', 'cane', or 'kain') refers to the tribute given to an overlord, usually paid in the form of foodstuffs such as butter or poultry. The obligation to provide the lord (and/or his military retinue) with a food and lodging when he/they travelled, or to render to him the equivalent value, was referred to as *coinnmed*. The term *cuid-oidhche* 'a night's due' (rendered into Scots in various forms such as 'Cuddiche') may have been a development of the practice of coinnmed. Chieftains could also expect their dependants to work on their estates.[154]

Men were required to join the military hosts of their lords when called upon. This service, called *slógad* or *slúagad* in early forms of Gaelic, was easily incorporated into the 'feudal order'. King Alexander II declared an ordinance in 1220 imposing heavy penalties upon those who disregarded this service, and further Acts in 1318, 1456, and 1481 sought to secure 'fencible men' for the Defence of the Realm.[155] Hosts could be raised at short notice in the Highlands by a series of messengers passing along the *crois-tàraidh* or *cranntàra* 'summoning stick' (known popularly in English as the 'fiery cross').

The obligatory payment of tribute to an acknowledged overlord was contrasted by Tiree poet Iain MacIlleathain in 1883, after a visit by the Napier Commission, with the unjust levying of taxes by the Duke of Argyll, who was represented as having usurped the previous rightful rulers:

> Ged tha an t-eilean cliùiteach seo
> Do'n Diùc 'toirt chìsean,
> Cha b' ann le ceart no cruaidh lannan
> A fhuaireadh e le shinnsre[156]

('Although this illustrious island pays taxes to the duke, it was not with justice, or by hard blades, that his ancestors acquired it.')

The chieftain was responsible for the welfare of his clan members. As a chieftain's strength was in the men who were in his command, it was in his interest to look after them. He would postpone or even cancel rent in times of scarcity and attend to the needs of the poor. When a number of the followers of Colin Campbell of Glenorchy in 1570 were raided, he promised that they would be recompensed and protected from his own savings: 'Spare neither my gear nor your own, for God leaving us our healths we will get gear enough.'[157]

Clan legends describe the *bord follaiseach*, a custom observed by the most generous clan chiefs which allowed strangers in need to eat at their tables for a year and a day without having to reveal their identity or origins. 'Gentlemen are very charitable to their poor: some will have 20 or [more at] every meal in the house.'[158] The role of the chieftain in feeding the hungry and supporting the needy is frequently met in Gaelic poetry, as in this ode to the chief of Clanranald in 1716:

Ga mhèid 's gun cost thu 'chìsean ris
Chan fhaic thu dìth air tuathanach;
Do bhantraichean 's do dhìlleachdain
On 's e do nì-se 'dh'fhuasglas orr';
Dèanamaid ùrnaigh dhìcheallach
Gun cùm an Rìgh a-suas duinn thu.[159]

('No matter what you have to spend, you ensure that no tenant is in need; widows and orphans are relieved by your wealth; let us make an earnest prayer that God will keep you in good health for us.')

The clan chieftain and members of his clan were expected to be mutually supportive and beneficial to one another. Commoners were obliged to assist the chieftain in his times of need as he was expected to support them in theirs. Martin Martin confirms the practice of praying for the welfare of the chieftain related in the verse above:

The Islanders have a great respect for their Chiefs and Heads of Tribes, and they conclude Grace after every Meal, with a Petition to God for their Welfare and Prosperity. Neither will they, as far as in them lies, suffer them to sink under any Misfortune; but in case of a Decay of Estate, make a voluntary Contribution on their behalf, as a common Duty, to support the Credit of their Families.[160]

Even after the defeat of Culloden there were exiled clan chiefs whose followers were making financial contributions for their upkeep, despite being burdened by taxes levied by the central government.[161]

While the chieftain was expected to be concerned with the welfare of his clan, individuals could also rely upon the support of the entire community. Seeking aid from neighbours was known in Gaelic as *faoighe* (borrowed into Scots as 'thigging'): 'It entailed no stigma upon the craver, and was by no means confined to the lower classes of society. On the other hand, refusal of the thing craved is represented as extremely dishonouring to the person refusing.'[162] The practice of faoighe is further explained in the context of a Perthshire glen in the nineteenth century:

While kinship near or far made it the duty of the comfortably-off to help those that were badly-off, usually through no fault of their own, it likewise filled the strugglers with such pride of independence that, however hardly tried, none of them took [to] the road as beggars going with meal-pokes from door to door. What a lonely woman did was, at clipping time, to go around the fanks *air faoigh ollamh*, in other words, to ask for puckles of wool, which she took home and spun and so turned into money. Men who drifted into helplessness often quartered themselves for the end of their days on well-to-do relations who did not grudge them their keep.[163]

The sense of reciprocation in reflected in such Gaelic proverbs as 'Beathaich thusa mise an-diugh agus beathaichidh mise thusa a-màireach' ('Feed me today and I'll feed you tomorrow').[164] Newly married couples commonly resorted to faoighe when attempting to gather the necessary equipment and livestock to support themselves. Like any social custom that relies upon honesty and integrity, however, it could be abused by those ready to take advantage of Highland generosity.

Many Gaelic proverbs display a profound distaste for deprivation and praise generosity to the poor and vulnerable: 'Dà rud nach còir a bhith falamh: goile an t-seann duine agus làmh an leanaibh bhig' ('Two things that should not be empty: the stomach of the old and the hand of the child'); 'Math ri seann duine, math ri an-duine, math ri leanabh beag: trì mathan nach téid am mugha' ('Doing good to the old, the infirm of mind, and the child: three kinds of goodness that cannot go wrong').[165] People relied upon each other to an enormous extent, for there were tasks which required the cooperation and coordination of everyone in the community. Everyone had a function and contribution to make: 'A dh'aindeoin cumadh an fhòid, gheibh thu àite 's a' chruaich dha' ('Despite the shape of the peat, you can find a place in the stack for it').[166] This was particularly true of agricultural work.

> The actual cultivation of the land was done by groups, either of joint tenants holding directly of the chief or of sub-tenants holding of his tacksmen. The custom of joint cultivation, of course, is not a peculiarly Gaelic feature and was common to most northern countries, but the system fitted in well with the social organization of the clan.[167]

Clans held large-scale celebrations at seasonal festivals. The festival of *Samhainn* (corresponding to the modern Hallowe'en) marked the end of the year and was the time when accounts were settled between partners in contracts. The winter tribute due to superiors was expected at this time, much of it consumed in large feasts.[168]

GENDER ROLES

Women were for the most part excluded from formal roles in the élite institutions of Gaeldom; they are therefore not always well represented in the documents written by men for institutions dominated by men. Women were explicitly barred from acting as clan chieftains, for example, and were not allowed to inherit land independently, as it would cause their parent clans to lose territory to rivals who would gain it as marriage dowry.[169]

> Even more so than in Ireland, the culture of the early modern Scottish Gàidhealtachd was imbued with a strong patriarchal ideology. [. . .] Indeed, so well entrenched was the ideology that it can make little sense to speak of a prescriptive patriarchy in relation to the Gàidhealtachd of this period. Within the boundaries of the culture, it

seemed natural and incontrovertible. In fact women at all levels of Gàidhealtachd society enjoyed considerably more freedom, or at any rate suffered somewhat less subordination, than we might be led to expect from prevailing cultural norms.[170]

Women did wield forms of informal power that are often invisible in official sources but discernible in less formal ones, particularly those created and transmitted by women through oral tradition. The obscurity of such sources has made the cultural history of women in the Gàidhealtachd difficult to write and it remains under-developed.[171] To get a more balanced sense of gender and women's roles in society, we need to tap a wide range of sources and be aware of the biases that come from texts created in particular contexts. As with men, the privileges and responsibilities of women, and the forms of power that they enjoyed, varied according to the social class to which they belonged.

Like most non-industrial societies, gender roles in Gaeldom were sharply defined, as reflected in the proverb 'Chan eil ìm ann am bò fir is chan eil treabhadh ann an each mnatha' ('A man's cow has no milk and a woman's horse cannot plough').[172] Women generally took a back seat to men in public life; this subordination is evident even in the transmission of oral tradition. Social etiquette (particularly as evidenced from the eighteenth century on) prohibited women from performing publicly in the presence of their husbands, as this could detract from the higher status of their male counterparts; they did, however, perform for children and thus tended to excel in genres appropriate for children, such as wonder tales, riddles, games, and nonsense rhymes. Women were also theoretically barred from being active performers of high-register material, such as Classical Gaelic poetry and Ossianic ballads.[173]

> Gaelic society, either during their own lives or in retrospect, seems to view women poets with suspicion. [. . .] When women whose names we know stepped out of line and began to compose 'bigger' songs, they came to be suspected of evil intent, witchcraft and the abuse of power.[174]

And yet, paradoxically, despite the apparent force of such theoretical restrictions, Highland women have enjoyed surprisingly prominent roles in the creation and transmission of Gaelic literature in nearly every century, even more so in Scotland than in Ireland. The compositions of female poets were clearly consequential to wider society by the end of the sixteenth century, and continued to persuade popular opinion in the War of the Three Kingdoms, the Jacobite Risings, the Crofters' Land Agitation, and the many social traumas in between. Women have often been the bearers of traditions once in the preserve of males long after men had abandoned them. The role of women as standard-bearers of tradition and even cultural champions should not be underestimated.[175]

Formal education was limited to the clan élite, which sometimes extended to females. Domhnall Gorm Òg, chief of the MacDonalds of Sleat, had his two daughters tutored by the ollamh Cathal MacMhuirich in the 1630s, probably to avoid their being educated in the Lowlands by the Protestant establishment.[176] Poems in the Classical style attributed to three women have survived, one the widow of Clan Nèill of Gigha, another may be a daughter of Campbell of Argyll, and the third of the house of Stewart;[177] composing Classical poetry, as these women did, required significant education. Several bardic poems exist which compliment female aristocrats for their patronage and sophistication using terms indicating mutual friendship and respect.[178]

As an informant whose memory reached back to the late eighteenth century reminds us, few women had the opportunity to receive education, particularly with the high demands made on women for economic survival:

> It was an unheard of thing for girls, except the daughters of 'gentlemen' to be sent to school [. . .] When could a woman find time for schooling with the clothing of the whole family dependent upon her knowledge and skill in working wool and flax; even the sewing thread had to be manufactured by her deft fingers. The women had also the care of the cattle to a great extent, and often times they were obliged to grind the meal before baking it. How could time be spared to read and write?[179]

The working of cloth was a specifically feminine activity, and the environment in which this was done may have been exclusive of males from very early times. Songs sung by women in this setting, and composed by them for these occasions, provide evidence of their own perspectives on Gaelic society. While most of the *òrain-luaidh* 'waulking songs' composed by women deal with their relationships with their families and with romantic interests, some of them also reveal political concerns. Examples can be cited which argue for backing one side of a dispute against another (especially against the interference of the central government). These 'demonstrate that some women, at that particular time and in these particular areas, were involved at least to some extent in public debates and in shaping political opinions among their people.'[180] Although waulking songs advocating a position on the 1745 Jacobite Rising were composed by Alasdair mac Mhaighstir Alasdair, he must have thought this female medium of communication one which would have an influence on men of standing via the women who transmitted highly politicised songs.

The primary social function of women was in producing descendants for her husband and clan. Anne Grant assures us that this was a contribution not be to undervalued:

> She borrowed a kind of sacredness from the tie which united her to her husband [. . .] independent of mental charms or personal attractions, was endeared to the husband by this tacit homage, and by a tie, more prevalent by far here, than in polished societies. She was the mother of his children; to her he was indebted for the link that connected him with the future descendants of his almost idolized ancestors.[181]

At an economic level, people were maintained by their parents in their youth and by their offspring in their old age. A good wife not only maintained domestic affairs properly, but raised children who would be of benefit to the entire family in coming years. Quite a number of proverbs relate to the importance of a wife in a successful household. 'Is e fortan no mì-fhortan fir bean' ('A man's wife is either his fortune or his misfortune'); 'Is fhearr bean ghlic na crann is fearann' ('A wise wife is better than a plough and land').[182] A man and his wife are a working unit who ideally work in unison for the same purpose. 'Am fear a labhras olc mu 'mhnaoi, tha e a' cur mì-chliù air fhèin' ('The man who speaks ill of his wife ruins his own reputation').[183] That women deserved their own place of respect in the home is observed in the proverb, 'Is e duine gun nàire a shuidheas ann an cathair bean an taighe' ('Only the shameless man would take the housewife's chair').[184]

The general social pattern was for a wife to move into the home of her husband and as an 'outsider' who had a powerful role in the family, she could be at the centre of tension and conflict (especially if the husband's extended family was also in the home).[185] Women are often represented as excessively haughty about their households with their female peers and this rivalry was a potentially destabilising force in society: 'Cha téid àrdan nam ban fon ùir' ('The pride of women cannot be buried').[186]

Giving birth to a man's children forged a strong link to him. The leniency about the legitimacy of children born out of wedlock gave many low-born women an incentive to become the mistresses of noblemen, or at least fantasise about the prospects. 'The desire to bear illegitimate children to some handsome aristocrat, or envy of women raped by a handsome aristocrat, is fairly common'[187] as a motif in women's songs. 'I would bear you five, or six, or seven sons' can be found in many women's songs, but the following song of a secret love affair is remarkably frank in its eroticism:

> Nam bu toigh leat siod, 'fhir bhàin,
> Bhiodh falt mo chinn 'gad chumail blàth;
> Gum biodh mo chìochan a' cumail dìon ort
> Ged rachadh mo riasladh 's mo chur gu bàs.
>
> Shaoilinn fèin nach bu pheacadh trom
> Ged shiùbhlainn fraoch leat is talamh lom
> Gach nì fos n-ìosal a bhiodh tu 'g iarraidh
> Bu leat do mhiann dheth 's chan iarrainn bonn.[188]

('If it be your pleasure, o fair-haired man, my hair could keep you warm, my breasts could give you shelter, even if I be harmed and put to death.')

('I wouldn't think it any serious sin if I was to travel heather and bare land with you; I would do secretly everything you want: have your desire, and I ask no payment.')

The nurse of a child also formed a very close bond with it and it was believed that certain traits could be transmitted through breast milk. According to a nineteenth-century tale, a number of Jacobite Highlanders were taken prisoner after their defeat at Culloden. General John Campbell, having heard Cumberland insult the ability of the Highland soldiers, bet than one of the prisoners could defeat the best swordsman from the English Hanoverian ranks. If the Highlander were to win, all of the prisoners under Campbell's charge were to be freed; otherwise, they would all be killed. The Highlander who accepted the challenge was missing a hand from the battle and sorely wounded, but was able to beat the larger and healthier Englishman. Campbell congratulated him with the words (in translation), 'Go home now and thank your mother, because she gave you such good milk.' Similarly, Domhnall Moireasdan says in his ode to the Lord of Coll, 'B' i do mhuime bhean chìche / Rinn do chuislean lìonadh' ('It was your wet-nurse who pumped up your veins').[189]

Many Gaelic legends portray a very special bond between heroes and their *muime* 'foster-mother, wet-nurse'.[190] The muime often gives the hero special training or knowledge when he is young, tools and guidance when he has grown to be a warrior, and support and healing when he is wounded or in distress. It is worthwhile to speculate why so much attention is paid to these characters and relationships. The institution of fosterage provided a means of connecting the lower-caste foster-parents with the higher-born aristocratic warriors. The frequent regard paid to this social bond in literature suggests that it allowed the audience, regardless of their social station, to maintain an imaginative link to the heroic and high-prestige elements of their own culture through identification with the muime. These stories and songs often convey tenderness between people of different rank but may also represent the wider concerns of a society frequently under siege.

Women are strongly associated with the fundamental principles of life and played prominent roles in the processes of birthing as *mnathan-glùine* 'mid-wives' and of death as *mnathan-tuiream* 'keening women'. These women were important enough to have had their livelihoods secured by their communities, as Catrìona Phearsan of Barra attested to Alexander Carmichael in 1872:

Bha bean-ghlùin agus bean-tuiream anns a chuile baile am Barraidh. Agus bha e mar fhiachaibh air muinntir a chuile baile fiar samhraidh agus fodar geamhraidh fhaicinn aig gach tè dha'n t-seòrsa gu àilgheas a' mhaoir air faobhar a' chlaidhe. Agus chan fhaodadh na daoine dìth no deireas 'fhaicinn air tè seach tè dhiubh seo, los gum bitheadh gach tè dhiubh murrach air a dleasdanas a dhèanadh dar a thigeadh e m'a coinneamh.[191]

Every village in Barra had a mid-wife and a keening-woman. And everyone in every village was obligated to supply each woman of this sort with summer grazing and winter fodder, to the satisfaction of the bailiff [promising on] the sword's edge. And the people would see to it that neither of these women would suffer want nor loss any more than her peers, so that each of them could carry out her responsibility when the time would come.

Whether the result was victory or defeat, women had an important role in the aftermath of battle. In the case of defeat, women searched amongst the corpses to find their kin and lament the dead in song. Keening gave women in an otherwise male-dominated society a chance to voice their anger, criticisms, and complaints publicly with relative impunity. The later prohibition of women from accompanying the corpse to the graveyard may have been a step taken in extinguishing this practice with its overtly pagan associations.[192]

Women celebrated the return of their men in victory with praise in song. An account of the journey of Edward I of England in the Highlands in 1296 mentions that the women of Strathearn 'came out to meet the king [. . .] and sang before him, as they used to do'.[193] Although they mourned their relations killed in combat, there is no suggestion that women questioned or rejected the warrior ethos of their society; they only wished that their male progeny and relations fight, and die, honourably. Women rarely took part in warfare directly but they are frequently represented in oral tradition as sending men into action with words of shame, vengeance, mockery, or provocation.[194] When Charles Stewart of Ardshiel showed reluctance to lead his clan for the Prince in the 1745 Rising, his wife rebuked him sharply, 'If you, Charles, are not willing to become Commander of the men of Appin, stay at home and take care of the house, and I will go myself and become their Commander.'[195] She is, in other words, implying that her cultural loyalty is greater than his and that he is more suited to women's work than she is. Upon hearing her taunt he agreed to lead them.

The power that women could wield, even if outside of formal institutions, is reflected in their considerable impact in the religious conflicts of the sixteenth and seventeenth centuries. Some noblewomen upheld Catholicism in their clan territories, despite the Protestant allegiances of their chieftain husbands, providing support for the poorly financed Counter-Reformation which fought a 'guerrilla war' against the officially sponsored Protestant movement. On the other hand, Protestant women could be just as pivotal in Catholic areas, as can be seen in the history of the church in MacKay territory.[196]

Women wielded the bulk of their power in domestic realm; female aristocrats managed the estates and aspects of clan affairs, especially when their husbands were away, as they frequently were. Unique evidence for the life of aristocratic women in the Highlands has been uncovered in the recently edited letters of Katherine Ruthven, second wife of Cailean Liath Campbell of Breadalbane:

> Katherine's surviving correspondence reveals a woman who was extremely active in all of the affairs in which her husband was involved. Historians have tended to assume a subordinate and relatively passive role for Scottish noblewomen within early modern society. The evidence concerning Katherine's activities supports a much more positive assessment of the part they played in the sixteenth century. In particular, the political importance of a wife to her husband has been underestimated. Lady Glenorchy demonstrates just how vital a wife could be in securing her husband's political goals.[197]

Non-aristocratic women performed a majority of the manual labour in the Highlands, especially work that men considered undignified, such as dealing with goats, sheep, poultry, and cattle. The changes of the eighteenth and nineteenth century had a disproportionately negative effect on women: more women than men travelled for seasonal work (often agricultural labour with serious physical demands) in the Lowlands, and those women left at home while their peers worked abroad (and their menfolk were recruited into the British regiments, returning home impaired if they returned at all) had ever increasing loads to shoulder.[198] Anne Grant wrote about those changes as they were visible in 1787:

> You Lowlanders have no idea of the complicated nature of Highland farming, and of the odd customs which prevail there. Formerly, from the wild and warlike nature of the men, and their haughty indolence, they thought no rural employment compatible with their dignity, unless, indeed, the plough. Fighting, hunting, lounging in the sun, music, and poetry, were their occupations [. . .] This naturally extended the women's province both of labour and management. The care of the cattle was particularly theirs. [. . .] The effect, you know, often continues when the cause has ceased; the men are now civilized in comparison to what they were, yet the custom of leaving the weight of everything on the more helpless sex continues, and has produced this one good effect, that they are from this habit less helpless and dependent. The men think they preserve dignity by this mode of management; the women find a degree of power or consequence in having such an extensive department, which they would not willingly exchange for inglorious ease.[199]

Such hardships and gender-based inequities have contributed to the high level of female emigration from the Gàidhealtachd to the present, making it even more difficult for communities to sustain themselves.

Chapter Five

FAMILY AND PERSONAL LIFE

Servants, labourers and workmen of different kinds, make up the far greater part of every great political society. But what improves the circumstances of the greater part can never be regarded as an inconveniency to the whole. No society can surely be flourishing and happy, of which the far greater part of the members are poor and miserable. It is but equity, besides, that they who feed, clothe, and lodge the whole body of the people, should have such a share of the produce of their own labour as to be themselves tolerably well fed, clothed, and lodged.

– Adam Smith, 1776,
An Inquiry into the Nature and Causes of the Wealth of Nations

Role models offer examples of human achievement. Stories about heroes can exemplify the values, ethics, beliefs, behaviours, deeds, and principles deemed to be important to a society. A culture propagates itself from one generation to the next, at least in part, by inspiring the youth to follow the precedents offered by role models. For generations Scottish educational institutions have deprived children of the role models in Gaelic oral tradition – historical figures as well as fictional characters – and replaced them with those of the anglophone world. From the standard school curricula it is nearly impossible to imagine how to be a successful and fully realised human being and live within the Gaelic world at the same time, if indeed the Gàidhealtachd is even acknowledged to exist.[1]

One of the last pan-Gaelic heroes, Alasdair mac Colla, has been remembered and celebrated in song and story to the present day for his leadership of Irish and Scottish Gaels in Royalist forces in the 1640s. A legend about his childhood, recorded from Donald Black of Glendaruel, Argyll, *c.*1860, demonstrates the common patterns of 'heroic biography': his birth is accompanied by omens, he is precocious, he is the subject of prophecy, and so on. These vivid events also serve as milestones of his coming of age as a great warrior.

~

According to some oral traditions, Colla MacDonald, who was commonly called 'Colkitto', was married to a daughter of the Laird of Auchinbreck. The first home in which he lived was in Aird Chìrean Beag in Glendaruel, and it was there that his son Alasdair was born.

164

The people of Glendaruel say that on the night that Alasdair mac Colla was born every sword that was in the house jumped a little out of its sheath and every gun's trigger snapped. His father was ready to drown him on that very night for fear that he would grow to be an evil man. But his nursemaid intervened on his behalf and she said that he would be a mighty warrior one day and enjoy great success. Alasdair was then allowed to live.

When Alasdair mac Colla was a sturdy, young lad, he used to travel with his nursemaid. One day they went to the garden and Alasdair caught a poison toad and began to eat it. The nursemaid took it away from him. He became very cross, and yelled, and caused a loud uproar.

His grandfather heard him and went to see what was bothering him. He asked the nursemaid, 'What does he want?'

The nursemaid said, 'He caught a toad and I took it away from him, as he wants to eat it.'

His grandfather said, 'Give it to him, give it to him, and let the one devil eat the other.'

And she had to give the toad back to him again, and he ate it. But it did not poison him.

In the old days, some people had a tradition that they kept on Hallowe'en in which they would perform a ritual to see what luck would come to them in the future. On one evening they were performing auguries in the house of Colkitto, and Alasdair mac Colla's nursemaid went out to the kiln with a ball of blue yarn to determine Alasdair's fate.

When she returned to the house, said she to Alasdair, 'You will perform heroic deeds and you will win every battle until you plant your war-banner at the Mill of Gocam-gò, but after that, you will fail.'

Not much attention was paid to what she said at that time, but Alasdair always remembered [the name] the Mill of Gocam-gò.[2]

We all require the basic necessities of life – food, clothing, shelter, and so on – to survive, but the ways in which we meet those needs and integrate them into the rest of our experience is shaped by tradition. Only in the minds of the heirs of the Industrial Revolution is life a harsh struggle of survival against hostile elements, an unrelenting ascent up Maslow's hierarchy of needs. The universe, in the worldview of even the most 'primitive' peoples, is teeming with significance and wonder: basic resources are endowed with personalities and woven into myth and custom, and people do not need to consume exorbitant amounts of resources to consider themselves creative, confident, and contented.

Foodways – the culinary practices of folklife – provide an excellent example of how culture transforms even the most fundamental of human biological imperatives into more complex patterns and systems of meaning. All people need to eat to survive, yet two different cultures in the same environment will create differing beliefs, behaviours and customs around the same foodstuffs: they will transform raw materials into unique diets; they will create tabus about certain foods or ways of preparing them; they may refrain from eating altogether during religious fasts or serve special dishes during certain holidays or rites of passage; they will assign special meanings to particular foods or associate them with mythological characters. The primal need for sustenance thus becomes interpreted and embellished in complex ways.

This chapter discusses a few of the essential aspects of personal and family life in Scottish Gaelic tradition. These practices and beliefs help to give individuals a sense of worth and purpose, nurturing them along lifetime of growth and change, and enabling them all to participate in the transmission and generation of meaning. Given the material preoccupations of our age, it may be useful to point out that aesthetic expectations, communal integrity, and the bounds of tradition were often more important considerations in Highland society than the modern notions of efficiency, productivity, and private property. These were precisely the reasons why many agents of the central government argued that Gaelic society needed to be reformed if not destroyed altogether.

NAMES AND NAMING

Personal names illustrate how the distinctions between Gaelic and anglophone cultures have become obscured by practices of translation and the assumptions taken by those unaware of the historical complexities of that translation. While people generally assume that their surname indicates something about the clan affiliation and ancestral territory of their family, 'surnames of the present day can be unreliable, and even misleading, as evidence of family origins.'[3]

There are several different naming schemes in Gaelic society which determine how an individual is named and addressed, depending largely on the context.

1. First name and/or nickname, used within the family and home community
2. *Sloinneadh* 'patrilineal descent', used amongst those familiar with the family of origin
3. First name and surname used in official documents and outside of the community

Children were generally expected to be named after their forebears; according to traditional practice, the first son was named after his grandfather and the second after his father. As a result, a small number of names tend to recur in most families. As George Henderson noted in 1911, 'I find with many that it is a matter of extreme importance to call a child by the name of a deceased ancestor.' This practice is called *togail an ainm* 'raising the name' in Gaelic.[4] There are also traces in tradition of giving children names according to when they were born or other propitious signs. 'It is alleged (in Arran) to have been an ancient Highland custom, before surnames, to call a child by the name of the first thing which attracted the notice of the baptismal party on their way to church.'[5] The name of a MacLean leader, Maol Ìosa (anglicised as 'Malise'), was said to have be given in a similar fashion:

> His first name is somewhat peculiar, and not common among the MacLeans or any other West Highland clan, and was given to him in this manner. The heir of Torloisk was a promising healthy boy, but the succeeding children of the then chief were dying young. The Chief was then advised by the sages of his race to give to his child the name of the first person whom he met on the way to have the child baptized. The first person encountered was a poor beggar man who had the name of Malise. A name given in this way was known as *ainm-rathaid*, or road-name, and was deemed as proof against evil.[6]

It is not uncommon for more than one child in a family to share the same first name and there was typically a profusion of the same first name in any particular community. To distinguish between all of these individuals of the same name adjectives were often added to their first name. These adjectives could refer to hair colour (such as 'Raibeart Ruadh' for 'Red-haired Robert'), relative age to distinguish between generations (such as 'Aonghus Òg' for 'Young Angus' or 'Domhnall Beag' for 'Little Donald'), distinctive features (such as 'Ailean Breac' for 'Pock-marked Allan' or 'Ruairidh Dall' for 'Blind Rory'), occupation (such as 'Niall Gobha' for 'Neil the Smith'), or the place of origin or fosterage (such as 'Iain Mùideartach' for 'Iain of Moydart' or 'Raghnall Gallda' for 'Foreign Ranald').[7] A nickname (*frith-ainm, far-ainm*, or *leas-ainm*) serves to identify a person uniquely and often eclipses the given first name of a person for life. It typically refers to a childhood anecdote, a distinguishing characteristic, or a memorable event. It is used most often within a community, but sometimes travels with the individual outside of his home area.

The *sloinneadh*, a line of (normally male) ancestors listed by first name, is the formal means of fully identifying a person in Highland society. A complete sloinneadh lists at least seven generations and sometimes more, suggesting the importance of ancestors in a person's own individual identity. A sloinneadh is, however, most useful to those who know the history of families in a community.

As already mentioned in Chapter Four, surnames were first used by the élite and arose as fossilised styles based on the name of the founder of a dynasty, such as MacDonald 'Son of Domhnall', MacNeill 'Son of Niall' and MacLean 'Son of Gille Sheathain'. There are other Highland surnames, however, which are derived from the epithet of the founder of a family, such as Gow (*Gobha*, 'Smith'), Roy (*Ruadh*, 'Red-haired'), and Cameron (*Camshron*, 'Crooked Nose').

Generally, only the élite used surnames as such before the eighteenth century; there was no particular need for surnames in the day-to-day lives of the commonality of the Highlanders. Edmund Burt remarked in the 1720s, 'Thus the surnames, being useless for distinction of persons, are suppressed, and there remain only the Christian names.'[8]

Surnames were little used in Gairloch in old times [. . .] To the present day surnames are little used in Gairloch when Gaelic is being spoken, and even in English a number of men are often called by the equivalents of their Gaelic names. [. . .] In each of these cases the individual is either a Mackenzie, Urquhart, or Macleannan, but is never so called by his neighbours.[9]

Although Highlanders knew a great deal about their ancestors and lines of descent, the surnames of the non-élite were easily lost and exchanged in the oral-dominant Highlands for a number of reasons. First, tenants and dependants were sometimes assigned (or assumed to have) the surname of their chieftain. 'When a person changed his name to that of some other clan, or powerful chief, he was said to accept the name and clanship (*ainm 's a chinneadhdas*).'[10] Second, some families assumed new surnames for purposes of enhancing their prestige or evading their past. Finally, a family who had relocated were sometimes given the surname of the chieftain dominant in their territory of origin, even if it had not been their own. A family who had emigrated from Mull might be assumed to be MacLeans by their new neighbours and so called, regardless of their actual ancestry.[11]

The intrusion of the paperwork of the state and various forms of bureaucracy imposed the need for universal surnames. Those who first committed those names to written form (usually parish ministers or estate managers) were not always literate in Gaelic and their writings were intended for an English-speaking readership. Attempts to render Gaelic into English without uniform principles resulted in ambiguities, corruptions and confusions. Names continued to change form into the nineteenth century. Some people removed the 'Mac' from their surname or exchanged it with '-son' to distance themselves from their Highland ancestry. An original Gaelic name such as 'MacGill'Ìosa' ('The Son of the Servant of Jesus') can be found today in numerous anglicised forms such as M'Gleish, MacLeish, Gillies, and Lees.[12]

What appears to be a single surname can have multiple origins. Even within the Highlands, a surname like MacGill'Ìosa could belong to numerous families derived from distinct founders who bore the same first name. Adding to the confusion are the 'false friends' that look like Highland names but originate elsewhere. The personal name 'Giles' was popular in France and came to the Lowlands as a surname in the Middle Ages; the name 'Leys' has its own history in the Lowlands. Both of these names can be easily mistaken as derived from the Gaelic surname MacGill'Ìosa.

The last Highland *clàrsair* 'Gaelic-harp player' and his family will serve as an example of naming practices. He is still known in Gaelic by his nickname 'An Clàrsair Dall' ('The Blind Harper') and his formal Gaelic name 'Ruaidhri Dall MacMhuirich' (given English form as Roderick Morison). The first few names in his *sloinneadh* are Ruaidhri Dall mac Iain mhic Mhurchaidh mhic Ailein mhic Iain Duibh. He came from a family called in Lewis 'Sliochd a' Bhreitheimh' ('The Progeny of the Lawman') because they had attended to legal matters for the MacLeods of Lewis and probably the Lords of the Isles before that.[13]

In Lowland Scotland, lairds were called by the land to which they had title, such as 'Lord of Leslie', 'Fairfield', and so on. This practice was adopted in the styles of Highland chieftains in English, especially because this allowed the heads of a clan with many branches to be distinguished from one another, such as 'MacLeod of Raasay' and 'MacLeod of Dunvegan'. These styles came into usage in Gaelic, both as surname-place compounds such as 'MacCoinnich Chinn t-Sàile' ('Mackenzie of Kintale'), and 'MacGriogair o Ruadhshruth' ('MacGregor of Roro'), and as title-place compounds such as 'Rìgh Innse Gall' ('King of the Hebrides'), 'Tighearna Labhair' ('The Laird of Lawers') and 'Fear Bhròlais' ('The Laird of Brolas'). It was more common in Gaelic, however, for chieftains to be called by a fossilised patronymic derived from their branch founder, sometimes in conjunction with the place name of the chieftain's seat. The chieftains of the branches of the MacDonalds, for example, were known by the styles 'Mac 'ic Ailein' ('MacDonald of Clanranald'), 'Mac 'ic Alasdair' ('MacDonald of Knoydart'), 'Mac Iain' ('MacDonald of Glencoe'), and so on.

FAMILY AND CLAN LIFE

Despite the disapproval of Lowland and English writers, there is little evidence to suggest that ordinary Highlanders wished to live in anything other than a kin-oriented society. A Gaelic proverb makes the analogy 'Is miann le triubhas a bhith a-measg aodaich, ach is miann leam fhéin a bhith a-measg mo dhaoine' ('Trousers like to be amongst clothes, but it is my wish to be amongst my people').[14] Life was more fulfilling and richer for sharing it: 'Is sona gach cuid an comaidh; is mairg a chromadh 'na aonar ('Everything shared brings happiness; pity he who stoops by himself').[15] The loosening of these ties has been distressing to many Gaels: 'In these modern times I often hear the horrid and unnatural assertion that it is disagreeable having one's relatives all round one. So much for the culture of the twentieth century!'[16]

Ancestry is a prevailing concern of many societies, for the characteristics of ancestors are believed to be passed on to their descendants. Inherited qualities, skills, and dispositions were thought to be overriding factors in life: 'Is buaine dùthchas na oilean' ('Inheritance is more lasting than what is learnt').[17] Gnomic lore underscores the obligation to respect ancestors and follow ancestral precedent: 'Cuimhnich air na daoine bhon tànaig thu' ('Remember the people from who you descend'); 'Lean gu dlùth ri cliù do shinnsre' ('Follow closely to the reputation of your ancestors').[18]

Values and proper conduct were reinforced by the repetition of traditional songs and tales. The Fian, in particular, were the celebrities and role models of Gaeldom who exemplified the virtues or behaviours listed in many Gaelic proverbs: 'Bha dorus Fhinn do'n ànrach fial' ('Fionn's door was always generous to the traveller'), 'Cha do thréig Fionn riamh caraid a làimhe deise' ('Fionn never abandoned his right-hand friend'), 'Cothrom na Féinne' ('The opportunity of the Fian', an expression meaning 'fair play'), and so on.[19]

Parents were responsible for the proper raising of their children: 'An leanabh a dh'fhàgar dha fhéin, cuiridh e a mhàthair gu nàire' ('The child who is left to himself will bring shame to his mother'). In practice, however, the extended kin-group and community were involved in the process. Parents were dependent upon their peers and children in their old age: 'Is mairg aig am bi comhdhaltas gann agus clann gun rath' ('Pity those without close compatriots and whose children have no success').[20]

Children were expected to respect their elders: 'Young people are bred, not only with a profound reverence for their parents, but with a kind of implicit confidence in the elders of their tribe.'[21] Being accused of disrespecting parents was an insult. The reverence for ancestors is demonstrated by the Highland custom of swearing by the hand of one's father or grandfather.[22]

It was vital to instil an understanding of honour in children while they were young so that they would not bring shame upon themselves and their kin: 'B' fhearr a bhith gun bhreith na bhith gun teagasg' ('It would be better to have never been born than to be untaught').[23] Another proverb, 'Ciall bà buachaille' ('The sense of a cow is [determined by] the herdsman'), was said of children who behaved poorly because of inadequate supervision.[24] Such discipline not only led to mastery of oneself, but success in life: 'Am fear a thug buaidh air fhéin, thug e buaidh air nàmhaid' ('The man who has conquered himself has conquered his enemy').[25]

On other hand, other gnomic lore suggests that children not be excessively restricted but be given a reasonable degree of freedom. The proverb 'Léintean farsaing do na leanaban òga' ('Loose shirts for the young children')[26] symbolises the importance of giving children freedom and room to grow according to their own needs. Another expression, 'Is fheairrde brà breacadh gun a ro-bhreacadh' ('It is best if the pecking of the quern is not overdone'), was used metaphorically of raising children: while it was necessary to chastise misbehaviour, it was recognised as counter-productive to be overly harsh.[27] The first schools to operate widely in the Highlands, established by the Society for the Propagation of Christian Knowledge in the early eighteenth century, broke with social precedent concerning punishment of children. 'What was likely to be new to many ordinary Highland people at this period was the idea that a complete stranger could enter the community and brutalise their children in the interests of teaching them English, arithmetic and the Catechism.'[28]

Children naturally like to be included in the activity of adults and were encouraged to participate in work and contribute to the efforts of the community, even if these were just symbolic gestures. 'The same philosophy appears in the practice of a child carrying a *ceann-rèidh*, a token sheaf of corn, on his back at the time when the harvest was being transferred to the barns for winter.'[29]

> The boys learned how to make and repair the milking and dairy utensils, to tend the flocks, shear [sic] the sheep, make and mend their own shoes; and to thatch, and make the heather and hair ropes so largely used by them; and perhaps the most desired part of their education was the shooting of a blackcock, the stalking of a deer, and the spearing of a salmon.

The girls learned to emulate their mothers in skill of the dairy work, as well as in spinning wool for future webs on the distaff, and knitting stockings and hose of brilliant hues and rare patterns. They learned to know the herbs that were medicinal for man and beast, and the different plants used in dyeing the colours of their tartans. They learned to become useful wives, following in the footsteps of their mothers, as helpmates in the struggle for existence, neither fearing the snows and storms of winter, nor ashamed of the tawning of the summer sun.[30]

Adults had plenty of responsibilities of their own. A good wife had be capable of not only doing many different kinds of tasks, but to 'multitask' them: 'Cas air creathail, làmh air cuigeil, comharradh air deagh bhean taighe' ('The signs of a good wife are a foot on the cradle and a hand on the spindle'). The value and importance of a wife in contributing to the family is attested to in the proverb, 'Is fhearr ban ghlic na crann is fearann' ('A prudent wife is better than a plough and land').[31] The husband was responsibile for providing her with the necessary resources: 'Cha dèanar banas-taighe air na fraighean falamh' ('Housekeeping can't be done with empty shelves').[32]

Extended families often lived together, sharing limited living quarters and material possessions. Each bed was typically shared by several family members and an endearing rhyme describes how they could arrange themselves geometrically: 'Tòin ri tòin / cadal nan ròn / Mionach ri màs / cadal nan spàin' ('Back to back is the sleep of the seals; front against back is the sleep of the spoons').[33] Poverty can be as much a state of mind as an objective measurement, and Reverend John Buchanan remarks on the attempts of Gaels to hold their heads high despite deteriorating conditions at the end of the eighteenth century:

> In defiance of the hardships these oppressed people suffer, they retain part of their former state and dignity, at their meetings and partings. They address one another by the title of gentleman or lady (*duin' uasal* or *a' bhean uasal*) and embrace one another most cordially, with bonnets off. And they are never known to enter a door without blessing the house and people so loud as to be heard, and embracing every man and woman belonging to the family. They both give and receive news, and are commonly entertained with the best fare their entertainers are able to afford.[34]

STAGES OF LIFE

Life is a constant process of growth, maturation, and revelation, from the joyous appearance of an individual at birth to the certainty of their loss at death. Every culture recognises different stages of life and has ways of marking the transition of the individual from one stage to the next, often by 'rite of passage' ceremonies. Most rites of passage can be analysed as consisting of three phases:

1. the separation of the individual from his previous environment and social role

2. the transition of the individual while in a state symbolically removed from profane reality, social norms and mundane time
3. the re-integration of the individual into the community, acknowledging his new state and the return to social norms

The period of transition is often viewed as a *liminal state* – a condition of being in-between – when normal restrictions and social constraints are relaxed. In Gaelic rites of passage, re-integration into the community typically includes the sharing of food and drink and the performance of song composed for the event.

Sacred Reality

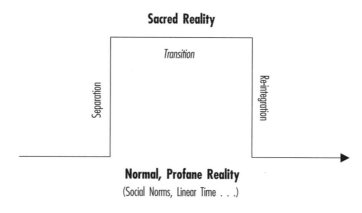

Figure 5.1: A schema of rites of passage

The most important rites of passage in Highland society centred on birth, baptism, marriage, and death. There was not a strict script for any of these events, but they tended to include a common set of elements used in similar patterns across Gaelic Scotland (and Ireland). While these were performed by people who had long been Christianised and considered themselves to be Christian, many of the beliefs and practices of these rites of passage reflect older cosmological traditions that were at odds with the strict interpretations of Christianity. While secular Gaelic society remained resilient, the church was not able to displace traditional practices from the scattered congregations in its remit. The customs documented in the seventeenth and eighteenth centuries were hybrids of ancestral traditions and prescribed church practices; tensions over control of such rituals and their meaning were particularly pronounced at birth and at death.[35]

The rituals surrounding birth typically included:

- Preparation (unlocking locks)
- Predictions about the child from day and hour of birth, other signs
- **Separation**
  - The child is born (separating him physically from his mother)

- **Transition**
  - First rites of welcome
  - Saining (providing magical protection to) mother and child

The process of giving birth was dangerous for obvious reasons: childbirth is a common cause of death of women in non-industrial societies. The *bean-ghlùine* 'midwife' was trained to assist with birthing and was usually a mother herself. The immediate physical danger of childbirth was paralleled by anxieties about the spiritual well-being of the mother and child. Women in childbed and newly born infants were believed to be particularly vulnerable to being stolen by the fairies and replaced with changelings (see Chapter Six). They were under constant supervision and had special rites and charms administered to them for their protection. The advantage of this anxiety and supervision is that any medical complications that a woman or infant might have would be quickly noticed and attended to. The child was not considered safe from Otherworld harm until he had been baptised, and his name was not said aloud until after it had been officially conferred upon him at the baptism.[36] 'A child's name must not be used till it gets it by baptism; it has no name till then. It is not safe from evil powers or the fairies till christened.'[37]

A child was often welcomed into the world by being plunged into cold water, the shock of which started him breathing. There were other common rites of welcome for infant and mother: fire was carried sun-wise around them as further protection from malicious beings; the first food given to an infant in some areas was the sap from a stick of ash, a custom reminiscent of many around the world in which a newborn is given a token of the Tree of Life. Others established gender roles: 'When a Male is born they put a sword or knife in his hand, and a spindle or a Rock i.e. Distaff into the hand of a female.'[38] Amongst the signs read about the baby's birth were those that indicated that he or she had the potential to heal other members of the community.[39]

An extensive passage on birth customs comes from John Ramsay of Ochtertyre in the late 1700s:

Thus it was a received notion that a lying-in woman [i.e., newly given birth] should never be left alone, for fear the fairies should steal her away, and substitute something in her room. Yet this notion, though seemingly ridiculous, was in the main sensible, since it secured her against the giddiness or neglect of her attendants. Before the Highlanders were disarmed it was common to have a broadsword half drawn at the head of the bed or below the bolster. And on the north-east coast it is the first business of a mid-wife to set a lighted candle at each corner of the bed; whilst in other [parts of Scotland] she takes a light or fiery peat and draws a circle thrice round the lying-in woman, moving it *deiseil* – i.e., according to the course of the sun. This rite was not, however, peculiar to this occasion, being used by the Highlanders in many of their superstitions.

In some districts, so soon as the child is born the midwife ties a straw round its middle and then cuts it in three pieces. A live coal, or some sparks of fire, are commonly thrown into the water in which the infant is first bathed; and in Skye they throw a little of the water into the fire. It is usual in Breadalbane to put the end of a new-cut ash stick into the fire, and to receive with a spoon the juice which then gushes out at the other end, a little of which is the first liquor put into the mouth of the new-born infant. It is uncertain whether this was done medicinally or with a superstitious view.[40]

The child's (and mother's) re-integration into the community was not complete until after the baptismal ritual was performed. This was reflected by the restriction of the mother from visiting the community: 'When a child was born the mother was never wanted in any house until her child had been baptized, as her entry meant very bad luck for the house so entered.'[41] Baptism was a rite of passage which gave the child its name and the recognition of its existence by the church. Due to the perennial shortage of clergy in the Highlands and the belief that children should be christened within a week and a day of being born, forms of lay baptism survived into the eighteenth century, if not later.[42]

The rites surrounding baptism commonly consisted of the following elements:

- **Separation**
  - Child is taken from home to church
    - Gift given to first person encountered
    - Omens read on journey (e.g., ainm-rathaid 'road-name')
- **Transition**
  - Child baptised
  - Child given name
- **Re-integration**
  - Baptism feast
  - Omens read about child's future
  - Visitors and friends give silver to child

Poem fourteen in Appendix A is a rare relic from a baptismal ceremony. It mentions the name given to the child, the baptism itself, and a traditional ritual for looking into the child's future (a theme also echoed in the tale of Alasdair mac Colla in the beginning of this chapter). Alexander MacBain notes some of the practices surrounding baptism in the late nineteenth century and strict observations of gender:

> In going to baptism with a child, take a piece of bread, and give it to the first person you meet. Some restrict this to the first man, if the child is a boy; to the first woman, if a girl. It is a bad sign if a child does not cry on being baptised. If a boy and a girl are baptised together, the boy must be baptised first, otherwise he would want his beard when grown up, and the girl would have it.[43]

The baptismal rite itself usually involved the *goistidh* 'gossip, godfather, sponsor' and *ban-ghoistidh* 'female gossip, godmother, female sponsor' of the child.

> The baptism of infants was considered a very important ceremony in Cantyre; for, in addition to its scriptural import, it was thought to be a temporal charm. Some people imagined that a child would not grow unless it were baptized, and all were of the opinion that it was bad luck to have an unbaptized child in the house. [. . .] The celebration of the baptism ceremony was attended with a great display of hospitality on the part of the parents, who invited their friends and neighbours to the christening feast. A jar of whisky having been provided, sponsors were chosen, whom they called 'goistie' and 'banna-goistie'. The care of the whisky was entrusted to the 'goistie', and the 'banna-goistie' (or female gossip) had the charge of the eatables. The infant was then given up by the 'bonheen' (ailing mother) to the company, and was carried away to the church or to the minister's house.[44]

Many heroic tales elucidate the processes of social maturation implicitly. The tales of the Fian derive at least part of their popularity because of their exploration of male development from youth to adulthood and of the alternating poles of existence between life in the 'wild' and life in domesticated society. The term *fian* is derived from the same Indo-European root which produces Latin *venari* 'to hunt' and English 'win'. 'In many cultures, hunting and warring in the wilderness constitute the designated vocation of the young male on the verge of manhood.'[45] There are references to games of the Fian which appear to be aggressive competitions between young men; initiation into Fian bands required passing strenuous tests.[46]

The summer months when the women would be tending and milking the cattle in the mountains were an ideal time for romantic trysts. The shielings serve as the setting of many songs of courtship.[47] Well into the twentieth century in some areas, courtship during the winter was commonly done in the homes of young women by 'bundling'. The daughter's family were better to be involved in the process of wooing than to try to avert the passions of youth. The more cautious parents inserted their daughter's legs into a securely tied stocking; with this precaution was in place, she was allowed to sleep with her sweetheart under their roof.[48]

> Till about forty or fifty years ago, bundling, or a young man and woman being put to bed together by their parents, was very common; but such were the customs and manners of the country, that if the woman was with child, the man was reckoned a scoundrel, and none would have any dealings with him if he did not marry her. On the other hand, if there was no child in the case, they dissuaded him from marrying, and thought there was no harm done.[49]

Other courtships happened without parental supervision and resulted in pregnancies. Although the church was increasingly censorious of sexual relations outside of marriage, secular Highland society did not burden women or their offspring with heavy stigmas until the nineteenth century.

> The common, as well as the better sort of people, court sweet-hearts at nights, over all this country. The unlocked doors yield those lovers but too easy access to their favourites. The natural consequences of their rencounters often occasion squabbles in kirk courts, in which minister and elders take cognizance of the fornication committed in the parish. [. . .] The woman, if she is pregnant by a gentleman, is by no means looked down upon, but is provided in a husband with greater eclat than without forming such a connection. Instead of being despised, numberless instances can be produced, where pregnant women have been disputed for, and even fought for, by the different suitors.[50]

The non-élite had a great deal of freedom in selecting partners, especially when families were not concerned about the political and economic consequences, and this became truer of the élite as well in the seventeenth century.[51]

> But there is hardly any country where parental authority is more passive than there. People marry very early, and without much regard to circumstances and hence their union is generally the effect of mutual liking [. . .] Nor have parents the same reasons for crossing their children's affections as in countries where there is a greater inequality of circumstances [. . .] It is, however, reckoned dutiful to consult them before entering into that state, because they may thereby expect their blessing, and a share of the little they have.[52]

In 1215 Canon Law sought to define and regulate marriage throughout Christendom, prohibiting unions within four degrees of kinship and requiring the presence of clergy and witnesses for the marriage to be recognised as 'regular'. A series of church pronouncements from the thirteenth century through the sixteenth century attempting to eradicate 'irregular' marriage practices demonstrates how difficult it was to convince people of such restrictions and enforce them, especially as the élite married within a fairly small pool of candidates. After the Reformation restrictions relaxed to allow unions greater than two degrees of kinship and by the eighteenth century the church stopping trying to police marriage practices altogether.[53]

The full set of Gaelic marriage customs consisted of several stages, each successive stage becoming increasingly binding (in social and legal terms) and involving a wider segment of the community. Wedding practices typically consisted of the following elements:

- *Còrdadh / Réiteach Beag* 'Initial proposal'
- **Separation:** *Réiteach (Mór)* 'Betrothal'
  - Parties meet at sacred mound or bride's house

176

- Verbal sparring and negotiations for dowry
- (If groom's spokesman successful) Bride sits with groom, drink from same glass
- Declaration of banns (in church or public place), make entry in registry book
- Ritual blackening/cleansing of bride and groom
- Faoighe 'thigging' to gather initial capital for family
- **Transition:** *Banais(-taighe)* 'Wedding ceremony'
  - Minister's blessing
  - Cake/bread broken over bride's head
  - Contention for good-luck token (kiss, oatcake, stocking, etc.)
  - Marriage feast
    - Toast to couple
    - Poetic contributions or contests
  - Dance
    - Bride's maids take away bride secretly to bed chamber
    - Groom's friends take away groom
  - Bedding of couple
    - Community puts couple into bed
    - Ritual counteraction against spells
- **Re-integration**
  - Married women place marriage mutch on bride
  - Bride is welcomed in verse

In normal circumstances, a man and woman would have been courting and mutually ready for marriage. The *còrdadh* and *réiteach beag* were the occasions when the suitor informed his sweetheart or her father that he intended to approach her family for a full, formal betrothal, called the *réiteach* (*mór*). In some cases, however, men went seeking brides whom they had never met, on the advice of others; such circumstances presented the possibility of failure during the negotiations of the réiteach. This ritual emphasised both the consent of the bride and her family to marry before public witnesses, and also fixed her *tochradh* 'dowry'.

In the most archaic observances, the réiteach was held on a high summit, suggesting the ancient sacred associations of the *sìdhean* 'fairy mound';[54] it was done otherwise at the home of the wooed woman once the suitor's party earned entrance. Negotiations were done on behalf of the suitor by the *gille-suiridhich* 'courtship-helper, best man', who would extol the virtues of his client eloquently and mediate the delicate arrangements between families so that the suitor himself could not be accused of being forward, overbearing, or acquisitive. The potential bride's family sometimes had their own spokesperson who fulfilled a similar function.

The réiteach was a humorous verbal game of skill in which the woman's family held off the suitor (and his spokesman) for as long as possible, pretending that they knew neither the purpose nor the subject of the suitor's visit. Rather than being a direct and explicit request for the daughter's hand in marriage, the gille-suiridhich played a verbal game in which the potential bride was represented as a possession of the father which the suitor had come to purchase, such as livestock or valuable goods. All of the women of the family, even community, would be offered to the suitor and rejected in turn, often with wry sarcasm. If the best man was successful and won the consent of the woman and her family, she sat down next to the suitor and drank from the same celebratory glass with him as the entire household toasted to their future together. The réiteach is depicted in a clan saga about two rival suitors in Argyll recorded in the mid nineteenth century:

> They knocked at the door and Mackellar cried, 'Who is there at the door?'
> Macvicar replied, 'A friend. Let us in.'
> Mackellar said, 'If you are friends, I will let you in,' so he opened the door and let them in.
> Then the goodwife arose and lighted the lamp. One of those that accompanied Macvicar took a bottle of whisky out of his pocket and said to the goodwife, 'Have you a quaich?' She said, 'Yes,' and she got a quaich for him. He filled the quaich and offered it to her, saying, 'Here, goodwife, drink to us.'
> She said, 'But I shall know first before I drink, why I am going to drink?'
> Macvicar of Dail-chruinneachd said, 'We are building a house in Dail-chruin-neachd and putting a [roof-]couple in it; we have one side of the couple, and we have heard that Mackellar of Mam has a tree that would make the other side of the couple; so we have come to try whether he will give it to us.'
> Mackellar inquired of what kind of wood the half-couple that he had was.
> 'It is oak,' said Macvicar.
> 'The couple that I have,' remarked Mackellar, 'is ash, and these kinds of wood do not fit each other. Oak lasts much longer than ash.'
> 'Ash,' rejoined Macvicar, 'lasts long also, if it is kept dry, but I rather suspect that your half-couple is oak too. I do not think that you have looked at it properly.' [. . .]
> 'She is there herself,' said the goodman, 'and ask her, first, if she is willing.'
> Macvicar's spokesman then said to Effie, 'And are you willing yourself, Effie?'
> Effie replied, 'If I had the goodwill of my parents, I should be very willing myself.'
> Her mother rejoined, 'If you agree yourselves I will not put between you.'
> 'And indeed, I will not put between them either,' said her father.[55]

The metaphor of the bride and groom as roof beams who uphold the structure of a house is an apt one that recurs in other dialogues recorded of the réiteach, for it symbolises how both rely upon each other to create the support and shelter of a household.[56] The successful conclusion of the réiteach moves the bride and groom into a liminal state between betrothal and marriage. As in many other cultures, the bride and groom were guarded and sometimes given ritual restrictions until the wedding occurred.[57] The couple began thigging after the betrothal was complete, but sometimes not until after the wedding itself.

The moon was believed to exert an influence over all living things so the luckiest time for a wedding was during a full moon. Tuesdays and Thursdays were also seen as favourable days for the réiteach and the wedding. Aeneas Mackintosh described how people in the Central Highlands celebrated weddings in the eighteenth century:

As soon as the partys have agreed upon the Day of Marriage the Clerk of the parish (sometimes the Parson) is sent for, and in the presence of their mutual Relations, a Writing called the Contract is signed, whereby the Parties bind themselves to marry, and in case of nonperformance (without just cause) to pay such a sum as is thought proper. The night before Marriage the Ceremony of feet washing is performed at the Bride and Bride Grooms own Lodgings; among the Men it is an excuse for drinking. Next morning, being dressed, the Bridegroom first (preceded by a Bag pipe,) having a young man on each side of him, next comes the Bride with her two Maids, proceed for Church; when the ceremony is over, and the partys come out, pistols and guns are fired over their heads by their acquaintances who then join, and a Cake broke over the Bride's head, when a great Struggle is made for a piece of it.

Upon their Return a Dinner is ready, Several Cows and Sheep being frequently killed for that purpose. When it is over the Bride Groom goes round the Guests with a plate, when every one gives according to his Inclination, and if the Bride and Bridegroom are liked, they get as much as will enable them to stock their farm. The Lord of the Manor frequently attends in order to encourage Matrimony, formerly for different Reasons (*vide Buchannon*) which custom was taken off by the intercession of Margaret, a pious and vertuous Queen, the Bridegroom paying one Merk (as *Marcheta Mulierum*). I have been frequently well entertained at them when a Company of young people have scampered to them from Moyhall.

The Country people sometimes dance to a pipe, but oftener to the fiddle. At the commencement and finishing of each Reel or Dance the Swains kiss their Nymphs. The fiddler receives one penny for each Dance. The Highlanders have a sort of Dance performed by two people, bearing a great Resemblance to the Spanish Fandango. The Company continue dancing and drinking till the hour for the young peoples going to bed, when the whole accompany them to the Barn (for they are not allowed to sleep in the house the first night). All the men remain on the outside till the Bride is undressed, then, (the Bridegroom being undressed) they kiss the Bride, and after untying the latch of the left shoe which they imagine will take away the power from Witches, of preventing the Man from performing the marriage Rites (*ut vim coeundi ni fallor viris tollerent*) and also lock the Door, the key of which is deliver'd to the Bride's Mother.

Next morning it formerly was the Custom to ty a Basketfull of Stones round the Man's neck to show his Strength, for the cutting away of which the young Woman had a sharp knife. It was and is still a Custom to make the husband drunk the second night, that the Wife might know how to treat him on similar occasions. The wedding continues several Days. If the young Couple are very poor, they frequently went round the country to Thigg, which is a gentle name for begging, when the farmers gave corn, and Shepherds sheep to stock the farm. The first work the married woman undertook was making her winding sheet, which put her in mind of mortality.[58]

The celebration of marriage and the concerns of reproduction were such community affairs that the whole party participated in the bedding of the new couple. William Stewart describes in the mid nineteenth century how the bride is stolen away during the dance to be bedded:

Wishing, if possible, to elude the public gaze, she attempts to steal away privately, when, observed by some vigilant eye, her departure is announced, and all push to the bridal chamber. The door is instantly forced open, and the devoted bride, divested of all her braws, and stripped nearly to the state of nature, is placed in bed in presence of the whole company. Her left stocking is then flung, and falls upon some individual, whose turn to the hymeneal altar will be the next. The bridegroom, next led in, is as rapidly demolished, and cosily stowed alongside of his darling. A bottle and glass being then handed to the bridegroom, he rewards the friendliness of those who come forward to offer their congratulations, with a flowing bumper. When the numerous levee have severally paid their court, they retire, and leave the young couple to repose.[59]

It was believed that jealous rivals of either bride or groom might employ magic to prevent the couple from conceiving children; the couple and their family and friends resorted to counter-spells and other practices to counteract such malicious intentions, as John Ramsay explains:

At the celebration of marriage there was a custom in some parts of the Highlands of leaving the latchet of the bridegroom's left shoe loose, and of putting a piece of silver under his heel. The purpose of it was to prevent the effect of charms and incantations.[60]

The last stages of the wedding ceremony are described in a song from nineteenth-century Cowal, along with a toast to the future of the young couple:

> *Nuair bha gach nì ullamh,*
> *Do'n leabaidh chaidh an cupall,*
> *Is chruinnich a' chuideachd ud uile le chéile;*
> *Le aighear, le furan,*
> *Le botal, le cupan,*
> *Tost leapaich gun tug iad 's gun cuir mi e 'n céill:*

> *'Gun gluais sibh 's an fhìrinn*
> *An ceumannan dìreach*
> *Bithibh stuaimeil is sìobhailt 's na dìobairibh céill;*
> *Ur sliochd-sa biodh lìonmhor*
> *Feadh glacan na tìre*
> *'S ur n-iar-oghachan chì sibh a' dìreadh ur ceum.*[61]

('When everything was ready, the couple went to bed and all of that company gathered together; With joy and hospitality, with a bottle and a cup, they gave a bedding-toast which I will recite for you:')

(' "May you travel in the truth on the straight path; be moderate and civil and never abandon reason; may your progeny be numerous throughout the land, and you will see your great-grandchildren following in your footsteps." ')

The mother of the bride greeted her the next morning and arranged her hair in the *bréid beannach* 'pointed coif', indicating her status as a married woman. After this ritual conferring of marital status some poet recited a blessing to her in verse, praising her beauty in the new headdress and giving her advice about marriage.

The following blessing was addressed to a bride on the day after her marriage, as she came forth with her maidens from the bridal bed. According to custom she gave a dram to all the bridal party, and in return each member of the party presented her with some article to be of future use, and the bard usually administered the blessing.[62]

Numerous proverbs suggest that people accepted death as the inevitable conclusion of the progression of life: 'Feumaidh an talamh a chuid fhéin' ('The earth, i.e., the grave, will get its own'); 'Am fear a gheibh gach latha bàs, 's e as fhearr a bhitheas beò' ('The man who finds death each day is the man who lives best').[63] People began preparing for their fate immediately after their wedding was over. 'It is a curious practice of newly married women to commence spinning and preparing linen for their shroud.'[64] Customs associated with death were particularly poignant, however, because they represented not just the next stage in the life of an individual but a potential crisis to an entire community.

Death and burial rituals in the Highlands tended to consist of the following elements:

- Portents of death seen or heard beforehand
- Last rites (if possible)
- **Separation I**
  - Death (i.e., soul is parted from body)
  - Clocks stopped, windows opened, mirrors covered or removed

- **Transition**
  - The body is prepared (closing eyes, washing, changing clothes)
  - Body is placed in coffin or bier
  - Wake
    - Body is watched especially at night
    - People pay respects to the deceased
    - Wake games, storytelling, keening, dance
- **Separation II**
  - Funeral procession from home to the burial site led by keening women, bagpipes or bell
- **Re-integration**
  - Body laid in the earth
  - Funeral feast

The transition from profane reality to sacred reality is represented by the stopping of clocks and the 'unseemly' social chaos that erupted at wakes. John Ramsay provides copious notes about funeral customs in the Highlands in the late eighteenth century:

No sooner did a person die than those about him lifted the body from the bed. And after being stretched, it was laid at full length on a board or plank of wood, set either on stools or two timber pins placed on the side of the wall; and above it, at some distance, another board was suspended from the roof, over which a plaid or other piece of cloth was thrown, which hung down like a canopy. When it became dark, candles or lights were set on the upper board. And it was also the custom to lay some iron, cheese, a plate with salt, and sometimes a green turf, on the dead person's breast. Some of these things were perhaps used to prevent the corpse from swelling; but the salt, the iron, and the cheese, intimate some purpose of superstition. [. . .]

Between this period and that of interment, the friends and neighbours of the deceased assembled at night in the chamber where the corpse was laid. This was called *Faire-mhairbh*, or the late wake. The manner in which the Highlanders formerly behaved on these occasions must appear to strangers indecent and unnatural. During this period, nothing went on in the house of mourning but dancing and other amusements. [. . .]

Upon the day of the burial, both men and women attended in great numbers. In old times it was the practice in the West Highlands (as it is still in Ireland) to hire women as mourners at the funerals of people of distinction. The females who were invited commonly sat in a cluster by themselves upon a neighbouring eminence till the corpse was brought out and laid upon two stools at the door. As soon as it appeared the women flocked around it, clapping their hands and raising hideous cries. And many of them tore their hair or head-dress, and shed tears plentifully.

The corpse was then put on a bier and carried successively by four men on their shoulders; the rest followed – a piper, or perhaps a number of pipers – playing some melancholy tune all the way before them. The chieftain's march was commonly the first played after they set out, and the last was one peculiarly plaintive [. . .] The women kept behind the men, bewailing at intervals, in broken extempore verses, the dead man; and praising him for his birth, his achievements in war, his activity as a sportsman, and for his generous hospitality and compassion to the distressed. This was called the *coronach* – i.e., the dirge. The women of each valley through which they passed joined in the procession, but they attended but a part of the way, and then returned. Even female passengers who accidently met the funeral joined in the coronach, though perhaps strangers to the deceased. [. . .]

As soon as the burial people approached the place of interment, two men were despatched before to mark out the grave. And when the corpse arrived, it was carried *deiseil* – i.e., according to the course of the sun – around the spot which had been chosen. After this ceremony, the body was laid down hard by; the pipers then gave over, the grave was dug, and the tartan plaid or other covering taken off. When the body was put into the earth, the women raised the coronach for a few minutes louder than ever, and then were silent. And after the grave was closed, the whole company sat down in the churchyard, and every person was served with meat, and liquor out of shells.

The coronach seems to have no connection with that mode of Christianity which was professed by the Highlanders before the Reformation. On the contrary, we are told the Popish clergy were at pains to discountenance it, as being highly indecent. [. . .] The coronach is not practiced now in any part of the Highlands or Isles. Upon the west coast, and in the neighbouring islands, it was common forty years ago; and it is said to have been last used in South Uist, which is inhabited by Roman Catholics. There is no tradition of its having been performed in the east Highlands for a century past. They have, however, some remains of its spirit in Mull, Skye, and St. Kilda. In the two former, the nearest female relations mourn in the house in extempore verses.[65]

As John Ramsay realised, Christianity had been against such 'heathenish' practices as the funeral keen (depicted in lines 11-12 of poem three of Appendix A) since the early medieval period. Two origin myths for the keen exist in early Gaelic literature, both attributing it to the goddess Bríg. The Irish penitentials, composed in the seventh and eighth centuries, express general disapproval of the keen, imposing penance on those who perform it according to their social status and that of the person keened, but made allowance for its continuation in society nonetheless.[66] Ramsay was slightly premature in his pronouncement of the extinction of keening, for there were still reports of its use in the nineteenth century.

The funeral wail, which contrasted strangely with the succeeding mirth, has fallen into disuse. Yet, so late as in the year 1824, a poor widow woman, in Morvern, followed the remains of her only son to the grave, and sang extemporaneously his lament, to an old plaintive air, enumerating all his virtues, from his own house to the place of interment nearly a mile distant, in beautiful and tender poetry.[67]

Given the feelings of loss and grief that would naturally surface at a funeral, the merriment of the wake often acted as a counterbalance, asserting the community's resilience and continuity in the face of death and the capricious forces of the Otherworld.[68] Patrick Campbell, a native of Argyll, tells us in the late eighteenth century that the church was unable to rival the devotion young people had for the traditional games and narratives performed at such occasions:

It was customary in the corner of the country where I was born, when the people assembled on any public occasion, particularly at late-wakes, to place their best [seanchaidh] in some conspicuous and centrical place, where he could best be heard in the house, but more frequently in a barn, where the corpse was kept; and after they were tired of playing games and tricks peculiar to that country, in which all the strength, alertness, and dexterity, were exerted to their utmost, the best orator began and continued till day-light, repeating Ossian's poems, and recounting the atchievements of his race, which exalted their minds and ideas to perfect enthusiasm. I myself, when a boy, was present on many of these occasions, and I well remember that I never observed a sermon by the greatest devotee, or any other discourse, picked up with half the avidity that the young people did these poems; and I have different times gone on a Saturday evening from school eight or ten miles off, to a friend's house to hear them repeated, and to learn them.[69]

Official church policy looked disapprovingly on the frivolity of funeral customs, as they detracted from the view of death as final and from the religious duties expected of believers. The Church of Scotland passed an act requiring the presence of a clergyman at the burial site, attempting to wrest control of this highly significant rite of passage from secular society:

For avoiding of all inconveniences we judge it best that neither singing nor reading be at the burial: For albeit things sung and read may admonish some of the living to prepare themselves for death, yet shall some superstitious think that singing and reading of the living may profite the dead. And therefore we think it most convenient that the dead be conveyed to the place of burial with some honest company of the kirk, without either singing or reading; yet without all kind of ceremony heretofore used, other than that the dead be committed to the grave, with such gravity and sobriety as those that be present may seeme to fear the judgments of God, and to hate sinne, which is the cause of death.[70]

The Synod of Argyll had already passed an act in 1642 against the practice of keening: 'ignorant poore women to howle their dead into the graves [. . .] a thing unseemly to

184

be used in any true Christian kirk.'[71] In Ireland the bagpiper was playing at part in funeral rituals as early as the sixteenth century,[72] and probably in Scotland shortly thereafter. The author of *A Collection of Highland Rites and Customs* (*c*.1685) shows them both accompanying the corpse: 'The women make a crying while the corps is carried and when they have done, the Piper plays after the corps with his great pipe.'[73] The description by the Reverend John Buchanan in the late 1700s describes both still at funerals in the Hebrides:

> Burials are preceded by the large bag-pipe, playing some mournful dirge. They continue playing till they arrive at the place of interment, while the women sing the praises of the dead, clasping the coffins in their arms, and lie on the graves of their departed friends [. . .]
>
> On those occasions, there is great profusion of meat and drink brought to the place of interment, where the expenses generally bear a proportion to the rank and fortune of the person deceased, to prevent the imputation of meanness; and they seldom separate while the cask contains any spirits to wash down their sorrow: which seldom happens before their griefs are converted into squabbles, and broken heads, which some of them carry home as marks of remembrance for their lost friends.
>
> They seldom display much mirth at late wakes, as they do in many parts of Scotland; but sit down with great composure, and rehearse the good qualities of their departed friend or neighbour. Their grief soon subsides after they are buried; and many have speedily replaced a lost wife by some of their former acquaintance.[74]

There were too many joys, and tasks, in life to let death trouble one for too long. A person might be advised to bring his grief to a closure with the proverb, 'Is fhada tha bàs do sheanmhar 'nad chuimhne' ('Your grandmother's death is long on your mind').[75] 'The ghost of a person who is grieved for too much by his nearest relative may return, for it is an act of insubordination against Providence to grieve too much for the dead.'[76]

SUSTENANCE

Discussion of the many varieties of Highland foodstuffs and means of sustenance throughout Gaelic history is beyond the remit of this work; it is relevant, however, to consider in brief the ways in which diet and sustenance are bound with cultural values and social customs and are reflected in literature. Like so many other aspects of Gaelic culture, the associations of foodstuffs reflect concepts of the noble/non-noble dichotomy. Noble foods include those associated with aristocratic life, especially the meat of wild game killed in the hunt, as well as those which had to be imported; non-noble foods included tubers, shellfish, and animals considered to be scavengers.[77]

Although Highlanders often had to obtain needed protein from marine life that was to be caught in rivers, lochs and coastal waters, they were considered low-status foodstuffs. This prejudice may be quite ancient, for the Roman writer Xiphilinus wrote of the tribes of Scotland, 'They eat no fish, though their waters teem with all kinds of them.'[78] As late as the 1720s Edmund Burt remarked, 'The meanest servants, who are not at board wages, will not make a meal upon salmon if they can get anything else to eat.'[79] The proverb 'Tha e air a dhol don fhaochaig' ('He has gone to the whelk-shell'),[80] said of someone showing stinginess, exemplifies the disdain shown to shellfish. Remarking in poetry that someone ate shellfish was understood to be an insult.[81]

A general dislike of tubers caused western Highlanders to resist the introduction of potatoes in the eighteenth century,[82] although they had to rely on such plants as silverweed in times of scarcity. An old Gaelic proverb reminded the hungry of this resource: 'Brisgean beannaichte earraich / Seachdamh aran a' Ghàidheil' ('The blessed silverweed of spring / The Highlander's seventh bread').[83]

The staples of the Highland diet were oats and milk, prepared in a wide variety of ways. The recurrence of cattle in Gaelic lore and legend is not surprising when one considers how dependent people were on dairy products. Mary Mackellar, a nine-teenth-century Lochaber poetess, describes how combinations of oats and milk were prepared and enjoyed:

Cattle were of so much importance to the Highlanders because they represented, in a special manner, their food supply. Milk, in its different forms, was their chief sustenance. Instead of the morning cups of tea, now indulged in by all classes of the community, they began the day by taking drinks of milk. Among the better classes, the morning drink (*deoch-maidne*) was what is known as "old man's milk," which was an egg switched into a glass of milk, with a little whisky added; and even the herd-boy got, if nothing better, a cup of whey to his piece of barley bread before turning out to tend the cows. When milk was scarce, the morning drink of the poorer people was *sughan*, which is the juice of oatmeal or bran steeped so long as to become sour, and in very hard times they took it to their porridge. *Sughan* was spoken of in song and story as a sign of poverty, as it indicated a scarcity of cows, and certainly it is not very palatable. [. . .] A careful housewife was much more lavish with her butter and cheese to her household than she would be with either her warm milk or cream, as she took great pride in the quantities of dairy produce in her "cellar" at the end of the season. Yet there were times when even the richest cream would be freely produced, and this was especially at the demands of hospitality. Water was never offered as a drink to the meanest wayfarer. *Deoch fhionna-ghlas* was the most effectual drink for quenching thirst. This "whitey-grey" mixture was milk and water in equal proportions, and the sour thick milk that was under the cream that was kept for butter was churned into a froth, and it made a cooling drink. It was called *sgathach*. When strangers had to be entertained, *fuarag* was made plentifully, and curds and cream were laid out with oatcake, butter, cheese and whisky. They made the yearning, or yeast, that turned the milk into curds, by putting milk and salt into the stomach of a calf. The he-calves were generally killed, and their stomachs supplied them for this purpose. *Fuarag* was made of the sour thick cream, churned into a froth, with a *lonaid* made for the purpose, and some oatmeal stirred into it. The meal made on the quern was considered by far the best for making it. This is a most delicious luxury, and a favourite with all classes.[84]

The Gaelic proverb 'Is fearr aon sine bà na bolla de'n mhìn bhàin' ('A single cow's teat is better than a bowl of meal')[85] reflects how much Highlanders trusted the nutrition of dairy products upon which they so heavily relied. Modern appraisals substantiate the logic of this trust. Although the Highland diet has been much maligned, commentators of the eighteenth and nineteenth centuries realised that the rural population, subsisting on traditional foodstuffs, was generally better fed than its urban counterpart. 'The basic Highland diet had much to commend it, as contemporary nutritional studies showed. [. . .] Moreover, the efficacy and healthfulness of the simple Highland diet has been repeatedly confirmed by researchers during the last few centuries.'[86]

People sought out diverse sources of nutrition to complement these staples, according to their local habitat and the time of year. 'Nuair a bhios a' chaora caol, bidh am maorach reamhar' ('When sheep are lean, shellfish is fat'), says one Gaelic proverb to coastal communities.[87] The period between Christmas and Saint Bridget's Day was known as *Earrach Beag nam Faochag* 'The Little Spring of the Whelks' because the whelk was in prime condition and was used to make a hearty soup.[88] A native of the Dornoch Firth describes the wealth of foodstuffs which he enjoyed as a child in the early nineteenth century:

> *Sgioladh*, which we pronounced 'skeeloo', are shelled kiln-dried oats. All the people of the neighbourhood had their oats ground into meal there. We also got skeeloo, and all the carrots we could eat, for pulling Boyd's annual crop of carrots near the mill; and in the vicinity was Place Calltuinn, an extensive grove of hazel trees, where hundreds of bushels of nuts must have been annually gathered by the scholars and others; for by custom and usage the nuts were common property. It amazes me now to think of our capacities for *sgioladh*, and nuts, carrots, turnips, peas and beans, the buds of the fir, *mucaigean* (the wild-rose apples or hips), and lots of other raw stuff. [. . .] Blaeberries by the basketful were gathered in the hollows of the hills southwest of Ardgay, but they also grew in satisfactory quantities, and of extra good quality and size, all along the firth. [. . .] The whole district, in the valleys, is excellent for fruit-growing; all the small garden fruit and berries were good, also apples and pears, and I have seen apricots ripen well as wall-fruit.[89]

Eggs were collected and eaten to supplement the diet; young people in particular were encouraged to eat raw eggs, after they had been tested for consumption by putting them into a container of water.[90] Whisky had been brought to the Scottish

Highlands by medieval monks but it became a useful supplement to the diet, providing a quick source of energy and warmth.[91] Notwithstanding the drinking binges reported of the élite, traditional medicine advocated moderation, as in the Gaelic adage about the amount of whisky to imbibe at a sitting: 'Aon ghloine, chan fheairrde 's mhisd; dà ghloine 's fheairrde 's cha mhisde; trì gloineachan 's misde 's chan fheairrde' ('One glass: neither better nor worse for it; two glasses, the better and no worse for it; three glasses, the worse and not better for it.').[92] Whisky was an essential ingredient in many cures but was equally important in imparting hospitality.

> In this, and many other parts of the highlands, a glass of whisky is drank the first thing in the morning, and you are seldom allowed the privilege of a refusal, however unaccustomed to such a mode of living; for a highlander would not think he had discharged the duties of hospitality, if he let you leave his house without it.[93]

Songs and tales illustrate the cultural significance of food, especially as representing notions of generosity and grandiosity (as in lines 9-12 of poem five in Appendix A). One such is a flyting between Nic Iain Fhinn, representing the MacNeills of Barra, and Nic a' Mhanaich, representing Clanranald, which enumerates foods associated with the élite and peasantry of Gaelic society as a means of praise and dispraise of their respective clans.[94] Nic a' Mhanaich insults the MacNeills by claiming that the inhabitants of Barra sustain themselves on fish:

> *Far am bi na sgait air fleòdradh*
> *Dallagan is sùilean rògach*
> *Giomaich 'gan tarraing à frògaibh*
> *Strùbain 'gan cladhach le'm meòirean*
> *Muirsgein 'gan tarraing à lònaibh.*

('Where the skates are left to marinate; [there are] dogfish with their creepy eyes, lobsters snatched from orifices, cockles being dug out by hand, razor-fish snatched from mudholes.')

Nic Iain Fhinn, however, counters by praising Barra for, amongst other things, its ability to grow crops. Her list of culinary items culminates in high-status provisions that would entice even the Irish to come to feast:

> *Tìr a' chorca, tìr an eòrna,*
> *Tìr uisge-beatha agus bheòire,*
> *Tìr ichinnich is òil i;*
> *Dh'fhàsadh peasair, dh'fhàsadh pònair,*
> *Dh'fhàsadh biolair air a lòintean*
> *Fàsaidh lìon air chnocain chòmhnard*

> *Gheobhadh Éireannaich an leòr innt'*
> *Nam foghnadh muc, ìm, is feòil dhaibh*
> *Sitheann mu seach agus ròsda*
> *'S mairtfheoil 'ga bruich, muc 'ga stòbhadh.*

('The land of oats and barley, a land of whisky and beer, of food and drink; peas and beans would grow there, and watercress on its ponds; flax grows on its smooth hillocks; the Irish would get their fill there, if they would be satisfied with pork, butter and meat, roasted venison in turn, with boiled beef and stewed pork.')

Besides reflecting social class, dietary habits were also commonly seen as markers of ethnic identity. Gaelic songs often insult Lowlanders (or fellow Highlanders following Lowland ways) by calling them 'kail-eaters'.[95] The Gaelic poet An Ciaran Mabach (†1688) composed a song while in Edinburgh in which Highland and Lowland difference are symbolised by foodstuffs, the deer exemplifying the Gaels themselves:

> *B' iad mo ghràdh-sa a' ghreigh uallach*
> *A thogadh suas ris an àird*
> *Dh'itheadh biolair an fhuarain*
> *'S air 'm bu shuarach an càl.*[96]

('Beloved to me is the proud deer-herd who would ascend to the summit, who would eat the watercress of the fountain, and would disdain the kale.')

More derisive is the poetry of Iain Lom celebrating the victory of Royalist forces under Alasdair mac Colla at the Battle of Inverlochy in 1645 and mocking the defeated Covenanters: 'Chuir thu ruaig air Ghallaibh glasa, 'S ma dh'òl iad càl gun d' chuir thu àsda e' ('You routed the pallid Lowlanders, and if they drank kail, you knocked it out of them').[97]

The traditional simplicity of the Highland diet, and the ability of Gaels to live on a minimal food supply, was renowned. George Buchanan noted in 1582:

In their food, clothing, and in the whole of their domestic economy, they adhere to ancient parsimony. [. . .] Of [oatcakes] they eat a little in the morning, and then contentedly go out hunting, or engage in some other occupation, frequently remaining without any other food till the evening.[98]

In opposition to their own frugality, they attributed to the English insatiable greed for expensive foodstuffs, as Edmund Burt noted in the 1720s:

By Accounts of the Plenty and Variety of Food at the Tables of the Luxurious in England, the People, who have not eaten with the English, conclude they are a likewise Devourers of great Quantities of Victuals at a Meal, and at other Times talk of little else besides Eating. [. . .] It is from this Notion of the People that my Countrymen, not only here [in the Highlands], but all over Scotland, are dignified with the title of *Poke Pudding*, which, according to the Sense of the Word among the Natives, signifies a Glutton.[99]

While the fundamentals of the Highland diet were sound, the cultural and economic marginalisation imposed from the mid eighteenth century onwards limited the ability of Highlanders to realise the potential of their own resources to maintain their quality of life:

What eighteenth- and nineteenth-century Establishmentarians failed to acknowledge, however, was that the quantity and quality of people's food supply was uncertain at best, and that the destruction of their lifestyle had stripped them of other elements necessary to health. [. . .] Thus the degradation of the industrial towns where they found work, no less than their destitution at home, deprived Highlanders of their traditionally simple but nutritious fare: milk, oats, potatoes, fish and a limited intake of meat. That deprivation proved a serious danger to health, in particular to the body's defence mechanism. Malnourished wherever they lived, Highlanders were prone to disease.[100]

HEALTH AND HAPPINESS

There is no single, absolute, and objective definition of health: culture sets expectations and perceptions about health and disease, and encourages tastes and behaviours that affect our mental and physical state positively or negatively. In the preamble of its 1948 constitution, the World Health Organization (WHO) defined health as 'a state of complete physical, mental and social well-being and not merely the absence of disease or infirmity'. This definition has since been extended to include the ability to lead a 'socially and economically productive life'. As in many other languages, the word *slàinte* indicates health in Gaelic but its root meaning is 'wholeness' and signifies a holistic concept of wellness.[101]

Factors other than the purely material were understood as influencing one's well-being. Illness and even death was attributed to the transgression of tabus (imposed by orthodox Christianity or 'pagan' ancestral tradition), the power of satire, the paralysis of fairy-shot, the malice of witchcraft, and the venom of the evil eye, amongst other things. These correspond to social stresses that have been confirmed as essential to maintaining sufficient immunity to fend off disease. Put the other way around, modern medicine continues to validate the efficacy of placebos and hence the ability of the body to heal itself given conducive mental, emotional, and environmental conditions.

The art of healing has deep roots in the Celtic world in general and in the prehistory of the British Isles more specifically. Thus far, archaeologists have found four Celtic tombs in Continental Europe containing sophisticated surgeon's instruments dating to the fourth and third centuries BC, including tools used to perform trepanation. The Roman writer Pliny displayed an interest in the medical cures of the Gauls in his *Natural History* (c.AD 78). The sick went to sacred healing sites, especially springs and wells, sometimes with carved objects representing the part of the body afflicted.[102] The early lives of the Gaelic saints include therapeutic miracles and the Christian approval of pagan healing sites and practices.[103] Saints Bridget and Columba remained closely associated with healing in Gaelic tradition, and as late as 1618 a healing miracle in Islay was said by a priest of the Counter-Reformation to win many converts back to the Catholic church.[104]

Dian Cécht was a Gaelic god personifying the powers of the physician who appears in a number of tales from as early as the eighth or ninth century AD.[105] He was invoked in Old Gaelic incantations for healing and continued to be remembered as a byword for medical skill in Classical Gaelic literature (as in line 20 of poem one of Appendix A). The Gaelic tale 'Cath Dédenach Maige Tuired' ('The Last Battle of Mag Tuired') was compiled in the twelfth century, drawing from materials as old as the ninth century. In one scene, Dian Cécht replaced the hand of Nuada, which had been struck off in battle, with an artificial silver hand. Dian Cécht's son Miach disliked this unnatural prosthesis and decided instead to heal Nuada's hand by means of a traditional charm. The charm worked, but this upstaging of his handiwork vexed Dian Cécht so much that he killed his son.

> Thereafter Miach was buried by Dian Cécht. Three hundred and sixty five herbs, corresponding to the number of his joints and sinews, grew through the grave. Then Airmed opened her mantle and separated those herbs according to their properties. But Dian Cécht came to her, and he confused the herbs, so that *no one knows their proper cures unless the Holy Spirit should teach them afterwards* [italics mine]. And Dian Cécht said 'If Miach be not, Airmed shall remain.'[106]

At the time at which this text was compiled, professional medicine in Europe, like all branches of learning, was under the aegis of the Christian church, which attempted to monopolise such skills for itself.[107] Although the tale acknowledges that a herb grows for each of the part of the body that might suffer affliction, the men of the church wanted to maintain control of the knowledge of their use and marginalise others. There is no evidence, for example, of woman physicians in the Gaelic medical order.[108]

As today, professional physicians enjoyed positions of prestige in Gaeldom, including the Scottish Gàidhealtachd. The first name *Mac-bethad* 'The Son of Life' was recorded in the twelfth-century *Book of Deer* from Aberdeenshire and may indicate the professional title for a physician.[109] The name took other forms in later periods, in Gaelic and in English, such as MacBeth, MacVey, Beaton and Bethune. A medical dynasty of this name was established in Scotland by an Irish immigrant coming with *tochradh nighean a' Chathanaich* 'the dowry of Ó Catháin's daughter' in the late thirteenth century and flourished for some four hundred years throughout Scotland.[110]

Patrick MacBeth was the chief physician and surgeon to Robert the Bruce and there is historical evidence that MacBeth (or 'Beaton') doctors continued to serve the kings of Scotland up to King James IV. Oral tradition asserts that their service to Scotland's royalty continued into the reign of King James VI.[111] Various branches of the MacBeth dynasty copied and compiled many of the twenty-nine Gaelic medical treatises that survive in Scotland.[112] These texts drew upon the successive layers of tradition that constituted medieval European medicine, beginning with the Greek philosophers, going through Muslim scholars and finally passing into the hands of medieval Christendom before being translated into Classical Gaelic. The manuscripts also contain the notes of doctors working in the field, as writing materials were expensive: a single book such as *Lilium Medicinae* required the hides of sixty milk cows. Although the MacBeths were the most illustrious family of formally trained Gaelic physicians, several others existed as well in close association with the learned classes, such as the MacLachlans of Craiginterve, the Ó Conachers of Lorn, and the Livingstons (MacDhuinnshléibhe) of Cowal.[113]

Unsurprisingly, the church could not maintain an exclusive monopoly on medicine and health. The traditional healing lore of the lower orders of the Scottish Gàidhealtachd, including 'wise women' who performed cures, survived well given that witchcraft persecution was minimal in the Highlands and did not threaten its practice as it did in so many other parts of Europe.[114] (Many of the folk-healers prosecuted as witches in the Lowlands, however, were native Highlanders.) Martin Martin commented in the late seventeenth century that Highlanders were adept at applying sound scientific principles to discover new remedies in the many resources around them:

> The inhabitants of [the Hebrides . . .] seem to be better versed in the Book of Nature, than many that have greater Opportunities of Improvement. This will appear plain and evident to the judicious Reader, upon a View of the successful Practice of the Islanders in the Preservation of their Health, above what the Generality of Mankind enjoys; and this is perform'd merely by Temperance, and the prudent use of Simples; which, as we are assured by repeated Experiments, fail not to remove the most stubborn Distempers, where the best prepar'd Medicines have frequently no Success. This I relate not only from the Authority of many of the Inhabitants, who are Persons of great Integrity, but likewise from my own particular Observation. And thus with Celsus, they first make Experiments, and afterwards proceed to reason upon the Effects. [. . .] Many of the Natives, upon occasion of sickness, are disposed to try Experiments, in which they succeed so well, that I could not hear of the least Inconvenience attending their Practice.[115]

The shortcomings of the medieval European traditions of medicine inherited by Gaelic physicians are well-known to modern doctors today and were also suspected by many contemporaries.[116] Martin Martin relates that Niall Beaton of Skye, an illiterate folk-healer of the long lineage of Beaton physicians, had greater faith in his own abilities than in the learned books so revered by his professional relations.[117]

> His great success in curing several dangerous Distempers, tho he never appeared in the quality of a Physician until he arrived at the Age of Forty Years, and then also without the advantage of Education. He pretends to judg of the various qualities of Plants, and Roots, by their different Tastes; he has likewise a nice Observation of the Colours of their Flowers, from which he learns their astringent and loosening qualities; he extracts the Juices of Plants and Roots, after a Chymical way, peculiar to himself, and with little or no charge.
>
> He considers his Patients Constitution before any Medicine is administered to them; and he has form'd such a System for curing Diseases, as serves for a Rule to him upon all Occasions of this nature.
>
> He treats Riverius's *Lilium Medicinae*, and some other Practical Pieces that he has heard of, with Contempt; since in several Instances it appears that their Method of Curing has fail'd, where his had good Success.[118]

Highland folk wisdom advocated dietary simplicity, exercise, and moderation. There is even evidence that people had a basic understanding of the ability of microscopic organisms to communicate contagion and of the importance of sanitary conditions for medical procedures.[119] A proverb about healthy living, attributed by some to the MacBeth physicians, advised:

> *Bith gu subhach geanmnaidh*
> *Moch-thràthach as t-samhradh*
> *Bith gu curraiceach brògach*
> *Brochanach 's a' gheamhradh.*[120]

('Awake early and be cheerful and temperate in the summer; in the winter, wear a head-cap and shoes, and eat plenty of porridge.')

Healers with a knowledge of medical herbs survived after the lines of professional Gaelic physicians died out and became even more vital in the eighteenth century as Highland communities became fragmented and poorly cared for. Reverend John Smith of Argyll noted in 1780 that 'The Highlanders, having seldom access to the help of the physician or surgeon, still perform very surprising and speedy cures by their knowledge of the herbs of the mountain. These they still gather "by the side of their secret stream".'[121] Alexander Campbell noted in the early nineteenth century, 'I have met with some of the herb-doctors (as some call them) of the Grampian mountains, possessed of no small share of practical knowledge in the healing art.'[122]

Healers used procedures other than just the ingestion of herbs to cure illness. In both Gaelic Scotland and Ireland perspiration was induced in simple structures similar to 'sweat-lodges' to speed the recovery of the sick. 'Intense sweating was often seen as the turning point during a fever and was termed *fallas-faochaidh*.'[123]

> When diseases, which are chiefly of the acute kind, make their attack on the Highlander, he endeavours to procure evacuation by vomit or stool, or profuse perspiration. If these fail, he takes no food, and trusts to nature for a cure. But, if he remains for any length of time in pain, or severe illness, superstitious practices are resorted to [. . .] charms, amulets and other means are employed to restore health to the system.[124]

Although Highlanders were clearly susceptible to periodic food shortages, exposure to new diseases and simple human failings, contemporary commentators describe their condition as no worse than that of other people. The anonymous author of a late seventeenth century tract noted, 'They are not much troubled with any Disease but feavours; wherof they die commonly.' To this entry, antiquarian Edward Lhuyd added that Highlanders were subject to 'in short all Diseases incident to other nations'.[125] Martin Martin makes frequent remarks about the health and longevity of Hebrideans.[126] James Robertson, a graduate of Edinburgh University, visited Skye in 1768 and remarked positively, 'Perhaps there is no part of the Inhabitable Globe where so few bodily imperfections are to be seen. [. . .] They are generally very healthy, and many of them live to a great old age.'[127] There was, in fact, a ritual performed to hasten the death of people who had lived too long![128]

At least some of the strength and resilience of Highlanders can be attributed to their positive mental and emotional outlook, starting from the self-esteem inculcated since youth: ''Se anacladh na h-òige a nì duine' ('It is the nurture of youth that makes a person').[129] People expected that life brought cycles of ease and difficulty, joy and sorrow: 'Reothart an-diugh agus conntraigh a-màireach' ('Spring-tide today and neap-tide tomorrow').[130] This buoyancy contributed to their overall health.

> They are great composers of songs, both of tunes and words, and are noted for gaiety, and an excessive fondness for singing and dancing. They work hard (being very industrious) all day, and dance the chief part of the night, as the best receipt for taking off fatigue. If hearsay may be credited, they verify the golden age, and must be the happiest people existing. They have dancing assemblies once a week, which are held in a barn. There are one of these assembly rooms at each end of the island, where the young and gay part of the inhabitants meet alternately. They have numerous fiddlers and pipers on the island, so that they are never at a loss for music. They have much health and little money amongst them, consequently ever gay and lively.[131]

By the early nineteenth century, many writers describe Highlanders as beginning to suffer physically and emotionally from the cultural repression imposed on them. This affected their well-being at the same time as their diet deteriorated from restricted access to their traditional foodstuffs and lifestyle. Excessive reliance on the potato escalated nutritional deficiencies, which undermined the effective absorption of an increased amount of cheap whisky. By the mid-nineteenth century, women and children were consuming a disproportionately low amount of available nutrients, accelerating poor health in succeeding generations. As the Highland population was introduced to new diseases by tourists and immigrants in the Highlands, seasonal migration to the Lowlands, and overseas military service, the immunity acquired during centuries of relative isolation was broken. Only in the late nineteenth century was there a systematic effort to improve the living conditions of and medical provisions for Highlanders, and even then it was resisted by landlords and the propertied classes.[132]

CLOTHING

The word 'tartan' is probably derived from the Old French word *tiretaine*, used to describe a cloth made of wool and linen.[133] The Gaelic word *breacan* 'the speckled one' has been in use since at least the eighth century to describe checked textiles worn as clothing or used as blankets and bedding.[134] The earliest example of woollen cloth found in Scotland was excavated near Falkirk and has been dated to the third century AD. The 'Falkirk Tartan' uses a combination of two natural colours of wool in a checked pattern to create four distinct blocks which repeat throughout the weave. An illustration in the *Book of Durrow*, drawn c.AD 675, seems to depict a cloak made of tartan cloth.

In the lengthy and labourious process of creating cloth, dyeing was the most problematic stage. It was nearly impossible to create two batches of wool whose colours matched exactly: the results depended on the proportions of wool, water, dye substance, and mordant (used to fix the dye in the wool), the stage of development at which plants were harvested, the length of time the wool was left in the dye, and a host of other factors which were hard for people using simple implements to control. Combining the different yarns into checked patterns was a natural solution for distributing the colours so that such irregularities were not immediately obvious. This technique, in fact, is found all around the world from the earliest times and has the added benefit of allowing weavers to design their own patterns.

There were several types of clothing worn in the Highlands before the development of the belted plaid, and sometimes well after. The oldest form, also worn in Ireland, was a cloak (*brat*) worn over a large and loose saffron shirt (*léine chróich*). The belted plaid probably evolved from this form of clothing, with a very long plaid taking the place of the cloak. It is rare to find references to the shirt-cloak style of dress in vernacular Gaelic songs, although I know of one example:

'S math thig mandal mu do dhruim
agus léine phreasach theann
mar ri claidheamh leathann crom
agus ceann chóig aisnean ann.[135]

('A mantle around your shoulders suits you well, with a tight-fitting, pleated shirt, along with a curved broadsword with a hilt of five ribs.')

Various forms of trews (*triubhas*) also have a long history of use in Gaelic Scotland and Ireland. They had a distinctive cut made to fit the legs snugly, as mentioned in a number of Gaelic poems and songs.[136] Trews were sometimes worn under the kilt, especially by men of wealth. Trews, which fit around the waist and come down to the thigh, calf, or ankle, must be distinguished from hose, which start at the foot and usually come up to the top of the calf. The earliest illustration of trews occurs in the *Book of Kells*, a manuscript probably created on the island of Iona in the eighth century (see Plate 5).

Professional warriors wore expensively produced battle gear, as mentioned by George Buchanan in 1582: 'Their defensive armour consists of an iron headpiece, and a coat of mail, formed of small iron rings, and frequently reaching to the heels.'[137] Armour and weapons are depicted on the medieval gravestones of many Highland warriors and described in a number of Gaelic poems[138] and runs in folk tales describing warriors preparing for battle.[139] A seventeenth-century poem describes the handsome warrior uniform of a seventeenth-century MacNaughton aristocrat, which included imported clothing:

Is ionmhainn leam Iain as òige
Calpa deas air thùs na tòrach;
'S math thug lùireach dhuit is gòirseid
Agus léine 'n anart Hòlaind
Còta goirid air a òradh
'S boineid bhreac nan caitein gorma
'S breacan nan triuchana bòidheach.[140]

('Iain the younger is beloved to me, whose fine calf would be in the vanguard of battle; a breastplate and gorget suit you well, along with a linen shirt from Holland, a gold-embroidered short coat, a blue-ribboned tartan bonnet, and a tartan plaid of resplendent stripes.')

The older style kilt, called *féileadh mór* in Gaelic, is a heavy cloth (about 5 feet wide by 15 to 20 feet long) pleated and held together at the waist with a belt. The excessive material was then folded around the body to keep the wearer warm in the extreme weather to which the Highlands are often subject (see Plate 18). The belted plaid seems to date from the sixteenth century, at the same time that Highland Scotland was becoming less tied to Irish fashions and standards, probably because innovations in wool-working made it easier to create such long pieces of cloth.

Highland looms at this period were upright and could only make narrow lengths of cloth. In order to get a cloth wide enough for the féileadh mór, two of these pieces of cloth had to be joined together.[141] In the 1720s the small kilt (*féileadh beag*), a single length of cloth with the folds sewn in place, was adapted from the older style. This lighter and shorter version of the kilt was more practical in some contexts, as it was less cumbersome and left the arms free. The féileadh mór continued to be used into the late 1700s, however, especially by soldiers, drovers, and travellers, as it could envelop the body in harsh weather and be used as bedding. These extra functions are mentioned in George Buchanan's account of Hebridean clothing:

> They delight in variegated garments, especially striped, and their favourite colours are *purpureum* (dark red, purple) and *caeruleum* (blue, green-blue). Their ancestors wore plaids of many different colours, and numbers still retain this custom, but the majority, now, in their dress, prefer a dark brown, imitating nearly the leaves of the heather, that when lying upon the heath in the day, they may not be discovered by the appearance of their clothes; in these, wrapped rather than covered, they brave the severest storms in the open air, and sometimes lay themselves down to sleep even in the midst of snow.[142]

While it may have been common to wear plaids of muted hues as camouflage, Highlanders did not abandon their love of bright colours in the sixteenth century. Such was the demand for dyes that woad was being imported to the Highlands from the fifteenth century, and Mexican cochineal (used to produce red) from the early seventeenth century. As we might expect, these rarer and more expensive colors were associated with nobility.[143] A waulking song from the seventeenth century reflects the continuing fondness for brilliance:

> Gun aithichinn do bhuidheann
> A' tighinn o'n mhòintich
> Air ghilead an léintean
> 'S air dheirgead an còta
> Air ghuirmead an triubhais
> 'S air dhuibhead am brògan.[144]

('I would recognise your troop coming from the moor by the whiteness of their shirts and by the redness of their coats, by the blueness of their trousers and the blackness of their shoes.')

Not everyone could afford these expensive colours: the most humble classes in the Highlands wore woollen plaids of a natural, off-white hue. As we might expect, social status is reflected in attire. A verse from a song written to Coinneach Òg (probably the fourth Earl of Seaforth, born in 1569) is in praise of his mother and refers to her social class by describing her clothing and work implements:

> *A Mhic Coinnich na biodh gruaim ort*
> *Cha do ghlac do mhàthair buarach*
> *No plaide bhàn air a gualainn*
> *Ach sìoda dearg is stròl uaine.*[145]

('Do not be downhearted, Mackenzie, your mother never grasped a cow-fetter nor did she wear a white plaid: she wore red silk and green cloth.')

Martin Martin, writing in 1695, gives us extensive and interesting details about early Highland clothing, including the evolution of older Gaelic styles into the kilt in the late sixteenth century. He also notes that class distinctions were becoming widely felt during the seventeenth century in the Highlands, with the upper classes imitating the styles of the Lowlands.

The first Habit wore by Persons of Distinction in the Islands, was the [*Léine-Chróich*], from the Irish word [*Léine*], which signifies a Shirt, and *Croich* Saffron, because their Shirt was dyed with that Herb: the ordinary number of Ells us'd to make this Robe was twenty four; it was the upper Garb, reaching below the Knees, and was tied with a Belt round the middle: but the Islanders have laid it aside about a hundred Years ago.

They now generally use Coat, Wastcoat, and Breeches, as elsewhere; and on their Heads wear Bonnets made of thick cloth, some blue, some black, and some grey.

Many of the people wear Trowis [i.e., trews]: some have them very fine woven like Stockings of those made of Cloth; some are colour'd, and others striped: the latter are as well shap'd as the former, lying close to the Body from the middle downwards, and tied round with a Belt above the Haunches. There is a square Piece of Cloth which hangs down before. The Measure for shaping the Trowis is a Stick of Wood, whose Length is a Cubit, and that divided into the Length of a Finger, and a half a Finger; so that it requires more skill to make it, than the ordinary Habit.

The Shoes antiently wore, were a piece of the Hide of a Deer, Cow, or Horse, with the Hair on, being tied behind and before with a Point of Leather. The generality now wear Shoes, having one thin Sole only, and shaped after the right and left Foot; so that what is for one Foot, will not serve the other.

But Persons of Distinction wear the Garb in fashion in the South of Scotland.

The Plad wore only by the Men, is made of fine Wool, the Thred as fine as can be made of that kind; it consists of divers Colours, and there is a great deal of Ingenuity requir'd in sorting the Colours, so as to be agreeable to the nicest Fancy. For this reason the Women are at great pains, first to give an exact Pattern of the Plad upon a piece of Wood, having the number of every Thred of the Stripe on it. The Length of it is commonly seven double

Ells; the one end hangs by the Middle over the left Arm, the other going round the Body, hangs by the end over the left Arm also : the right Hand above it is to be at liberty to do any thing upon occasion. Every Isle differs from each other in their Fancy of making Plads, as to the Stripes in Breadth, and Colours. This Humour is as different thro the main Land of the Highlands, in so far that they who have seen those Places, are able, at the first View of a Man's Plad, to guess the Place of his Residence.

When they travel on foot, the Plad is tied on the Breast with a Bodkin of Bone or Wood (just as the Spina wore by the Germans, according to the Description of C. Tacitus:) the Plad is tied round the middle with a Leather Belt. It is pleated from the Belt to the Knee very nicely: this dress for Footmen is found much easier and lighter than Breeches, or Trowis.

The antient Dress wore by the Women, and which is yet wore by some of the Vulgar, called [*Earasaid*], is a white Plad, having a few small Stripes of black, blue, and red; it reach'd from the Neck to the Heels, and was tied before on the Breast with a Buckle of Silver, or Brass, according to the Quality of the Person [see Plate 17]. I have seen some of the former of a hundred Marks value; it was broad as any ordinary Pewter Plate, the whole curiously engraven with various Animals, &c. There was a lesser Buckle, which was wore in the middle of the larger, and above two Ounces weight; it had in the Center a large piece of Chrystal, or some finer Stone, and this was set all round with several finer Stones of a lesser size.

The Plad being pleated all round, was tied with a Belt below the Breast; the Belt was of Leather, and several Pieces of Silver intermix'd with the Leather like a Chain. The lower end of the Belt has a Piece of Plate about eight Inches long, and three in breadth, curiously engraven; the end of which was adorned with fine Stones, or Pieces of Red Coral. They wore Sleeves of Scarlet Cloth, clos'd at the end as Men's Vests, with Gold Lace round 'em, having Plate Buttons set with fine Stones. The Head-dress was fine Kerchief of Linen strait about the Head, hanging down the Back taper-wise; a large Lock of Hair hangs down their Cheeks above their Breast, the lower end tied with a Knot of Ribbands.[146]

As Martin Martin notes, weavers in particular areas tended to use particular patterns and thus you could infer the place to which a person belonged if you were familiar with the local styles of tartan. This is quite different from the claim that each clan had its own tartan. Clan affiliation, especially when going to battle, was indicated by wearing sprigs of plants or trees. These were called *suaicheantas* in Gaelic and were originally, at least in part, a means of magical protection from harm in warfare.

What formed a more conspicuous distinction, every clan wore a badge on the side of the bonnet, which ascertained the tribe of each individual. This badge was always of some plant or tree that does not shed the leaf, otherwise the distinction could not exist in winter. The Grants have the fir or pine – the Macleods the juniper – the Frazers the yew – the Macintoshes the box – the Mackenzies the holly – the Macdonalds the crimson heath.[147]

Within Highland society, the use of imported dyes and the foreign luxury garments (such as silken shirts and gloves) indicated social status. Distinctive materials and styles of clothing also served as visible markers of ethnic identity, differentiating Gaelic society from the Lowlands and England. Although tartan was once widespread in Scotland, by the sixteenth century it was becoming restricted to the Highlands and seen as a sign of the conservatism of Gaelic society. Bishop John Leslie commented in 1578 that Scottish Highlanders 'preserve completely unchanged the ancient form of dress and lifestyle', a remark echoed by others in this period. This notion fed into the paradigm of Scottish Jacobitism even in the seventeenth century, which represented itself as restoring to Lowland Scotland what it had lost from contact with England by tapping into the reservoir of primordial Scottishness retained in the Highlands.

The Battle of Glen Fruin in 1603 was represented in popular tradition, in both Gaelic and Scots sources, as a conflict between Highlands and Lowlands. In a contemporary Gaelic song about the event Lowland forces are epitomised by their clothing, 'luchd nan ad dubha' ('the folk of black hats') and 'luchd-chleòc' ('Cassock-wearing folks').[148] Poets in the seventeenth century criticised chieftains for spending excessive time and money in the Lowlands and England; their wearing of foreign fashions was seen as a sign of their estrangement from Highland cultural norms and their assimilation into Anglo-British society. MacDonald poet Iain Lom boldly reprimands Lord MacDonell *c.*1665 by suggesting he set aside his foreign cassock and attire himself in tartan trews and kilt.

> *Gur fada leam an Sasann thu*
> *'S a bhith 'gad chreach le spòrs.*
>
> *B' fhearr leam còt' is breacan ort*
> *Na pasbhin chur air cleòc.*
>
> *Is tu bhith falbh gu h-aigeannach*
> *An triubhas chadaidh chlò.*[149]

('It seems to me you've been away long in England, ruining yourself with gambling; I would prefer a kilt and jacket on you than a cassock shut with pins, and for you to stride in trews of tartan cloth.')

Tartan was a salient emblem of Highland warriors in the seventeenth century when they became major players in British politics for the first time. When Jacobite forces won the Battle of Killiecrankie on 27 July 1689, celebratory literature (whether written in English or Gaelic) played up the sight of warriors in their kilts and tartan. The *Grameid* states, 'The clans were drawn up in saffron array. Glengarry's men were in scarlet hose and plaids crossed with a purple stripe; Lochiel was in a coat of three colours; the plaid worn by MacNeil of Barra "rivalled the rainbow".'[150] Gaelic songs commemorating the event are no less enthusiastic for the tartan-arrayed Jacobite combatants. Probably the most popular of these, composed by the MacLean poet Iain mac Ailein mhic Iain, describes the Jacobite forces as simply 'luchd nam breacan' ('the tartan crew'); the defeated Hanoverian forces are described as 'luchd Beurla is cleòca' ('the people of the English language and cassocks').[151]

The tartan and the kilt were powerful symbols of masculinity and militarism in the Scottish Highlands. The Act of Proscription (1746) attempted to defuse the military capacity of the Highlands by outlawing the wearing of tartans and kilts by civilian males.[152]

no Man or Boy [. . .] shall, on any Pretence whatsoever, wear or put on the Clothes commonly called Highland Clothes [that is to say] the Plaid, Philebeg, or little kilt, Trowse, Shoulder Belts, or any Part whatsoever of what peculiarly belongs to the Highland Garb; and that no Tartan, or party-coloured Plaid or Stuff shall be used for Great Coats, or for Upper Coats.[153]

This legislation names both the big and small kilts explicitly, showing that the féileadh beag was already in common use among Highlanders by this time and considered an element in the martial gear of the Gaelic warrior. John Ramsay had no doubt about the intention or impact of the Act of Proscription:

That the pride of the Highlanders might be exceedingly mortified, and one of their most striking distinctions taken away, their favourite dress was likewise forbidden, under severe penalties. Nothing, indeed, seemed to hurt their spirits more, or to give them a meaner appearance, than this regulation, the wisdom of which might be questioned.[154]

Chapter Six

BELIEF SYSTEMS AND COSMOLOGY

Magic was important to many in the medieval church because it was already believed in by the peoples to whom its missionaries came, and because some of this belief gave hope and supported happiness. The church had need of these peoples. It too supported this hope and happiness; and it could find echoes of this magic, furthermore, when it looked for them, within its own dispensation. Much magic was, then, rescued in the service of human aspiration, and, certainly, in defiance of certain aspects of reason and regulation.

– Valerie Flint, *The Rise of Magic in Early Medieval Europe*

Iona, the most successful of the three monasteries founded by Saint Columba, was a headquarters for missionary work and a renowned centre of European learning. Columba remained the most revered saint of the Scottish Highlands, despite the later adoption of Saint Andrew in the Lowlands, and was the subject of many hymns, incantations, and pious legends. His successors and disciples were amongst the most energetic 'soldiers of Christ' in Europe.

Despite the authority of the church throughout Scotland and the reverence paid to Columba throughout Gaeldom, a tale was told in Iona, the very heart and birthplace of Scottish Christianity, which casts doubt upon the ability of the 'new faith' to maintain a complete stranglehold over truth. The first sketch of this tale occurs in a twelfth-century biography of the saint written in Middle Gaelic, but many of the more interesting details were only recorded from oral tradition by travellers and scholars in the eighteenth and nineteenth centuries.[1]

⁓

Columba and his men set out to build a church in Iona. Each time they built it to a certain height, however, what was built in the day tumbled down in the night. Columba received a divine message that no building would ever be erected success-fully until a human being was buried alive in the foundation.

Columba had a companion named Odhran who offered himself up to be the sacrifice. After Odhran was buried for three days, Columba ordered that the ground be dug so that they could see Odhran. Odhran arose and said to the astonished spectators:

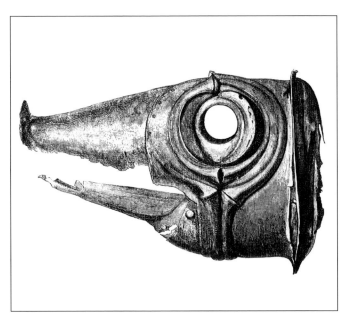

1. (*left*) A battle trumpet in the shape of a boar's head from *c.* AD 100, found in Deskford, Banffshire. Picture reproduced from *Scotland in Pagan Times* by Joseph Anderson (1883).

2. (*below*) The Hunterston Brooch, the finest example of its kind, was created *c.* AD 700, probably at Dunadd, the capital of Dál Riata. It displays a fusion of Gaelic, Pictish and Anglo-Saxon art styles. Picture reproduced from *Scotland in Early Christian Times* by Joseph Anderson (1881).

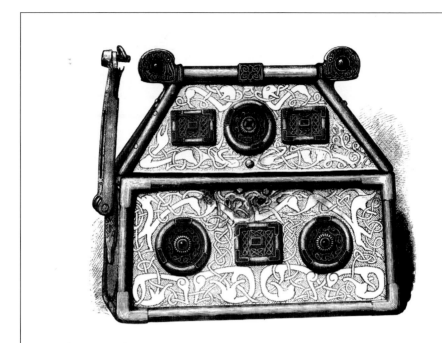

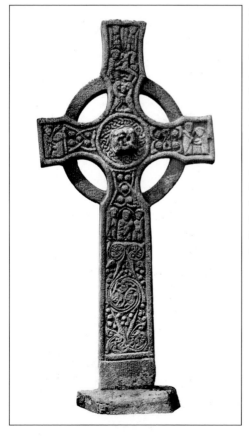

3. (*above*) The eighth-century portable shrine known in English as the Monymusk reliquary. It is believed by many to be the shrine associated with St Columba known in Gaelic as the *Brecbennach* 'The peaked and decorated one', carried by Robert the Bruce into the Battle of Bannockburn in 1314. Picture reproduced from *Scotland in Early Christian Times* by Joseph Anderson (1881).

4. (*left*) The cross at Kildalton, Islay, probably fashioned in late eighth century containing several scenes from Old Testament stories. Note also the decorative elements that reflect La Tene art styles. Picture reproduced from *The Carved Stones of Islay* by Robert C. Graham (1895).

5. (*above left*) The figure of a warrior wearing short breeks in the *Book of Kells*, probably created on the Island of Iona c. AD 800. Picture reproduced from *A Smaller Social History of Ancient Ireland* by P. W. Joyce (1906).

6. (*above right*) An early Christian carved stone with ogham inscribed on its side from Bressay, Shetland. Picture reproduced from *Scotland in Early Christian Times* by Joseph Anderson (1881).

7. (*left*) The chapel dedicated to St Odhran on Iona, probably built by Somerled or his son in the twelfth century. It was built on a burial ground also associated with Odhran probably in use at an earlier date. Picture by Michael Newton.

8. (right) A nineteenth-century depiction of a fourteenth-century engraved graveslab from the island of Iona for Giolla Brighde MacKinnon. Picture reproduced from *Archaeologia Scotica: Sculptured Monuments in Iona & the West Highlands* by James Drummond (1881).

9. (far right) Gravestone found in ruined chapel at Finlaggan, Islay, with inscription to Domhnall Mac Giolla Easpaig, probably from the mid sixteenth century. Picture reproduced from *The Carved Stones of Islay* by Robert C. Graham (1895).

10. A graveslab in Keills, Knapdale, probably from the late fifteenth century. An inscription on the stone refers to a father and son, the latter named as 'Alan', possibly from a family of harpers. Note that the detail on the harp is very similar to the ornament on Queen Mary's Harp (11). Picture reproduced from *Archaeologia Scotica: Sculptured Monuments in Iona & the West Highlands* by James Drummond (1881).

11. (*left*) The finest surviving early *clàrsach*, referred to as 'Queen Mary's Harp'. It was probably made in the late fifteenth century by craftsmen using West Highland artistic styles and preserved by the Robertsons of Lude in Perthshire. Picture reproduced from the *Proceedings of the Society of Antiquaries of Scotland* 15 (1880–1).

12. (*below*) A page from the early sixteenth-century manuscript known as the *Book of the Dean of Lismore*. Compiled in Breadalbane, it is the most important surviving collection of medieval Scottish Gaelic poetry. This page contains an elegy to Fionn mac Cumhaill attributed to Ossian. Picture reproduced from *The Dean of Lismore's Book* by the Rev. Thomas McLauchlan (1862).

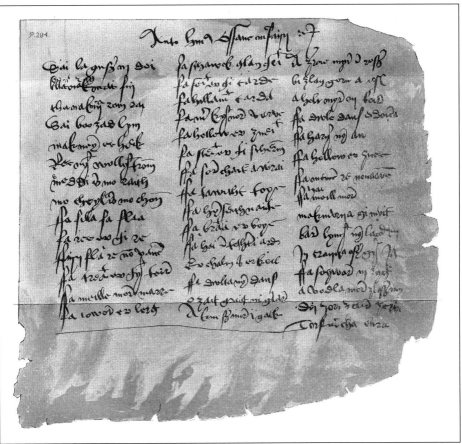

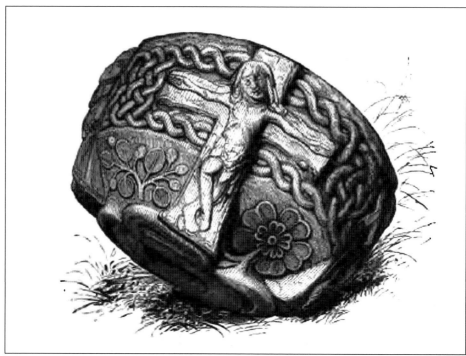

13. A baptismal font from Borline, Skye, with an inscription date 1530 naming the probable patron, Iain MacLeod. Picture reproduced from *Scotland in Early Christian Times* by Joseph Anderson (1881).

14. A crannog in Loch Freuchie near Amulree in Perthshire, at which local tradition sets '*Laoidh Fhraoich*' ('The Lay of Fraoch'). Picture by Michael Newton.

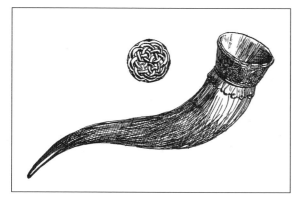

15. (*left*) The drinking horn used in the inaugural ceremony of the MacLeods of Dunvegan. Picture reproduced from the *Proceedings of the Society of Antiquaries of Scotland* 46 (1913).

16. (below) A nineteenth-century reproduction of the family tree of the Campbells of Glenorchy as drawn in 1635 by George Jamesone. Picture reproduced from *Records of Argyll* by Lord Archibald Campbell (1885).

17. (*right*) An engraved silver brooch owned by a member of the MacNabs who emigrated to Canada, later put in the care of the Breadalbane Folklore Centre. Picture by Michael Newton.

18. (*below*) An illustration of Highlanders at the market in Inverness. Their position below the 'urban' mercantile classes implies their subordinate status. The men demonstrate three different styles of wearing the plaid. Picture reproduced from *Letters from a Gentleman in the North of Scotland* by Edmund Burt (1754). Thanks to Hugh Cheape for the original illustration.

19. (*top*) A reconstructed thatched
house in the Kingussie Folk
Museum in Badenoch. Note the
peat smoke rising from the thatched
roof. Picture by Michael Newton.

20. (*above*) An illustration of the
inside of a weaver's cottage in Islay.
Picture reproduced from *A Tour in
Scotland and Voyage to the Hebrides
in 1772* by Thomas Pennant (1774).

21. (*above*) Daily activities on
the isle of Skye: two women
work a quern (grinding corn)
while a group of women sing a
waulking (or 'fulling') song as
they pound the tweed with their
feet. Married women wear
mutches but the unmarried
maidens have their heads bared.
The shepherd — excluded from
these activities — gazes into the
distance. Picture reproduced
from *A Tour in Scotland and
Voyage to the Hebrides in 1772* by
Thomas Pennant (1774).

22. (*right*) An illustration of two
women working the quern to
grain their corn. Picture reproduced from *Leabhraichean
Sgoile Gàidhlig Leabhar III*
edited by Domhnall Mac a' Phì
(1922).

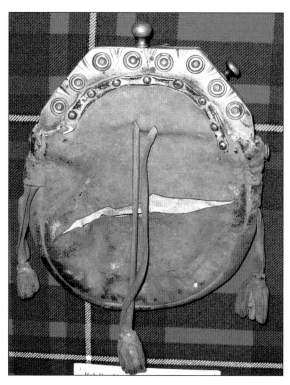

23. (*left*) The sporran once belonging to Rob Roy MacGregor, now kept in the Breadalbane Folklore Centre. Picture by Michael Newton.

24. (*below left*) The title page of the first anthology of Gaelic poetry, usually called the *Eigg Collection*, published in 1776 by Raghnall Dubh MacDonald. This copy of the Eigg Collection was owned by the Inverness-shire poet Kenneth MacKenzie.

25. (*below right*) The title page of the first collection of Gaelic proverbs, published by Donald Macintosh in 1785.

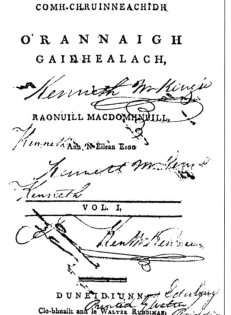

COMH-CHRUINNEACHIDH

O'RANNAIGH

GAIDHEALACH,

RAONUILL MACDOMHNUILL,

Ann. N. Eilean Eigg

VOL. I.

DUNEIDIUNN

Clo-bhuailt and le WALTER RUDDIMAN,

M,DCC,LXXVI.

A

COLLECTION

OF

GAELIC PROVERBS,

AND

FAMILIAR PHRASES;

Accompanied with

AN ENGLISH TRANSLATION,

Intended to facilitate the Study of the LANGUAGE;

ILLUSTRATED WITH NOTES.

TO WHICH IS ADDED,

THE WAY TO WEALTH,

BY DR. FRANKLIN,

TRANSLATED INTO GAELIC.

BY DONALD MACINTOSH.

Ge d' dh' ùignichear an sean-fhocal, cha bhreugaichear e.

EDINBURGH:

Printed for the AUTHOR, and fold by Meffrs. DONALDSON, CREECH, ELLIOT, and SIBBALD, Bookfellers, Edinburgh; JOHN GILLIES, Perth; JAMES GILLIES, Glafgow, and by all the Bookfellers in Town and Country.

M,DCC,LXXXV.

26. (*above*) An illustration
from the title page of the
tune collection *Airs and
Melodies Peculiar to the
Highlands of Scotland and
the Isles* by Captain Simon
Fraser (1816). It awards the
nation's musical laurels to
the fiddle (represented by
Neil Gow) and the *clàrsach*
(represented by a modern
orchestral harp, rather than
the older Gaelic
instrument); the bagpipe is
relegated to the rural
background. Several of the
functions of Gaelic song
are portrayed – milking
and rowing – as well as the
popular subject of hunting.
Thanks to John Purser for
the illustration.

27. (*right*) A portrait of the
pioneer folklorist John
Francis Campbell of Islay,
known in Gaelic as *Iain òg
Ìle*. Picture reproduced
from *Records of Argyll* by
Lord Archibald Campbell
(1885).

> *Chan eil flathas mar a theirear*
> *Chan eil Ifrinn mar a dh'aithrisear*
> *Chan eil saoi suthann sona*
> *Chan eil daoi dona duthann.*

('Heaven is not what they say, nor is Hell as reported; the good are not eternally happy, nor are the bad eternally miserable.')

At this unwelcome pronouncement, Columba quickly called out to his companions:

> *Ùir! Ùir air sùil Odhrain*
> *Mun dùisg e 'n corr carmaisg*
> *Dh'fhios oidheim a thoirt dhan chuideachd,*
> *Dh'fhios toibheim a thoirt dha bhràithribh!*

('Earth, earth, put earth over Odhran's eyes before he rouses any more confusion, which would reveal secrets to the company and bring scandal to his brethren!')

Odhran was covered up with soil and was not disturbed again. The building was finished and dedicated to him (see Plate 7).

~

In even approaching the subject of ancestral Gaelic beliefs, it becomes immediately apparent that we are separated not only by a gulf of *mentalité* but of language. The words that we use carry with them connotations and assumptions which were not held by people in the past and which obscure our understanding of their experience and perceptions. The word 'supernatural', for example, assumes a worldview which has carefully marked out beings, forces and phenomena which are 'natural' and those which could only be explained as something beyond nature.

> No absolute boundaries were believed to exist between the supernatural and the natural; indeed, the natural world was conceived as a direct manifestation of supernatural order. Spiritual forces, divine or demonic, infused material creation and were active in the operations of the physical world. [. . .] The sharp separation of the spiritual world and religious belief from the physical world and scientific rationalism, which is such a fundamental feature of modern Western culture, is a relatively recent product of Europe's movement toward modernity.[2]

These conceptual chasms are widened by differences in language. Although the elements of the English term 'supernatural' have been translated into a new Gaelic compound word with the same implication, *os-nàdarra*, in traditional usage these phenomena were referred to as *ana-ghnàthaiche,* meaning simply 'unusual' or 'extraordinary'.[3]

What people may today call 'superstition' and the 'supernatural' is not one phenomenon to be accounted for entirely by any one explanation or totalising theory, be it pagan survivals, folk memories of past races, embodiments of natural forces, coded language for social issues, or psychic phenomena. Belief systems are interlocking ontological complexes, operating at multiple levels simultaneously for differing purposes. They are dynamic paradigms which vary over time as well as area and a single individual may even hold contradictory beliefs without any sense of cognitive dissonance. Belief systems can absorb successive strata of ideas and practices which are active and activated in particular contexts for specific audiences. They are thus fraught with difficulties for those who attempt to analyse them and may offer a number of differing interpretations for any particular set of data.

As in many other spheres of Gaelic folklife, most writers in the past have generally approached Highland beliefs with assumptions of deficiency: that is, they are assumed to exist because 'primitive' people were not yet granted the gifts of modern science and logic which eradicate the need for such forms of 'irrational' thought. There are solid arguments against such condescending assumptions. The essentials of science – observation, experimentation, cause-and-effect reasoning, and so on – are used in even the most 'primitive' cultures. Folk beliefs serve the purposes for which they were developed very well and people often resort to them even when they can choose other more 'modern' solutions to their problems. The tradition-bearers from whom such material was gathered were said time and again by folklorists to be sharp-minded and perceptive individuals, as John Gregorson Campbell noted in the nineteenth century:

> The writer has thankfully to acknowledge, and he cannot but remember with pleasure, the readiness and courtesy, and in very many cases the great intelligence with which his inquiries have been answered. Some of his informants have shown a quickness and retentiveness of memory which he could not but envy, and an appreciation of, and an acquaintance with, ancient lore that seemed to him to indicate in those who were strangers to the world of letters powers of mind of a high order.[4]

To dismiss such individuals as 'ignorant' or 'naive' is to discount the legitimacy of their experience and to deny the fact that the concepts and categories which influence our perception of 'reality' are socially constructed. Previous generations as well as tradition-bearers of recent times deemed this cultural knowledge worthy of transmitting. Even in the modern era, when the 'bright light' of science and technology has penetrated the furthest corners of the globe and the brain, people cling to non-rational modes of explanation and belief, and reinvent mythic narratives, because in fact they seem to be endemic to human consciousness.[5] Furthermore, as Valerie Flint observes in the opening quote, they can also have positive and empowering functions in the lives of individuals.

When we read oral narratives of the 'supernatural' closely we find a language full of potent symbols and metaphors that relate to the ineffable, the mysterious, the profound, and the mundane, creating a conceptual matrix of relationships between humankind and the cosmos. 'These motifs make for a satisfying vivid narrative, but one that demands no more of the hearer than suspension of disbelief in the existence of a hidden, nearby world of the supernatural. [. . .] such a willingness to forgo natural scepticism paid rich dividends in terms of access to a shared symbolic universe.'[6] While these narratives are expressed in terms of a cultural heritage specific to Gaeldom they also have international parallels because they are rooted in human consciousness and social realities.

> To be able to understand them and what they tell us, we require to be aware of and alert to the way they carry reference to socio-political and cosmological traditions in Ireland [and Scotland] on the one hand, and to archetypal patterns of a universal human provenance on the other.[7]

Ancestral Gaelic belief systems include a wealth of concepts, customs, rituals, and texts, few of which I have space to examine here.[8] This chapter will explore the interaction between sacred and secular in the history of Scottish Gaelic society, the concept of the Otherworld, the female figure(s) associated with landscape and life forces, and cosmological principles in leadership and the social order.

Sacred and Secular in Gaelic History

It is beyond question that the pagan Celts had their own myths, pantheons, religious institutions and orders, but it is very difficult to reconstruct the pre-Christian Celtic world with much certainty: only short, and often fragmentary, pagan inscriptions in Celtic languages remain and conclusive translations have been elusive; the Classical authors often obscure as much as they illuminate, exaggerating Celtic traits and practices, and projecting their own biases, agendas, and rejected shadow-selves into the texts; later documents produced by Celtic scribes generally tell us more about the agendas of the Christianised élite than they do of pagan religion or even of contemporary folk beliefs derived from pre-Christian times.

Early Christian tales claiming to depict the confrontations between saints (especially Patrick and Columba) and druids (and other pagans) need to be read sceptically; they bear the influence of similar scenes from Christian literature and serve not the purposes of history (or ethnography) but the claims of the church for ultimate dominance. The pagan characters, in other words, are essentially puppets controlled by the Christian scribes to underscore the triumph of Christianity over the 'old religion'.[9] This is not to deny that they may bear some resemblance to the pagan Celtic world and simultaneously validate Christianity and ancestral Gaelic traditions. In Muirchú's biography of Saint Patrick, composed in Old Gaelic in the late seventh century, the druids prophesy of the coming of the saint using the 'dark riddles' for which they were renowned:

> Adze-head will come, the end of his staff bent,
> from his house, with a perforated head, he will chant abominations,
> from his table, in the front of his house,
> all of his household will respond to him, 'So be it, so be it.'[10]

By predicting the arrival of Patrick and the ultimate victory of the new religion, the ability of the druids to predict the future is acknowledged, but so is the certainty of their own downfall.

The early churchmen sought to create a literary canon that would claim legitimacy for the church in Gaelic society and revalidate the connections between the past and present, despite the fractures caused by its very presence. The stories of the lives of saints first began to be written in Latin in the seventh century, with translations into Gaelic beginning shortly thereafter. This undertaking, along with the compilation of legal, historical and poetic tracts by the same Christian intelligentsia, formed the foundation of a lasting literary and intellectual legacy of the church in Gaeldom. The later accomplishments and self-confidence of this tradition belie its tentative and experimental genesis.

Detailed analysis of these early texts suggests that the authors were conscious of their role in creating an authoritative literature legitimising the role of the church as the exclusive custodian of knowledge in an oral-dominant culture with a strong sense of the pre-Christian past. Saint Patrick is portrayed in the early lives as a champion of the written word, which is used to transmit his authority and to act as a weapon against paganism. He sanctions the documentation of Gaelic law – the verbal codification of society itself – an act which allows it to come under the control and custodianship of the Christian literati. Some scenes in the lives of Patrick depict him as reviving dead heroes from the pagan past, but the information shared by the resurrected characters serves to foretoken Christianity and accede to its inevitability. Patrick's mission was not just to establish Christianity but also to inaugurate a new mode of knowledge representation – literacy – which would supersede the older oral mode. Patrick's heirs continued to justify this new mode in their writings.[11]

The figure of Saint Columba is even more deeply implicated in the Gaelic verbal arts across Scotland and Ireland than was Patrick: he is frequently described as a singer and performer, and (according to one text) his childhood friends gave him his nickname after he joined them in the singing of the psalms; more poems were put in the voice of Columba than any other saint, especially on the theme of exile; when the men of Ireland threatened to eliminate the profession of poetry, he returned from Scotland to intercede on behalf of the poets at the Convention of Druim Cett (*c.*AD 575); 'Amra Choluim Chille', one of the oldest surviving poems in the Gaelic language (*c.*AD597), acquired the aura of a sacred incantation, copied and glossed for centuries after its composition. The result of Columba's intercession in the craft of traditional poetry was to uphold it within the standards of the church and co-opt it for Christianity.[12]

The intervention of monastic scribes in Gaelic oral tradition – transcribing, transforming, and editing oral performance into written text – is often paralleled metaphorically in early Christian literature in the treatment of acts of communication and performance. In one scene from the *Life of Columba* (as written by Adomnán, his successor in Iona), Columba and his followers were sitting beside Lough Key in Ireland when they were approached by a poet named Crónán. Columba dismissed him quickly, which caused his disciples to ask of him:

'Why did you not ask, before the poet Crónán left us, that he should sing us a tuneful piece of his own composition, as custom allows?'

The saint answered, 'Why ask such a pointless question? How could I have asked for a merry song from that unhappy fellow, who even now has reached the end of the line so soon? His enemies have murdered him.'

Columba had no sooner spoken than they heard a man shout from the other side of the river, 'That poet who left you a little while ago safe and well has in the past hour been attacked on the road and killed by enemies.'[13]

Although Crónán was a common Gaelic name, it is also a word that means 'tune' or 'humming' and, in Scottish Gaelic, 'a simple song of praise';[14] it is probably the origin of the English word 'croon'. By denying Crónán, the human embodiment of low-status, secular song itself, the opportunity to manifest his art, Columba hastens his death and thus symbolically asserts his authority over secular verbal arts. By thwarting the composition of a praise poem, of which he would have no doubt been the subject, Columba also remains detached from the messy web of poet-patron relationships that characterised secular Gaelic society.[15]

In the early literature of the saints, they sometimes express disapproval of aspects of secular culture or at least a desire to deprioritise them in comparison to religious responsibilities. In a text produced by the *Céili Dé* 'Servants of God' in the eighth century, a musician appropriately named *Cornán* 'Little-Horn' expresses his wish to play for the pious Mael Ruain. The puritanical saint, however, sends him the reply, 'These ears are not inclined to the music of the earth, so that they may be inclined to the music of heaven.'[16] The idea that a person should deny himself the pleasures and vanities of this world so that he does not become distracted from the obligations of true religion recurs across the history of Christendom, particularly when reformers wish to purge the church from worldly excesses and society from practices that are incompatible with Christian ideals.

The social institution of the *díberg* and *fían*, usually translated as 'brigands' in modern English, drew particular censure of the church. These two terms appear interchangeably in early sources, with members of such bands referred to collectively as *maic báis* 'sons of death'. Bands of brigands were made up of two kinds of members: élites (mostly male) who had matured out of fosterage but had not yet inherited land and become members of the settled community, and men for whom brigandage was a chosen occupation. Gangs of warrior-hunters lived outside of the geographical bounds and social norms of conventional society, often preying on the settled community and, later, monasteries. The díberg and fían appear to be orders derived from older Indo-European 'wolf cults' in which warriors fostered a close symbolic association with wolves. Terms such as *mac-tíre* could be equally applied to warriors and wolves, and brigands were said to assume the appearance or behaviour of wolves. The church saw such practices as violent and aberrant, especially as they threatened the members and property of the church itself. It thus classed druids, satirists and brigands together as enemies of the church and attempted to minimise their access to legal redress and economic resources.[17]

The early lives of the saints portray them getting the upper hand on brigands and sometimes even converting them to the new faith. A scene from the *Life of Columba* demonstrates how even brigands, once reformed, could invoke the power of the saint:

> Certain men, wicked and bloodstained from a life as brigands, were protected by songs that they sang in Gaelic in praise of St Columba and by the commemoration of his name. For on the night they sang these songs, they were delivered from the hands of their enemies, who had surrounded the house of the singers, and escaped unhurt through flames and swords and spears.[18]

Adomnán here makes explicit that the song was in Gaelic and thus that Christian songs had been established in the vernacular tongue.

The church in Ireland eventually celebrated its success in exterminating organised paganism, even if it could not transform secular society as thoroughly as it desired. *Féilire Oengusso*, a poetic calendar probably composed in the ninth century commemorating saints' days, contrasted the decay of pagan monuments and sites with the flourishing state of the Christian church:

> The [Christian] Faith has increased,
> it will endure until Doomsday,
> the guilty pagans are borne away,
> their settlements abandoned. [. . .]

> The ancient fortresses of the pagans
> to which title had been gained by long habitation,
> are empty and without worship
> like the place where Lugaid dwelt. [. . .]

> Though it was far-flung and splendid,
> paganism has been destroyed:
> the kingdom of God the Father
> has filled heaven, earth, and sea.[19]

Surviving evidence indicates that by the ninth century the formal institutions of paganism – the druids in particular – had been marginalised throughout the Gaelic world, with the élite eager to participate in the mainstream of European Christendom and its perceived benefits. 'Folk' rituals explicitly in honour of the old gods, however, survived into at least the eleventh century, even if they no longer were aspects of an organised religious tradition performed by druids.[20]

On the other hand, Christianity inevitably takes on features of local culture wherever it goes and must represent itself in terms that its host culture can understand (especially when such features do not contradict the essentials of Christianity and conversion is a matter of choice and not force). 'The culture engaged in becoming dominant, in this case the culture of the early European Christian Church, had both to make concessions and invent attractions if its aims were to be fulfilled.'[21] In a letter to the Pope *c.*604 the Irish missionary Columbanus, based in Luxeuil, asserted that 'the one hundred and fifty authorities of the council of Constantinople, who determined that churches of God established among pagan barbarians should live according to their own laws as they had been taught by their fathers'.[22] This was one of a number of precedents allowing local custom to survive the transition to Christianity, especially after explicitly pagan elements were expurgated.

Christianity adapted to local conditions in Gaeldom by adopting vernacular architecture for church buildings, sometimes on top of or next to ancient pagan sites. We should not assume that this indicates a desire to co-exist harmoniously with paganism, as it is more likely an assertion of victory over paganism or a means of supervising practices on-site. The way in which the 'High Cross' was fashioned and ornamented, possibly first in Iona itself before spreading to Ireland and mainland Scotland,[23] is indicative of the mark made by native Gaelic culture on the image of the divine. Elements of Celtic La Tène art appear on some of the early crosses of Scotland (including Pictish territory), which also feature depictions of the activities and members of aristocratic society, such as hunters and harpers (see Plate 4). Churches were not centres of religion alone: Iona became the burial site of the kings and other leading magnates of Scotland, which illustrates that secular and spiritual authority were intertwined.

The same dynasties that wielded secular power were also those that became the leaders of religious institutions, with succession determined in the same manner. The socio-economic value, or 'honour-price', of members of religious orders was calculated by mirroring their position in secular society. Certain legal concepts and aspects of social organisation were adopted in the church's own structure and operation: free/unfree status and clientship, usually applied to people, were extended to churches and relationships between monasteries and churches.[24]

Literacy and literary practices also reflect a blending of the native and the foreign. The Roman alphabet was adopted by scribes for writing in the vernacular, but the script and orthographical conventions were refashioned to suit the particular needs of the Gaelic language. The Latin verses composed by Gaelic scribes were influenced by native metrical devices and rhetorical styles at the same time that aspects of Latin poetry were being assimilated into Gaelic poetic traditions.[25] The Gaelic notes in the twelfth-century *Book of Deer* from Aberdeenshire exemplify how native literary genres could be exploited in religious institutions: the monastery was said to be named by Saint Columba after the tears shed by Saint Drostan upon their parting, a characteristic origin legend relying upon the creative interpretation of place names.[26]

Sector	Church Influenced by Culture	Culture Influenced by Church
Physical Presence	Native building materials and layout; Some churches built on old pagan sites; Ornamental style and themes reflect native tastes	Buildings primary focus for religious activity; Lands granted by kings to churches; Christian monuments proliferate
Literacy, Literature	Script and orthography modified for Gaelic; Metres and rhetoric in Latin influenced by Gaelic poetry; Church becomes patron of native literature, centre of education	Literacy introduced; Druidism and paganism exterminated; Literature of Christianity and Classical worlds introduced, provide new literary models; Church becomes literary patron, limits subjects of literature
Social organisation	Religious clergy drawn from and chosen by established élite; Legal status and privileges of clergy mirror secular practice; Churches designated as free/unfree, structured in clientship relationships	Church attempts to limit violence; Church becomes patron of legal codification, influences formulation and practice of law

Table 6.1: Some aspects of early native-Christian interaction

Despite charges of paganism or barbarity that others may have claimed against them, the Gaels certainly saw themselves as a Christian people by the time of the Viking invasions. From their initial onslaughts in the year 794 (according to the Annals of Ulster) the Norse were referred to as 'gentiles', contrasting them to the Christianised peoples of Gaeldom. Only in the later ninth century was this religious label replaced with an ethnic one to describe the Norse. Even the seventeenth-century *History of the MacDonalds* recalled that 'the Danes were no Christians'.[27]

Like other peoples who accept Christianity, the Gaels sought a means of salvaging the essence of their origin legends and redeeming their forefathers. Amongst ancestors and mythological characters were the old Gaelic gods, who were later known collectively as *Tuatha Dé Donann* 'the people of the Goddess Donann'. Although pagan pantheons in other cultures were typically unseated by Christian reformers who claimed that they were demons or larger-than-life human beings from the past, the Gaels attempted first to find a theological loop-hole through which to absolve their divine ancestors. Their solution, unique to early European converts, was to claim them as a branch of the human race untouched by the Fall of Adam and Eve in the Garden of Eden. They still exist, said such scholars, in a state of grace beyond sin and age in a timeless paradise where they can see us but we, because of our fallen state, cannot see them. This notion was repeated in some literary texts throughout the medieval period, although it was also joined by more conventional claims that the beings living in the hills and under the seas were fallen angels or the delusions of demons. This remarkable effort by scholars to produce 'a hybrid, composite culture which would be both wholly Irish [i.e., Gaelic] and wholly Christian' allowed for the continuous development of literary characters and themes influential throughout all levels of society with roots consciously planted in the pre-Christian past.[28]

The cautious interest in native tradition which early scholars projected upon the founding saints is exemplified by a tale probably composed in the seventh century, possibly within living memory of Saint Columba. The saint, in this tale, is approached by a young man who clearly indicates that he has come from the Otherworld, having lived a series of lives as a stag, a salmon, a seal, a wolf, and a human. He describes the animals and people who live under the sea – one of the locations where the Otherworld was said to be – but then is stopped by Columba.

> 'That is enough', said Columba. Columba arose as his followers watched, and went aside to speak with him and to ask him about the heavenly and earthly mysteries. While they were together thus for half the day, or from one hour to the next, Columba's followers watched them from a distance. When they parted, they saw that the youth was suddenly hidden from them. They did not know whither he went nor whence he came. When Columba's followers were asking him to reveal to them something of what had passed between them, Columba told them that he could not relate to them even a single word of anything that he had been told; and he said that it was better for mortals not to know it.[29]

Columba is thus represented as the great editor of native tradition, exposed to it himself but protecting his followers from it for their own good. Columba thought it best not to relay the tales told to him of the Otherworld just as the author of this text itself keeps us, the readers, at a safe enough distance to prevent us from overhearing anything dangerous.

The Celtic saints were the subject of literature – formal biography, local oral legends, and hymns, amongst other genres – for over a thousand years. The portrayal of these characters and their confrontation with paganism and secular societies changed greatly over this time span as Gaelic culture itself changed. The earliest texts depict a harsh and rather uncompromising stance as the proponents of Christianity sought dominance over rival forms of authority and power. By the twelfth century, however, with formal pagan religious institutions a dim memory and secular culture reformed within a Christian framework, the saints were remodeled in a kinder, gentler image that makes them conciliatory intermediaries between paganism and Christianity. Confusion has resulted by allowing the later portraits of the 'romanticised' saints, remembering pagan times and characters nostalgically, to obscure the earlier portraits of the saints as severe, ascetic reformers of both sacred and secular culture.[30]

The participation of Scottish Gaels in mainstream European Christendom is demonstrated by their involvement in the crusades, beginning with the First Crusade in the late eleventh century. Many clans kept prized artefacts from these journeys, including the *bratach shìdhe* 'fairy banner' of the MacLeods and the *clach dhearg* 'red stone' of the Stewarts of Ardvorlich.[31] Many Gaelic hero-tales recorded in the modern period recall the 'Turks' amongst foreign peoples bested by Highland warriors. We have brief poetic records of the Fifth Crusade from the pens of Muireadhach Albanach Ó Dálaigh and Gille-Brighde Albanach, apparently the only two of four travelling Gaelic companions (including an Irish prince) who survived the experience.[32]

During the twelfth and thirteenth centuries new monastic orders attempted to reform the church in both Scotland and Ireland (as discussed in Chapters One and Three). This deprived Gaelic scholarship and literature of important intellectual bases and demoted certain aspects of Gaelic religious life. The arts found new patronage with the rise of powerful clans and many older features of native spiritual tradition continued at a vernacular level.

The local élite were entrenched in the church by the eighth century and secular and sacred society remained interwoven throughout the medieval period. Once established, the same families tended to remain established in religious institutions as patrons and/or staff. The Gaelic clergy maintained the same marital and reproductive customs as secular society, including concubinage, resulting in hereditary lineages of churchmen. Surnames such as 'Mac a' Phearsain' ('MacPherson', 'the son of the parson'), 'Mac an t-Sagairt' ('MacTaggart', 'the son of the priest'), and 'Mac an Aba' ('MacNab', 'the son of the abbot') are relics of such practices. There was considerable overlap in the social and educational background of the native learned orders and the church, such as a grounding in Classical Gaelic and Latin, allowing for professionals to change sides of the sacred–secular divide as needed. Highland churchmen followed secular fashions in clothing and grooming; wearing long hair, in the manner of Gaelic aristocrats, drew the criticism of their Lowland peers. Gaelic clergy 'were integrated into society as a whole, and exhibited the values, traits and behaviour of the secular Gaelic world'.[33] Chieftains were praised or criticised by poets according to their support of both professional poetic schools and churches (as in lines 81-2 of poem one in Appendix A).

The Lords of the Isles provided the support for some of the most dynamic religious centres of Gaelic Scotland between the late twelfth and early sixteenth centuries. A distinctive form of stone sculpture was developed and produced under their patronage, an accomplishment unique for such a late period, 'for nowhere else within the late-medieval British Isles do we find the richly carved and decorated free-standing stone crosses which formed so conspicuous a part of the output of these craftsmen'.[34] The grave slabs of Highland warriors and aristocrats ornamented with symbols of power and prestige are still to be found in churchyards and burial grounds (see Plates 8, 9, and 10). Operating within the orbit of such workshops were artisans producing materials for secular society, such as harps, armour, weapons, and mason work.[35]

Saint Columba remained a powerful figure in religious consciousness throughout Scotland, especially amongst Gaels, and his relics were used in battle to ensure victory for the Scots. A brief account of a clash between Scots and Vikings in the early tenth century illustrates this:

> The men of Alba fought this battle steadfastly, moreover, because Colum Cille was assisting them, for they had prayed fervently to him, since he was their apostle, and it was through him that they received faith. [. . .] their battle-standard in the van of every battle would be the Crozier of Colum Cille – and it is on that account that it is called the *Cathbuaid* 'Battle-Triumph' from then onwards; and the name is fitting, for they have often won in battle with it, as they did at that time, relying on Colum Cille.[36]

The use of Columba's relics by Robert Bruce has already been mentioned in Chapter One. A prayer in Latin from the early twelfth century, probably composed in the Lowlands, emphasises the enduring relationship between Scotland and Ireland and the church's desire to maintain its influence over political affairs:

> Holy Columba, our father, born of mother Ireland,
> given by Christ's command to be the church's light,
> may what we have written for you be pleasing to you, we pray [. . .]
> May the king shape his royal acts according to the rule of law,
> for when the king is ruled by law, the realm is kept from harm.[37]

The island of Inchcolm (*Innis Choluim* in Gaelic) in the Firth of Forth is named after Columba, probably after a monastery dedicated to the saint was built there by King Alexander in the year 1123. The Inchcolm Antiphoner is a unique manuscript containing plainchant from the late thirteenth or early fourteenth century belonging to this monastery, a chance survival providing a window into sacred medieval Scottish music.[38] One of the hymns in Columba's praise invokes his protection from English brigands:

> Father Columba, splendour of our ways,
> receive your servants' offerings.
> Save the choir which sings your praise
> from the assaults of Englishmen
> and from the taunts of foes.[39]

An ode composed by Muireadhach Albanach Ó Dálaigh to the Virgin Mary illustrates how native sensibilities informed religious expression. He praises her physical features according to Gaelic standards of beauty, giving her blue eyes, white teeth, and long, curly, blonde hair, and making frequent use of tree metaphors. Instead of the usual rewards a poet expects for his work, Muireadhach asks Mary to grant him entrance to the eternal feast held in her fort (*dún*), images mirroring Gaelic aristocratic life.[40]

In folk tradition, and indeed in many later literary works, the accoutrements of the saints and many items associated with the office of the clergy gained an independent aura and character of holy power in their own right. This was a European-wide phenomenon that saw saint's relics, baptismal water, and even religious books used in the working of magic, a practice that the church encouraged, within certain limits.[41] Items associated with local saints, such as Saint Faolan of Breadalbane, bestowed special privileges and responsibilities upon those who inherited them and used them for healing and other purposes.

The hand-bell, the aural companion of the saint in Scotland, introduced a new audio component to religious experience. Iron hand-bells, dating from as early as the Iona mission of the seventh and eighth centuries, still survive in central Scotland where missionaries converted the Picts.[42] As John Purser has recently demonstrated, many bells can play three different notes and simple melodies can be produced by striking the sides in a particular order.[43] Later traditions made bells out to be autonomous agents whose magical powers worked on behalf of God and the community, after ensuring their own integrity. Adomnán's bell, for example, was said to have the power to curse disobedient kings.[44]

The incorporation of native characters and beliefs into popular religion is exemplified by the transformation of Brighid (known in English as 'Brigit' or 'Bridget'). Saint Brighid seems to have inherited little that is known about the Celtic goddess of this same name;[45] whatever their relationship, she emerged in the early Christian period to become one of the most important holy figures of Gaeldom. Sites were dedicated to her in Scotland as well as Ireland. An apocryphal Gaelic story about her nursing the new-born Jesus elevated her in Gaelic tradition to the status of *muime Chrìosda* 'the foster-mother of Christ', making her closer to Christ than any other mortal apart from the Virgin Mary.[46] The *sloinneadh* 'ancestry' of Brighid was recited as an incantation to protect the speaker from harm, similar to the chants dedicated to the memory of Columba previously cited.[47] The desire for native lore to enjoy the same prestige as the 'imported' lore of the Bible, so marked in the early Christian period, persisted in some communities virtually to the present.

The fairs and holy days commemorating the Celtic saints were an enduring legacy of these figures in the ordinary lives of Highlanders. Some of these were very local affairs dedicated to saints obscure outside the immediate area. The 'Peace of the Fair' that held during these events created a temporal sanctuary from violence and legal prosecution. 'Annual fairs were held on holy days, and dedicated to a saint. They would come under the protection of the saint and thus have the same status as one of his (or her) relics.'[48] Some of the fairs were held on sites that incorporated (or were centred on) ancient sacred features, such as standing stones, fairy mounds and holy wells.[49]

It would be natural to assume that the Protestant Reformation instigated great cultural and social upheaval, but even here we must exercise caution in interpreting the dynamics in both sacred and secular domains. As in previous eras, the church had to adapt to the prevailing norms of Gaelic society and infiltrate from the top down.

> The long-term success of Protestantism and its ability to put down roots depended upon the conversion of the Gaelic aristocracy. The dominant position of the chiefs and their massive influence within the kin-based society was recognised by the Protestant ministers.[50]

The efforts of Archibald Campbell, the fifth Earl of Argyll, in advancing the Reformation in the Highlands has already been noted in Chapter Three. Amongst other efforts, he provided the patronage necessary for John Carswell to translate the *Book of Common Order* into Classical Gaelic. Carswell pitched his work to the high standards of the professional poets, knowing that this landmark in Gaelic literature would draw their attention. The production of texts in Classical Gaelic presumes a literate readership and indeed many of the native literati were finding employment in the reformed church.[51]

Carswell's text was intended to be inclusive of both Gaelic Scotland and Ireland: 'Protestantism was to embrace both areas, since it could be readily allied to the Gaelic culture which both countries shared as part of their common inheritance throughout the Middle Ages.'[52] He strove not just to translate this cornerstone text but to make it compatible with the sensibilities of Gaelic culture. His dedicatory epistle to the Earl of Argyll displays an understanding of the rhetoric of Gaelic panegyric and a blessing he composed for the book itself makes it resemble a poet on his courtly tour. His ability to create and employ new theological terminology invested Gaelic with the ability to express the concepts of the reformed church nearly simultaneously with the Lowlands and enriched its high-register prose for generations to come.[53]

Most of the Highlands were not so well served as some areas of Argyll: the immediate result of the Reformation in Scotland was the creation of a virtual religious vacuum which left most Highlanders even more poorly served than before.[54] In the year 1618, just half a century later, an Irish Franciscan argued that the Catholic Church should allocate resources in its Counter-Reformation efforts to administer to the many Gaels who had been abandoned throughout so much of Scotland:

> Gaelic is the language used in the greater part of Scotland, as that is the language spoken in all but three of the dioceses, and there is not a secular or regular priest in the country who knows that language; it is equally true that a very great number of

Gaelic-speaking Scots are blind concerning the truth faith or have strayed from it, not through any malice of their own but through sheer ignorance, as they had nobody to impart the teaching of the church to them; for a long time no one has been found who would go to Scotland to instruct these people, and, consequently, they are half-pagan in as much as very many of them have never been baptized.[55]

The Irish Franciscans argued that they needed to carry out the missionary work in Gaelic Scotland, for Lowlanders were not only incapable of speaking the language and understanding cultural norms, but were indifferent at best to the spiritual needs of Highlanders.[56]

There is a lasting and mutual enmity between the Anglo-Scots and the Gaelic-speaking Scots; furthermore, the Anglo-Scots do not know Gaelic, and there is only one priest among them who has a knowledge of that language; there is as much difference in mode of life and outlook between the Anglo-Scots and the Gaelic-speaking Scots as there is between the Scots and the Greeks, and, indeed, the Anglo-Scots would be about as useful as the Greeks in helping the people in the Highlands and the Isles; the Scots' colleges at Rome, Paris, and Douai have been established about thirty years, and yet not one priest has come from them during that time to labour in the Gaelic-speaking districts.[57]

The central government attempted to use religious affiliation as a means of bringing about and expressing political allegiance and social conformity to the emerging British state, asserting the authority of its institutions above those of Rome. The consequences of the 'confessional' role of religion were such that some Highland aristocracy were accused of strong-arming their followers into the politically expedient denomination for non-spiritual reasons. The phrase 'creideamh a' bhata bhuidhe' ('the religion of the yellow-stick') in Gaelic oral history attests to chieftains forcing their clansmen into church; it was used to describe Lachlann MacLean (†1687) driving the people of Coll to the Catholic church, but it remains more firmly associated with Protestantism.[58]

Despite the attempt by the central government to exploit religion for political purposes, religious affiliation did not determine political allegiances in the Gàidhealtachd nor were Gaelic political arguments typically expressed in confessional terms, even at the era of the Jacobite movement.[59] 'On the evidence at our disposal, it would seem that within the bonds of a shared culture, a common Gaelic identity, warm personal relationships, social inequalities, and theological disparity could all co-exist.'[60] A great deal, if not the majority, of the military might and intellectual propaganda of the Royalist and Jacobite movements, for example, was provided by Highland Protestants.[61]

The ultimate triumph of the Reformation over the Catholic faith and Counter-Reformation efforts was neither as final nor as inevitable to contemporary observers as it might seem in retrospect. Catholic priests were still attending to Highlanders in

Campbell-dominated Kintyre in the early 1700s, aided and abetted by Catholic contacts amongst the Campbells themselves.[62] In some areas Catholics have remained stubbornly committed to their faith to the present day despite generations of marginalisation.

The acknowledgment of the separation of the reformed church of Scotland from its former connections to European Christendom is given traditional narrative form in a Gaelic tale about Michael Scot. Scot was an important intellectual figure in the early thirteenth century who had been born in Fife, although he spent most of his life on the continent of Europe. The authority of the Catholic Church was conveyed in Gaelic by the saying 'fios na h-Inid às an Roimh' ('knowledge of Shrovetide comes from Rome').[63] The debate over the date of Easter had been a cause of dissension amongst early Christians in the British Isles, with some churches only conforming to a uniform date for Easter in the seventh century.[64] According to the tale recorded in nineteenth-century Argyll, Scot was chosen to travel to Rome. After winning several verbal contests, Scot managed to wrest 'fios na h-Inid', the method of determining Easter, from the Pope, allowing Scots to operate church customs independently.[65] It may be significant that this task was accomplished by a Lowlander otherwise rare in Gaelic tradition and in some versions of the tale it is the Devil himself that Scot rides to reach his goal.[66] This hardly reads like a rousing endorsement of Protestantism in its Highland heartland.

Few non-élite Highlanders were literate in Gaelic before the nineteenth century and so religious teaching relied to a large degree on traditional oral genres, much as in the rest of Europe. 'The singing of metrical psalms was one method employed by Calvinist communities throughout Europe to spread the Protestant message among the non-literate.'[67] 'Laoidh MhicEalair' ('MacKellar's Hymn'), a virtual summary of the Bible in 132 verses,[68] was said to have been so popular that many people learnt and sang it all by heart. Like several other early hymns, it is sung to a 'semi-recitative air such as is associated with the Ossianic Lays'.[69] Despite the opposition of many clerics to Ossianic ballads, the use of the melodies of these prestigious musical and poetic genres elevated religious song. Dugald Buchanan, who was likewise said to have composed secular songs in his youth, evangelised his fellow Highlanders by recourse to native song traditions. His 'Latha a' Bhreitheanais' ('Day of Judgment') is sung to 'the semi-recitative class [of airs] to which Ossianic ballads and poems of the narrative order' were sung.[70]

Tunes were not the only elements borrowed from the secular song tradition into the sacred. The old image of the Highland warrior was moulded into the soldier of Christ. Poem nine in Appendix A, 'Am Meangan' ('The Branch'), is a remarkable example of how the conventions of the Gaelic panegyric code and aspects of ancestral cosmology were reworked to serve Christian subjects. The image of Jesus as a beautiful, verdant, fertile, self-renewing, sheltering branch are derived from the sacred tree standing as the *axis mundi* in Gaelic tradition (discussed below); beside him is the well-spring of eternal youth, another primal archetype with a history long predating Christianity.

There is little doubt that the majority of Gaels accepted the Protestant church in a confessional sense, but it does not necessarily follow that everyone strictly observed its religious discipline or even understood the theological ramifications in detail. That is, we should not assume that the way in which the Protestant church, especially in its Presbyterian form, was prescribed accurately reflected what was always happening in the hearts and minds of its flocks, especially with the shortage of trained Gaelic-speaking ministers in the Highlands.[71]

Reverend John Walker was sent by the General Assembly to assess the state of the kirk in the Highlands in 1765. He claimed that, despite the efforts of the government and the Church of Scotland to promote Protestantism among the Gaels, 'the Popish religion is visibly on the increase.' This was due, he claimed, to the excessive size of parishes, the spiritual ignorance of the Highlanders, and the missionary work by Catholic priests. 'In some parts of the Highlands, the inhabitants have quitted the Protestant Religion [. . .] merely by being left destitute of the ministry and assistance of the Protestant Clergy.' Highlanders were easy prey for Catholicism, he maintained, because they lacked proper education and because they venerated their ancestors and tradition excessively, 'powerful Arguments, of which, the Priests never fail to make proper use, and are very successful ones, in persuading them to return to the Superstitions of the Church of Rome.'[72] Although Walker's comments exaggerate the situation to advance his own interests, they underscore the church's previous lack of investment in the Highlands.

As we have seen in previous chapters, despite disapproval from the clergy many ordinary Highlanders stuck tenaciously to some Gaelic traditions and customs to recent times. The independence of mind amongst common clansmen seems to have kept them resistant to the exclusive authority claimed by ministers, who were largely drawn from the aristocratic and tacksmen classes of Gaelic society. Simon Fraser observes in his notes to the song 'Coma Leam am Ministeir' ('I don't care much for the minister') in his 1816 collection of Highland music:

> The Highlanders, it would seem, were as much inclined as others to resist the authority assumed by the clergy, in extorting confessions, and venting public reproofs, &c, as the words to this air appear to intimate, and they felt particularly sore upon this point, if the clergyman was a worthless person himself.[73]

Similar complaints about both ministers and legal authorities were expressed in the song 'Am Ministeir 's Am Bàillidh', recorded no later than 1770 from an Argyllshire source before becoming popular throughout the Hebrides.[74]

While the era of the Moderate ministers lasted, and before the fabric of Gaelic life was too deeply rent, secular culture still continued with much of the vitality that it had in earlier times. By the end of the eighteenth century, however, the Puritan model of the 'inner community' which turned its back on the vanity of the world began to fuel the impulses of many within the Evangelical movement. The great discontinuities in

Gaelic folklife only become pronounced in the nineteenth century in the midst of social calamity and upheaval, affecting Gaels regardless of religious affiliation. Having internalised the notion that the Highlands were a missionary field like Asia or America, awaiting the civilising influences of the anglophone world,[75] secular Gaelic tradition was assessed as deficient by some such as Patrick Grant, a Baptist minister from Strathspey:

'S an t-seann seanchas, bha Gàidheil ainmeil
A-measg dhaoine, b'ainmig an leithid ann,
Le gaisg' is cruadal, is creach air uairibh,
Is bha am fuil cho uaibhreach a' toirt buaidh dhaibh ann,
Gun tuigse, gun chiall ac', mu thimcheall siorraidheachd [. . .]

B'e ar cleachd o'r n-òige bhith aotrom gòrach
Gun neach a' seòladh dhuinn slighe nas fearr;
Bhitheadh tional mòr anns na taighean-òsda dhinn
Bhitheadh seinn air òrain, bhitheadh spòrsa is gàire [. . .]
Le cainnt ro dhìomhan mu thimcheall Fianntaibh [. . .]

Bhitheadh eagal mòr orra roimh na bòcain
Is iad a' faicinn mòran diubh nach bitheadh ann;
Bhitheadh gisriag is orthaichean is seachnadh chòmhlaichean
Is mòran seòlaidhean ann 'nan ceann;
Bhitheadh aca Sìdheachan anns gach sìdhean
A bheireadh sìos leò mnathan is clann;
Is bhitheadh iad cuid a' bruadair 's an sluagh 'ga mhìneach –
Is gun ghuth air Bìobull bhith idir ann.

Nach truagh ri innseadh gum biodh na mìltean
De anamain prìseal cho anabarra dall
Is gun tèid iad dìreach an aghaidh na fìrinn
Is nach creid iad nì dheth a bhith gu an call;
Sibhse a tha cuir Bhìobull is luchd teagaisg fìrinneach
Dh'ionnsaigh Innseanach fada thall:
Nach cuir sibh pairt dhiubh 's gach eilean Gàidhealach
Oir is truagh bu bhràth dhuinn ma bhitheas sinn mall.[76]

('The Gaels were famous in traditional lore, there were few of their kind: with great feats and hardiness, and an occasional foray, their vainglorious blood brought them victory, but they lacked sense and understanding of the eternal [. . .]')

('It was our habit since youth to be light-hearted and foolish, lacking anyone to show us a better way; we would gather together in the public houses and there would be the singing of songs, merriment and laughter [. . .] with vain and idle talk about the Fian [. . .]')

('Ghosts were feared greatly and they saw many things which did not exist; they had superstitions, and charms, and the avoiding of omen-encounters, and many such practices; they believed that fairies dwelt in every fairy hillock who would take women and children down with them; and some would have dreams which others would interpret – and there was not a single mention of the Bible.')

('Terrible to say, but there were thousands of precious souls which were exceedingly blind and in direct opposition to the truth and they did not believe that any of it was to their loss; o all of you who are sending Bibles and honest missionaries to the Indians so far away: will you not send some of them into the Gaelic islands, for the judgment against us will be harsh if we react slowly.')

The denunciation of various expressions of secular culture – music, poetry, and so on – by the extreme ascetics had a stultifying effect on cultural self-esteem given that the greatest accomplishments of previous generations had been primarily in these domains.

Some characteristics of the Free Church services may be noted [. . .] There is an air of settled gloom on the faces of many of the people – intensified on the Sabbath day. It seems to partake of a religious character. The ministers, catechists, and elders nearly all oppose dancing and every kind of music. Surely they are short-sighted! A sort of fatalism is the most apparent result of the religion of the natives of Gairloch. It has a depressing effect when illness comes.[77]

Rather than blame the theology itself, however, we need to consider the broader social context. Somhairle MacGill-eain, the celebrated twentieth-century poet, was at pains to emphasise that Calvinism did not mute all oral tradition in his family, and that he was 'very sceptical of the Scottish writers who seemed to attribute most of Scotland's ills to Calvinism.'[78]

The Presbyterian Gaelic immigrants of Cape Breton, in the eastern Maritimes of Canada, provide us with a contrast to the anti-secular tendencies which emerged in the Highlands. At the same time that many communities in Scotland were discouraged from indulging in worldly pleasures, the vibrant musical traditions of the Canadian communities, which sided with the Free Church in the Disruption of 1843, suffered no noticeable deterioration.[79]

Protestant ministers, especially the Moderates, were amongst those most responsible for salvaging oral traditions and maintaining the Gaelic language itself. Elements of the supernatural, such as the second-sight, survived even amongst the Evangelicals as a sign of their godliness. Some of the sites used for communion services had strong pre-Christian associations.[80] 'The protestant churches in the Highlands had an ambivalent attitude towards supernatural events.'[81]

During the eighteenth and nineteenth centuries, the secular institutions of Gaelic society were effectively eradicated; only religious institutions remained to any degree in Highland hands but even they internalised many of the external assumptions of Gaelic inferiority. Native society largely lost its élite, the people who should have helped it navigate through a period of intense suffering and cultural disorientation. Without alternative sources of prestige and an articulate challenge to the ideology of Improvement through the anglicisation prescribed in school and church, the symbiotic dialectic between secular and sacred in Gaelic life was broken.[82]

THE OTHERWORLD OF THE SÌDH

As we have already seen, the Gaels had their own gods and panoply of myths when Christianity arrived. By the eighth century Gaelic texts referred to these divine beings as *áes-síde* 'the people of the *sìdh*' collectively and associated them with *sìdhean* 'burial mounds, fairy hillocks'.[83] An archaic Old Gaelic hymn says that the Irish considered them to be gods before the coming of Christianity: 'Darkness covered the people of Ireland who worshipped the síde.'[84] Although the earliest explanation offered by Christianised Gaelic scholars for their origins was as a race of humans untouched by the Fall of Adam and Eve, there was no single, consistent account for them accepted by all medieval scholars. Instead, different writers explored various means of fitting them into Christian cosmology, also claiming them to be fallen angels, demons, or delusions, interpretations which survived into the modern era.[85]

One of the fullest statements about them in early texts occurs in 'Serglige Con Culainn' ('The Wasting-Sickness of Cú Chulainn') from about the tenth century, in which the writer seemingly repents of repeating tales which had been inspired by

> the people of the síde. For before the coming of the Faith the demons had great power, so that they did bodily battle with humans, and revealed delights and mysteries to them, as though they were eternal. And so they were believed in. And so the ignorant call those apparitions síde, and áes-síde.

There is an intentional double entendre in this name which will be discussed below, but suffice it to say that *sìdh(ean)* survives to the present to describe the Otherworld in Scottish Gaelic and *sìdhichean* (plural) its denizens. The English term 'fairy' has connotations of its own, now typically calling to mind small, winged creatures with strange skin. The *sìdhiche* (singular) of Gaelic tradition looks for all purposes like a human, which makes it all the more dangerous; hence I will generally retain the Scottish Gaelic terms in this text and only use 'fairy' sparingly.

It is not until the later burst of 'pseudohistorical' creativity in the late tenth and eleventh centuries that the old gods as a corporate entity – i.e., as a 'Gaelic pantheon' – were given a specific and unambiguous name *Tuatha Dé Donann* 'the People of the Goddess Donann'.[86] The term 'Tuatha Dé Donann' is thus a literary construct which had greatest currency amongst the intelligentsia and became particularly entrenched in the legendary accounts of the waves of settlement of Ireland compiled in *Lebor Gábala Érenn* 'The Book of the Taking of Ireland' and traditions derived from it. Material about the Tuatha Dé Donann circulated in Scotland in textual and oral form to some extent, particularly in areas under the influence of the bardic schools. The Macleans of Mull were amongst the last patrons of the professional poets and in the year 1700 Edward Lhuyd noted several manuscripts in the possession of Reverend John Beaton of Mull which included materials such as the tale 'Cath Maige Tuired' and genealogies of the Tuatha Dé Donann.[87]

They seemed to have been getting more attention amongst the Scottish literati than John Carswell thought proper, for they are denounced explicitly in his dedicatory epistle of 1567. They had diminished greatly by the time they appear in vernacular tradition, however. They are comical figures in the satirical poetry of Iain mac Ailein Maclean of Mull who flourished in the first half of the eighteenth century.[88] An elegy from about the same period to MacAllister of Loup in Kintyre mentions them in a serious historical context.[89] They meet and are killed by Fionn mac Cumhaill and his men in a tale collected in Barra in 1859, an act which parallels their displacement from Gaelic oral tradition by the Fian.[90]

Many of the individual Gaelic deities faded very slowly in oral tradition, sometimes after leaving their names on places in the landscape. The Tuatha Dé Donann were said to have driven out an earlier people, the Fir Bolg, whose name was given to an Iron Age fort on the island of St Kilda, 'Dùn Fir Bholg'. Duncan Campbell says that even in early-nineteenth-century Perthshire, tales of the sea god Manannan were told:

> Of course I believed when a boy in the céilidh myth, and in that myth Diarmid was made the pupil of Mannanan [sic] Mac Lir, the weird magician who owned and gave his name to the Isle of Man – *Eilean Mhannain*, as we called it in Glenlyon.[91]

Manannan received votive offerings in the ocean and was named in charms well into the nineteenth century.[92] Nemain, one of the early Gaelic goddesses who appears as a consort of kings and a demon of battle, said to be the queen of the fairies in some Lowland traditions, survived in the name of NicNiven as distant as Shetland.[93]

Fionn mac Cumhaill seems to have originally been a god of the men of Leinster who gained the characteristics of wisdom and prophecy from the cult figure Find File of the Boyne valley. His name is related to Vindonnus of the Continental Celts and Gwynn ap Nudd of the Welsh. The church seems to have created an illustration of him on an eighth-century stone cross foretelling the coming of Christianity, about the same time that the first story about his 'thumb of knowledge' was written down.[94] Although songs and stories about Fionn and his men proliferated throughout Gaeldom and have survived into the present, the memory of his origin amongst the gods seems to have left no trace in Scottish Gaelic oral tradition.

From the earliest sources, the realm of the pagan gods was depicted as one of eternal youth, beautiful women, opulence, and inexhaustible food and drink, characteristics that continued to be associated with the Otherworld in Scottish Gaelic oral tradition. Like many utopian visions of the divine, it represents human desire and wish-fulfilment. One of the oldest surviving depictions of the Otherworld describes how Angus mac Óg tricked the Dagda out of his residence, the megalithic chamber now called 'Newgrange', in the Boyne valley. 'That is a wonderful land. There are three trees there perpetually bearing fruit, and an everlasting pig on the hoof and a cooked pig, and a vessel with excellent liquor; and all of this never grows less.'[95] The banqueting hall of the gods set a precedent by which the hospitality of mortals was measured, with similar imagery used in Gaelic poetry of chieftains' halls (see line three of poem three in Appendix A).

From the earliest sources there is some implied association between the sìdh and the dead, as the ancient megalithic tombs were the residences of the Gaelic gods in early texts such as that quoted above. An ode as old as the seventh century to a Leinster king says that he 'reached the realms of the dead [. . .] under the worlds of men', which is where the Otherworld was commonly described to be.[96] By the seventeenth century the ancestral dead of humankind were commonly said to be seen amongst the sìdh, perhaps as an aspect of the accommodation of Gaelic tradition to Christian cosmology. In his famous treatise *The Secret Commonwealth*, Robert Kirk wrote in 1692:

There Be manie places called Fayrie hills, which the [Highlanders] think impious and dangerous to peel or discover, by taking earth or wood from them, superstitiously believing the souls of their predecessors to dwell there. And for that end (say they) a Mote or Mound was dedicate beside everie Churchyard, to receave the souls, till their adjacent Bodies arise, and so become as a Fayrie-hill.[97]

Although the sìdh originated as the realm of the immortal gods, distinct from humankind, it often functions in vernacular oral tradition as a counterpart to human society and the human experience. By means of comparison and contrast, tales about the Otherworld and its inhabitants allow us to explore what it means to be human, in the same way that modern science fiction discusses the human experience by comparing and contrasting us with robots and 'little green men' from outer space.

It seems to have been understood by storytellers and their audiences for centuries that the sìdh were in many respects mirror images of humankind. Robert Kirk also commented about the sìdhichean:

They are distributed in Tribes and Orders; and have children, Nurses, marriages, deaths and burials, in appearance even as we [. . .] their apparell and speech is like that of the people and countrey under which they live: so are they seen to wear plaids and variegated garments in the high-lands of Scotland.[98]

Some of the stories themselves indicate an awareness that oral narratives could be used a means of commenting on the human predicament. In one tale told all over Gaelic Scotland and Ireland, commonly known as 'Dùn Bhurg ri theine' ('Dùn Burg is on fire'), a human woman tricks her Otherworldly assistants into leaving her home by claiming that their home is ablaze. As they run outdoors, they say:

> Mo bhean 's mo phàisdean,
> Mo chàise 's mo ghogan ìme,
> Mo mhic 's mo nigheanan
> 'S mo chisteachan móra mine
> Mo chìr 's mo chàrdan
> An snàmh 's a' chuigeal
> Mo bhò 's a' bhuarach
> 'S na cuachan bainne
> Eich 's na h-iallan
> Cliabhan 's cinnean
> 'S an talamh 'cur roimhe
> M' ùird 's m' innean
> Dùn Bhurg ri theine –
> 'S ma loisgear Dùn Bhurg
> Loisgear mo mhùirn
> 'S mo mhireadh.[99]

('My wife and my children, my cheese and my butter-keg, my sons and my daughters, my big chests of meal, my comb and my wool-cards, thread and distaff, my cow and the fetter, horses and traces, harrows and hoard, and the soil breaking before it, my hammers and my anvil, Dùn Bhurg on fire – and if Dùn Bhurg is burnt, my joy and my merriment will be burnt.')

There could hardly be a more mundane enumeration of domestic concerns, and indeed this tale has been shown to be a parable about housekeeping.[100]

Many aspects of fairy lore seem to belong to the dark underbelly of the psyche. Stories of the sìdh were used to discuss a range of social stresses, anxieties, abuses, jealousies, and inequalities between individuals, families, the sexes, and the classes, and anything else that needed to be expressed in ambiguous verbal expression. In a highly interdependent society where most people in a community were closely related, it was not prudent to interfere too strongly in people's affairs or judge them too directly. Supernatural tales allowed people to use 'coded language' to discuss such matters, as well as to recount tales that prescribed social norms and expectations.

Fairies belong to the margins, and so can serve as reference points and metaphors for all that is marginal in human life. Their mostly underground existence allows them to stand for the unconscious, for the secret, or the unspeakable, and their constant eavesdropping explains the need sometimes to speak in riddles, or to avoid discussion of certain topics. [. . .] Viewed as a system of interlocking units of narrative, practice, and belief, fairy legend can be compared to a database: a premodern culture's way of storing and retrieving information and knowledge of every kind, from hygiene and child care to history and geography.[101]

Many of the deeds attributed to the sìdhichean – abduction, infanticide, murder, rape, theft – were more likely the fault of humans whom the tales exonerated. Redirecting the blame to the alien sìdhichean was socially convenient: it prevented an escalating cycle of punishment, vengeance, hatred, and reprisals; it provided a scapegoat for those who exploited their positions of privilege, whether of class or gender; it provided a form of wish-fulfilment for those living in unsatisfying circumstances; it provided an alibi for those with addictions or with a slim hold on reality when sober; it gave a label to those who were seen as socially or sexually deviant. Reading 'fairy' tales with this in mind can make for grim and grisly work.[102]

Consider a common tale about a woman who was out with the cattle one day when she was kidnapped by sìdhichean. She was taken to their home in the sìdhean and commanded to make bread from the meal in the meal-chest; once she had used up all of the meal, they promised, she would get payment and be allowed to return home. Even though she worked as hard as she could all day baking bread, the chest would always be full the next morning. She was so heartbroken that she burst into tears. There was an old woman in the sìdhean who had also been abducted when she was young who had lost all hope of escaping. This old woman took pity on her and told her the secret of making the meal-chest empty: she was to return the last sprinkling of meal to the chest, rather than make a bannock from it. Sure enough, the next morning the chest was empty and the chief of the sìdh gave her a payment and allowed her to leave, although he called after her as she departed, 'My blessing on thee, but my curse on the mouth who taught you [the secret].'[103] Some women were, as a matter of fact, kidnapped to become wives by force;[104] even many housewives who entered marriage willingly must have resented the drudgery and thankless labour which they were obligated to do. The tale seems to be one of wish-fulfilment, of dreaming of escape back to a previous life.

Another crucial strand in the complex of sìdh belief relates to abnormalities, defects and handicaps. Many of the classic characteristics of children claimed to be change-lings ('impostors' left by the sìdh after they had kidnapped 'real' infants) correspond closely to well-documented symptoms of genetic abnormalities which can include webbed fingers or toes, scaly skin, large and unusual ears, and cleft palates.

Traits that are linked – ravenous appetite, irritability, failure to thrive, small size – are logically associated with infectious illness [. . .] and with a range of disorders that effect a child's ability to properly digest food. [. . .] Finally, the withered appearance of the changeling so frequently commented upon in these tales may simply be the appearance of a very ill infant, or it may be the result of specific disorders that actually affect the thickness and pigmentation of the skin.[105]

The birth of a child should be a cause for joy and celebration: a mother's realisation that the infant that she carried through pregnancy and labour was abnormal and unable to ever flourish must have been emotionally traumatic. Changeling tales seem to reflect and/or guide a mother's grieving process, from denial through guilt and anger to acceptance, particularly by distancing herself psychologically from the child by representing him as an alien creature.[106] Kirk Session registers from the eighteenth century contain records of charity being given to changelings, suggesting 'a system of social security, with "changelings" – presumably those who are at risk of abandonment due to mental and physical disability – regarded as the most deserving'.[107] This evidence documents those who were functional enough to have survived into adulthood; traditional tales suggest that without such support, or in more extreme cases, children were abandoned and allowed to die.

Consider the common story in which a tailor – usually an outsider to the community and therefore a suitable scapegoat for blame – recognises that a woman's child is really a changeling:

'And what am I do to with him?' asked the woman.

'Take him', said the tailor, 'to the neighbouring ravine, and throw him over the bank into the water below.'

The woman did as she was told, but no sooner had the child touched the water than he became a little grey man. He rose to his feet in a great rage and scrambled up the steep side of the ravine, threatening the woman with vengeance if he overtook her. But she took to her heels as fast as she could, and never looked behind her until she arrived at the house, where she found her own child laid at the door before her.[108]

The anger of the changeling is a projection of the woman's own guilt about infanticide, which is done by drowning or abandonment in the water. Finding a healthy child at home is either wish-fulfilment or another attempt at bearing a child which is successful.

Although these various interpretative methods are useful in understanding how the concept of the Otherworld operated in oral narrative and informed daily life, they are not entirely adequate to explain the full range of beliefs and behaviours of the past. There was more to this ancestral universe of discourse and practice than we can ascribe to mass hallucination, ignorance, or a willing suspension of disbelief. The writers who developed and employed narratives of the sìdh for over a millennium were not simply using them as euphemisms for violence or birth defects but were legitimising dynasties, explaining the success and failure of rulers, and even mobilising society for political action.[109] The 'confessions' transcribed from witchcraft trials, however they were produced, reveal that much of the archaic symbolism of Gaelic cosmology survived in Scottish folk life but was being subverted by church and state to impose greater central authority and a change of *mentalité* upon the populace.[110]

GODDESS OF LIFE AND LANDSCAPE

One of the most powerful and enduring 'personalities' of Gaelic cosmological tradition is the *Cailleach*, an archaic female figure associated with the landscape, wild nature, elemental forces, and geotectonic powers. She seems to belong to the oldest layer of surviving belief in oral tradition, although the Norse may have contributed to and reinforced the imagery and symbolism around her.[111] Her oldest recorded name is *Cailleach Bhéarra* from her association with the Beara peninsula in the south-west tip of Ireland. She is known by this name in Scotland as well, although the place name is usually reinterpreted as the adjective *beur* 'keen, sharp, pointed, witty'. She was never fully adopted by any pan-Gaelic institution, so she is also known by a variety of names rooted in the local landscape or referring to her rough appearance and behaviour. Differing regions have elaborated some of her character-istics and neglected others. Unlike the gregarious sìdhichean, the only company she keeps is that of wild creatures or cattle.

It has been speculated that the other female goddesses in Gaelic tradition ultimately derive from her; as new clusters of feminine figures evolved, patterns of symbols were left in successive strata of cultural developments.[112] The Great Mother of Indo-European and early Celtic mythology and her bovine aspect/companion are early incarnations of the feminine goddess which can still be traced in Gaelic tradition.[113] The Gaels developed goddesses of death, war and irrepressible sexuality at an early period known as Mórrígan, Badhbh, and Nemain.[114] The Gaelic literati developed territorial sovereignty goddesses who conferred legitimacy upon kings, looked after their interests, and warned of their deaths.[115] Despite the distinctiveness of these manifestations of the divine feminine in successive cultural layers, there are themes, images, and functions that connect them and were continually reworked and reimagined by both vernacular verbal artists and professional intelligentsia of the Gaelic world.

Gearóid Ó Crualaoich has identified four major themes in narratives about the Cailleach (besides her role as the archetype of the sovereignty goddess), all of which are well attested in Scottish Gaelic oral tradition:[116]

1. She creates and dominates landscape
2. She has extraordinary traits and behaviours, linking her with wild nature
3. She is able to restore her youth periodically, thus living forever
4. She is eventually in conflict with and displaced by Christianity and modern society

Stories about her creation or use of features of the landscape survive from wherever Gaelic was spoken in Scotland in recent generations. 'She is associated with places along the whole west coast of Argyllshire, each district claiming her as a native, and pointing to the spots she frequented.'[117] The standing stones on Craigmaddy Moor near Glasgow are called in Lowland Scots 'The Auld Wife's Lifts'. Loch Awe, Loch Tay, and Loch Ness were said (in separate, local tales) to have been formed when she forgot to replace a flagstone lid on a magical well-spring. Myriad mountain ranges and islands were said to have been formed by her, including the mountains of Ross-shire, the Hebrides and Ailsa Craig. She washed her clothing in the giant whirlpool of Coire Bhreacan and covered the mountains with snow when she lifted her plaid.[118]

She set about building a bridge across the Sound of Mull, commencing at the Morvern side, and was on her way, with a creelful of stones on her back for the purpose, when the creel strap (*iris mhuineil*) broke, and the burden fell to the ground. The stones with which the basket was filled (and it must have been one of no small capacity) form the remarkable cairn called *Càrn na Caillich* (the old wife's heap of stones).[119] She intended to put a chain across the Sound of Islay, to prevent passage of ships that way, and the stones are pointed out on the Jura side to which the chains were to be secured. *Beinn na Caillich*, a hill in Kildalton parish, Islay, is called after her, and a furrow down its side, called *Sgrìob na Caillich*, was made by her, as she slid down in a sitting posture. In the parish of Stralachlan and Strachur, in Cowall, Argyllshire, there is also a hill called after her, *Beinn Chailleach Bheur*.[120]

She was said to be so large that even the most awe-inspiring features of the landscape were insignificant to her:

> *Crù-lochan beag dorcha domhainn*
> *An aon loch as doimhne air domhan*
> *Ràinig a' mhuir mhór an glùn domh*
> *'S ràinig Crù-lochan an tòn domh.*[121]

('Little, dark, deep Crù-lochan is the deepest loch in the world: the great sea comes only to my knee and Crù-lochan reaches my buttocks.')

She was said to be so old that she could recall previous eons of geological development of the landscape. A song attributed to her in South Uist recalls the ancient Celtic theme of land being overcome by water;[122] her subsistence on uncooked foods underlines her primal associations with the wild:

> *Duair a bha an fhairge mhór*
> *'Na coille choinnich ghlais*
> *Bha mis' am mhùirneig òig*
> *Bu bhiadh miamh maidne dhomh*

Duileasg leac o Haigeir
Agus creamh à Sgòth
Uisge à Loch a' Cheann Dubhain
Is iasg às an Ionbhaire mhóir
B' iad siud mo ragha beatha-sa
Am fad 's a bhithinn beò.[123]

('When the great sea was a grey, mossy forest, I was a merry young maiden and my wholesome morning meal was the dulse of the rock of Agir, the wild garlic of Sgoth, the fresh water of Loch a' Cheann Dubhain and the fish of Ionbhaire Mór: that was my chosen way of life for as long as I lived.')

The second theme, that of her association with wild nature, is particularly expressed by her association with extreme weather and the undomesticated animals of the wilderness. Weather and calendar lore associated with her was collected by Katherine Grant in the late nineteenth century:

'The Cailleach is going to tramp her blankets to-night,' might be the remark of a neighbour when an unusually heavy wintry storm was imminent. 'The Cailleach has thrown her mallet under the holly,' would be the cheerful observation made when the storms of the vernal equinox were exhausted, and snowy cloud islets lay becalmed in the blue abysses of air. 'The Cailleach is milking her goats to-night; don't you hear the milking-lilt?' (*Sruth-bleoghan.*) This when the hurricane was at its height, and the thunder of the billow rose in unison with the voice of the winds; and foam-crested waves rolled into cove, and cave, and creek around the shore.[124]

She was known as Cailleach Bheathrach in the Braes of Mar[125] and as Cailleach Beinne Bhric in the central Highlands. She had a herd of deer that she milked and accompanied through the moorland, protecting them from human hunters: as the Cailleach represents the forces undomesticated by humankind, so are her livestock the untamed deer who live in the high, wild places.[126] She was said to sing a song as she travelled:

Cailleach Beinne Bhric, ho ró,
Bhric ho ró, Bhric ho ró,
Cailleach Beinne Bhric, ho ró,
Cailleach mhór an fhuarain àird.

Cha leiginn mo bhuidheann fhiadh
Mo bhuidheann fhiadh, mo bhuidheann fhiadh
Cha leiginn mo bhuidheann fhiadh
A dh'iarraidh shlige dhuibh an tràigh.[127]

('Cailleach Beinne Bhric ho ró . . . The great Cailleach of the high well-spring.')

('I would not let my herd of deer . . . seek out the shellfish of the tide.')

Legends about Cailleach Beinn a' Ghlotha (called 'the Wife of Ben-y-Ghloe' in English sources) in nineteenth-century Atholl demonstrate her connection with the ferocious powers of the natural world which were indifferent if not hostile to human interests:

> There is great talk of a witch that still haunts Ben-y-gloe. She is represented as of a very mischievous and malevolent disposition, driving cattle into morasses, where they perish, and riding the forest horses by night, till covered with mire and sweat, they drop down from fatigue and exhaustion. She has the power of taking the shape of an eagle, raven, hind, or any other animal that may suit her purpose. She destroys bridges, and allures people to the margin of the flood, by exhibiting a semblance of floating treasures, which they lose their lives in grasping at.[128]

Themes three and four, her cyclic restoration of youth and ultimate dethronement, are neatly illustrated in a tale from the island of Mull, which had a complex of place names memorialising her presence:

> It was here, on the banks of Loch Bà, that the legendary 'Cailleach Bheur' closed her career of a thousand years. This famous hag, the legend relates, immersed herself in the waters of Loch Bà at intervals of a hundred years, an ordeal which always gave her a new lease of life. The charm was of no avail, however, should a bird or beast of the field happen 'to greet the early morn' before the hag had bathed herself in the elixir of life. One morning when the cycle had been spun out to its last moments, the hag was slowly descending the beautiful slopes beyond Loch Bà. She had just gained the bank, whose sandy lips the little wavelets kissed, and was about to take the plunge which would have changed the 'withered' dame into the handsome maid, when, alas! the distant barking of a shepherd's dog, welcoming the first grey streaks of the summer morning, echoed and re-echoed among the hills. The hag stood and listened. The last grain of sand in the centenary glass trickled out, and the charm was broken. The hag now felt the effects of hoary age, she staggered, reeled, and dropped down dead.[129]

The place name *Loch Bà* 'the Loch of the Cow' is significant in that cattle are commonly associated with the Indo-European Mother Goddess. An early text about Cailleach Bhéarra explicitly gives her the appellation *Boí/Buí*. It is also noteworthy that the Otherworld was often portrayed as accessible through bodies of water such as lochs. The need to acknowledge the primacy of the Cailleach is broken by a shepherd's dog, which symbolises the domestication of animals and landscape. Thus usurped, she loses her ability to restore herself.[130]

Like many other personifications of wild nature, she was not always friendly to humankind but was unpredictable and uncontrollable. In her role as territorial goddess, however, she was generally seen to favour kindreds with a right to own land, and act out her dislike of usurpers, which may be implied in the following passage from the late nineteenth century:

> In olden times almost every Highland hamlet had its hag, or *cailleach*. These extraordinary beings – whatever they were – according to a common tradition, all frequented the wildest, weirdest, and most solitary parts of the districts where they were to be found, but yet very often such places as drovers, packmen, and travellers generally had from time to time to pass. An interesting feature of the belief in them was that while some of them were considered inimical, particularly to members of certain clans, others were looked upon as friendly. The parish of Urquhart and Glenmoriston, about a hundred years ago or so, contained no less than five or six of those 'cailleachs', most prominent among whom was *Cailleach a' Chràich* (the Hag of the Cràach). [. . .] According to one tradition Cailleach a' Chràich's pet aversion was the Clan Macmillan. There is some evidence, however, to show that members of the Clan Macdonald were particularly the objects of her malice and spite. In an old song one of them says regarding her:

> > *Cha téid mi an rathad*
> > *A dh'oidhche no na latha*
> > *Chan eil deagh bhean an taighe*
> > *'S a' Chràich.*
> >
> > *Tha i trom air mo chinneadh*
> > *'Gam marbhadh 's 'gam milleadh;*
> > *'S gun cuireadh Dia spiorad*
> > *Nis fhearr ann.*[131]

('I won't take the road by night or by day, there is no guid-wife in the Cràach.')

('She's hard on my clan, killing and destroying them; may God replace her with a better spirit.')

COSMOLOGY AND SOCIAL ORDER

As in other societies, ancestral Gaelic cosmology asserted that the stability and well-being of human society depended upon a proper relationship with the divine order. Many concepts, beliefs, customs, and practices reflect the desire to reassert social order and realign it with the forces of the Otherworld. This is implicit in early texts about the sìdh in which the two possible meanings of the word – 'Otherworld' and 'peace' – were brought together to imply the cause and effect of sacred rule:

First, that legitimate kingship has its source in the Otherworld, and, secondly, that the reign of the righteous king is marked by peace (as well as plenty) in the land. That is as much to say that 1 *síd* denotes the source of *fír flathemon* ['prince's truth'], and 2 *síd* its symptom. [. . .] The ideology of kingship is matched by the symbols and rituals which surround the office, and especially by those attending the election and consecration of the king.[132]

The common use of ancient burial mounds, 'fairy knolls', and sacred trees in the ruler's inauguration reinforce the conceit that he is connected in a special way to the Otherworld. In order for this connection to work in his favour, rather than against him, he must uphold the ideals of leadership, especially truth.

The human order was especially reasserted in a periodic *oenach* 'assembly, festival'[133] in early Gaelic tradition. The cyclic revivification of the community reinforced symbolic parallels between human society and the Otherworld, linked together by the ancestral dead:

One might express the triad's unity by saying that society, affirmed and symbolized by the *oenach*, derives its legitimacy from the traditions received from ancestors who have departed into the Otherworld; or that the *oenach* establishes a link between the life of the *tuath* and the transcendent validity of an eternal state of which both death and immortality are aspects.[134]

The beliefs and rituals surrounding the oenach drew a number of analogies between the 'two worlds':[135]

1. Tribal assemblies were often held at sites sacred to divine characters and sometimes at burial mounds explicitly called sidhean
2. Tribal assemblies were often held at sacred times (such as Bealltainn or Samhainn), precisely those times when the Otherworld was most accessible to this world
3. Time and space in the Otherworld has a transcendent quality of unification and omnipresence, just as tribal assemblies unified the populace in place and time.
4. Feasting was a feature of the Otherworld as well as of assemblies
5. Just as the Otherworld granted truth and peace to the righteous ruler, so were tribal assemblies regarded as sanctuaries from violence or criminal persecution
6. Just as the Otherworld is beyond sin and guilt, normal social restrictions were temporarily lifted at assemblies, allowing for a taste of the 'sexual liberation' often depicted in the Otherworld
7. The king who is given divine endorsement by the Otherworld is the master of the oenach and the connection between the tribe and the Otherworld

The divine personage most significant to Irish society was the sovereignty goddess personifying the island of Ireland as a whole, or specific territories within it. Under names such as Ériu, Fódla, and Banbha, she conferred legitimacy upon the men who became king by union with her.

> Where the region is also a kingdom, the goddess embodies not merely its fertility but also its sovereignty, and from this nexus comes one of the most prolific of Celtic myths, that of the solemn union of the ruler and his kingdom. It is much older than the Celts, but among them it found a congenial and remarkably productive context. [. . .] Because of its enduring resonance, the myth was often used to eulogise individual rulers or to justify the ambition of political dynasties. Bereft of her rightful mate and ruler the kingdom became widowed, impoverished and decrepit, reflecting the material and political misfortunes of the land and its people, and this is graphically highlighted in numerous tales and poems in which the woman becomes repulsively old and ugly only to be restored to radiant youth and beauty by the act of intercourse with her new ordained partner.[136]

It is particularly in this notion of the potential immortality of her restored youth and vigour that we can see how patriarchal society appropriated and adapted the Cailleach Bhéarra archetype to legitimise itself.[137]

As extensive research on oral folklore by Patricia Lysaght has revealed,[138] the *ban-sí* 'banshee' of Irish oral tradition is derived from the territorial goddess of sovereignty and can take different forms associated with specific functions. She is attached to a native Gaelic family who produce the rightful rulers of her territory; she foretells the death of her 'mate', sometimes by appearing to him in a ford where she is washing his blood-soaked clothes; she keens his death; she has associations with bodies of water and the landscape in general.

These symbolic complexes expressing the connections between human society and the divine Otherworld so richly developed in Ireland, especially by the literati, have parallels in Scotland, although they sometimes appear meagre or less cohesive by comparison or are taken in a slightly different direction. There are a number of reasons to explain why the concept of a territorial goddess gets little attention in the élite Scottish Gaelic literature of the filidh: the territorial claims of Gaelic-speaking leaders in Scotland were unstable and the landmass was not as neatly delimited as Ireland; the dynasty of Scottish kings became alienated from their Gaelic origins and thus did not seek legitimising texts of this nature; professional poets were trained in Irish bardic colleges to learn a canon of material relating to Irish mytho-history but few equivalent institutions with a specifically Scottish remit operated. The result may have been a sense of geographical marginalisation and cultural ambiguity amongst the literati.[139]

The oral narratives in Scottish Gaelic tradition, however, provide us with evidence that variations of these concepts and practices operated on the ground in a more vernacular form, namely:

1. Beliefs about *A' Bhean-Nighe* 'Washer Woman' who is seen washing the bloody clothes of the man whose death she foretells, whose family to which she is attached
2. Beliefs about other tutelary beings belonging to specific noble families who look after their interests and who foretell and mourn their deaths
3. Beliefs that the state of the landscape and its produce reflected the righteousness of the ruler
4. Gaelic poetry addressed to the landscape concerned about the social order
5. Continuation of the symbols of marriage with the sovereignty goddess in inaugural rituals

Scottish narratives about the bean-nighe show that she is the same character as the ban-sí and 'washer at the ford' of Irish tradition.[140] Surviving tales recounting sightings of her had a remarkable range, from Islay to Lewis. In some texts, she is associated with the raven and the term *Baobh*, which reflect the images of the ancient Gaelic war-goddesses. She can also be referred to as the *Caoinea(cha)g* 'the crying, keening one', since she laments the death of the man to whom she is attached. The bean-nighe attached to the Macleans of Loch Buidhe sang their death dirge.[141]

According to a tale collected by Alexander Carmichael in the late nineteenth century, the caoineachag was heard weeping on several successive nights before the Massacre of Glencoe, giving a warning to some families who were able to escape. A fragment of her song went:

> *Tha caoineachag bheag a' bhròin*
> *A dortadh deòir a sùla*
> *A' gul 's a' caoidh cor Clann Domhnaill:*
> *Fàth mo leòin nach d' éisd an cumha!*[142]

('The little caoineachag of sorrow is weeping tears from her eye, crying and lamenting the fate of Clan Donald: that the lament was not heard hurts me!')

Several other types of preternatural beings seem to have had similar attachments and roles, especially the *gruagach* 'long-haired one'. Throughout the Gaelic-speaking world, milk offerings were made to the gruagach on particular stones. 'There is hardly a district in the Highlands which does not possess a *leac gruagaich* [. . .] whereupon the milk libation was poured.'[143] The gruagach was often credited with watching after the cattle herd from which the milk came and many were specifically assigned to 'families of name and note'.[144] An example was recorded in Islay in 1859, referring to this being with the English equivalent 'brownie':

The small island of Inch, near Easdale, is inhabited by a brownie, which has followed the MacDougalls of Ardincaple for ages, and takes a great interest in them. He takes care of their cattle in that island night and day, unless the dairymaid, when there in summer with the milk-cattle, neglects to leave warm milk for him at night in a knocking-stone in the cave, where she and the herd live during their stay in the island. Should this perquisite be for a night forgot, they will be sure in the morning to find one of the cattle fallen over the rocks with which the place abounds.[145]

The white cows in Gaelic tradition which feed people in their time of need and provide guidance at critical times are also likely to derive from the ancestral goddess figure.[146] She plays a role in the tale of the origins of the Macintyres of Glennoe:

According to tradition, the Macintyres came from one of the Western Isles. They lived for some time south of Ben Cruachan. They tried on several occasions to drive their cattle through the passes of that mountain, but were always stopped and turned back by a spirit that acted as guardian of the mountain. This spirit, however, was by no means unfriendly to them. He told them that they had been taking the wrong passes, and directed them to the pass or opening that led to Glennoe. He also told them to follow a white cow that they had in their herd, and to build a house for themselves on the first spot on which the cow would lie down to rest. They followed his advice. The result was that they settled in the beautiful valley of Glennoe.[147]

The idea that the land and the plants and animals on the land flourish under a goodly ruler and wither under a bad ruler is an ancient belief found in most cultures with a 'cult' of kingship. This notion is reflected, for example, in a poem from the early fourteenth century anticipating the return of the galloglass chieftain Eòin MacSuibhne to the home of his ancestors at Castle Sween in Knapdale:

> *Fáilte ag sruthaibh Sléibhe Monaidh*
> *ré Mac Suibhne Sléibhe Mis* [. . .]
> *Léigid géaga a nglúine fútha*
> *feartha fáilte rér bhflaith ceóil;*
> *measa sláinte coll gach calaidh,*
> *trom a bhfáilte i n-aghaigh Eóin.*[148]

('The streams of Scotland's moorside welcome MacSweeny of Sliabh Mis [. . .] branches bend their knees to welcome our melodious prince; wholesome hazelnuts of every harbour give a weighty welcome to Eóin.')

Duncan Campbell noted in the late nineteenth century that 'Highlanders mortally hated William and Mary' and saw the effects of their misrule manifest physically in the late seventeenth and early eighteenth centuries:

On the 8th March, 1702, a widow woman in Camusvrachdan, in Glenlyon, astonished her neighbours by the news of the King's death. She had no visible means of information, was far from being suspected of witchcraft, and still she asserted the truth of what she said with wonderful pertinacity. On being pressed for reason, she replied, 'My cow gave me twice the milk I ever had from her at any time for the last seven years.' By subsequent information it was discovered William had died on the precise day.[149]

Indeed, many Jacobite songs exploit similar claims. When Prince Charles Edward Stewart was born in 1720, his anticipated return to Scotland was depicted as restoring the bounty of the land:

> Bidh gach tulach 'na iomairibh réidh
> 'S fàsaidh cruithneachd air aodainn shliabh [. . .]
> Cuiridh coille trom-bhlàth os ar cionn
> Cuiridh 'n talamh gun airceas de bharr
> Tacar mara cur làin 's gach lion.[150]

('Every hillock will become smooth fields and wheat will grow on hillsides [. . .] the forest above us will produce fruit, the land will yield harvest without stint, the provision of the sea fill every net.')

Rob Donn Mackay of Sutherland declared that livestock, crops, and and the weather all improved upon Charles's arrival in Scotland.[151] When the prince died in 1788, however, William Ross says that the land went into a state of mourning:

> Tha gach beinn, gach cnoc 's gach sliabh
> Air am faca sinn thu 'triall
> Nis air chall an dreach 's am fiabh
> O nach tig thu 'chaoidh nan cian.[152]

('Every mountain, hill and moor-side on which we saw you travelling has now lost its beauty since you will never ever return.')

In seventeenth-century Ireland, the concept of the sovereignty goddess was given new life and purpose in the political *aisling*, a prophetic poem in which the female personification of Ireland laments her forlorn state but expects her reunion with her rightful spouse (the king). While this genre did not emerge in the same configuration in Gaelic Scotland, especially because of the lack of a national sovereignty goddess as noted above, poets did compose verse with similar themes and concerns, especially on behalf of the Jacobite cause.[153] While the Irish aisling invokes the embodiment of Ireland in order to facilitate a dialogue, similar poems in Scottish Gaelic address features of the landscape directly (cutting out the 'middle-woman', as it were).[154] Gaelic poets in both Scotland and Ireland had a long literary tradition of such poetic conversations (illustrated in poem seven of Appendix A).

In times of crisis, particularly after Culloden, Scottish poets composed versified dialogues with the landscape that lamented the fall of the old Gaelic order and, sometimes, its hopeful return. This was not merely a literary convention, for it was used for centuries during which time the landscape was seen as a living and divine entity inextricably bound with its human community. In a dialogue between a poet and the ruins of Inverlochy Castle, composed no later than the late eighteenth century, the castle is made to say:

> *Bha uair a bha mi àlainn ùr*
> *Rìghrean is flaithean ann mo mhùr;*
> *Nam faiceadh tusa féin an lò*
> *Cha b' iongnadh leat an diugh mo bhròn.*
>
> *Ach thréig na tréin a b'fhéile gnàthas*
> *Is dh'fhàg iad mise falamh fàs*
> *Gun neach 's an t-saoghal ga bheil suim*
> *Ged chìte mi 'nam làraich luim.*[155]

('There was a time when I was fresh and beautiful, with kings and princes inside my ramparts; if you had seen that day yourself, you would not be surprised at my sorrow today.')

('But those most generous warriors have fled, and they have left me empty and abandoned, with no one in the world who cares, even though I am a bare ruin.')

It is not just for the sake of the warriors, kings and princes as individuals that the castle (and the human author) grieves, but the traditional society to whom they were patrons and paragons.

As already discussed in Chapter Four, the inauguration of kings and chieftains contained symbols and customs relating to the endorsement of the Otherworld and the sovereignty goddess, namely the location of the ceremony (a burial mound or *bile* 'sacred tree'), the drink of sovereignty, and the rod of sovereignty (*slat tighearnais*).

These beliefs and practices reinforced the association between the social order and the Otherworld in a manner similar to the 'classic Irish' model outlined above. A supplementary cosmological paradigm evolved independently in Gaelic Scotland out of the symbol of the sacred tree as *axis mundi* 'the world pillar' or *ompholos* 'cosmic navel' that stands at the centre of the universe connecting the heavens with the earth. This is arguably the most enduring and evocative symbol in Gaelic culture, to be found from the prehistoric era (in archaeological and place-name evidence) to the modern era in song and story. Religious traditions all around the world, including Christianity, have revered trees or symbols derived from tree imagery.

The conviction has remained through the ages that at the ompholos lies an ultimate source of ever-renewing vitality and regeneration symbolised by the Tree of Life. [. . .] It is apparent that around this widespread symbol a mythology and cultus have developed centred in the belief in the renewal of life in its various forms of manifestation in nature, the universe and in the human species.[156]

It is believed that the word 'druid' has some relation to the word 'tree' and that trees played some part in their religious rites, although we can do little more now than speculate on these connections. Three trees feature in the early Gaelic text describing the Otherworld 'inside' of Newgrange given above. Cosmological trees feature in early Irish texts and some early tribal names imply association with or even ancestry from trees.[157]

There are a number of trees in Scotland that were sacred in pre-Christian times, sometimes close to a place name containing the early Celtic term *nemeton* 'sacred site' or a later derivative.[158] Most notable of these is the yew at Fortingall, thought to be between three and five thousand years old, which is near the nemeton name 'Duneaves' and the traditional centre of Scotland.[159]

Many of the sites sanctified by the Celtic saints had sacred trees. According to local tradition, Saint Columba went to the island of Bernera off the south-west corner of Lismore. He blessed a large yew tree there and, like the descriptions of so many other sacred trees, it was preternaturally large: 'Under the shadow of the branches a thousand people could shelter.' Columba foretold that the men who injured it would suffer a threefold death, a prophecy which came true in the nineteenth century. Yet, despite this damage, it recovered and still sprouts anew.[160]

Although many other sacred trees in Scottish legend and landscape could be listed, what is important is the archetype of the *bile* which these instances manifest: the tree is the central pillar of the world that provides access between this world and the Otherworld; it is full of life force, verdant, fresh, self-renewing; it offers shelter and protection; it is strong and steadfast, straight and true. Scottish Gaelic cosmological tradition projects the archetype of the bile in various forms in different spheres of life and culture.[161]

Cultural Sphere	Projection
Spatial	Sacred tree serves as centre of ceremony (inauguration, ritual, etc.)
Human	King or chieftain
Family	Family tree of geneaology
Symbols of office	Rod/sceptre of king/poet
Society	Social order imagined in tree form

Table 6.2: Projections of the sacred tree archetype in Gaelic cosmology

Gaelic poetry abounds with tree kennings. Humans are to the animal world what trees are to the plant world: it is an elementary analogy that has been discovered independently many times. Like trees, people are erect and tall (the tallest beings in many ecosystems); trees have branches and roots, people have arms and legs; trees have sap, people have blood; trees have leaves, people have hair; and so on. A poet would seek the most striking images and strongest assertions for the subject of his praise. One of the many vivid examples of this in Gaelic verse is an elegy to Iain Molach MacKenzie of Applecross *c.*1685:

> *A' chraobh thu b' àirde anns a' choille*
> *Thar gach preas bha thu soilleir*
> *A' cumail dìon air an doire*
> *Le d' sgèimh ghuirm fo bhlàth dhuilleag;*
> *Cha b'e 'mhàin Clanna Choinnich*
> *Bhiodh mun cuairt dhuit mu Challuinn*
> *Bhiodh gach fine agus sloinneadh*
> *A' teachd le càirdeas 'ad choinneamh:*
> *Bhiodh fir Éireann 's nan eilean mu d' bhòrd.*[162]

('You were the highest tree in the forest, visible above every bush, protecting the grove with your verdant beauty of blooming foliage; it was not only the Mackenzies who would gather around you on Hogmanay: every people and lineage would come to meet you in friendship; the men of Ireland and the islands would gather around your table.')

Iain Molach is equated with the sacred *bile*: his excellence makes him literally outstanding, and he provides sanctuary and provision to all those who seek it. This imagery serves very well to complement Gaelic ideals of hospitality and clientship, and it was co-opted by Christian poets in praise of Jesus (see poem nine in Appendix A).

Tree kennings and metaphors were applied to people generally, not exclusively the élite. They were also extended by equating groups of people to forests or the branches of a tree (see Plate 16). Indeed, family genealogy was already discussed using tree terminology – *cráeb coibnesa* 'branches of kinship' – in early texts[163] and it appears in a poem in praise of Aonghus MacDonald of Islay in the thirteenth century.[164] In a song by William Ross in praise of Gearrloch and its people *c.*1783, he names Eachann Ruadh as the trunk of the tree of the MacKenzies growing there:

> *O là Raon Flodden nam beum trom*
> *A shocraich bonn na fiùbhaidh –*
> *Gu h-uallach dosrach, suas gun dosgainn*
> *Uasal on stoc mhùirneach.*[165]

('From the day of the Battle of Flodden of the heavy blows, which secured the root of the timber – proudly branching, growing up without any defects, nobly from the delicate trunk.)

Of particular significance in Gaelic cosmology are the terms *craobh-shìdhe* and *crann-shìdhe*, both meaning 'tree/branch of peace/the Otherworld', which connect the tree archetype operating at different levels. These terms could be used of the physical manifestation of the sacred tree. They are also used as kennings for the ruler, emphasising both his role as peacemaker and his connection to the Otherworld. They additionally refer to the symbols of the offices of ruler and poet, as well as the idealisation of the overarching social order. Murchadh MacKenzie uses this kenning in his elegy to Domhnall Gorm Òg MacDonald of Sleat (†1643):

> An sgeula thàinig air tuinn,
> A Dhé, nach bu dàil do'n aiseag,
> Gun do eug an Triath ùr glan
> Rìoghchrann-sìthe nan Eilean.[166]

('The tidings have come across the waves, o God, it was no friendly tryst for the messenger: that the fresh, young ruler has died, the kingly sìdh-branch of the Hebrides.')

In early texts, the identity of Otherworld beings was sometimes signalled by their possession of a magical branch. By the eleventh century the royal sceptre and the musical Otherworld branch had merged as a single symbol in tradition and royal officials were often portrayed as bearing a *cráeb-shíde* as a mark of their position.[167] The significance of the white rod given to the newly consecrated ruler in the course of his inauguration also draws on the tree archetype.

> It is undeniably a symbol of the sacred wisdom of which we have seen the otherworldly hazel tree as source. In the inauguration, the poet gives sacred wisdom to the king in symbolic form. [. . .] The underlying concept behind the ritual is evident: sacred wisdom is the basic component of sovereignty.[168]

Chapter Four has already provided depictions of inaugural ceremonies in which the white rod of sovereignty was given to the new ruler. This bestowal (and the accompanying cattle-raid) is probably what the poet Iain Lom MacDonald is referring to when he says to Sir Ewan Cameron of Lochiall, who became chief of his clan in 1647 at the age of eighteen, 'Fhuair thu garbh-bhata cuillin / Cheud là dhearbh thu bhith 'd dhuine' ('You took a hazel rod / on the first day you proved yourself to be a man').[169] An even more explicit statement comes from the self-consciously antiquarian verses celebrating the repeal of punitive post-Culloden acts after the conclusion of the American Revolution. The poet Domhnull MacKenzie refers to Campbell of Argyll as 'slat chaol bhàn o chrann nan ollamh' ('a slender white rod from the branch of the master-poets'), to which he adds the comment 'an emblem of peace', affirming the continuing connection with the concept of sìdh.[170]

The tree archetype, with its overarching structure and self-renewing life force, is finally abstracted to represent society in proper order. This is represented graphically in a poem written in 1756 by the Reverend James McLagan, a leader in the efforts to document Gaelic oral tradition who later became chaplain to the Black Watch during their engagement in the American Revolutionary War. In this piece to troops departing to fight in the Seven Years' War, he describes the idealised condition that their victory will bring, drawing upon the image of the axis mundi:

> 'N sin gabhaidh Craobh na Sìth' le freumh
> Teann-ghreim de'n doimhne-thalmhainn
> Is sìnidh geugan gu ruig Nèamh,
> Gach àird le sèimh-mheas 's geal-bhlàth.
> Bidh ceilear èibhinn eun 'na meanglain
> 'S daoine le'n cloinn a' sealbhachadh,
> Toradh 's saothair an làmh gun mhaoim
> Fo dhubhar caomh a dearbh sgàil.[171]

('Then the roots of Tree of Peace will take a firm hold of the earth's depths and its branches will stretch to Heaven, delicate fruits and white blossoms extending in every direction; the merry music of birds will sound in its branches, with families settling, the produce of their labour unfailing under its soft shadow.')

Similar symbolism is used by Iain Lom MacDonald in the crisis following the assassination of the young chief of the MacDonalds of Keppoch and his brother in 1663. He made his case for persecuting the assassins to the other branches of the MacDonalds by resorting to the archetype of the craobh-shìdhe:

> Chuir sinn romhainn craobh-shìdhe
> Chumadh dìon oirnne gu leòr;
> Cha bu chòir dhuinn bhith strìth rith'
> Am fad cian bhiomaid beò
> Mas sinn féin a chuir sìos i
> B' olc a shìothlaidh sud oirnn
> Tuitidh tuagh oirnn à Flaitheas
> Leis an sgathar na meòir.[172]

('We placed a craobh-shìdhe before us which would give us plenty of protection; we should not be fighting against it for as long as we live; if we were the ones who felled it, that bodes ill for us: an axe will fall from Heaven which will sever limbs.')

Iain Lom is lamenting not only the deaths of the persons involved, but the disruption of the social contract, invoking its sacred origin and function, and warning of the divine retribution they were liable to pay for its violation. The tree imagery is concrete, macabre, and ambiguous; the 'limbs' to be lopped off could be interpreted as human limbs, offices of the chieftaincy, or branches of the clan (another example appears on lines 77–8 of poem ten of Appendix A).

The archetype of the sacred tree as axis mundi thus provided a cohesive and compelling cosmological model for Scottish Gaelic culture into relatively recent times, conceptually connecting humankind and the Otherworld at multiple levels simultaneously. The central place of the tree in ancestral Gaelic tradition endowed it with special significance that was activated in many contexts, including inauguration and rites of passage. As we shall see in Chapter Eight, a story about the ruination of the Great Caledonian forest provided a framework for understanding changes in the Highland landscape itself. Even after this mythic wood was largely deforested, the concept of the tree itself remained deeply rooted in the Gaelic psyche.

Chapter Seven

SONG, MUSIC, AND DANCE

To dance is human, and humanity almost universally expresses itself in dance. Dance interweaves with other aspects of human life, such as communication and learning, belief systems, social relations and political dynamics, loving and fighting, and urbanization and change. It may even have been significant in the biological and evolutionary development of the human species.

– Judith Hanna, *To Dance is Human*

The first, and sometimes only, contact that many people have with the Gaelic language is through music. Many of us remember that initial experience as exciting, enchanting, and spellbinding. Enthusiasm for the primal power and magical efficacy of music is shared by Gaelic tradition itself: from the earliest texts, music is depicted as having an irresistible effect on people, putting them to sleep, bringing them joy, or inciting them to battle.

In all human societies, music is seen as a kind of magic,[1] and Gaeldom is no exception. Besides being used to influence human emotions, music can be used to communicate with the Otherworld and to provide a form of aural protection from malevolent supernatural beings. The power of music flows in both directions, for the Otherworld also uses music to communicate with us. Even within living memory many Gaelic tunes, songs, and dances have been said to have been learnt from members of the Otherworld. As in many other cultures, the Otherworld was seen as the source of human creativity and artistic genius and in oral narrative this shadowy realm can serve as a metaphor for the unconscious.[2]

These ideas about the source of human creativity and talent are reflected in a tale collected in the Outer Hebrides in the late nineteenth century about the MacIntyre bagpipers of South Uist.

∿

The MacIntyres practised from sun-up to sun-down in order to achieve success. At the time, there was the MacIntyre father and his three sons, two who were normal, and one who was a bit daft. The daft son didn't play the bagpipes at all, he only did farm work.

There is a loch in Smearclait which is called Loch Briste and they say that the bagpipers created the loch by their constant walking back and forth with the bagpipes.

But at this time it was a green level field, that was used as a cattle enclosure. All of the village's cattle were kept in the enclosure and they drew lots as to who would watch it each night, two at a time. The daft son and a neighbour girl were chosen this particular day to guard the cattle for the night.

As they watched that night, they saw the fairy knoll opening. He asked the girl to give him the brooch-pin she had stuck in her blouse so that he could go into the knoll whilst it was open. She wasn't willing, so they argued, and at last he snatched it from her suddenly and took it anyway. He left her at the gate and went into the fairy knoll, putting the pin into the door.

As soon as he entered they asked him where he was going, or what art he was seeking. 'Bagpipe music is the art I am seeking,' said he. An older man said that he should come over to him and that he would give it to him. 'Come over and open your mouth, and I will put my tongue in around your cheeks.' And that's what he did.

Then the old man gave him a bagpipe and asked if he already knew a tune or if they should teach him one. He answered that he did know a tune: he composed it right then and there, and played it for them without needing any help. This is the tune he composed:

Tha 'n crodh laoigh air aodann Chorra-Bheinn [. . .]

Then he left the knoll and took the pin out from the door with him. He reached the girl at the gate where he had left her. He gave her back the pin and left for home. He opened his father's chest and he took out his bagpipe while everyone else was still asleep. He went out of the house to the kiln, behind the main house, and began to play the bagpipe, which woke up his father and brothers. They were expecting an Irish bagpiper to be coming to challenge them to a competition at the time and assumed that he had come.

'Do you hear that music?' asked the sons.

'Yes,' answered the father.

'We might as well put our bagpipes into storage,' they said.

'Hold on,' said the father. 'I can't mistake the sound of my son's fingers.'

'That can't be true,' said one son. 'He hasn't touched the bagpipes, or even a chanter, since he was born.'

'That doesn't mean anything,' the father answered. 'Go and peek inside and I'll bet you that you'll see that it is my son who is playing that music.'

They arose and looked in and saw clearly that it was their brother who was playing the bagpipes and walking back and forth in the kiln. 'It's not the Irishman at all, but our own daft brother – we might as well give up the bagpipes altogether. He's the one with the talent.'

A short while thereafter the Irish bagpiper arrived. He and the brothers went to the level field where Loch Briste is today to hold a musical competition between them. A great crowd from the southern end of the country gathered there. When they heard the bagpipers play they realised that the Irishman was going to beat the Highlanders; the women in the crowd stabbed the air-bag of the Irishman's bagpipe with their brooch-pins. The holes in the air-bag made him work so hard to inflate it that he soon fell down dead. It is said that the Irish bagpiper was buried there in Smearclait.[3]

~

Amongst other things, this curious tale suggests that memories of the Irish connection to Highland bagpiping, even its supremacy over it in previous eras, have been annihilated and buried. This is only one of the fascinating aspects of the history of song, music, and dance in Highland society that have been obscured and distorted in the modern era but which can be recovered by a careful study of Gaelic tradition.

Song, music and dance are universal phenomena: every culture around the world practises its own genres of artistic expression constructed from melody, rhythm, bodily movement, and other features. Despite the common proverb that 'Music is a universal language', however, art forms such as music are practised and interpreted in ways that are very specific to a culture's own aesthetic standards. A song that sounds happy in one society, for example, can sound melancholy in another. Each culture has its own standards by which it judges and creates expectations for artistic expressions, and only by trying to 'get inside' of those culturally specific parameters can we hope to understand them on their own terms.

Song, music, and dance provide compelling, visceral examples of tradition in action. As we often experience them at an early age in the context of the wider community, they can give us a tangible feeling of connection to the past. Many people invest a great deal of personal value in such traditions, believing them to represent the 'timeless and unchanging soul of a people'. Given that people often celebrate their culture through song, music, and dance it is not surprising that these art forms are typically seen as embodying a people's identity itself. Detailed historical research often reveals, however, that they have been subjected to sudden and radical changes in the recent past which are downplayed by our need to see them as emblems of continuity and persistence.[4]

Music and dance have taken many different forms in Gaelic society through the ages, some of which would be hardly recognisable to us today. Apart from genres of Gaelic song which have been growing increasingly rare, most of the 'traditional' Highland music and dance now performed took their current forms only in the nineteenth century and virtually none of it is older than the eighteenth century. It has been similarly noted of the 'ancient' music of Gaelic Scotland's closest relation, Ireland:

Although Irish dance music and song are usually easily identifiable as such by listeners, they share stylistic features with the folk music of Scandinavia, Brittany, and Scotland, as well as England. Indeed, for all the nationalist weight placed on it by patriots, Irish traditional music is not the product of an isolated island population. Rather, it derives from a rich history of musical exchange with European music, especially popular dance music. This was music demanded and appreciated by urban Irish audiences from the eighteenth century to the present. As Seán Connolly points out in his study of pre-Famine Irish society, travelers' accounts from eighteenth-century Ireland chronicle the movement of popular European dances and the music that accompanied them from the urban centers of Ireland where they made their first appearance to the more rural areas of Ireland.[5]

Like Ireland, Gaelic Scotland was also connected to European centres of innovation via noble families and networks of trade, labour, and ideas. The bagpipe was adopted in the Highlands no earlier than the fifteenth century and the modern violin as recently as the seventeenth century. Yet, over time, such novelties offered new possibilities to creative performers and communities could adopt or adapt them if they could be fit into prevailing standards and notions of taste. It is only in the modern period, as tradition has been transformed into commodity, that the forces of the global marketplace threaten to overshadow the relevance of the local community and its independence as a participant in the creation and transmission of the meaning of its own musical legacy.[6]

The recent creation of the idea of 'Celtic music' as an ancient and seamlessly unified tradition provides a modern example of the distortions that happen in the invention and marketing of heritage. Labelling music as 'Celtic' invokes the misleading associations of Celticism discussed in Chapter Two. Each of the Celtic communities has distinctive musical traditions that have been evolving along separate paths for so many generations that they seldom have much in common with one another (unless it is through the modern influences of radio and audio recordings). There are many significant divergences even between the closest of these relations, the Scottish and Irish Gaels.[7] The music usually featured as 'Celtic' in mass media is derived directly from the mainstream of Western European music, especially the dance music of the seventeenth through nineteenth centuries. Although regional variations of such music existed in broad swathes of Europe, much of it was lost during the processes of industrialisation and urbanisation in the nineteenth century. It is only by accidents of history and geography that some of the places in which it survives best happen to have Celtic associations. Finally, those elements of Celtic music traditions which are most indigenous – such as òran-luaidh or iorram, in the case of Gaelic Scotland – tend to get far less airplay than those which are derived from the last several centuries of mainstream European dance and art music (which, it must be remembered, only entered the Gaelic community as the old order was collapsing). When the more archaic musical survivals are performed or recorded by modern musicians, they tend to be played on or accompanied by modern instruments in modern tunings and modern rhythms which tend to undermine the distinctive older styles.

The interpreters of tradition have always had to negotiate between the forces of innovation and conservatism, but they normally did so in the past so by reference to the standards of their home communities. The pervasive song tradition provided stylistic criteria and numerous points of reference for musical innovations in Gaeldom, including the popular dance music that accompanied the introduction of the violin. Even dance was connected and responsive to local aesthetics rooted in the song tradition. Chapter Three examined Gaelic poetry from the standpoint of literature and its social context; this chapter will begin by examining the musical component of the poetic tradition and aspects of its performance.

SONG

The most fundamental musical instrument is the human voice and the oldest form of human-produced music is song. Song exerts a dominating and unifying influence on the musical idioms and traditions in most folk cultures. Highland musical traditions are best approached from a grounding in the Gaelic song tradition.

Human societies have evolved in relationship to their natural environments and humankind has often closely observed and imitated animals. The songs of birds in particular attract the attention of many cultures for their musicality. There are many Gaelic songs and rhymes that mimic birds and other animals, often using words that describe their behaviour or speculate on their thoughts.[8] A song imitating the swan sung in many parts of the Gàidhealtachd in numerous variants to the present day was first documented in Argyll in the eighteenth century:

> *Guidh ég ì, guidh ég ó*
> *Sgeula mo dhùnach*
> *Guidh ég ì*
> *Rinn mo léire*
> *Guidh ég ó*
> *Mo chasan dubh*
> *Guidh ég ì*
> *'S mì féin glé gheal*
> *Guidh ég ó.*[9]

('*Guidh ég ì, guidh ég ó*, The tale of my woe, *Guidh ég ì*, which has ruined me, *Guidh ég ó*, my feet are black, *Guidh ég ì*, while the rest of me is white, *Guidh ég ó*.')

Each verse is here interjected by a strain of the chorus, which consists solely of *vocables* (words with no semantic meaning) which imitate the sound of the swan.

Until fairly recently, all Gaelic poetry was meant to be performed rather than just read on the page; although there were different styles, structures, and musical idioms, song and poetry formed a continuum from chanting to musical singing. This is reflected in terms associated with the performance of song in Gaelic – *gabh, can, labhair* and *abair* – which are equally valid for prose, song and poetry.[10] The term *seinn* relates to musical performance, whether of the human voice or any instrument.

There are a number of factors which make a definitive analysis of the song traditions of previous centuries in any society elusive. Until fairly recently, the words of songs were transcribed for literary purposes only, without much detail about the way in which the song was actually sung. In the case of *luinneagan* 'choral songs', for example, the choral refrain and the way in which it intersected solo lines was not well documented. The musical aspect of the delivery of poetry is crucial for understanding the metre and style of the song,[11] but the surviving evidence about songs no longer in active circulation is often incomplete. The gradual evolution of genres also complicates our ability to make conclusive generalisations over long periods of time: a particular verse form may originate with an associated structure for a specific function, but eventually develops its own independent existence. New compositions may extend the previous restrictions of the form, distinct genres may influence one another, and songs originally composed in one genre may be drawn into another tradition which is flourishing and allows for a degree of adaptation.

Within the variety of styles in the native Gaelic song tradition, there is a tension between the heavy rhythmic pulse of the work-song genre (also present to a degree in the port-à-beul genre) and the natural speech cadences which dominate other genres. The differences between these genres are accentuated by the prestige gap associated with them and the internal strains seem to have accelerated in the seventeenth century, when élite poetry was losing its system of patronage and previously segregated strands of tradition came into closer regular contact. The higher social status of the literary tradition, with its emphasis on the text, has generally enabled it to exert its influence on the rhythmic irregularities and melodic complexities of the sub-literary work-song style, so that most categories of Gaelic songs are normally sung according to the natural speech rhythms of the Gaelic language itself.[12] 'The broad general principle is that the rhythm in which a song is sung is determined by the rhythm in which it would be spoken.'[13] While a beautiful melody has always been appreciated, poetry was generally intended for communication, with the song as a powerful medium for telling a story. Donald Campbell, in his 1862 *Treatise on the Language, Poetry and Music of the Highland Clans* notes, 'The airs of the historical poems were, properly speaking, not melodies, but a musical and pleasing style of reciting poetry.'[14] Unlike the modern emphasis on the music, in Gaelic tradition the ideal was for the words to remain unobscured by the melody. In his introduction to the 1884 *Killin Collection*, editor Charles Stewart notes, 'The words occupy the first place, the music only the second [. . .] The words and music implicitly follow the idiosyncrasies of the language.'[15] The terms *luinneag, fonn, sèis(t)* and *caoin* refer both to chorus vocables and the tune, as 'the separate concepts of words and music of a song did not exist.'[16]

Vernacular Gaelic song-makers generally composed new song-poems to pre-existing airs and choruses in a very organic and unselfconscious way, as Lucy Broadwood observed in 1911:

A Highland singer usually knows nothing of the origin of the tunes which he sings, though he often knows the name of the poet, old or new, whose words he repeats, and may indeed have composed the poem himself. 'There is nothing like these beautiful songs which are handed on from mouth to mouth; but most of all it is the beauty of the *words! There is nothing in the world* like these splendid words!' cried a singer of the Loch Morar district to the writer, with passionate enthusiasm. As a rule, Highlanders use the tunes as vehicles for their verse and are frequently almost unaware what tune they are using. Ask the singer of an original poem whether he composed the air to it and he will sometimes answer that he is not sure how much he 'may have made' and how much is like something that he 'may have heard somewhere'. At other times he will show where he has adapted an old tune to suit his own words.[17]

The Gaelic language has a number of features which complicate the relationship between melody and words but which make a close correspondence all the more powerful and integral to the native speaker. Unlike English, the length of vowels are important in Gaelic: they can be short or long (according to the amount of time that they are held) and their lengths are phonemically significant. The only difference between the words *bàs* 'death' and *bas* 'palm', for example, is the length of time for which the 'a' is held. This vowel system, along with regular initial-syllable stress and other features, causes speech utterances to conform to particular rhythmic patterns which are usually observed when the song is sung. It is the long notes (long vowels and diphthongs) which receive melodic ornamentation.[18]

The terms *dàn* and *laoidh* refer to the syllabic poetry of the filidh (as discussed in Chapter Three). The degree to which they derive from native or Latin poetic forms is debated; regardless, they were adopted as the primary form for the high-register literature of the filidh by the twelfth century. With the eradication of the professional poetic order in the eighteenth century, only fragments of the sung syllabic tradition survived into the twentieth century, mostly Ossianic ballads and religious hymns. It is difficult to be certain how accurately these items reflect the practices of earlier eras, especially because the accompanying *clàrsach* 'Gaelic harp' tradition died out in the eighteenth century.

> In its musical aspect, *dàn* was a chant sung in free rhythm with a constant shifting of the musical accent as determined by variations in the number and positions of stresses. This chanting could be accompanied on the harp, but what the nature of this accompaniment was there is now no means of knowing.[19]

The term *amhran* or *òran* describes a song tradition that appears to have derived from the mainstream of medieval European music. This song form has regular rhythmic stress and (usually) four musical phrases such as AABA. It is often associated in Gaelic tradition with performers referred to as *aos-theud* 'string-players' and *luchd-ealaidh* 'artists'.[20] Its connection with wider European tradition is indicated by the themes it shares with the European minstrel tradition but most especially by melodic kinship:

> The type of air just described is found, not only in Gaelic Scotland and Ireland, but also in Lowland Scotland, England, and on the continent of Europe. Furthermore, variants of individual airs can also be very widely distributed. [. . .] In short, *amhran* belongs to a musical tradition that is international. It has historical affinities with the mediaeval *chanson*, and in Gaelic there may have been a time when it was considered suitable only for the more personal and informal themes of life, in particular the theme of love.[21]

Information gathered by Dr James Garden of King's College, Aberdeen, on behalf an English antiquarian in the year 1692 sheds some interesting light on the performers and performance contexts for poets in the seventeenth century. This account correctly distinguishes between the file, the highest-ranked poet who composed high-register Classical Gaelic verse for an aristocratic patron, and the bard, a lower-ranked poet who performed the poetry of the file and composed in vernacular Gaelic:

> A *bard* in common Irish [i.e., Gaelic] signifies a little poet or a rhymer; they used to travel through countries and coming into a house salute it with a rhyme called in Irish *beannachadh bàird* 'the bard's salutation', which is only a short verse or rhyme touching the praise of the master and mistress of the house. [. . .] The inferior sort, otherwise called beggars, makes few or no verses of their own, but only makes use of such as has been composed by others [. . .] He that's extraordinary sharp of these bards is named *fili*, i.e. an excellent poet; these frequent only the company of persons of quality and each of them has some particular person whom he owns his master.[22]

Besides poets belonging to the professional orders the account mentions groups of female performers who seem to fulfil the role of Gaelic minstrels:

> There used likewise 9 or 10, sometimes 11 or 12, women to travel together, who as they came to any house, two and two together, sang one of those songs these fili had made. They had ordinarily a violer with them who played on his fiddle as they sang; when they had done singing, then they danced. These were named *amhranaich*, i.e., singers.[23]

The work-song tradition, exemplified by luinneagan, was omnipresent in the lives of commoners. These songs are by nature of low social prestige and in the vernacular form of Scottish Gaelic, usually sung with a group chorus. Their primary function is to accompany or direct work with a regular beat, even if their texts range from the historical to the personal. In these rhythmically driven songs the natural speech patterns of Gaelic – especially syllable emphasis and vowel length – can become forcibly altered, resulting in what is often called the 'wrenched accent'. As most of the tasks sung to are very old and the tunes very archaic, the form and style of these songs are likely to be very ancient indeed, even if the words themselves have been continually altered, augmented, and replaced through the centuries.[24]

The oldest strata of luinneagan have choral refrains consisting entirely of vocables; it seems likely that words became increasingly common in refrains composed during the seventeenth and eighteenth centuries.[25] While vocables in choruses do not carry any semantic weight, they are nonetheless not random or insignificant. 'Gaelic singers feel a close association between the vocable refrain and the melody of the song – as if the vocables had a definite mnemonic function as far as the music is concerned.'[26] The vocable chorus helps to provide an approximate encoding of the melody of the associated song.

> When Scottish Gaelic poetry first began to appear in print in the eighteenth century, and the authors or collectors wished to indicate to readers to what airs the poems were sung, they needed to do no more than to give the (usually meaningless) words of the chorus as the 'tune'. Gaelic readers then were sufficiently acquainted with the chorus of Gaelic to be able to recognize what air was meant immediately from this as a rule; whereas many modern readers would require that the tune be written in staff notation or in sol-fa.[27]

While the vowels do not have exact melodic pitches, the general rule is that front vowels ('e' and 'i') correspond to high pitches while back vowels ('a', 'o', and 'u') correspond to low pitches.[28]

Many travellers and scholars in the Highlands commented on the use of song in communal and individual labour:

> Over all the Highlands and in the Isles there are various kinds of songs which are sung to airs suited to the nature of the subject. But on the western coast, from Lorne and in all the Hebrides, *luinneag*s are most in request. These are in general very short and of a plaintive cast, analogous to their best poetry, and they are sung by women, not only at their diversions, but also during almost every kind of work where more than one person is employed, as milking cows and watching the folds, fulling of cloth, grinding of grain with the quern or hand-mill, cutting down of corn, or peeling oak-bark, and hay-making. The men, too, have *iorram*s, or songs for rowing, to which they keep time with their oars, as the women likewise do in their operations whenever their work admits of it. When the same airs are sung in their hours of relaxation, the time is marked by the motion of a napkin which all the performers lay hold of. In singing, one person leads the band, but in a certain part of the tune he stops to take breath, while the rest strike in and complete the air by pronouncing to it a chorus of words and syllables, generally of no signification.

These songs greatly animate every person present, and therefore, when labourers appear to flag, a *luinneag* is commonly called for, which makes them for a while forget their toil and work with redoubled ardour. In travelling through the Highlands in harvest, the sound of these little bands on every side [. . .] has a most pleasing effect on the mind of a stranger.[29]

A number of *òrain-bhuana* 'reaping songs' survive. One of these recounts bands of MacDonalds and MacLeods striving against one another in the harvest field. 'While working with all their might to be first at the other end of the field which they were reaping, [they] sang this song with so much fervor that they unconsciously cut themselves with their sickles.'[30]

There is a huge corpus of female choral work songs sung while fulling tweed, called *òrain-luaidh* 'waulking songs' (see Plate 21). Males were excluded from this activity, allowing the expression of exclusively female topics and concerns. Sarah Murray of Kensington, touring the Highlands in 1803, was impressed by the energy and musicality of the people she met, who held a *luadh* 'cloth fulling' exercise on her behalf.

At Ulva House one night after supper, there being a party of ladies and gentlemen, a fulling song was proposed, to give me an idea of the tunes of such songs. Handkerchiefs were made use of to imitate the see-saw motion of the fullers. Some of the ladies had very good voices: they sung the song and the rest joined in the chorus, all of us see-sawing the handkerchiefs held in our hands, which linked us together in a circle around the table. It is not to be imagined what an effect the Gaelic music has upon Highlanders: when rowing, grinding, fulling, or at any other laborious work, their tunes and songs seem to invigorate every nerve in their bodies.[31]

The òrain-luaidh genre drew to it a number of songs from other traditions, such as rowing songs, clan panegyrics, and Ossianic ballads, that would have otherwise been lost. Women sang *òrain-bhleoghainn* 'milking songs' as they sang to the cattle, which soothed them and encouraged them to give more milk. Mothers and nurses sang children to sleep with *tàlaidhean* 'lullabies', many of which are tragic and sorrowful in nature, suggesting that they were just as important as a catharsis for the mother as they were as sedatives for the baby.

Men had their own repertoire of songs suited for masculine tasks and social contexts. Early Gaelic sources mention the *dòrd*, a group chorus sung by the Fian with low throaty voices as they clashed their spears.[32] Men who lived near waterways would have known a large number of rowing songs.

They are sung on board of ships and buirlings by the sailors, when they row or work, to deceive the time. The subject is generally the life and actions of some chief or relation. The language is such, as to express the sentiments and actions described; the music, expression, and strokes of the oars, coinciding in such exact time, both the sailor and passenger forget their hardships and fatigue, even in the most inclement seasons.[33]

There seem to have been different song styles to choose from according to the speed and rhythm of the rowing. The rowers sang the chorus of the song, while the verses were sung by a soloist at the helm of the boat, who announced his intentions by shouting, 'Suidheam air stiùir is èigheam creagag!' ('I shall sit at the helm and I'll call out the rowing!')[34]

When the modern violin arrived in Scotland in the seventeenth century it came with a new style of dance music which, once reshaped by native musical sensibilities, evolved into distinctively Scottish forms, particularly the reel and strathspey. These tunes, primarily instrumental and played specifically for dancing, are referred to in Gaelic as *puirt* (plural, singular *port*). As they became 'verbalised' in song form (known as *port-à-beul* 'mouth-tune') for the purposes of memorising and teaching, they acquired the rhythms and cadences of Gaelic speech. The Scotch-snap, one of the most distinctive features of Scottish dance music, accords directly with Gaelic speech rhythms.[35] These ditties, however, are not considered true poetry according to the high standards of Gaelic poetry (such as found in the genres of dàn, laoidh, etc.), but mnemonic verbalisations, sung for dancers if instruments are not available.[36]

> It is perhaps not sufficiently realised, even today, that this strathspey-and-reel type of music is a comparatively late importation, that it has quite a different ancestry from indigenous folk-song, and that great harm can be done by imposing its style on folk-song.[37]

Probably the oldest recorded words to a port-à-beul in Gaelic tradition, recorded by Eoghan MacDiarmaid no later than 1770 from a St Kilda source, is a reel whose words describe eagles lamenting a blackcock, connecting Gaelic music back to bird-song;[38] it must have been popular in a number of communities, for it was recorded two centuries later from Maighread NicAoidh of Harris by the School of Scottish Studies.[39] With the popularity of the new styles of dance, a very large repertoire of puirt-à-beul developed in Gaelic, many humorous, some absurd, a few bawdy, and most rhythmically interesting. Once the style emerged, new songs were composed that were not directly connected to dance.[40] Vocal dance music also evolved in Gaelic Ireland, where it is called *portaireacht bhéil*.[41]

Ritual activity – rites of passage, calendar customs, daily routines, magical acts – were accompanied by songs, chants, invocations, and incantations. Very few categories of these ritual texts have survived as they did not attract the attention of early folklorists,[42] apart from those printed by Alexander Carmichael in his monumental volumes of *Ortha nan Gàidheal / Carmina Gadelica*. The verbatim integrity of Carmichael's texts has been seriously called into question, with the suspicion that he has reworked these to a large extent even if each item is based on an irrecoverable core he retrieved from oral tradition in the nineteenth century.[43] There are many Duain Challuinn (songs performed on Oidhche Challuinn, such as poem twelve of Appendix A), but only a small number of other ritual songs have been recorded by folklorists in the twentieth century.

All told, song was a normal and ubiquitous element in Gaelic life which included all members of the community. 'The occasions for singing were so numerous that Gaelic song – and the social and affective content of the verses – has over generations inevitably made up a large part of the inner verbal dialogue among many traditional Gaels.'[44] Some of these occasions were driven by practical aims, such as communal labour; at other times, singing was simply a means of entertainment and communal fellowship, at céilidhs and other social events. A singer forms a personal association with a song not just because of its content or author, but also from how and when he learnt it and from whom. Gaelic communal song has multiple simultaneous functions, serving as 'an integrating force at all levels of traditional society'.[45]

Like any folklore genre, Gaelic songs typically exist in variants reflecting regional differences and personal styles. The fact that songs can be found in different forms does not mean, however, any change is seen as equally valid: 'in each society limits are placed on musical creativity.'[46] Gaelic musical tradition has its own aesthetic logic which determines what changes fall within its accepted parameters of variation, and which go beyond them:

> The fact that an air could assume so many forms does not mean that it could assume any form. Some things were possible within the tradition: other things were not [. . .] All we are entitled to ask is whether a version of a song is consistent with the tradition, and then to ask how good it is, judging by the musical standard of what is best in the tradition.[47]

In the vernacular tradition, the practice has been for songs to be sung unaccompanied and in unison; the effect of instrumental backing would be to detract from the words. 'They are of sufficient merit in themselves to be heard without additional harmony. [. . .] The traditional songs of the Hebrides are never accompanied nor sung in parts.'[48] A large corpus of songs was the normal inheritance of all Gaels for centuries and would have formed an essential foundation in the unconscious training of Highland musicians.

Musical Instruments

As we've already seen in the case of song, the natural world was a source of inspiration for Gaelic musicians, especially bird-song. Martin Martin mentions how bird-song was imitated on a wind instrument: 'The Gawlin is a Fowl less than a Duck [. . .] the Piper of St. Kilda plays the Notes which it sings, and hath composed a Tune of 'em which the Natives judg to be very fine Musick.'[49]

There was little effort made to standardise the plethora of instruments in medieval Europe, which assumed a multitude of shapes and forms.[50] Interpreting musical terminology from the period presents many challenges: the same term was sometimes used to refer to different instruments, and some terms became obsolete before the musical instrument or technique that they described could be documented sufficiently for us to understand them unambiguously. Surviving illustrations (in manuscripts or on sculptures) are not always clear and there has been debate as to whether these accurately depict native instruments or were copied from generic 'templates' floating around European Christendom.[51] It is not until the later medieval period that evidence becomes plentiful and less ambiguous.

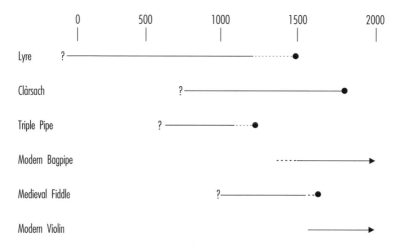

Figure 7.1: Timeline of important pan-Gaelic musical instruments

Wind instruments have a particularly ancient lineage in human cultures: amongst the oldest surviving instruments are flutes made from animal bones, such as the two-holed bone flute found in Skara Brae in Orkney dating to *c.*2300 BC. The Gaelic term *cuisle* referred to wind instruments in general.[52] Animal horns, referred to as *adharc, corn,* or *buabhall* (singular) in Gaelic,[53] have an ancient history of use, especially in war. Curved metal horns may have been made in imitation of animal horns. A fragment of a side-blown bronze horn found in Wigtownshire, dated to the eighth century BC, resembles bronze horns found in Ireland. The carnyx was a trumpet used by Celts and other Iron Age peoples to terrify their enemies in battle. A group of carnyx players is depicted on the famous Gundestrup Cauldron. A particularly good example of a carnyx, in the shape of a boar's head, was found in Banffshire, dated to *c.*AD 100 (see Plate 1). A set of similar boar-head carnyxes was discovered in 2004 in the trenches of a Gallo-Roman temple in the south of France, dated to the first century BC.[54]

The term *crott* or *cruit* appears in Gaelic sources by the eighth century as a generic term referring to a plucked stringed instrument. This initially referred to an instrument we now call the 'lyre', that is, an instrument containing strings lying parallel to the frame, usually resting over a bridge on one end.[55] The lyre was well known in the wider Celtic world, probably borrowed at an early date from the Greeks. It appears on coins of the Celtic west before the Roman conquest and a stone sculpture of a Celtic musician (complete with torc) holding a seven-stringed lyre has been found in northern France, dated to the time of the Roman invasion.[56] Probable fragments of early lyres (and related accoutrements) have been found in Argyll, Lewis, and Orkney,[57] and lyres are depicted on several stone sculptures in Ireland and Gaelic Scotland carved between the eighth and eleventh centuries.

Stringed instruments were significant in heroic societies because they were used to accompany songs, especially panegyric, performed in royal courts. The high status of the *cruitear* 'player of the cruit' is reflected in early Gaelic law tracts: while other musicians derived their legal standing from that of their patron, only the cruitear was granted legal status regardless of his employment, the highest legal status possible for a non-noble. Similarly, the cruitear was allocated a seat in the royal court near the ruler himself and next to the royal poet while other musicians were located on the far side of the hall.[58] The Gaelic term *timpán* was also used to refer to the lyre. The lyre was widespread in Ireland until it fell out of use in the fifteenth century or shortly thereafter, but by the high medieval period it seems to have already been rare in Scotland.[59]

The *clàrsach* 'Gaelic harp' is different from the lyre in that its limbs form a triangle and the strings are perpendicular to the sound board. The clàrsach was a much more versatile and audible instrument than the lyre because the design sustained a greater amount of tension, and hence more strings, and it contained a resonating chamber. Based on surviving evidence, the clàrsach seems to have originated amongst the Picts and been borrowed by the both the Gaels and Brythonic peoples of Scotland. The earliest depictions, dated to the eighth and ninth centuries, are found in eastern Scotland, the territory of the Picts; in fact, between the eighth and fifteenth centuries, all but two portrayals of stringed instruments in Scotland are of the clàrsach, whereas in Ireland (and early Gaelic Scotland), the lyre is the prevailing musical instrument depicted. Triangular harps do not begin to appear in Ireland until the eleventh century, and even afterwards they are rare.[60] Unlike the other professional fields which relied heavily upon imported talent from Ireland, native Scottish families dominated the playing of the clàrsach in Scotland.[61]

By the fifteenth century two different types of strings were used in Scotland, metal on the clàrsach and gut (common in the rest of Europe) on the non-Gaelic harp, each lending itself to a particular technique of playing.[62] John Mair's 1521 *History of Great Britain* refers to these: 'For musical instruments and vocal music the Wild Scots use the harp, whose strings are of brass, and not of animal gut; and on this they make most pleasing melody.'[63] George Buchanan provides more useful details in his 1582 account:

They are exceedingly fond of music, and employ harps of a peculiar kind, some of which are strung with brass, and some with catgut. In playing they strike the wires either with a quill, or with their nails, suffered to grow long for the purpose; but their grand ambition is to adorn their harps with great quantities of silver and gems, those who are too poor to afford jewels substituting crystals in their stead.[64]

Three complete clàrsaich produced in Gaelic Scotland survive, probably produced in the workshops of the Lords of the Isles during the last century of their reign. The most elegant of these, the so-called 'Queen Mary' harp, is ornamented with interlace, fabulous beasts, and split-palmette leaves characteristic of the West Highland art style not paralleled in Ireland (see Plate 11). Similar clàrsaich appear on several grave slabs in the Lordship of the Isles (see Plate 10).[65] It is likely that the clàrsach displaced the lyre in Ireland, but its ascendancy was short-lived: it was an élite (rather than a 'folk') instrument which relied upon the native system of patronage. With the loss and assimilation of the aristocracy throughout Gaeldom, the tradition of the clàrsach was lost in the eighteenth century, although modern proponents have been attempting to reconstruct it.

Five stone crosses carved between the ninth and twelfth centuries in Ireland and Scotland depict musicians playing triple-pipes, a wind instrument with three reed pipes of different lengths. These instruments may have enjoyed high status in some context, given how rare it is for instruments to appear on stone crosses. The Gaelic term *píopaí* is a loanword from a Latin-derived language which probably referred to reed aerophones; the foreign origin of the word suggests that it was used for a wind instrument that had been also imported.[66] It may be relevant that a Roman carving near the Antonine Wall depicts double pipes. The launeddas of Sardinia is a similar triple-pipe instrument which has survived into the modern era; the Gaelic triple-pipe, however, seems to have become extinct by the late Middle Ages.[67]

The bagpipe, a wind instrument with a melody chanter and one or more drones using a bag of animal skin as an air reservoir, developed its modern form in the towns of Continental Europe during the twelfth century, stimulated by economic prosperity and contact with the Islamic world. The bagpipe appeared in England by the thirteenth century and shows up in Lowland Scotland about a century later. Scotland had many trading and political links with Continental Europe, so the bagpipe may have come directly from the Continent with the people recruited to establish the burghs of the Scottish Lowlands. On the other hand, the English royal court provided patronage for bagpipers by 1285–6 (during the reign of Edward I)[68] and by the reign of King James III (1452–88) English bagpipers were finding paid work in the Scottish royal court.[69] The bagpipe probably did not arrive in the Highlands, however, until at least the fifteenth century.[70]

Like other pre-modern instruments, the bagpipe did not have a single, fixed form, but was constructed according to available resources, local traditions, and the whims of individual bagpipe makers. By the late sixteenth century small and large forms of the bagpipe, corresponding roughly to the modern parlour pipes and Highland bagpipe, were in use in Lowland Scotland, but there was no sense that there was anything specifically 'Highland' about the latter.[71] As late as the mid nineteenth century, bagpipe-makers in Edinburgh offered six distinct varieties of bagpipes. The Highland bagpipe is still called *a' phìob mhór* 'the big pipe' in Gaelic, recalling its original single drone. Over the next several centuries, the second and third drones were added.[72]

Before the introduction of the modern fiddle, the trump (also known as the 'mouth harp', 'Jew's harp', or 'jaw harp') was the instrument mostly common used to accompany dancing. The trump could be produced inexpensively by local smiths and was easy to play. The early witchcraft trials provide us with an important window into the life of the non-élite and these frequently mention the use of the trump for dancing. The first textual record of the word 'reel', signifying a dance, occurs in the North Berwick witchcraft trial of 1598 when a trump provided the musical accompaniment. Richard James, an Oxford scholar who travelled around the Highlands in 1618, mentions the use of the trump as well as the playing of Gaelic battle songs on the bagpipe, but makes no reference to the fiddle: 'the instruments with which they make mirth are Iewes harpes wch they call trumps and great lowd bagpipes uppon which they plaie and tune battails and combats and other such songes as they have.'[73]

A primitive form of the fiddle (a stringed instrument played with a bow) was played throughout medieval Europe. Its name in most languages is derived from the medieval Latin term *vidula*. It existed in a wide variety of forms with two to six strings and no standard tuning.[74] The Old Gaelic term *fidil* (modern Scottish Gaelic *fidheall*) first appears in a poem about the Fair of Carman in Ireland in a low-status context, transcribed in a manuscript dated *c.*1160.[75] There is scant surviving evidence about this instrument, however, so it is unlikely to have played a prominent role in élite Gaelic society.

The modern violin was fashioned in Italy in the sixteenth century and made its way into Gaelic Scotland and Ireland during the seventeenth century, along with the new forms of dance music for which it was particularly well suited.[76] The new instrument was similar enough to the old for the Gaelic term to remain unchanged (*fidheall*), making it difficult for us now to determine from textual sources which instrument was being referred to. The fiddle was truly a folk instrument which the non-élite ranks of society could afford to build and learn to play, independent of any system of patronage. Martin Martin, for example, wrote of Lewis: 'They are great Lovers of Musick; and when I was there they gave an Account of eighteen Men who could play on the Violin pretty well, without being taught.'[77]

By the late eighteenth century, a wide array of instruments was available in the Highlands, especially for those who could afford them. In the economically prosperous parts of the Gàidhealtachd, such as Highland Perthshire, dance ensembles formed in the eighteenth century which paired the fiddle with other instruments, such as the cello. The Gow family were particularly successful proponents of the dance music ensemble and applied Continental musical styles in their bass accompaniment.[78] Such instrumental pairings are reflected in the occasional Gaelic verse, as in a song from

Kintail: 'Chuala mise clàrsach theud / Fidheall is beus ag co-sheinn' ('I've heard the stringed clàrsach / the fiddle and cello playing together').[79]

Apart from the incidental pounding accompanying work songs, there is little surviving evidence of percussion in Scottish Gaelic tradition. The term *crannan* appears in the 1776 Eigg Collection with a footnote explaining it to be a drum (apparently a hollow wooden cylinder), but it is otherwise unattested in Gaelic.[80] The tenth-century Pictish stone at Lethendy depicts a musical ensemble which may include a drum.[81] The absorption of British and Continental military practices brought the word *drumma* 'drum' into Gaelic by the early eighteenth century, but its use until then, like that of the Highland bagpipe, was to conjure the mood of war and to send signals to troops within the context of military operations (rather than musical performance *per se*). Such is the import of a reference in Iain Dubh's poem on the 1715 Jacobite Rising, where he describes the sounds of war:

> *Bu lìonmhor nan campa*
> *Guth galltromp is pìoba*
> *Fairgne na druma*
> *Cur an curaids am fiacha.*[82]

('In their camps there were many sounds of trumps and bagpipes, the beating of the drums, to assert their courage.')

Musical instruments were not used by European militaries to coordinate the precise movement of soldiers, i.e., marching in time, until the late eighteenth century.[83] The late development of the use of rhythm in music for synchronising group movement is also true for dance.

Each of these different instruments was suited to a particular kind of music and advocates developed distinctive styles and genres for them. While there was certainly symbiotic collaboration between the practitioners of these various traditions, there was also jealousy and rivalry between them as they competed for status and patronage.

MUSICAL TRADITIONS

The sound of musical instruments, especially the clàrsach, is frequently in the implicit 'soundtrack' running in the background of élite Gaelic story and song. A run in a story recorded in Tiree in 1863 describes the clàrsach's peerless capacities for transcendent musical performance:

> *Tha cruit chànranach chiùil aige*
> *A sheinneadh puirt agus duanagan cadail*
> *Nach robh an sìdh-bheinn,*
> *No an sìdh-dhùn,*

> No am bugh na bòcthuinn,
> No an teach Mhanainn,
> Aon cheòl cànranach cadail a b' àillidh na e
> Chuireadh mnathan-sìdh,
> Fir ghointe,
> Agus mnài-siubhla
> 'Nan siorran suain 's nan troma chadal.[84]

('He has a harp of sweet-murmuring music that would play tunes and sleep-ditties, and there was not in a fairy mountain, nor in a fairy fortress, nor in the breaking of the surging sea-wave, nor in the house of Manannán, any murmuring sleep-music more wondrous than it, which would put fairy women, wounded men, and women in childbirth into a deep and heavy slumber.')

Although it is natural to be sceptical of such hyperbolic depictions, several writers substantiate the ability of even simple music to put Highlanders into fits of ecstasy or passions of dancing, as Robert Kirk noted in his tract *The Secret Commonwealth*:

Finally, Irish-men, our Northern-Scottish, and our Athol men are so much addicted to and delighteth with harps and music, as if like King Saul they were possessed with a foreign spirit, only with this difference: that music did put Saul's play-fellow asleep, but roused and awakened our men, vanquishing their own spirits at pleasure, as if they were impotent of its powers, and unable to command it; for we have seen some poor beggars of them chattering their teeth for cold, that [as] soon [as] they saw the fire, and heard the harp, leapt through the house like goats and satyrs.[85]

The clàrsach was played by the trained *clàrsair* (plural *clàrsairean*); it was the aural demonstration of the chieftain's ability to maintain his household in the traditional manner, adding to the ambiance of the ruler's domain and hence to his standing (code C.3). One of the more graphic depictions of the clàrsach in the chieftain's hall occurs in the elegy for Sir Lachlann MacLean of Duart (†1649):

> 'N àm na fàire bhith glasadh
> Bhiodh a' chlàrsach 'ga creachadh:
> Cha bhiodh ceòl innt' an tasgaidh
> Ach na meòir 'ga thoirt aiste
> Gun leòn làimhe gun laige
> Gus 'm bu mhiannach leibh cadal gu fòill.[86]

('When the horizon would begin to turn grey, the clàrsach would be exploited until it had no music left in it, the fingers drawing music out of it, effortlessly and constantly, until you wished to spend a while in sleep.')

Many aspects of the professional clàrsairean followed the precedents set by the filidh, even if musicians could not quite achieve the same economic and social standing as their poetic peers. By the early thirteenth century, music was taught and learnt aurally using a mnemonic system called *canntaireachd*, rather than written notation.[87] The clàrsair often exhibited the same haughty pride and sense of entitlement as the file. Sir Duncan Campbell of Glenorchy (†1513) composed a satirical elegy on the death of the clàrsair Lachlann MacBhreatnaich, enumerating the excessive demands he made of his many patrons.[88] The clàrsair travelled with a servant who, like the modern 'roadie', looked after him and his instrument.[89] Also similar to the file was the clàrsair's *cuairt* 'travelling circuit' from the hall of one chieftain to the next. When the clàrsair Lachlann Dall died, Sìleas na Ceapaich lamented that he would no longer be bringing her news from her far-scattered MacDonald relations.[90] Some of these parallels between the filidh and clàrsairean may have resulted from scions of poetic dynasties entering into the musical field: Ruaidhri Ó Dálaigh (†1469) of the illustrious family of poets is an early Irish clàrsair.[91]

Like the filidh, a clàrsair required extensive and expensive training, and the office of clàrsair tended to be inherited from father to son over several generations if not centuries. The Stewart kings provided patronage for MacBhreatnaich clàrsairean who were based in Galloway, members of which appear on the royal payroll into the early sixteenth century.[92] The Lords of the Isles employed the MacGhilleSheanaich clàrsairean, who were granted land in Kintyre near the estate of the MacMhuirich filidh. By the early seventeenth century, a little more than a century after the forfeiture of the Lords of the Isles, only one MacGhilleSheanaich clàrsair remained and the family's lands had been greatly reduced. The family seems to have lost its ability to find employment as professional harpers by the mid seventeenth century, but they were already branching into other professional fields, such as law, medicine, and the church.[93]

We know the names of some of the clàrsairean maintained by Highland chieftains at certain periods, giving us episodic glimpses into the musical life of the élite: Campbell of Argyll had a MacVicar clàrsair in the mid sixteenth century; MacLeod of Dunvegan seem to have been employing a hereditary line of clàrsairean at the same time; the Lamonts had MacEwen clàrsairean by 1434, but they are last attested in 1661; a member of this MacEwen family seems to have come to Atholl *c.*1460, where his descendants continued to find the patronage of the Earls of Atholl and various branches of the Robertsons into the late seventeenth century; the Earl of Sutherland had a clàrsair in 1602; one Grant chieftain had a clàrsair in the 1620s and 1630s; MacLean of Duart had a MacNeill clàrsair in 1674, though he was gone by 1716; Campbell of Achinbreck had a MacIndeor clàrsair at the end of the seventeenth century. Ruaidhri Dall Morison, the last Gaelic clàrsair whose poetry survives, was initially in the employ of Iain Breac MacLeod of Dunvegan, and later Iain MacLeod of Talisker acted as his patron. Ruaidhri died *c.*1714, but his pupil Murdoch MacDonald was clàrsair to MacLean of Coll until his death in 1738.[94]

The limited economic means of most Scottish chieftains may have made it necessary for many poets to be able to perform their own compositions as well as accompany themselves on the clàrsach. Even in Ireland, however, it may not have been uncommon for filidh to have some musical ability.[95] A number of professional Scottish poets played the harp. Gille-Bríde Albanach was gifted a clàrsach by an Irish patron sometime before 1242. Gille-Críst MacBhreatnaich asked in one poem for a clàrsach from Tomaltach MacDiarmada of Magh Luirg in Ireland, and thanked him for it in a later one.[96]

It may have been impractical, if not impossible, however, for a single person to be both a fully trained file and clàrsair: Gille-Críst MacBhreatnaich was nick named 'Brúilingeach' for a looser form of rhyme than that required by the most stringent rules of syllabic poetry; Ruaidhri Dall Morison composed verse in vernacular language and styles which he set to traditional melodies, but may not have composed original melodies at all.[97] It was recorded in Ireland that the file preferred to conduct the performance of his compositions by men of a lower station, the clàrsair and bard, as the *Memoirs of the Marquis of Clanricarde* relate:

> The action and pronunciation of the poem in presence [. . .] of the principal person it related to was performed with a great deal of ceremony in a concert of vocal and instrumental music. The poet himself said nothing, but directed and took care that everybody else did his part right. The bards having first had the composition from him, got it well by heart, and now pronounced it orderly, keeping even peace with a harp, touched upon that occasion; no other musical instrument being allowed of for the said purpose than this alone.[98]

Just as aristocrats composed 'amateur' syllabic poetry, so do we find aristocrats playing the clàrsach as a sign of their rank and learning without making it their profession. Indeed, the tract *A Collection of Highland Rites and Customs* (c.1685) states, 'Most part of the Gentry play on the Harp.'[99] King James I was said to have been a talented musician on a number of instruments, including the harp.[100] Chieftain Iain Garbh MacLean of Coll (c.1596–post-1670) played on the clàrsach and composed the tune 'Caoineadh Rìoghail' ('Royal Lament') on the death of King Charles I in 1649.[101] Branches of the Robertsons in Highland Perthshire were patrons of the clàrsach tradition for several generations, and numerous chieftains of these families seemed to play as well. John Robertson of Lude (1667–1731), probably taught by a MacEwen clàrsair, seems to have been the last member of the family to play the clàrsach.[102]

As in the rest of early Europe, Gaelic music was strongly tied to vocal song traditions. During the fifteenth century, élite European musical schools were beginning to disconnect instrumental music from the song tradition and develop it for its own sake; although many melodies derived from their older song sources, they became arranged, embellished, and transformed in new ways specific to the instruments on which they were played, no longer limited by the range or characteristics of the human voice.[103] This innovating trend seems to have stimulated the creation of a new genre of clàrsach music in Scotland, composed for instrumental performance rather than simply accompanying the voice. The term *port* was used in a technical sense for these compositions, the earliest of which seems to date from the 1570s. Many of these melodies show the conscious use of recurring melodic motifs and incrementally ornamented variations of a common theme. Their asymmetric structure suggests that they were not intended to accompany either song or dance. These musical pieces drew the interests of Lowland musicians who notated many of them in manuscripts of lute music. Despite this promising start, the burst of creativity amongst clàrsairean seems to have declined by the second half of the seventeenth century: not only was patronage of the clàrsach waning and the prestige of the bagpipe on the up-swing, but people's attention was being drawn to other new forms of European music, especially music associated with social dancing.[104] The clàrsair must have guarded his status and privileges as jealously as the professional poets did theirs; in fact, the file also had a vested interest in the security of the clàrsach tradition, given that it was integral to the performance of professional poetry.

The bagpipe made its way to Gaeldom by the sixteenth century, having already been in use in England and the Scottish Lowlands. The earliest illustrations of the 'Great Highland Bagpipe' were made not in Scotland but in Ireland, such as the well-known woodcut by John Derricke *c.*1578 depicting a troop of warriors led by a bagpiper. A portrait of four Irish people at the English court in the mid sixteenth century by Lucas de Heere also includes the bagpipes.[105] While the accuracy of the features of the bagpipes in these illustrations has been rightly questioned, they draw our attention to two important facts which have been obscured in the histories of the 'Highland' bagpipe: first, that the instrument was common to Scotland and Ireland, and second, that its functions in Gaeldom were initially as military tools, not musical instruments.

The bagpipes would have been an obvious element of cultural interchange between Scots and Irish Gaels. It was only in the nineteenth century that artificial distinctions between Scottish Gaelic and Irish musical traditions began to be imposed on historical and literary evidence in the cause of nationalist myth-making on both sides. The preposterous lengths to which nineteenth-century Scottish writers went to avoid Irish associations is demonstrated by the story invented by the influential Reverend Dr Norman MacLeod to account for the origins of the most celebrated of bagpiping dynasties, the MacCrimmons of Skye. According to MacLeod, the family was founded by an Italian immigrant from Cremona; in fact, their name may be derived from the common Gaelic name *Crimthan* 'fox', which was Saint Columba's original name.[106]

As illustrated in the tale at the beginning of this chapter, Gaelic sources generally acknowledge Irish connections to Scottish bagpipe traditions. An account of bagpipe music published by Angus Mackay in 1838 states that one of the earliest MacCrimmon bagpipers was sent for musical instruction to Ireland;[107] the Rankin bagpipers to the MacLeans of Duart, who established a college of piping at Cill Bhrianain, were also said to have received their musical training in Ireland.[108] Gaelic tradition furthermore indicates that Irish bagpipers, who played the same instruments as their Scottish counterparts, came to visit them, sometimes in musical competitions.[109] As a matter of record we know of Highland bagpipers who also played the 'Union' bagpipe,[110] later renamed the 'Uilleann' bagpipe to give it a distinctly Irish identity. Early sources, therefore, do not reflect the strong divisions later asserted between Irish and Scottish branches of the tradition.

The early bagpipe, however, was not represented, and apparently not perceived, by the Highland élite as a musical instrument *per se*, as was the clàrsach, but rather as an implement of warfare used to lead soldiers, intimidate enemies, and send battle signals. These were precisely the functions of the contemporary trumpet, used throughout medieval Europe to make announcements and invoke particular moods for events.[111] Like the trumpet, the bagpipe carried the banner of the aristocrat with whom the player was associated. An Irish adaptation of the story of Fieracas, which may date from as early as the fifteenth century, contains what is probably the first comment about the bagpipe in Gaelic literature. It clearly states the function of the bagpipe in war: 'sinnter adharca agus píba agaibh do tinol bur sluaigh' ('Let horns and bagpipes be played by you to gather your host'). The first historical evidence of Irish bagpipers begins in 1544, when they appear amongst the muster rolls of soldiers. The bagpiper then seems to become an essential element in Irish military forces; many of these early sources compare the bagpipe to the trumpet.[112]

Early sources about Scottish bagpipes are consistent with this Irish evidence. A French author, probably employed in the forces of Queen Mary of Guise during the Battle of Pinkie in 1547, wrote that the Highlanders 'encouraged themselves to arms by the sound of their bagpipes'.[113] In his 1582 tract on the Western Isles, George Buchanan, at the end of a list of Highland weapons, states simply, 'Instead of a trumpet, they use a bagpipe.'[114]

Unlike the clàrsach, the bagpipe does not appear in any Classical Gaelic verse. Although it is named in many vernacular poems well into the early eighteenth century, it is usually in the formula 'pìob agus bratach' ('bagpipe and war-banner'), that is, as accoutrements of battle, not as a musical instrument. Furthermore, until the eighteenth century, when the sound of the bagpipe is mentioned in Gaelic poetry, it is usually described in terms of texture and sound effects, not melody: *gleadhraich* 'rattling', *nuallanaich* 'bellowing', *sgal* 'blast, shriek', *spreigeadh* 'incitement, stirring', *torman* 'rumbling, murmuring', and so on.[115] The ability of the bagpipes to convey messages by mimicking Gaelic song has remained a common theme in Highland tradition, as numerous nineteenth-century sources recorded:

> Of old the Highlanders believed that their pipers could actually communicate all requisite tidings by making the instrument almost speak the same as if by words. There are several traditions of parties having been rescued from danger and death by the distant warning notes of the *pìob mhór*. In this there is nothing incredible to any

who know the surprising execution with which pipers of skill can handle their chanters.[116]

This is not to deny that the bagpipe can play exquisite music in the present and that players were skilled enough, and possessed instruments capable enough, to do so in the distant past. It is important to realise that the early bagpipe faced a well-entrenched monopoly of the clàrsach and the file in Gaelic society, many of whom saw it an unwelcome upstart. Advocates of the bagpipe helped to make it accepted as a musical instrument worthy of the patronage of the élite by adapting some of the institutional trappings of the schools of the filidh and clàrsairean, utilising some of the same teaching methods, playing and composing in established genres, and using Gaelic poetry itself to assert a niche for the bagpipe.

The first surviving evidence of an antagonism to the bagpipe comes from a poem attributed to the professional poet Niall Mór MacMhuirich (*c.*1550–*c.*1630), who was then probably in the service of the Clanranald branch of the MacDonalds. According to John MacKenzie, who made a large collection of Gaelic poetry in the early nineteenth century and the traditions connected to them,

> Neil had lately returned to his father's house from the bards' college, in Ireland, from whence, along with the stores of genealogical and other lore with which he had stored his head, he had in addition, brought over a back-burden of the small-pox, and was lying asleep, on a settle bed, at the back of the house near the fire, when John and Donald McArthur, two pipers, came in, and sitting down on the bed-stock, began tuneing their pipes preparatory to playing. The horrid and discordant sound of the pipes roused the bard, who, bursting with indignation, in the true style of his profession, began to inveigh against the pipers, in the following mock genealogy of the bag-pipe. It would appear from this, as well as from hints in other poems, that the bag-pipe was never a favourite with the bards; but was rather regarded by them as trenching on their province. [. . .] Neil's father on hearing the poem to the end exclaimed, '*Math thu féin, a mhic, tha mi faicinn nach bu thuras caillt' a thig thu dh'Éirinn*', i.e., 'Well done, my son, I see your errand to Ireland has not been lost.'[117]

This satire describes the bagpipe in unambiguously negative terms, including animal imagery 'aodroman muice air a shéideadh gu h-ana-mhór' ('A pig's bladder greatly inflated'), sexual innuendo 'Ball Dhomhnuill is dos na pìoba' ('Donald's penis and the bagpipe's drones'), and nefarious associations 'Do-cheòl do bhith 'n Ifrinn ìochdrach' ('Bad music from the depths of Hell').[118] We should be cautious about interpreting this evidence too generally, however: Niall Mór composed this satire to the two brothers specifically on this occasion, rather than making a wider statement about the bagpipes. Satires were also composed against poor clàrsairean which contain similar imagery.[119]

Niall Mór's satire is generally seen as the first in a series of poems debating the merits and defects of the bagpipe and other instruments. The next surviving poem to make a statement about the bagpipe was composed by Gilleasbuig na Ceapaich, chieftain of the MacDonalds of Keppoch from 1670 to his death in 1682 and a prolific poet in vernacular registers and styles. Gilleasbuig begins with a defensive gesture which indicates some previous attack on the bagpipe, perhaps the earlier satire by Niall Mór:

> 'S mairg do dhi-moil ceòl is caismeachd
> Prosnadh slòigh go gaisgeachd threun
> Mór-phìob leis an dùisgear gach misneach
> A torman mòid is misde beum.
>
> Mo ghaol clàirseach, ro ghaol pìob,
> Mì-thlachd leam an tì do chàin;
> Olc an duais aig ceòl droch-comain,
> Bonn-chluas aig ollamh ri dàn.
>
> Cha bhi mi di-moladh an dàin
> Ach 's ann bu mhaith an dàn 's an t-sìth;
> Air a nàmhaid cha deachaidh an dàn
> Riamh cho dàna is chuaidh i.[120]

('Woe to the one who dispraises music and war-signal, a war-band incited to brave heroism; beats are greater and more powerful from the drone coming from the great bagpipes, by which all courage is aroused.')

('Although I love the clàrsach, more do I love the bagpipe: the one who complains of the bagpipe annoys me; poor gratuity is an evil payment for music, [like] a deaf ear turned to a professional poet engaged in dàn.')

('I will not dispraise dàn, but dàn is best in times of peace; dàn was never as bold against an enemy as was the sound of the bagpipe.')

Gilleasbuig draws a strong contrast between the clàrsach (and dàn, the syllabic poetry which it accompanied) and the bagpipe, and in doing so attempts to find specialised niches for them both so that they are not in direct competition. This resolution through specialisation is echoed in several other poems composed in the late seventeenth and early eighteenth centuries. Gilleasbuig's final full stanza is suggestive of how the bagpiping tradition succeeded by assimilating the aesthetics of Gaelic poetic tradition:

'*Bhean bhinn-fhoclach nach breun sturt*
Chiùin chaoin-fhoclach, 's nìor breug sin
Labhras go sèimh air gach modh
'*S a bréid air slinneanaibh fir.*

('The woman of melodious speech is never a rotten huff; she is gentle and softly spoken, that is no lie; She speaks carefully in each measure, with her kerchief across a man's shoulders.')

There is a long history of anthropomorphising instruments in Gaelic tradition, particularly as the female partners of their male players. Here the bagpipe's ability to speak is not just a reference to its use as a signalling device but a reflection of the strong general emphasis on the song tradition in Gaelic music: while the clàrsach *accompanied* song, the bagpipe could *speak* it. The poem subtly trumps the clàrsach's cachet at the same time as it asserts the gentle femininity of the bagpipe, such as describing the attached war-banner as a woman's kerchief.

Gilleasbuig's poem initiates the debate in earnest, with the authors of successive pieces taking the side of the bagpipes, the clàrsach, or the fiddle into the second half of the eighteenth century.[121] In fact, the debate probably only ceases because the clàrsach tradition became extinct shortly before the system of native patronage evaporated altogether with the capitulation and assimilation of the Gaelic aristocracy. One of the last tributes to the clàrsach is a song attributed to Sìleas na Ceapaich in which she speaks to it, saying:

B' annsa na fiodhull is beus,
Orgain cha téid mi g'a luaidh,
'*S b'e mo roghainn thar gach ceòl*
Fuaim do theud throimh d' bhòrdaibh cruaidh.[122]

('Dearer to me than the fiddle and cello – without even mentioning the organ – my preference above all other music, is the sound of your strings through your solid beams.')

The prestige of the bagpipe in general was no doubt enhanced by its functions in battle during a time when the intensity of warfare was escalating.[123] However, multi-instrumentalist musicians, and bagpipers who worked closely with professional poets and musicians, played a pivotal role in transforming the status of the bagpipe by adapting for it techniques and repertoire derived from the clàrsach tradition. We know of several important chieftains who employed harpers and bagpipers simultaneously in the seventeenth century, such as Campbell of Argyll, Grant of Freuchie, and MacLeod of Dunvegan.[124] Musicians who played these instruments sometimes belonged to the same family: according to one tradition, the first MacCrimmon employed as a musician by the MacLeods of Dunvegan was actually a clàrsair, not a bagpiper;[125] members of the Mac an Deòir family of Perthshire were employed by the Campbells of Achinbreck as both clàrsairan and bagpipers in the seventeenth century.[126] Some aristocratic musicians played both instruments, such as Raghnall mac Ailein òig of Eigg (fl. *c*.1700).[127]

Like the file, professional bagpipers became the full-time employees of chieftains, granted lands rent-free near their estates and were responsible for performing at the chieftain's request, as the tract *A Collection of Highland Rites and Customs* (*c*.1685) recorded: 'Pipers are held in great Request so that they are train'd up at the Expence of Grandees and have a portion of Land assignd and are design'd such a man's piper.'[128] Like the filidh and clàrsairean, professional bagpipers prided themselves on their social rank and expected to be treated accordingly. Edmund Burt related a couple of anecdotes from the 1720s which illustrate the self-regard of the bagpiper, such as this account which mentions his *gille* 'servant':

> His gilly holds the pipe till he begins; and the moment he has done with the instrument, he disdainfully throws it down upon the ground, as being only the passive means of conveying his skill to the ear, and not a proper weight for him to carry or bear at other times. But, for a contrary reason, his gilly snatches it up – which is, that the pipe may not suffer indignity from its neglect.[129]

The legacy of the MacCrimmons has been well established in Highland tradition, if rather overplayed by those whose claims of authority have been backed up by association with them. Like the filidh, the MacCrimmons maintained a college of bagpiping at Borreraig in Skye which operated into the 1770s;[130] attempts to establish a new college of piping under MacCrimmon leadership continued into the early nineteenth century.[131] It cannot be doubted that the MacCrimmons were central in the development of bagpipe music as an art form in its own right: perhaps the first surviving claim that bagpipe music had attained a high level of musical achievement is expressed in a song by Màiri nighean Alasdair Ruaidh (post-1666) in which she praises the playing of Pàdraig Mór MacCrimmon:

> *Ach pìob nuallach mhór*
> *Bheireadh buaidh air gach ceòl*
> *An uair a ghluaiste i le meòir Phàdraig.*[132]

('The great, bellowing bagpipe that outshone every sort of music when it was played by Patrick's fingers.')

It is less well known, however, that there were other families of professional bagpipers all around the Scottish Gàidhealtachd: the MacArthurs, employed by the MacDonalds in Sleat and North Uist;[133] the Rankins, employed by the Macleans of Duart;[134] the MacKays, employed by the MacKenzies of Gairloch;[135] the Mac-Gregors, probably a branch of the leading family of that name in Perthshire;[136] the Macintyres, employed across a wide range of Gaeldom, including Badenoch, Perthshire, Argyll, Skye;[137] and others. Many of these families have élite origins. The MacGregor bagpipers of Fortingall were called *Clann an Sgeulaiche* 'the children of the storyteller', demonstrating that they were members of the Gaelic intelligentsia before becoming bagpipers:

> These men were, for many generations, pipers, fiddlers, musical composers, and poets. One of them piped to his chief and clan at the Battle of Glenfruin, and commemorated the victory over the Colquhouns of Luss by the piobaireachd 'Mult dubh an earbuill ghil.'[138]

As the Battle of Glenfruin took place in 1603[139] and members of Clann an Sgeulaiche dominated the bagpipe scene well into the nineteenth century,[140] the family enjoyed a musical legacy at least two centuries long.

Formal bagpipe instruction was traditionally conducted not through the medium of written notation, but the aural mnemonic system *canntaireachd*; the fact that the term first appears in the thirteenth century in association with the clàrsach indicates that some technology transfer must have happened between these traditions. There are also indications that a number of the tunes that became adopted into the bagpipe tradition had originally been played on the clàrsach.[141]

The difference between the meanings of words in English and Gaelic to describe bagpipe music is a common source of confusion. The Gaelic word *pìobaireachd* was borrowed as 'pibroch' into Scottish English in the first half of the eighteenth century.[142] In English, 'pibroch' refers to the 'classical' music of the bagpipes, a formal, highly structured and stylised form of composition which consists of a theme (the *ùrlar*) and a number of increasingly ornamented variations. In Gaelic, however, pìobaireachd refers to bagpipe music generally; the high-register genre of bagpipe music is referred to with the term *ceòl mór*, distinct from the less formal tradition, which has strong associations with dancing, referred to with the term *ceòl beag*.[143]

There are Gaelic songs which are strongly associated with the bagpipe tradition. Most of them commemorate important events of clan history or the clan élite, some of them as early as the sixteenth century, if not earlier. This was a formative period for the bagpipes in Gaeldom, but it was also a period of great musical creativity and political turbulence. John Ramsay of Ochtertyre, in his introductory essay to the 1784 *A Collection of Highland Vocal Airs*, remarked on the popularity of these clan songs: 'But a very peculiar species of martial music was in the highest request with the Highlanders. It was sometimes sung, accompanied with words, but more frequently performed on a bagpipe.'[144] This once again confirms the important grounding that Gaelic musical traditions have in the song tradition, and hence in the language itself.

In the communities where the continuities of Gaelic language and music have been strongest to recent times, such as South Uist, the airs of these songs have been understood to be central in the interpretation and playing of ceòl mór.[145] While traditional Gaelic songs provide the ùrlar for many of the ceòl mór pieces played by pibroch players to the present, the modern arrangements and styles are significantly different from the simple metres and tunes of these songs. Several bagpiping dynasties enjoyed the stable patronage of leading chieftains during the seventeenth century, and several aristocrat-bagpipers also flourished during this period. There can be little doubt that in such circumstances professional bagpipers would have followed the lead of the clàrsairean in developing an elevated style of music for the enjoyment of the native élite in their leisure hours, abstracted and refined from the song form; indeed, the technique of variations on themes in clàrsach puirt is paralleled directly in pibroch music. This does not account for all of the development of the modern form, however: as a growing body of recent research indicates, the patronage system established in the late eighteenth century – the competition circuit, in particular, judged by a panel of non-Gaelic-speaking bourgeoisie – altered it significantly and divorced it from the original settings and styles natural to Gaelic music.[146]

The bagpipe was not limited to élite players or patrons: there were many forms of the bagpipe and many genres of bagpipe music, suited to different functions and contexts. John Ramsay of Ochtertyre noted, 'The large bagpipe is their instrument for war, for marriage, or funeral processions, and for other great occasions. They have also a smaller kind, on which dancing tunes are played.'[147] The bagpipe was also used to accompany mundane labour, as Edmund Burt testifies in the 1720s: 'Sometimes they are incited to their work by the sound of a bagpipe; and by either of these they proceed with great alacrity, it being disgraceful for any one to be out of time with the sickle.'[148]

The modern violin was introduced to Gaeldom at the same time that the native intelligentsia, including professional musicians, were losing the support of the aristocracy; these circumstances must have increased the hostility of clàrsairean and bagpipers to the fiddle, in addition to its association with a new style of music which appealed to the non-élite. In fact, when the clàrsair Ruaidhri Dall Morison first heard a fiddler playing music originally composed for the clàrsach, he is said to have remarked contemptuously, 'Masa ceòl fidileireachd, tha gu leòr siud dheth' ('If fiddling is music, that is enough of it'). He was said to have composed the tune 'Fuath nam Fidhleirean' ('Contempt of the Fiddlers') as a satire on such fiddlers.[149]

The fiddle (and its advocates) thus entered the poetic-musical fray already ongoing between the clàrsach and bagpipe. Surviving evidence suggests that similar strategies were taken to accommodate the fiddle to Gaelic musical precedents and to find a unique niche for it. One again, we can see social mediators who enriched the fiddle tradition by adapting pre-existing tunes, genres, and techniques, especially aristocratic musicians who played multiple instruments and families who had players of numerous instruments in them. Chieftain's halls were frequented by players of these instruments who also allowed for these musical exchanges. Lachlann mac Theàrlaich òig MacKinnon of Skye, for example, was a poet, a clàrsair, and a fiddler who spent time in the home of Iain MacLeod of Talisker, who was popular with a wide variety of poets and musicians.[150] Alexander Cummings played both bagpipe and fiddle to the Laird of Grant in the mid seventeenth century.[151] The pre-eminence of the fiddle in Atholl probably owes something to the long cultivation of the clàrsach in the area.[152]

Grant of Sheugly in Glen Urquhurt (fl. early 1700s), who played clàrsach, bagpipe, and fiddle, composed a Gaelic song about the rivalry between these instruments which seems to fit into the poetic debate already discussed. Captain Simon Fraser's influential 1816 collection *The Airs and Melodies peculiar to the Highlands of Scotland and the Isles*, reaching back a century in musical tradition, preserved a summary of it which was only printed in English translation:

> In appreciating the qualities of each instrument, he supposes that they had quarreled, and that he was called upon to decide the contest. In addressing a verse to his pipe, he observes 'how it would delight him, on hearing the sound of war, to listen to her notes, in striking up the gathering, to rally round the chief, on a frosty spring morning, whilst the hard earth reverberated all her notes, so as to be heard by the most distant person interested.' To the harp he says – 'The pleasure which thy tones afford are doubled, whilst accompanying a sweet female voice, or round the festive board, inspired by love or wine, I reach beyond my ordinary capacity, and feel the pleasure of pleasing.' But to his violin, which he calls by the literal name of Mary, George's Daughter, and seems to have been his favourite, though held cheap by other combatants, he says, 'I love thee, for the sake of those who do, – the sprightly youth and bonny lasses, – all who declare, that, at a wedding, dance or ball, thou, with thy bass in attendance, can have no competitor. – thy music having the effect of electricity on those who listen to it,' – and on thus receiving their due share of praise, their reconciliation is convivially received.[153]

What remains of this lost work suggests the three instruments can be reconciled by specialisation: the bagpipe is to serve military interests, the clàrsach is to play art music for the gentry, and the fiddle is to play for the dances and merriment of the commonality. This resolution is reflected in other contemporary sources. Fraser was a fiddler himself and his collection seems aimed to further the cachet of the instrument,[154] as the cover of his book indicates (see Plate 26).

In the Highlands the fiddle was truly a 'folk' instrument, free to operate independently of the élite, particularly in its function as the chosen instrument of the dance. Although the fiddle entered with a repertoire of new dance tunes, these eventually became assimilated within the wider set of pre-existing aesthetics of Gaelic music; in fact, being a vernacular rather than an élite tradition, the gravitational pull of Gaelic speech and song rhythms may have been even stronger for the fiddle than the clàrsach and bagpipe.[155] Not only was the new style of dance music adapted to Gaelic aesthetics by encoding it as port-à-beul, but other pre-existing genres of Gaelic song could also be adapted for the fiddle. Captain Fraser's command of Highland fiddle style was complimented with the remark, 'I never heard any one make the fiddle *speak Gaelic* so beautifully.'[156]

The Gaelic song tradition was so distinctive and so influential on the wider instrumental tradition that Martin Martin claimed that Lowland performers were not able to hide the origins of tunes that they had borrowed from the Highlands:

> There are several of 'em, who invent Tunes very taking in the South of Scotland, and elsewhere; some Musicians have endeavoured to pass for first Inventers of them by changing their Name, but this has been impracticable; for whatever Language gives the modern Name, the Tune still continues to speak its true Original: and of this I have been shew'd several instances.[157]

Despite the trend of Western music to divorce instrumental music from its roots in the song tradition, Gaelic tradition has maintained a strong belief in the grounding of music in song, as Charles Stewart noted in the late nineteenth century:

> I was much struck by a remark I heard made a few days ago, by one of our very best reel players, to a class of young men who were learning the violin, and which was to this effect: 'Every old reel and strathspey, being originally a "port-a-beul", has its own words. Now, if you wish to play with genuine taste, keep singing the words in your mind when you are playing the tune.[158]

The Gaelic language has thus been long perceived as a vital asset in the ability to interpret and perform Highland music.

DANCE

As in the case with music, efforts to trace and analyse the early history of dance are complicated by the incomplete and inexact documentary record as well as the shifting sands of language itself. Accounts before the nineteenth century seldom provide anything more than the vague impressions of the observer, which are often coloured by ethnocentric biases, and even at the end of nineteenth century few dances had been recorded with the precision of modern dance notation. Dance terms are notoriously fickle, jumping back and forth between languages and changing meaning and nuance. It is common for a word to refer at one time to a specific form of dance and at another to dancing in general, or vice versa; it can also refer to the kind of music associated with a dance genre. The most common terms for dance – 'jig', 'reel', 'strathspey', and 'hornpipe' – share some or all of these complications, which can render textual sources tenuous.

It is often pointed out that the two words used for 'dance' in Scottish Gaelic are loanwords: *dannsa* (or *damhsa*) was borrowed from French (either directly or via English), while *ruidhle* is a Germanic or Norse borrowing (from a word which gives us 'whirl' in modern English).[159] This does not mean, however, that dance was unknown to Scottish Gaeldom before contact with these cultures or that it lacked a concept to describe some type of dancing: it merely suggests that new words were borrowed in Gaelic after being exposed to new styles and functions of dance and that older terms were displaced and forgotten.

Not only is dance – bodily movement responding to music – universal, but there is sufficient evidence to demonstrate that early Celtic peoples practised forms of dance similar to contemporary European peoples. Dancers are represented on a terracotta vase from the late seventh century BC found in Sopron-Burgstall (Hungary); the bronze couch accompanying burial from the sixth century BC is decorated with pairs of dancers holding short swords; bronze figures found at the Gallo-Roman temple at Neuvy-en-Sullias appear to have portrayed members of group choral dances.[160]

Like the other performing arts, dance is a highly dynamic form of expression capable of responding to cultural changes without leaving much of a trace in the written record. The dances performed at any one time in a given community may be complex hybrids of diverse elements from different sources and time periods. Although the Gàidhealtachd has been more closely integrated into the rest of Europe during the last two centuries and hence more impacted by the increasingly rapid changes in dance fads, it has never been immune to the innovations emanating from élite European culture. In fact, many of the elements of dance now considered to be characteristically 'Scottish' or 'Highland' were incorporated from or stimulated by the fashions of the European aristocracy, especially those in the French and English courts.

Dance can be classified according to a number of different characteristics, including function, the number of people in a dancing 'unit', the degree of spontaneity, the movements of the parts of the body involved in executing the dance, the 'figure' traced on the ground during the course of the dance, the relationship between the dance and the music, and so on. As we shall see, social and aesthetic changes amongst the élite had wide-sweeping repercussions on the forms and functions of dance throughout medieval Europe.

Although in modern European culture we assume a direct correlation between dance movement and musical rhythm and phrase length, no close association need exist. On one extreme, musical accompaniment may merely provide the mood for the dance, not its 'pulse' or timing. Music and dance can also be contrastive. On the opposite extreme is percussive dance, where the movement of the dance is not only synchronised to the music but provides an essential rhythmic element of it.

Dances tend to be categorised according to the number of people involved in them in a wide variety of cultures: solo dances, couple dances, and group dances (usually in circles or chains). Most solo dances serve to emphasise the individual strength, dexterity, and/or grace of the dancer. Vestiges of a Highland 'pyrrhic' (imitating or preparing for acts of war) dance survive in 'Dannsa a' Chlaidheimh' ('The Sword Dance'), also known as 'Gille Chaluim' from the associated port-à-beul. The style of the sword dance was altered significantly during the nineteenth century, and little is known of the content of other pyrrhic dances whose names were recorded in the eighteenth and nineteenth centuries, such as 'Mac an Fhorsair' ('The Son of the Game-Keeper'), 'Dannsa na Biodaig' ('The Dirk Dance'), 'A' Bhonaid Ghorm' ('The Blue Bonnet'), and 'Buailidh mi thu 's a' cheann' ('I will strike you on the head').[161] Typical are the cryptic notes left by Alexander Campbell in his 1804 book of poetry: '*A' Cuthaich chaoil dubh*, is a kind of wild fantastic dance that requires great strength and agility to go through the various steps and movements, and is danced by one man.'[162]

Many early solo and couple dances imitate animals or act out dramatic scenes. In 'Dannsa nan Tunnag' ('The Dance of the Ducks'), dancers hop on their hunkers in a circle like ducks, a physically demanding activity which is clearly related to similar dances in other parts of Europe such as Cossack dancing.[163] 'Marbhadh na Béiste Duibhe' ('The Killing of the Otter'), is a pantomime in which one dancer, portraying a hunter, pursues an object representing an otter, which is manipulated by another cast-member who extends the hunt for as long as possible and moves the prey through the audience, much to their amusement.[164] Early observations about the combination of music and dance to provide a simple form of drama in rural Scottish society were provided by none other than the philosopher Adam Smith:

> In the country it frequently happens, that a company of young people take a fancy to dance, though they have neither fiddler nor piper to dance to. A lady undertakes to sing while the rest of the company dance: in most cases she sings the notes only, without the words, and then the voice being little more than a musical instrument, the dance is performed in the usual way, without any imitation. But if she sings the words, and if in those words there happens to be somewhat more than ordinary spirit and humour, immediately all the company, especially all the best dancers, and all those who dance most at their ease, become more or less pantomimes, and by their gestures and motions express, as well as they can, the meaning and story of the song. This would be still more the case, if the same person both danced and sung.[165]

Some of these dramatic dances appear to have no higher purpose than group entertainment; others seem to be integral to the rituals of special occasions. Seasonal festivals celebrating or ensuring the success of sowing or reaping often incorporated pantomimes enacting these activities.

In every folk culture in Europe there is a dance-drama which ritually enacts the death and rebirth of the solar year and symbolises the cycles of fertility upon which agricultural efforts were dependent. The day on which this dance-drama is performed and its particular form may change from region to region, but the general scenario of conflict, death, and resurrection is widespread. In the Scottish Gàidhealtachd, the dance was generally known as 'Cailleach an Dùdain' ('The Hag of the Mill-dust'), clearly a form of the Cailleach discussed in Chapter Six. There are records of this dance being performed on New Year's Eve, Michaelmas, and Bealltainn. The drama unfolded in a three-stage sequence: first, the Cailleach and a man appear in a scene of confrontation, both bearing weapons; second, after a pitched battle, the Cailleach is struck down dead by the man; third, the man regrets her death and brings her back to life. The drama represents man's harnessing of nature through agriculture: man, the agriculturalist, grapples with the forces of nature and with his farming implements strikes down the corn; most of the corn is ground to dust in the mill, but some of its seed is saved to return to the ground to grow again and begin the cycle anew.[166] As in many other similar customs, the fertility and regenerative powers of nature are echoed in the bawdy words and movements of the dance.

The first surviving description was based on the dance as it was performed in the central Highlands in the eighteenth century.

> If a female, the character assumed is *a' C[h]ailleach*, or old wife; and the person who dances is dressed in a very grotesque stile, having a bunch of keys hanging by her apron-string, and a staff to support her, for she affects to be very stiff, and lame of one leg. When the tune strikes up, she appears hardly able to hobble on the floor; by degrees, however, she gets on a bit, and as she begins to warm, she feels new animation, and capers away at a great rate, striking her pockets, and making her keys rattle; then affecting great importance as keeper of the good things of the store-room, ambry, and dairy. Meanwhile some of the company present join the person who plays the tune, and sings words suitable to the character the dancer assumes – generally some nonsense of a comic cast with which the matron, or Cailleach, seems wonderfully delighted. The names of the tunes and words that I have heard played and sung to this dance, are: [*an t-Seann Ruga Mhór*], *Cailleach an* [*Dùdain*], *Cailleach* [*an Stòpain-Fhalaimh*], and several others that I do not at present recollect.[167]

The large set of keys worn by the Cailleach figure symbolise her position of power and pre-eminence, as reflected in the Gaelic proverb 'Is math nach eil iuchraichean an domhain fo chrios na h-aon mhnatha' ('It is good that the keys to all of the world are not under the girdle of just one woman').[168] As in any folklore, the dance absorbed local colour and variations emerged in different communities. In the eastern Highlands of Perthshire, the figure of the Cailleach in the dance was combined with a character from local legend, a Fergusson woman nicknamed 'an t-Seann Ruga Mhór' ('The Old, Female Brute') who attacked McCombie of Glenshee in revenge for his mistreatment of her clansmen. Although four verses of it were preserved in the late nineteenth century, the rest of it was deemed 'scarcely refined enough for ears polite of the present day'.[169]

Father Allan MacDonald left a description of the dance as performed in late-nineteenth-century Eriskay, by which time some of the sexual content had been teased out:

Two take part in the dance – an old man and an old trembling shivering hag (a man dressed in punch attire does her part). The old hag comes in trembling and quivering with a stick in her hand and her husband similarly armed. They fight with the sticks – dancing all the time. Finally the old man thrusts his stick into her body and she falls down dead. The old man beats his hands and howls most atrociously as it occurs to him that he has murdered the old woman. The sudden change from anger and animosity to broken-heartedness for the loss of his partner in life is ridiculous. He bends down over her only to find out more surely that she is dead. The lamentation is heart-rending. Again and again he bends over her and again his sorrow is only intensified. He bends down and touches her boot and the foot rises a little and quivers away most singularly. The old man regains a little confidence. He bends down again and touches the other foot, and it too begins to shake incessantly. At these signs of returning life he bursts out into hysterical laughter. He touches the hands one by one. They too begin to quiver. The old carlin stretched out on the floor with her two feet and two hands quivering looks ridiculous to a degree and the spectators nearly drown the piper with their uproar. The old man then bends down and touches her hair and up she springs with renewed life and they both rush into each other's arms most gleefully.[170]

A tune entitled 'Cailleach an Dordan' was transcribed *c.*1740 in the MacFarlan manuscript (and about a century later in the Angus Fraser manuscript[171]), but it was not until the late nineteenth century that Alexander Carmichael recorded the words of one variant of the song. They employ clever double-entendres to describe the erotic overtones of the dance as well as the process and result of harvesting itself:

> *Chailleach an dùdain, dùdain, dùdain,*
> *Chailleach an dùdain, cùm do dheireadh rium.* [. . .]
> *Chailleach an dùdain, cùm do chùl rium.* [. . .]
> *Chailleach an dùdain, cùm do cheathramh rium.* [. . .]
> *Chailleach an dùdain, null e, nall e.* [. . .]

('O Hag of the mill-dust, mill-dust, mill-dust,
O Hag of the mill-dust, keep your backside to me [or, supply me with your harvest]. [. . .]
O Hag of the mill-dust, face away from me [or, supply me with your crop]. [. . .]
O Hag of the mill-dust, keep your thigh to me [or, supply me with your grain]. [. . .]
O Hag of the mill-dust, take it over, bring it back. [. . .]')[172]

Descriptions of two other Highland dance-dramas related to agricultural customs survive. One of these was entitled 'Croit an Droighinn' ('The Thorny Croft'). In it a farmer complains about the poor land he must plough, interspersing comments about his sexual exploits and his escape from forced recruitment in the Battle of Bothwell Bridge in 1679. It thus appears to be a classic example of 'low' entertainment.[173] Two verses of a peat-cutting dance for two survive from Badenoch.[174]

Dance has been integral to religious ritual from earliest times. The 'choral dance' in particular has been the dance par excellence for collective religious experience in cultures around the world. Any number of dancers can join together in a ring (or, alternatively, a chain) and step together in a circular motion as they accompany themselves in song. These choral songs are often arranged in verse and chorus structure, with a lead singer calling out the verses and the group responding with the chorus. The Christian church had a long and complex relationship with the choral dance, attempting in early centuries to incorporate dance into the liturgy. *The Acts of John*, dated to *c.*AD 160, describes Jesus as being surrounded by his disciples singing in a ring-dance at the Last Supper. Dance was said by Epiphanius, a fourth-century bishop in Cyprus, to be an essential element in the celebrations of Palm Sunday: 'once again perform the choral dances [. . .] ye who dwell in Zion, dance ring dances.'[175] The carole evolved from sung-dances which accompanied seasonal festivities.

Choral dances were also already part of the pre-Christian customs of northern Europe and had strong associations with both sex and death: 'From the 4th century well into the 18th century, there were many prohibitions against dancing for the dead in graveyards, particularly against dances which were ribald and indecent, or which involved drinking and feasting.'[176] One such reprimand against pagan Celtic dance customs was issued by St Caesarius (*c.*470–543), bishop of Arles in Gaul:

There are some people who come to the birthday festivals of the martyrs for this sole purpose, that they may destroy themselves and ruin others by intoxication, dancing, singing shameful songs, leading the choral dance, and pantomiming in a devilish fashion.[177]

From church records we know that the choral dance was practised in medieval Scotland as well and may even be graphically represented in medieval manuscripts and monuments.[178] The Diocese of Aberdeen prohibited the choral dance and 'indecent and shameful games/dances' in the church and graveyard in the thirteenth century. Similar bans were enacted in Scotland into the seventeenth century.[179]

Nonetheless, forms of the choral dance continued to be practised in Gaelic Scotland into the nineteenth century, sometimes with sexually explicit content.[180] 'An Dannsa Mór' ('The Big Dance'), last performed on the island of Eigg, appears to be descended from the choral dance. Any number of men can dance in the ring as they sing together on the chorus; two men take turns singing and acting out the verses.[181] Alexander Carmichael describes a carole to Saint Brighid sung as a choral dance during the proceedings of her festival: 'As the grey dawn of the Day of Bride breaks they form a circle and sing the hymn of "Brìde bhòidheach muime Chorr Chrìosda" ["Beauteous Brìde, choice foster-mother of Christ"].'[182] Once universal, the choral dance now survives only in a few corners of Europe, such as the Faroe Islands.

During the High Middle Ages, the nobility of feudal Europe developed social norms and forms of behaviour and etiquette that asserted an increasing distinction between themselves and the peasantry. These changes were reflected in the styles and forms of dance, especially in the creation of highly formalised dances for couples in the aristocratic courts:

> Two opposite poles developed in Europe in this last medieval phase between the twelfth and fourteenth centuries: the peasants, or the populace at large, stood for the earthiness and crude joy, while the nobility replaced the primary impulses with refinement and polished sparkle. [. . .] the court dance was subjected more and more to rules.[183]

The presumptions of sophistication, self-control, and grace assumed by the nobility and exhibited in their formal dance are still reflected in modern English words derived from feudal court-life: 'courtship', 'courteous', 'courtesy', 'curtsey', and so on. These new forms of dance developed alongside new genres of instrumental music meant to accompany them.

In the 15th and 16th centuries, a great dance movement swept throughout the courts of Europe, accompanied by a surge of creation of new musical forms. Essentially, this movement had two aspects. One was the creation of a variety of new court dances, performed by the nobility themselves as a form of aristocratic amusement and, more than this, a means of educating courtiers in social deportment and grace. The second was the development of a number of major entertainments, or spectacles, which ultimately gave rise to the art of ballet in France.[184]

The contrasts emerging between the aristocracy and the peasantry as relating to the characteristics and context of dance can be outlined in summary:

Characteristic	Peasantry	Aristocracy
Dancing unit	Choral (ring) dance; all members of the community could participate	Couple and solo dances performed after receiving formal training
Musical accompaniment	Songs sung by dancers	Professional instrumentalists
Movements	Spontaneous, informal, simple	Formally predefined choreography of increasing complexity; exercise of self-discipline and poise
Space / Location	Generally outdoors, free of spatial limitation	Generally indoors, limited space and freedom of movement
Clothing	Loose garments which permitted freedom of movement	Elaborate costume and jewellery which restricted movement

Table 7.1: Trends in medieval dance developments

The leader in dance, the arbiter of style, and the teacher of courtly manners was the dancing master who made his living training the youth in the arts of court life. Many dancing masters provided their own musical accompaniment while training their pupils; the modern violin was a popular choice, as was the smaller, more portable version of the instrument, the 'kit' or 'pochette'.[185] With the invention of the printing press, manuals that included the instructions for dances and accompanying tunes allowed for a set of standards to be distributed and adopted across the courts of Europe.

The growing psychological distance between the aristocracy and the animal world brought disfavour upon dances which imitated animals or were associated with them; ritual dances associated with the harvest, fertility, or other aspects of the crude life of the peasantry were also scorned by the élite.[186] The lower classes and the growing ranks of the bourgeoisie were inevitably influenced by the aesthetics of the élite, and in attempting to affect their manners also sought to master the new dance styles and repertoire. In such social conditions, the older forms of dance gradually lost their appeal and audiences.

Even if it took time for these developments to reach Gaelic Scotland, most of them eventually had an impact on Highland dance traditions, especially in locales with strong connections to France, the innovating centre of Europe dance. Not only were the royal courts of Scotland and France closely tied for a period, but many Highland leaders had family connections in France and some continued to send their sons there for education. These connections remained influential, especially in areas that remained Catholic, well into the eighteenth century.[187] The fluid intercourse between the classes of Highland society in the pre-modern era allowed such developments amongst the élite to be quickly transmitted throughout Gaelic culture.

The term 'reel' first appears in Scottish sources in the sixteenth century to refer to a weaving figure in dance, where dancers pass each other on alternating sides. The term also came to refer to specific dances that included this figure-of-eight movement, usually for three or four people, as well as a particular style of dance music (usually in 4/4 time signature) associated with these dances. The figure of the Scottish reel corresponds directly to the English 'hey' and both are likely to have derived from the French *hay d' Alemaigne* during the sixteenth century. The linear reel only penetrated the Lowlands and the eastern Highlands; in the western Highlands and Hebrides the geometry of the circle remained dominant in the figure of the dance, probably due to the legacy of the choral dance.[188] The reel remained the dominant form of social dance in many Gaelic communities into the twentieth century, and balls and public performances often consisted of nothing else.[189]

The first evidence of the galliard (Italian *gagliarda*, French *gaillarde*, Spanish *gallarda*) comes from late-fifteenth-century Lombardy. It was essentially a dance of courtship in which the man and woman pursue one another in turn, demonstrating their dexterity and agility. The galliard consists primarily of leg thrusts and leaps performed in 6/8 time, generally arranged in groups of five known by the French term *le cinq pas*. The figure of the galliard is open, allowing movement forward, backward, sideways and diagonally.[190] It was popular in aristocratic courts of the sixteenth century and was known in England by 1541. There are two galliards specifically associated with Mary Queen of Scots which may have been composed by her.[191] The galliard is likely to have been a key influence on the leg movements of Highland dance.[192]

These new forms of dance emerging in the courts of Renaissance Europe were social – not ritual or dramatic – in nature. They were increasingly governed by the rhythm of the music rather than just reflecting its mood or enacting the story conveyed by the words of a song. As perceptions about the purpose and form of dancing changed, so were the new, imported terms *dannsa* and *ruidhle* used to refer to it. From the seventeenth century onwards Gaelic poetry reflects a growing awareness of the role of social dance as an indicator of a person's station in society. The assembled company in the noble household of one òran-luaidh is described as:

Daoin' uaisle mu bhòrdaibh dùmhail	C.5
Ruidhleadh mu seach air an ùrlar	C.3
Le pìob mhór nam feadan dùmhail	
Le pìob bheag nam feadan siùbhlach.[193]	

('Aristocrats around the tightly packed planks reeling in turn on the floor to the great bagpipes of the dense drones and to the small bagpipes of the lively drones.')

In another, a household of MacDonalds is praised for their athletic figures, polite manners and polished dancing style:

Ach luchd nan leadan 's nan cùl donna	C.5, E.3
'S nan calpannan geala troma	E.4
Dhianadh an danns' air am bonnaibh	C.3, E.2
Dhianadh an ùmhlachd le'm boineid.[194]	E.8

('People with long, flowing, brown locks of hair and fair, well-built calves who would dance on the front of their feet and show respect with their bonnets.')

Social dancing began to spread widely in Scottish society in the late seventeenth century as religious restrictions loosened, but it, and the allied art of fiddle music, flourished most fully in the eighteenth century. The strathspey, the most distinctively Scottish form of dance music, appears to have developed in the early eighteenth century.[195] Alexander Campbell wrote in 1798 that social dance and dance music had been evolving local characteristics around the Highlands:

The reel seems prevalent in the Braes of Athol, and over the west part of Perthshire, and is pretty universal throughout Argyleshire. The strathspey seems peculiar to the great tract of country through which the river Spey runs. Through the North-Highlands, and western Isles, a species of melody, partaking somewhat of the reel, and strathspey, seems more relished by the natives, to which they dance, in a manner peculiar to these parts of the Hebrides. The Athol reel is lively, and animating in a high degree. The strathspey is much slower, better accentuated [. . .] The movements to the former are spirited, yet less graceful.[196]

Dance schools became established in Lowland burghs from the mid seventeenth century onwards, often teaching manners, music and the French language as well as dance to the youth of upwardly mobile families. At the end of class term, pupils performed at dance balls open to the public, which served as effective advertising for the dance schools. Dance masters emphasised their training in, and ongoing connections to, the dance traditions of Paris and London.[197] French influence on Scottish dance is reflected in the pervasive use of French terminology as well as ballet technique: indeed, some of the dance masters at Scottish schools taught French dances.[198] During the later eighteenth century dancing masters began to bring their lessons to the countryside, including rural Ireland and the Scottish Highlands.[199] An English traveller in the late eighteenth century confirms that showcases for students also performed in the Gàidhealtachd:

In the evening there was a dancing-school ball at the inn, to which we were politely invited, and where we had again an opportunity of hearing Neil Gow, and observing the superiority of the highlanders to our countrymen in dancing; some of the children who we saw dance this evening, would have cut no disgraceful figure on the stage.[200]

Francis Peacock, dancing master in Aberdeen from 1747 to 1807, wrote a manual on dancing in 1805 in which he makes explicit the role of dance in refining Scotland's youth in the manners of the 'cultured' world:

And with what a sensible pleasure do we behold the elegant and engaging deportment of a young lady, whose natural fine form has been improved by a proper cultivation of all those graces which are characteristic of dignity and ease? Such a one, when compared with the uninstructed, pretty, bashful rustic, just emerged from the country – how striking the contrast! Yet, perhaps, the native qualities of the latter may be equal to those of the former; only the opportunities for improving them have been neglected. [. . .] I may here observe, that there cannot be a greater proof of the utility of Dancing, than its being so universally adopted, as a material circumstance in the education of the youth of both sexes, in every civilized country. Its tendency to form their manners, and to render them agreeable, as well in public as in private; the graceful and elegant ease which it gives to the generality of those who practise it with attention, are apparent to every one of true discernment.[201]

Peacock mentions that many of his students were from the Gaelic-speaking Highlands (which then extended into Aberdeenshire) and islands and that some of them were such excellent dancers that he 'thought them worthy of imitation'.[202] With the help of a contemporary (probably the scholar Ewen MacLachlan, librarian of King's College) he provided pre-existing Gaelic terms for many dance steps and movements.[203]

Elizabeth Grant of Rothiemurchus noted in the early nineteenth century that 'all Highlanders considering this art as essential in the education of all classes and never losing an opportunity of acquiring a few more flings and shuffles'.[204] In fact, Alexander Stewart, the minister for Moulin Parish in Perthshire, lamented in the *Old Statistical Account for Scotland* (published 1791–9) that the older Highland recreations were becoming displaced by the new training offered by dancing masters:

> It is observable that those gymnastic exercises, which constituted the chief pastime of the Highlanders 40 or 50 years ago, have almost totally disappeared. At every fair or meeting of the country people, there were contests at racing, wrestling, putting the stone, and on holidays, all the males of a district, young and old, met to play at football, but oftener at shinty. These games are now practised only by school-boys, having given place to the more elegant, though less manly, amusements of dancing, which is become very common, especially on holidays.

The role of dancing schools in creating a successful 'Highland gentleman' passed into the Gaelic storytelling canon itself. A tale recorded by Hector MacLean in 1859 in North Uist tells of a rustic shepherd's son from Skye who went to live with his uncle in Perth. While in the Lowland city, he attended a dancing school for three years and became an expert dancer. He was eventually taken by a sea-captain to dance balls in a large town where he won the hearts of female sophisticates and the bride of his choice.[205] It is significant, however, he gains both the art of dancing and rewards from it outwith the Gàidhealtachd.

Amongst the innovations of cosmopolitan dancing masters in the second half of the eighteenth century were dances which focus on the precise and elaborate movements of the feet in rhythm with the music. These are now generally referred to as 'step-dances', although at the time they were called variously 'high dances', 'hornpipes', or 'jigs' (regardless of the specific time signatures).[206] Just as composers sought to create ever more embellished variations of musical themes, so did dancing masters and their students create ever more ornate variations of rhythmic foot movements in complex combinations: steps, shuffles, hops, slides, taps, twists, kicks, springs, and so on. An English traveller observed a ball in the Dalmally Inn in 1804 in which the dance master, with austere command of his students, demonstrated a dance movement local to Glenorchy:

> The company consisted of about fourteen couple[s], who all danced the true Glen Orgue Kick. I have observed that every district of the Highlands has some peculiar

cut; and they all shuffle in such a manner as to make the noise of their feet keep exact time. Though this is not the fashionable style of dancing, yet, in such districts, it had not a bad effect. But I shall never forget the arrogance of the master; his mode of marshaling his troops, his directions, and other manoeuvres were truly ridiculous; he felt himself greater than any adjutant disciplining his men, and managed them much in the same manner.[207]

Step-dance spread widely throughout Europe and colonial America, especially in areas served by dance masters, until it fell out of fashion in the early nineteenth century. England became even more accomplished for step-dance than France in the late eighteenth century and the names of some step-dances performed in Scotland (such as the Liverpool Hornpipe and the Lancashire Hornpipe) indicate their origins in England.[208] Like any kind of folklore, it took very little time for dances introduced to the Gaelic community to evolve local forms, as long as there wasn't a dance master requiring strict adherence to external standards. Styles and repertoires absorbed local influences and were strongly impacted by available material resources. Into the nineteenth century most Gaels in the Scottish Highlands lived in homes with mud-packed floors and did not own hard-soled shoes; the conditions in North America, where shoes and wooden floors were more widely available and similar dance traditions flourished in neighbouring communities, facilitated immigrant Gaels in developing step-dance as a percussive dance form.[209]

Gaelic dance music initially developed for the fiddle was soon adapted for the trump and the bagpipe[210] and sung as Gaelic mouth music. Alexander Campbell noted the use of port-à-beul in 1815 while conducting fieldwork in North Uist:

> I witnessed for the first time, persons singing at the same time they dance: and this is called dancing to [puirt-à-beul], being a succedaneous contrivance to supply the want of a musical instrument. [. . .] the men and women sing a bar of the tune alternately; by which they preserve the accent and rhythms quite accurately – the effect is animating: and having words correspondent to the characters of the measure.[211]

This and similar scenes illustrate how community members of all ages, classes, and abilities could be active participants in their own culture. They serve to remind us that various genres of music and dance were closely interrelated in Gaelic folklife before they were fragmented, fossilised, and taken under the aegis of numerous specialised institutions based in the urban Lowlands that were dominated by the anglicised élite. While this new patronage allowed certain forms of the arts derived from Gaelic tradition to survive, they did so in forms and contexts increasingly alienated from each other and influenced by the aesthetics of Anglo-British culture. In depictions such as this dance in North Uist we see glimpses, however fleeting, of high-spirited, self-assured Highland communities which sang and danced without worrying about the future of their tradition.

Chapter Eight

HUMAN ECOLOGY

To restore any place, we must also begin to re-story it, to make it the lesson of our legends, festivals, and seasonal rites. Story is the way we encode deep-seated values within our culture. Ritual is the way we enact them. We must ritually plant the cottonwood and willow poles in winter in order to share the sounds of the vermillion flycatcher during the rites of spring. By replenishing the land with our stories, we let the wild voices around us guide the restoration we do. The stories will outlast us.

– Gary Paul Nabhan *Cultures of Habitat*

Coille Dhubh Raithneach (known in English as 'the Black Wood of Rannoch'), one of the last stands of old-growth forest in Highland Perthshire, is home to rare species of lichens, fungi, plants, and animals. If you were to travel from these lush woodlands on the shore of Loch Rannoch westwards you would soon end up in the bogs and marshes known in Gaelic as 'Madaigein na Mòin' and in English as 'Rannoch Moor'. Here, and in other wetlands around Scotland, the stumps and limbs of trees over 4,000 years old – the victims of the agricultural revolution – have been preserved in acidic waters, bearing silent testimony to vanished forests.[1]

Gaels have speculated for many centuries about the fate of Scottish woods. The destruction of the 'Great Caledonian Forest', as it is often called in English, was most often explained by a tale about the Vikings and their jealousy of Scottish forests, recorded in many places in the Gàidhealtachd. The story accords with portrayals of the Vikings as a hostile, alien, and pagan anti-image of the Gaels in oral tradition.

The place name 'Lochlann' which appears in tales of the Vikings can be translated roughly as 'Scandinavia' but it is also an exotic region of the imagination. It is notable that the story begins not in some small locale particular to the Highlands but is set in Scotland as a whole, portraying it as a cohesive country covered in trees. The storyteller does root the tale in the landscape in a specific way: he asserts that the grave of the king's daughter authenticates the truth of the tradition.

~

In the old days Scotland was entirely covered in forests of Scots pine. The King of Lochlann saw this and became greatly jealous of the Scots, since the Norse were ruining their own resources, and he decided that he would burn down all of Scotland's forests.

This is how it happened. He sent his daughter to be schooled in the Black Arts and when her training was complete, he sent her ashore in Scotland with a load of fire. With this load she began to set fire to all of Scotland's forests. She had not made much progress when the Scots saw that she wasn't a Christian being, and so they tried to see if there was some means of capturing her.

In spite of their various tactics they could not catch her. 'Dubh a' Ghiuthais' ('Black Scots-Pine') was the name that the Scots gave her on account of how black she was from the smoke of the pine that she was burning. If they did manage to get close to her, she would fly upwards and as soon as she gained great height a cloud would enclose itself around her and hide her from everyone on the ground.

She was causing a great deal of destruction this way and the Scots were puzzled about how she could be killed. One day there was a man from Loch Broom who thought of a tactic to destroy her, and its like was never heard of before. This man said that since her youth Dubh a' Ghiuthais had kept company with livestock and that if the young of each sort of animal could be separated from their mothers at the moment that the people saw Dubh a' Ghiuthais in the cloud, that she would descend to the earth.

This is how it happened. A great herd was gathered at Achadh Bad a' Chruiteir in the Braes of Kildonan in Loch Broom and when the people saw the cloud in which Dubh a' Ghiuthais was, they quickly separated the young animals from their mothers and then there arose a great commotion! Every cow was lowing, every mare was neighing, every sheep and goat was bleating, and every sort of animal was searching for its own kind.

Dubh a' Ghiuthais heard this noise and commotion in the field and she descended. No sooner did she touch her foot to the ground than she was shot with an arrow. She fell down dead there and no one knew who would bury her. There were two Norse ships at that time in Camusnagaul and having heard the news of the king's daughter's death, the two crews went to seek her corpse.

They put it into a wicker coffin and carried it to their ship. They stretched open the sails but no sooner did they open them than a storm arose worse than any ever seen before. They had to return. The next day, they set off but a storm arose as terrible as it had been before. No matter how often they would attempt to depart, the same ill luck met them. They finally gave up and buried her in Kildonan.

They sailed from there to Lochlann and on the way they caught the fairest wind for sailing that they had ever encountered. They told the king what had happened. He was greatly grief-stricken, especially because his daughter's remains were not in the soil of Lochlann.

He sent the same two ships back again loaded with the soil of Lochlann. They reached Kildonan. As soon as they arrived they put the soil on land and they placed Dubh a' Ghiuthais in it. And anyone who wishes to may see her grave to this very day.

I have now told the story about Dubh a' Ghiuthais and if I have told a falsehood, it is because a falsehood was told to me.[2]

~

The study of human ecology allows us to analyse how material culture, economic practices, cultural values, social institutions, and mental concepts are interconnected and mutually reinforcing in a society's relationship with its environment. There is nothing predetermined, inevitable or even 'natural' about the ideology that informs a particular culture's notion of its place in the world and its relationship to its surroundings. Every cultural configuration does, however, have ramifications for its impact on the environment.

> A society's symbols and images of nature express its collective consciousness. They appear in mythology, cosmology, science, religion, philosophy, language, and art. Scientific, philosophical, and literary texts are sources of the ideas and images used by controlling elites, while rituals, festivals, songs, and myths provide clues to the consciousness of ordinary people. [. . .] Viewed as a social construction, nature as it was conceptualized in each social epoch (Indian, colonial, and capitalist) is not some ultimate truth that was gradually discovered through the scientific processes of observation, experiment, and mathematics. Rather, it was a relative changing structure of human representations of 'reality'.[3]

Language provides the raw materials for consciousness and perception. The words we use to describe the world and our relationship to it, and the meanings associated with those words, strongly affect the ways in which we interpret, and create meaning from, the data coming from our sensory organs about our surroundings. Words and their associations connect to narratives and beliefs intrinsic to the construction of culture and ultimately provide explanations and rationales about social institutions and practices.[4] Consider words we use in modern English and the assumptions underlying them such as 'development', 'weeds', 'pests', 'dirt', 'resource', 'waste', 'creation of wealth', 'productive', and so on. They all relate in various ways to a worldview in which nature is merely a desacralised warehouse of resources and humankind is uniquely privileged above the rest of creation to exploit it at will.

For the vast majority of our existence as a species, humankind has lived comfortably as hunter-foragers without perceiving any distinction between ourselves and 'nature', or between home and 'wilderness'. Paleolithic humans, and hunter-forager societies surviving into the present, have enjoyed a remarkably stable and symbiotic relationship with their environment.[5] The worldviews of these societies share a core of features which underpin their ecological practices:[6]

- They regard nature as a benevolent mother figure
- They conceive of nature as a living and sacred system

- They infer that the sacred can be manifest in many forms
- They understand that metaphor and symbol are the means of accessing the sacred
- They believe that time is synchronous, folded into an eternal present
- They understand that ritual is essential to maintain the natural order

The pioneers of the Neolithic agricultural revolution, mastering the cultivation of grain after the end of the last Ice Age, instigated a paradigm shift in several different parts of the world nearly simultaneously. Once people became dependent upon agriculture, they were compelled to intervene in natural processes: they converted the forests into fields, maintained knowledge about astronomical and climactic events, and harnessed massive amounts of human and animal labour to cultivate the fields. With the agricultural way of life, people formed permanent settlements, accumulated goods, stratified themselves into hierarchical and specialised castes, and grew crops to feed a variety of domesticated animals. This was not a straightforward improvement over the hunter-forager, however, for these changes were accompanied by the rise of warfare, disease, class inequality, and a general decline in the quality of life.[7]

The agricultural revolution thus brought about fundamental changes in the organisation of society, the classification of knowledge, and the relationship to the environment. Humankind became self-conscious of itself and of how culture differentiated it from nature. Human consciousness only perceived 'wilderness' after the post-agricultural human efforts to create permanent settlements and cultivate fields created the distinction. 'Boundaries were drawn between the natural and the cultural, and conceptual restructuring was inevitable.'[8] These boundaries were physical, such as the contrast between domesticated space and 'wild' nature, but they had abstract and symbolic associations as well.

> Such metaphorical divisions and limits can be explored in different communities since the countryman recognises the quintessential division between the cultivated land of the settlement and the land beyond. In the Highlands this may be instantly recognisable or identifiable as the 'head-dyke' of the township, a physical division introduced or imposed in crofting agriculture, but standing metaphorically for divisions created by the mind, for a synchronic division between settled and waste land, tamed and untamed, or a diachronic and meaningful division between occupied and unoccupied land, controlled and wild, and rich in vocabulary and terminology.[9]

The terms we use to discuss nature in modern English bear more recent influences as well. The word 'wilderness' is derived from Old English *wild dēor* 'wild deer', as these creatures typify the inhabitants of 'untamed' nature. The word 'landscape' is itself a comparatively recent coinage, having been imported from Dutch into English by élites in the seventeenth century whose appreciation for the countryside had been transformed by new fashions in visual art.

The initial appeal of rural scenery was that it reminded the spectator of landscape pictures. Indeed the scene was only called a 'landscape' because it was reminiscent of a painted 'landskip'; it was 'picturesque' because it looked like a picture. The circulation of topographical art in which human figures were absent or unimportant thus preceded the appreciation of rural landscapes and determined the form it took.[10]

Seldom, however, do even radical revolutions manage to eradicate pre-existing features of cultures entirely: ecological paradigm shifts generally happened slowly and left behind 'cultural residue' from earlier phases.[11] Although Gaelic culture went through the agricultural revolution millennia ago, many of the general features of the Paleolithic worldview regarding nature and humankind's relationship to it survived to a surprising degree. The stature of the Cailleach and the central place of the sacred tree in Gaelic cosmology attest to this. In examining the meaning and function of the description of nature in early Gaelic poetry, Maria Tymoczko observes:

> The intermingling of human activities with statements about plants, animals, and the elements is characteristic of much early Irish nature poetry. This suggests an outlook which did not rigidly demarcate human beings from the rest of the natural order. Humanity does not seem estranged or alienated in this type of nature poetry.[12]

Perhaps the endurance of an archaic ecological outlook in the Scottish Highlands in particular is not surprising given the marginal role of agriculture in the poor soils and the great reliance upon pastoralism. Indeed, Lowlanders are often stereotyped in later Gaelic tradition as stooping field-workers.[13] The opposition Gaeldom perceived between itself and its Lowland neighbours, who were steadily developing an urbanised environment and mercantile economy, may have also contributed to Highland conservatism. The necessities of survival in the Highlands were turned into virtues by contrast to the Lowlands and the symbolic features of the landscape of the Highlands were used as badges of identity for the Gaels as a whole.[14]

Nature, land use and the landscape itself have influenced the Gaelic language in many ways, such as providing metaphors and analogies applicable to a wide range of circumstances. Local characteristics of the landscape have made an impact on the usages of the Gaelic language. In the eastern Highlands, for example, the words *s(h)ìos* and *s(h)uas*, which mean 'down' and 'up' respectively in the rest of Gaeldom, came to mean 'east' and 'west' respectively because of the slope of the central mountains.[15] If there is a Gaelic equivalent to the proverbial fourteen words for snow in the Inuit language(s), it would probably be the set of terms to distinguish between different types of heights. A recent survey of the Gaelic names of mountains and peaks in Perthshire alone identifies twenty different terms designating specific shapes and characteristics.[16]

As discussed in Chapter Three, the Gaelic literary tradition has long been dominated by the poet-patron relationship and the function of literature to uphold the legitimacy of particular rulers and dynasties, as well as wider social institutions. As a result, the amount of literary evidence directly relevant to the study of human ecology in the Scottish Gàidhealtachd, especially as expressed and composed by the non-élite, committed to writing before the eighteenth century is limited. By comparing different types of evidence and analysing the continuities between élite and non-élite traditions in both Scotland and Ireland we can recapture some of the dominant patterns and themes.

The tale of Dubh a' Ghiuthais, for example, attests to the importance of forests and the wilderness generally in Gaelic culture, as well as the ambiguities that were felt about the consequences of the agricultural revolution and later activities that impacted the environment.

> Tradition is consistent and widespread over the Highlands that woods were once extensive and no longer are so. [. . .] The traditions themselves serve to provide an insight into a symbolic role for woodland in the culture of the Gaelic Highlands. [. . .] They indicate that the woods were inseparably part of the cultural heritage of the area and that there was an innate understanding of environmental issues since the loss of trees was interpreted as a disaster and an upsetting of the natural order.[17]

That the loss of the forests is blamed on the archetypal non-Gael, the Viking, underscores the importance of woods and the need to exonerate Gaeldom from such wrongdoing. Similar traditions in Ireland indicate a parallel cultural impulse.[18]

Even cultures that utilise agriculture have been capable of staying intimately attached and finely tuned to their local environment. We can call 'indigenous' those cultures whose way of life and identity are specific to their locale.

> Traditional societies are socialized to existence in a specific place. That is to say, the most Traditional societies are indigenous in the sense that they believe they belong to the space they occupy [. . .] Generation after generation expends energy thinking about what it means to be a people of a forest or desert, and that thinking process develops a conservatism about the ecology which is both healthy and, in the long term, necessary for survival.[19]

It is no accident that biological diversity is declining in concert with the loss of diversity in human languages and cultures. Many contemporary scholars who argue that a sustainable future depends, in fact, upon our ability to maintain and nurture diversity of all sorts point out the historical interdependencies between nature and culture.

> Cultural diversity and biological diversity are not only related, but often inseparable, perhaps causally connected through coevolution in specific habitats. Research has shown quite striking correlations between areas of biodiversity and areas of highest

linguistic diversity, allowing us to talk about a common repository of what we will call biolinguistic diversity: the rich spectrum of life encompassing all the earth's species of plants and animals along with human cultures and their languages.[20]

This chapter will begin to explore how words, concepts, phrases, and entire narratives in Gaelic encode, transmit, and reinforce particular ways of thinking about the relationship between people and nature. These elements in Gaelic culture – oral tradition most specifically – encourage particular ways of 'reading the landscape' and perpetuate Gaelic ecological ideals and a sense of place and belonging for the individual and the community. These factors have shaped Scottish Gaelic culture and made it indigenous to its habitat in the Highlands and Islands.

HUMAN-NATURE MIRRORING

Besides mere economic resources, nature has provided humankind with symbolic reference points to define itself by comparison and contrast. It is inevitable that a culture's perceptions of nature are coloured by the mental categories and standards that it creates to explain and systematise itself.

> The work of many anthropologists suggests that it is an enduring tendency of human thought to project upon the natural world (and particularly the animal kingdom) categories and values derived from human society and then to serve them back as a critique or reinforcement of the human order, justifying some particular social or political arrangement on the grounds that it is somehow more 'natural' than any alternative. [. . .] the universal belief in analogy and correspondence made it normal to discern in the animal world a mirror image of human social and political organization.[21]

Some of the fundamental organisational features of Gaelic society – such as hierarchy, leadership, and fosterage – are projected upon the natural world, with the analogies between humankind and the natural world appearing in many forms at many levels of abstraction.

Parallels perceived by Gaels between trees and human beings have already been mentioned in Chapter Six. The anatomy of the tree is seen in Gaelic as analogous to the human body, and terms used for parts of the human body are also used of trees. Most words for trees were also used as kennings for people, such as *crann, craobh, faillean, fiùbhaidh, fiùran, fleasgach, gasan, geug(ag), ògan(ach)*, and *slat*. A poem of praise by Donnchadh Bàn Macintyre for the Earl of Breadalbane exemplifies the use of these tree kennings: 'gur deas am fiùran / Air thùs nan gallan thu' ('You are a handsome branch / In the forefront of the saplings.')[22]

People are also frequently described or analysed by way of tree metaphors in Gaelic. The expression 'Bha e 's an fhiodh' ('It was in the timber')[23] is used metaphorically to explain how a person's personality or behaviour is explained by their heredity. The importance of good child-rearing was expressed by proverbs such as 'Lùb am faillean is chan fhairtlich a' chraobh ort' ('Bend the sapling and the tree won't defy you').[24] The aggressive and expansionist nature of the ash tree could be attributed to a person with the expression 'Thachair ludh an uinnsinn fhiadhaich dhà; cinnidh e gu math ach millidh e a' chraobh a bhios an taice ris' ('The way of the wild ash befell him; it grows well but destroys the tree that is next to it').[25] These examples demonstrate that the parallels between trees and humans are seen as operating in both directions, not just a projection of human traits onto the natural world.

Chapter Three has already mentioned how praise and satire can be expressed in Gaelic literature by association with particular plants and animals that have positive and negative connotations. While there are many examples of poems that invoke particular species in order to praise or satirise a human subject, the most exhaustive litany used for panegyric appears in Sìleas na Ceapaich's poem on the death of Alasdair MacDonald of Glengarry *c.*1721. One excerpt from her enumeration of kennings reads:

Bu tu 'm bradan anns an fhìoruisg'	F.2
Fìreun às an eunlainn as àirde	F.2
Bu tu leoghann thar gach beathach	F.2
Bu tu damh leathann na cràice [. . .]	F.2
Bu tu 'n t-iubhar às a' choillidh	F.1
Bu tu 'n darach daingeann làidir	F.1
Bu tu 'n cuileann, bu tu 'n droigheann	F.1
Bu tu 'n t-abhall molach blàthmhor	F.1
Cha robh meur annad de'n chritheann	≠F.1
Cha robh do dhlighe ri feàrna	≠F.1
Cha robh do chàirdeas ri leamhan.[26]	≠F.1

('You were the salmon in fresh water, the eagle from the highest eyrie – you were a lion above all creatures; you were the stout stag of the antlers [. . .]')

('You were the yew in the forest; you were the strong and steadfast oak; you were the holly, you were the blackthorn; you were the rough, blossoming apple tree; there wasn't a trace of aspen in you; you had no connection with the alder; you had no relation to the elm.')

By assertion and negation, literature such as this reveals a classification of animals and trees into noble and non-noble categories in Gaelic tradition. This particular song was quite popular in the eighteenth-century Highlands. A satire on Doctor Samuel Johnson was composed and modelled on this song after he drew the ire of several prominent Highland literati by claiming that there was no history of a Gaelic literary tradition. As if to prove him wrong by drawing upon native literature, Seumas Macintyre, chieftain of the Macintyres, responded with a scathing caricature of Johnson which mirrors Sìleas's song but in reverse:

Gur tu an losgann sleamhainn tarr-bhuidh	F.2
'S tu màigein tàirgneach nan dìgean	F.2
Gur tu dearc-luachrach a' chàthair	F.2
Ri snàg 's ri màgaran mìltich;	
'S tu bratag sgreataidh an fhàsaich	F.2
'S tu 'n t-seilcheag ghrànda bhog lìtheach [. . .]	F.2
Cha bu tu 'n droigheann no 'n cuileann	−F.1
No 'n t-iubhar fulannach làidir	−F.1
Chan eil mìr annad de'n darach	−F.1
No de sheileach dearg nam blàran;	−F.1
Tha 'chuid as mò dhiot de chritheann	F.1
Ìngnean sgithich 's làmhan feàrna –	F.1
Tha do cheann gu lèir de leamhan	F.1
Gu h-àraidh do theanga 's do chàirein.[27]	F.1

('You're the slimy, yellow-bellied toad; you're the barbed crawler of ditches; you're the lizard of the swamp that creeps and crawls through the grass; you're the horrid caterpillar of the wasteland; you're the filthy, sticky, gooey snail [. . .]')

('You wouldn't be the blackthorn or holly, or the strong, hardy yew; there isn't a trace of the oak in you, or of the red willow of the fields; you are made mostly of aspen, with whitethorn fingernails and alder hands – your head is made entirely of elm, especially your tongue and your gums.')

The assignment of non-noble status to particular species of the natural world does not necessarily mean that there was any attempt to persecute them or eliminate them from existence. The very existence of such a dichotomy is threatened unless both sides are maintained and continue to stand in opposition to one another.

The rulers of Gaelic society were generally men who had been born into that role. Assumptions about leadership and group behaviour were sometimes projected onto nature as well, for some groups of animals (and marine creatures) are described as following a particular leader. Martin Martin, for example, relayed the following belief about the herring:

The Fishers and others told me, that there is a big Herring almost double the size of any of its kind, which leads all that are in a Bay, and the Shoal follows it wherever it goes. This Leader is by the Fishers call'd the King of Herring, and when they chance to catch it alive, they drop it carefully into the Sea; for they judg it Petty Treason to destroy a Fish of that name.[28]

He also recorded a similar belief about otters:

The Hunters say, there is a big Otter above the ordinary size, with a white Spot on its Breast, and this they call the King of Otters; it is rarely seen, and very hard to be kill'd: Seamen ascribe great Virtues to the Skin; for they say that it is fortunate in Battle, and that Victory is always on its side.[29]

Alexander Carmichael observed that according to Gaelic tradition the principle of leadership was ubiquitous in nature:

The people say that all creatures have a *ceann-snaoth*, 'head-chief'. A certain fish is *ceann-snaoth nan iasg*, 'the head-chief of the fish'; a certain bird is *ceann-snaoth nan ian*, 'head-chief of the birds'; a certain cow or bull *ceann-snaoth nan nì*, 'head-chief of the nowt'; a certain horse, *ceann-snaoth nan each*, 'the head-chief of the steeds'; and a certain deer, *ceann-snaoth nam fiadh*, 'head-chief of the deer'.[30]

This idea is sometimes alluded to in Gaelic wonder tales when the protagonist is in animal form: being a natural-born leader, he or she is inevitably the chief of the pack or flock. As in many other traditions, the oak was known by the kenning *rìgh na coille* 'the king of trees'; the salmon by the kenning *rìgh nan iasg* 'the king of fish'; and so on.

As we have seen in Chapter Four, the vertical stratification in Gaelic society was complemented by horizontal interdependencies, not the least of which was fosterage. The bonds between *muime* 'foster-mother' and *oide* 'foster-father' are portrayed as being particularly strong. These ideas inform the use of the terms *(ban-)altruim* 'nurse-maid' and muime for homeland in Gaelic literature, as do the ancient ideas about the goddess of a territory who is the protector and provider of the people who are dependent upon the chieftain she has married.

Extensive use of the symbolism of land as mother is made in a poem composed by Domhnall Siosalach *c.*1800 when he was forced to leave his home in Strathglass. The poem is composed in a dialogue between the poet and the mountain, called 'A' Chìoch' because of its breast-like shape:

Chuir mo bhan-altrum cùl rium	øG.4
Chaill mi 'n cupan 'bha fallainn.	øC.2
Fhuair na Frisealaich còir ort	
'S chaidh mis' 'fhògar le m' aindeoin.	øC.6

Ceithir bliadhna 's a fichead:
Bha mi siud air do bhainne [. . .]

'S tric a bha mi gu h-uallach
Air do ghualainnean geala [. . .]

(an sin fhreagair a' bheinn)
De tha 'cur air mo phàiste
Rinn mi àrach gun ainnis?[31]

('My nurse-maid has turned her back on me: I have lost a wholesome drink.')

('The Frasers have taken control of you and I have been forced out.')

('Twenty-four years: that is the time I fed on your milk [. . .]')

('Many is the time I was playful on your fair shoulders [. . .]')

('(Then the mountain replied) What is bothering my child that I raised without experiencing dearth?')

The entire landscape is understood in anthropomorphic terms in Gaelic. Many words for topographical features are actually the same as those for human body parts: *ceann* 'head, end', *aodann* 'face, surface', *gualann* 'shoulder, mountain ridge', *bràigh* 'upper chest, uplands', *cìoch* 'breast, pointed hills', *druim* 'back, mountain ridge', *tòn* 'buttocks, eminence', *bod* 'penis, stone pillar', *fèith* 'vein, bog-channel', and others. This practice reinforces the sense of the landscape as a living entity.[32] A stanza from a variant of the song 'Òran na Comhachaig' makes analogies between human and landscape features explicit:

> *Loch mo chridhe sin, Loch Tréig*
> *Loch mu'm faighear féidh is earb*   D.2
> *'G am bheil an slios farsuing réidh*
> *Mar gum biodh an taobh aig mnaoi.*[33]

('Loch Tréig, my beloved loch, the loch around which deer are found; it has a long, smooth side, just like the side of a woman.')

The ability to relate the structure and operation of human society to nature provided a rhetorical framework for discussing it equivalent to what we would now call an ecosystem. In other words, some poets describe the dynamics of their local environment in similar terms to how they describe the functioning of their human community. Indigenous cultures realise that there is no easy division between the human actors, animal inhabitants, and the natural landscape which forms the backdrop of heroic endeavours. The health of the human community and nature are intimately connected.

Aspects of these ideas appear in the song 'Cumha Choire an Easa', a lament composed by Iain Dall MacAoidh *c.*1696 on the death of Colonel Robert Mackay. It is in the form of a dialogue between the poet and the corry often visited by the Colonel and his men, especially while hunting. The first two stanzas in this excerpt are in the voice of the corry, while the last is in the voice of the poet:

> *Is e sin mise, Coire an Easa,*
> *Tha mi 'am sheasamh mar a b'àbhaist;*
> *Ma tha thusa 'nad fhear ealaidh*
> *Cluinneamaid annas do làimhe.* [. . .]

> *Mo chreach, mo thùirse, is mo thruaighe*
> *'Ga chur 's an uair-sa dhomh an ìre*
> *'Mhuinntir a chumadh rium uaisle*
> *Bhith 'n-diugh 's an uaigh d'am dhìth-sa.* [. . .] øC.5

> *Is grianach d' ursainn féin, a Choire,*
> *Is gun fhéidh a' tèarnadh gu d' bhaile;* øD.2
> *Is iomadh neach d'am b'fhiach do mholadh* B.2
> *Do chliath chorrach bhiadhchar bhainneach.*[34]

('That is me, Coire an Easa – I stand as I always have; if you are a poet, let us hear the splendour of your art [. . .]')

('What is related to me now is my ruination, my sorrow and my anguish: that the people who kept me ennobled are today sent away from me into the grave [. . .]')

('Your own door-post is unshadowed, o corry, since no deer descend to your homestead; many a person considered the praise of your jagged, fertile, milk-producing flanks to be worthwhile.')

Implicit in the imagery of this poem is the idea that the corry fulfils a similar role to that of a chieftain: it is worthy of bardic praise, endowed with the qualities that ennoble a human subject; it is a patron, being a host to many guests, both human and animal; it is intrinsically part of the larger ecosystem relevant to the resources and operations of the human community.

The poetry of ecosystems was arguably taken to its artistic apogee in Gaelic by Donnchadh Bàn Macintyre in his famous poem in praise of the mountain Beinn

Dobhrain, composed between 1751 and 1766 using the metrical structure and music of ceòl mór.[35]

> Duncan Bàn transfers images from the eulogy of chiefs and allies them figuratively to the mountain [. . .] As one becomes familiar with Moladh Beinn Dobhrain one soon realises that the poem is not concerned simply with a mountain in the geological or geographical sense, but is even more a celebration of the life and way of life it supports; the flora and fauna, and especially the deer and the men who hunt the deer are all part of a continuum – an ecological system if I may use the term – sustained by and on the mountain [. . .] it is the hunt that enshrines the organising principle of the system.[36]

The exquisite word-painting of 554 lines opens explicitly as a panegyric and there are clear echoes of the descriptions of a chieftain's hall, bright, resplendent, and well-stocked with food for inhabitants and guests. Also notable is the metaphor of the land as nurse-maid. Donnchadh Bàn's poem inspired imitators, but many Highlanders consider his poetic achievement never to have been excelled.

A Sense of Place and Belonging

The embedding of communal history in the Gaelic notion of landscape makes it a kind of living library of tradition. Tradition-bearers make allusion to the lore encoded in the landscape as a source of authority and a touchstone of identity, and these links have reinforced the connection between people and place and the primacy of the local community in the past. These patterns in the Gaelic literature and culture of Ireland and Highland Scotland are rooted in beliefs about the territorial goddess and her marriage to the human ruler, although they have been generalised to the community at large:

> It seems then that it is the sacred wedding of territory to chief – and by extension of territory to kin – which is at the heart of the passion for place in Irish life and literature. Parallel with this bonding, of course, was the bonding of each free family group with its own particular inherited land. Down to our own day each field, hill and hillock was named with affection [. . .] There is a sense in which place finally becomes co-extensive in the mind, not only with personal and ancestral memories, but with the whole living community culture. If one's day to day pattern of living is found good, the feeling of identification with its place of origin is accordingly enhanced. Community becomes place, place community.[37]

The density of Gaelic place names on the landscape and the intimate knowledge most Gaels had of that landscape has been frequently noted by scholars wherever Gaelic was spoken, from Loch Lomond to Lewis. Every discernible feature – each stone, clump of trees, pool, bend in a stream, notch in a ridge, and so on – had a distinctive name to identify it. This allowed for the names of many people and events to be attached to the natural features of the landscape. William J. Watson, for example, himself a native of Easter Ross, relied upon the local knowledge of tradition-bearers wherever he did fieldwork collecting Gaelic place names, such as in Menteith:

> The Gael is acquainted with the name of each place in the region to which he belongs, not as they have been mangled by the English language, but as they have been transmitted of old. 'I am familiar,' said Parlan MacPharlain to me as we sat on Loch Venachar side, 'with every stone and ditch and hillock between Callendar and Inversnaid.' And he spoke truly. Parlan has died, and there's no one to replace him.[38]

This irrevocable sense of loss of local lore and communal knowledge has recurred in communities across the Highlands since the early twentieth century with the passing of the last local speakers of Gaelic with an intimate acquaintance with the land. In the early twentieth century Murdoch McNeill stated that the inhabitants of Colonsay had a similarly minute level of knowledge of their terrain and the names on it:

> The places in Balnahard had formerly been so well named in detail that the people without difficulty could apportion the land out as they sat on Cnoc a' Chreagain, yes, even to the breadth of the handle of a *caibe* [a kind of spade].[39]

There were a multitude of mundane reasons for this detailed topographic datastore: allocating lots (especially for the so-called 'run-rig' agricultural system), marking territorial boundaries, describing the location of livestock, navigating by land and by sea, and so on. These practical functions engaged with cultural memory and imagination through the medium of place names. Amongst the materials gathered to attest to the authenticity of Macpherson's *Ossian* is the testimony of Ùisdean MacDonald, recorded in the year 1800. Ùisdean considered Gaelic place names in the Highlands as suitable evidence for the historicity of the Fian:

> There are names of hundreds of places in the Highlands where the Fian lived and frequented; the monuments, and their significances, corresponding to Ossianic lore that has been passed down from generation to generation, are still to be found [. . .] The meanings of the names of places and people cannot be explained in any other language but Gaelic.[40]

Place names appear in literature and oral tradition in many ways and for many reasons. They can implicate the appearance and shape of the landscape; they can invoke the memories of the community and narratives about the history of place; they can be aesthetically pleasing merely for their own sound. Creators of Gaelic literature certainly made them an essential ingredient in their work. Thomas Sinton (1855–1923), minister of Glengarry and Dores, published a collection of Gaelic poetry from Badenoch and recalled how frequently place names occurred in them:

It is probable that mostly all the names connected with every countryside in the Highlands have been fashioned into rhyme. The heights enumerated in this catalogue belong to that portion of the Monadh Liath range, lying between Kingussie and Craig Dhubh:

> *Creag Bheag Chinn a' Ghiùbhsaidh,*
> *Creag Mhór Bhail' a' Chrothain,*
> *Beinne Bhuidhe na Stròine,*
> *Creag an Lòin aig na croitean* [. . .][41]

Place names were woven into songs celebrating familiar territory such as the summer pastures, as Sinton further observed:

Each year, when Beltane came round, the crofters' township presented a scene of busy preparation for the glens. Then happy groups would set out for their appointed sheilings, driving their cattle, sheep, and goats to the upland grazing, and ever and anon joining in some blithe chorus as the above; wherein favourite pastoral resorts would be enumerated, in so far as the rhythm of their names could be got to fall in with the measures of the tune.[42]

The love of place and the creation of litanies of place names is already apparent in Gaelic literature as long ago as the eleventh and twelfth centuries in texts such as *Buile Shuibhne*, the *Metrical Dindshenchas*, and *Acallam na Senórach*. In fact, the use of place names is a characteristic feature of traditional Gaelic literature which departs significantly from the conventions of modern literary style.

Indeed, some older Gaelic verse is little more than a string of place names tricked out with epithets to make up the meter. [. . .] However much an ability to tolerate – even enjoy – lists of things in poetry may be regarded as a sign of true devotion to the art, the topomania of the seanachies surely stretched that tolerance to the limit.[43]

Lists of place names often occur after the phrase 'Chì mi' ('I see / can see') in Scottish Gaelic verse. The numerous places named by the poet can seldom be seen physically from a single vantage point, however. Even if the verses incorporating these place names were composed during the poet's travels through the landscape, they are recounted and recited in a stationary performance – such as a céilidh – in which physical movement is impossible. Indeed, in an early, influential poem making heavy use of place names in this manner ('Òran na Comhachaig', discussed further below), the poet is so old that he is hardly able to walk. Rather than taking these assertions of the sightings of places literally, we could instead interpret them as the internal vision of the poet (and performer) reconstructing his ancestral territory with the mental map created by the performance itself, reaffirming his identification with people and place. The implication that sight and knowledge are related and can be connected through poetry takes us back to the ancient functions of the Celtic poet.[44]

It was this intimacy with and connection to place that caused so much longing and melancholy to those who emigrated, willingly or unwillingly, from the Highlands. When people departed, they took with them this lore of the local landscape, a store of knowledge which features in some oral narratives as a kind of passport proving their origin in a given community. One example is set in North America when two soldiers in British regiments met during the Seven Years' War. This tale was originally given in Gaelic; although I have translated the dialogue, I leave the place names in their original form:

One man was older than the other, and he looked it. But both of them were quite genteel, and had Highland features in their faces. The older man turned to the younger and asked him, 'Where are you from?'

The younger man answered, 'From Europe.'

'Europe is a big place' said the first man. 'To which country in Europe do you belong?'

'Britain.'

'Britain is still quite large,' said the first man. 'From which part of Britain do you come?'

'Scotland.'

'Now we're getting close to one another,' said the first man. 'From which region of Scotland?'

'Perthshire.'

'We're closing in on each other for certain,' said the first man. 'What part of Perthshire?'

'Glen Dochart.'

'Name some places in the glen,' said the first man.

The second man answered,

'Eas a' Ghraig is in Leathad Charaidh
And Sgaoil a' Chasaidh is in Ard Choille
And Caibeal na Fairge is in Ard Chloinne
Tom an Taghain and Meall na Samhna
And Tom an Suidhe are in Innis Eóghain
Dal Chlachaig is in Both Uachdair
And stags are on Cruachain Beinne Móire.'

The first man responded,

'Allt an Tuairnear is in Leac Uachdarach

And it is swift when it begins to move,
But the king will go under the shovel
Before he reaches Suidhe, even if he is quick.'
The second man said, 'You forgot Both Bhainne.'
'There is a treasure in Sìth Bhruach,
Whenever it will be discovered –
It will never be taken,
It is in the trout's haunt.'[45]

Much of the interest in this tale comes from the challenges issued by each man to the other in increasingly fine levels of detail about local lore, moving from the visible (in high places) to the hidden. There are other tales in Gaelic oral tradition on this subject of people who meet each other far from home and prove their identity by means of rhymes of local place names.[46]

The cultural prominence of place lore is particularly developed in the élite literary tradition of Ireland. The knowledge of the origin of place names and the stories associated with them was considered such an important branch of learning that the early Gaelic literati had a special term for it: *dindshenchas* (spelled *dinnsheanchas* in modern Scottish Gaelic[47]). Dinnsheanchas usually claims to explain the way in which a place received its name even though most of these derivations are linguistically unlikely and serve merely as a vehicle for telling a story. Early forms of dinnsheanchas occur in the earliest literature surviving from the Gaelic world, such as the origin legends of the Laigin, the *Tripartite Life of Patrick*, and the *Martyrology of Oengus*.[48] There are hundreds of items of prose and poetry in the catalogue of dinnsheanchas dating back to at least the eleventh century that an aspiring poet was expected to learn associated with the important sites of Ireland.[49] Although there is some evidence to suggest that this learned, literary genre had some counterparts in Scotland no complete corpus of dinnsheanchas relating to Scotland such as there is for Ireland has survived.

While not always reliable in terms of formal history, the prevalence of such lore in vernacular oral tradition attests to a keen interest in local history. George Brown, one of the last Gaelic tradition-bearers of Deeside, was typical of those generations which inherited this store of local knowledge.

His fund of this kind of lore seemed inexhaustible. There was not within the district the ruins or site of an old church or chapel regarding which he had not gleaned some legend. The names of hills, glades, glens, corries, streams, and even pools and rapids in the river, had each its legend which accounted for its origin or related some circumstance connected with it.[50]

Donald MacDonald of Lewis provides evidence that such tales did indeed root in the landscape oral tradition that would have vanished otherwise:

In every part of the island there are stones and mounds and river fords, whose names signify that once upon a time warriors had met there in deadly conflict, and if one makes enquiry at the local ceilidh, the tale of what happened there is sure to be told [. . . some particular story] has only persisted because there are two topographical features which have acted as a perpetual reminder of the event.[51]

As the Gaelic sense of place is one in which communal history is embedded in the place names attached to landscape features, it depends to a great degree upon understanding the language in which the place names were coined. The poet Gilleasbuig MacIain warned of the consequences of the Education Act of 1872 shortly after its enactment: a day might come when people would not be able to understand or even pronounce the names of the places around them. His admonition portrays the features of the landscape, especially the mountains, as animate beings lamenting the estrangement of the Gaels from their homeland on account of their capitulation to anglophone culture:

> Ochan nan och! an caochladh truagh
> 'S a' Ghàidhealtachd thig 's gach taobh mun cuairt
> Ma théid a cànain chaoin 'na suain
> Le cion an t-sluaigh a labhras i!
>
> Luchd-àiteachaidh nan gleann 's nan stùc,
> Thaobh ainm gach nì is àite 's an dùthaich
> An teangaidh Ghalld' chan urrainn lùb
> Bidh iad gun tùr, gun aithne orr'!
>
> Gach creag is sliabh, gach stùc is càrn
> Gach lag is cnoc, is slios, is learg
> Gach glaic is tulaich, eas, is allt:
> Bidh iad gu dall is aineolach! [. . .]
>
> Chan aithne 'chainnt, 's cha tuig a fuaim
> Bho nì no àit' a tha mu'n cuairt,
> Oir reic am parantan, mo thruaigh!
> Iad uil' le'n uaill 's le'n amaideachd.
>
> Rinn tràillean dhiubh do'n t-Sas'nach mhór
> 'S an toirt fo chìs do chainnt a bheòil;
> A' Ghàidhealtachd 'chur fo chleòc –
> Nach cian an ceò a chaidleas oirr'! [. . .]

301

Beinn Cruachan fhéin as guirme snuadh,
Bidh 'cridh' fo chràdh ri tuireadh truagh
A chionn 's nach cluinn i chaoidh gu buan
Ach goileam cruaidh nan Sasannach.

Beinn Ghlòdh nan eag – cha bheag an t-ioghn'
A cridh' bhith goirt 's fo sprochd a' caoin'
'S nach cluinn i 'chànain mhilis chaoin
Bh' aig luchd a gaoil, na h-Athallaich.

'S Beinn Labhr', bidh i 'na lasair dheirg –
Ri luchd an fhoghluim bidh i 'm feirg,
A chionn 's gun mheall an sluagh le'n ceilg
'Gan cur an geimhlean Sasannach.

Gach creag is stac, gach sgorr is stùc,
Togaidh am fonn le co-sheirm ciùil
Gu tiamhaidh trom le mulad is tùrs
Chionn cainnt na dùthch' nach maireann i:

M'an tachair siud, a luchd mo spéis,
Grad éiribh suas ri guaillibh 'chéil'
A' boideachadh gu daingeann treun
Nach strìochd, nach géill, 's nach tachair e.

Nach ceadaich sibh gum bi 'nur dùthaich
A' chànain ghaoil 'ga chùr air chùl
Le tràillean leibideach gun fhiù
D'an ainm 's d'an cliù bhith fasanta.[52]

('Alas and alas! What terrible change could come into the Gàidhealtachd from all sides if its delightful language is laid to rest because of the lack of people who speak it!')

('O inhabitants of the glens and peaks, the Lowland tongue can't pronounce the names for things and places in our homeland: it can't understand or recognise them!')

('Every craig and moor, every peak and cairn, every hollow and hillock, side, and slope, every defile and knoll, waterfall and stream: people will be blind and ignorant! [. . .]')

('They won't recognise the language, or understand the sound of the things and places around them, since their parents sold it all – alas! – in their pride and foolishness.')

('They were made slaves to the great Englishman and yoked to his speech; the Gàidhealtachd was put under a veil – long does the mist cover it! [. . .]')

('Even Ben Cruachan of greenest hue has a broken heart and grieves mournfully since it will never again hear anything but the harsh chatter of English.')

('It is not surprising that jagged Ben-y-Gloe has a broken heart and that she keens sadly, since she cannot hear the sweet, gentle language of her beloved Atholl-folk.')

('And Ben Lawers will be incensed – she will be angry at the educational authorities since they deceived people treacherously, putting them into English chains.')

('Every craig, precipice, peak, and cliff, they will raise a wailing, sad chorus in their sorrow because the tongue of the homeland perished.')

('Before any of that happens, o beloved people, rise up in support of each other, giving solemn and steadfast vows, that you will never submit, and that it will not come to pass.')

('Never allow your country to turn its back on its language because of worthless, contempuous slaves to the fashion of the day.')

Not only did place names record the memory of bygone days, they helped to foster an ongoing connection between the dead and living. The attachment to homeland was exemplified by the desire to be buried amongst one's ancestors. Just as ancestry provided the idea of heritage and identity, so did continuous occupation of land and burial in it underscore claims of belonging to it.

Just as the nominal sense of place may be located within the wider, verbal character of the Irish tradition, so too the funereal sense may be seen as part of a larger configuration. [. . .] Granted that this is the case, it is hardly surprising that graveyards hold such a privileged position in our landscape and literature. [. . .] A multiplicity of texts [. . .] link place, death and identity.[53]

A preoccupation with proper burial, and what may seem today to be a morbid fixation on bodies lost at sea, is expressed in many Gaelic elegies (codes H.2 and H.4). One such example occurs in the lament for Sir Iain MacLean and the downfall of the MacLeans, composed by Mairearad nighean Lachlainn in 1716:

Och is mis' th' air mo sgaradh
Nach tug iad thu thairis
Dhol air tìr air an Ealaidh
Dhol fo dhìon anns a' charraig
Ann an reilig nam manach   H.2
Mar ri d' athair is do sheanair,
Is ioma treun laoch a bharrachd
Far am faodamaid teannadh mu d' chàrnan.[54]

('Och, how I am grieved that they did not take you across to land in Ealaidh, to be sheltered in the stone and go into the holy burial ground along with your father and grandfather, and many other brave warriors, where we would be able to gather around your cairn.')

As we have already seen in the case of the choral dance, the graveyard has been an important ceremonial site since ancient times because of the presence of the ancestral dead there. Many people noted the continuing stress Highlanders put on having their corpse laid to rest amongst their relations.

> Of all people Highlanders think most of the reverence due to their dead, and of the privilege of being under the shadow of the old place of worship while living, and when dead of being buried in ancestral graves. In their minds old churches and churchyards seem to unite the living with the dead of many generations.[55]

This idea is reflected in the legend of Dubh a' Ghiuthais at the beginning of the chapter when the King of Lochlann sent the soil of his country for the burial of his daughter. It is further illustrated by an anecdote from the easternmost edge of nineteenth-century Highland Perthshire:

> Lately, a woman aged ninety-one, but in perfect health, and in possession of all her faculties, went to Perth from her house in Strathbraan, a few miles above Dunkeld. A few days after her arrival in Perth, where she had gone to visit a daughter, she had a slight attack of fever. One evening a considerable quantity of snow had fallen, and she expressed a great anxiety, particularly when told that a heavier fall was expected. Next morning her bed was found empty, and no trace of her could be discovered, till the second day, when she sent word that she had slipt out of the house at midnight, set off on foot through the snow, and never stopped home till she reached home, a distance of twenty miles. When questioned some time afterwards why she went away so abruptly, she answered, 'If my sickness had increased, and if I had died, they could not have sent my remains home through the deep snows. If I had told my daughter, perhaps she would have locked the doors upon me, to prevent my going out in the storm, and God forbid that my bones should lie at such a distance from home, and be buried among *Goill na Machair* [the non-Gaels of the Lowlands].'[56]

Graveyards have been central features in many rituals and community celebrations throughout the history of Gaelic culture. Early sources such as the *Metrical Dind-senchas* mention celebrations and races being held around ancestral graves in medieval Ireland,[57] a practice that continued into recent times in Scotland. One of the events of the festival of Michaelmas as it was observed in Iona, Rum, and South Uist was to hold a race at the burial ground.[58] The gathering-place of the Stratherrick Frasers was Tom na h-Iùbhraich, a site containing a sacred yew tree and ancient burial ground. The clan met there for pronouncements of law and horse races, and the sìdhichean were said to inhabit it. The associations between the graves of ancestors and the sìdh were remarked upon by Robert Kirk:

> There be many places called Fairie-hills, which the mountain people think impious and dangerous to peel or discover by taking earth or wood from them, superstitiously believing the souls of their predecessors to dwell there. And for that end (say they) a mote or mount was dedicate[d] beside every church-yard, to receive the souls till their adjacent bodies arise, and so become as a Fairy-hill.[59]

The early Irish law tracts describe a procedure which was to be carried out by a person wishing to assert an ancestral right of occupation against someone else currently occupying that land. The first step of the procedure was a symbolic statement of the hereditary title to the land: the claimant was to enter the land by passing over the graves of ancestors that mark the boundary of the territory and were believed to protect it. As we saw in the tale about Saint Columba and Odhran in Chapter Six, this ritual reflected a belief in the continuing presence and power of the dead in the landscape.

> The role of the grave, *fert*, in [the legal procedure known as] *tellach* may depend upon a belief that the dead do not merely survive but take an active part in the affairs of the living. [. . .] The remains of the Christian dead might be indeed 'remains', *reliquiae* (OIr. relic); but it was not thought that a Christian soul entirely abandoned his place of burial. [. . .] The reason why the tract on *tellach* requires the claimant to enter the land over the *fert* is now clear. This is an act which is only safe if the claimant is indeed what he claims to be, a man with hereditary right in the land, and therefore a kinsman of the person buried in the *fert*. The buried man was thought to repel outsiders, not kinsmen.[60]

A belief in the lingering presence of the dead in graveyards continued in the Gàidhealtachd well into the twentieth century.[61] The right to occupy land was understood traditionally to come through ancestral channels, just as personal qualities were inherited from predecessors. These ancient ideas about heritage and its associa-tion with the landscape are echoed in the Gaelic phrase 'cladh na sinnsearachd' ('the trench of ancestry'). This refers literally to the physical channel that contains the dead but is also used metaphorically of the connection to one's ancestors and what one inherits from them.[62]

In Gaelic culture people belong to places, rather than places belonging to people. The phrase 'Buinidh mi do . . .' meaning literally 'I belong to . . .' is used to express the enduring ties and association of the place of one's birth. Gaelic has several words with a common root which are used for the interconnected concepts of one's heredity, identity, homeland, and inherited rights and duties: *dù*, *dùthaich*, and *dùthchas*. The ineffable quality of these terms, and the matrix of ideas and feelings that they evoke, has been noted since the sixteenth century.[63] John MacInnes explains the difficulty in translating these terms into English with their culturally specific nuances and associations:

> The native Gael who is instructed in this poetry carries in his imagination not so much a landscape, not a sense of geography alone, nor of history alone, but a formal order of experience in which these are all merged. The native sensibility responds not to 'landscape' but to 'dùthchas'. And just as 'landscape', with its romantic aura, cannot be translated directly into Gaelic, so 'dùthchas' and, indeed, 'dùthaich' cannot be translated into English without robbing the terms of their emotional energy. The complexity involved can be appreciated by reflecting on the range of meaning: 'dùthchas' is ancestral or family land; it is also family tradition; and, equally, it is the hereditary qualities of an individual.[64]

The words themselves are rooted in the soil. The Gaelic root term *dù(th)* originally means 'place'. It is derived from the Indo-European root *(gh)dhō(n)* meaning 'earth', which is also the origin of the Greek word *chthon*. From the definition 'place' the term 'dùth' acquired the meanings 'inheritance', 'entitlement', and 'duty', as land was inherited and a person's privileges and obligations were largely based on possession of land. Personal identity and commitments were abstracted from these titles by the eighth century so that 'dùth' acquired more metaphysical usages that had been idealised from these concrete meanings, such as 'native', 'natural', 'appropriate', and 'proper'.[65] An example related to landscape comes from a poem composed *c.*1692 to the exiled chieftain of the MacLeans in which the author Iain mac Ailein mhic Iain boasts 'Cha dùth do Ghall àrd bheann a dhìreadh' ('It is not natural/native/fitting for a Lowlander to climb a high mountain.').[66]

The Gaelic term *dùthaich* is derived from 'dùth' but refers specifically to land. Its primary meaning was originally 'hereditary land' but it acquired a wider range of usages in the medieval period, especially the native land of an individual but also 'region' and 'territory' on a larger scale.[67] There are nicknames for regions in the Highlands which reflect the notions of patrimony and clan territory: *Dùthaich MhicAoidh* is the common Gaelic byname for the Reay country in the north of Sutherland, for example, being the ancestral lands of the MacKay dynasty.

Arguably the most abstract and complex of the terms derived from 'dùth' is *dùthchas.* This term originally had a narrow range of concrete meanings, primarily 'hereditary right or claim' and secondarily 'native land'. However, this too acquired further metaphysical usages relating to the individual such as 'hereditary trait', 'innate quality', 'inalienable right', and 'familial tradition' by the early medieval period. The flexible and fluid quality of 'dùthchas' made it particularly useful for discussing the customs, values, beliefs, and duties prescribed by tradition, especially when they were perceived to be challenged or threatened.[68] A wide range of meanings and usages of 'dùthchas' have continued in Gaelic to the present day.

Dùthchas is used to conjure the sense of place and attachment to it in a version of the Deirdre story written in the Glenmasan manuscript, which was copied by a scribe in southern Argyllshire *c.*1500 who had access to older manuscripts. The themes of exile and homeland seem to have been expanded by the Scottish writers in comparison to the Irish versions of the tale.[69] The main male characters discuss their anticipation of returning to Ireland after many years of exile in Scotland:

'*Is ferr duthchas ina gach ní,*' *ar Fergus,* '*uair ni h-aibinn do neoch maithes da méd, muna fhaice a duthchas.*'
'*Is fír sin,*' *ar Naisi,* '*doigh is annsa lem pen Ere ina Alba ge mad mó do maith Alban do gebhainn.*'[70]

'Dùthchas is better than everything else,' said Fergus, 'for no amount of wealth can bring happiness to someone if he cannot see his *dùthchas* (i.e., native land).'
'That is true,' said Naoise, 'for Ireland is dearer to me than Scotland, even though I have enjoyed far more of the wealth of Scotland.'

Distinct shades of meanings of 'dùthchas' can appear in the same text and thus reinforce its ability to evoke abstract associations. A song composed by Lachlann mac Theàrlaich Òig MacKinnon *c.*1705 laments the lack of commitment amongst the chieftains of Skye to maintain the customary privileges that had been enjoyed by the native Gaelic poets. He specifically mentions the recently deceased Tormod MacLeod of Berneray '*a chum an dùthchas suas*' ('who kept ancestral tradition alive') and the chieftain of the MacKinnons '*Gan dùthchas cian an Srath*' ('whose ancient homeland was Strath').[71] It can be used in a more general sense about hereditary traits, as when Iain Lom said of villainous men, such as those who had committed the assassination of the heirs of Keppoch, '*Dha'm bu dùthchas an t-olc*' ('Have evil as their dùthchas').[72]

The powerful emotive qualities in such words and the unspoken intricacies that lay hidden in their depths embedded in the corpus of Gaelic literature, often remain dormant until they are reawoken by social crisis. This is precisely what we see in Gaelic poetry responding to the calamities of the eighteenth and nineteenth centuries (such as in lines 74, 80, and 82 of poem 10 of Appendix A). The Napier Commission report of 1884 observed that many Highlanders felt that Clearances were a violation of the traditional understanding of 'dùthchas' and customary practice relating to tenure, even though these norms and expectations had never been recognised by the central government.

> The opinion was often expressed before us that the small tenantry of the Highlands have an inherited inalienable title to security of tenure in their possessions while rent and service are duly rendered – an impression indigenous to the country though it has never been sanctioned by legal recognition, and has long been repudiated by the action of the proprietors.[73]

The linguistic and literary patterns evident in the history of 'dùthchas' in Gaelic Scotland are paralleled in Gaelic Ireland, where it was understood as 'embodied, internalised history, both individual and collective, which is therefore forgotten as history, until activated by the appropriate context'.[74] There too it reinforced a sense of belonging and gave strength to those attempting to defend their rights to their homeland.

The Aesthetics of Landscape

Before the Romantic movement forever changed popular perceptions of the wilderness, English travellers in the Highlands expressed their fear of and disgust for its 'unimproved' state. The idea that higher civilisations progressed by 'conquering' nature meant by contrast wilderness was the condition of 'primitive' societies living in a state of savagery. Even after spending a considerable amount of time in the Highlands Edmund Burt remarked on the civility of the Gaelic élite despite the influence of their environment:

> So in the Highlands I have met with some lairds, who surprised me with their good sense and polite behaviour, being so far removed from the more civilized part of the world, and considering the wildness of the country, which one would think was sufficient of itself to give a savage turn to a mind most humane.[75]

Immediately after the defeat of the Jacobites in 1746 a proposal for 'civilising that Barbarous People' saw the landscape itself as an obstacle to the domestication of the people themselves, for 'the numbers of woods, mountains, and Secret Glens [. . .] are also great allurements to incite that perverse Disposition that reigns amongst all Ranks of them, stimulated by the Rudeness of their Nature, unrestrained by Law or Religion.'[76] Nor were the opinions of many Lowlanders much different. In a letter to a friend Robert Burns commented during travels in the Highlands in 1787, 'I write this on my tour through a country where savage streams tumble over savage mountains, thinly overspread with savage flocks, which starvingly support as savage inhabitants.'[77]

Highlanders themselves did not perceive their own landscape in these terms, of course. Edmund Burt also tells us that Highlanders maintained pride in their origins in the mountains despite the boasts of the Lowlanders about the superior qualities of their habitat: 'As the Lowlanders call their part of the country the land of cakes, so the natives of the hills say they inhabit a land of milk and honey.'[78] The oldest surviving vernacular Gaelic songs exult in the pastoral way of life, especially during the summer when women and children followed the cattle to the shielings. Many waulking songs from the seventeenth century also delight in the beauty and fecundity of nature, particularly as manifested in the foliage and fruits of the trees and the birds and animals which were sheltered by them. An example from Lochaber includes typical images:

> *Thoir mo shoraidh gu Ceann-trà*
> *Far bheil fàileadh a' bharraich;*
>
> *Far am bheil doireachan dlùtha*
> *Is cnothan a' lùbadh gach meangain;*
>
> *Far am bi a' mhil 's an t-samhradh*
> *'Sileadh bho gach crann do'n darach;*
>
> *Far am bi 'n crodh-laoigh a' bàirich*
> *Tighinn gu pàirceannan a' bhainne.*[79]

('Take my greetings to Kintra, where the foilage is fragrant, where there are dense groves and nuts weighing down every tree limb, where honey drips from every branch of the oak in the summer, where the calves are bellowing as they come to the milk-rich fields.')

A keen eye for nature is particularly evident in songs featuring hunting: the focus of the poetic text itself can parallel the mind of the hunter reading the environment for signs of his prey. According to tradition, Domhnall mac Fhionnlaigh nan Dàn was a hunter who spent his time in the mountains of Lochaber in the late sixteenth century. His attachment to the deer and the mountains was so strong that his last request was to be buried in the hide of the last deer he killed with his face towards the hunting hill.[80] A long poem attributed to him usually called 'Òran na Comhachaig' ('The Song of the Owl'), most of which is in the form of a dialogue between himself and an aged owl, was popular throughout the central Highlands and contains many keen observations of the life of the deer and the historical resonances of the landscape. It paints a picture of a man at home in wild nature and at peace with the company of the archetypal wild creature, the deer,[81] as illustrated by a few excerpts from this lengthy poem:

> *Nuair bhùireas damh Beinne Bige*
> *'S a bheucas damh Beinn na Craige*
> *Freagraidh na daimh ud d'a chéile*
> *'S thig féidh a Coire na Snaige.*

Bha mi on rugadh mi riamh
An caidreabh fhiadh agus earb:
Chan fhaca mi dath air bian
Ach buidhe riabhach is dearg. [. . .]

Cha do chuir mi dùil 's an iasgach,
Bhith 'ga iarraidh leis a' mhaghar;
'S mór gum b' annsa leam am fiadhach
Siubhal nan sliabh anns an fhoghar.

Is aoibhinn an obair an t-sealg
Aoibhinn a meanma is a beachd;
Gur binne a h-aighear 's a fonn
Na long is i dol fo beairt.

Fad a bhithinn beò no maireann
Deò de'n anam ann mo chorp
Dh'fhanainn am fochair an fhéidh:
Sin an spréidh an robh mo thoirt.[82]

('When the stag of Beinn Bheag bellows and the stag of Beinn na Craige roars, those stags will call to each other and deer will emerge from Coire na Snaige.')

('Ever since I was born I have always been in the company of deer; the only skin colour that I have ever seen is speckled yellow and red [. . .]')

('I never had an interest in fishing, to go seeking it with bait; I greatly prefer the deer-chase, travelling the moors in the autumn.')

('Hunting is joyful work: joyful it is in spirit and contemplation; sweeter is its music and mood than that of equipping a ship.')

('For as long as I live, as long as there is a spark of life in my body, I will stay in the company of the deer: that is the herd in which I put my esteem [i.e., rather than cattle].')

The final stanza in this excerpt seems to be a rejection of the agricultural revolution, a sentiment echoed to a degree in many of the Ossianic ballads popular in the Highlands which extol the hunter-warrior lifestyle of the Fian.[83]

The bulk of the poetry praising nature and place which survives in Scottish Gaelic was produced after the forced severance of people from their homes during the Clearances when entire communities became aware of their ties to the lands from having lost them. By the early nineteenth century, many poets had begun to absorb the influences of Macpherson's *Ossian* and the Romantic movement.[84] It is valid to ask how 'native' the sentiments and style of the post-Clearance poetry may be.

Even before the Clearances, there were authors whose expressions of their experiences of nature, and especially of exile and loss, established literary conventions which were picked up and developed on a larger scale at later periods. Such authors include Christian missionaries working in foreign lands, prisoners, hostages, outlaws, foresters, drovers, people moving up to the shielings for summer and back down for winter, and exiles of age, illness, and political circumstances. Surviving samples of early poetry of these sorts, in which nature and landscape feature as primary subjects, suggest a long line of continuity and development despite the lack of provision in the poet-patron patronage system for it.

There can be no doubt that it was emotionally difficult for the early Celtic saints to leave their communities in the cause of missionary work, so much so that it was considered a form of 'white martyrdom'. Poems cast in the voice of Saint Columba after his migration to Scotland, though first composed some four centuries after his death, formed the early canon of the Gaelic literature of exile:

> These poetic sentiments of love of country and longing for return became an established feature of Columban tradition, as shown, for instance, by their incorporation into the sixteenth-century Life of the saint, *Betha Colaim Cille*. Indeed, the poems retained their resonance as emigration from Ireland continued through the centuries.[85]

Poetry which delights in nature and praises place is used to adorn medieval Gaelic tales, such as those about the Fian. A poem about the island of Arran, detailing the wealth of animals and plants to be found there, was inserted into the twelfth-century anthology *Acallam na Senórach*.[86] Two medieval poems in praise of place were put into the mouth of Deirdre: one of these depicts the natural beauty and fecundity of the glen in Scotland where she and her lover Naoise took refuge, which some traditions name as Glen Etive; another poem praises a string of places in Scotland where they found food and shelter while on the run.[87]

Rob Donn MacKay (1714–78) was a drover and prolific poet who enjoyed the company of local gentry, especially when out on the moors hunting the deer. Except for droving expeditions, he spent his entire life in the parish of Durness in Sutherland. Although most of his poetry was edited and published several times in the nineteenth century, a minister of Durness of the late nineteenth century noted with disappointment that one song, 'Òran nam Beanntaichean' ('The Song of the Mountains'), popular with the older natives of the parish, had never been printed. The reason, he explained, was simple:

> There is very little poetry in it – only a string of names – of interest only to natives of the district, or to the topographist. Among the many evils consequent upon the

removal of the people from the interior to the sea coast may be included the loss of a large number of place-names. In this song the bard makes honourable mention of every hill and glen and knoll and corrie where he was wont in early days to follow the deer, and one can easily understand how the old people should preserve intact this rather lengthy composition, not because of any merit in the song, but by reason of the many happy associations which were recalled to their minds by the mere mention of these places.[88]

This song, composed between 1761 and 1768, is a typical Gaelic song in praise of place and the deer of the hills, but one which would not appeal to modern literary tastes. Thus it has been that many men of letters have not thought that humble songs of this sort – specific to a particular community and its environs, and hence quite relevant to our understanding of a sense of place and landscape – were worthy of being documented in the past.

From the endearing verses celebrating life in the summer shielings we can expect that people had many fond memories of their early years there and waxed nostalgically about them when they were too old and weak to climb the hills. Mairearad MacGregor, a native of Atholl, states her preference for the Highlands over the Lowland towns by reference to aspects of the landscape and pastoral lifestyle[89] in an eighteenth-century song:

> *Fhir a shiubhlas uam thar a' Bhealaich*
> *Thoir uam soraidh gu Taobh Loch Eireachd*
> *Gu Beinn Udlamain 's am bi 'n eilid*
> *Gu Bràigh an Sgulain 's gu Loch an t-Searraich.*
>
> *Là na h-imrich nuair a dh'fhalbhainn*
> *Rachainn timcheall air a' mheanbh-chrodh*
> *Leiginn m' anail air a' Gharbh-Dhùn*
> *'S air Lùb Bad Chearc gun caidlinn an-moch.*
>
> *Nuair a théid mi mach mu'n chabhsair*
> *Leam chan éibhneas ceòl nan àrd-chlag:*
> *An crodh a' geumnaich mach mu'n àiridh*
> *'S a' ghrian a' teàrnadh fo sgéith Beinn Eallar.*[90]

('O man who travels away from me over the pass, take my greeting to Loch Errocht, to Beinn Udlamain where the deer hinds are, to Bràigh an Sgulain and to Loch an t-Searraich.')

('When I would set off on the day of flitting, I would go around the calves, catch my breath at Garbh-Dhùn, and sleep late at Lùb Bad Chearc.')

('When I set out around the city streets, the music of the bells is no joy to me: [I prefer] the lowing of the cattle on the shieling as the sun sets over Ben Alder.')

The exile of old age is a common cause of nostalgia for a lost landscape. Early examples of this theme are Domhnall mac Fhionnlaigh nan Dàn's 'Òran na Com-hachaig' and Donnchadh Bàn Macintyre's 1802 'Cead Deireannach nam Beann' ('Final Farewell to the Mountains').[91] A lesser known but interesting specimen is 'Cead an Ùghdair do Dhùn Éideann is do na Beanntaibh Gàidhealach' ('The Author's Farewell to Edinburgh and to the Mountains of Gaeldom') by Iain MacGregor, a native of Glenlyon born in the mid eighteenth century. MacGriogair's verse covers a sweeping vista of the pinnacles visible from the vantage point of Arthur's Seat in Edinburgh, where he resided in the latter part of his life, and many far beyond the reaches of eyesight. MacGriogair invokes the Gaelic forms of the place names of the landscape, emphasising the enduring legacy of Gaelic throughout Scotland:

> Chì mi Beinn Laomainn shuas
> Air an luidh an cuailean bàn;
> Beinn Lìde 's gach beinn ri taobh –
> Tha iad man aon aois ri càch –
> Gun dì-chuimhn' air a' Bheinn Mhóir
> 'S air Beinn Dobhrainn nan damh cràcach
> Air Gleann Urchaidh 's air Gleann Lìomhann:
> Siud an tìr an d' fhuair mi m' àrach. [. . .]

> Cha téid mi gu tuath nas fhaide
> Pillidh mi air ais 's gun gluais mi
> Air mo thuras 's théid mi dhachaidh,
> Chan fhan mi fo fhasgadh nam fuar-bheann.[92]

('I can see Ben Lomond out west on which the white coverlet lays, Ben Ledi and each mountain next to it – they are all about the same vintage – without forgetting about Benmore or Beinn Dobhrain of the antlered stags, or Glenorchy or Glenlyon: that is the land where I was raised [. . .]')

('I will no longer go north; I will commence and return on my travel and I will go home; I will not remain in the shelter of the cold mountains.')

As discussed in Chapter Six, the imagery of nature was employed in early Gaelic literature as an implicit commentary about a ruler's exercise of leadership. It was an oblique form of praise to a ruler to praise the beauty, fertility, and bounty of his lands as this signified that the land-goddess was rewarding his territory favourably for his good leadership. As people were implicated in place, the praise or dispraise of a place generally had the same implications for its inhabitants by association. A poem ostensibly in praise of Kintyre from the early eighteenth century provides a suitable example, for it begins by praising the land and ends by praising its native sons, Clan Donald:

> *Soraidh soir uam gu Cinn-tìre*
> *Le caoine dìsle agus fàilte*
> *Gun àrd no ìosal a dhearmad*
> *Eadar an Tairbeart is Abhart.*
>
> *Banaltra Galldachd is Gàidhealtachd*
> *Ge do thréig i nis a h-àbhaist*   øB.3
> *Bha drùdhadh gach tìr d'a h-ionnsaigh,*
> *Is cha dùraig aon neach a fàgail.* [. . .]
>
> *Is e a glòir 's a sgèimh thar gach aoinni,*
> *A h-uaisle flathail rìoghail stàtail:*   C.1
> *'S an cùirtibh maiseach meadhrach mùirneach*   C.1
> *Bha an sinnseara cliùiteach 'gan àiteach.*   A.4
>
> *Clann Domhnaill na féile is an t-suaircis*   B.1, B.8
> *'Gam buaine ceannas nan Innse:*   B.5
> *Is cian bunadh na tréibhe as uaisle*
> *'S an tìr mhaisich bhuadhaich rìoghail.*[93]   C.6

('Send a greeting eastwards from me to Kintyre with sincerity and a welcome, without neglecting places high or low between Tarbert and Dunaverty.')

('She is the nurse-maid of Gael and non-Gael, although she no longer follows the customs that once drew all lands toward her; no one would wish to leave her [. . .]')

('Her crowning glory above all is her royal, stately aristocracy: renowned ancestors inhabited joyous, delightful, resplendent courts.')

('Clan Donald of generosity and civility, who long held sway over the islands: the foundation of that noblest kindred is ancient in that lovely, royal, propitious land.')

Although this poem opens with the praise of the natural features and creatures of Kintyre and spends most of its verses on this topic, the ultimate aim may have been to please a MacDonald patron.

Pre-modern Gaelic aesthetics of nature and landscape are reflected in the song 'Smeòrach Chlann Domhnaill' ('The Mavis of Clan Donald'), composed by Iain MacCodrum. MacCodrum was born *c.*1693 in the west of North Uist and showed exceptional promise as a poet from an early age despite lacking formal education or even the ability to read. His mastery of Gaelic oral literature was evident, however, in that he could recite Ossianic ballads for hours and was said to have been the foremost expert on them in the Western Isles. He composed this song no later than 1755, several years before he was appointed as the last official poet of a clan chieftain.[94] MacCodrum assumes the voice of the mavis which can soar high to gain a bird's eye view of clan territory and sing sweetly in its praise:

> *Smeòrach mis' air mullach beinne*
> *'G amharc gréin' is speuran soilleir*
> *Thig mi stòlda 'chòir na coille –*
> *Bidh mi beò air treòdas eile.* [. . .]
>
> *Ma mholas gach eun a thìr féin*
> *Cuim thar éis nach moladh mise?*
> *Tìr nan curaidh, tìr nan cliar*
> *An tìr bhiadhchar fhialadh mhiosail.*
>
> *'N tìr nach caol ri cois na mara*
> *An tìr ghaolach chaomhach channach*
> *An tìr laoghach uanach mheannach*
> *Tìr an arain bhainneach mhealach.*
>
> *An tìr riabhach ghrianach thaitneach*
> *An tìr dhìonach fhiarach fhasgach*
> *An tìr lèanach ghèadhach lachach*
> *'N tìr 'm bi biadh gun mhiadh air tacar.*
>
> *An tìr chròiceach eòrnach phailte*
> *An tìr bhuadhach chluaineach ghartach*
> *An tìr chruachach sguabach dhaiseach*
> *Dlùth ri cuan gun fhuachd ri sneachda.*[95]

('I am a mavis on the peak of the summit looking at the sun and clear sky; I will go calmly to the forest, and find another livelihood [. . .]')

('If every bird praises its own territory, why indeed should I not do the same? The land of warriors and of poets, the land abounding with food, generosity, and admirers.')

('The land with generous fields around the coastline, the beloved, mild, attractive land, the land abounding with calves, lambs, and kids, the land of bread, milk, and honey.')

('The land of many colours, sunshine, and satisfaction, the snug, grassy, sheltered land, the land of meadows, geese, and ducks, the land full of food without need to hoard.')

('The land abounding with seaweed, barley, and plenty, the superb land of meadows and tilled fields, the land abounding with corn-stacks, sheaves, and heaps of grain, close to the sea without the cold of snow.')

By choosing the symbol of the forest, MacCodrum draws upon its many rich associations, including its ability to represent a family, clan, or community. He characterises North Uist as a land of milk and honey, overflowing with natural resources and wealth. His verses are not unlike those of the flytings of female poets boasting of the superiority of their clans (such as the excerpt from the poetic match between Clanranald and MacNeill poetesses given in Chapter Five). There are also strong similarities between his portrayal of North Uist and the ways in which the filidh idealised land in Classical Gaelic poetry: the old poetic order indicated a preference for a moderate climate and a balance between 'domesticated' land and 'wastelands', coastland and interior lands.[96]

In a song in praise of the Duke of Atholl composed *c.*1785, when clan estates forfeited after Culloden were restored to select Highland chieftains, Iain MacGregor relates the wide diversity of terrain and plant life in Atholl:

> 'S fad 's gur leathann do chrìochan
> Nan iarrteadh an tomhas,
> Gun gabhadh iad bliadhna
> 'S cha dèanadh e 'n gnothach;
> Oir is farsaing gach fàsach
> 'S gach àiridh tha 'd mhonadh,
> Gach srath agus bràighe,
> Gach beinn àrd agus coire.

> 'S coillteach, badanach, luachrach C.6
> Feurach, fuaranach, fallain,
> Lùbach, lurach, na bruachan
> Deas is tuath do Uisg' Gharaidh:
> Lusach, seilleanach, sguabach,
> Gun ghruaim ann an talla: C.6
> Is leat Dùn Chaillean nam fuar bheann A.3
> Gu Druim Uachdar a' chathaidh.[97] A.3

('The bounds of your territory extend far and wide: if there was ever a desire to measure them, it would take a year, and even that would not be sufficient; every wild space is expansive, as are all of the shielings that are in your moorland, every strath and brae, every high mountain and corry.')

('Both north and south sides of the River Garry are full of forests, thickets, rushes, grass, fresh water springs: thriving, beautiful, and full of bends [in the river], plants, bees, and sheaves of corn, without displeasure in any hall; yours is Dunkeld of the cold mountains to Drumochter of the snow-drift.')

By way of contrast, a poem composed by Alasdair mac Mhaighstir Alasdair *c.*1745 when he was expelled from his home in Eignig provides an example of the negative portrayal of landscape:

> *Dh'fhalbh mi à nathrachan creagach*
> *Làn conaisg 's de phreasaibh sgrogach*
> *Bioran droighinn ann 'dam bhriogadh*
> *Roimh 'm chliabh gu neimhneach 'dam bhrodadh* [. . .]

> *Ghabh mi comhnaidh an Inbhir Aoidhe*
> *Bail' ionmholta solta gaolach*
> *'S e gu solach torrach maoineach*
> *Mùirneach sò-ghràdh'ch forach faoilidh.*[98]

('I have left the stony, serpentine place, full of gorse and shriveled bushes, where there are thorn spikes in front of my chest to stab me, poking me with poison [. . .]')

('I took residence in Inbhir Aoidhe, a praiseworthy settlement full of kindness; sunny, fertile, prosperous, joyous, easily loved, hospitable.')

While this poem does tell us about the kinds of natural features that were felt to be either praiseworthy or detestable, it is little more than a reflection of Alasdair's anger at being turned out of his home in Eignig and his relief at finding refuge in Inbhir Aoidh.

These contrasts alert us to the fact that nature imagery can be used for rhetorical purposes without necessarily reflecting Gaelic aesthetics of nature. In other words, images of nature can be harnessed by poets as a vehicle for expressing their own feelings without telling us much about what they think about nature *per se.*[99] Classic examples of this rhetorical exploitation of nature symbolism come from immigrant Gaelic poets in North America, where the same forests are represented as either gloomy and doom-laden, or fair and fruitful, according to the message they wish to convey to their audience. Such compositions tell us little directly, however, about typical Gaelic attitudes towards trees and forests in general.

Highland aristocrats enjoyed the freedom to travel widely, to hunt wild game in the hills, and to engage in various sorts of activities in their own territory and far beyond it. In Gaelic literature the nobility are commonly depicted as frequenting the wilderness. This close association embues wild nature with the noble associations of the native aristocracy, given that this was seen to be their 'natural habitat'. A poem by Iain Dubh MacDonald, probably for Captain Raghnall of Clanranald when he was in France in 1716, makes a succinct allusion to this. Iain Dubh said of the clan, 'Gum b'fhearr linn thu bhith sealgaireachd / Air fearann garbh nam Mòraireach' ('We would prefer that you were hunting on the rough terrain of the Morar-men').[100]

A more elaborate example of the noble associations of wilderness comes from a song composed by Gilleasbuig Ruadh MacDonald ('An Ciaran Mabach'), brother to MacDonald of Sleat, when he was being treated by doctors in Edinburgh before he died in 1688. Like Domhnall mac Fhionnlaigh nan Dàn, Gilleasbuig looks back fondly on his life as a hunter and his affection for the deer, anthropomorphising them as his companions. He and the deer take a dim view of life in the Lowland community by contrast:

> B' iad mo ghràdh-sa a' ghreigh uallach
> A thogadh suas ris an àird
> Dh'itheadh biolair an fhuarain
> 'S air 'm bu shuarach an càl;
> 'S mise féin nach tug fuath dhuibh,
> Ged a b' fhuar am mìos Màigh –
> 'S tric a dh'fhulaing mi cruadal
> 'S móran fuachd air ur sgàth. [. . .]

> B' i mo ghràdh-sa a' bhean uasal
> Dha nach d' fhuaras riamh lochd,
> Nach iarradh mar chluasaig
> Ach fior ghualainn nan cnoc.[101]

('Beloved to me is the proud deer-herd who would ascend to the summit, who would eat the watercress of the fountain, and would disdain the kale; I myself never bore you [deer] ill will, even if the month of May was frigid; very often did I endure hardship and cold for your sake [. . .]')

('Beloved to me is the noblewoman [i.e., the deer hind] on whom no fault was ever found, and who never sought any other pillow than the actual shoulder of the hill.')

Poetess Màiri nighean Alasdair Ruaidh was closely associated with the household of the MacLeods of the Dunvegan in the late seventeenth and early eighteenth centuries, an era in which they were under great pressure to assimilate into anglophone society. She was said by tradition to have nursed five MacLeod chieftains and two Mackenzie chieftains of Applecross.[102] Her poetry reminded them that despite such outside forces they were expected to stay loyal to their ancestral territory and customs:

Cha b'e Machair nan Gall a chleachd thu fo d' bhonn
Gionach no sannt Pàrlamaid:
Bu roghainn dhut gleann, faghaid 'na deann   D.2
Tadhal nam beann àrda dhut.[103]

('The Lowlands were not your inclination, nor the greed and ambition of politics: you would prefer to be in a glen in pursuit of the hunt, frequenting the high mountains.')

Vernacular Gaelic oral tradition asserts that the lower ranks of society also perceived the Highland landscape as their own native habitat. A song from the Battle of Killiecrankie in 1689 constrasts Lowland and Highland forces in stereotyped polarities as 'Bodaich machair' a bhuachair / no sìol uasal nan Garbh-Chrìoch' ('The churls of the Lowland dung-plains / or the noble folk of the Highlands').[104] In a song from the 1745 Jacobite Rising, the clans are described as coming from 'garbh-shlios nam beann' ('the rough slopes of the mountains').[105] The ethnic identification with landscape was sometimes expressed as an opposition between Highlands and Lowlands, such as the aforementioned seventeenth-century boast, 'Cha dùth do Ghall àrd bheann a dhìreadh' ('It is not natural/native/fitting for a Lowlander to climb a high mountain'). This sentiment is echoed in the proverb 'Anail a' Ghàidheil: air a' mhullach' ('The Gael draws his breath at the summit (of the mountain)').[106] Such oppositions became much more common in poetry decrying the Clearances: Gaels often complained that the new landscapes to which they were driven were totally unnatural and unsuited to them. After leaving Knoydart in 1798 for Glengarry, Ontario, Iain mac Dhomhnaill mhic Aonghuis MacDonald recalled his life in the Highlands wistfully:

Nuair a bha mi aig baile,
Dh'éirinn bealach is beinn,
Cha robh mùchadh air m' anail   E.2
No maille 'nam cheum,
'S ann a bhithinn cho cridheil
Cur geall-ruith agus leum
'S fhada chithinn bhuam sealladh
'N àm cromadh na gréin.[107]

('When I was at home, I would climb hill-pass and mountain; I had no shortness of breath or slowness of step; I would be so happy of heart, running at top speed and leaping; I could see far into the distance when the sun was setting.')

Just as human culture has not imprinted wilderness with physical divisions, neither do social restrictions and limitations apply there. The wilderness is thus depicted in many literatures as the place of lovers' trysts, where romance could flourish despite the complications at home. In many Gaelic songs too, women state that they would gladly leave their homes to join their sweethearts even if they had to live in the wild to do so. After her own family assassinated her lover Griogair Ruadh MacGregor in 1570, Marion Campbell stated:

> 'S mór a b' annsa bhith aig Griogair
> Air feadh coille 's fraoich
> Na bhith aig baran crìon na dalach
> An taigh cloiche 's aoil.[108]

('I would much more prefer to be married to Griogair living in the forest and heath than to be married to the little baron of the river-meadow in a lime-painted stone house.')

WILDERNESS AND SURVIVAL

Much of the material in this chapter to this point has reflected the anthropocentric perceptions of nature and landscape in Gaelic culture: projecting names relating to the human body and social history onto the landscape, interpreting natural phenomena in terms of the leadership of a human ruler, praising or disparaging land according to what it has to offer human inhabitants, and so on. We should now consider the ways in which Gaelic culture perceived and interpreted nature independent of human history and needs.

The ability to describe the sights, sounds, and cycles of nature, without any implications for humankind or guest appearances by human characters, is attested from almost the beginning of Celtic literature in the British Isles: many examples in both Gaelic and Welsh date to between the seventh and tenth centuries AD.[109] The idea of 'Celtic nature poetry' composed by isolated monks contemplating the wilderness around them was popularised by scholars in the early twentieth century, but such a simplistic context and function for this literature is no longer accepted by contemporary scholars. It has been argued that some of these poems were simply linguistic or metrical exercises for students. It remains to be explained adequately, however, why so many poets should choose nature as the subject of their verses and write about it with such a keen eye and ear.[110]

A vernacular proverb (mentioned in Chapter Three) lists the masterpieces of several genres of Scottish Gaelic literature, including 'Moladh Loch Cé' ('The Praise of Loch Key'). Loch Key is in the county of Roscommon in Ireland and was home to monastic scholars in the medieval period. Although there does not seem to be any surviving evidence of the song-poem in praise of Loch Key mentioned in the proverb, its acknowledgment as an exemplar of nature panegyric suggests that such a genre existed in pre-modern Gaeldom, even if only a few samples of it have been preserved. Several other poems were committed to writing in the eighteenth century in praise of the beauty of specific locales whose titles consist of the term *moladh* 'praise' followed by a place name, including 'Moladh Chinn Tìre' ('The Praise of Kintyre', early eighteenth century),[111] 'Moladh Eas Mòrair' ('The Praise of the Waterfall of Morar', *c.*1745),[112] 'Moladh Choille Chros' ('The Praise of Cross Wood', *c.*1745),[113] 'Moladh Ghearrloch' ('The Praise of Gairloch', 1783),[114] and the aforementioned 'Moladh Beinn Dobhrain' ('The Praise of Ben Dorain'). There are also songs in praise and dispraise of the river Mashie from the mid eighteenth century, composed by Lachlann MacPherson, the tacksman of Strathmashie (see item seven of Appendix A).

Like other indigenous societies, pre-modern Gaeldom saw nature as animate and populated by preternatural forces and beings. There are fragments about a curious tradition of composing poems in praise of the beauty of a place in order to appease the potentially hostile supernatural beings there. A visitor to Ireland in 1756 commented, 'There is a custom among the country people, to enjoin every one that passes this mountain, to make some verses to its honour, otherwise, they affirm, that whoever attempts to pass it without versifying, must meet with misfortune.'[115] Martin Martin recorded what seems to be a related custom about a valley in South Uist in the late seventeenth century:

> The Natives who farm it come thither with their Cattle in the Summer-time, and are possessed with the firm Belief that this Valley is haunted by Spirits, who by the Inhabitants are call'd the great Men; and that whatsoever Man or Woman enters the Valley without making first an entire Resignation of themselves to the Conduct of the great Men will infallibly grow mad. The words by which he or she gives up himself to these Men's Conduct are comprehended in three Sentences, wherein the glen is twice named, to which they add that it is inhabited by these great Men, and that such as enter depend on their Protection.[116]

In the nineteenth century Alexander Carmichael transcribed a short poem and related tradition from this area. The poem is a short invocation that recounts some of the marvels of the glen and seeks the protection of the 'great ones' there.[117] This and other evidence confirms that Gaelic tradition retained the concept of wilderness as something beyond human control and exploitation, places that humankind must leave alone to remain the domain of non-human beings.

Iain MacCodrum's song 'Smeòrach Chlann Domhnaill' discussed above was composed to the melody and metre of an even older song said to have been sung by a seal-woman lamenting her relations who had been killed by seal hunters. This song formed part of a local legend about the MacCodrums. The MacCodrums carried the Gaelic nickname *sliochd nan ròn* 'the seal-people' because they were said to be descended from the seals.

> It was said, for example, that a woman of the name of MacCodrum, possibly a relative of the bard, was regularly seized with pains at the time of the annual seal hunt, out of sympathy, as was supposed, with her kith and kin. It was even darkly suggested that

the MacCodrums could and did sometimes assume the form of seals, and that several of them had lost their lives in that way. [. . .] Their traditions show at least two features which are generally characteristic of totemism. The first of these is belief in descent from the totem animal [. . .] The second is a tabu against killing it: no one bearing the name of MacCodrum would kill a seal or eat seal flesh; it is even probable that they would not use the skin or oil of the seal in any way. The MacCodrums lived in close proximity to sea-girt rocks where seals bred in thousands.[118]

The practice of totemism places limitations on the human exploitation of nature and engenders an empathy for animals on which the population is dependent for survival. That this and other traces of totemism could be found in the eighteenth-century Highlands again attests to Gaelic adaptation to the local environment and continued sensitivity to the limitations of its resources.

Some of the Classical Gaelic poetry of the filidh demonstrates an unusually keen appreciation of rough, undomesticated land,[119] and, as demonstrated above, vernacular Gaelic poetry provides evidence for a continued high regard for wilderness and 'unimproved' land amongst segments of Scottish Gaeldom. The remnants of archaic Gaelic beliefs associated with wild nature and landscape are probably preserved best in a few surviving oral narratives that make use of mythical characters, symbols, and scenarios. Such narratives can implicitly express ineffable truths and communicate intuitive, non-rational modes of understanding of the wilderness and humankind's relationship to it.

The 'forest primeval' was the archetypal wilderness and oral tradition in many locales across the Highlands recalled a time when woods were plentiful.[120] As we saw in the tale of Dubh a' Ghiuthais, which opened this chapter, the loss of that feature of the Scottish landscape was seen as a calamity and blamed on the jealous enemies of the Gaels, the Vikings.

There are other narratives which affirm the importance of the wilderness and of limiting humankind's encroachment upon it. This was often expressed in stories in which places are described as being inhabited by preternatural beings who seem to both embody the place itself and act to protect it. This is yet another strand in the complex of beliefs about the sìdh, for they are often associated with the wilderness and elemental forces. The sìdh inhabit the undomesticated space outside of human control and appear in colours associated with nature.

> This is usually beyond the bounds of the *baile* 'human habitation and arable land', on the moorland, in the glens, and among the mountains. The fairies are creatures of the wild; the colours of their clothes are the colours of the vegetation, in growth and decay, and merge with that of their surroundings, almost like camouflage.[121]

This aspect of folklore about the sìdh belongs to the paradigm shifts resulting from the agricultural revolution and connects to other aspects of the lore of supernatural beings, including the Cailleach, *ùruisg*, and *glaistig*.

In Gaelic tradition, they are the supernatural representatives, often guardians, of wilderness and the untamed, alternatively to be respected or feared, or at least to be placated and kept at a distance. Typical of the landscape of the Highland wilderness would be the glacial feature of the 'fairy mound' or *sìthean* to be avoided and bypassed while recognised. [. . .] Respect is always given to the spirits of the wild as tutelary beings and even deities.[122]

One narrative in which preternatural beings force the human community to retreat from their exploitation of nature ends with a single verse recording the injunction:

The mountain stretch at Corri-Dho which is known as *Taigh Mór na Seilg* ['The Big House of the Hunt'] was the haunt of a male goblin known as Dàibhidh and of a female spirit named Mór. These two strongly objected to the right which the Glen Urquhart tenantry had of grazing their cattle in summer on the shielings of Corri-Dho, and they were repeatedly seen driving away the Glen Urquhart herds. At last Dàibhidh was so thoroughly roused that he pulled a great fir tree up by the roots and, with the assistance of Mór, chased the Urquhart men and their bestial for many miles, until he sent them over the Glenmoriston march beyond Achnagoneran. Dàibhidh's words on the occasion are still remembered:

> *Is leam-s' Doire-Dhamh is Doire-Dhàibhidh*
> *Is Boirisgidh bhuidh' nan alltan*
> *Is Ceann a' Chnoc mòr le fiodh is le fàsaich*
> *A bhodaichibh dhubh dhaithte, togaibh oirbh!*

('Doire-Dhamh and Doire-Dhàibhidh are mine, and bright Boirisgidh of the streams, and wide Ceanacroc with its woods and wilderness – Go away, you worthless churls!')

And the Urquhart carles did take themselves away, and never again showed face in Corri-Dho.[123]

In some tales the Cailleach stops human hunters from killing too many of the deer, an animal with which she has close associations. Given the role of the deer in symbolising the wilderness in general, her actions may have a wider significance and implications. In one tale a hunter named Donald Cameron – a very common name perhaps representing the archetypal Highlander – was said to be hunting deer alone in the hills of Lochaber. The glaistig of this tale is the Cailleach by another name.

During the sunrise of a quiet morning, he was sitting on the deer-path on the mountain with his trusty, slender gun on his knee, waiting until the 'proud deer-herd' would descend from the summit of the mountain to drink their morning beverage from the pure springs that erupt from under the side of the mountain. He eventually saw them emerging from the mist that hid the rocky ridge above him, being driven by the great Glaistig. She suddenly noticed him and before the foremost deer came within shot of the hunter, she cried out to him, 'You are too hard on my hinds, Donald! You must not be so hard on them!'

Donald was quick-witted and so he answered her with this swift reply: 'I have never killed a hind where I could find a stag.'

He allowed the hinds to pass, with the Glaistig trailing them, and she never bothered him again.[124]

The activity of the deer in this tale seems to make visible the operation of the many elements of the ecosystem and their reliance upon one another to function properly. That the Cailleach was indeed concerned in oral tradition with the integrity and health of the wider environment as a whole is indicated by another tale in which the Cailleach makes an appearance. It is merely a brief episode but is arresting and hauntingly foreboding:

A hunter was one day returning from Beinn Bhric and when he reached the bottom of the mountain, he thought he heard a sound like the cracking two rocks striking each other, or like the grating of a stag's horns when he rubs them against a rock. He continued walking until he came within sight of a large stone that lay at the side of the road, and there he saw at the base of the stone a woman with a green shawl around her shoulders. She held a deer shank in each hand and was constantly striking them together. Even though he realised that she was a glaistig, he was bold enough to say to her, 'What are you doing there, poor woman?'

But the only answer that he got was, 'Since the forest was burnt! Since the forest was burnt!' And she kept repeating this refrain for as long as he could hear her.[125]

As explained in Chapter Six, the Cailleach's natural home is at the top – not bottom – of the mountain; her deer herd are represented in this tale only by the bones of a dead animal; the road is a sign of human impact and 'progress'; the man is noted as being unusually lacking in fear of her. The beating of the bones in the Cailleach's hands echoes the practice of the striking of the palms in the rituals of keening: it is clear that she is mourning the forest, which represents the wilderness in general. The tale indicates that humankind's adoption of modern rationality has dethroned the Cailleach and hence she can no longer function as a protector of nature.

There are also Gaelic traditions about the concern shown by supernatural beings of the wilderness for the indigenous human community. In the Braes of Mar, on the far eastern fringe of the Highlands, the Cailleach Bheur was said to have given a forewarning of the conversion of shielings into deer forests and grouse-shootings during the Clearances:

Nan robh fios aig cloinn nan Gàidheal
Dé bu phrìs do bharr an fhraoich
No do ubh na circe
Bu daoir' bhiodh cearc na bò
'S bu daoir' bhiodh gleann na strath.[126]

('If the Gaels only knew the value of the top of the heather, or of the hen's egg, fowl would be more valuable than cattle, and the glen more valuable than the strath.')

Although some aspects of Gaelic tradition represent the Cailleach's attitudes towards humankind as capricious or simply indifferent, in others she includes the human community in her interests, in addition to animal and plant life.

The 'nature tales' of the Cailleach can be thought of as encoding a principle which is reinstated and reaffirmed by being continually retold in oral tradition: a principle of the sacrality of nature and of the need to recognise it as important in its own right, keeping human exploitation within certain limits. In many of the traditions recorded and literature composed in the eighteenth and nineteenth centuries, on the other hand, the sudden assault of 'Improvement' upon the Highland landscape (and cultural imagination) is represented as destroying the habitat of preternatural beings if not the beings themselves.[127] Duncan Taylor, a retired army officer who had worked with General Wade to construct a network of roadways through the Highlands, went on to construct a road through Glenlochay and Làirig an Lochain in Breadalbane. Local poet Aonghas Caimbeul composed a song in praise of his accomplishment, remarking that

B' i Comh-sheilg an t-àite béisteil
Gus an deach thu fhéin 'ga còir [. . .]
Thug thu 'n rathad 's cha b'e 'n-diugh e
Às na cùiltibh bha 's an fhròig –
An t-àite b' àbhaist bhith o thùs
'Na chuilidh ùruisgean nan còs.[128]

('Comh-sheilg was a beastly place until you entered it [. . .] Some time ago you brought the road out of the marshes and dark recesses; the place that was from the beginning a sanctuary for hole-lurking *ùruisgs*.')

The Gaelic panegyric code is subverted in this ode to praise Duncan's conquest of nature using many of the same motifs used in the praise of chieftains. This shift in attitudes is indicative of the environmental and cultural transformations under way in the post-Culloden era.

The image of wilderness and 'unimproved' landscapes was essentially a negative one in the Evangelical movement dominant in the late-eighteenth-century Highlands, having been associated with the 'pre-enlightened' state of Gaeldom.[129] This new religious rhetoric of nature, in which Christianity was portrayed as taming both the savage inhabitants and habitat, was an absorption of external stigmas about Gaeldom which eclipsed the earlier positive associations of nature which appear in a small number of the transitional religious poems of the eighteenth century. The poem by Marairead Cameron which praises Jesus with use of tree imagery (poem nine in Appendix A), for example, draws its power from the ancient symbolism of the sacred tree but has few surviving parallels.

Despite these tumultuous changes in the landscape and in conceptions of nature in the Highlands, some Gaels remained firmly rooted in and attached to their ancestral homes. Using Perth to symbolise the urban Lowland world and its material advantages, an old Gaelic proverb stated 'B'fhearr am meug a bhiodh 's a' Ghàidhealtachd na am bainne blàth a bhiodh am Peairt' ('It would be better to have whey in the Highlands than to have warm milk in Perth.').[130] In other words, despite the attractions of the Lowlands and its financial benefits, many Gaels saw a commitment to remaining in the Highlands as a virtue.

The necessity of co-existence with the wilderness was understood intuitively in Gaelic culture and encoded in mythic form in Gaelic narrative. While the wilderness stands in contrast to domesticated space, humankind was still represented as dependent upon the benefits that emerge from the wilderness: deer from the forest, fish from the sea, water from the mountains, human creativity from the mysterious depths of the unconscious.[131] We ignore at our own peril the counsel of ecologists who bluntly warn that the destruction of the wilderness will ensure our own extinction: 'Humankind's apparent success in dominating and transforming wilderness into civilization not only endangers the web of life itself but fundamentally diminishes our humanity, our potential for a fuller and richer human beingness.'[132]

CONCLUSIONS

Many statements testify to the way a community's elders, leaders, and educators explicitly acknowledge the importance of their language as an expression of their whole society and history. They see language as the means of transmitting the story of the great journeys, wars, alliances, and apocalyptic events of their past; it is the chief mechanism of their rituals; it is the means of conveying ancient myths and legends, and their beliefs about the spirit world, to new generations; it is a way of expressing their network of social relationships; and it provides an ongoing commentary on their interaction with the landscape.

– David Crystal, *Language Death*

It is not surprising that James Macpherson chose the literature of the Fian as the basis of his *Ossian*: we see in these prose and poetic narratives some of the finest aspirations and most compelling heroic, and tragic, characters of Gaeldom, personifications of traditional virtues but also human failings, defending their territory and traditions from antagonists and invaders. Prowess in battle was only one of many attributes needed in a leader and championed in Gaelic culture. The many qualities of Fionn mac Cumhaill, a popular role model for Highlanders, are enumerated in an elegy attributed to Ossian, preserved in the early-sixteenth-century *Book of the Dean of Lismore* (see Plate 12):

> He was a *file*, and a prince,
> A ruler over all rulers,
> Fionn, princely ruler of the Fian,
> He was a ruler over all lands. [. . .]

> Talented in many skills,
> He was a mighty horseman
> He was an *ollamh* for his behaviour
> He was expert at all music. [. . .]

> He was the subject of poets and poems
> He was the leader of battle
> He was an *ollamh* for his behaviour
> He was refined to women. [. . .]

> Fionn did not withhold from any man
> Even if he had little ale;
> He did not cast out of his house
> Any man who entered it.[1]

Fionn represents not a war-mad savage nor a poet lost in misty dreams, but a magnanimous, educated, and broadly accomplished person, even if tales do not hide those flaws which make him human.

Macpherson was not the first to recast the Ossianic cycle in Scotland, nor was he the first to see in the Ossianic ballads a lost Gaelic Golden Age. The *Book of the Dean of Lismore* itself, compiled by churchmen with Campbell patronage in the very centre of Scotland, contains many poems about the Fian, including several not found in Ireland.[2] Amongst them is 'Laoidh Dhiarmaid' ('The Lay of Diarmaid') a well-known tragedy which was reimagined by a Scottish poet in Glenshee, probably in the fifteenth century, even then on the eastern border of the Gàidhealtachd.[3] In his manuscript history of the Campbells of Craiginish, Alexander Campbell wrote *c.*1720 of the traditions surrounding the Fian:

> There are many fabulous accounts built in the old Irish and Highland tales upon the atchievments of these great men [. . .] It will not be thought unreasonable that they & their Children, born and brought up in this unbounded freedom, may have many grains of allowance given to their actions far surpassing the common rate of mankind. I am not by this to train the Reader in to a belief [in] all the incredible stuff that is handed about of them, but I am well persuaded that they exceeded any thing we have seen.[4]

While Highland society remained intact, oral tradition – songs, stories, proverbs, phrases, words, and so on – transmitted and regenerated Gaelic culture across countless generations. This is not to claim that there has always been only one single oral tradition for all Gaels at all times, for it has been as diverse and multi-layered as the many regions, communities, kin-groups, social strata, and individuals who have contributed to it and participated in it. Particular poets have argued that their patrons were better suited to be leaders than others, and invented lineages to back up those claims, just as local storytellers have woven stories to explain how their clans were displaced by less-deserving rival clans. Transcendent above and beyond such variations, however, the emergent themes of Gaelic oral tradition offer particular ways of seeing the world and convey self-esteem, a sense of place, and a unifying sense of identity to its participants, especially through high-register story and song.

> Throughout the whole range of the poetry conventional images pass before us like waves on the sea, endlessly recurring, formed in the same creative matrix, each a reflection of others, each one individual. They remind us of those that have passed;

328

they prepare us for those that are to come. The rhetorical systems which contain these elements, interlocking and lighting up, as it were, in their entirety no matter where we make contact, could not fail to keep alive the unity of the Gaelic nation.[5]

Despite whatever might be assumed today about the 'impoverished' material culture, natural environment, or economic conditions of the Gaelic world, Highlanders show time and again in their own cultural expressions that they are intelligent, resourceful, confident, and resilient people, capable of adapting new ideas from the outside world and creating new ideas which others have found worthy of imitation. Is it any wonder, then, that Gaels were willing to fight, with words and weapons, in order to defend their culture, even when their options were narrowing and the odds were stacked against them? Were they wrong to assume that once cultural institutions were taken out of their hands and into the hands of English speakers who disdained their language and culture that their very existence would be threatened?

As a child I heard about Gaelic in Kintyre and Arran and Perthshire. Argyll was famous for 'having the best Gaelic'. We knew people from Ross-shire and Sutherland who spoke Gaelic. Because of that we had a sense of the Gàidhealtachd as an unbroken cultural and linguistic area [. . .] it gave us the sense of belonging to a much wider community and strengthened our Gaelic identity in the face of the Anglicising policies of formal education. [. . .] Through such sources we were able to add a whole dimension to our experiences as Gaels. Legend and song, music and poetry opened up a perspective on Gaelic history that was denied to generations of us in our formal schooling.[6]

Once spoken throughout Scotland and Ireland, Gaelic was pushed to the margins and excluded from the corridors of power and privilege. With all of the work a day concerns and calamities of the modern world – all of the pressing 'practical' issues which require our limited attention and resources – does such a small and intangible thing matter? This question is asked of many languages and cultures on the brink of extinction.

There are no such practical incentives for learning the Haida language. It will not get you a job. And Haida poetry, like English poetry, is not an easy commodity to sell in the contemporary world. Why does it matter? It matters because a language is a lifeform, like a species of plant or animal. Once extinct, it is gone forever. And as each one dies, the intellectual gene pool of the human species shrinks. The big, discontinuous brain to which we all in our way contribute, and on which we all depend, loses a part of itself that it cannot rebuild.[7]

Gaelic matters in Scotland just as every language matters to its own community and environment. An indigenous culture is one society's response to its own environmental, material, intellectual, and spiritual resources and needs, it is not a claim for a universal solution for all societies. We diminish our own humanity by denying the humanity of others; we diminish our own choices by denying choices to others; we diminish our well-being as a planet by restricting the diversity and freedoms of local cultures. It is ethnocentric and narcissistic to think that we know best how other peoples can meet their own needs and realise their own potential, and that we have an exclusive claim to the criteria to be used to evaluate others' aspirations.

Such have been the damaging presumptions which have been applied to Gaelic in the past, and often even into the present. Despite centuries of aggressive attempts to annihilate it, however, Gaelic – the only language spoken continuously throughout the history of Scotland, once spoken by its founders and kings – still persists and holds the promise of reconnecting the ties of continuity severed in the past. The assimilation of traditional communities is not a simple matter of painlessly extracting one language and culture and transplanting an inherently superior replacement: the process can induce breaks between generations in families, discontinuities in a community's sense of place and self-confidence, and fractures in a person's identity and self-esteem.

> The deterioration of self-identity, and even more its total loss, bring with them an acute trauma. They promote the disintegration of the community and place it, in the last instance, in situations of alienation and of easy subjugation, where it is incapable of orienting itself sufficiently to act on its own behalf. In this way, while not implying a negation of the processes of change, possession of a sense of identity is an essential prerequisite for any group to exist and act on its own behalf.[8]

This loss of the soul of a culture is powerfully described by Iain Crichton Smith, envisioning what it would mean for his native community to be bereft of Gaelic:

> I imagine those who lose their language dying in the same way as the language dies, spiritless, without pride. One imagines the tourist then entering a world which would truly be inferior to his own. One imagines the beggars of the spirit, no longer real people in a real place. They will be shadows cast by an imperialistic language that is not their own. For if they speak a language that is not their own they are slaves in the very centre of themselves. They will have been colonised completely at the centre of the spirit, they will be dead, exiles, not abroad but in their own land, which will not reflect back the names they have given it.[9]

During the past several centuries of European imperialism, it was claimed that indigenous peoples were less deserving than the imperial races because their cultures were primitive, their economies undeveloped, their lands unimproved, and their very beings inferior. The manifest destiny of empires, it was argued, was to take over the lands of native peoples and rule them according to superior conceptions and methods. If the current state of the planet is a reflection of the stewardship of those supposedly superior races, that is condemnation enough. Although the meek may yet inherit the earth, the assertive have already squandered much of that inheritance during a minuscule blip of the history of humankind.

The concerted and sustained attack on the Gaelic language since the opening of the seventeenth century has usually been an attack on Highland culture itself, attempting to weaken the resolve of Gaels to sustain their traditions. Although many fled or capitulated in the face of hostile, hegemonic forces, others attempted to make creative use of traditional culture itself to resist domination and preserve their self-worth and self-determination.

Like many other cultures in a desperate struggle to survive, prophetic stories and songs nourished hopes that a day would come when the Gaels would return to their proper place of respect in the Scottish nation. Allusions to a saviour figure in Gaelic literature, in fact, have been argued to appear as early as the twelfth century, when Anglo-Normans took over so many of Scotland's national institutions.[10] Prophecies were prominent in the Gaelic songs composed to raise the spirits of Highlanders during the Jacobite Risings of the eighteenth century, assuring them that victory would not only restore the rightful king to the throne but bring an end to their persecution and allow for a new Gaelic Golden Age. Even after those aspirations were dashed on the field of Culloden elements of these prophecies were reformulated from time to time in hopeful expectation that some action – agitating for land reform, fighting in British regiments, or escaping through emigration – would bring relief.[11]

After a long struggle, Scotland's first Chair of Celtic was established at the University of Edinburgh in 1882. In the 1883 augural lecture to celebrate the achievement, the first holder of the chair, Donald MacKinnon, remarked on this significant milestone in the regaining of ground which had been lost to Gaelic:

> The history of the foundation of the Chair, of the difficulties which had to be surmounted, and of the success which finally crowned the efforts of the founder, have been a wonder to many. But perhaps even a greater wonder is that the institution of a Celtic Chair in Scotland has been delayed until now. [. . .] I would be prepared to maintain that the Gaelic language might, with advantage to the community, be used more largely in school and college than it has been. With exceptional opportunities for forming a judgment upon this question, I have long been of the opinion – an opinion based on the nature of the case, and on such experience as is available – that a policy which systematically ignores the native language in the schools, and which administers large grants of public money without taking security that the teacher is able to understand the children, cannot be defended on educational grounds.[12]

MacKinnon concluded the inaugural address by acknowledging the many years of campaigning and fundraising done by Professor Blackie, connecting his calling to an old Highland legend of the Fian (here referred to with the alternative form *Féinne*):

The Féinne were laid spell-bound in a cave which no man knew of. At the mouth of the cave hung a horn, which if ever any man should come and blow three times, the spell would be broken, and the Féinne would arise, alive and well. A hunter, one day wandering in the mist, came on this cave, saw the horn, and knew what it meant. He looked in and saw the Féinne lying asleep all round the cave. He lifted the horn and blew one blast. He looked in again, and saw that the Féinne had wakened, but lay still with their eyes staring, like that of dead men. He took the horn again, blew another blast, and instantly the Féinne all moved, each resting on his elbow. Terrified at their aspect, the hunter turned and fled homewards. He told what he had seen, and, accompanied by friends, went to search for the cave. They could not find it; it has never again been found; and so there still sit, each resting on his elbow, waiting for the final blast to rouse them into life, the spell-bound heroes of the old Celtic world.[13]

This prophecy challenges us to find that place of inner strength from which we can awaken the gifts left to us by our predecessors. It dares us to have the courage to reinvigorate a venerable tradition, one which can connect us to the best of what has come before us. It warns that creating a better future requires exertion and persistence, but it also reassures us that the possibility of renewal lies waiting for those who seek it.

APPENDIX A: GAELIC POETRY SAMPLER

This appendix contains a small sampling of the range of genres, subjects, and themes of the Scottish Gaelic poetic canon. I have chosen the items below according to several criteria: they do not appear in any of the anthologies of Scottish Gaelic literature that have appeared since the 1990s, few have been previously edited or translated into English, and most relate to significant historical events or circumstances relevant to the subjects in this book. I have attempted to represent the geographical breadth of Scottish Gaeldom and even include an item from Cape Breton.

These poems are given in approximate chronological order. Lines in the Gaelic texts are marked with the taxonomic codes of the Gaelic panegyric code given in Chapter Three.

1. PRAISE OF EÒIN DUBH MACGREGOR

This eulogy to Eòin Dubh MacGregor (†1519) of Glen Strae, one of several to this chieftain in the *Book of the Dean of Lismore*, is an excellent example of the syllabic praise poetry of the filidh in Classical Gaelic.[1] The Clan Gregor's claims to royal ancestry, as in their motto 'Is rìoghail mo dhream' ('My race is royal'), is clear in this poem and in the recurrence of the name Malcolm (used of three kings of Scotland) amongst MacGregor chieftains. Eòin's triumph over hostilities emanating from both Lowland adversaries and Highland rivals underlines his leadership skills in adverse conditions. Eòin is not just a 'hard man': he has knightly virtues, such as mercy, generosity to church and poets, and physical allure. There are ample allusions to the mytho-historical canon, as in the reference to the Greek ancestor of the Gaels and the Gaelic god of healing (Céacht), and the many comparisons to the Fian, especially the characters Fionn mac Cumhaill and Oscar.

1	*Ríoghacht ghaisgidh oighreacht Eòin*	G.1
	is aistreach dá dheoin a ghníomh	B.2
	Ní nach fhuil 'na bhriocht do chách	
	fuair iona riocht a sáth ríogh.	B.6

5	*MacGriogóir na gcraoiseach ngéar*	D.5
	taoiseach as tréan ar gach tír:	B.5, B.9
	Idir thóir agus creich Ghall	D.1
	is dóigh a bheith go mall mín.	B.1
9	*Éinrinn ghaisgidh Gaoidheal nGréag*	F.4, A.1, A.4
	leis nár maoidheadh méad a chlú;	B.2
	Fear as fearr ágh agus iocht	B.5, B.1
	an lámh a tír sliocht an rú.	F.6, B.6
13	*Seabhag déidgheal na dtrí ngleann*	F.2, A.1
	leis an léigthear geall gach gníomh;	
	Lámh as cródha i gcathaibh cniocht,	F.6, B.9, D.1
	flath as córa don t-sliocht ríogh.	B.1, B.6
17	*Ar mhac Phádraig na ngruaidh ndearg*	A.4, E.3
	'n uair ásas fearg i n-uair éacht	
	Na h-álaidh do-bheir 'na diaidh	D.1
	nocha slánuigh an liaigh Céacht.	
21	*Ua Mhaoil Choluim na ndearc gcorr,*	A.4, E.3
	ní sgaradh ré ór gan díth;	B.1
	Giolla dámhach sochrach seang	E.1
	an lámh as fearr um gach ní.	F.6, D
25	*Aicme Ghriogóir timchioll Eòin*	A.4
	ní mír ceilte a bhfeoil 's a bhfíon;	C.2
	Drong bhreathach ar nach léir locht:	C.1
	badh greathach gort mar a mbíodh.	D.1
29	*Clann Griogóir an dream nach tréith,*	≠B.9
	'n-am nach beidis réidh ré rígh;	øG.2
	Goill, giodh fuileachtach na fir,	
	ní chuireadh siad sin i mbrígh.	
33	*Ní mó leó Gaoidheil ná Goill,*	B.5
	na saoirfhir ó chloinn an ríogh;	B.6
	Aicme Ghriogóir na gcolg gcruaidh	A.4, D.5
	ó bhorb shluagh ní ghabhadh sníomh.	B.9

37	*Branán foirne na bhfear bhfial*	B.6, B.1
	oighre Ghriogóir na srian n-óir;	A.4, D.3
	Olc do dhuine ara ndéin creach:	
	meisde do neach théid 'na thóir.	D.1
41	*Flath Ghlinne Líomhunn na lann*	A.1, A.3, D.5
	sgiath bhríoghmhor nach gann ré cléir;	D.5, B.2
	Lámh mar Osgar is gach cath:	F.6, D.1
	is dá as cosmhail an flath féin.	
45	*Urraim einigh dá ghruaidh dheirg*	B.1, E.3
	do fhuair gan cheilg mar as cóir	
	Ar dhíolmhanacht do gach neach,	B.1
	ar thiodhlacadh each is óir.	B.1
49	*MacGriogóir an teaghlaich ghrinn*	A.4
	ní h-iongnadh linn 'na chúirt cliar;	B.2, C.1
	Ní fhoil coimmeas dá ucht geal	E.4
	acht an fear 'gá roibh an Fhian.	
53	*Ag sin trí freiteacha Finn:*	
	breith a ghill rí facas riamh;	B.3
	Lámh badh mhath iorghail i ngreis;	F.6, D.1
	dob ionmhain leis fuileach fiadh.	D.2
57	*Cosmhail a mhín is a mhodh*	B.1
	ris an rígh 'gá robh an Fhian;	B.6
	Ré h-ádh Mheic Ghriogóir na gcreach	A.2, D.1
	do-bheir rádh gach neach a mhian.	B.1
61	*Math as cubhaidh a rosg gorm*	E.3
	ré mac Cumhaill na gcorn bhfiar;	A.2, C.2
	Ionann a n-uabhar fá fhíon	C.2
	agus a rún ag díol chliar.	B.2
65	*Ionann a suirghe is a sealg*	E.1, D.2
	riú is ceard na bhFian:	
	Atá an rath ar sliocht an rú	B.6
	is math a gclú is a gciall.	B.2, B.8

69	*Eineach is eangnamh is iocht*	B.1
	do ceangladh ar a sliocht riamh;	B.3
	Fíon agus ciar agus mil	C.1
	a mian sin le sealgaibh fiadh.	D.2

73	*Fine Eòin as gasta gníomh*	
	iad mar mhacaibh ríogh na bhFian;	B.6
	Agus Eòin mar an Fionn fàidh	
	'na chionn ar gach dáimh dá riar.	B.2

77	*Giodh oirdhearc libh flaitheas Finn*	B.5
	do caitheadh ré linn na bhFian;	
	'S ar mhac Phádraig atá an rath:	
	do sháruigh sé gach math riamh.	B.4

81	*MacGriogóir na dtochar dteann,*	D.1
	ceann sochar ceall agus cliar;	B.2
	Taobh seang ara mbraitheadh bean,	E.1
	ó Ghleann Sraithe na bhfear bhfial.	A.3, B.1

85	*Córaide dhúinn breith le Eòin*	G.2
	is neithe dá dheoin do-ní	B.5
	Ag tiodhlacadh each is óir	B.1
	fá seach, mar as cóir i rígh.	B.6

89	*Rí nimhe mac Muire Óigh*	
	dlighidh mar as dóigh mo dhíon;	
	Mo bhreith san chathair gan cheilt	
	i bhfeil Athair mheic an Ríogh.	

(1–4) Eòin has inherited a warrior kingdom: he causes word of his deeds to travel far; no others can accomplish it even by magic; he completely satisfies his kingdom's qualifications as king.

(5–8) MacGregor of the sharp spears, mightiest war-leader over each land in both chasing and plundering non-Gaels; his nature is to be gentle and steady.

(9–12) The solo star of the Gaels from Greece, he does not boast of his fame; best in battle and most merciful, he is the hand of the land of princes.

(13–16) White-toothed hawk of the three glens [Glen Strae, Glen Lyon and Glen Orchy] who weighs in on every wager; the bravest hand in knights' battles, most even-handed prince of the royal race.

336

(17–20) When in trying times anger flushes the red cheeks of Patrick's son, not even the surgeon Céacht can heal the wounds that he delivers.

(21–24) Grandson of Malcolm of the stately eyes who gives away his gold generously, a slender, alluring young man, the best hand at everything.

(25–28) Clan Gregor encircles John and all see their meat and wine; a faultless, perceptive people who bring uproar wherever they go.

(29–32) Clan Gregor show no weakness if they disagree with a mighty lord; even if non-Gaels promise to draw blood, they are rendered worthless.

(33–36) They are not intimidated by either Gaels or non-Gaels, these nobles of royal ancestry; Clan Gregor of the hard blades, fierce troops do not make them wince.

(37–40) Gregor's heir of the golden bridles is the leader of the generous men; it is bad for any man to raid him, and even worse for anyone to go in pursuit of him.

(41–44) The prince of Glen Lyon of the blades, a mighty shield, generous to poets; a hand like Oscar in battle, yes, he [Oscar] is very like this prince.

(45–48) His magnanimity has won honour for his ruddy cheek, as is proper, since he has been generous to all, gifting horses and gold.

(49–52) MacGregor of the handsome household, it is not surprising that poets are in his hall; no one can compare to his bright breast except the leader of the Fian [i.e., Fionn].

(53–56) These are Fionn's three resolutions: no judgment of his sureties ever needed to be seen; his hand was good in a fight; he enjoyed the hunting of deer.

(57–60) His gentility and his manners are like those of the king of the Fian; during the prosperous career of the cattle-raiding MacGregor, each person need only speak to have his wish.

(61–64) His blue eye is a good match to [Fionn] mac Cumhaill of the curved drinking horns; they are alike in their refinement in wine and their goodwill in paying poets.

(65–68) They are alike in their wooing and in their hunting; the Fian's vocation suits them; fortune favours the line of prince, their reputation and judgment are good.

(69–72) Bounty and prowess and compassion are forever bound to their lineage; their wishes are for wine and wax candles, honey and hunting.

(73–76) Eòin's kindred of excellent deeds are like the young Fian, and Eòin is like the seer Fionn, rewarding every poet band.

(77–80) Although you may consider Fionn's leadership of the Fian to have been illustrious, Patrick's son is the fortune one; he has excelled other nobles.

(81–84) MacGregor of the hard skirmishes, provider of churches and poets, whose lean shape would attract the attention of a woman, from Glen Strae of the generous men.

(85–88) It is right for us to side with Eòin, who acts of his own will, gifting horses and gold to each person in turn, as is proper in a king.

(89–92) King of Heaven, son of the Virgin Mary, whose duty is my protection, take me to the [Heavenly] City where God the Father dwells.

2. 'I HATE . . .'

By enumerating a number of complaints, this didactic poem (in the rhetorical mode *teagasg*) serves to illustrate cultural mores and norms.[2] This poem is ascribed to 'Màiri nan Dàn', indicating a female endorsement for these standards, but it clearly has some connection to much older verses such as those recorded in the *Book of the Dean of Lismore*.[3]

1	'S fuath leam ceann-bheairt gun bhith cruaidh;	–D.5
	'S fuath leam sluagh nach buail creach;	–D.1
	'S fuath leam an cogadh no 'n sìth	
	Duine nach cuir nì mu seach.	–B.1
5	'S fuath leam bhith athaiseach a' triall;	
	'S fuath leam cléir air am miann bean;	
	'S fuath leam bhith 'n comann luchd-sgleò;	
	'S fuath leam bhith ri òl gun ghean.	–C.2

9	*Allta domhain ri droch shìd'*	
	'S fuath leam e gun chlachan-tairis;	
	'S fuath leam teanga leam-leat, mhìn	
	'S fuath leam balach breun aig banais.	–B.6
13	*'S fuath leam fleasgach is nì aig'*	–B.1
	Bhith 'na aonar a' fanachd;	
	'S fuath leam leabaidh gun bhriodal;	–E.1
	'S fuath leam cìochan gun bhainne.	
17	*Òganach suairce ri suirgheadh*	
	Air mnaoidh shuilbhear nan rosg mall,	E.3
	Nuair nach faigheadh e a chuid,	
	'S fuath leam a chuid bhith air chall.	
21	*'S fuath leam oinnseach gun òran,*	–C.3
	o-chòn gun tinneas,	
	Taigh mór gun aoidheachd,	–C.2
	Teudan gun bhinneas.	–C.3
25	*Cagar ri bodhar,*	
	Lobhar an còisridh,	
	Céile carrach	
	Cladhaire bòsdail.	–B.9
29	*Ban-tighearna labhar,*	–B.8
	Abhal gun ubhal,	
	Ceann-feadhna gealtach,	–B.9
	'N cearcall nach lùbadh –	
33	*Earradh gun iarrtas,*	–D.5
	Fiadhtachd gun fheòraich,	–B.1
	Aigne bhith sgaoilte	
	Aig fear nach saoilte bhith gòrach.	–B.8

(1–4) I hate a helmet that is not hard; I hate a warrior band that does not raid cattle; I hate a man who does not save some wealth in peace or war.

(5–8) I hate to travel at a slow pace; I hate clergy who lust for women; I hate to be in the company of idle talkers; I hate drinking without merriment.

(9–12) I hate a deep stream without stepping-stones in bad weather; I hate a two-faced smooth talker; I hate an obnoxious lad at a wedding.

(13–16) I hate a wealthy bachelor who remains single; I hate a bed without sweet-talk; I hate breasts that have no milk.

(17–20) A gentleman who courts an attractive, doe-eyed maiden: if he cannot get his share, I hate for his share to be lost.

(21–24) I hate a songless lass, and grumbling without a cause; a great house that is not hospitable, strings that do not produce melody.

(25–28) Whispering to the deaf, a leper at a party, a deceitful marriage partner, a boastful coward.

(29–32) A talkative peeress, a fruitless apple-tree, a skittish leader, the hoop that does not bend.

(33–36) Unwanted wares, unwarranted anger, a man with an unhinged mind who is not expected to be foolish.

3. ELEGY TO SIR DÙGHALL CAMPBELL

This terse elegy for Dùghall Campbell of Achadh nam Breac ('Auchinbreck') of Argyll first appeared in the 1776 *Eigg Collection* published by Raghnall Dubh MacDonald (see Plate 25). There were two chieftains of this name, one who lived 1617 to 1643, and another who lived from 1645 to *c.*1660. This short piece offers an evocative portrayal of the members and activities of the chieftain's hall, and, by portraying how it has declined in his absence, indirectly indicates what he was expected to support during his reign.

1	*'S uaigneach a-nochd Cathair Dhùghaill*	øC.5
	Chuaidh dùnadh ri ceòl 's ri aighear	øC.3
	Am brugh-sìdh amhlaidh deòraidh	øC.1
	Gun seirm, gun chòisir, gun tathaich.	øC.3, øC.5
5	*Gun chlàirseach 'gheinn de'n fhiodh chùbhraidh*	øC.3
	Gun seanchaidh, gun fhilidh-leabhair	øC.3
	Gun fhear-dàn' anns a' bhrugh òirdheirc	øC.1
	Gun mhnài bhinn-cheòl, gun lèigh-cabhair.	øC.3

9	*A Dhùghaill òig mhic Dhonnchaidh chliùitich*	A.2, A.4, B.2
	'S i do chùis bu mhòr ri h-iomradh	B.2
	Basraich bhan fo ghàirich leanabh	H.5
	'S truagh am bannal ud mu d' thimcheall.	H.5

(1–4) Dùghall's seat is lonely tonight: it has been closed to music and merriment; the fairy mound is like an exile, without music, retinue or visitors.

(5–8) Without a harp made of blocks of the fragrant wood, without an historian, or a book-learned high poet; without a performing poet in the bright hall, without singing women, or a helpful physician.

(9–12) O young Dubhghall son of renowned Donnchadh, to speak of you is a weighty matter; the sound of women striking their palms, the wail of children, sorrowful is the group that surrounds you.

4. SONG ABOUT THE MASSACRE OF GLENCOE

This song about the 1692 Massacre of Glencoe (one of a number of variants) was probably preserved by one of the many MacDonald tradition-bearers who migrated to Nova Scotia in the early nineteenth century.[4] It is attributed to Aonghus mac Alasdair Ruaidh. It is in *iorram* metre and was sung to the same tune as Màiri nighean Alasdair Ruaidh's song 'Gur muladach sgìth mi'.[5] In perpetrating the massacre Campbell of Glenlyon was unenthusiastically carrying out government orders under duress. Although the poem is a bitter indictment of the Campbells, the 'vengeance' called for by the MacDonald poet is capital punishment via the 'Maiden' (a guillotine) under the supervision of the civil authorities, rather than clan feuding.

1	*'S mi 'am shuidh' air a' chnocan*	
	Chaidh mo léirsinn an olcas	
	Is mi mar aon mhac an trotain air m' fhàgail.	
4	*Tha mi 'coimhead a' ghlinne*	
	Far am bu aighearach sinne	
	Gus an d' aom oirnn an fhine 'n robh 'n fhàilinn.	
7	*Rinn na Duibhnich oirnn leadairt*	
	Bha 'n fhuil uasal 'ga leagail	B.6
	'S bha Gleann Lìomhann 'na sheasamh mar cheannard.	A.1

10	*Ach nam b' ionnan d' ur macnas*	
	'S nuair bha mise 'nur taice	
	Nàile! Rachadh iad dhachaidh 'nan deann-ruith.	D.1
13	*Bhiodh MacFhilip le 'bhrataich*	D.5
	Air tùs na fine neo-ghealtaich	≠B.9
	Ged a fhuair iad an nasgadh le ainneart.	
16	*A MhicEanraig nam feadan*	A.2, D.5
	'S tric a bha mi 's tu beadradh	
	Leis a' mhuinntir a ghreas do'n taigh-shamhraidh.	
19	*Bha Clann Iain nan gadhar*	A.2, D.2
	Rinn na h-uaislean a thadhal	C.5
	'S iad 'gan riasladh le cuthach gun chairdeas.	øG.2
22	*Dh'fhàg sibh marcaich' 'n eich uaibhrich*	D.3
	Reubt' air ruighe nan ruadh-bhoc	H.1
	Ann an sneachda trom fuar nam beann arda.	
25	*Dh'fhàg sibh làraichean dubha*	øC.1
	Far am b' àbhaist duibh suidhe	
	'N comann luchd an fhuil bhuidhe chais amhlaich.	E.3
28	*Fhir Bhail' Fhearna nam badan*	A.1, A.3
	Bu cheann-fheadhn' thu air brataich	B.5, D.5
	Is chaidh smùid chur ri d' aitreabh 'na smàlaibh.	
31	*Bha do cho-bràthair guailte*	H.1
	Deagh fhear Baile nam Fuaran	
	Leam is goirt e, 's an uair air dhroch càradh.	
34	*Ach mas deònach le'r Rìgh e*	
	Bidh là eile 'ga dhìol sin	
	Agus Maighdeanan lìobhte 'cur cheann diubh.	
37	*Bidh na Tuirc air an dathadh*	F.2
	'S bidh Rìgh Uilleam 'na laidhe	
	'S bidh cùird mhór air an amhaich dhen ain-toil.	

40   *B' e mo rogha sgeul éibhneis*
     Moch Di-Luain is mi 'g éirigh
     Gun robh againn Rìgh Seumas 's na Fraingich.

43   *Chiteadh iomain ball achaidh*
     Air fir mheallt' nam balg craicinn
     Loisg ar n-arbhar 's ar n-aitreabh 's a' gheamhradh.

(1–3) I sit on the hillock, my eyesight failing me, left behind like an only son.

(4–6) I gaze at the glen where we were once merry, until the blemished clan descended upon us.

(7–9) The Campbells massacred us, noble blood was shed, under the supervision of Campbell of Glenlyon.

(10–12) If only you prospered as you did when I was with you, they would be driven off in a rush!

(13–15) MacKillop would have his war-banner in the vanguard of the valiant clan, even though they were oppressed by violence.

(16–18) O Henderson of the bagpipe chanters, often did we sport and play with those folk who hastened to the summer abode.

(19–21) Clan Donald of Glencoe, owners of greyhounds, who called upon the nobility, were torn asunder by inhumane insanity.

(22–24) You left the horseman of the proud spirited chargers gored on the shielings of the roe-bucks in the cold, heavy snows of the great mountains.

(25–27) You left charred ruins where you were once seated in the company of the people of flowing, ringleted, blonde hair.

(28–30) O tacksman of Baile Fhearna of the thickets, you were the war-bannered war-leader, and your abode was burnt to ashes.

(31–33) Your friend, the tacksman of Baile nam Fuaran, was consumed by fire; an ill hour it was that grieves me.

(34–36) But if the king grants it, a day to avenge it will come when the sharpened Maiden will behead them.

(37–39) The boars [Campbells] will be stained and King William brought down, and heavy cords around their necks bringing them misery.

(40–42) It would be my wish to hear good news as I awoke on Monday morning that we had King James and the French.

(43–45) The false men of skin bags who burnt our corn and our homes in the winter would be driven back.

5. SONG TO AILEAN OF MOYDART

This anonymous song was composed in praise of Ailean of Moydart, the fourteenth chief of Clanranald who fell at Sheriffmuir in 1715.[6] It was popular in Uist and has continued to be popular, in a more 'domesticated' form, in Cape Breton.[7] Although it has the appearance of having originated as a man's song it was preserved as a waulking song (in *luinneag* metre) and exhibits the non-linear shift in focus typical of this form. It is sung as repeated couplets (1+2, 2+3, etc) followed by the chorus (which is not given here), each line connected by 'a' or 'ea' assonance in the penultimate syllable.

1	*Chì mi, chì mi, chì mi thallad,*	
	Chì mi na féidh air a' bhealach,	D.2
	'S an gìomanach fhéin 'gan leanailt	D.2
	Le 'ghunna caol 's le 'mhìol-choin sheanga	D.5, D.2
5	*Dhìreadh bheann 's a theàrnadh bhealach*	
	Dh'fhàgadh tu an damh donn gun anail	D.2
	Air an fhraoch a' call na fala	
	Bhiodh do mhiol-choin sgìth 'gan leanailt	D.2
9	*Bhiodh do ghillean sgìth 'gan tarraing*	G.1
	Anns an anmoch tigh'nn gu d' bhaile	
	Far am faighte féidh gun ghainne.	C.2
	Òl is ceòl is comhradh tairis	C.2, C.3
13	*'S beag an t-iongnadh tu bhith smiorail*	
	'S tu mac-oighre Mac 'ic Ailein	A.4
	Ogha 's iar-ogha nam fear fearail	A.4
	Dhèanadh euchd an streup nan lannaibh	D.1

17	'S car do thu do MhacLeòid na h-Earadh	G.2
	'S do Mhac Dhomhnaill Duibh o'n darach	G.2, A.3
	'S tha thu 'd bhràthair do na fearaibh	
	Dhèanadh éirigh leat gu h-ealamh	G.2
21	'N t-àrmann treun b' e fhéin an ceannard	B.9, B.5
	'S an laoch gleust' o Ghleanna Garadh	A.1
	Dhèanadh reubadh air na Gallaibh	D.1
	Latha Raon Ruairidh fhuair sibh an ceannas	D.1
25	Chuir sibh ruaig gu luath 'nan deannaibh	D.1
	Sgathadh ghualann, chluas is cheannaibh.	D.1

I see deer yonder in the pass and the hunter chasing them with his narrow gun and slender hounds; climbing mountains and descending the passes, you would leave the brown stag breathless and losing blood on the heather; your hunting hounds would grow tired chasing them and your gillies would grow tired hauling them in the twilight coming to your abode, where there would be no limit to deer meat, and drinking and music and gentle conversation; it is no wonder that you are manly! You are the heir of Clanranald, grandson and great-grandson of the virile men, who achieve great deeds in the contest of blades; you are related to MacLeod of Harris and to Lochiall of the oaks; you are brother to those men who would rise immediately to your aid; the brave soldier is himself the leader, and the accomplished hero from Glengarry who would tear apart the non-Gaels; you were given leadership at the Battle of Killiecrankie and sent them running off in haste, lopping off shoulders, ears and heads.

6. CHARM OF LASTING LIFE GIVEN TO AILEAN OF MOYDART

According to a tradition preserved in South Uist and recorded by the folklorist Calum MacLean (of the School of Scottish Studies, University of Edinburgh) from Domhnall MacIntyre in 1959, the following charm was recited over Ailean of Moydart before he went to the Battle of Sheriffmuir in 1715 by a wise woman in Benbecula.[8] The charm did not work when a bullet struck him, it was said, because he lacked absolute confidence in its power – surely a warning to all who lack faith in native tradition.

1	Sian a chuir Brìghid m'a dalt,	G.5
	Sian a chuir Moire m'a mac,	G.5
	Sian a chuir Mìcheal m'a sgéith,	G.5
	Sian a chuir Mac Dhé mu Chathair Nèamh.	G.5

5   *Sian ro chlaidheamh,*
Sian ro shaighead
Sian ro fhraoich 's ro bhà
Sian ro shìthich,
Sian ro shaoidhtich,
Sian ro bhlìdhtich.

11   *Sian ro bhaoghal bàthaidh,*
Sian ro sgrìob na roide ruaidhe,
Sian ro reubadh luathas na Finne.

14   *Cochall Chaluim Chille mar riut*   G.5
Is cochall Mhìcheil mhìl umad   G.5
Is cochall Chrìosd, a ghràidh, 'gad chumail G.5
Gad dhìon bho do chùlaibh
Bho do chùlaibh gu d' aghaidh
Bho mhullach do chinn gu d' urla
Is gu dubh-bhonn do chaise.

21   *Is eilean thu air muir*   F.4
Is tulaich thu air tìr   F.4
Is fuaran thu am fàsach   F.4
Is slàinte tu dh'an tinn.   E.1

25   *Is mór eagal am beatha dhaibh-san*   B.4
A chitheadh a' cholann mu'n téid an t-sian
Oir tha cobhair Chaluim Chille mar riut G.5
Is tha cochall Mhìcheil mhìl umad   G.5
Is a sgiath mhór 'gad dhìdeann.

(1–4) A charm that Brighid put on her fosterling [i.e., Christ], that Mary put on her son, that Saint Michael put on his shield, that the Son of God put around the City of Heaven.

(5–10) A charm against sword, arrow, rage and folly; a charm against fairy folk, wizards, and wasters.

(11–13) A charm against drowning, the wound of red bog-myrtle, and furious blows of the Fian.

(14–20) May the armour of Columba be with you, the armour of valiant Saint Michael be around you, and the armour of Christ protect you, my beloved, shielding you in front and back, from the top of your head to the soles of your feet.

(21–24) On the sea, you are an island; on land, you are a hillock; in the wilderness, you are a well-spring; you are health to the sick.

(25–29) Those who see your charmed body will be in fear of their lives, since you are allied with Columba and the armour of valiant Saint Michael is around you and his great shield protects you.

7. PRAISE AND CENSURE OF MASHIE

These two short poems[9] on the river Mashie, a tributary of the mighty Spey, were composed by Lachlann MacPherson (*c*.1723–*c*.1795), the tacksman of Strathmashie, who assisted his kinsman James Macpherson in collecting Ossianic materials in the Highlands. The Mashie ran near Strathmashie house and when in spate could be dangerous, flooding and carrying away house and goods. These short songs were probably sung to the air of 'Mhnathan a' Ghlinne Seo'.

Moladh Mathaisidh ('Praise of Mashie')

1   *Mhathaisidh bhòidheach gheal,*
     Bhòidheach gheal, bhòidheach gheal,
     Mhathaisidh bhòidheach gheal,
     B' ait leam bhith làmh riut.

5   *Nuair a rachainn 'am shiubhal*
     B' e siud mo cheann-uidhe
     Na bh' air bràigh Choire Bhuidhe
     Agus ruigh Allt na Ceardaich.

9   *Gum bu phailt bha mo bhuaile*
     Do chrodh druim-fhionn is guaill-fhionn
     Mar siud 's mo chuid chuachag
     Dol mun cuairt dhoibh 's an t-samhradh.

(1–4) Fair, beautiful Mashie [4 times] I love to be beside you.

(5–8) When I would set off to travel, my destination would be the Brae of Coire Buidhe and the shieling of Allt na Ceardaich.

(9–13) My cattle-fold was well stocked with cattle of white backs and white shoulders, and likewise are my [plentiful] share of cuckoos flying around you in the summer time.

Mi-moladh Mathaisidh ('Censure of Mashie')

1   *Mhathaisidh fhrògach dhubh,*
     Fhrògach dhubh, fhrògach dhubh,
     Mhathaisidh fhrògach dhubh,
     'S mór rinn thu 'chall domh.

5   *Rinn thu m' eòrna a mhilleadh*
     'S mo chuid ghabhrag air sileadh
     Is cha d' fhàg thu sguab tioram
     Do na chinnich do bharr dhomh.

9   *Cha robh lochan no caochan*
     A bha 'ruith leis an aonach
     Nach do chruinnich an t-aon làn
     A thoirt aon uair do shàth dhut.

13   *Rinn thu òl an taigh Bheathain*
     Air leann 's uisge-beatha
     'S garbh an tuilm sin a sgeith thu
     'S a ghabhail-rathaid Di-Màirt oirnn.

(1–4) Black, crater-pitted Mashie [4 times], you have brought me great destruction.

(5–8) You spoiled my barley, my sheaves of corn have fallen, and you left not a single dry sheaf of all of my harvest for me.

(9–12) There was no lochan or streamlet that ran down the hill that did not gather altogether in order to satisfy your thirst.

(13–16) You went to drink ale and whisky in Beaton's house and savagely discharged the contents, taking leave of us on Tuesday.

8. 'It Was In A Dream'

This poignant song of unrequited love is one of the most powerful in Gaelic, full of stark images of intense emotion, ranging from sorrow to erotic sexuality, from vengefulness to stoic grief.[10] It is in the voice of a sailor who draws on marine symbolism; it was most likely composed in the eighteenth or early nineteenth century, although there is no way to be sure of a date of composition. Alan Bruford (of the School of Scottish Studies, University of Edinburgh) recorded it in 1965 from Mrs

Archie Munro of the island of South Uist. She was our one and only source for this beautiful jewel. It is in *meòrachadh* 'remembrance' mode and in *òran* metre.

1   *Sann a' bhruadar mi raoir:*
      An eal' air a' chuan, is i 'snàmh,
     'S a h-aghaidh gu tìr –
      Bha mo leannan is mi fhìn mar sgaoil.

5   *Gur e mis' tha fo ghruaim*
      Bidh mi sineach a' luaidh an-dràst'
     Gur e stoirm is droch uair
      Tha 'gad shìor-chumail bhuam-s', a ghràidh.

9   *Tha mo làmhan cho sgìth*
      Is nach urrainn dhomh inns' an-dràst'
     Is mi ri tarraing nan ròp
      Is ri cumail nan seòl an àird.

13   *Tha 'n léine ri m' chùl*
      Cho fliuch 's nì burn no sàl
     Is mi ri iarraidh dol sìos
      Far bheil nighean mo ghaoil a' tàmh.

17   *Gur e brìodal do bheòil*
      A mheall mi 's mi òg is faoin
     Ach nam faighinn mo mhiann
      Bhiodh m' acraichean a' triall do chuim.

21   *Thug thu gealladh as ùr*
      'S chaidh an comann air chùl a bha -
     Gura fhada bho'n uair
      A mheall iad thu bhuam-s' a ghràidh.

25   *Cha toir mi ort binn*
      Ach innis an fhìrinn réidh -
     Cha bhi naidheachd ri inns'
      Aig fear eil' orm fhìn mu d' dheidhinn.

(1–4) I saw it in a dream last night: A swan afloat on the ocean with her face to the shore as I was torn from my beloved.

(5–8) Let me speak of it now and of the sadness I feel – a storm and wild weather held you far away from me.

(9–12) I can hardly express it: my hands are so weary from handling the ropes and keeping the sails erect.

(13–16) The shirt on my back is drenched, soaking wet, and I want to go down to where my darling girl abides.

(17–20) It was the sweet nothings of your mouth that deceived me when I was young and naive, but if I had my wish my anchors would be ripping your flesh.

(21–24) You have taken a new vow and turned your back on our love – such a long time ago they turned you against me.

(25–28) I will not pass judgment on you but tell me the honest truth – I will not allow another man to speak ill of me for your sake.

9. 'THE BRANCH'

This song[11] was composed by Marairead Cameron, who was born at the farm of Clashgour, Glen Orchy. She seems to have retired to Callander. This song is remarkable but hardly typical in its praise of Christ using very powerful tree imagery (often with erotic undertones), reflecting the harnessing of the Gaelic panegyric code and traditional cosmology for religious purposes. It also indicates the rich natural environment in which the author lived in Argyllshire, Lochaber, and Stirlingshire, whose natural flora is more abundant than most of the Hebrides.[12]

1	*Bho bhonn* Iesse *bhrist a-mach*	
	Am Faillein gasda, ùr;	F.1
	Fìor chrann uaine, taghta, luachmhor	F.1
	'S airidh e air cliù;	B.2
	Meangan uasal, torach, buadhmhor	B.6, E.1
	'S e gach uair fo dhrùchd	E.1
	A gheugan dosrach sìnte suas	F.1
	'S iad tarraing uaithe sùigh.	
9	*Seo an Crann am measg nan crann*	F.1
	Air àrdachadh gu mòr	
	Faillein sùghmhor, maiseach, cùbhraidh	E.1
	Taitneach, ùrar, òg;	E.1
	Àlainn, ciatach, 's e mo sgèimheach	E.1
	Miannaicht' air gach dòigh	E.1
	Gun fheachd' no fiaradh, ruaidh' no crìonadh	≠E.1, ≠E.5
	Gun ghaoid, gun ghiamh, gun ghò.	

17	*Meangan prìseil, miann na frìthe*	F.1
	'S e gu dìreach 'fàs	E.5
	E air sìneadh mach a gheugan	E.4
	'S iad gu lèir fo bhlàth;	E.1
	Nach mothaich tart ri àm an teas	
	Nach searg 's nach seac gu bràth	E.1
	Aig uisge sèimh tha e a' tàmh	
	'S cha tiormaich meud an tràsg'.	
25	*Tha abhainn fhìorghlan 'ruith m'a chrìochaibh*	
	De'n fhìor-uisg' shoilleir, bheò	
	'Cur subhachais an cridh' gach aoin	
	A gheabh dhi taom r'a òl;	
	Tha slàint' as ùr na 'dhuillich chùbhraidh	E.1
	Dh'anam brùit' fo leòn;	
	Beatha 's ìoc-shlàint dhoibhs' fo 'n iargain;	E.1
	'S dream gun lùths gheabh treòir.	
33	*Meangan cliùiteach 's e air lùbadh*	F.1, B.2
	Le ùr-mheas chum an làir	E.1
	Toirt toraidh thruim gach àm 's a' bhliadhn'	E.1
	'S gu sìorruidh a' toirt fàis;	E.1
	Tha e bhrìoghmhor 's mòr a mhìlseachd	E.1
	Do gach linn is àl;	B.1
	'S gach eun tha glan am measg na coill	
	Gheibh iad fo'n chraoibh seo sgàil.	B.1
41	*Crann ro thaitneach 'sgaoil ro fharsaing*	F.1, E.1
	Mach o chuan gu cuan;	
	'S ann fo 'sgàile gheabhar fasgadh	B.1
	Taitneach do luchd-cuairt.	C.5
	Tha 'àirde ruigheachd chum nan nèamh	
	'S thar nèamh nan nèamh a bhuaidh	
	Tha 'mhaise 's àilleachd a' toirt barr	E.1
	Air gach crann dh'fhàsas suas.	B.4
49	*Crann ro bhrìoghar e da-rìreadh*	F.1, E.2
	Bho'n sruth mìltean buaidh;	
	Nas mils' gu mòr na 'mhil 's na cìribh	E.1
	Tha 'n ìoc-shlaint a thig uaith;	
	Tha sruithean sòlais ruith gach lò uaith;	
	Do'n anam leòinte, thruagh,	B.1
	'S na h-uile h-aon a nì dhiubh òl	
	Bidh aca sòlas buan.	B.1

57	*Crann ro luachmhor, nach gabh gluasad*	F.1, E.2
	'S nach luaisg an doinionn àrd;	E.2
	Cha dean stoirm a fhrèumhan fhuasgladh	E.2
	'S cha chaill e 'shnuadh no 'bhlàth.	E.1
	E suidhichte air slèibhtibh Isreil	E.2
	Le làimh an Ti is Àird';	G.5
	'S cha tèid am feasd a ghearradh sìos	
	No chaoidh a spìon' as 'àit'	E.2
65	*An crann is rìomhach o'n stoc is rìoghail'*	F.1, B.6
	Tha 's an fhrìth a' fàs;	
	Gach crann 's an fhrìth a' tarraing brìgh uaith	B.1
	Neirt is sùigh gach là;	E.2
	Fo dhubh'r a gheugan gheabh na fèumaich	B.1
	Beatha, rèite, 's blàths;	
	Fo sgàil a thròcair thig gach seòrsa	B.1
	'S bidh iad beò gu bràth.	
73	*S e 'n sgeul is prìseil' chaidh riamh innseadh*	B.2
	'S e 'na fhìrinn bhuain	
	Gur e an tì so Righ nan Rìghrean	B.6
	Sìth is glòir a shluaigh;	
	Strìochdaidh cinnich dhà is treubhan	D.1
	'S bheir fo ghèill gach sluagh	D.1, B.4
	Is slòigh nan nèamhan bheir gu lèir dhà	
	Urram 's gèill bhith-bhuan.	

(1–8) The fine young shoot broke out from Jesse's trunk; the precious, green, chosen, true branch; he deserves praise; a noble fertile triumphant branch, eternally dewy, his leafy branches stretched upwards, drawing moisture from them.

(9–16) This is the greatly exalted branch amongst branches, a sappy, elegant, fragrant branch, pleasant, fresh, young; beautiful, handsome, he is my handsome one, desirable in every way; without contortion, defect or withering, stainless, faultless, honourable.

(17–24) Precious branch, darling of the forest, growing straight, stretching his blooming branches outward; they don't register thirst during the heat, never dry up or wither; He dwells at calm water and won't desiccate despite poor weather.

(25–32) A pure stream of pure clear living water runs around his bounds putting cheer in everyone's heart who takes a drink from it; renewed health is in his fragrant leaves for the battered wounded soul; Life and healing for those in pain, and listless people will find strength.

(33–40) Renowned branch which is bent towards the ground with fresh fruit, giving a heavy harvest all year long and constantly giving growth; he is superb, his sweetness is great, to every generation and race; and every bird in the wood that is pure will find shade beneath this tree.

(41–48) Very pleasing branch which spread so wide outwards, from sea to sea; shelter is found is under his shade, shelter that pleases travellers; his height reaches to the heavens and his virtue excels the heaven of heavens; his beauty excels all other upward-growing trees.

(49–56) Excellent tree he is truly, from whom stream thousands of virtues; far sweeter than honey in the comb is the medicine that comes from him; streams of solace run from him daily for the wounded, wretched soul; everyone who drinks from them will have lasting solace.

(57–64) Priceless branch that cannot be budged, which the high gale does not toss; no storm can untie his roots and he won't lose his flower or colour; he is situated on the slopes of Israel by the hand of the Highest One; he will never be cut down or ever be rooted out.

(65–72) The beautiful branch from the most royal stock that grows in the forest; every tree in the forest draws strength and moisture from him every day; under the shadow of his branches the needy will get life, warmth and comfort; under the shade of his mercy all kinds come and they will be alive forever.

(73–80) The most precious story ever told, and it is the eternal truth: that this one is the King of Kings; peace and glory of his host; nations will submit to him and he will defeat every legion; the heavenly hosts will submit totally to him honour and deference forever.

10. A Song to the Big Sheep

This song was composed by Donnchadh Buidhe Chisholm of Strathglass *c.*1800 before he emigrated to Nova Scotia.[13] Although not the earliest Clearance protest, it is one of the harshest and most detailed. Like many others of this period, it castigates the aristocracy for evicting Highlanders, who proved their effectiveness in the British regiments, in favour of sheep. It contrasts the conditions and leaders of the past, including local Catholic priests, unfavourably with the new regime. It ends by cursing the sheep and the men who own them with a list of ailments. Due to its excessive length (128 lines), only a portion is given here.

1   *G'e h-aon rinn an duanag, chaidh e tuathal an tòs,*
    Nach do chuimhnich na h-uaislean dha'm bu dual a bhith mòr;   –B.1, –B.3
    Nam biodh feum air neart dhaoin' ann an caonnaig no'n tòir   G.1, D.1
    'S iad a sheasadh an cruadal, 's lannan cruaidhe 'nan dòrn. [. . .]   D.1, D.5

29   *Gur a tric tha mi 'smaointinn air an dùthaich a th' ann*
    Tha 'n-diugh fo na caoirich, eadar raointean is ghleann,   –C.6
    Gun duine bhith làthair dhe'n àlach a bh'ann   øG.1
    Ach coin agus caoirich 'gan slaodadh gu fang.

33   *'S ann tha adhbhar a' mhulaid aig na dh'fhuirich 's an àit'*
    Gun toil-inntinn gun taic ach fo chasan nan Gall;
    Bhon a dh'fhalbh an luchd-eaglais bha freasdalach dhaibh
    Cò a ghabhas an leth-sgeul nuair bhios iad 'nan càs?   øB.1

37   *Gur lìonmhor sonn àlainn chaidh àrach bho thùs*
    An teaghlach an àrmainn a bha tàmh an Cnoc Fhionn   A.4, A.2, A.1
    'S bhon a dh'fhalbh na daoin' uaisle, chaidh an tuath air an glùin   øB.1
    'S gum bheil iad bhon uair sin gun bhuachaille cùil. [. . .]   øB.5

45   *Dh'fhalbh na cinn-fheadhna b' fhearr èisdeachd 's a' chùirt*   øB.1
    An ceann-teaghlaich bu shine dhe'n fhine b'fhearr cliù;   A.4, B.2
    Tha gach aon a bha taitneach air an tasgadh 's an ùir
    'S iad mar shoitheach gun chaptain, gun acfhuinn, gun stiùir. [. . .]   øB.5

69   *Chan eil buachaillean aca no taic air an cùl*   øB.5
    Bhon a leigeadh fir Shasainn a[m] fasgadh an Dùin
    'S e naidheachd is ait leam mar thachair do'n chùis
    Gun do shleamhnaich an casan a-mach dhe'n ghrunnd.

73   *Tha mi an dòchas gun tionndaidh a' chùis mar as còir*
    Gun tig iad a dh'ionnsaigh an dùthchais bho thòs;   B.3
    Na fiùranan àlainn chaidh àrach ann òg   F.1
    Gun cluinneam sibh 'thàmh ann an àros nam bò.   C.1

77   *Ged a thuit a' chraobh-mhullaich 's ged a fhrois i gu barr*   F.1
    Thig planndais a stoca an toiseach a' bhlàiths;
    Ma gheibh iad mo dhùrachd mar a dhùrachdainn daibh
    Bidh iad shuas an Cnoc Fhionn 's e bhur dùthchas an t-àit'   A.1, B.3

81	*Agus Iain Chnoic Fhionn, bith-sa misneachail treun,*	A.1, B.9
	Glac dùthchas do sheanar, 's gu meal thu a stéidh;	B.3
	An t-àit' robh do sheòrsa, bhon òige gu'n eug,	
	Am mac an ionad an athar, suidh 's a' chathair 's na tréig. [. . .]	
89	*Dh'fhalbh gach toil-inntinn a bh'aig ar sinnsreadh bho thòs,*	øB.3
	'S e mo bharail nach till iad ris na linntinnean òg';	
	Chan eil fiadhach ri fhaotainn ann an aonach nan ceò;	øD.2
	Chuir na caoirich air fuadach buidheann uallach nan cròc. [. . .]	øD.2
97	*Leam is duilich mar thachair, nach d' thàinig sibh nall*	
	Mun deachaidh ur glacadh le acanan teann;	
	Nam biodh uachdaran dligheach 'na shuidh air ur ceann	
	Cha rachadh ur sgapadh gu Machair nan Gall.	
101	*Cha b' i 'Mhachair bu taitneach le na Glaisich dhol ann*	
	Nuair a thigeadh an samhradh, ach bràighe nan gleann	
	Bhiodh aran, ìm, agus càise, 'gan àrach gun taing	
	Crodh-laoigh air an àirigh, bliochd is dàire anns an àm.	C.6
105	*Chan eil 'nur ceann-cinnidh ach duine gun treòir*	–B.5
	Tha fo smachd nan daoine-uaisle chuireas tuathal a shròn	–B.5
	Nach iarradh dhe'n t-saoghal ach caoirich air lòn	–G.1
	An àite na tuatha a bha buan aig a sheòrs.	
109	*Sgrìos air na caoirich às gach taobh dhen Roinn Eòrp*	
	Cloimh is cnàmhag is caoile, at 'nam maodal is cròic,	
	Gabhail dalladh 'nan sùilean, agus mùsg air an sròin	
	Madadh ruadh agus fireun a' cur dìth air a' phòr.	

(1–4) Whoever composed a song and forgot the nobility, whose duty was to be great, he went wrong from the start: if there was call for men's brawn, whether in a scrape or a chase, they are the ones who would stand to the challenge with iron swords in their hands. [. . .]

(29–32) Often do I think about this country that is today occupied by sheep, both field and glen; none of the old population remain, only dogs herding the sheep to the fank.

(33–36) Those who have stayed behind have reason to be sad, lacking support and happiness, oppressed by the non-Gael; since the churchmen who ministered to them have departed, who will listen to their complaint when they are sore pressed?

(37–40) There is many a winsome youth who was reared in the warrior-family who inhabited Knockfin; since the native gentry have departed, the peasantry have been brought to their knees, and have been ever since without a shepherd. [. . .]

(45–48) The chieftains who were best at hearing judgments in the court have departed, along with the head of the most renowned household; each one deserving of praise has been buried, and the people are like a vessel without a captain, rigging, or rudder. [. . .]

(69–72) They have no shepherd or support since the English have been let inside of the chieftain's abode; the tale of this matter is strange to me: their feet slipped from under them.

(73–76) I hope that the matter will be resolved so that justice prevails and they will return to their original *dùthchas*; those handsome saplings who were raised there, may I hear them inhabiting the grand hall.

(77–80) Although the top-most tree has fallen, and it has been stripped completely, new growth from its stock will come with the return of warmth; if they are granted all that I would hope for them they will be up on Knockfin, as that is their *dùthchas*.

(81–84) John of Knockfin, take courage: seize your grandfather's *dùthchas*, and make use of his foundation; sit on the seat appropriate to you, from father to son, from birth to death, and do not abandon it. [. . .]

(89–92) Every joy that our ancestors enjoyed from time immemorial has vanished and I do not expect them to return as they were; no hunting is allowed on the moor and the sheep have banished the noble, antlered band [i.e., the deer]. [. . .]

(97–100) I am very sorry about what has happened, and that you did not emigrate before you were constrained by harsh restrictions; if you were ruled by the rightful chieftains you would not be driven off to the Lowlands.

(101–104) It is not to the Lowlands that the Strathglass folk would wish to go when the summer comes, but into the hills; they would live independently on bread, butter, and cheese, calves would be in the shielings, dairy and calving all in good time.

(105–108) Your chieftain is worthless, controlled by élite who point him in the wrong direction and whose only wish is to put sheep on the hill in place of the peasantry that his kind had always known.

(109–112) Destruction to the sheep from every part of Europe: mange, consumption and distemper on them, may they suffer swelling in their guts and horns, blindness in their eyes, and gore in their noses; may their brood be devastated by foxes and eagles.

11. Dispraise of the Tobacco Pipe

This poem[14] was probably part of a local debate on the virtues and vices of tobacco, of which Highlanders were said to be excessively fond as early as the seventeenth century. The author, Domhnall Dubh, was the tacksman of Tom na Craoibh in Strath Braan, Perthshire, early in the nineteenth century, attesting to the resilience of Gaelic on the Lowland border. The song is in the rhetorical mode of *mì-mholadh* 'dispraise' and it contains anti-smoking sentiments which are strikingly familiar in the present.

1 *Pìob thombac: pìob gun tlachd!*
  Cha bhithinn-s 'gam thachd fo m' shròn leath'
 Dhèanainn a spairt 's ann fo m' chas
  'S bheirinn srac 's a gheòt di.

5 *Cha bhithinn 'gam phian' 'ga glanadh 's 'ga lìon'*
  Toileachadh miann na feòl leath'
 Cha bhithinn dhi 'm thràill a dh'oidhch' agus là
  'S cha toir i dhomh dàil Dì-Domhnaich.

9 *Cha bhithinn-s' ri strì a' call mo bhrìgh*
  Caitheamh mo nì le gòraich
 Ceò fo m' shùil agus toit rium dlùth,
  Is miosa na cùl na òtraich.

13 *Gur lachdann am maol, le casan ro chaol,*   −E.3, −E.4
  Neul an aoig tha comhl' rith'   −E.1
 Bu duine gun chiall thug cumhachd di riamh
  'S ann aige bha miann na gòraich.

17 *Chan eil oisinn no iùc an sporan gu chùl*
  Às nach toir i gu dlùth na gròtan   −C.2
 'S nan dèanadh i feum ach ceò chur ri speur
  Cha chunntainn fhéin an corr rith'.

21 *Cha bhi mi 's an tìm nas faide ga binn*
  'S iomadh caileag dhonn ghrinn gheibh toit di
 'S nam bithinn-s' na h-àit' cha leiginn i 'm dhàil
  'S cha tugainn-se fàilt' no pòg di.

(1–4) Tobacco pipe: miserable pipe! I would not allow myself to be choked by its smoke: I would smash it under my feet and break it into tiny pieces.

(5–8) I would not be pained to clean it and stuff it, satisfying the pleasures of the flesh with it; I would not be a slave day and night to it; it will not delay me on a Sabbath day.

(9–12) I would not struggle, losing my energy, wasting my money on foolishness, smoke around my eyes and smoke clinging to me smelling worse than the midden.

(13–16) A discoloured forehead and undernourished limbs, along with a deathly hue, only a senseless man has surrendered his power to it! Isn't he a man whose wishes are foolish?

(17–20) There is no corner or nook anywhere in a sporran from which it will not extract money, and it was never of any use, except for sending smoke skywards; I make no further account of it.

(21–24) I will no longer be condemned by it; there is many a fair young maid who takes a puff from it and if I were in her place I wouldn't let it near to me! I would not welcome nor kiss it!

12. HOGMANAY SONG

The custom of composing and reciting ditties in order to gain permission into homes for food and drink on *Oidhche Challuinn* 'Hogmanay, New Year's Eve' was universal in the Highlands. This song[15] probably comes from Lochaber and mentions many aspects of the Oidhche Challuinn ritual.

1	*Thàinig mis' a-nochd do'n dùthaich*	
	A dh'ùrachadh na Calluinn.	
	Cha ruig mi leas a bhith 'ga innse:	
	Bha i ann ri linn ar sinnsear.	B.3
5	*Tigh'nn deiseal air an fhàrdaich,*	
	'S bualadh le fàilt' aig an doras;	C.2
	Mo dhuan a ghabhail aig a' chomhla	
	'Cur deoch m' eòlais air gach aineol.	C.2
9	*Pìos de chaisean-uchd 'nam phòca*	
	Chaidh a ròstadh ann an cabhaig –	
	Gheibh a' bhean e – 's i as fiach e –	
	Làmh a' riarachadh nam bonnag.	F.6, C.2
13	*Leis an achd a th'anns an dùthaich*	
	Cha bhi dùil againn ri dràma	
	Ach beagan de thoradh an t-samhraidh	
	Tha mi an geall air leis an aran.	
	A' Challuinn seo!	

(1–4) I've come tonight to this place to revisit Hogmanay; I need not explain it, it has existed since the times of our ancestors.

(5–8) Travelling sunwise around the house and striking the door in welcome; I recite my ditty in front of the door before I drink to the friendship of each stranger.

(9–12) A piece of singed-sheepskin in my pocket which was burnt in a hurry – the housewife will have it as she well deserves – the hand that supplies the bannocks.

(13–17) With the laws enacted in this country we cannot expect a dram, only some of the summer's produce which I crave, along with the bread, on this Hogmanay!

13. 'OVERCOME THE ROGUES'

This song[16] was one of a number of compositions by Gilleasbuig Mac Iain in defense of Gaelic after the 1872 Education Act. The rhetorical mode is *brosnachadh* 'incitement', drawing strongly from the language of traditional battle songs and illustrative of how old poetic styles could be applied to modern circumstances. Gilleasbuig's response to the overturning of the status of Gaelic in the Highlands is to overturn the school-masters as though they were themselves children. The first quatrain (lines 1–4) is the chorus.

1   *Cuiribh glùn, cuiribh glùn*
    Cuiribh glùn air na bodaich
    Gach maighstir sgoile ruinn chuir chùl
    Cuiribh glùn air mar sgoilear.

5   *Tha ri'r cànain iad cur cùl*
    Agus diùlt' bhith 'ga teagaisg
    Chum 's gum fògair às an dùthaich
    Chainnt is rùnaich do'r n-anam.

9   *'N d'rinn an nàdurrachd a chall?*
    'N d'rinneadh Galld' iad is Sas'nnach
    Is gur miannach leo ar clann
    Thoirt 'nan deann-ruith do Shasann.

13 *Oir gun teagamh 's e tha annt'*
    Luchd na feall is a' bhrathaidh
    A tha toileach Tìr nam Beann
    Bhith fo cheannsal do Shasann.

17   *Cha toil leinn agus chan ail*
      Bhith 'nar tràillean do bhodaich
      Tha air ar cànain ri tàir
      Is gun àite aic' 'nar sgoilean.

21   *'S i ar cànain fuil nan Gàidheal*
      A chur blàths ann an anam
      Ach an tobair mu nì tràgh'
      Théid le'n càirdeas iad seachad.

25   *Thoill na bodaich seo le cinnt'*
      Air an cinn a bhith 'n crochadh
      Chionn 's gu bheil e réir an gnàths'   B.3
      Sliochd nan Gài'il bhith dort 'm fola.   D.1

29   *'Cuiribh às daibh gu ro luath*
      An geur ruag' (deir na bodaich)
      'Do America m'a thuath
      Thar a' chuain às ar fochair!'

33   *'S toigh leinn, iad bhith teagasg Beurl'*
      Gu ro eudmhor 'nar sgoilean
      Ach cha toil ar cànain féin
      Iad bhith feuchainn di 'n doruis.

(1–4) Overcome the rogues [3 times], every school-master who has turned his back on us, overcome the rogues as though they were students.

(5–8) They have turned their backs on our language and refused to teach it in order to remove it from the land, the language most beloved to our souls.

(9–12) Did nature make a mistake? Were they [our children] born Lowland or English? They would like to rush our children off to England.

(13–16) They are without a doubt people of deceit and fraud who wish the Highlands to be under the domination of England.

(17–20) We have no wish to be slaves to rogues who despise our tongue and have not given it a place in our schools.

(21–24) Our language is the lifeblood of the Gaels, which puts warmth in the soul; but before the well is exhausted, their relationship will become estranged.

(25–28) These rogues certainly deserved to be hanged; it is the tradition of High-landers to spill blood.

(29–32) 'Banish them immediately and completely', say the rogues, 'over the sea to North America; get them out of our presence!'

(33–36) We certainly want them to teach English in our schools, but we don't like our own language to be cast out of the door.

14. CHRISTENING SONG

These verses were recorded by Charles Dunn in Cape Breton.[17] He noted that the subject's father was from the Lake Ainslie area and that the mother was a MacKay, but no further information on the item's origin was known. Songs composed for baptisms and christenings seem to be very rare. It opens with a reference to a traditional form of augury in which shoes are thrown over a house to see which direction they point.[18] The rhetorical mode is *beannachadh* 'blessing' and it seems to be in the father's voice.

1	*Ceann nam bròg do Chloinn 'ic Aoidh;*	
	An ceannard do'n chinneadh rìoghail,	B.6
	Sìol nan Domhnallach bha ainmeil	A.4, B.2
	Choisinn buaidh troimh na linntean.	D.1
5	*Lite choirce, bainne blàth*	
	Cìoch do mhàthar dhuit gun dìobradh –	
	Siud an lòn a gheibh am pàiste	
	Gus an amhlaich e 'chuid fhiaclan.	
9	*Gun do bhàist mi leis a' chlèir thu*	
	'S thug mi 'Seumas' ort dà rìreamh	
	Ainm an oifigich bu threuna	A.4, B.9
	Tharraing geur-chlaidheamh 'nar sinnsreadh.	D.5, A.4

(1–4) Shoe tips pointing to the MacKays: the chieftain of the royal clan; the Clan Donald, which is famous for winning victories throughout the ages.

(5–8) Oatmeal and warm milk, the unfailing milk of your mother's breast – that is what is provided to the child until his teeth come in.

(9–12) I have had you baptised by the clergy, and indeed, 'James' is your name, the name of the most valiant officer who ever drew a sword amongst our ancestors.

NOTES

INTRODUCTION

1 His name is properly 'Oisean' in its original Gaelic form. The anglicised form 'Ossian' has, however, for better or worse, become well established.
2 John L. Campbell 1999: 182–3; the translation is mine.
3 *Ibid.*: 181.
4 R. L. Thomson 1970: 179–80.
5 I will be using the term 'Ossianic' to refer to texts about the Fian whether or not they are ascribed to Oisean in Gaelic tradition.
6 Donald Meek 2007b: 145, 148–9.
7 William Gillies 1987.
8 John F. Campbell 1994a, vol. 2: 528.
9 John G. Campbell 1891: 3.
10 Richard Sher 1991: 212–15.
11 Ian McGowan 1996: 101, 102.
12 Ronald Black 2001: 292–9.
13 Such as Donald Meek 1991.
14 Paul Bohannan 1995: 150.

CHAPTER ONE: THEMES IN SCOTTISH HISTORY

1 Geoffrey Ward 1996: 48.
2 Archibald Campbell 1889: 11–12.
3 J. R. N. MacPhail 1914: 10, 11, 46.
4 Quoted in Edward Cowan 2000b: 1.
5 John L. Campbell 1994: ix. (First edition in 1984.)
6 Ian Armit 2005: 18–25.
7 Barry Cunliffe 1997: 21.
8 Ian Armit 2005: 69; William Gillies 2007a: 53.
9 The hypothetical branches and stages of development of the Goidelic family are taken from Breandán Ó Buachalla 2002: 9. The centuries for these stages are estimates.
10 Ian Armit 2005: 101–12.
11 *Ibid*: 106–14.
12 William Gillies 2007a: 55.
13 Katherine Forsyth 1997: 2; William Gillies 2007a: 57.
14 W. F. H. Nicolaisen 1996: 15–19.
15 Alex Woolf 1998; Sally Foster 2004: 35.
16 Ewan Campbell 1999: 7, 12; Alex Woolf 2002.
17 Ewan Campbell 1999: 9, 12–15, 53.
18 William Watson 1926: 390, 459–60, 436; W. F. H. Nicolaisen 1996: 6–10; Sally Foster 2004: 20.
19 Derick Thomson 1989: 107–8; John Koch 2005: 1447–8.
20 Ewan Campbell 1999: 20–1, 43–50.

21 John Bannerman 1989: 127; Sally Foster 2004: 37–8.
22 Kim McCone 1990: 226–32; John Carey 1999a: 21; Donald Meek 2000: Chapter Eight.
23 Stephen Driscoll 2002: 32–3; Sally Foster 2004: 88.
24 Alfred Smyth 1984: 177–9; Michael Lynch 1991: 22–3; Sally Foster 2004: 35–6.
25 Alex Woolf 2007: 43.
26 Stephen Driscoll 2002: 12, 28–32.
27 Alex Woolf 2005: 206; *idem* 2007: 956.
28 Alfred Smyth 1984: 177–9; Michael Lynch 1991: 22–3; Stephen Driscoll 2002: 35–45; Sally Foster 2004: 107–8.
29 A process described in Alex Woolf 2007: 312–50.
30 Alan Bruford 2000: 66.
31 Dauvit Broun 1998a: 9. See also Sally Foster 2004: 108–9.
32 Alfred Smyth 1984: 231–3; Michael Lynch 1992: 44; Domhnall Uilleam Stiùbhart 2005: 49–52.
33 I. F. Grant and Hugh Cheape 1987: 60–1; Domhnall Uilleam Stiùbhart 2005: 545.
34 G. W. S. Barrow 1989: 74.
35 W. D. H. Sellar 1989: 6.
36 G. S. Barrow 1981: 14.
37 I. F. Grant and Hugh Cheape 1987: 54–5; R. A. Houston and W. W. J. Knox 2001: 87–8, 118.
38 Steve Boardman and Alasdair Ross 2003: 15–16.
39 W. D. H. Sellar 1989: 7; Steve Boardman 2003: 97.
40 W. D. H. Sellar 1989: 5–6; Steve Boardman and Alasdair Ross 2003: 16.
41 John Bannerman 1993: 23.
42 G. W. S. Barrow 1989: 70.
43 R. Andrew McDonald 2000: 181–3; Steve Boardman and Alasdair Ross 2003: 16.
44 A. A. M. Duncan 1975: 197; R. A. Houston and W. W. J. Knox 2001: 160.
45 R. Andrew McDonald 2000: 174–80.
46 *Ibid*: 34–6.
47 Keith Stringer 2000.
48 Sally Foster 2007: 47.
49 Michael Lynch 1991: 63; Sally Foster 2007: 46.
50 Gilbert Márkus 2007a: 95.
51 W. D. H. Sellar 1989; G. W. S. Barrow 1989: 73–4.
52 Hamish Henderson 1989: 265.
53 W. J. Watson 2004: 198.
54 Hector MacQueen 2003: 76–8.
55 Alison Cathcart 2002: 164–5.
56 Michael Lynch 1991: 118–9; John Bannerman 1993: 38.
57 Dauvit Broun 1998a: 10–11.
58 William Ferguson 1998: 40–3.
59 I. F. Grant and Hugh Cheape 1987: 82; John Bannerman 1998: 10; Wilson McLeod 2004: 43.
60 John Bannerman 1977: 216, 233; I. F. Grant and Hugh Cheape 1987: 92, 101, 117; Wilson McLeod 2004: 40–54; Domhnall Uilleam Stiùbhart 2005: 67.
61 Wilson McLeod 2002b: 32.
62 John Bannerman 1977.
63 This genealogical chart was compiled primarily from information in Jean Munro and R. W. Munro 1986 and David Stevenson 1994.
64 James Hunter 1999: 136; Domhnall Uilleam Stiùbhart 2005: 96, 118–19.
65 Jean Munro 1981: 29–31.
66 Jean Munro 1981: 32–3; I. F. Grant and Hugh Cheape 1987: 115; James Hunter 1999: 143.
67 I. F. Grant and Hugh Cheape 1987: 112–15; Alison Cathcart 2002; Aonghas MacCoinnich 2002: 149–53.
68 Alison Cathcart 2002: 181, 184.
69 Philip Smith 1994: 17–19.
70 Jean Munro 1981: 35; James Hunter 1999: 164–5; Aonghas MacCoinnich 2002: 146–9.

71 I. F. Grant and Hugh Cheape 1987: 108–11; Gordon Menzies 2001: 104–11; Aonghas MacCoinnich 2002.

72 Aonghas MacCoinnich 2002: 143–6.

73 Jane Ohlmeyer 1998: 133; Robert Dodgshon 1998: 105–6; Aonghas MacCoinnich 2002: 156.

74 Edward Cowan 1979: 152.

75 I. F. Grant and Hugh Cheape 1987: 109; Jane Ohlmeyer 1998: 135; Aonghas MacCoinnich 2002: 145.

76 Edward Cowan 1979: 141, 150–1.

77 Quoted in Jane Dawson 1998: 291 (I have modernised the spelling).

78 I. F. Grant and Hugh Cheape 1987: 110; Martin MacGregor 2006:114–16, 132–50.

79 Martin MacGregor 2006: 124, 155, 165–8.

80 David Stevenson 1994: 30–1, 34–9.

81 David Stevenson 1994: 40–7; Martin MacGregor 2006: 126–9, 167–9.

82 Martin MacGregor 2006: 129–31, 180–1.

83 Quoted in Charles Withers 1988: 113 (I have modernised the spelling).

84 Allan Macinnes 1996: Chapter Four.

85 John L. Campbell 1945: 45–6.

86 *Ibid*: 43, 46–9; Charles Withers 1988: 120–2; Michael Lynch 1991: 304; Dòmhnall Uilleam Stiùbhart 1996: 84.

87 John L. Campbell 1945: 50–1; Geoffrey Plank 2006: 13.

88 Michael Lynch 1991: 327–34.

89 *Idem* 2001: 349–52.

90 William Gillies 1991: 32–6; Hugh Cheape 2000.

91 Geoffrey Plank 2006: 45, 70.

92 *Ibid*: 54.

93 Marianne McLean 1991: 20; Allan Macinnes 1996: 212–3; *idem* 2002; Geoffrey Plank 2006: 45, 63, 67, 70.

94 William Gillies 1991: 40.

95 Margaret McKay 1980: 6.

96 Ian McGowan 1996: 49–50.

97 *Ibid*: 22–3. (The italics are mine.)

98 Alexander Allardyce 1888, vol. 2: 396, 502.

99 Geoffrey Plank 2006: 4–7, 104–8.

100 Peter Stearns and Herrick Chapman 1992: 72–9.

101 Eric Richards 2000: 39, 43, 54–5, 57, 60.

102 Michael Kennedy 2002: 18.

103 I. F. Grant and Hugh Cheape 1987: 227–31; James Hunter 1999: 239–42, 267.

104 For a history of the use of 'clearance' in this sense, see Eric Richards 2000: 5–7.

105 Patrick Campbell 1937: 49.

106 See James Hunter 2000: 1–30 for critiques of these standard approaches.

107 John L. Campbell 2000: 210.

108 Andrew MacKillop 2000; Michael Newton 2003a.

109 Typical eighteenth-century protest songs can be found in Michael Newton 1999: 246–53; *idem* 2001a: 43–7, 52–9, 88–93.

110 Michael Newton 2001a: 60–6.

111 Eric Richards 2000: 288–90.

112 Ruth Megaw and Vincent Megaw 1999: 44–5; Colin Kidd 1999: 212–13; Geoffrey Plank 2006: 8.

113 John MacInnes 2006: 364–5, 372.

114 *Ibid*: 368.

115 Douglas Ansdell 1998: 63–5, 127–34; John MacInnes 2006: 436–9.

116 Colin Kidd 1993.

117 Victor Durkacz 1983; Derick Thomson 1994: 259–61; John MacInnes 2006: 116–17.

118 *The Scottish-American Journal* 13 January 1881.

119 Perhaps most explicitly and eloquently in numerous BBC Radio nan Gàidheal interviews with Dr John MacInnes, such as the series 'Air Mo Chuairt', first broadcast in the summer of 2008.

120 James Hunter 1999: Chapter Eight; Eric Richards 2000: Chapter Eighteen.
121 *Western Isles Socio-Economic Overview*, Department for Sustainable Communities, September 2007 (http://www.cne-siar.gov.uk/factfile/socioeconomicoverview.htm).
122 Anita Quye et al 2004: *passim.*

CHAPTER TWO: IDENTITY AND ETHNICITY

1 Michael Newton 1999: 86–9.
2 Audrey Smedley 1993.
3 Barry Cunliffe 1997: 2; John Haywood 2001: 16.
4 Barry Cunliffe 1997: 6–8.
5 *Ibid*: 10–11; John Collis 1999.
6 George Buchanan 1827: 103–4.
7 Barry Cunliffe 1997: 16, 25.
8 *Ibid*: 137–40, 146, 154–9, 268–74.
9 T. M. Charles-Edwards 1993: 2.
10 *Ibid*: 477.
11 John Gillingham 1992: 396–7; Rees Davis 1993.
12 Colin Kidd 1993: 66.
13 John MacInnes 2006: 38–40.
14 W. J. Watson 1993: 100, 172–3.
15 Wilson McLeod 2002: *passim.*
16 W. J. Watson 1959: 362. See also *The Celtic Magazine* 2 (1877): 191.
17 John MacInnes 2006: 39.
18 Wilson McLeod 1999; *idem* 2000.
19 John MacInnes 2006: 359.
20 Harald Haarmann 1999: 64.
21 Quoted in Harald Haarmann 1999: 66. Note that 'race' is used here in the pre-eighteenth century sense of 'line of descent' rather than the modern, pseudo-biological notion of race.
22 T. M. Charles-Edwards 1998: 76.
23 *Ibid*: 77; Alan Bruford 2000: 53.
24 Francis Byrne 1973: 8; T. M. Charles-Edwards 1996: 722–3; Alex Woolf 2002: 12.
25 Quoted in Dauvit Broun 2007: 49. The story that Picts took Irish wives goes back at least as far as Bede *c.*731.
26 Martin MacGregor 2007a: 37–43.
27 John MacInnes 2006: 38.
28 Rees Davies 1994: 9.
29 Martin MacGregor 2000a: 79.
30 Andrew Simmons 1998: 19. Burt says that this ethnolinguistic identification followed the usage of the church, but it is likely to be as much a product of internal perceptions.
31 Alexander MacRae 1899: 249.
32 *The Highlander* 18 December 1875.
33 Quote and discussion in Rees Davies 1994: 14–15.
34 Quoted in Victor Durkacz 1983: 49.
35 An overview of the poetic response can be found in Wilson McLeod 2003a.
36 William Shaw 1972: x–xi.
37 John Carey 1994: 2–3, 11, 13, 15.
38 *Idem* 1990; *idem*: 1994: 9.
39 John Carey 1994.
40 Wilson McLeod 2004: 114–15.
41 Edward Cowan 1984: 121–4.
42 William Ferguson 1998: 36–42.
43 John L. Campbell and Derick Thomson 1963: 25–6.
44 *Ibid*: 28.

45 Duncan Campbell 1910: 136–7.
46 Colm Ó Baoill 1979: line 129.
47 Michael Newton 2001a: 58–9.
48 Quoted in Hume Brown 1891: 271.
49 Wilson McLeod 2004: 119–21.
50 Wilson McLeod and Meg Bateman 2007: xxv.
51 William J. Watson 1959: xxxi; W. D. H. Sellar 2000. However, see also Alex Woolf 2005.
52 William Gillies 1994: 145.
53 *Idem* 1999.
54 *Idem* 1976–8: 276–7; W. D. H. Sellar 1981: 108–9.
55 Rees Davies 1993: 3.
56 John Gillingham 1992: 394.
57 *Ibid*: 405.
58 Dauvit Broun 2007: 69–71.
59 *Ibid*: 64, 72–8.
60 Quoted and discussed in Martin MacGregor 2007a: 10, 15.
61 Quoted and discussed in *ibid*: 7–8.
62 G. W. S. Barrow 1989: 78–9.
63 Martin MacGregor 2007a: 14, 19.
64 Quoted in Ulrike Morét 2000: 61.
65 Dauvit Broun 2007: 56.
66 Martin MacGregor 2007a: 20–4.
67 Roger Mason 2002: 104.
68 Æneas J. G. MacKay 1892: 48–50.
69 Martin MacGregor 2007a: 31.
70 *Ibid*: 33–7.
71 Quoted in Ulrike Morét 2000: 71. This comment is paralleled in the travelogue by Taylor, the Water-Poet, who says that when Scottish gentry of any origin came to the Highland to hunt that they adopted Highland clothing. See Hume Brown 1891: 120.
72 Roger Mason 2002: 110–12; Martin MacGregor 2007a: 33.
73 James Cranstoun 1885–7: 280–1.
74 Rodger Cunningham 1987: 53.
75 Jane Dawson 1998: 270.
76 Donald Meek 1989a: 137, 145; Martin MacGregor 2007a: 32.
77 Jane Dawson 1998: 289.
78 J. D. Young quoted in Charles Withers 1988: 59. Thanks to Iain MacKinnon for pointing this and the following text out to me.
79 Andrew Simmons 1998: 272.
80 Cosmo Innes 1839: 29.
81 For his background, see Hector MacQueen 2003: 92.
82 This would read in modern English: 'I understand, elf, that you do not love Irish (i.e., Gaelic), but it should be the language of all true Scotsmen; it was the good language of this land and caused the Scottish nation to multiply and spread; while we read that your treasonous forefather Gospatrick made Irish and Irishmen decline, through his treason he brought in Englishmen (to Scotland), and you would do the same yourself if you were to succeed him.'
83 Arthur Williamson 1982: 37, 53; Rees Davies 1997: 12.
84 Quoted in Arthur Williamson 1982: 41.
85 Quoted in Ulrike Morét 2000: 62.
86 Quoted in Aonghas MacCoinnich 2006: 219.
87 Quoted in *idem* 2002: 145.
88 Aonghas MacCoinnich 2002: 140; *idem*: 2006: 218.
89 See W. D. H. Sellar 2000: 244–7 for the identification of Olbhair and related forms with Olaf.
90 William Mackay 1905: 40.
91 William J. Watson 1959: lines 4632–9; William Gillies 1976–8: 261.

92 Craig must here be referring to a hypothetical 'pure Gaelic', implying high-register usages, rather than Gaelic in general given that vernacular Gaelic survived well into the twentieth century in these areas.
93 C. Sanford Terry 1909: 61–2, 288–9; Edward Cowan 2000a: 259–60.
94 Quoted in Nancy Dorian 1981: 18.
95 Colm Ó Baoill 1979: 100–3. I have not attempted to modernise or regularise the orthography. I have modified the translation. The letters to the right refer to the Gaelic panegyric code discussed in Chapter Three.
96 Michael Newton forthcoming.
97 Anne Grant 1811, vol 1: 27–9.
98 William Gillies 1991: 20–1.
99 John L. Campbell 1984: 118–19.
100 John Mackenzie 1841: 373.
101 Robert Clyde 1998: 181; Geoffrey Plank 2006: 70, 96, 108.
102 John L. Campbell 2000: 197.
103 Norman Scarfe 2001: 174, 175.
104 Henry MacKenzie 1805: 43, 50.
105 William Ferguson 1998: 245.
106 Henry MacKenzie 1805: 65.
107 Anne Grant 1811, vol. 2: 126–7.
108 Quoted in James Hunter 1999: 302.
109 Duncan Campbell 1910: 119–20.
110 Thomas Newt 1791: 125.
111 Colin Kidd 2003: 7.
112 *Idem.* 1995: 50.
113 *Ibid*: 62.
114 John Pinkerton 1787: 67, 68.
115 Krisztina Fenyo 2000: 28–31.
116 Quoted in *ibid*: 40.
117 *Ibid*: 40–2.
118 *The Scotsman* 26 July 1851 quoted in *ibid*: 77–8.
119 Colin Kidd 2003: 8.
120 Donald Meek 2004.
121 Andrew MacKillop 2001: Chapters Four and Five.
122 Robert Clyde 1995: 163–5; Andrew MacKillop 2001: 9, 107, 114, 156, 226–9.
123 Quoted in the *Scottish-American Journal* 14 November 1868.
124 *Mac-Talla* 18 July 1896. See also Michael Newton 2003b: 109–12.
125 A few examples can be found in Donald Meek 2003a: 101–25; Gilleasbuig Mac-na-Ceardaich 2004: 244–5, 271–3.
126 Quoted in Ronald Black 1986: 3.
127 *An Gàidheal* 1 (1872): 276–7.
128 The *Scottish-American Journal* 10 October 1872.
129 Quoted in the *Scottish-American Journal* 21 December 1876.
130 Murray Pittock and Isla Jack 2007.
131 John L. Campbell 1978: 1.
132 *An Gàidheal* 1938: 116.
133 Iain Crichton Smith 1986: 37, 49.
134 Discussed in Martin MacGregor 2007a: 19, 33; Arthur Williamson 1996.
135 Aspects of this thesis are explored in Rodger Cunningham 1987.

CHAPTER THREE: LITERATURE AND ORAL TRADITION

1 *The Celtic Monthly* 15 (1907): 128.
2 John MacInnes 2006: 3.

3 Wilson McLeod and Meg Bateman 2007: 208 (I have altered the translation slightly).
4 Quoted from and discussed in Joan Radner 1990: 175–6.
5 John Shaw 2000: 18–19.
6 Based on Morton Bloomfield and Charles Dunn 1989: 32, 57 (I have altered the schema).
7 John F. Campbell 1994b, vol. 1: xi.
8 Proinsias Mac Cana 1980: 23–4.
9 See John Shaw 1999 for discussion of spoken genres.
10 Alexander Nicholson 1996: 211 with discussion in Appendix V. John Francis Campbell recorded a variant listing other tales (see Alan Bruford 1969: 163).
11 John Shaw 2000: 14.
12 John F. Campbell 1994a, vol. 1: 34.
13 Donald MacAulay 1976: 46.
14 John Shaw 2000: 22.
15 Donald Meek 1990: 352.
16 John F. Campbell 1994a, vol. 2: 202.
17 Morton Bloomfield and Charles Dunn 1989: 11.
18 Alan Bruford 1969: 60.
19 Somhairle Mac Gill-eain 1985: 251.
20 James Ross 1961: 38; Barbara Hillers 2007: 163.
21 John F. Campbell 1994a, vol. 1: 204–5.
22 John Shaw 2000: 38.
23 Proinsias Mac Cana 1980: 3, 5, 7, 9; Charles Dunn and Morton Bloomfield 1989: 60–1; Wilson McLeod 2004: 100; Donald Meek 2007a: 255, 258.
24 Gearóid Ó Crualaoich 2003: 20–1.
25 John Koch and John Carey 2003: 13.
26 *Ibid*: 18.
27 These are the forms of the word in early forms of Gaelic. In Classical Gaelic they are *file* (singular) and *filidh* (plural), and in modern Scottish Gaelic *filidh* (singular) and *filidhean* (plural). I have attempted to use the forms appropriate to the period in question.
28 J. E. Caerwyn Williams and Patrick Ford 1992: 21–7.
29 John Koch 2005: 997.
30 T. M. Charles-Edwards 1998: 722.
31 Liam Breatnach 1987; Katherine Simms 1998: 238.
32 J. E. Caerwyn Williams and Patrick Ford 1992: 67–9, 79, 87–8.
33 Thomas Owen Clancy 1998: 108–13, 115–16, 144.
34 Colm Ó Baoill 1972–4: 387–8.
35 Margaret Dobbs 1958: 50, 54, 55; Benjamin Hudson 2007.
36 Thomas Owen Clancy 2000: 100–2; John Koch 2005: 1577.
37 Kenneth Jackson 1972: 96.
38 Dauvit Broun 1998a: 194.
39 John Bannerman 1989; *idem* 1996.
40 Katherine Simms 1998: 242–6.
41 *Ibid*: 241–9; *idem* 2007; Wilson McLeod and Meg Bateman 2007: 68–75.
42 Katherine Simms 1998: 250.
43 Thomas Owen Clancy 1998: 236–41, 309; Wilson McLeod and Meg Bateman 2007: 74–91.
44 John Carey 1997; Katherine Simms 1998: 250.
45 Although 'bardic poetry' has become the conventional term for referring to the syllabic poetry of the *filidh* in Classical Gaelic, it is an inaccurate designation given that the bard was an inferior rank of poet who did not compose in the *dán díreach* metres. The emphasis of these academies was to sustain poetry at the highest levels, i.e., *filidheacht*. See John MacInnes 2006: 273; Wilson McLeod and Meg Bateman 2007: xxxiv.
46 This term was coined in Brian Ó Cuiv 1980: *passim*.
47 Wilson McLeod 2004: 114.
48 Derick Thomson 1968a; William Matheson 1970: 186–7; John Bannerman 1977: 234; *idem*: 1991: 7.

49 Wilson McLeod 2004: 70–8.
50 Derick Thomson 1968a: 61–5; John Bannerman 1998: 96–7.
51 Wilson McLeod 2004: 33–5, 63–70; John MacInnes 2006: 235–8.
52 James Ross 1953–5: 231–2; Roibeard Ó Maolalaigh 2006.
53 John Higgitt 2000: 336; Martin MacGregor 2007b: 214–15.
54 See many important points of discussion in Donald Meek 1998.
55 R. L. Thomson 1970: 179.
56 Donald Meek 1998: 58–60.
57 Wilson McLeod 2004: 201–3.
58 Colm Ó Baoill and Donald MacAulay 2001; Wilson McLeod and Meg Bateman 2007: xlii–xliv.
59 John MacInnes 2006: 233.
60 Derick Thomson 1989: 146–7, 152–3; Colm Ó Baoill and Meg Bateman 1994: 10.
61 This is a very old Gaelic term for the collective body of artists; its use in the singular is innovative.
62 Derick Thomson 1989: 107, 127, 145, 148; *idem* 1992: 157, 160; Wilson McLeod 2004: 67.
63 William Gillies 1991 discusses a sample of this material.
64 Hugh Cheape 2004: 19; Ronald Black 2007a: *passim*.
65 Ronald Black 1989: 167.
66 Derick Thomson 1963: 276, 281–2, 301–2.
67 Donald Meek 2004c; *idem* 2007a: 257, 259; John Shaw 2007a: 347–8.
68 Michael Newton 2003b; Donald Meek 2007a: 253–5.
69 John Shaw 2007a.
70 Thomas McKean 2007; Michelle MacLeod and Moray Watson 2007.
71 Ronald Black 1977: 342–3.
72 John Bannerman 1989.
73 Mark Zumbuhl 2006: 13 (my translation).
74 This description is based on Eleanor Knott 1960; Osborn Bergin 1970; William Gillies 1989; Katherine Simms 1998; Liam Breatnach 2007; Damian McManus 2007.
75 Derick Thomson 1994: 259.
76 Wilson McLeod 2004: 99.
77 Martin Martin 1716: 115–16.
78 Quoted and discussed in Joan Radner 1990: 177.
79 Wilson McLeod and Meg Bateman 2007: 110–13 (I have altered the translation).
80 Colm Ó Baoill and Meg Bateman 1994: 23–5; Wilson McLeod and Meg Bateman 2007: xli–xlii; Martin MacGregor 2007b: 213.
81 Wilson McLeod 2004: 66–9; John MacInnes 2006: 233–40.
82 John L. Campbell and Derick Thomson 1963: 33; Derick Thomson 1968a: 68.
83 Herbert Campbell 1926: 190.
84 Damian McManus 1991.
85 Mary Beith 1995: 60–1.
86 Derick Thomson 1968b; Wilson McLeod and Meg Bateman 2007: 228–33.
87 Proinsias Mac Cana 1980: 3–5.
88 'The Dornoch Firth', *The Scottish-Canadian* 22 January 1891.
89 John Shaw 2007c: 35.
90 *Idem* 2000: 15; *idem* 2007c: 35.
91 John F. Campbell 1994a, vol. 1: 5.
92 Alexander MacDonald 1914: 252.
93 James Logan 1876: 237–8.
94 John Dewar 1964: 259.
95 John Shaw 2000: 14, 22–5.
96 George Henderson 1904–5: 352.
97 James Ross 1961: 35. See item 11 in Appendix A for an example relating to tobacco.
98 Thomas McKean 1997: 145.
99 Mary MacKellar 1886: 225–6.
100 John MacInnes 2006: 244.

101 Martin Martin 1716: 13–14, 106–7.
102 John Shaw 1992; John MacInnes 2006: 340–55.
103 Frances Tolmie 1997: 234–5; John L. Campbell 1999: 85–8.
104 William Mackenzie 1891–2: 99.
105 William Gillies 1987; John MacInnes 2006: 187, 202.
106 Henry MacKenzie 1805, Appendix: 10; John Shaw 1992: 150–6; Alan Bruford and D. A. MacDonald 2003: 15–16; John Shaw 2007b: xiii.
107 John Shaw 2007c: 37.
108 Eoghan Mac a' Phì 1938: 105.
109 *Tocher* 38 (1983): 8.
110 Quoted in Linda Dégh 1982: 60. Alan Bruford 1968: i–ii defines 'motif' more strictly as a structural element abstracted from the 'details' that are used to embody it.
111 T. M. Charles-Edwards 1999.
112 Máire Ní Annracháin 2007 offers an insightful analysis of these in Gaelic poetry.
113 Wilson McLeod and Meg Bateman 2007: 242–3.
114 My classification is based primarily on observations in James Ross 1957 and Donald Meek 1995: 26–33.
115 This is my attempt to use only the textual aspects of Barre Toelken 1996: 31–49 and reconcile it with Rosemary Zumwalt 1998.
116 Alan Bruford and D. A. MacDonald 2003: 98–106.
117 John Shaw 2007b: xiv.
118 Proinsias Mac Cana 1980: 27, 29–30, 73–81; J. E. Caerwyn Williams and Patrick Ford 1992: 37–9.
119 Linda Dégh 1972: 62–76.
120 Alan Bruford 1969: 5, 8; J. E. Caerwyn Williams and Patrick Ford 1992: 122–6.
121 John MacInnes 2007a: 70.
122 Alan Bruford 1969: 243.
123 This is mostly from Alan Bruford and D. A. MacDonald 2003: 12–14.
124 Alan Bruford 1969: 23, 34–5, 213; Alan Bruford and D. A. MacDonald 2003: 16–17.
125 Barbara Hillers 2007: 157.
126 Alan Bruford 1969: 182–204; John MacInnes 2007a: 71; *idem* 2007b: 82.
127 John F. Campbell 1994a, vol. 2: 408.
128 John MacInnes 2006: 48–63; *idem* 2007a. For a good selection of these, see John Dewar 1964.
129 Domhnall Uilleam Stiùbhart 2007: 130.
130 Aonghas MacCoinnich 2002: 158.
131 Eric Creegen 2004: 112.
132 This list is based on William Matheson 1970: 149–68; *idem*: 1993; Roibeard Ó Maolalaigh 2006; John MacInnes 2006: 186, 217, 224, 237–40, 288–304. There is debate over the technical nuances of these terms but it may not be reconcilable, given that terms may have been used in different contexts over time and evolved independent usages accordingly.
133 James Ross 1953–5.
134 William Gillies 2007b: 222.
135 John MacInnes 2006: 170, 226, 275.
136 Roibeart Ó Maolalaigh 2006.
137 William Matheson 1983: 130.
138 The end-rhyme scheme is approximate in the case of this poem, however.
139 James Ross 1953–5: 218, 219, 231; Alan Bruford 1990: 70–1; Leeman Perkins 1999: 350–6; John MacInnes 2006: 238–41.
140 The extent to which extempore composition actually happened has been hotly debated: see Alan Bruford 1990: 72 and the references therein.
141 Morton Bloomfield and Charles Dunn 1989: 6–7.
142 Some of these are discussed in Terence McCaughey 1989b: 110–19.
143 Ronald Black 2001: xv–xix; William Gillies 2006.
144 Research done for his 1976 doctoral dissertation at the University of Edinburgh, presented to the Gaelic Society of Inverness in 1978 and printed in John MacInnes 2006: 265–319.
145 Ronald Black 2001: xix.

146 John MacInnes 2006: 275.
147 Wilson McLeod 2004: 215–9; Pía Dewar 2006; John MacInnes 2006: 12–17, 22–6, 270–3, 275–7.
148 I am grateful to Ronald Black of Edinburgh University for the exercises he assigned in applying the panegyric code while I was his student. His classification can be seen in Ronald Black 2001: 525–7.
149 Gearóid Ó hAllmhuráin 1999; Colm Ó Baoill 2003.
150 Domhnall Uilleam Stiùbhart 2007: 124.
151 Wilson McLeod 2003a.
152 Hector Cameron 1932: 180–1.
153 William Gillies 1989: 248–9; Wilson McLeod 2004: 114–15; John MacInnes 2006: 29.
154 Donald Meek 2004a: 17–18, 20–2.
155 John F. Campbell 1994a, vol. 2: 529.
156 *An Teachdaire Gàidhealach* 1836: 228–9.
157 John Shaw 2003; *idem* 2007c: 38; Domhnall Uilleam Stiùbhairt 2007: 128.
158 Calum Nicolson n.d.: 15.
159 Alexander Allardyce 1888: 408–9.
160 Duncan Campbell 1910: 120.
161 John Francis Campbell 1994a, vol. 1: 4, 6, 10–16, 26.
162 Domhnall Uilleam Stiùbhart 2007: 136.
163 Angus Peter Campbell 1986: 103.
164 John Shaw 2003.

CHAPTER FOUR: CLAN SOCIETY

1 John L. Campbell 2000: ii.
2 Allan Macinnes 1996: 40–6.
3 Donald Macpherson 1878: 371–2.
4 I know of three variants of this tale in print: Henry Whyte 1907, vol. 2: 67–9; *The Celtic Annual* 1910: 54–6; Calum Iain MacLeòid 1977: 51–2. There are also variants of the tale attributed to other clan chieftains.
5 John Bannerman 1988: 5–6.
6 Michael Lynch 2001: 93–4.
7 R. W. Munro 1981: 122.
8 Andrew Simmons 1998: 191–2.
9 Alexander Nicolson 1996: 69.
10 Martin Martin 1716: 97.
11 J. R. N. MacPhail 1914: 45.
12 Martin Martin 1716: 103–4.
13 Aonghas MacCoinnich 2002: 153–5; John MacInnes 2006: 27–8.
14 Allan Macinnes 1996: 18.
15 Quoted in Robert Dodgshon 1998: 95.
16 Archibald Campbell 1889: 4.
17 Norman MacLeod 1910: 74.
18 Nerys Patterson 1994: 11–12; R. W. Munro 1981: 121; I. F. Grant 1961: 11–12.
19 Quoted in I. F. Grant 1961: 130.
20 Æneas J. G. MacKay 1892: 45–6.
21 Quoted in I. F. Grant 1961: 27.
22 Andrew Simmons 1998: 200.
23 Thomas Pennant 1998: 751–2.
24 I. F. Grant and Hugh Cheape 1987: 219.
25 Aonghas MacCoinnich 2002: 135
26 John L. Buchanan 1997: 21.
27 John Bannerman 1977: 224.
28 Calum MacPhàrlain 1908: 56.

29 Alexander Nicolson 1996: 110.
30 *Ibid*: 134.
31 Anne Grant 1811: 51.
32 Allan Macinnes 1996: 32–3; Alison Cathcart 2006: 93–4.
33 Norman B. Aitchison 1994: 63.
34 Proinsias Mac Cana 1981: 456.
35 Alison Cathcart 2006: 212–14.
36 *Ibid*: 159–62.
37 There is some debate as to the nearness of relation and the origin of the system. See Dáibhí Ó Cróinín 1995: 63–71.
38 Alison Cathcart 2006: 69–71.
39 Rosemary Ommer 1986: 128; W. D. H. Sellar 1989: 13–4; John Bannerman 1998: 86.
40 John Bannerman 1977: 221, 225–6.
41 Anne Grant 1813: 256.
42 Ronald Black 2007b.
43 Thomas Owen Clancy 2003: 85.
44 *Ibid*: 88–9.
45 John Bannerman 1989: 120–1; Thomas Owen Clancy 2003: 102–3.
46 J. R. N. MacPhail 1914: 23–4.
47 Martin Martin 1716: 102.
48 R. C. Macleod 1927, vol. I: xiv.
49 Frederick MacLeod 1912–13: 115.
50 Ewan Campbell 2003: 52–5; Thomas Clancy 2003; Elizabeth FitzPatrick 2003.
51 Donncha Ó Corráin 1972: 37.
52 Martin Martin 1716: 101–2.
53 Alison Cathcart 2006: 60–9, 75–77.
54 Alexander Nicolson 1996: 323, 237, 201.
55 Anne Grant 1811: 206.
56 Annie MacKenzie 1964: xxii.
57 James Clark 1900, vol 1: 182–3.
58 David Caldwell 2003: 70–1.
59 R. W. Munro 1981: 121.
60 The background to this can be found in Hugh Barron 1972–4: 38–9; *The Celtic Magazine* 7 (1882): 49–51.
61 Martin MacGregor 1998.
62 Nerys Patterson 1994: 29; Alison Cathcart 2006: 25.
63 John L. Campbell 1975: 57.
64 Alison Cathcart 2006: 112.
65 W. D. H. Sellar 1989: 12.
66 Alison Cathcart 2006: 82.
67 Alexander MacDonald 1924–5: 281.
68 Alexander Nicolson 1996: 248.
69 Alexander MacDonald 1924–5: 288.
70 Herbert Campbell 1926: 200.
71 Nerys Patterson 1994: 310–1; Domhnall Uilleam Stiùbhart 1999: 235–7.
72 Mary Mackellar 1888: 146.
73 Neill Martin 2006: 91–107.
74 Angus Matheson 1952: 374.
75 Nerys Patterson 1994: 211, 288, 311–15.
76 T. M. Charles-Edwards 1993: 24–5.
77 Alison Cathcart 2006: 98–101.
78 R. W. Munro 1981: 126; Allan Macinnes 1996: 11–2, 51; Robert Dodgshon 1998: 11, 34–6; Alison Cathcart 2006: 85–90.
79 Alison Cathcart 2006: 119.
80 R. W. Munro 1981: 1267.

81 Allan Macinnes 1996: 10; Robert Dodgshon 1998: 34, 40; Alison Cathcart 2006: 126.
82 Martin Martin 1716: 109.
83 Donald Meek 1978: no. 642.
84 Liam Breatnach 1996: 113.
85 John Lane Buchanan 1997: 21.
86 Robert Dodgshon 1998: 94.
87 Rosemary Ommer 1986: 126.
88 Colmán Etchington 1996: 131.
89 William J. Watson 1927–8: stanzas 4–5.
90 Jean Munro and R. W. Munro 1986: 21–7.
91 The charter and an insightful discussion of it are given in Ronald Black 1992: 53.
92 Jean Munro and R. W. Munro 1986: 165–8.
93 Steve Boardman 2003: 98–9.
94 Robert Dodgshon 1998: 44.
95 Andrew Simmons 1998: 226.
96 R. W. Munro 1981: 124; Peter McQuillan 2004: 79.
97 Peter McQuillan 2004: 23–4, 43, 69–81. Aspects of this will be further explored in Chapter Eight.
98 This discussion is based on Allan Macinnes 1996: 15–18; Robert Dodgshon 1998: 32–6, 44–7; Alison Cathcart 2006: 132–5.
99 Quoted in Robert Dodgshon 1998: 46.
100 Archibald Campbell 1889: 36.
101 Anne Grant 1811: 306, 302.
102 This is actually just one of three separate origins for the name rendered in English as 'MacNair'.
103 Michael Newton 1999: 122–3.
104 Fergus Kelly 1988: 1.
105 R. A. Houston and W. W. J. Knox 2001: 42.
106 *Idem* 1997: 190–1.
107 Michael Lynch 1991: 42.
108 Derick Thomson 1968a: 58–60.
109 J. R. N. MacPhail 1914: 24–5.
110 Derick Thomson 1992b: 113–18, 207–10; John F. Campbell 1994b, vol. 1: xxxv; Alexander Nicolson 1996: 429.
111 James Carmichael Watson 1940: 171.
112 Alison Cathcart 2006: 126–8.
113 Donald Meek 1978: no. 488.
114 Alexander Allardyce 1888, vol. 2: 419.
115 Thomas Pennant 1998: 752.
116 David Stewart 1885: 41–3.
117 Sarah Murray 1799: 228–9.
118 Alexander Nicolson 1996: 93, 113.
119 *Ibid*: 156.
120 Donald Meek 1978: no. 30.
121 Robert Dodgshon 1998: 8.
122 James Logan 1876: 46–7.
123 Quoted in William Matheson 1970: liii.
124 Iain MacIlleathain and Maletta NicPhàil 2005: 82.
125 John MacInnes 2006: 41.
126 Aonghas MacCoinnich 2002: 160–1.
127 Alexander Nicolson 1996: 247, 244.
128 John MacInnes 2006: 52.
129 Pàruig Mac-an-Tuairneir 1813: 220.
130 Æneas J. G. MacKay 1892: 45.
131 E. G. Cody 1888: 91.
132 Martin Martin 1716: 104.

133 Alexander Allardyce 1888, vol 2: 408.
134 William J. Watson 1937: lines 909–10.
135 Alexander Nicolson 1996: 368, 369.
136 William J. Watson 1914–19: 221; Wilson McLeod and Meg Bateman 2007: 150–2.
137 George Henderson 1898: 283.
138 Duncan Campbell 1984: 215; Ronald Black 2000: 10.
139 Martin MacGregor 1998: 25–6.
140 Thomas Pennant 1998: 747–8.
141 J. R. N. MacPhail 1914: 51.
142 Colm Ó Baoill and Meg Bateman 1994: 174.
143 Charles MacDonald 1997: 38–9. See also Alison Cathcart 2006: 68–9.
144 Annie MacKenzie 1964: lines 1701–6.
145 Pàruig Mac-an-Tuairneir 1813: 311–14; Alexander Nicolson 1996: 41, 250, 258, 430, 438; Michael Newton 1999: 114–15.
146 Anne MacKenzie 1964: lines 735–8, 2852; Ronald Black 2001: 176.
147 Anne Grant 1811: 118.
148 Iain MacIlleathain and Maletta NicPhàil 2005: 145.
149 Colm Ó Baoill 1997: lines 223–30.
150 Thomas Pennant 1998: 752.
151 Alexander Nicolson 1996: 233.
152 Aonghas MacCoinnich 2002: 156.
153 Norman B. Aitchison 1994: 69.
154 I. F. Grant 1961: 87, 216; Allan Macinnes 1996: 20; Robert Dodgshon 1998: 66; Alex Woolf 2007: 25.
155 W. D. H. Sellar 1989: 17.
156 Donald Meek 1995: 126.
157 R. W. Munro 1981: 119.
158 John L. Campbell 1975: 45.
159 Colm Ó Baoill 1994: 32; Ronald Black 2001: 76.
160 Martin Martin 1716: 209–10.
161 Rosemary Ommer 1986: 125;
162 William J. Watson 1937: 273.
163 Duncan Campbell 1910: 65.
164 Iain MacIlleathain and Maletta NicPhàil 2005: 156.
165 *Ibid*: 30, 83.
166 *Ibid*: 155.
167 I. F. Grant 1961: 44.
168 Nerys Patterson 1994: 126–7.
169 Alison Cathcart 2006: 15–16.
170 Domhnall Uilleam Stiùbhart 1999: 233–4.
171 Michael Lynch 2001: 647. Hence this section and details about female roles in and contributions to Gaelic culture in this volume generally are briefer than they ideally should be.
172 Iain MacIlleathain and Maletta NicPhàil 2005: 98.
173 John Shaw 2007c: 35; Barbara Hillers 2007: 158, 162.
174 Colm Ó Baoill 2007: 313.
175 Alan Bruford 1996; John MacInnes 2007: 89.
176 Domhnall Uilleam Stiùbhart 1999: 241.
177 Thomas Owen Clancy 1996: 55.
178 Hugh Cheape 1987: 66.
179 Quoted in Hugh Cheape 1987: 68–9.
180 Domhnall Uilleam Stiùbhart 1999: 239.
181 Anne Grant 1811: 50.
182 Alexander Nicolson 1996: 260, 272.
183 Alexander Nicolson 1996: 16.
184 Iain MacIlleathain and Maletta NicPhàil 2005: 124.

185 Richard Jenkins 1991: 305.
186 Alexander Nicolson 1996: 141. See Lisa Bitel 1996: Chapter Seven and Joan Radner 1990: 182–4 for this theme in early Gaelic literature.
187 Somhairle MacGill-eain 1985: 125. See also Anne Frater 1999: 77–8.
188 Angus Matheson 1952: 360.
189 Colm Ó Baoill 1997: 38.
190 See the observations and speculations (many of which would be discounted by modern scholars) in John F. Campbell 1994b, vol 2: 500–4.
191 Alexander Carmichael 1987, vol. 5: 344.
192 Angela Bourke 1993: 161; Alan Bruford 1996: 63.
193 Quoted and discussed in John MacInnes 2006: 241.
194 *Idem* 2007: 76.
195 John Dewar 1964: 167.
196 Domhnall Uilleam Stiùbhart 1999: 240–2.
197 Jane Dawson 1997: 22.
198 Hugh Cheape 1987: 67–8; Domhnall Uilleam Stiùbhart 1997: 235, 243.
199 Anne Grant 1845: 229–30.

Chapter Five: Family and Personal Life

1 My thanks to Allan MacDonald, Alastair McIntosh and Domhnall Uilleam Stiùbhart for discussion on these points. See further John MacInnes 2006: 163, 181.
2 Angus Matheson 1958: 12–14.
3 William Matheson 1973: 3.
4 George Henderson 1911: 19.
5 William Mackenzie 1914, vol. 2: 116.
6 John G. Campbell 1895: 29.
7 William Matheson 1973: 1.
8 Andrew Simmons 1998: 198.
9 John H. Dixon 1886: 110–11.
10 John G. Campbell 1895: 18. The Gaelic expression is ambiguous, but I parse it as meaning 'his name and kinship'.
11 William Matheson 1973: 3–4.
12 George Black 1946: 306, 421, 469–70.
13 William Matheson 1970: xxxvii, 186–92.
14 Alexander Nicolson 1996: 308.
15 *Ibid*: 321.
16 Osgood MacKenzie 1949: 59.
17 Alexander Nicolson 1996: 247.
18 *Ibid*: 173, 333.
19 *Ibid*: 61, 109, 171.
20 *Ibid*: 32, 301.
21 Anne Grant 1813: 47.
22 John L. Campbell 1975: 90; Alexander Nicolson 1996: 332; Ronald Black 2005: 331.
23 Alexander Nicolson 1996: 59.
24 Donald Meek 1978: no. 365.
25 Alexander Nicolson 1996: 19.
26 *Ibid*: 335.
27 Iain MacIlleathain and Maletta NicPhàil 2005: 81.
28 Ronald Black 2001: 411.
29 Iain MacIlleathain and Maletta NicPhàil 2005: 101.
30 Mary Mackellar 1888: 152.
31 Iain MacIlleathain and Maletta NicPhàil 2005: 29, 33.

32 Alexander Nicolson 1996: 103.
33 Iain MacIlleathain and Maletta NicPhàil 2005: 50.
34 John Buchanan 1997: 43.
35 Gearóid Ó Crualaoich 1998: 176.
36 Margaret Bennett 1992: 6–30.
37 Alexander MacBain 1888: 20.
38 John L. Campbell 1975: 77.
39 Mary Beith 1995: 94.
40 Alexander Allardyce 1888, vol. 2: 422–3.
41 William Mackenzie 1914, vol. 2: 310.
42 Alexander MacDonald 1914: 140–1; Alexander Carmichael 1928, vol. 1: 60–1, 114–15; John L. Campbell 1975: 79–81; Mary Beith 1995: 98–9.
43 Alexander MacBain 1888: 20.
44 *Notes and Queries* 21 January 1871.
45 Joseph Nagy 1987: 163.
46 Nerys Patterson 1994: 124–5.
47 James Ross 1961: 32.
48 Margaret Bennett 1992: 94.
49 James Hall 1807, vol. 2: 441–2.
50 John Buchanan 1997: 46–7.
51 Domhnall Uilleam Stiùbhart 1999: 235, 243.
52 Alexander Allardyce 1888, vol. 2: 420.
53 Fiona M. MacDonald 2005: 59–61; Neill Martin 2006: 78–80. My discussion of marriage customs is based largely on these two texts.
54 Neill Martin 2006: 102.
55 John Dewar 1964: 62–3.
56 Neill Martin 2006: 94, 97.
57 Fiona MacDonald 2005: 66–7; Neill Martin 2006: 81, 130.
58 Aeneas Macintosh 1892: 33–4.
59 William G. Stewart 1851: 192.
60 Alexander Allardyce 1888, vol. 2: 422. See also Alexander MacBain 1888: 20.
61 Archibald Brown 1908: 182.
62 William Mackenzie 1878–9: 30. See also Lachlan Shaw 1882, vol. 3: 136; Alexander Carmichael 1928, vol. 2: 212–13; Michael Newton 1999: 118–19; Michael Hunter 2001: 128.
63 Alexander Cameron 1894, vol. 2: 477.
64 James Logan 1876: 375.
65 Alexander Allardyce 1888, vol. 2: 427–31.
66 Kaarina Hollo 2005: 83–5.
67 Baron Teignmouth 1836: 195. See also Thomas Sinton 1906: 225–6; Alexander Carmichael 1954, vol. 5: 338.
68 Gearóid Ó Crualaoich 1998: 191–7.
69 Patrick Campbell 1937: 176.
70 From the *Compendium of the Laws of the Church of Scotland*, quoted in Baron Teignmouth 1836: 197.
71 John L. Campbell 1975: 86–7.
72 Breandán Breathnach 1996: 71.
73 John L. Campbell 1975: 86.
74 John Buchanan 1997: 73–4.
75 Alexander Nicolson 1996: 9.
76 Alexander MacBain 1888: 240. See also *Folklore Journal* 3 (1885): 281.
77 Terence McCaughey 1989b: 110, 111–14, 118.
78 William J. Watson 2004: 57.
79 Andrew Simmons 1998: 68.
80 Iain MacIlleathain and Maletta NicPhàil 2005: 128.
81 James Ross 1961: 26; Terence McCaughey 1989b: 118.

82 Michael Newton 2001a: 60–6.

83 Margaret Bennett 2001: 56; Ronald Black 2005: 302.

84 Mary Mackellar 1888: 147–8.

85 *Ibid*: 149.

86 Robert Mathieson 2000: 98.

87 Iain MacIlleathain and Maletta NicPhàil 2005: 107.

88 Ronald Black 2005: 540.

89 *The Scottish-Canadian* 22 January 1891; 19 March 1891.

90 Iain MacIlleathain and Maletta NicPhàil 2005: 52.

91 Robert Mathieson 2000: 103.

92 Mary Beith 1995: 115.

93 Thomas Garnett 1811, vol. 1: 120.

94 John L. Campbell and Francis Collinson 1977: 114–17.

95 Colm Ó Baoill 1979: 227.

96 Colm Ó Baoill and Meg Bateman 1994: 178.

97 *Ibid*: 110.

98 R. W. Munro 1961: 42.

99 Andrew Simmons 1998: 63–4.

100 Robert Mathieson 2000: 100, 102.

101 See discussion in *ibid*: 78–80.

102 Barry Cunliffe 1997: 198–9; Miranda Green 1999.

103 Mary Beith 1995: 36–40.

104 Cathaldus Giblin 1964: 89.

105 Such as 'Tochmarc Étaíne' and the Pseudo-Historical Prologue to the Senchas Már.

106 Whitley Stokes 2004: section 35. I have altered the translation slightly for readability.

107 Mary Beith 1995: 41–3; Robert Mathieson 2000: 82–7.

108 Mary Beith 1995: 48.

109 On the other hand, it was used during the conversion of Christianity of those leading a Christian life, in distinction to brigands and enemies of society (*maic báis*). See Kim McCone 1990: 219.

110 Mary Beith 1995: 45–7; John Bannerman 1–11.

111 John Bannerman 1998: 53, 82.

112 *Ibid*: 98–119.

113 Derick Thomson 1968a: 61–5; Mary Beith 1995: 45–57; Robert Mathieson 2000: 85.

114 Mary Beith 1995: 84; Robert Mathieson 2000: 87.

115 Martin Martin 1716: x–xi, 197.

116 Robert Mathieson 2000: 88. In this regard, the original author of the *Collection of Highland Rites and Customes* c.1685 noted that Highlanders 'abhor physic and bloudletting and so they have few or no physicians'. The Reverend John Beaton, descended from the dynasty of MacBeth/Beaton medics, struck through this line on the manuscript. He also noted the recent introduction of a 'superstitious' principle of curing illness. See John L. Campbell 1975: 70–1.

117 Mary Beith 1995: 56.

118 Martin Martin 1716: 197–8.

119 Mary Beith 1995: 79–83

120 John L. Campbell 1975: 72; Alexander Nicolson 1996: 68. This was first published in a short form in John Smith 1780: 80.

121 John Smith 1780: 76.

122 Alexander Campbell 1804: 231.

123 Iain MacIlleathain and Maletta NicPhàil 2005: 148.

124 Alexander Campbell 1802, vol. 1: 202.

125 John L. Campbell 1975: 70–1.

126 Martin Martin 1716: 11, 78, 195, 202, 232, 234.

127 *West Highland Free Press* 31 July 1998.

128 John L. Campbell and D. S. Thomson 1963: 52–3; Ronald Black 2005: 132, 388–9.

129 Iain MacIlleathain and Maletta NicPhàil 2005: 33.

130 *Ibid*: 141.
131 Sarah Murray 1803: 377.
132 Robert Mathieson 2000: 102–144, 225–32.
133 Hugh Cheape 1995: 3.
134 I derive this from the fact that it appears in the text 'Fled Bricrenn', which is dated to about the eighth century.
135 Angus Matheson 1952: 353. My translation.
136 See, for example, Ronald Black 2001: 82, 174; Wilson McLeod and Meg Bateman 2007: 148.
137 R. W. Munro 1961: 43.
138 There is an elaborate description of the war gear of Campbell of Argyll in the sixteenth century in Wilson McLeod and Meg Bateman 2007: 148–50.
139 Several are listed in Alan Bruford 1969: 184–6.
140 Colm Ó Baoill and Meg Bateman 1994: 170.
141 I. F. Grant 1961: 227. This was first explained to me by James MacDonald Reid.
142 R. W. Munro 1961: 42–3. Thanks to Hugh Cheape for pointing out complexities of colour in this passage.
143 Anita Quye et al. 2004.
144 John Macrury 1888–9: 146.
145 Angus Matheson 1952: 320.
146 Martin Martin 1716: 206–9.
147 Anne Grant 1811: 243–4.
148 Michael Newton 1999: 212.
149 Annie Mackenzie 1964: lines 1566–71.
150 Hugh Cheape 1995: 18.
151 Colm Ó Baoill and Meg Bateman 1994: 184, 190.
152 Ronald Black 2001: 456–7.
153 John Gibson 1998: 265–6.
154 Alexander Allardyce 1888, vol. 2: 501.

CHAPTER SIX: BELIEF SYSTEMS AND COSMOLOGY

1 Early versions of the tale are given and discussed in Richard Sharpe 1995: 360–2 and Joseph Nagy 1997: 281–4. The version given here is a collation of Sarah Murray 1803, vol. 2: 219–20, Alexander Carmichael 1928, vol. 2: 338–41, and Alexander Nicolson 1996: 419–20.
2 Michael Bailey 2007: 3.
3 John MacInnes 2006: 459.
4 Ronald Black 2005: lxxxiv.
5 See, for example, the introduction to Raphael Samuel and Paul Thompson 1990.
6 Angela Bourke 2000: 165–6.
7 Gearóid Ó Crualaoich 2003: 12.
8 The fullest treatment of Scottish Gaelic belief systems to date is Ronald Black 2005.
9 See, for example, Kim McCone 1990: 32–4, 229–32.
10 Quoted and discussed in Joseph Nagy 1997: 46–7.
11 *Ibid*: 10, 21, 25, 38–9, 47–8, 93.
12 *Ibid*: 106, 146, 155, 162.
13 Richard Sharpe 1995: 144–5.
14 John L. Campbell 1975: 49; John MacInnes 2006: 261–2.
15 Joseph Nagy 1997: 153, 164.
16 John Carey 2000: 249.
17 Kim McCone 1990: 203–32; Máire West 1997.
18 Richard Sharpe 1995: 111; Joseph Nagy 1997: 149–50. The songs are described in Latin as *scoticae*, which I have translated as 'Gaelic' rather than the usual 'Irish', which is too tied to the identification of a modern nation-state.

19 John Carey 2000: 189–91.
20 *Idem* 1999a: 21.
21 Valerie Flint 1991: 407.
22 Quoted in John Carey 1996: 53.
23 Ewan Campbell 1999: 40–1.
24 Donald Meek 2000: 152–4.
25 Gilbert Márkus 2007b: 92–3.
26 Thomas Owen Clancy 2007: 127.
27 J. R. N. MacPhail 1914: 6.
28 This paragraph is based on John Carey 1999a: 10–37; the quote is from page 11.
29 The story is given in full in *idem* 2002: 57–61. See discussion in *idem* 1999a: 5–6.
30 Donald Meek 2000: 161–94.
31 Alan Macquarrie 1981: 130–1.
32 Thomas Owen Clancy 1998: 263–74.
33 Martin MacGregor 1998: 17–18.
34 *Ibid*: 10.
35 Keith Sanger and Alison Kinnaird 1992: 63–5; Martin MacGregor 1998: 11, 20–3.
36 Quoted in Thomas Owen Clancy 1999: 27.
37 *Idem* 1998: 185.
38 John Purser 2007: 44–9.
39 Thomas Owen Clancy 1998: 318.
40 Wilson McLeod and Meg Bateman 2007: 18–31.
41 Valerie Flint 1991: 254–328.
42 John Purser 2006.
43 *Idem.* 2007: 42–3.
44 Thomas Owen Clancy 1999: 13.
45 Lisa Lawrence 2003.
46 *Tocher* 39 (1985): 110–13 has a version of the tale recorded from Donald MacIntyre of South Uist in 1960.
47 An example recorded in 1965 from Donald MacQueen of South Uist is given in *Tocher* 48/49 (1995): 429–30.
48 Ronald Black 2000: 10.
49 *Ibid*: 18, 22, 43.
50 Jane Dawson 1994: 247.
51 *Ibid*: 237; Donald Meek 1998: 51; Martin MacGregor 1998: 30; Wilson McLeod 2004: 197–9.
52 Donald Meek 1998: 40.
53 *Ibid*: 43, 55.
54 Terence McCaughey 1989: 188–9; Jane Dawson 1994: 245–6; Wilson McLeod 2004: 196–7; Fiona A. MacDonald 2006: 15–18, 55–96.
55 Cathaldus Giblin 1964: 15.
56 Wilson McLeod 2004: 211; Fiona A. MacDonald 2006: 88–90.
57 Cathaldus Giblin 1964: 90.
58 Ronald Black 2007b.
59 Wilson McLeod 2004: 197–9.
60 John MacInnes 2006: 434–5.
61 Terence McCaughey 1989: 182–7; John MacInnes 2006: 432–3.
62 Fiona A. Macdonald 1995: 20.
63 Neill Martin 2006: 119.
64 Donald Meek 2000: 134–9.
65 Archibald Campbell 1889: 46–53.
66 Ronald Black 2005: 162–3.
67 Jane Dawson 1994: 242.
68 Ronald Black 2001: 134–43. 427–8.
69 George Henderson 1912: 20.

70 From an undated article from *An Deó-Ghréine* in my files.
71 Domhnall Uilleam Stiùbhart 2003; Michael Newton 2003c: *passim.*
72 Quoted in Robert Clyde 1995: 60–1.
73 Simon Fraser 1986: 102 (note 42).
74 Derick Thomson 1992b: 126–7; Michael Newton 2003c: 30–1.
75 Donald Meek 1989b; *idem* 2007b: 143–4; John MacInnes 2006: 368–72.
76 Pàdruig Grannd 1842: 107–9;
77 John Dixon 1886: 121.
78 Somhairle MacGill-eain 1985: 10. See also Douglas Andsell 1998: 131–4.
79 John Gibson 1998: 200–1.
80 John MacInnes 2006: 441–2, 456.
81 Douglas Andsell 1998: 136.
82 John MacInnes 2006: 436–41.
83 Tomás Ó Cathasaigh 1977–9; John Carey 1999a: 27–8.
84 H. Wagner 1981: 1.
85 John Carey 1999a.
86 *Idem* 1980; Sharon MacLeod 1998–9. Note that I am here using the first form to emerge 'Donann' rather than the later 'Danann'.
87 John L. Campbell and D. S. Thomson 1963: 39, 45, 49.
88 Derick Thomson 1994: 4–5; Colm Ó Baoill 1997: 111; *idem* 2001: 40, 42, 44.
89 William J. Watson 1959: line 4503.
90 John F. Campbell 1994a, vol. 1: 438–44.
91 Duncan Campbell 1910: 552.
92 Ronald Black 2005: 219, 390–1.
93 Lizanne Henderson and Edward Cowan 2001: 15–16, 77–8, 161.
94 James MacKillop 1998: 230–1; Dáithí Ó hÓgáin 1990: 213–15.
95 John Koch and John Carey 2003: 145.
96 *Ibid*: 52. Thanks to John Carey for pointing this text out to me.
97 Michael Hunter 2001: 85.
98 *Ibid*: 79, 80.
99 Archibald Campbell 1889: 64.
100 Áine O'Neill 1991.
101 Angela Bourke 2000: 32, 33.
102 Ronald Black 2005: xxxv–lxxxi.
103 There are variants of this in James MacDougall 1910: 158–61; Alan Bruford and Donald A. MacDonald 2003: 342–4; Ronald Black 2005: 36.
104 Ronald Black 2005: lxvi–lxxvi.
105 Susan Eberly 1991: 238–9.
106 *Ibid*: 231–3.
107 Ronald Black 2005: lxiii.
108 James MacDougall 1910: 157.
109 William Mahon 2000; Gearóid Ó Crualaoich 2003: 38–67.
110 Lizanne Henderson and Edward Cowan 2001: 118–38.
111 Gearóid Ó Crualaoich 2003: 83.
112 *Ibid*: 82–8.
113 H. Wagner 1981: 5, 6; Sharon Paice MacLeod 1998–9; Hilda Ellis Davidson 1999.
114 Máire Herbert 1999.
115 Patricia Lysaght 1999.
116 Gearóid Ó Crualaoich 2003: 89.
117 John G. Campbell 1914–15: 413.
118 Katherine Grant 1925: 4–9; Eleanor Hull 1927: 247–50.
119 There is a rhyme about this, attributed to the Glaisteag, in John Smith 1964: 94.
120 John G. Campbell 1914–15: 416.
121 *Ibid*: 414; Ronald Black 2005: 368.

122 John Carey 1999b.
123 Alexander Carmichael 1928, vol. 2: 283 with readings from the variant in John Smith 1964: 94–5. There is a verse of a similar import from Tiree in John G. Campbell 1914–15: 415.
124 Katherine Grant 1925: 4. For Gaelic texts, see Katherine Grant 1911: 129–39.
125 John Grant 1876: 61–2.
126 John MacInnes 2006: 497.
127 James MacDougall 1910: 240; Alexander Carmichael 1954, vol. 5: 168–77. The identity of Cailleach Beinne Bhric with Cailleach Bheur is underlined in that the Cailleach of the Mull tale below sings this same song.
128 William Scrope 1883: 160–1.
129 John Mac Cormick 1923: 65. There are fuller and more interesting texts in Gearóid Ó Crualaoich 2003: 113–19; 240–4.
130 Gearóid Ó Crualaoich 2003: 114–19.
131 Alexander MacDonald 1896–7: 34–5.
132 Tomás Ó Cathasaigh 1977–9: 140, 148.
133 This is the Irish form. In Scottish Gaelic it is spelled *aonach*.
134 John Carey 1986–7: 13.
135 *Ibid*: 13–15.
136 Proinsias MacCana 1997: 620–1.
137 John Carey 1999b: 35; Gearóid Ó Crualaoich 2003: 28, 38–42.
138 Patricia Lysaght 1999.
139 Wilson McLeod 2004: 136–42.
140 Patricia Lysaght 1999: 157.
141 Sithiche 1912; Alexander Carmichael 1954, vol. 5: 272–84; Ronald Black 2005: 22–3, 234–9.
142 Alexander Carmichael 1928, vol. 2: 245.
143 *Ibid*, vol. 2: 306.
144 Alexander MacBain 1888: 13.
145 John F. Campbell 1994a, vol. 1: 61.
146 John MacInnes 2006: 79–80, 441.
147 Alasdair MacLean Sinclair 1891–2: 291. See also James MacDougall 1910: 198–201.
148 Wilson McLeod and Meg Bateman 2007: 226.
149 Duncan Campbell 1984: 83–4.
150 John L. Campbell 1984: 4–6.
151 William Gillies 1991: 23.
152 John L. Campbell 1984: 286.
153 Michael Newton forthcoming.
154 *Idem* 2009.
155 Lachlan MacKinnon 1960: 22.
156 E. O. James 1968: 246, 245.
157 A. T. Lucas 1963: 17–20; Francis Byrne 1973: 182; Alden Watson 1981.
158 William J. Watson 2004: 244–5; G. W. S. Barrow 1998: 56–9.
159 William J. Watson 2004: 247–8; John MacInnes 2006: 23.
160 Ian Carmichael 1948: 42–3.
161 This general assertion was first made in 1978 in John MacInnes' seminal article on Gaelic panegyric code and developed further in Michael Newton 1998. See John MacInnes 2006: 284.
162 Colm Ó Baoill and Meg Bateman 1994: 176.
163 T. M. Charles-Edwards 1993: 28.
164 Wilson McLeod and Meg Bateman 2007: 90–1.
165 Ronald Black 2001: 308–9.
166 William Watson 1959: 221.
167 Kaarina Hollo 1995: 18, 23; Ann Buckley 1995: 33–4.
168 Alden Watson 1981: 12.
169 Annie MacKenzie 1964: lines 2320–1.
170 Domhnull MacCoinnich 1785: §23.

171 Michael Newton 2001a: 125.
172 Annie MacKenzie 1964: lines 1070–7.

Chapter Seven: Song, Music, and Dance

1 Bruno Nettl 1983: 40.
2 Michael Newton 1998–9; John MacInnes 2006: 466–7.
3 Translated and adapted from Allan McDonald 1908. Thanks to Hugh Cheape for pointing this text out to me and providing me with a copy.
4 Scott Reiss 2003: 149–50, 153–4.
5 Sally K. Sommers Smith 2003: 105.
6 Scott Reiss 2003: 155–8.
7 See for example Alan Bruford 1973.
8 Some of these can be found in Alexander Nicolson 1996: 195 and John Smith 1964: 11–15, 17–18. For more about the connection between birds and Gaelic music, see John Purser 2007: 22.
9 John Smith 1780: 148. I have attempted to modernise the spelling of his vocables.
10 Alan Bruford 1990: 61. Only a subset of these may be active in any particular dialect, however.
11 William Matheson 1983: 131–2.
12 James Ross 1953–5: 237.
13 William Matheson 1955: 78; exceptions are discussed on 79. For the most recent and complete analysis (in Gaelic), see Mòrag Nic Leòid 2002. There are also very valuable notes about Gaelic song style in Anne Lorne Gillies 2005: xxvii–xxxi.
14 Donald Campbell 1862: 154.
15 Charles Stewart 1884: 154.
16 John MacInnes 2006: 218. See also Margaret Shaw 1986: 76. For this use of the term *caoin*, see John Shaw 2000: 15.
17 Francis Tolmie 1997: ix.
18 I owe many of these observations about song aesthetics to Allan MacDonald of Glenuig and John MacInnes of the School of Scottish Studies.
19 William Matheson 1970: 149.
20 Alan Bruford 1990: 68; William Matheson 1993: 4.
21 William Matheson 1970: 152.
22 Michael Hunter 2001: 125. I have modernised the spelling. This information probably came from a native of Speyside. See *ibid*: 128.
23 *Ibid*.
24 John L. Campbell and Francis Collinson 1969: 237; John MacInnes 2006: 251.
25 James Ross 1953–5: 233–4, 239.
26 John MacInnes 2006: 213.
27 John L. Campbell and Francis Collinson 1969: 236–7.
28 James Ross 1956–7: 2.
29 Alexander Allardyce 1888, vol. 2: 410–11.
30 Frances Tolmie 1997: 235.
31 Sarah Murray 1803, vol. 2: 377.
32 Ann Buckley 1995: 31–2; Ríonach Uí Ógáin 1995: 81.
33 William Shaw 1972: 123–4.
34 Alexander Nicolson 1996: 134.
35 John Shaw 1992–3: 44–6.
36 This low ranking of the port-à-beul genre has been more clearly articulated in Gaelic Nova Scotia; the adoption and promotion of puirt by the choirs of An Comunn Gàidhealach may have served to elevate their perceived status in twentieth-century Scotland. See Heather Sparling 2000.
37 William Matheson 1955: 69.
38 Derick Thomson 1992b: 156–7.
39 This recording was featured on a BBC Radio nan Gàidheal programme presented by Jo MacDonald.

40 John Ross 1961: 20–2.
41 Ríonach Uí Ógáin 1995: 84.
42 I am making a distinction here between songs that describe or mention ritual activities and those actually sung in the performance of the ritual itself.
43 John MacInnes 2006: 477–91; Donald Meek 2007c.
44 John Shaw 2000: 13.
45 John Shaw 2000: 27.
46 Bruno Nettl 1983: 36.
47 William Matheson 1955: 76.
48 Margaret Shaw 1968: 72.
49 Martin Martin 1716: 71–2.
50 Stuart Eydmann 2007: 194.
51 Frank Harrison 1986: 255–6.
52 Seán Donnelly 1981: 19.
53 Noel Hamilton 1988: 289.
54 John Purser 2007: 21–9.
55 Keith Sanger and Alison Kinnaird 1992: 13.
56 J. V. S. Megaw 1997: 664–73.
57 John Purser 2007: 29.
58 John Bannerman 1991: 1; Ann Buckley 1995: 36–7.
59 John Bannerman 1991: 9; Keith Sanger and Alison Kinnard 1992: 32–3. The term itself continued to be used in Gaelic poetry and song, but probably referred to the clàrsach rather than the lyre.
60 Keith Sanger and Alison Kinnaird 1992: 12–30.
61 John Bannerman 1991: 6.
62 Keith Sanger and Alison Kinnaird 1992: 42–5.
63 Æneas J. G. MacKay 1892: 50.
64 R. W. Munro 1961: 43–4.
65 John Bannerman 1991: 9–12; Keith Sanger and Alison Kinnaird 1992: 53–68.
66 Seán Donnelly 1981: 20.
67 Noel Hamilton 1988: 289; Breandán Breathnach 1996: 6–7; *Piping Times* 21 (2006): 30–3; John Purser 2004: 224–5; *idem* 2007: 29, 35–6.
68 Keith Sanger, personal communication.
69 Hugh Cheape 1999: 44.
70 Seán Donnelly 1981: 20–1; *idem* 1982: 57; Breandán Breathnach 1996: 69–72; Hugh Cheape 1999: 35–7, 42–4.
71 Keith Sanger, personal communication.
72 Hugh Cheape 1999: 13–14, 62.
73 John Dunbar 1962: 36.
74 Stanley Sadie 2001, vol. 8: 767–75; Mary Anne Alburger 2007: 239.
75 Breandán Breathnach 1996: 6.
76 Breandán Breathnach 1996: 6, 79–80; Mary Anne Alburger 2007: 242, 246–8.
77 Martin Martin 1716: 14.
78 John Purser 1994: 3.
79 William MacKenzie 1878–9: 104.
80 William J. Watson 1959: 319.
81 John Purser 2007: 35–6.
82 Colm Ó Baoill 1994: lines 446–9.
83 Niall MacKenzie 2002. Edmund Burt noted that when attempting to recruit Highlanders in the 1720s the bagpipe was played, as it was 'more agreeable to the people than a drum' (Andrew Simmons 1998: 39. See also p. 222.)
84 John G. Campbell 1886–7: 70; John F. Campbell 1994b, vol. 1: 471.
85 Michael Hunter 2001: 99. I have modernised the spelling and punctuation.
86 Colm Ó Baoill 1979: lines 250–5.
87 John Bannerman 1991: 12–13.

88 William J. Watson 1937: 14–21; John Bannerman 1991: 6–7; Keith Sanger and Alison Kinnaird 1992: 39.

89 Keith Sanger and Alison Kinnaird 1992: 118.

90 Colm Ó Baoill 1972: lines 1273–92.

91 Keith Sanger 2008: 9.

92 John Bannerman 1991: 6; Keith Sanger and Alison Kinnaird 1992: 82.

93 William Matheson 1970: lxxii–lxxiii; John Bannerman 1991: 7; Keith Sanger and Alison Kinnaird 1992: 112–16, 162.

94 Keith Sanger and Alison Kinnaird 1992: 73–4, 86, 116–135, 149–50.

95 Keith Sanger 2008: 5.

96 William J. Watson 1937: 32–59; John Bannerman 1991: 6–8; Keith Sanger and Alison Kinnaird 1992: 39–40.

97 William Matheson 1970: 151–3, 164–7.

98 Quoted in Eleanor Knott 1960: 58. I have modernised the spelling and punctuation.

99 John L. Campbell 1975: 49.

100 Keith Sanger and Alison Kinnaird 1992: 81; John Purser 2007: 73.

101 Keith Sanger and Alison Kinnaird 1992: 123–4; Colm Ó Baoill 1997: xxv–xxx.

102 Keith Sanger and Alison Kinnaird 1992: 150.

103 I. F. Grant and Hugh Cheape 1987: 130–1; Keith Sanger and Alison Kinnaird 1992: 174; Leeman Perkins 1999: 113–16, 757–75.

104 Keith Sanger and Alison Kinnaird 1992: 174–89.

105 H. F. McClintock 1950: plates 19 and 26.

106 Hugh Cheape 1999: 22; *idem* 2002a: 11–12. It is also possible that the name is a by-form of *MacGuirmein* (probably originally MacGilleGhuirmein, anglicised as 'Blue'), which is close to the form in which it was recorded in the *Wardlaw Manuscript*, 'Macgurmen' (William Mackay 1905: 379).

107 Hugh Cheape 2002a: 19–20.

108 Neil Rankin Morrison 1934–6: 61.

109 *Ibid*: 68.

110 Such as John MacGregor IV and Malcolm MacGregor, bagpipers to the Highland Society of London in the early nineteenth century. See Frank Buisman 2001: xxxi.

111 Leeman Perkins 1999: 106–9.

112 Sean Donnelly 1981: 20–4.

113 Hugh Cheape 1999: 65.

114 R. W. Munro 1961: 43.

115 Michael Newton and Hugh Cheape forthcoming.

116 Alexander MacGregor 1852: 2.

117 John MacKenzie 1841: 67.

118 The poem has most recently been edited and translated in Wilson McLeod and Meg Bateman 2007: 278–81.

119 Derick Thomson 1974–6: 23. See also the satires on Irish pipers in Seán Donnelly 1984: 55–7.

120 Colm Ó Baoill and Meg Bateman 1994: 160–3.

121 Several others are translated and discussed in Michael Newton and Hugh Cheape forthcoming.

122 Colm Ó Baoill 1972: lines 1345–8.

123 Hugh Cheape 1988: 2–3; Michael Newton and Hugh Cheape forthcoming.

124 William Forsyth 1900: 276; Keith Sanger and Alison Kinnaird 1992: 117–19.

125 John Bannerman 1991: 13.

126 Keith Sanger and Alison Kinnaird 1992: 117–19.

127 *Ibid*: 153; Frank Buisman 2001: xxv.

128 John L. Campbell 1975: 49.

129 Andrew Simmons 1998: 222.

130 Alexander Nicolson 1994: 37, 84, 128–31.

131 Frank Buisman 2001: xxvii–xxviii.

132 James Carmichael Watson 1934: lines 502–4.

133 Frank Buisman 2001: xxii–xxix.

134 Neil Rankin Morrison 1934–6.

135 John Dixon 1886: 41–43, 56–7, 177–9.

136 Hugh Cheape 1988; Frank Buisman 2001: xxix–xxxi.

137 Joshua Dickson 2006: 84–5.

138 Duncan Campbell 1888: 212–13.

139 Michael Newton 1999: 190–215.

140 Hugh Cheape 1988.

141 William Matheson 1970: 155, 157, 165; Keith Sanger and Alison Kinnaird 1992: 186–90.

142 Allan MacDonald 1995: Chapter One.

143 I. F. Grant and Hugh Cheape 1987: 131–3; Joshua Dickson 2006: 7–9.

144 Patrick McDonald 2000: 12.

145 Allan MacDonald 1995; Joshua Dickson 2006: 18–24, 138–53.

146 Allan MacDonald 1995; John Gibson 1998.

147 Patrick McDonald 2000: 11.

148 Andrew Simmons 1998: 213.

149 William Matheson 1970: 164, 167, 181; Keith Sanger and Alison Kinnaird 1992: 181.

150 I. F. Grant and Hugh Cheape 1987: 180–1; William Matheson 1970: lxi–lxvi.

151 I. F. Grant and Hugh Cheape 1987: 181.

152 Keith Sanger and Alison Kinnaird 1992: 151–2.

153 Simon Fraser 1986: 100 (note 3).

154 William Matheson 1955: 69–71.

155 John Shaw 1992–3.

156 Simon Fraser 1986: iv. Italics as in original text.

157 Martin Martin 1716: 200.

158 Charles Stewart 1884: x.

159 George Emmerson 1972: 10–11, 151; Derick Thomson 1994: 56; Breandán Breathnach 1996: 356. Noel Hamilton 1988: 290.

160 J. V. S. Megaw 1997: 659; Frank Harrison 1986: 254–5.

161 Robert MacLagan 1901: 103–5; George Emmerson 1972: 153, 155–6, 161, 186–92, 229, 245; Simon Fraser 1986: 101; Derick Thomson 1994: 56; J. F. Flett and T. M. Flett 1996: 21–8, 44–8. The Angus Fraser manuscript (NLS Adv. MS 73.1.5–6) also mentions a pyrrhic dance called *Fir-chlis*, which is also the name for the Aurora Borealis.

162 Alexander Campbell 1804: 263.

163 J. F. Flett and T. M. Flett 1952–5: 119–20; George Emmerson 1972: 38; Breandán Breathnach 1996: 42–3; James MacDonald Reid 2001.

164 J. F. Flett and T. M. Flett 1952–5: 119–20, 125.

165 Quoted in *idem* 1956: 84–5.

166 This analysis draws heavily upon Ronald Black 1998: 148–51.

167 Alexander Campbell 1804: 262–3.

168 Alexander Nicolson 1996: 307.

169 Charles Ferguson 1896–7: 101.

170 Quoted in J. F. Flett and T. M. Flett 1952–5: 115.

171 Angus Fraser 1996: 16.

172 Quoted in J. F. Flett and T. M. Flett 1952–5: 116–7; Ronald Black 1998: 149–50. This tune is in 6/8 time, whereas the tune to *an t-Seann Ruga Mhór* seems to have been in 2/4 time.

173 Alexander Campbell 1804: 265–8; Ronald Black 1998: 151–2.

174 Thomas Sinton 1906: 4; J. F. Flett and T. M. Flett 1956: 86–7.

175 Richard Kraus 1969: 47–8.

176 *Ibid*: 54.

177 Valerie Flint 1991: 269.

178 Alan Newell 2005.

179 George Emmerson 1972: 19; Michael Newton 2006: 230.

180 John MacInnes 2006: 226–9, 241–4, 248–64; Michael Newton 2006.

181 J. F. Flett and T. M. Flett 1952–5: 120–24; Derick Thomson 1994: 58; James MacDonald Reid 2001.

182 Alexander Carmichael 1928, vol. 1: 167.
183 Walter Sorell 1967: 45.
184 Richard Kraus 1969: 64.
185 Mary Anne Alburger 2007: 246–51.
186 Carolyn Merchant 1989: 40–2; Keith Thomas 1996: 36–50.
187 John MacInnes 2006: 254; George Emmerson 1972: 78, 144, 150–1, 162, 163.
188 J. F. Flett and T. M. Flett 1972; George Emmerson 1972: 151–2; Breandán Breathnach 1996: 37–8.
189 George Emmerson 1972: 154; Maggie Moore 1994: 18; John Gibson 1998: 112–13, 135.
190 Curtis Sachs 1937: 358–61; George Emmerson 1972: 44–5.
191 John Purser 2007: 118.
192 George Emmerson 1972: 45, 151, 257; Frank Harrison 1986: 260–1; Michael Newton 2006: 231.
193 John L. Campbell and Francis Collinson 1969: lines 287–90.
194 *Ibid*: lines 822–5.
195 J. F. Flett and T. M. Flett 1967: 1–2; *idem* 1972: 94–6; George Emmerson 1972: 173–6; John Gibson 1998: 112, 114; Mary Anne Alburger 2007: 253–9; Evelyn Hood, Joan Henderson and Alastair MacFadyen 2007: 508–12.
196 Quoted in J. F. Flett and T. M. Flett 1972: 96.
197 Eveyln Hood 1994; J. F. Flett and T. M. Flett 1996: 1–6.
198 George Emmerson 1972: 151, 163; J. F. Flett and T. M. Flett 1996: 6.
199 Breandán Breathnach 1996: 49–54; Evelyn Hood, Joan Henderson and Alastair MacFadyen 2007: 509–13.
200 Thomas Garnett 1811, vol. 2: 72.
201 Francis Peacock 1805: 14–15, 25.
202 *Ibid*: 86.
203 That these Gaelic terms seem to have been in circulation, at least in the central Highlands, is suggested by their appearance in William G. Stewart 1860: 101–2.
204 Quoted in I. F. Grant 1961: 352.
205 John F. Campbell 1994b, vol. 2: 230–7.
206 George Emmerson 1972: 155–9, 211–13; J. F. Flett and T. M. Flett 1996: 1, 4–8; Breandán Breathnach 1996: 43–5. According to the Angus Fraser manuscript (NLS Adv. MS 73.1.5–6), completed in 1848, these types of dances and footwork were referred to with the Gaelic terms *alt-cheum, bonn-bhreabadh, caismeachd,* and *ceumadh.*
207 Colonel Thornton quoted in George Emmerson 1972: 158.
208 *Ibid*: 211–22; J. F. Flett and T. M. Flett 1996: 40–3.
209 Thanks to James MacDonald Reid, in particular, for these observations. Barry Shears (personal communication) adds the caveats that one of the areas in Nova Scotia which produced some of the best dancers still had homes with dirt floors into the 1970s, and that many dancers wore soft-soled shoes derived from the native moccasin.
210 John Gibson 1998: 110–18, 133–6.
211 Quoted on Joshua Dickson 2006: 18.

CHAPTER EIGHT: HUMAN ECOLOGY

1 John Fowler 2002: 4–6.
2 The original Gaelic tale was contributed by Iain Moireaston, probably a native of Loch Broom, and printed in *An Gàidheal* 1 (1872). The translation is mine.
3 Carolyn Merchant 1989: 19, 25.
4 *Ibid*: 11–12, 19–26, 70–4; Max Oelschlaeger 1991: 9–11.
5 For commentary on modern survivals, see Hugh Brody 2000.
6 Max Oelschlaeger 1991: 12.
7 *Ibid*: 15, 21–9.
8 *Ibid*: 28, 32.
9 Hugh Cheape 2002b: 13.

10 Keith Thomas 1998: 265.
11 Max Oelschlaeger 1991: 7, 27, 30, 37, 50–1.
12 Maria Tymoczko 1983: 26.
13 John MacInnes 2006: 40.
14 There is something of a parallel in the self-identification with pastoralism in the Old Testament. See Max Oelschlaeger 1991: 48.
15 I was reminded of this lately in a conversation with my friend Anthony Dilworth.
16 John Stuart-Murray 2006.
17 Hugh Cheape 1993: 54.
18 For further discussion see Michael Newton 1998: Chapter Four; *Idem* 2003d.
19 John Mohawk 1990: 94.
20 David Nettle and Suzanne Romaine 2000: 13.
21 Keith Thomas 1996: 61.
22 Angus MacLeod 1978: lines 5268–9.
23 Iain MacIlleathain and Maletta NicPhàil 2005: 113.
24 Alexander Nicolson 1996: 336.
25 *Ibid*: 405.
26 Ronald Black 2001: 102–4.
27 *Ibid*: 294–6.
28 Martin Martin 1716: 143.
29 *Ibid*: 159.
30 Alexander Carmichael 1928, vol. 2: 360.
31 Colin Chisholm 1883: 225–6.
32 Liam Mac Mathúna 1989–90.
33 Thanks to Pat Menzies for giving me her transcription from one of the McLagan manuscripts.
34 William Watson 1959: lines 3222–5, 3230–3, 3265–5. See also the variant in Colm Ó Baoill and Meg Bateman 1994: 206–12.
35 Angus MacLeod 1978: 196–225. For background information about the poem, see Ronald Black 2001: 490–3.
36 William Gillies 1977: 45–6.
37 Seán Ó Tuama 1985: 23, 28.
38 Translated from William J. Watson 1934: 233.
39 Murdoch McNeill 1910: 81. Thanks to Hugh Cheape for this reference.
40 Translated from William J. Watson 1929: 134, 135.
41 Thomas Sinton 1906: 2.
42 *Ibid*: 11.
43 Patrick Sheeran 1988: 192.
44 Maria Tymoczko 1983.
45 Seumas MacDhiarmaid 1913; William J. Watson 2002: 177.
46 Michael Newton 2009.
47 The term seems to have been revived in a Scottish Gaelic context first by William J. Watson in 1904. See William J. Watson 2002: 44.
48 Brian Ó Cuív 1989–90: 91, 96–9.
49 Proinsias Mac Cana 1988: 332–3; Brian Ó Cuív 1989–90: 93, 102–5; J. E. Caerwyn Williams and Patrick Ford 1992: 34–5.
50 John Michie 1908: 150.
51 Donald MacDonald 2004: 142.
52 *An Gàidheal* 3 (1874): 143–4. Discussed in Wilson McLeod 2003c: 114–17.
53 Patrick Sheeran 1988: 203.
54 William J. Watson 1959: lines 3746–53; Ronald Black 2001: 70.
55 Duncan Campbell 1910: 170.
56 Hector Mackenzie 1885: 392.
57 Ellen Ettlinger 1952–4.
58 Alexander Carmichael 1928, vol. 1: 207; Thomas Pennant 1998: 252, 272.

59 Michael Hunter 2001: 85. I have modernised the spelling and punctuation.
60 T. M. Charles-Edwards 1993: 262–5.
61 John MacInnes 2006: 432, 441, 463.
62 Alexander Carmichael 1972, vol. 6: 42.
63 Peter McQuillan 2004: 9, 39, 80.
64 John MacInnes 2007: 279.
65 Peter McQuillan 2004: 25, 38, 46–7.
66 Pàruig Mac-an-Tuairneir 1813: 111.
67 Peter McQuillan 2004: 77, 90–1.
68 *Ibid*: 32, 38, 43–4, 50, 60.
69 Donald MacKinnon 1905–8: 4–6.
70 *Ibid*: 108.
71 William J. Watson 1959: lines 3925, 3987; Ronald Black 2001: 30, 34.
72 Annie MacKenzie 1964: line 1111.
73 Quoted in R. W. Munro 1981: 123.
74 Peter McQuillan 2004: 182.
75 Andrew Simmons 1998: 270.
76 Quoted in Charles Withers 1988: 64.
77 Robert Burns 1855: 348.
78 Andrew Simmons 1998: 268.
79 Mary MacKellar 1886: 215.
80 *An Gàidheal* 5 (1876): 330.
81 John MacInnes 2006: 476, 497.
82 William J. Watson 1959: lines 6691–8, 6711–22. An independent variation of the entire poem has been edited and translated in Wilson McLeod and Meg Bateman 2007: 392–405. See general discussion in Pat Menzies 2006.
83 Pat Menzies 2006: 92–5.
84 Donald Meek 2003b.
85 Máire Herbert 2005: 131.
86 Wilson McLeod and Meg Bateman 2007: 304–7.
87 *Ibid*: 306–13.
88 Adam Gunn 1899: 63–4.
89 See also states this in a song written while at a girl's school in Perth. See Michel Byrne 2007: 113.
90 Thomas Sinton 1906: 11–12.
91 Angus MacLeod 1978: lines 5512–99.
92 Iain MacGhrigair 1818: 19.
93 William J. Watson 1959: lines 4912–19, 4988–95.
94 William Matheson 1938: xvii, xix, xxiv–xxviii.
95 *Ibid*: lines 621–4, 629–44.
96 Wilson McLeod 2003b: 98–9, 106–7.
97 Iain MacGhrigair 1801: 56–7.
98 Derick Thomson 1996: 168–9.
99 Meg Bateman 2003: 81–3; Donald Meek 2003b: 10–11.
100 Colm Ó Baoill 1994: lines 480–1; Ronald Black 2001: 72.
101 Colm Ó Baoill and Meg Bateman 1994: 178–80.
102 James Carmichael Watson 1934: xii, xiv.
103 William Matheson 1965: 165.
104 Angus MacDonald and Archibald MacDonald 1911: 78.
105 *Ibid*: 97.
106 Alexander Nicolson 1996: 47.
107 From an undated copy of a clipping from a Gaelic column in a Montreal newspaper given to me by Kenneth McKenna.
108 William J. Watson 1959: lines 6487–90; Martin MacGregor 2000b: 143.
109 Maria Tymoczko 1983: 17–19; John Koch 2005, vol. 4: 1345.

110 *Ibid*: 1346–7.

111 William J. Watson 1959: lines 4911–99.

112 John Mackenzie 1841: 160. See notes in Ronald Black 2001: 461–2.

113 William J. Watson 1959: lines 2299–330. See notes in Ronald Black 2001: 461–2.

114 Ronald Black 2001: 304–9.

115 Charles Smith quoted in Máire Mac Neill 1962: 137.

116 Martin Martin 1716: 85–6.

117 Alexander Carmichael 1954, vol. 5: 386–7. This tradition appears to be closely related to that of sailors needing to respond to poetic challenges from *na Fir Ghorma* 'The Blue Men (of the Minch)' before being allowed to pass safely. See Ronald Black 2005: 107.

118 William Matheson 1938: xl–xlii.

119 Wilson McLeod 2003b: 112.

120 Michael Newton 2003d: 182–7.

121 John MacInnes 2006: 461–2.

122 Hugh Cheape 2002b: 13–14.

123 William MacKay 1914: 425–6. The original has *Ceann a' chnoc mhór* but the English translation is 'great Ceanacroc'. I have therefore altered the Gaelic adjective accordingly.

124 Translated from James MacDougall 1910: 256.

125 Translated from *Ibid*: 248.

126 John Grant 1876: 62.

127 Lizanne Henderson and Edward Cowan 2001: 24–30, 193–208.

128 Aonghas Caimbeul 1785: 108–11.

129 Donald Meek 2003b: 23–8.

130 Iain MacIlleathainn and Maletta NicPhàil 2005: 157. I have emended it slightly to agree with the form in which it appears in the Charles Robertson manuscript collection of the National Library of Scotland.

131 John MacInnes 2006: 497–9.

132 Max Oelschlaeger 1991: 4.

Conclusions

1 Neil Ross 1939: lines 2429–32, 2437–40, 2453–6, 2533–6.

2 Donald Meek 2004a: 14–17.

3 Martin MacGregor 2007b; Donald Meek 1990.

4 Herbert Campbell 1926: 195.

5 John MacInnes 2006: 29.

6 *Ibid*: xxiv–xxvi.

7 Richard Bringhurst 2008: 30.

8 Miguel León-Portilla 1990: 9.

9 Iain Crichton Smith 1986: 70.

10 *Ibid*: 19–22, 31.

11 Michael Newton forthcoming.

12 Donald MacKinnon 1883: 3, 28.

13 *Ibid*: 36.

Appendix A: Gaelic Poetry Sampler

1 Gaelic text from William J. Watson 1937: 204–10. The translation is mine.

2 *Highland Monthly* 1 (1890): 755–6. This was copied from the MacColl manuscript, a very valuable folklore collection which has since been lost.

3 See Wilson McLeod and Meg Bateman 2007: 358–63.

4 *Mac-Talla* 9 (5 April 1901).

5 *Celtic Monthly* 19 (1911): 180.

6 *Mac-Talla* 2 (29 June 1893). It was probably contributed by Rev. Angus MacDonald who compiled the 'Killearnan Collection' manuscript now housed in Edinburgh University Library.
7 John Shaw 2000: 234–6.
8 *Saga Och Sed* (1959): 75–8.
9 *Celtic Magazine* 1 (1875): 26.
10 *Tocher* 52 (1996): 139–40.
11 It does not appear in her 1785 collection of poetry *Òrain Nuadh Ghàidhealach*, but is given in full in the 1894 book of Gaelic hymns edited by Archibald MacCallum. Five verses of it, with the melody, appear in Francis Tolmie's appendix to *The Gesto Collection*.
12 Biographical information from *The Northern Chronicle* 26 April 1882.
13 *Celtic Magazine* 10 (1885): 344–6.
14 *Northern Chronicle* 4 February 1885.
15 Donald MacPherson 1868: 154. There is an even longer and more interesting example in Iain MacIlleathain and Maletta NicPhàil 2005: 165–6.
16 *The Highlander* 28 October 1876.
17 *An Teangadóir* 4 (1957): 2.
18 See Ronald Black 2005: 559–60, 599–600; Thomas Owen Clancy 2003: 105.

BIBLIOGRAPHY

AITCHISON, NORMAN B., 'Kingship, Society, and Sacrality: Rank, Power, and Ideology in Early Medieval Ireland', *Traditio* 49 (1994), 45–75.

ALBURGER, MARY ANNE, 'The Fiddle' in John Beech, et al. (eds), *Oral Literature and Performance Culture*, Scottish Life and Society 10 (Edinburgh: John Donald, 2007), 238–73.

ALLARDYCE, ALEXANDER (ed.), *Scotland and Scotsmen in the Eighteenth Century*, 2 vols (Edinburgh and London: W. Blackwood and Sons, 1888).

ANSDELL, DOUGLAS, *The People of the Great Faith: The Highland Church 1690–1900* (Stornoway: Acair, 1998).

ARMIT, IAN, *Celtic Scotland* (Edinburgh: Birlinn, 2005).

BAILEY, MICHAEL, *Magic and Superstition in Europe* (Lanham: Rowman & Littlefield, 2007).

BANNERMAN, JOHN, 'The Lordship of the Isles' in Jennifer Brown (ed.), *Scottish Society in the Fifteenth Century* (London: Palgrave Macmillan, 1977), 209–40.

— 'The Scots Language and the Kin-based Society' in Derick Thomson (ed.), *Gaelic and Scots in Harmony* (Glasgow: University of Glasgow, 1988), 1–19.

— 'The King's Poet and the Inauguration of Alexander III', *Scottish Historical Review* 68 (1989), 120–49.

— 'The Clàrsach and the Clàrsair', *Scottish Studies* 30 (1991), 1–17.

— 'MacDuff of Fife' in Alexander Grant and Keith Stringer (eds), *Medieval Scotland* (Edinburgh: Edinburgh University Press, 1993), 20–38.

— 'The Residence of the King's Poet', *Scottish Gaelic Studies* 27 (1996), 24–35.

— *The Beatons* (Edinburgh: John Donald, 1998).

BARRON, HUGH, 'Notes on Bards', *Transactions of the Gaelic Society of Inverness* 48 (1972–4), 1–61.

BARROW, G. W. S., *Kingship and Unity* (Edinburgh: Edinburgh University Press, 1981).

— 'The lost Gàidhealtachd of medieval Scotland' in William Gillies (ed.), *Gaelic and Scotland / Alba agus a' Ghàidhlig* (Edinburgh: Edinburgh University Press, 1989), 67–88.

— 'The Uses of Place-names and Scottish History – Pointers and Pitfalls' in Simon Taylor (ed.), *The Uses of Place-Names* (Edinburgh: Scottish Cultural Press, 1998), 54–74.

BATEMAN, MEG, 'Cruth na Tìre ann am Bàrdachd Ghàidhlig an 18mh Linn' in Wilson McLeod and Máire Ní Annracháin (eds), *Cruth na Tìre* (Dublin: Coiscéim, 2003), 69–89.

BEITH, MARY, *Healing Threads: Traditional Medicine of the Highlands and Islands* (Edinburgh: Polygon, 1995).

BENNETT, MARGARET, 'Plant Lore in Gaelic Scotland' in R. J. Pankhurst and J. M. Mullin (eds), *Flora of the Outer Hebrides* (London: Natural History Museum Publications, 1991), 56–60.

— *Scottish Customs from the Cradle to the Grave* (Edinburgh: Polygon, 1992).

BENOZZO, FRANCESCO, *Landscape Perception in Early Celtic Literature* (Aberystwyth: Celtic Studies Publications, 2004).

BERGIN, OSBORN, *Irish Bardic Poetry* (Dublin: Dublin Institute for Advanced Studies, 1970).

BITEL, LISA, *Land of Women: Tales of Sex and Gender from Early Ireland* (Ithaca: Cornell University Press, 1996).

BLACK, GEORGE, *The Surnames of Scotland* (New York: New York Public Library, 1946).

BLACK, RONALD, 'The Genius of Cathal MacMhuirich', *Transactions of the Gaelic Society of Inverness* 50 (1976–8), 327–65.

— 'The Gaelic Academy: The Cultural Commitment of the Highland Society of Scotland', *Scottish Gaelic Studies* 14 (1986), 1–38.

— 'The Gaelic Manuscripts of Scotland' in William Gillies (ed.), *Gaelic and Scotland / Alba agus a' Ghàidhlig* (Edinburgh: Edinburgh University Press, 1989), 146–74.

— *Cothrom Ionnsachaidh: Gaelic Grammar and Exercises* (Edinburgh: University of Edinburgh, Department of Celtic, 1992).

— *Gaelic Ethnography*, Honour's Coursebook prepared for the Department of Celtic, University of Edinburgh, 1998.

— 'Scottish Fairs and Fair-Names', *Scottish Studies* 33 (2000), 1–75.

— *An Lasair: Anthology of Eighteenth Century Scottish Gaelic Verse* (Edinburgh: Birlinn Ltd, 2001).

— *The Gaelic Otherworld* (Edinburgh: Birlinn Ltd, 2005).

— 'Alasdair mac Mhaighstir Alasdair and the New Gaelic Poetry' in Susan Manning (ed.), *The Edinburgh History of Scottish Literature*, vol. 2 (Edinburgh: University of Edinburgh Press, 2007a), 110–24.

— 'The Quern Dust Calendar: The Religion of the Yellow Stick', *West Highland Free Press* (8 June 2007b).

BLOOMFIELD, MORTON AND CHARLES DUNN, *The Role of the Poet in Early Societies* (Cambridge: Boydell & Brewer, 1989).

BOARDMAN, STEVE, 'The Campbells and charter lordship in medieval Argyll' in Steve Boardman and Alasdair Ross (eds), *The Exercise of Power in Medieval Scotland* c. *1200–1500* (Dublin: Four Courts Press, 2003), 95–117.

— AND ALASDAIR ROSS (eds), *The Exercise of Power in Medieval Scotland* c. *1200–1500* (Dublin: Four Courts Press, 2003).

BOHANNAN, PAUL, *How Culture Works* (New York: Free Press, 1995).

BOURKE, ANGELA, 'More in Anger than in Sorrow: Irish Women's Lament Poetry', in Joan Radner (ed.), *Feminist Messages: Coding in Woman's Folk Culture* (Urbana: University of Illinois Press, 1993), 160–82.

— *The Burning of Bridget Cleary* (New York: Penguin Books, 2000).

BREATHNACH, BREANDÁN, *Folk Music and Dances of Ireland*, new edition (Cork: Ossian Publications, 1996).

BREATNACH, LIAM (ed.), *Uraicecht na Ríar: The Poetic Grades in Early Irish Law* (Dublin: Dublin Institute for Advanced Studies, 1987).

— 'Law', in Kim MacCone and Katherine Simms (eds), *Progress in Medieval Irish Studies* (Maynooth: Department of Old Irish, 1996), 107–22.

— 'On satire and the poet's circuit' in Cathal G. Ó Háinle and Donald Meek (eds), *Unity in Diversity: Studies in Irish and Scottish Gaelic Language, Literature and History* (Dublin: Trinity College, 2004), 25–36.

BRINGHURST, ROBERT, *The Tree of Meaning* (Berkeley: Counterpoint, 2008).

BRODY, HUGH, *The Other Side of Eden: Hunters, Farmers, and the Shaping of the World* (New York: Four Point Press, 2000).

BROUN, DAUVIT, 'Defining Scotland and the Scots before the Wars of Independence' in Dauvit Broun, Richard Finlay and Michael Lynch (eds), *Image and Identity: The Making and Remaking of Scotland through the Ages* (Edinburgh: John Donald, 1998a), 4–17.

— 'Gaelic literacy in eastern Scotland between 1124 and 1249' in Huw Pryce (ed.), *Literacy in Medieval Celtic Societies* (Cambridge: Cambridge University Press, 1998b), 183–201.

— 'Attitudes of *Gall* to *Gaedhel* in Scotland before John of Fordun' in Dauvit Broun and Martin MacGregor (eds), *Mìorun Mòr nan Gall, 'The Great Ill-Will of the Lowlander'? Lowland Perceptions of the Highlands, Medieval and Modern* (Glasgow: University of Glasgow, 2007), 49–82.

BROWN, ARCHIBALD, *The History of Cowal* (Greenock: Telegraph Printing Works, 1908).

BROWN, HUME (ed.), *Early Travellers in Scotland* (Edinburgh: David Douglas, 1891).

BRUFORD, ALAN, *Gaelic Folk-Tales and Mediæval Romances* (Dublin: The Folklore Society of Ireland, 1969).

— 'The Sea-divided Gaels: Some Relationships Between Scottish Gaelic, Irish and English Traditional Songs', *Éigse Cheol Tíre* 1 (1973), 4–27.

— 'Song and recitation in early Ireland', *Celtica* 21 (1990), 61–74.

— 'Workers, weepers and witches: the status of the female singer in Gaelic society', *Scottish Gaelic Studies* 17 (1996), 61–70.

— 'What happened to the Caledonians?' in E. J. Cowan and R. Andrew McDonald (eds), *Alba: Celtic Scotland in the Medieval Era* (East Linton: Tuckwell Press, 2000), 43–68.

— AND D. A. MACDONALD, *Scottish Traditional Tales* (Edinburgh: Birlinn Ltd, 2003).

BUCHANAN, GEORGE, *The History of Scotland* (Glasgow: Blackie, Fullarton & Co., 1827).

BUCHANAN, JOHN LANE, *Travels in the Western Hebrides* (Waternish: Maclean Press, 1997 [1793]).

BUCKLEY, ANN, ' "and his voice swelled like a terrible thunderstorm . . .": Music as Symbolic Sound in Medieval Irish Society' in Gerard Gillen and Harry White (eds), *Irish Musical Studies* 3 (Blackrock: Irish Academic Press, 1995), 13–76.

BUISMAN, FRANK, 'MacArthur and MacGregor Pipers', in F. Buisman, R. D. Cannon and A. Wright (eds), *The MacArthur-MacGregor Manuscript of Piobaireachd (1820)* (Glasgow: University of Glasgow, 2001), xxii–xxxi.

BURNS, ROBERT, *The Complete Works of Robert Burns*, ed. Allan Cunningham (Boston: Phillips, Sampson and Co., 1855).

BYRNE, FRANCIS, *Irish Kings and High-Kings* (New York: St. Martin's Press, 1973).

BYRNE, MICHEL, 'Mairearad Ghriogarach: sùil thòiseachail air bana-bhàrd air dìochuimhne', *Scottish Gaelic Studies* 23 (2007), 85–122.

CAIMBEUL, AONGHAS, *Òrain Nuadh Ghàidhleach* (Dun-eidin: R. Fleming, 1785).

CALDWELL, DAVID, 'Finlaggan, Islay – stones and inauguration ceremonies' in Richard Welander, David Breeze and Thomas Clancy (eds), *The Stone of Destiny: artefact & icon* (Edinburgh: Society of Antiquaries of Scotland, 2003), 61–76.

CAMERON, ALEXANDER, *Reliquae Celticae : Studies in Gaelic Literature*, 2 vols, ed. A. MacBain and J. Kennedy (Inverness: Northern Chronicle, 1892, 1894).

CAMERON, HECTOR (ed.), *Na Baird Thirisdeach* (Stirling: The Tiree Association, 1932).

Campbell, Alexander, *A Journey from Edinburgh through parts of Northern Britain*, 2 vols (London: A. Strahan, 1802).

— *The Grampians Desolate* (Edinburgh: John Moir, 1804).

Campbell, Angus Peter, 'The Moving Picture' in Malcolm MacLean and Christopher Carrell (eds), *Às an Fhearann / From the Land* (Edinburgh: Mainstream Publishing, 1986), 99–103.

Campbell, Archibald (ed.), *Craignish Tales*, Waifs and Strays of Celtic Tradition 1 (London: David Nutt, 1889).

Campbell, Donald, *A Treatise on the Language, Poetry and Music of the Highland Clans* (Edinburgh: D. R. Collie, 1862).

Campbell, Duncan, *The book of Garth and Fortingall* (Inverness: Northern Counties Publishing Company, 1888).

— *Reminiscences and Reflections of an Octogenarian Highlander* (Inverness: Northern Counties Publishing Company, 1910).

— *The Lairds of Glenlyon* (Perth: Clunie Press, 1984 [1886]).

Campbell, Ewan, *Saints and Sea-kings: The First Kingdom of the Scots* (Edinburgh: Historic Scotland, 1999).

— 'Royal inaugurations in Dál Riata and the Stone of Destiny' in Richard Welander, David Breeze & Thomas Clancy (eds), *The Stone of Destiny: artefact & icon* (Edinburgh: Society of Antiquaries of Scotland, 2003), 43–60.

Campbell, Herbert (ed.), *Miscellany of the Scottish History Society* (Edinburgh: Scottish History Society, 1926).

Campbell, John F. (ed.), *Popular Tales of the West Highlands*, 2 vols (Edinburgh: Birlinn Ltd, 1994a [1860]).

— *More West Highland Tales*, 2 vols (Edinburgh: Birlinn Ltd, 1994b [1940, 1960]).

Campbell, John G., 'Sgeulachd air Sir Uallabh O'Corn', *Transactions of the Gaelic Society of Inverness* 13 (1886–7), 69–83.

— *The Fians; or, Stories, Poems & Traditions of Fionn and his Warrior Band*, Waifs and Strays of Celtic Tradition 4 (London: David Nutt, 1891).

— *Clan Traditions and Popular Tales of the West Highlands and Islands*, Waifs and Strays of Celtic Tradition 5 (London: David Nutt, 1895).

— 'The Sharp-witted Wife', *Scottish Historical Review* 12 (1914–15), 413–17.

Campbell, John L., *Gaelic in Scottish Education and Life* (Edinburgh: The Saltire Society, 1945).

— 'The Letter sent by Iain Muideartach, Twelfth Chief of Clanranald, to Pope Urban VIII, in 1626', *Innes Review* 4 (1955), 110–16.

— 'Some Notes on Scottish Gaelic Waulking Songs', *Éigse* 8 (1956), 87–95.

— (ed.), *A Collection of Highland Rites and Customs* (Cambridge: D. S. Brewer, 1975).

— 'Notes on Hamish Robertson's "Studies in Carmichael's *Carmina Gadelica*" ', *Scottish Gaelic Studies* 13 (1978), 1–17.

— (ed.), *Òrain Ghàidhealach mu Bhliadhna Theàrlaich / Highland Songs of the Forty-Five*, Scottish Gaelic Texts 15 (Edinburgh: Scottish Gaelic Texts Society, 1984 [1933]).

— *Canna: The Story of a Hebridean Island*, 3rd edn (Edinburgh: Canongate, 1994).

— *Songs Remembered in Exile*, 2nd edn (Edinburgh: Birlinn Ltd, 1999).

— *A Very Civil People*, ed. Hugh Cheape (Edinburgh: Birlinn Ltd, 2000).

— and Francis Collinson (eds), *Hebridean Folksongs*, 3 vols (Oxford: Clarendon Press, 1969, 1977, 1981).

— AND D. S. THOMSON, *Edward Lhuyd in the Scottish Highlands 1699–1700* (Oxford: Clarendon Press, 1963).

CAMPBELL, PATRICK, *Travels in North America*, ed. William Ganong (Toronto: The Champlain Society, 1937).

CAREY, JOHN, 'The Name "Tuatha Dé Danann" ', *Éigse* 18 (1980), 291–4.

— 'Time, Space, and the Otherworld', *Proceedings of the Harvard Celtic Colloquium* 6/7 (1986–7), 1–27.

— 'Otherworlds and Verbal Worlds in Middle Irish Narrative', *Proceedings of the Harvard Celtic Colloquium* 8/9 (1988–9), 31–41.

— 'The Ancestry of Fénius Farsaid', *Celtica* 21 (1990), 104–12.

— 'The Waters of Vision and the Gods of Skill', *Alexandria* 1 (1991), 163–85.

— *The Irish National Origin-Legend: Synthetic Pseudo-History* (Cambridge: University of Cambridge, 1994).

— 'Saint Patrick, the Druids, and the end of the world', *History of Religions* 36 (1996), 42–53.

— 'The Three Things Required of a Poet', *Ériu* 48 (1997), 41–58.

— *A Single Ray of the Sun: Religious Speculation in Early Ireland* (Andover: Celtic Studies Publications, 1999a).

— 'Transmutations of Immortality in "The Lament of the Old Woman of Beare" ', *Celtica* 23 (1999b), 30–7.

— *King of Mysteries: Early Irish Religious Writings*, 2nd edn (Dublin: Four Courts Press, 2000).

— 'The Lough Foyle Colloquy Texts', *Ériu* 52 (2002), 53–87.

CARMICHAEL, ALEXANDER (ed.), *Ortha nan Gàidheal / Carmina Gadelica*, 6 vols (Edinburgh: Scottish Gaelic Texts Society, 1900–71).

CARMICHAEL, IAN, *Lismore in Alba* (Perth: D. Leslie, 1948).

CATHCART, ALISON, 'Crisis of Identity? Clan Chattan's Response to Government Policy in the Scottish Highlands *c.*1580–1609' in Steve Murdoch and A. MacKillop (eds), *Fighting for Identity: Scottish Military Experience c.1550–1900* (Leiden: Brill, 2002), 163–84.

— *Kinship and Clientage: Highland Clanship 1451–1609* (Leiden: Brill, 2006).

CHARLES-EDWARDS, T. M., *Early Irish and Welsh Kinship* (Oxford: Oxford University Press, 1993).

— 'Language and Society among the Insular Celts AD 400–1000' in Miranda Green (ed.), *The Celtic World* (London: Routledge, 1996), 703–36.

— 'The context and uses of literacy in early Christian Ireland', in Huw Pryce (ed.), *Literacy in Medieval Celtic Societies* (Cambridge: Cambridge University Press, 1998), 62–82.

— 'Geis, prophecy, omen, and oath', *Celtica* 23 (1999), 38–59.

CHEAPE, HUGH, 'The Role of Women in Traditional Celtic Society in Scotland', *Journal of Agricultural Museums* 8 (1987), 63–9.

— 'MacGregor Pipers', *Proceedings of the Pìobaireachd Society Conference* 15 (1988), 1–12.

— 'Woodlands on the Clanranald Estates', in T. C. Smout (ed.), *Scotland since Prehistory* (Edinburgh: Scottish Cultural Press, 1993), 50–63.

— *Tartan*, 2nd edn (Edinburgh: National Museums of Scotland, 1995).

— *The Book of the Bagpipe* (Belfast: Appletree Press, 1999).

— 'Doubts and Delusions of Charlie's Year', *Cencrastus* 65 (2000), 41–5.

— 'The MacCrimmon Piping Dynasty and its Origins', *Transactions of the Gaelic Society of Inverness* 62 (2002a), 1–23.

— 'Environment', unpublished text for Sabhal Mór Ostaig Environment and Material Culture Studies course, 2002b.

— 'Gaelic Genesis', *Scottish Book Collector* 7:9 (Winter 2004), 15–23.

CHISHOLM, COLIN, 'Òrain agus Sgeulachdan Shrath-Ghlais', *Transactions of the Gaelic Society of Inverness* 10 (1883), 220–39.

CLANCY, THOMAS OWEN, 'Women Poets in Early Medieval Ireland', in Katherine Simms and Christine Meek (eds), *The Frailty of Her Sex? Irishwomen in their European Context* (Dublin: Four Courts Press, 1996), 43–72.

— (ed.), *The Triumph Tree: Scotland's Earliest Poetry AD 550–1350* (Edinburgh: Canongate, 1998).

— 'Columba, Adomnán and the cult of saints in Scotland' in Dauvit Broun and Thomas Owen Clancy (eds), *Spes Scotorum / Hope of Scots: Saint Columba, Iona and Scotland* (Edinburgh: T. & T. Clark, 1999), 3–33.

— 'Scotland, the "Nennian" recension of the *Historia Brittonum*, and the *Lebor Bretnach*', in Simon Taylor (ed.), *Kings, Clerics and Chronicles in Scotland, 500–1297* (Dublin: Four Courts Press, 2000), 87–107.

— 'Kingmaking and images of kingship in medieval Gaelic literature' in Richard Welander, David Breeze and Thomas Clancy (eds), *The Stone of Destiny: artefact & icon* (Edinburgh: Society of Antiquaries of Scotland, 2003), 85–106.

— 'A Fragmentary Literature: Narrative and Lyric from the Early Middle Ages' in Thomas Owen Clancy and Murray Pittock (eds), *The Edinburgh History of Scottish Literature*, vol. 1 (Edinburgh: Edinburgh University Press, 2007), 123–31.

CLYDE, ROBERT, *From Rebel to Hero: The Image of the Highlander, 1745–1830* (East Linton: Tuckwell Press, 1995).

CODY, E. G. (ed.), *Bishop Leslie's Historie of Scotland* (Edinburgh: Scottish Texts Society, 1888).

COLLIS, JOHN, 'George Buchanan and the Celts in Britain' in Ronald Black, William Gillies and Roibeard Ó Maolalaigh (eds), *Celtic Connections: Proceedings of the Tenth International Congress of Celtic Studies* (East Linton: Tuckwell Press, 1999), 91–107.

COWAN, EDWARD, 'Clanship, kinship and the Campbell acquisition of Islay', *Scottish Historical Review* 58 (1979), 132–57.

— 'Myth and Identity in Early Medieval Scotland', *Scottish Historical Review* 63 (1984), 111–35.

— 'The Discovery of the Gàidhealtachd in Sixteenth-century Scotland', *Transactions of the Gaelic Society of Inverness* 60 (2000a), 259–84.

— 'The Invention of Celtic Scotland' in E. J. Cowan and R. Andrew McDonald (eds), *Alba: Celtic Scotland in the Medieval Era* (East Linton: Tuckwell, 2000b), 1–23.

CRAIG, K. C. (ed.), *Sgeulachdan Dhunnchaidh* (Glasgow: Alasdair Matheson & Co., 1944).

CRAM, ISOBEL, 'Step dancing' in Evelyn Hood (ed.), *Scotland's Dances* (Edinburgh: Scottish Arts Council, 1994), 23–5.

CRANSTOUN, JAMES (ed.), *The Poems of Alexander Montgomerie* (Edinburgh: Scottish Text Society, 1885–7).

CREGEEN, ERIC, *Recollections of an Argyllshire Drover and other West Highland Chronicles*, ed. Margaret Bennett (Edinburgh: Birlinn, 2004).

CRYSTAL, DAVID, *Language Death* (Cambridge: Cambridge University Press, 2000).

CUNLIFFE, BARRY, *The Ancient Celts* (London: Penguin Books, 1997).

CUNNINGHAM, RODGER, *Apples on the Flood: The Southern Mountain Experience* (Knoxville: University of Tennessee Press, 1987).

— 'Post the Lost Past: Malcolm Chapman's *The Celts*', *Journal of Appalachian Studies* 2 (1996), 263–76.

DAVIDSON, HILDA ELLIS, 'Milk and the Northern Goddess', in Sandra Billington and Miranda Green (eds), *The Concept of the Goddess* (London: Routledge, 1999), 91–106.

DAVIES, REES, 'The English State and the "Celtic" Peoples 1100–1400', *Journal of Historical Sociology* 6 (1993), 1–13.

— 'The Peoples of Britain and Ireland 1100–1400: 1. Identities', *Transactions of the Royal Historical Society Series* 6.4 (1994), 1–20.

— 'The Peoples of Britain and Ireland 1100–1400: 2. Names, Boundaries and Regnal Solidarities', *Transactions of the Royal Historical Society Series* 6.5 (1995), 1–20.

— 'The Peoples of Britain and Ireland 1100–1400: 3. Laws and Customs', *Transactions of the Royal Historical Society Series* 6.6 (1996), 1–23.

— 'The Peoples of Britain and Ireland 1100–1400: 4. Language and Historical Mythology', *Transactions of the Royal Historical Society Series* 6.7 (1997), 1–24.

DAWSON, JANE, 'Calvinism and the Gàidhealtachd in Scotland' in Andrew Pettegree, Alastair Duke and Gillian Lewis (eds), *Calvinism in Europe 1540–1620* (Cambridge: Cambridge University Press, 1994), 231–53.

— (ed.), *Campbell Letters, 1559–1583* (Edinburgh: Scottish History Society, 1997).

— 'The emergence of the Scottish Highlands' in Brendan Bradshaw and Peter Roberts (eds), *British Consciousness and Identity* (Cambridge: Cambridge University Press, 1998), 259–300.

DÉGH, LINDA, 'Folk Narrative' in Richard Dorsan (ed.), *Folklore and Folklife* (Chicago: University of Chicago Press, 1982), 53–83.

DEWAR, JOHN, *The Dewar Manuscripts, Volume One*, ed. John MacKechnie (Glasgow: William MacLellan, 1964).

DEWAR, PÍA, 'Kingship imagery in Classical Gaelic panegyric for Scottish chiefs' in Wilson McLeod, James Fraser and Anja Gunderloch (eds), *Cànan & Cultar / Language and Culture: Rannsachadh na Gàidhlig 3* (Edinburgh: Dunedin Academic Press, 2006), 39–56.

DICKSON, JOSHUA, *When Piping Was Strong: Tradition, Change and the Bagpipe in South Uist* (Edinburgh: John Donald, 2006).

DIXON, JOHN H., *Gairloch in North-west Ross-shire* (Edinburgh: Co-operative Printing Co., 1886).

DOBBS, MARGARET, 'Notes on the Lists of Irish Historic Tales', *The Journal of Celtic Studies* 2 (1958), 45–55.

DODGSHON, ROBERT, *From Chiefs to Landlords* (Edinburgh: Edinburgh University Press, 1998).

DONALDSON, WILLIAM, *The Jacobite Song: Political Myth and National Identity* (Aberdeen: Aberdeen University Press, 1988).

DONNELLY, SEÁN, 'The Warpipes in Ireland – I', *Ceol* 5.1 (1981), 19–24.

— 'The Warpipes in Ireland – II', *Ceol* 5.2 (1982), 55–9.

— 'The Warpipes in Ireland – III', *Ceol* 6.1 (1983), 19–23.

— 'The Warpipes in Ireland – IV', *Ceol* 6.2 (1984), 54–8.

DORIAN, NANCY, *Language Death: The Life Cycle of a Scottish Gaelic Dialect* (Philadelphia: University of Pennsylvania Press, 1981).

DRISCOLL, STEPHEN, *Alba: The Gaelic Kingdom of Scotland, AD 800–1124* (Edinburgh: Historic Scotland, 2002).

DUNBAR, JOHN, *History of Highland Dress* (Edinburgh: Oliver & Boyd, 1962).

DUNCAN, A. A. M., *The Edinburgh History of Scotland: Scotland, the Making of the Kingdom*, vol. 1 (Edinburgh: Mercat Press, 1975).

DURKACZ, VICTOR, *The Decline of the Celtic Languages* (Edinburgh: John Donald, 1983).

EBERLY, SUSAN, 'Fairies and the Folklore of Disability: Changelings, Hybrids, and the Solitary Fairy' in Peter Narváez (ed.), *The Good People: New Fairylore Essays* (Lexington: The University Press of Kentucky, 1991), 227–50.

ELLIS, STEVEN, 'The collapse of the Gaelic world, 1450–1650', *Irish Historical Studies* 31 (1999), 449–69.

EMMERSON, GEORGE, *Ane Celestial Recreatioun: A Social History of Scottish Dance* (Montreal: McGill-Queen's University Press, 1972).

ETCHINGTON, COLMÁN, 'Early Medieval Irish History', in Kim MacCone and Katherine Simms (eds), *Progress in Medieval Irish Studies* (Maynooth: Department of Old Irish, 1996), 123–54.

ETTLINGER, ELLEN, 'The Association of Burials with Popular Assemblies, Fairs and Races in Ancient Ireland', *Études Celtique* 6 (1952–4), 30–61.

EYDMANN, STUART, 'Diversity and Diversification in Scottish Music' in John Beech, et al. (eds), *Oral Literature and Performance Culture*, Scottish Life and Society 10 (Edinburgh: John Donald, 2007), 193–212.

FENYO, KRISZTINA, *Contempt, Sympathy and Romance: Lowland Perceptions of the Highlands and the Clearances During the Famine Years, 1845–1855* (East Linton: Tuckwell Press, 2000).

FERGUSON, CHARLES, 'Sketches of the Early History, Legends, and Traditions of Strathardle – No. V', *Transactions of the Gaelic Society of Inverness* 21 (1896–7), 69–105.

FERGUSON, WILLIAM, *The Identity of the Scottish Nation: An Historic Quest* (Edinburgh: Edinburgh University Press, 1998).

FITZPATRICK, ELIZABETH, 'Leaca and Gaelic Inauguration Ritual in Medieval Ireland' in Richard Welander, David Breeze and Thomas Clancy (eds), *The Stone of Destiny: artefact & icon* (Edinburgh: Society of Antiquaries of Scotland, 2003), 107–21.

FLETT, J. F. AND T. M. FLETT, 'Some Hebridean Folk Dances', *Journal of the English Folk Dance and Song Society* 7 (1952–5), 112–27, 182–4.

— 'Dramatic Jigs in Scotland', *Folk-Lore* 67 (1956), 84–96.

— 'The Scottish Country Dance: Its Origin and Development I', *Scottish Studies* 11 (1967), 1–11.

— 'The History of Scottish Reel as a Dance-Form: I', *Scottish Studies* 16 (1972), 91–120.

— 'The History of Scottish Reel as a Dance-Form: II', *Scottish Studies* 17 (1973), 91–107.

— *Traditional Step-Dancing in Scotland* (Edinburgh: Scottish Cultural Press, 1996).

FLINT, VALERIE, *The Rise of Magic in Early Medieval Europe* (Princeton: Princeton University Press, 1991).

FORSYTH, KATHERINE, *Language in Pictland* (Utrecht: de Keltische Draak, 1997).

FORSYTH, WILLIAM, *In the Shadows of Cairngorm* (Inverness: The Northern Counties Publishing Company, 1900).

FOSTER, SALLY, *Picts, Gaels and Scots* (Edinburgh: Historic Scotland, 2004).

— 'The Topography of People's Lives: Geography until 1314' in Thomas Owen Clancy and Murray Pittock (eds), *The Edinburgh History of Scottish Literature* vol. 1 (Edinburgh: Edinburgh University Press, 2007), 44–51.

FOWLER, JOHN, *Landscapes and Lives: The Scottish Forest Through the Ages* (Edinburgh: Canongate, 2002).

FRASER, ANGUS, *The Angus Fraser Collection of Scottish Gaelic Airs* (Skye: Taigh na Teud, 1996).

Fraser, James, 'Hagiography' in Thomas Owen Clancy and Murray Pittock (eds), *The Edinburgh History of Scottish Literature*, vol. 1 (Edinburgh: Edinburgh University Press, 2007), 103–9.

Fraser, Simon, *The Airs and Melodies Peculiar to the Highlands of Scotland and the Isles*, 2nd edn (London, Ontario: Scott's Highland Services, 1986 [1874]).

Fraser-Mackintosh, Fraser, 'The Depopulation of Aberarder in Badenoch, 1770', *The Celtic Magazine* 2 (1877), 418–26.

Frater, Anne, 'Women of the Gàidhealtachd and their Songs to 1750' in Elizabeth Ewan and Maureen Meikle (eds), *Women in Scotland c.1100–c.1750* (East Linton: Tuckwell Press, 1999), 67–79.

Garnett, Thomas, *Observations on a Tour through the Highlands and Part of the Western Isles*, 2 vols (London: John Stockdale, 1811).

Giblin, Cathaldus, *Irish Franciscan Mission to Scotland, 1619–1646* (Dublin: Assisi Press, 1964).

Gibson, John, *Traditional Gaelic Bagpiping, 1745–1945* (Edinburgh: NMS Publishing, 1998).

Gillies, Anne Lorne, *Songs of Gaelic Scotland* (Edinburgh: Birlinn, 2005).

Gillies, William, 'Some aspects of Campbell history', *Transactions of the Gaelic Society of Inverness* 50 (1976–8), 256–95.

— 'The Poem in Praise of Ben Dobhrain', *Lines Review* 63 (1977), 42–8.

— 'Heroes and Ancestors' in Bo Almqvist, Séamas Ó Catháin and Pádraig Ó Héalaí (eds), *The Heroic Process* (Dún Laoghaire: The Glendale Press, 1987), 57–74.

— 'Gaelic: The Classical Tradition' in R. D. S. Jack (ed.), *The History of Scottish Literature*, vol. 1 (Aberdeen: Aberdeen University Press, 1989), 245–62.

— 'Gaelic Songs of the 'Forty-Five', *Scottish Studies* 30 (1991), 19–57.

— 'The Invention of Tradition, Highland Style' in A. A. MacDonald, Michael Lynch and Ian Cowan (eds), *The Renaissance in Scotland* (New York: E. J. Brill, 1994), 144–56.

— 'The "British" Genealogy of the Campbells', *Celtica* 23 (1999), 82–95.

— 'On the Study of Gaelic Literature' in Thomas Owen Clancy and Sheila Kidd (eds), *Litreachas & Eachdraidh: Rannsachadh na Gàidhlig 2* (Glasgow: Celtic Department, University of Glasgow, 2006), 1–32.

— 'The Lion's Tongues: Languages in Scotland to 1314' in Thomas Owen Clancy and Murray Pittock (eds), *The Edinburgh History of Scottish Literature*, vol. 1 (Edinburgh: Edinburgh University Press, 2007a), 52–62.

— 'Gaelic Literature in the Later Middle Ages: *The Book of the Dean* and Beyond' in Thomas Owen Clancy and Murray Pittock (eds), *The Edinburgh History of Scottish Literature*, vol. 1 (Edinburgh: Edinburgh University Press, 2007b), 219–25.

Gillingham, John, 'The Beginnings of English Imperialism', *Journal of Historical Sociology* 5 (1992), 392–409.

Gordon, Anne, 'Death and Associated Customs' in John Beech, Owen Hand, Mark Mulhern and Jeremy Weston (eds), *The Individual and Community Life*, Scottish Life and Society: A Compendium of Scottish Ethnology 9 (Edinburgh: John Donald, 2005), 104–17.

Grannd, Pàdruig, *Dàin Spioradail*, 6th edn (Elgin: P. Macdonald, 1842).

Grant, Anne, *Essays on the Superstitions of the Highlanders of Scotland . . .* (London: Longman, Hurst, Rees, Orme and Brown, 1811).

— *Letters from the Mountains*, 2 vols, 6th edn (London: Longman, Brown, Green and Longmans, 1845).

GRANT, JOHN, *Legends of the Braes of Mar*, 2nd edn (Aberdeen: Alexander Murray, 1876).

GRANT, KATHERINE, *Aig Tigh na Beinne* (Glasgow: Alexander McLaren & Sons, 1911).

— *Myth, Tradition and Story from Western Argyll* (Oban: Oban Times, 1925).

GRANT, I. F., *Highland Folk Ways* (London: Routledge & Kegan Paul, 1961).

— AND HUGH CHEAPE, *Periods in Highland History* (London: Shepheard-Walwyn, 1987).

GREEN, MIRANDA, 'The Celtic Goddess as Healer' in Sandra Billington and Miranda Green (eds), *The Concept of the Goddess* (London: Routledge, 1999), 26–40.

GUNN, ADAM, 'Unpublished songs of the Reay Country', *Celtic Monthly* 13 (1899), 62–4.

GWYNN, EDWARD, *The Metrical Dindshenchas*, 5 vols (Dublin: Dublin Institute for Advanced Studies, 1991 [1903–35]).

HAARMANN, HARALD, 'History' in Joshua Fishman (ed.), *Handbook of Language & Ethnic Identity* (Oxford: Oxford University Press, 1999), 60–76.

HALL, JAMES, *Travels in Scotland by an Unusual route*, 2 vols (London: J. Johnson, 1807).

HAMILTON, NOEL, ' "Ancient" Irish Music' in Gordon MacLennan (ed.), *Proceedings of the First North American Congress of Celtic Studies* (Ottawa: University of Ottawa, 1988), 283–91.

HARRISON, FRANK, 'Celtic Musics: Characteristics and Chronology' in K. H. Schmidt and R. Ködderitzsch (eds), *History and Culture of the Celts* (Heidelberg: Carl Winter, 1986), 252–63.

HAYWOOD, JOHN, *Atlas of the Celtic World* (London: Thames & Hudson, 2001).

HENDERSON, GEORGE (ed.), *Leabhar nan Gleann* (Edinburgh: N. Macleod, 1898).

— 'The Fionn Saga', *The Celtic Review* 1 (1904–5), 193–207, 352–66.

— *Survival in Beliefs among the Celts* (Glasgow: J. Maclehose, 1911).

— 'Arthurian Motifs in Gadhelic Literature' in Osborn Bergin and Carl Marstrander (eds), *Miscellany presented to Kuno Meyer* (Halle: Max Niemeyer, 1912), 18–33.

HENDERSON, HAMISH, 'The Ballad and Popular Tradition to 1660' in R. D. S. Jack, *The History of Scottish Literature*, vol. 1 (Aberdeen: Aberdeen University Press, 1989), 263–84.

HENDERSON, LIZANNE AND EDWARD COWAN, *Scottish Fairy Belief* (East Linton: Tuckwell, 2001).

HERBERT, MÁIRE, 'Transmutations of an Irish Goddess' in Sandra Billington and Miranda Green (eds), *The Concept of the Goddess* (London: Routledge, 1999), 141–51.

— 'Becoming an Exile: Colum Cille in Middle-Irish Poetry' in Joseph Nagy and Leslie Jones (eds), *Heroic Poets and Poetic Heroes in Celtic Tradition* (Dublin: Four Courts Press, 2005), 131–40.

HIGGITT, JOHN, *The Murthly Hours: Devotion, Literacy and Luxury in Paris, England and the Gaelic West* (London: The British Library, 2000).

HILLERS, BARBARA, 'Storytelling and the International Folktale in Scotland' in John Beech, et al. (eds), *Oral Literature and Performance Culture*, Scottish Life and Society 10 (Edinburgh: John Donald, 2007), 153–70.

HOLLO, KAARINA, 'Conchobar's "Sceptre": The Growth of a Literary Topos', *Cambrian Medieval Celtic Studies* 29 (1995), 11–25.

— 'Laments and lamenting in early medieval Ireland' in Helen Fulton (ed.), *Medieval Celtic Literature and Society* (Dublin: Four Courts Press, 2005), 83–94.

HOOD, EVELYN, 'The Dancing Masters, Dancies & the Scientific Professors' in Evelyn Hood (ed.), *Scotland's Dances* (Edinburgh: Scottish Arts Council, 1994), 14–16.

—, JOAN HENDERSON AND ALASTAIR MACFADYEN, 'Scottish Traditions of Dance' in John Beech, et al. (eds), *Oral Literature and Performance Culture*, Scottish Life and Society 10 (Edinburgh: John Donald, 2007), 505–30.

HOUSTON, R. A. AND W. W. J. KNOX (eds). *The New Penguin History of Scotland* (London: Penguin Books, 2001).

HUDSON, BENJAMIN, 'Tracing Medieval Scotland's Lost History' in Sharon Arbuthnot and Kaarina Hollo (eds), *Fil súil nglais / A Grey Eye Looks Back* (Ceann Drochaid: Clann Tuirc, 2007), 63–72.

HULL, ELEANOR, 'Legends and Traditions of the Cailleach Bheara or Old Woman (Hag) of Beare', *Folklore* 38 (1927), 225–54.

HUNTER, JAMES, *Last of the Free: A Millennial History of the Highlands and Islands of Scotland* (Edinburgh: Mainstream Publishing, 1999).

— *The Making of the Crofting Community*, 2nd edn (Edinburgh: Birlinn, 2000).

HUNTER, MICHAEL, *The Occult Laboratory: Magic, Science and Second Sight in Late Seventeenth-Century Scotland* (Woodbridge: Boydell Press, 2001).

INNES, COSMO (ed.), *Collectanea de Rebus Albanicis* (Edinburgh: Iona Club, 1839).

JACKSON, KENNETH, *Gaelic Notes in the Book of Deer* (Cambridge: Cambridge University Press, 1972).

JAMES, E. O., 'The Tree of Life', *Folklore* 79 (1968), 241–9.

JENKINS, RICHARD, 'Witches and Fairies: Supernatural Aggression and Deviance Among the Irish Peasantry', in Peter Narváez (ed.), *The Good People: New Fairylore Essays* (Lexington: The University Press of Kentucky, 1991), 302–35.

KELLY, FERGUS, 'The Old Irish Tree List', *Celtica* 11 (1976), 107–24.

— *A Guide to Early Irish Law* (Dublin: Dublin Institute for Advanced Studies, 1988).

— *Early Irish Farming* (Dublin: Dublin Institute for Advanced Studies, 1997).

KENNEDY, MICHAEL, *Gaelic Nova Scotia: An Economic, Cultural and Social Impact Study* (Halifax: Nova Scotia Canada, 2002).

KIDD, COLIN, *Subverting Scotland's Past* (Cambridge: Cambridge University Press, 1993).

— 'Teutonic Ethnology and Scottish Nationalist Inhibition, 1780–1880', *The Scottish Historical Review* 74 (1995), 45–68.

— *British Identities Before Nationalism: Ethnicity and Nationhood in the Atlantic World 1600–1800* (Cambridge: Cambridge University Press, 1999).

— 'Race and the Scottish Nation, 1750–1900' 7th BP Prize Lecture (Edinburgh: Royal Society of Edinburgh, 2003).

KNOTT, ELEANOR, *Irish Classical Poetry* (Dublin: At the Sign of the Three Candles, 1960).

KOCH, JOHN (ed.), *Celtic Culture: A Historical Encyclopedia*, 5 vols (Santa Barbara: ABC-CLIO, 2005).

— AND JOHN CAREY (eds), *The Celtic Heroic Age*, 4th edn (Aberystwyth: Celtic Studies Publications, 2003).

KRAUS, RICHARD, *History of the Dance in Art and Education* (Englewood Cliffs: Prentice-Hall, 1969).

KRISTELLER, PAUL, '"Creativity" and "Tradition," ' in Peter Kivy (ed.), *Essays on the History of Aesthetics* (University of Rochester Press, 1992), 66–74.

LAWRENCE, LISA, 'Pagan Imagery in Early Lives of Brigit: A Transformation from Goddess to Saint?' in *Proceedings of the Harvard Celtic Colloquium* 16/17 (2003), 39–54.

LEERSSEN, JOEP, 'Wildness, Wilderness, and Ireland: Medieval and Early-Modern Patterns in the Demarcation of Civility', *Journal of the History of Ideas* 56 (1995), 25–39.

— *Mere Irish and Fíor Ghael: Studies in the Idea of Irish Nationality*, 2nd edn (Cork: Cork University Press, 1996).

LEÓN-PORTILLA, MIGUEL, *Endangered Cultures* (Dallas: Southern Methodist University Press, 1990).

LOGAN, JAMES, *The Scottish Gael, or Celtic Manners as Preserved among the Highlanders*, 2nd edn, ed. Alexander Stewart (Edinburgh: Maclachlan and Stewart, 1876).

LUCAS, A. T., 'The Sacred Trees of Ireland', *Journal of the Cork Historical and Archaeological Society* 68 (1963), 16–53.

LYNCH, MICHAEL, *Scotland: A New History* (London: Pelico, 1991).

— (ed.), *Oxford Companion to Scottish History* (Oxford: Oxford University Press, 2001).

LYSAGHT, PATRICIA, 'Aspects of the Earth-Goddess in the Traditions of the Banshee in Ireland' in Sandra Billington and Miranda Green (eds), *The Concept of the Goddess* (London: Routledge, 1999), 152–65.

MAC-AN-TUAIRNEIR, PÀRUIG (ed.), *Comhcruinneacha de Dh'Òrain taghta Gàidhealach* (Edinburgh: T. Stiubhard, 1813).

MAC A' PHÌ, EOGHAN (ed.), *Am Measg nam Bodach* (Glaschu: An Comunn Gàidhealach, 1938).

MACAULAY, DONALD (ed.), *Nua-Bhàrdachd Ghàidhlig* (Edinburgh: Canongate, 1976).

MACBAIN, ALEXANDER, 'Highland Superstition', offprint from *Transactions of the Gaelic Society of Inverness* 14 (1888).

MAC CANA, PROINSIAS, *The Learned Tales of Medieval Ireland* (Dublin: Dublin Institute for Advanced Studies, 1980).

— '*Regnum* and *Sacerdotium*: Notes on Irish Tradition', *Proceedings of the British Academy* 65 (1981), 443–79.

— 'Placenames and Mythology in Irish Tradition: Places, Pilgrimages and Things' in Gordon MacLennan (ed.), *Proceedings of the First North American Congress of Celtic Studies* (Ottawa: University of Ottawa, 1988), 319–41.

— 'Celtic Religion and Mythology' in Venceslas Kruta, et al. (eds), *The Celts* (New York: Rizzoli, 1997), 616–27.

MACCOINNICH, AONGHAS, ' "His Spirit was given only to warre": Conflict and Identity in the Scottish Gàidhealtachd *c.*1580–*c.*1630' in Steve Murdoch and A. MacKillop (eds), *Fighting for Identity: Scottish Military Experience c.1550–1900* (Leiden: Brill, 2002), 133–61.

— ' "Kingis rabellis" to "Cuidich 'n Rìgh"? Clann Choinnich: the emergence of a kindred, *c.*1475–*c.*1514' in Steve Boardman and Alasdair Ross (eds), *The Exercise of Power in Medieval Scotland c.1200–1500* (Dublin: Four Courts Press, 2003), 175–200.

— ' "Mar Phòr san Uisge": Ìomhaigh Sìol Torcail an Eachdraidh' in Michel Byrne, Thomas Clancy and Sheila Kidd (eds), *Litreachas & Eachdraidh: Rannsachadh na Gàidhlig 2, Glaschu 2002* (Glasgow: Roinn na Ceiltis, 2006), 214–31.

MACCOINNICH, DOMHNULL, *Oran Gairdeachais Dhomhnuill MhicCoinnich* (Glasgow: R. Chapman and A. Duncan, 1785).

MAC CORMICK, JOHN, *The Island of Mull* (Glasgow: Alex MacLaren & Sons, 1923).

MACDHIARMAID, SEUMAS, 'Ainmean-Àitean an Gleann Dochart', *People's Journal* (25 Oct 1913).

MACDONALD, ALEXANDER, 'Scraps of Unpublished Poetry and Folklore from Glenmoriston', *Transactions of the Gaelic Society of Inverness* 21 (1896–7), 22–36.

— *Story and Song from Loch Ness-side* (Inverness: Northern Counties Publishing Company, 1914).

— 'Social Customs of the Gaels', *Transactions of the Gaelic Society of Inverness* 32 (1924–25), 272–300.

MacDonald, Allan A., 'The Relationship between Pibroch and Gaelic Song: Its Implications on the Performance Style of the Pibroch Urlar', unpublished Master's Thesis, University of Edinburgh (1995).

MacDonald, Angus and Archibald MacDonald, *The Macdonald Collection of Gaelic Poetry* (Inverness: Northern Counties Publishing Company, 1911).

MacDonald, Charles, *Moidart: Among the Clanranalds*, ed. John Watt (Edinburgh: Birlinn, 1997).

MacDonald, Donald. *Tales and Traditions of the Lews*, 2nd edn (Birlinn: Edinburgh, 2004).

Macdonald, Fiona A., 'Irish Priests in the Highlands: Judicial Evidence from Argyll', *Innes Review* 66 (1995), 15–33.

— *Mission to the Gaels: Reformation and Counter-Reformation in Ulster and the Highlands and Islands of Scotland 1560–1760* (Edinburgh: John Donald, 2006).

MacDonald, Fiona M., 'Courtship, Marriage and Related Folklore' in John Beech, Owen Hand, Mark Mulhern and Jeremy Weston (eds), *The Individual and Community Life*, Scottish Life and Society: A Compendium of Scottish Ethnology 9 (Edinburgh: John Donald, 2005), 59–73.

MacDougall, James, *Folk Tales and Fairy Lore*, ed. George Calder (Edinburgh: John Grant, 1910).

MacFarlane, Malcolm, 'The Bagpipe', *Guth na Bliadhna* 5 (1908), 350–80.

Mac Gill-eain, Somhairle, *Ris a' Bhruthaich: The Criticism and Prose Writings of Sorley MacLean*, ed. William Gillies (Stornoway: Acair Ltd, 1985).

MacGhrigair, Iain, *Òrain Ghàelach* (Edin-bruaich: A. Mac Neill, 1801).

— *Òrain nuadh Ghàelach nach robh riamh an cloth-bhualadh* (Dun-eudainn: R. Meinearach, 1818).

MacGregor, Alexander, *The Lays and Laments of the Gael* (Edinburgh, 1852).

MacGregor, Martin, 'Church and culture in the late medieval Highlands' in James Kirk (ed.), *The Church in the Highlands* (Edinburgh: Scottish Church History Society, 1998), 1–36.

— ' "Làn-mara 's mìle seòl": Gaelic Scotland and Gaelic Ireland in the Later Middle Ages' in *A' Chòmhdhail Cheilteach Eadarnàiseanta / Congress 99: Cultural Contacts within the Celtic Community* (Inverness: Lewis Recordings, 2000a), 77–97.

— ' "Surely one of the greatest poems ever made in Britain": The Lament for Griogair Ruadh MacGregor of Glen Strae and its Historical Background' in Edward Cowan and Douglas Gifford (eds), *The Polar Twins* (Edinburgh: John Donald, 2000b), 115–53.

— 'The Statutes of Iona: text and context', *The Innes Review* 57 (2006), 111–81.

— 'Gaelic Barbarity and Scottish Identity in the Later Middle Ages' in Dauvit Broun and Martin MacGregor (eds), *Mìorun Mòr nan Gall, 'The Great Ill-Will of the Lowlander'? Lowland Perceptions of the Highlands, Medieval and Modern* (Glasgow: University of Glasgow, 2007a), 7–48.

— 'The Book of the Dean of Lismore and Literary Culture' in Thomas Owen Clancy and Murray Pittock (eds), *The Edinburgh History of Scottish Literature*, vol. 1 (Edinburgh: Edinburgh University Press, 2007b), 209–18.

MacIlleathain, Iain and Maletta NicPhàil, *Seanfhacail is Seanchas* (Stornoway: Stornoway Gazette Group, 2005).

MacInnes, Allan, *Clanship, Commerce and the House of Stuart, 1603–1788* (East Linton: Tuckwell Press, 1996).

— 'The British Military-Fiscal State and the Gael: new perspectives on the '45' in Colm Ó Baoill and Nancy McGuire (eds), *Rannsachadh na Gàidhlig 2000* (Aberdeen: An Clò Gàidhealach, 2002), 257–70.

MacInnes, John, *The Kyles of Bute and Glendaruel* (Oban: Oban Times, 1904).

MacInnes, John, *Dùthchas nan Gàidheal: Selected Essays of John MacInnes*, ed. Michael Newton (Edinburgh: Birlinn, 2006).

— 'The Gaelic Hero-Tales' in John Beech, et al. (eds), *Oral Literature and Performance Culture*, Scottish Life and Society 10 (Edinburgh: John Donald, 2007a), 64–81.

— 'Gaelic Panegyric Verse' in John Beech, et al. (eds), *Oral Literature and Performance Culture*, Scottish Life and Society 10 (Edinburgh: John Donald, 2007b), 82–94.

MacIntosh, Aeneas, *Notes descriptive and historical principally relating to the parish of Moy in Strathdearn and the town and neighbourhood of Inverness* (London: n.p., 1892).

MacKay, Æneas J. G. (ed.), *John Major's History of Greater Britain* (Edinburgh: Scottish History Society, 1892).

MacKay, William (ed.), *Chronicles of the Frasers: The Wardlaw Manuscript* (Edinburgh: Scottish History Society, 1905).

MacKay, William, *Urquhart and Glenmoriston* (Inverness: Northern Counties Publishing Company, 1914).

MacKellar, Mary, 'Unknown Lochaber Bards', *Transactions of the Gaelic Society of Inverness* 12 (1886), 211–26.

— 'The Sheiling: Its Traditions and Songs, I', *Transactions of the Gaelic Society of Inverness* 14 (1888), 135–53.

MacKenzie, Annie (ed.), *Òrain Iain Luim / Songs of John MacDonald, Bard of Keppoch*, Scottish Gaelic Texts 8 (Edinburgh: Scottish Gaelic Texts Society, 1964).

MacKenzie, Hector, 'Characteristic Anecdotes of the Highlanders', *Celtic Magazine* 10 (1885), 388–96.

MacKenzie, Henry (ed.), *Report of the Committee of the Highland Society of Scotland appointed to inquire into the Nature of the Authenticity of the Poems of Ossian* (Edinburgh: Edinburgh University Press, 1805).

MacKenzie, John (ed.), *Sàr Obair nam Bàrd Gàelach; or, The beauties of Gaelic poetry and lives of the Highland bards* (Glasgow: McGregor, Polson & Co., 1841).

MacKenzie, Niall, 'Scottish Gaelic caismeachd, Irish caismirt, and the emergence of cadenced marching', *Scottish Language* 21 (2002), 60–71.

MacKenzie, Osgood, *A Hundred Years in the Highlands* (London: Butler & Tanner, 1949).

MacKenzie, William, 'Leaves from my Celtic Portfolio', *Transactions of the Gaelic Society of Inverness* 8 (1878–9), 18–32, 100–28.

— 'Gaelic Incantations, Charms, and Blessings of the Hebrides', *Transactions of the Gaelic Society of Inverness* 18 (1891–2), 97–182.

— *The Book of Arran*, 2 vols (Glasgow: Hugh Hopkins, 1914).

MacKillop, Andrew, *'More Fruitful than the Soil': Army, Empire and the Scottish Highlands, 1715–1815* (East Linton: Tuckwell Press, 2000).

MacKillop, James, *Dictionary of Celtic Mythology* (Oxford: Oxford University Press, 1998).

MacKinnon, Donald, *Celtic Chair Inaugural Address* (Edinburgh: MacLachlan & Stewart, 1883).

— 'The Glenmasan Manuscript', *Celtic Review* 1 (1905–8), 3–17, 104–31.

MacKinnon, Lachlan, *Cascheum nam Bard, Earrann III*, 2nd edn (Inverness: Highland Printers, 1960).

MacLagan, Robert, *The Games & Diversions of Argyleshire* (London: David Nutt, 1901).

MacLeod, Angus (ed.), *Òrain Dhonnchaidh Bhàin / Songs of Duncan Ban Macintyre*, Scottish Gaelic Texts 4 (Edinburgh: Scottish Gaelic Texts Society, 1978 [1952]).

MacLeod, Frederick, 'Relics Preserved in Dunvegan Castle, Skye', *Proceedings of the Society of the Antiquarians of Scotland* 47 (1912–13), 99–127.

Macleod, Michelle and Moray Watson, 'In the Shadow of the Bard: The Gaelic Short Story, Novel and Drama Since the Early Twentieth Century' in Ian Brown (ed.), *The Edinburgh History of Scottish Literature*, vol. 3 (Edinburgh: Edinburgh University Press, 2007), 273–82.

MacLeod, Norman, *Reminiscences of a Highland Parish* (London: Alexander Strahan, 1867).

— *Caraid nan Gàidheal* (Edinburgh: John Grant, 1910).

Macleod, R. C., *The Macleods of Dunvegan from the Times of Leod to the End of the Seventeenth Century*, 2 vols (Edinburgh: T. and A. Constable, 1927).

MacLeod, Sharon Paice, 'Mater Deorum Hibernensium', *Proceedings of the Harvard Celtic Colloquium* 18/19 (1998–9), 340–84.

MacLeòid, Calum Iain, *Sgial is Eachdraidh* (Glasgow: Gairm, 1977).

Mac Mathúna, Liam, 'The Topographical Vocabulary of Irish: Patterns and Implications', *Ainm* 4 (1989–90), 144–64.

Mac-na-Ceardaich, Gilleasbuig, *An t-Òranaiche / The Gaelic Songster* (Alba Nuadh: Sìol Cultural Enterprises, 2004 [1879]).

MacPhail, J. R. N. (ed.), *Highland Papers*, vol. 1 (Edinburgh: Scottish History Society, 1914).

MacPhàrlain, Calum (ed.), *Binneas nam Bard* (Stirling: A. Mac Aoidh, 1908).

Macpherson, Donald, 'The ClanDonald of Keppoch', *The Celtic Monthly* 4 (1878), 368–75, 424–4.

Macquarrie, Alan, 'The Crusades and the Scottish Gàidhealtachd in Fact and Legend' in Lorraine Maclean (ed.), *The Middle Ages in the Highlands* (Inverness: Inverness Field Club, 1981), 130–41.

— 'Kings, Lords and Abbots: Power and Patronage at the Medieval Monastery of Iona', *Transactions of the Gaelic Society of Inverness* 54 (1987), 355–75.

MacQueen, Hector, 'Survival and success: the Kennedys of Dunure' in Steve Boardman and Alasdair Ross (eds), *The Exercise of Power in Medieval Scotland c.1200–1500* (Dublin: Four Courts Press, 2003), 67–94.

MacRae, Alexander, *The History of the Clan MacRae* (Dingwall: A. M. Ross & Company, 1899).

Macrury, John, 'A Collection of Unpublished Poetry', *Transactions of Gaelic Society of Inverness* 15 (1888–9), 140–51.

Mahon, William, 'The Aisling Elegy and the Poet's Appropriation of the Feminine', *Studia Celtica* 34 (2000), 249–70.

Márkus, Gilbert, 'Gaelic under Pressure: A 13th-century charter from East Fife', *The Journal of Scottish Name Studies* 1 (2007a), 77–98.

— 'Saving Verse: Early Medieval Religious Poetry' in Thomas Owen Clancy and Murray Pittock (eds), *The Edinburgh History of Scottish Literature*, vol. 1 (Edinburgh: Edinburgh University Press, 2007b), 91–100.

MARTIN, MARTIN, *A Description of the Western Islands of Scotland* (London, 1716).

MARTIN, NEILL, 'The Gaelic Rèiteach: Symbolism and Practice', *Scottish Studies* 34 (2006), 77–158.

MASON, ROGER, 'Civil Society and the Celts: Hector Boece, George Buchanan and the Ancient Scottish Past' in Edward Cowan and Richard Finlay (eds), *Scottish History: The Power of the Past* (Edinburgh: Edinburgh University Press, 2002), 95–120.

MATHESON, ANGUS, 'Gleanings from the Dornie Manuscripts', *Transactions of Gaelic Society of Inverness* 41 (1952), 310–81.

— 'Traditions of Alasdair mac Colla', *Transactions of the Gaelic Society of Glasgow* 5 (1958), 9–93.

MATHESON, WILLIAM (ed.), *The Songs of John MacCodrum*, Scottish Gaelic Texts 2 (Edinburgh: Scottish Gaelic Texts Society, 1938).

— 'Some Early Collectors of Gaelic Folk-song', *The Proceedings of the Scottish Anthropological and Folklore Society* 5 (1955), 67–82.

— 'Further Gleanings from the Dornie Manuscripts', *Transactions of Gaelic Society of Inverness* 45 (1965), 148–95.

— (ed.), *An Clàrsair Dall: Òrain Ruaidhri Mhic Mhuirich agus a Chuid Chiùil / The Blind Harper: The Songs of Roderick Morison and his Music*, Scottish Gaelic Texts 12 (Edinburgh: Scottish Gaelic Texts Society, 1970).

— *Highland Surnames* (Glasgow: An Comunn Gàidhealach, 1973).

— Review of Ó Baoill 1979, *Scottish Gaelic Studies* 14 (1983), 129–36.

— *Gaelic Bards and Minstrels*, Scottish Tradition 16 (Edinburgh: School of Scottish Studies, 1993).

MATHIESON, ROBERT, *The Survival of the Unfittest: The Highland Clearances and the End of Isolation* (Edinburgh: John Donald, 2000).

McCAUGHEY, TERENCE, 'Protestantism and Scottish Highland Culture' in James Mackey (ed.), *An Introduction to Celtic Christianity* (Edinburgh: T. & T. Clark, 1989a), 172–205.

— 'Bards, Beasts and Men' in Donnchadh Ó Corráin (ed.), *Sages, Saints and Storytellers* (Maynooth: An Sagart, 1989b), 102–21.

McCLINTOCK, H. F., *Old Irish & Highland Dress*, 2nd edn (Dundalk: Duldalgan Press, 1950).

McDONALD, ALLAN, 'Pìobairean Smearcleit', *Celtic Review* 5 (1908), 345–7.

McDONALD, PATRICK, *A Collection of Highland Vocal Airs* (Edinburgh: Taigh na Teud, 2000 [1784]).

McDONALD, R. ANDREW, 'Rebels without a Cause? The Relations of Fergus of Galloway and Somerled of Argyll with the Scottish Kings, 1153–1164' in E. J. Cowan and R. Andrew McDonald (eds), *Alba: Celtic Scotland in the Medieval Era* (East Linton: Tuckwell Press, 2000), 166–86.

— 'Old and new in the far North: Ferchar Maccintsacairt and the early earls of Ross, c.1200–1274' in Steve Boardman and Alasdair Ross (eds), *The Exercise of Power in Medieval Scotland c.1200–1500* (Dublin: Four Courts Press, 2003), 23–45.

McGOWAN, IAN (ed.), *Journey to the Hebrides* (Edinburgh: Canongate Books, 1996).

McKAY, MARGARET (ed.), *The Rev. Dr John Walker's Report on the Hebrides* (Edinburgh: John Donald, 1980).

McKean, Thomas, *Hebridean Song-Maker: Iain MacNeacail of the Isle of Skye* (Edinburgh: Polygon, 1997).

— 'Tradition and Modernity: Gaelic Bards in the Twentieth Century' in Ian Brown (ed.), *The Edinburgh History of Scottish Literature*, vol. 3 (Edinburgh: Edinburgh University Press, 2007), 130–41.

McKone, Kim, *Pagan Past and Christian Present in Early Irish Literature* (Maynooth: An Sagart, 1990).

McLean, Marianne, *The People of Glengarry* (Montreal: McGill-Queen's University Press, 1991).

McLeod, Wilson, 'Galldachd, Gàidhealtachd, Garbhchriochan', *Scottish Gaelic Studies* 19 (1999), 1–20.

— 'Gàidhealtachd and Galldachd: Some Further Notes', *Scottish Gaelic Studies* 20 (2000), 222–4.

— 'Anshocair nam Fionnghall: Ainmeachadh agus ath-ainmeachadh Gàidhealtachd na h-Albann' in Colm Ó Baoill and Nancy McGuire (eds), *Rannsachadh na Gàidhlig 2000* (Aberdeen: An Clò Gàidhealach, 2002a), 13–24.

— '*Rí Innsi Gall, Rí Fionnghal, Ceannas Gàidheal*: Sovereignty and Rhetoric in the Late Medieval Hebrides', *Cambrian Medieval Celtic Studies* 43 (2002b), 25–48.

— 'Gaelic Poetry as Historical Source: Some Problems and Possibilities' in Edna Longley, Eamonn Hughes and Des O'Rawe (eds), *Ireland (Ulster) Scotland: Concepts, Contexts, Comparisons*, Belfast Studies in Language, Culture and Politics 7 (Belfast: Queen's University, 2003a), 171–9.

— 'Réidh agus Aimhréidh: Sùil air Cruth na Tìre ann am Bàrdachd nan Sgol' in Wilson McLeod and Máire Ní Annracháin (eds), *Cruth na Tìre* (Dublin: Coiscéim, 2003b), 90–120.

— 'Language Politics and Ethnolinguistic Consciousness in Scottish Gaelic Poetry', *Scottish Gaelic Studies* 21 (2003c), 91–146.

— *Divided Gaels: Gaelic Cultural Identities in Scotland and Ireland c.1200–c.1650* (Oxford: Oxford University Press, 2004).

— and Meg Bateman (eds), *Duanaire na Sracaire / Songbook of the Pillagers: Anthology of Scotland's Gaelic Verse to 1600* (Edinburgh: Birlinn Ltd, 2007).

McManus, Damian, *A Guide to Ogam* (Maynooth: An Sagart, 1991).

— 'The bardic poet as teacher, student and critic: a context for the Grammatical Tracts' in Cathal G. Ó Háinle and Donald Meek (eds), *Unity in Diversity: Studies in Irish and Scottish Gaelic Language, Literature and History* (Dublin: Trinity College, 2004), 97–124.

McNeill, Murdoch, *Colonsay: One of the Hebrides* (Edinburgh: n.p., 1910).

McNish, Neil, *The True Method of Preserving the Gælic Language* (Edinburgh: George Douglass, 1828).

McQuillan, Peter, *Native and Natural: Aspects of the Concepts of 'Right' and 'Freedom' in Irish* (Cork: Cork University Press, 2004).

Meek, Donald (ed.), *The Campbell Collection of Gaelic Proverbs and Proverbial Sayings* (Inverness: Gaelic Society of Inverness, 1978).

— 'Gàidhlig is Gaylick anns na Meadhon Aoisean' in William Gillies (ed.), *Gaelic and Scotland / Alba agus a' Ghàidhlig* (Edinburgh: Edinburgh University Press, 1989a), 131–45.

— 'Scottish Highlands, North American Indians and the SSPCK: Some Cultural Perspectives', *Records of the Scottish Church History Society* 23 (1989b), 378–96.

— 'The Death of Diarmaid in Scottish and Irish Tradition', *Celtica* 21 (1990), 335–61.

— 'The Gaelic Ballads of Scotland: Creativity and Adaptation' in Howard Gaskill (ed.), *Ossian Revisited* (Edinburgh: Edinburgh University Press, 1991), 19–48.

— (ed.), *Tuath is Tighearna / Tenants and Landlords*, Scottish Gaelic Texts Society vol. 18 (Edinburgh: Scottish Gaelic Texts Society, 1995).

— 'The Reformation and Gaelic culture: perspectives on patronage, language and literature in John Carswell's translation of "The Book of Common Order" ' in James Kirk (ed.), *The Church in the Highlands* (Edinburgh: Scottish Church History Society, 1998), 37–62.

— *The Quest for Celtic Christianity* (Edinburgh: The Handsel Press, 2000).

— (ed.), *Caran an t-Saoghail / The Wiles of the World: Anthology of 19th Century Scottish Gaelic Verse* (Edinburgh: Birlinn Ltd, 2003a).

— ' "Nuair Chuimhnicheam an Cuilithionn" : Àite Samhlachail na Tìre is Cruth na Tìre ann am Bàrdachd Ghàidhlig na Naoidheamh Linn Deug' in Wilson McLeod and Máire Ní Annracháin (eds), *Cruth na Tìre* (Dublin: Coiscéim, 2003b), 1–38.

— 'The Scottish tradition of Fian ballads in the middle ages' in Cathal G. Ó Háinle and Donald Meek (eds), *Unity in Diversity: Studies in Irish and Scottish Gaelic Language, Literature and History* (Dublin: Trinity College, 2004a), 9–24.

— 'Religion, Riot and Romance: Scottish Gaelic Perceptions of Ireland in the 19th century' in Cathal G. Ó Háinle and Donald Meek (eds), *Unity in Diversity: Studies in Irish and Scottish Gaelic Language, Literature and History* (Dublin: Trinity College, 2004b), 173–93.

— 'The Sublime Gael: The Impact of Macpherson's "Ossian" on Literary Creativity and Cultural Perception in Gaelic Scotland', in Howard Gaskill (ed.), *The Reception of Ossian in Europe* (London: Thommes, 2004c), 40–66.

— 'Gaelic Literature in the Nineteenth Century' in Susan Manning (ed.), *The Edinburgh History of Scottish Literature*, vol. 2 (Edinburgh: University of Edinburgh Press, 2007a), 253–66.

— ' "Craobh-Sgaoileadh a' Bhìobaill agus an t-Soisgeil': A Gaelic Song on the Nineteenth-Century Christian Missionary Movement' in Sharon Arbuthnot and Kaarina Hollo (eds), *Fil Súil nglais / A Grey Eye Looks Back: a Festschrift in honour of Colm Ó Baoill* (Ceann Drochaid: Clann Tuirc, 2007b), 143–62.

— 'Faking the "True Gael"? *Carmina Gadelica* and the Beginning of Modern Gaelic Scholarship', *Aiste* 1 (2007c), 76–106.

MEGAW, J. V. S., 'Music Archaeology and the Ancient Celts', in Venceslas Kruta et al. (eds), *The Celts* (New York: Rizzoli, 1997), 658–73.

MEGAW, RUTH AND VINCENT MEGAW, 'Celtic Connections Past and Present: Celtic Ethnicity Ancient and Modern' in Ronald Black, William Gillies and Roibeard Ó Maolalaigh (eds), *Celtic Connections: Proceedings of the Tenth International Congress of Celtic Studies* (East Linton: Tuckwell Press, 1999), 19–81.

MENZIES, GORDON (ed.), *In Search of Scotland* (Edinburgh: Polygon, 2001).

MENZIES, PAT, 'Òran na Comhachaig' in Michel Byrne, Thomas Owen Clancy and Sheila Kidd (eds), *Litreachas & Eachdraidh / Literature and History* (Glasgow: University of Glasgow Celtic Department, 2006), 83–96.

MERCHANT, CAROLYN, *Ecological Revolutions: Nature, Gender, and Science in New England* (Chapel Hill: University of North Carolina Press, 1989).

MICHIE, JOHN, *Deeside Tales*, 2nd edn (Aberdeen: D. Wyllie & Son, 1908).

MILLIKEN, WILLIAM AND SAM BRIDGEWATER, *Flora Celtica: Plants and People in Scotland* (Edinburgh: Birlinn, 2004).

MOHAWK, JOHN, 'Distinguished Traditions', in John Clark (ed.), *Renewing the Earth: The Promise of Social Ecology* (London: Green Print, 1990), 91–6.

MOORE, MAGGIE, 'Cape Breton Dancing' in Evelyn Hood (ed.), *Scotland's Dances* (Edinburgh: Scottish Arts Council, 1994), 17–21.

MORÉT, ULRIKE, 'Historians and Languages: Medieval and Humanist Views of Celtic Britain' in Terry Brotherstone and David Ditchburn (eds), *Freedom and Authority* (East Linton: Tuckwell Press, 2000), 60–72.

MORRISON, NEIL RANKIN, 'Clann Duiligh: Pìobairean Chloinn Ghill-Eathain', *Transactions of the Gaelic Society of Inverness* 37 (1934–6), 59–79.

MUNRO, JEAN, 'The Lordship of the Isles' in Lorraine Maclean (ed.), *The Highlands in the Middle Ages* (Inverness: Inverness Field Club, 1981), 23–37.

— AND R. W. MUNRO (eds), *Acts of the Lords of the Isles* (Edinburgh: Scottish History Society, 1986).

MUNRO, R. W. (ed.), *Monro's Western Isles of Scotland and Genealogies of the Clans, 1549* (Edinburgh: Oliver and Boyd, 1961).

— 'The Clan System – Fact or Fiction?' in Lorraine Maclean (ed.), *The Highlands in the Middle Ages* (Inverness: Inverness Field Club, 1981), 117–29.

MURRAY, SARAH, *A Companion and Useful Guide to the Beauties of Scotland* (1799).

— *A Companion and Useful Guide to the Beauties In the Western Highlands of Scotland and in the Hebrides*, 2 vols (1803).

NABHAN, GARY PAUL, *Cultures of Habitat: on Nature, Culture, and Story* (Washington D.C.: Counterpoint, 1998).

NAGY, JOSEPH, 'Fenian Heroes and their Rites of Passage' in Bo Almqvist, Séamas Ó Catháin and Pádraig Ó Héalaí (eds), *The Heroic Process* (Dún Laoghaire: The Glendale Press, 1987), 161–82.

— *Conversing with Angels & Ancients: Literary Myths of Medieval Ireland* (Ithaca: Cornell University Press, 1997).

NETTL, BRUNO, *The Study of Ethnomusicology* (Urbana: University of Illinois Press, 1983).

NETTLE, DANIEL AND SUZANNE ROMAINE, *Vanishing Voices* (Oxford: Oxford University Press, 2000).

NEWELL, ALAN, 'An Insular Dance – the dance of the Fer Cengail?', *Archaeology Ireland* (Summer 2005), 36–9.

NEWTE, THOMAS, *Prospects and Observations on a Tour in England and Scotland* (London, 1791).

NEWTON, MICHAEL, 'The Tree in Scottish Gaelic Literature and Tradition', unpublished PhD thesis, University of Edinburgh (1998).

— '*Bha mi 's a' chnoc*': Creativity in Scottish Gaelic Tradition', *Proceedings of the Harvard Celtic Colloquium* 18/19 (1998–9), 312–39.

— (ed.), *Bho Chluaidh gu Calasraid / From the Clyde to Callander* (Stornoway: Acair, 1999).

— *We're Indians Sure Enough: The Legacy of the Scottish Highlanders in the United States* (Richmond: Saorsa Media, 2001a).

— 'In Their Own Words: Gaelic Literature in North Carolina', *Scotia* 25 (2001b), 1–28.

— 'Jacobite Past, Loyalist Present', *e-Keltoi* 5 (2003a), 31–62. http://www.uwm.edu/Dept/celtic/ekeltoi/volumes/vol5/5_2/newton_5_2.pdf

— ' "Becoming Cold-Hearted Like the Gentiles Around Them": Scottish Gaelic in the United States 1872–1912', *eKeltoi* 2 (2003b), 63–132. http://www.uwm.edu/Dept/celtic/ekeltoi/volumes/vol2/2_3/newton_2_3.pdf

— ' "Vain, Hurtful, Lying, Worldly tales": Creed, Belief, and Practice in the life of Argyll Highlanders, in Scotland and America', *Argyll Colony Plus* 17 (2003c), 25–42.

— 'Coille Mhòr Chailleann ann am Beulaithris nan Gàidheal', in Wilson McLeod and Máire Ní Annracháin (eds), *Cruth na Tíre* (Dublin: Coiscéim, 2003d), 180–194.

— 'Dancing with the dead: ritual dances at wakes in the Scottish Gàidhealtachd' in Wilson McLeod, James Fraser and Anja Gunderloch (eds), *Cànan & Cultur / Language & Culture: Rannsachadh na Gàidhlig* 3 (Edinburgh: Dunedin Academic Press, 2006), 215–34.

— ' "Chì Mi Cuimhneachan Sgrìobhte Nach Gabh Leughadh Le Coigreach": Aiteam agus Àite, Dùthaich agus Dùthchas' in Richard Cox (ed.), *Dualchas is Àrainneachd* (Ceann Drochaid: Clann Tuirc, 2009).

— 'Prophecy and Cultural Conflict in Gaelic Tradition', *Scottish Studies* (forthcoming).

— AND HUGH CHEAPE, ' "The Keening of Women and the Roar of the Pipe": From Clàrsach to Bagpipe (*c.*1600–1782)', *Ars Lyrica* (forthcoming).

NÍ ANNRACHÁIN, MÁIRE, 'Metaphor and Metonymy in the Poetry of Màiri nighean Alasdair Ruaidh' in Sharon Arbuthnot and Kaarina Hollo (eds), *Fil súil glais / A Grey Eye Looks Back* (Clann Drochaid: Clann Tuirc, 2007), 163–74.

NIC LEÒID, MÒRAG, 'An Ceangal a tha eadar Faclan agus Ceòl ann an Òrain Ghàidhlig' in Colm Ó Baoill and Nancy McGuire (eds), *Rannsachadh na Gaidhlig 2000* (Aberdeen: An Clò Gàidhealach, 2002), 35–44.

NICOLAISEAN, W. F. H., *Scottish Place-Names* (London: Batsford, 1976).

— *The Picts and their Place-names* (Rosemarkie: Groam House Museum, 1996).

NICOLSON, ALEXANDER, *History of Skye*, 2nd edn, ed. Alasdair Maclean (Portree: Maclean Press, 1994).

— (ed.), *Gaelic Proverbs* (Edinburgh: Birlinn Ltd, 1996 [1881]).

NICOLSON, CALUM, *Calum Ruadh: Bard of Skye*, Scottish Tradition Series 7 (Edinburgh: School of Scottish Studies, n.d.).

Ó BAOILL, COLM (ed.), *Bàrdachd Shìlis na Ceapaich c.1660–c.1729 / Poems by Sileas MacDonald c.1660–c.1729*, Scottish Gaelic Texts 13 (Edinburgh: Scottish Gaelic Texts Society, 1972).

— 'Scotland in early Gaelic literature', *Transactions of the Gaelic Society of Inverness* 48 (1972–4), 382–94.

— 'Inis Moccu Chein', *Scottish Gaelic Studies* 12 (1976), 267–70.

— (ed.), *Eachann Bacach agus Bàird Eile de Chloinn Ghill-Eathain / Eachann Bacach and Other MacLean Poets*, Scottish Gaelic Texts 14 (Edinburgh: Scottish Gaelic Texts Society, 1979).

— (ed.), *Iain Dubh* (Aberdeen: An Clò Gàidhealach, 1994).

— (ed.), *Duanaire Colach, 1537–1757* (Aberdeen: An Clò Gàidhealach, 1997).

— *MacLean Manuscripts in Nova Scotia* (Aberdeen: Aberdeen University Department of Celtic, 2001).

— 'The Oldest Songs of the Gael' in Edna Longley, Eamonn Hughes and Des O'Rawe (eds), *Ireland (Ulster) Scotland: Concepts, Contexts, Comparisons*, Belfast Studies in Language, Culture and Politics 7 (Belfast: Queen's University, 2003), 65–76.

— 'Sìleas na Ceapaich' in Thomas Owen Clancy and Murray Pittock (eds), *The Edinburgh History of Scottish Literature*, vol. 1 (Edinburgh: Edinburgh University Press, 2007), 305–14.

— AND MEG BATEMAN (eds), *Gàir nan Clàrsach / The Harp's Cry: An Anthology of seventeenth-century Gaelic Poetry* (Edinburgh: Birlinn Ltd, 1994).

— AND DONALD MACAULAY, *Scottish Gaelic Vernacular Verse to 1730: A Checklist*, 2nd edn (Aberdeen: Celtic Department of the University of Aberdeen, 2001).

Ó BUACHALLA, BREANDÁN, ' "Common Gaelic" Revisited' in Colm Ó Baoill and Nancy McGuire (eds), *Rannsachadh na Gàidhlig 2000* (Aberdeen: An Clò Gàidhealach, 2002), 1–12.

Ó CATHASAIGH, TOMÁS, 'The Semantics of "Síd" ', *Éigse* 17 (1977–9), 137–55.

Ó CORRÁIN, DONNCHA, *Ireland Before the Normans* (Dublin: Gill and Macmillan, 1972).

Ó CRÓINÍN, DÁIBHÍ, *Early Medieval Ireland* (London: Longman Group, 1995).

Ó CRUALAOICH, GEARÓID, 'The "Merry Wake" ' in James S. Donnelly, Jr. and Kerby A. Miller (eds), *Irish Popular Culture, 1650–1850* (Dublin: Irish Academic Press, 1998), 173–200.

— *The Book of the Cailleach* (Cork: Cork University Press, 2003).

Ó CUÍV, BRIAN, 'A mediaeval exercise in language planning: Classical early modern Irish' in E. F. Konrad Koerner (ed.), *Progress in linguistic historiography* (Amsterdam: Benjamins, 1980), 23–34.

— 'Dinnshenchas – the Literary Exploitation of Irish Place-names', *Ainm* 4 (1989–90), 90–106.

OELSCHLAEGER, MAX, *The Idea of Wilderness: From Prehistory to the Age of Ecology* (New Haven: Yale University Press, 1991).

Ó HALLMHURÁIN, GEARÓID, 'Amhrán an Ghorta: The Great Famine and Irish Traditional Music', *New Hibernia Review / Iris Éireannach Nua* 3:1 (1999), 19–44.

Ó HÓGÁIN, DÁITHÍ, *Myth, Legend and Romance: An Encyclopædia of the Irish Folk Tradition* (London: BCA, 1990).

OHLMEYER, JANE, ' "Civilizing of those Rude Partes': Colonization within Britain and Ireland, 1580s–1640s' in Nicholas Canny and Alaine Low (eds), *The Origins of Empire* (Oxford: Oxford University Press, 1998), 124–47.

OMMER, ROSEMARY, 'Primitive accumulation and the Scottish clann in the Old World and the New', *Journal of Historical Geography* 12 (1986), 121–41.

Ó MADAGÁIN, BREANDÁN, 'Functions of Irish Song in the Nineteenth Century', *Béaloideas* 53 (1985), 130–216.

Ó MAOLALAIGH, ROIBEARD, 'On the Possible Origins of Scottish Gaelic *iorram* "rowing song" ', in Michel Byrne, Thomas Owen Clancy and Sheila Kidd (eds), *Litreachas & Eachdraidh: Rannsachadh na Gàidhlig 2* (Glaschu: Roinn na Ceiltis Oilthigh Ghlaschu, 2006), 232–88.

O'NEILL, ÁINE, ' "The Fairy Hill is on Fire!" (MLSIT 6071)', *Béaloideas* 59 (1991), 189–96.

Ó TUAMA, SEÁN, 'Stability and Ambivalence: Aspects of the Sense of Place and Religion in Irish Literature', in Joseph Lee (ed.), *Ireland: Towards a Sense of Place* (Cork: Cork University Press, 1985), 21–33.

PATTERSON, NERYS, *Cattle Lords & Clansman*, 2nd edn (Notre Dame: University of Notre Dame Press, 1994).

— 'The English Just Are – I', *Planet: The Welsh Internationalist* 114 (1995), 72–7.

— 'The English Just Are – II', *Planet: The Welsh Internationalist* 115 (1996), 84–90.

PEACOCK, FRANCIS, *Sketches Relative to the History and Theory but more especially to the Practice of Dancing* (Aberdeen: J. Chalmers, 1805).

PENNANT, THOMAS, *A Tour in Scotland and Voyage to the Hebrides, 1772,* ed. Andrew Simmons (Edinburgh: Birlinn, 1998 [1774–6]).

— *A Tour in Scotland, 1769* (Edinburgh: Birlinn, 2000 [1771]).

PERKINS, LEEMAN, *Music in the Age of the Renaissance* (New York: W. W. Norton, 1999).

PINKERTON, JOHN, *A Dissertation on the Origin and Progress of the Scythians or Goths* (London: John Nichols, 1787).

PITTOCK, MURRAY AND ISLA JACK, 'Patrick Geddes and the Celtic Revival' in Susan Manning (ed.), *The Edinburgh History of Scottish Literature*, vol. 2 (Edinburgh: University of Edinburgh Press, 2007), 338–46.

PLANK, GEOFFREY, *Rebellion and Savagery: The Jacobite Rising of 1745 and the British Empire* (Philadelphia: University of Pennsylvania Press, 2006).

PURSER, JOHN, 'Traditional Music & Dance' in Evelyn Hood (ed.), *Scotland's Dances* (Edinburgh: Scottish Arts Council, 1994), 3–4.

— 'Listening to Picts' in E. Hickmann, I. Laufs and R. Eichmann (eds), *Studien zur Musikarchäologie IV Orient-Archäeologie* 15 (2004), 221–39.

— 'Hand-bells of the Celtic Church in Scotland', *Transactions of the Gaelic Society of Inverness* 63 (2006), 267–91.

— *Scotland's Music*, 2nd edn (Edinburgh: Mainstream, 2007).

QUIN, E (ed.), *Dictionary of the Irish Language* (Dublin: Royal Irish Academy, 1983).

QUYE, ANITA, HUGH CHEAPE, JOHN BURNETT, ESTER S. B. FERREIRA, ALISON N. HULME AND HAMISH MCNAB, 'An Historical and Analytical Study of Red, Pink, Green and Yellow Colours in Quality 18th- and Early 19th-Century Scottish Tartans' in Jo Kirby (ed.), *Dyes in History and Archaeology* 19 (London: Archetype Publications, 2004), 1–12.

RADNER, JOAN, ' "Men Will Die": Poets, Harpers, and Women in Early Irish Literature' in A. T. E. Matonis and Daniel F. Melia (eds), *Celtic Language, Celtic Culture* (Belmont: Ford & Bailie, 1990), 172–86.

REID, JAMES MACDONALD, *Dance in the Gaelic Culture* (unpublished manuscript), 2001.

REISS, SCOTT, 'Tradition and Imaginary: Irish Traditional Music and the Celtic Phenomenon' in Martin Stokes and Philip Bohlman (eds), *Celticisms: from Center to Fringe in Europe* (Lanham: Scarecrow Press, 2003), 145–69.

RICHARDS, ERIC, *The Highland Clearances* (Edinburgh: Birlinn, 2000).

ROBINSON, CHRISTINE AND ROIBEARD Ó MAOLALAIGH, 'The Several Tongues of a Single Kingdom: The Languages of Scotland, 1314–1707' in Thomas Owen Clancy and Murray Pittock (eds), *The Edinburgh History of Scottish Literature*, vol. 1 (Edinburgh: Edinburgh University Press, 2007), 153–67.

ROSS, JAMES, 'The Sub-Literary Tradition in Scottish Gaelic Song-Poetry. Part I. Poetic Metres and Song Metres', *Éigse* 7 (1953–5), 217–39; 8 (1956–7), 1–17.

— 'A Classification of Gaelic Folk-Song,' *Scottish Studies* 1 (1957), 1–42.

— 'Folk Song and Social Environment', *Scottish Studies* 5 (1961), 18–39.

ROSS, NEIL, *Heroic Poetry from the Book of the Dean of Lismore*, Scottish Gaelic Texts 3 (Edinburgh: Scottish Gaelic Texts Society, 1939).

SACHS, CURTIS, *World History of the Dance* (New York: Norton, 1937).

SADIE, STANLEY (ed.), *The New Grove Dictionary of Music and Musicians*, 2nd edn (London: Macmillan Publishers, 2001).

SAMUEL, RAPHAEL AND PAUL THOMPSON (eds), *The Myths We Live By* (London: Routledge, 1990).

SANGER, KEITH, 'Irish Harpers BC, before Carolan that is', unpublished paper presented to 2008 Kilkenny Harp School.

— AND ALISON KINNAIRD, *Tree of Strings / Crann nan Teud* (Temple: Kinmor Music, 1992).

SCARFE, NORMAN (ed.), *The Highlands in 1786* (Woodbridge: Boydell Press, 2001).

SCOTT, PAUL (ed.), *Scotland: A Concise Cultural History* (Edinburgh: Mainstream Publishing, 1993).

Scrope, William, *Days of Deer-Stalking in the Scottish Highlands* (Glasgow: Thomas Morison, 1883).

Sellar, W. D. H., 'Highland Family Origins – Pedigree Making and Pedigree Faking' in Lorraine Maclean (ed.), *The Middle Ages in the Highlands* (Inverness: Inverness Field Club, 1981), 103–16.

— 'Celtic Law and Scots Law: Survival and Integration', *Scottish Studies* 29 (1989), 1–27.

— 'The Ancestry of the MacLeods Reconsidered', *Transactions of the Gaelic Society of Inverness* 60 (2000), 233–84.

Sharpe, Richard (ed.), *Life of St Columba* (London: Penguin Books, 1995).

Shaw, John, 'Scottish Gaelic Traditions of the Cliar Sheanchain', in C. Byrne, Margaret Harry and P. Ó Siadhail (eds), *Celtic Languages and Celtic Peoples: Proceedings of the Second North American Congress of Celtic Studies* (Halifax: St Mary's University, 1992), 141–58.

— 'Language, Music and Local Aesthetics, Views from Gaeldom and Beyond', *Scottish Language* 11/12 (1992–3), 37–61.

— 'The Ethnography of Speaking and Verbal Taxonomies: Some Applications to Gaelic' in Ronald Black, William Gillies, and Roibeard Ó Maolalaigh (eds), *Celtic Connections: Proceedings of the 10th International Congress of Celtic Studies* (East Linton: Tuckwell Press, 1999), 309–23.

— (ed.), *Brìgh an Òrain / A Story in Every Song* (Montreal & Kingston: McGill-Queen's University Press, 2000).

— 'Gaelic Cultural Maintenance and the Contribution of Ethnography', *Scotia* 27 (2003), 34–48.

— 'The Collectors: John Francis Campbell and Alexander Carmichael' in Susan Manning (ed.), *The Edinburgh History of Scottish Literature*, vol. 2 (Edinburgh: University of Edinburgh Press, 2007a), 347–52.

— *Na Beanntaichean Gorma / The Blue Mountains* (Montreal: McGill-Queen's University Press, 2007b).

— 'Storytellers in Scotland: Context and Function' in John Beech, et al. (eds), *Oral Literature and Performance Culture*, Scottish Life and Society 10 (Edinburgh: John Donald, 2007c), 28–41.

Shaw, Lachlan, *The History of the Province of Moray*, ed. J. F. S. Gordon, 3 vols (Glasgow: Thomas Morison, 1882).

Shaw, Margaret, *Folksongs and Folklore of South Uist*, 3rd edn (Aberdeen: Aberdeen University Press, 1986).

Shaw, William, *An Analysis of the Gaelic Language* (Menston: The Scolar Press, 1972 [1778]).

Sheeran, Patrick, 'Genius Fabulae: The Irish Sense of Place', *Irish University Review* 18 (1988), 191–206.

Sher, Richard, 'Percy, Shaw, and the Ferguson "Cheat": National Prejudice in the Ossian Wars' in Howard Gaskill (ed.), *Ossian Revisited* (Edinburgh: Edinburgh University Press, 1991), 207–45.

Simmons, Andrew (ed.), *Burt's Letters from the North of Scotland* (Edinburgh: Birlinn, 1998 [1754]).

Simms, Katherine, 'Literacy and the Irish bards' in Huw Pryce (ed.), *Literacy in Medieval Celtic Societies* (Cambridge: Cambridge University Press, 1998), 238–58.

— 'Muireadhach Albanach Ó Dálaigh and the Classical Revolution' in Thomas Owen Clancy and Murray Pittock (eds), *The Edinburgh History of Scottish Literature*, vol. 1 (Edinburgh: Edinburgh University Press, 2007), 83–90.

SINCLAIR, ALASDAIR MACLEAN, 'The Macintyres of Glennoe', *Transactions of the Gaelic Society of Inverness* 18 (1891–2), 289–94.

SINTON, THOMAS, *The Poetry of Badenoch* (Inverness: Northern Counties Publishing Company, 1906).

SITHICHE, 'A' Bhean-Nighe', *Guth na Bliadhna* 9 (1912), 195–221, 333–66.

SMEDLEY, AUDREY, *Race in North America: Origin and Evolution of a Worldview* (Boulder: Westview Press, 1993).

SMITH, IAIN CRICHTON, *Towards the Human* (Edinburgh: MacDonald Publishers, 1986).

SMITH, JOHN, *Galic Antiquities Consisting of a History of the Druids . . .* (Edinburgh, 1780).

SMITH, JOHN (convener), *Aithris is Oideas: Traditional Gaelic Rhymes and Games* (London: University of London Press, 1964).

SMITH, PHILIP, 'On the Fringe and in the Middle: The MacDonalds of Antrim and the Isles, 1266–1586', *History Ireland* 2.1 (Spring 1994), 15–20.

SMITH, SALLY K. SOMMERS, 'Interpretations and Translations of Irish Traditional Music' in Maria Tymoczko and Colin Ireland (eds), *Language and Tradition in Ireland* (Amherst: University of Massachusetts Press, 2003), 101–17.

SMYTH, ALFRED P., *Warlords and Holy Men: Scotland AD 80–1000* (Edinburgh: Edinburgh University Press, 1984).

SORELL, WALTER, *The Dance Through the Ages* (London: Thames & Hudson, 1967).

SPARLING, HEATHER, *Puirt-a-beul: An Ethnographic Study of Mouth Music in Cape Breton*, unpublished MA thesis. (York University, 2000)

STEARNS, PETER AND HERRICK CHAPMAN, *European Society in Upheaval: Social History Since 1750* (New York: MacMillan Publishing Company, 1992).

STEVENSON, DAVID, *Highland Warrior: Alasdair MacColla and the Civil Wars* (Edinburgh: The Saltire Society, 1994).

STEWART, CHARLES, *The Killin Collection of Gaelic Songs* (Edinburgh: n.p., 1884).

STEWART, DAVID, *Sketches of the Characters, Institutions and Customs of the Highlanders of Scotland*, revised edn (Inverness: A. & W. Mackenzie, 1885 [1822]).

STEWART, WILLIAM G., *The Popular Superstitions and Festive Amusements of the Highlanders of Scotland*, 2nd edn (Edinburgh: Oliver and Boyd, 1851).

— *Lectures on the Mountains; or the Highlands and Highlanders of Strathspey and Badenoch as they were and as they are* (London: Saunders, Otley and Co., 1860).

STIÙBHART, DOMHNALL UILLEAM, *An Gàidheal, A' Ghàidhlig agus A' Ghàidhealtachd Anns an t-Seachdamh Linn Deug*, unpublished PhD thesis (Edinburgh University, 1996).

— 'Women and Gender in the Early Modern Western Gàidhealtachd' in Elizabeth Ewan and Maureen Meikle (eds), *Women in Scotland c.1100–c.1750* (East Linton: Tuckwell Press, 1999), 233–50.

— 'The genesis and operation of the Royal Bounty scheme 1725–30', *Records of the Scottish Church History Society* 33 (2003), 63–142.

— *Rìoghachd nan Eilean* (Dùn Blathain: Clò Hallaig, 2005).

— 'Uses of Historical Traditions in Scottish Gaelic' in John Beech, et al. (eds), *Oral Literature and Performance Culture*, Scottish Life and Society 10 (Edinburgh: John Donald, 2007), 124–52.

STOKES, WHITLEY, 'The Second Battle of Moytura', 2004, http://www.ucc.ie/celt/published/T300011/index.html

STRINGER, KEITH, 'Reform Monasticism and Celtic Scotland: Galloway, *c.*1140–*c.*1240' in E. J. Cowan and R. Andrew McDonald (eds), *Alba: Celtic Scotland in the Medieval Era* (East Linton: Tuckwell Press, 2000), 166–86.

STUART-MURRAY, JOHN, 'Differentiating the Gaelic Landscape of the Perthshire Highlands', *Scottish Studies* 34 (2006), 159–77.

TEIGNMOUTH, BARON (CHARLES JOHN SHORE), *Sketches of the Coasts and Islands of Scotland*, 2 vols (London: John Parker, 1836).

TERRY, C. SANFORD (ed.), *De Unione Regnorum Britannia Tractatus* (Edinburgh: Scottish History Society, 1909).

THOMAS, KEITH, *Man and the Natural World: Changing Attitudes in England, 1500–1800* (Oxford: Oxford University Press, 1996 [1983]).

THOMSON, DERICK, 'The MacMhuirich Bardic Family', *Transactions of the Gaelic Society of Inverness* 43 (1963), 276–304.

— 'Gaelic Learned Orders and Literati in Medieval Scotland', *Scottish Studies* 12 (1968a), 57–78.

— 'The Harlaw Brosnachadh: An early-fifteenth-century literary curio' in James Carney and David Greene (eds), *Celtic Studies: Essays in memory of Angus Matheson* (London: Routledge & Kegan Paul, 1968b), 147–69.

— 'Niall Mór MacMhuirich', *Transactions of the Gaelic Society of Inverness* 49 (1974–6), 9–25.

— *An Introduction to Gaelic Poetry*, 2nd edn (Edinburgh: Edinburgh University Press, 1989).

— 'The Seventeenth-century Crucible of Scottish Gaelic Poetry', *Studia Celtica* 26–27 (1992a).

— (ed.), *The MacDiarmid Manuscript Anthology*, Scottish Gaelic Texts 17 (Edinburgh: Scottish Gaelic Texts Society, 1992b).

— (ed.), *The Companion to Gaelic Scotland*, 2nd edn (Glasgow: Gairm, 1994).

— (ed.), *Alasdair mac Mhaighstir Alasdair: Selected Poems*, Scottish Gaelic Texts New Series 1 (Edinburgh: Scottish Gaelic Texts Society, 1996).

THOMSON, R. L. (ed.), *Foirm na h-Urrnuidheadh*, Scottish Gaelic Texts 11 (Edinburgh: Scottish Gaelic Texts Society, 1970).

TOELKEN, BARRE, *The Dynamics of Folklore*, 2nd edn (Logan: Utah State University Press, 1996).

TOLMIE, FRANCES, *One Hundred and Five Songs of Occupation from the Western Isles of Scotland* (Lampeter: Llanerch Publishers, 1997 [1911]).

TUAN, YI-FU, *Topophilia: A Study of Environmental Perception, Attitudes, and Values* (New York: Columbia University Press, 1974).

TYMOCZKO, MARIA, ' "Cétamon": Vision in Early Irish Seasonal Poetry', *Eire-Ireland* 18 (1983), 17–39.

UÍ ÓGÁIN, RÍONACH, 'Traditional Music and Irish Cultural History' in Gerard Gillen and Harry White (eds), *Irish Musical Studies*, vol. 3 (Blackrock: Irish Academic Press, 1995), 77–100.

WAGNER, H., 'The Origins of Pagan Irish Religion', *Zeitschrift Für Celtische Philologie* 38 (1981), 1–28.

WARD, GEOFFREY (ed.), *The West: An Illustrated History* (Boston: Little, Brown and Co., 1996).

WATSON, ALDEN, 'Kings, Poets, and Sacred Trees', *Études Celtiques* 18 (1981), 165–79.

WATSON, JAMES CARMICHAEL (ed.), *Òrain us Luinneagan le Màiri nighean Alasdair Ruaidh / Gaelic Songs of Mary MacLeod*, Scottish Gaelic Texts 9 (Edinburgh: Scottish Gaelic Texts Society, 1934).

— 'Cathal Mac Muireadhaigh Cecinit' in Eòin Ó Riain (ed.), *Féil-Sgrìbhinn Eóin Mhic Néill / Essays and Studies Presented to Professor Eoin MacNeill* (Dublin: Three Candles, 1940), 166–79.

WATSON, WILLIAM J., 'Classical Gaelic Poetry of Panegyric in Scotland', reprinted and supplemented from *Transactions of the Gaelic Society of Inverness* 29 (1914–19), 194–235.

— 'Marbhnadh Donnchaidh Duibh', *An Deo-Gréine* 12 (1916–17), 132–4.

— 'Unpublished Poetry – III', *Scottish Gaelic Studies* 2 (1927–8), 75–91.

— (ed.), *Rosg Gàidhlig* (Stirling: An Comunn Gàidhealach, 1929).

— 'Cor na Gàidhealtachd air an la an diugh' in *The Active Gael* (Glasgow: Archibald Sinclair, 1934), 231–50.

— (ed.), *Bàrdachd Albannach O Leabhar Deadhan Lios-Móir / Scottish Verse from the Book of the Dean of Lismore*, Scottish Gaelic Texts 1 (Edinburgh: Scottish Gaelic Texts Society, 1937).

— (ed.), *Bàrdachd Ghàidhlig: Specimens of Gaelic Poetry, 1550–1900*, 3rd edn (Stirling: An Comunn Gàidhealach, 1959).

— *Scottish Place-Name Papers* (London: Steve Savage Publishers, 2002).

— *The History of the Celtic Placenames of Scotland* (Edinburgh: Birlinn, 2004 [1926]).

WEST, MÁIRE, 'Aspects of díberg in the tale Togail Bruidne Da Derga', *Zeitschrift für celtische Philologie* 49–50 (1997), 950–64.

WHITHERS, CHARLES, *Gaelic Scotland: The Transformation of a Culture Region* (London: Routledge, 1988).

WHYTE, HENRY, *Naigheachdan Fìrinneach*, 2 vols (Paisley: Alexander Gardner, 1907).

— 'Cumha Teaghlach a' Mhàim', *The Celtic Monthly* 16 (1908), 78–9.

WILLIAMS, J. E. CAERWYN AND PATRICK FORD, *The Irish Literary Tradition* (Cardiff: University of Wales Press, 1992).

WILLIAMSON, ARTHUR, 'Scotland, Antichrist and the Invention of Great Britain' in John Dwyer, Roger Mason and Alexander Murdoch (eds), *New Perspectives on the Politics and Culture of Early Modern Scotland* (Edinburgh: John Donald, 1982), 34–52.

— 'Scots, Indians and Empire: The Scottish Politics of Civilization 1519–1609', *Past & Present* 150 (1996), 46–83.

WOOLF, ALEX, 'Pictish matriliny reconsidered', *Innes Review* 49 (1998), 147–67.

— 'The 'When, Why & Wherefore' of Scotland', *History Scotland* 2 (2002), 12–16.

— 'The origins and ancestry of Somerled: Gofraid mac Fergusa and "The Annals of the Four Masters" ', *Mediaeval Scandinavia* 15 (2005), 199–213.

— *From Pictland to Alba, 789–1070* (Edinburgh: Edinburgh University Press, 2007).

ZUMBUHL, MARK, 'Contextualising the Duan Albanach' in Wilson McLeod, James Fraser and Anja Gunderloch (eds), *Cànan & Cultar / Language and Culture: Rannsachadh na Gàidhlig* 3 (Edinburgh: Dunedin Academic Press, 2006), 11–24.

ZUMWALT, ROSEMARY, 'A Historical Glossary of Critical Approaches', in John Foley (ed.), *Teaching Oral Traditions* (New York: Modern Language Association, 1998), 75–94.

INDEX